Teach Yourself® Microsoft® Publisher 2000

Teach Yourself® Microsoft® Publisher 2000

Lee Musick and Edward Willett

IDG Books Worldwide, Inc.
An International Data Group Company

Foster City, CA • Chicago, IL • Indianapolis, IN • New York, NY

Teach Yourself® Microsoft® Publisher 2000

Published by
IDG Books Worldwide, Inc.
An International Data Group Company
919 E. Hillsdale Blvd., Suite 400
Foster City, CA 94404
`www.idgbooks.com` (IDG Books Worldwide Web site)

ISBN: 0-7645-3401-7

Printed in the United States of America

10 9 8 7 6 5 4 3 2 1

1P/RT/RS/ZZ/IN

Distributed in the United States by IDG Books Worldwide, Inc.

Distributed by CDG Books Canada Inc. for Canada; by Transworld Publishers Limited in the United Kingdom; by IDG Norge Books for Norway; by IDG Sweden Books for Sweden; by IDG Books Australia Publishing Corporation Pty. Ltd. for Australia and New Zealand; by TransQuest Publishers Pte Ltd. for Singapore, Malaysia, Thailand, Indonesia, and Hong Kong; by Gotop Information Inc. for Taiwan; by ICG Muse, Inc. for Japan; by Intersoft for South Africa; by Eyrolles for France; by International Thomson Publishing for Germany, Austria and Switzerland; by Distribuidora Cuspide for Argentina; by LR International for Brazil; by Galileo Libros for Chile; by Ediciones ZETA S.C.R. Ltda. for Peru; by WS Computer Publishing Corporation, Inc., for the Philippines; by Contemporanea de Ediciones for Venezuela; by Express Computer Distributors for the Caribbean and West Indies; by Micronesia Media Distributor, Inc. for Micronesia; by Chips Computadoras S.A. de C.V. for Mexico; by Editorial Norma de Panama S.A. for Panama; by American Bookshops for Finland.

For general information on IDG Books Worldwide's books in the U.S., please call our Consumer Customer Service department at 800-762-2974. For reseller information, including discounts and premium sales, please call our Reseller Customer Service department at 800-434-3422.

For information on where to purchase IDG Books Worldwide's books outside the U.S., please contact our International Sales department at 317-596-5530 or fax 317-596-5692.

For consumer information on foreign language translations, please contact our Customer Service department at 800-434-3422, fax 317-596-5692, or e-mail rights@idgbooks.com.

For information on licensing foreign or domestic rights, please phone +1-650-655-3109.

For sales inquiries and special prices for bulk quantities, please contact our Sales department at 650-655-3200 or write to the address above.

For information on using IDG Books Worldwide's books in the classroom or for ordering examination copies, please contact our Educational Sales department at 800-434-2086 or fax 317-596-5499.

For press review copies, author interviews, or other publicity information, please contact our Public Relations department at 650-655-3000 or fax 650-655-3299.

For authorization to photocopy items for corporate, personal, or educational use, please contact Copyright Clearance Center, 222 Rosewood Drive, Danvers, MA 01923, or fax 978-750-4470.

Library of Congress Cataloging-in-Publication Data

Musick, Lee, 1955-
Teach Yourself Micrososft Publisher 2000 / Lee Musick and Edward Willett.
p. cm.
Includes index.
ISBN 0-7645-3401-7 (alk. paper)
1. Microsoft Publisher. 2. Desktop publishing. I. Title Microsoft Publisher 2000. II. Willett, Edward, 1959- Title.
Z253.532.M53 M88 2000
686.2'25445369--dc21 99–049494
CIP

ABOUT IDG BOOKS WORLDWIDE

Welcome to the world of IDG Books Worldwide.

IDG Books Worldwide, Inc., is a subsidiary of International Data Group, the world's largest publisher of computer-related information and the leading global provider of information services on information technology. IDG was founded more than 30 years ago by Patrick J. McGovern and now employs more than 9,000 people worldwide. IDG publishes more than 290 computer publications in over 75 countries. More than 90 million people read one or more IDG publications each month.

Launched in 1990, IDG Books Worldwide is today the #1 publisher of best-selling computer books in the United States. We are proud to have received eight awards from the Computer Press Association in recognition of editorial excellence and three from Computer Currents' First Annual Readers' Choice Awards. Our best-selling *...For Dummies®* series has more than 50 million copies in print with translations in 31 languages. IDG Books Worldwide, through a joint venture with IDG's Hi-Tech Beijing, became the first U.S. publisher to publish a computer book in the People's Republic of China. In record time, IDG Books Worldwide has become the first choice for millions of readers around the world who want to learn how to better manage their businesses.

Our mission is simple: Every one of our books is designed to bring extra value and skill-building instructions to the reader. Our books are written by experts who understand and care about our readers. The knowledge base of our editorial staff comes from years of experience in publishing, education, and journalism — experience we use to produce books to carry us into the new millennium. In short, we care about books, so we attract the best people. We devote special attention to details such as audience, interior design, use of icons, and illustrations. And because we use an efficient process of authoring, editing, and desktop publishing our books electronically, we can spend more time ensuring superior content and less time on the technicalities of making books.

You can count on our commitment to deliver high-quality books at competitive prices on topics you want to read about. At IDG Books Worldwide, we continue in the IDG tradition of delivering quality for more than 30 years. You'll find no better book on a subject than one from IDG Books Worldwide.

John Kilcullen
Chairman and CEO
IDG Books Worldwide, Inc.

Steven Berkowitz
President and Publisher
IDG Books Worldwide, Inc.

Eighth Annual Computer Press Awards 1992

Ninth Annual Computer Press Awards 1993

Tenth Annual Computer Press Awards 1994

Eleventh Annual Computer Press Awards 1995

IDG is the world's leading IT media, research and exposition company. Founded in 1964, IDG had 1997 revenues of $2.05 billion and has more than 9,000 employees worldwide. IDG offers the widest range of media options that reach IT buyers in 75 countries representing 95% of worldwide IT spending. IDG's diverse product and services portfolio spans six key areas including print publishing, online publishing, expositions and conferences, market research, education and training, and global marketing services. More than 90 million people read one or more of IDG's 290 magazines and newspapers, including IDG's leading global brands — Computerworld, PC World, Network World, Macworld and the Channel World family of publications. IDG Books Worldwide is one of the fastest-growing computer book publishers in the world, with more than 700 titles in 36 languages. The "...For Dummies®" series alone has more than 50 million copies in print. IDG offers online users the largest network of technology-specific Web sites around the world through IDG.net (http://www.idg.net), which comprises more than 225 targeted Web sites in 55 countries worldwide. International Data Corporation (IDC) is the world's largest provider of information technology data, analysis and consulting, with research centers in over 41 countries and more than 400 research analysts worldwide. IDG World Expo is a leading producer of more than 168 globally branded conferences and expositions in 35 countries including E3 (Electronic Entertainment Expo), Macworld Expo, ComNet, Windows World Expo, ICE (Internet Commerce Expo), Agenda, DEMO, and Spotlight. IDG's training subsidiary, ExecuTrain, is the world's largest computer training company, with more than 230 locations worldwide and 785 training courses. IDG Marketing Services helps industry-leading IT companies build international brand recognition by developing global integrated marketing programs via IDG's print, online and exposition products worldwide. Further information about the company can be found at www.idg.com.

1/24/99

Credits

Acquisitions Editor
Andy Cummings

Development Editors
Valerie Perry
Katharine Dvorak

Technical Editor
Ed Hanley

Copy Editors
Dennis Weaver
Michael D. Welch

Project Coordinator
Cindy Phipps

Book Designers
Daniel Ziegler Design, Cátálin Dulfu, Kurt Krames

Quality Control Specialist
Marianne J. Santy

Proofreading and Indexing
York Production Services

About the Authors

Lee Musick is the Marketing Manager for Indianapolis-based INTEC & Company, Inc., where he uses the computer to produce catalogs, sales flyers, and product brochures. He also oversees the corporate Web site. In addition to his day job, Lee also freelances as a technical editor for IDG Books Worldwide, having reviewed over a dozen books. He was also the revision author for *The Internet Directory for Dummies, 3rd Edition*, and wrote the PhotoDraw section of *the Microsoft Office 2000 9-in-1 for Dummies.* When not glued to his computer at work or home, he is affixed to the seat of his Harley or involved in youth community service projects. Feel free to drop him a message at lmusick@inetdirect.net.

Edward Willett is a full-time writer of fiction and non-fiction. He's the author of three young adult science fiction books (most recently *Andy Nebula: Interstellar Rock Star*) as well as several computer books and children's science books. He writes a weekly science column for newspapers and radio and hosts a weekly TV show about computers and the Internet. He is also a professional actor and singer. Ed and his wife live in Regina, Saskatchewan, Canada.

For the past twenty-some years, my wife Denise has been an inspiration for me. My kids, Kyle, Kevin, and Kourtney, have kept me young much longer than I had hoped or planned. And finally, to my mom and dad, not only did you give me life, but you taught me how to live. This is for you. — LM

Welcome to Teach Yourself

Welcome to *Teach Yourself*, a series read and trusted by millions for a decade. Although you may have seen the *Teach Yourself* name on other books, ours is the original. In addition, no *Teach Yourself* series has ever delivered more on the promise of its name than this series. That's because IDG Books Worldwide has transformed *Teach Yourself* into a new cutting-edge format that gives you all the information you need to learn quickly and easily.

Readers have told us that they want to learn by doing and that they want to learn as much as they can in as short a time as possible. We listened to you and believe that our new task-by-task format and suite of learning tools deliver the book you need to successfully teach yourself any technology topic. Features such as our Personal Workbook, which lets you practice and reinforce the skills you've just learned, help ensure that you get full value out of the time you invest in your learning. Handy cross-references to related topics and online sites broaden your knowledge and give you control over the kind of information you want, when you want it.

More Answers . . .

In designing the latest incarnation of this series, we started with the premise that people like you, who are beginning to intermediate computer users, want to take control of your own learning. To do this, you need the proper tools to find answers to questions so you can solve problems now.

In designing a series of books that provide such tools, we created a unique and concise visual format. The added bonus: *Teach Yourself* books actually pack more information into their pages than other books written on the same subjects. Skill for skill, you typically get much more information in a *Teach Yourself* book. In fact, *Teach Yourself* books, on average, cover twice the skills covered by other computer books — as many as 125 skills per book — so they're more likely to address your specific needs.

... In Less Time

We know you don't want to spend twice the time to get all this great information, so we provide lots of time-saving features:

- ▶ A modular task-by-task organization of information: any task you want to perform is easy to find and includes simple-to-follow steps
- ▶ A larger size than standard makes the book easy to read and convenient to use at a computer workstation. The large format also enables us to include many more illustrations — 500 screen illustrations show you how to get everything done!
- ▶ A Personal Workbook at the end of each chapter reinforces learning with extra practice, real-world applications for your learning, and questions and answers to test your knowledge
- ▶ Cross-references appearing at the bottom of each task page refer you to related information, providing a path through the book for learning particular aspects of the software thoroughly
- ▶ A Find It Online feature offers valuable ideas on where to go on the Internet to get more information or to download useful files
- ▶ Take Note sidebars provide added-value information from our expert authors for more in-depth learning
- ▶ An attractive, consistent organization of information helps you quickly find and learn the skills you need

These *Teach Yourself* features are designed to help you learn the essential skills about a technology in the least amount of time, with the most benefit. We've placed these features consistently throughout the book, so you quickly learn where to go to find just the information you need — whether you work through the book from cover to cover or use it later to solve a new problem.

You will find a *Teach Yourself* book on almost any technology subject — from the Internet to Windows to Microsoft Office. Take control of your learning today, with IDG Books Worldwide's *Teach Yourself* series.

Teach Yourself

More Answers in Less Time

Search through the task headings to find the topic you want right away. To learn a new skill, search the contents, chapter opener, or the extensive index to find what you need. Then find — at a glance — the clear task heading that matches it.

Learn the concepts behind the task at hand and, more important, learn how the task is relevant in the real world. Time-saving suggestions and advice show you how to make the most of each skill.

After you learn the task at hand, you may have more questions, or you may want to read about other tasks related to the topic. Use the cross-references to find different tasks to make your learning more efficient.

Ultimately, people learn by doing. Follow the clear, illustrated steps presented with every task to complete a procedure. The detailed callouts for each step show you exactly where to go and what to do to complete the task.

Creating a Table

When you create a table in Publisher, it's just like creating a picture, text, or WordArt frame. There's a button in the toolbar for creating a table frame. Once the frame is drawn, the dialog box that asks for the number of rows and columns comes up automatically.

Clicking in a table frame will not only highlight the frame, but on the top and left sides of the frame, you see the row and column control boxes. These not only indicate the width of a column or height of a row, but they are used to select the entire line of cells.

When Publisher creates a table, it's like many small text frames lined up in the number of rows and columns that you specify. You'll notice the table by the light gray lines that outline each cell. By default, these lines won't print unless you assign them a border. Likewise, the outside border won't print until you specify a border for it.

Because each cell contains a single paragraph, you can move your cursor from cell to cell by using the Tab key to go to the next cell, and Shift+Tab to back up a cell. As you press the Tab key, the cursor moves from left to right. When you reach the end of a row, the cursor starts at the leftmost cell of the next row. Shift+Tab works just the opposite.

Text that you place within a cell automatically wraps within the width of the cell. The row height will automatically change as you add text. The only time that the height will not change is when you have locked the table, something that gets explained later in this chapter under "Merging and Splitting Cells."

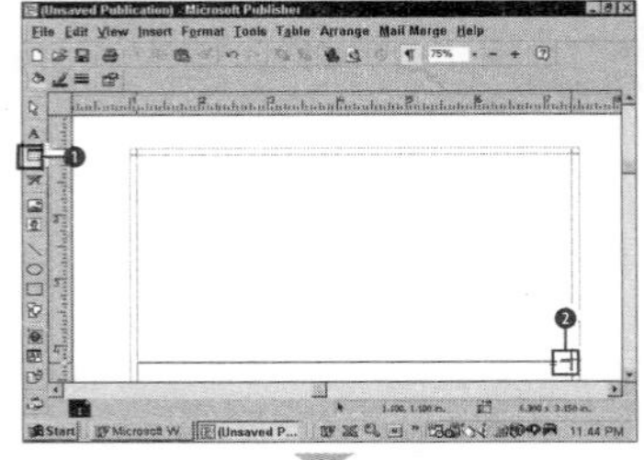

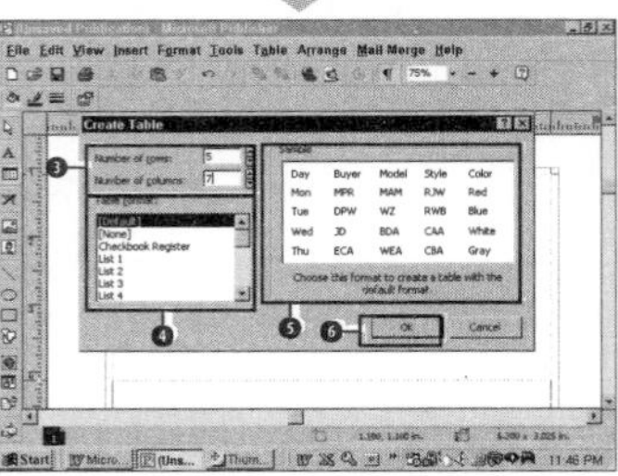

1. Click the Table Frame tool.
2. Draw a frame on the page that will hold the table.
3. After the frame is drawn, the Create Table dialog box appears. Indicate the number of rows and columns in the table.
4. You can choose a preformat from the "Table format" list.
5. The Sample window shows what the preformatted table looks like.
6. Click OK to have the table appear in the frame.

CROSS-REFERENCE

Learn how to create text and picture frames back in Chapter 6.

186

Go to this area if you want special tips, cautions, and notes that provide added insight into the current task.

The current chapter name and number always appear in the top right-hand corner of every task spread, so you always know exactly where you are in the book.

Working with Tables

CHAPTER 10

So, now that you know what tables are and that they can exist in your document, what kinds of things can you do with tables? Probably the most widely used application is making a calendar. You can forgo the wizard and make your own tables with seven columns and about five rows. That should take care of most months.

Organized lists of figures that compare yearly totals, monthly sums, or daily averages are also good applications. Post the swim team events, the swimmers, and their time. Organize a golf tournament and use a table to assemble the foursomes and their tee times. Create a product listing for items that you sell or collect. List your Beanie Babies, their names, birthdays, and value.

How about names and offices for your company or organization? Make one column for a person's name, another for their position in the company, secretary's name, phone extension, and so on. You get the idea — now let's get to it.

TAKE NOTE

USE TABLES IN WEB PAGES

Tables in Publisher will translate to HTML tables when published to a Web page. Don't hesitate to use them.

7 *The table is created to fill the frame with the number of rows and columns in Step 3.*

8 *Each cell contains an End of File symbol (choose View➪Show Special Characters to view them).*

9 *To select a row or column, click the buttons at the top of the columns or to the left of the rows.*

10 *This button selects all rows and columns.*

11 *Enter text into the cells. Note that the text will wrap within the cell.*

12 *Also notice that the row expands to accommodate the text in a given cell.*

13 *You can also have multiple paragraphs within a cell.*

14 *Notice that the frame will expand to accommodate the table.*

FIND IT ONLINE

To learn how to accurately and effectively display statistics, check out the resources at **http://ubmail.ubalt.edu/~harsham/statistics/REFSTAT.HTM.**

187

Use the Find It Online element to locate Internet resources that provide more background, take you on interesting side trips, and offer additional tools for mastering and using the skills you need. (Occasionally you'll find a handy shortcut here.)

Who This Book Is For

This book is written for you, a beginning to intermediate PC user who isn't afraid to take charge of his or her own learning experience. You don't want a lot of technical jargon; you *do* want to learn as much about PC technology as you can in a limited amount of time. You need a book that is straightforward, easy to follow, and logically organized, so you can find answers to your questions easily. And, you appreciate simple-to-use tools such as handy cross-references and visual step-by-step procedures that help you make the most of your learning. We have created the unique *Teach Yourself* format specifically to meet your needs.

Personal Workbook

It's a well-known fact that much of what we learn is lost soon after we learn it if we don't reinforce our newly acquired skills with practice and repetition. That's why each *Teach Yourself* chapter ends with your own Personal Workbook. Here's where you can get extra practice, test your knowledge, and discover ideas for using what you've learned in the real world. There's even a Visual Quiz to help you remember your way around the topic's software environment.

Feedback

Please let us know what you think about this book, and whether you have any suggestions for improvements. You can send questions and comments to the *Teach Yourself* editors on the IDG Books Worldwide Web site at **www.idgbooks.com**.

Personal Workbook

Q&A

1. Tables, like any text or image, have to reside in what type of container?
2. When you add columns or rows to a table, what do you run the risk of having happen to the table?
3. What technique does Publisher offer to accommodate headers and subheads that span across several columns?
4. When you remove a diagonal line from a cell, what happens to the contents of both halves?
5. When you resize columns and rows, what useful Publisher feature can you use to ensure that the borders of columns and rows will be placed in an exact location on the page?
6. To be sure that you are only changing the width of one column or height of one row in addition to the one next to it, what key do you press while dragging the border?
7. What other program in the Microsoft Office Suite can you use to aid you in creating tables in Publisher?
8. When using the Table AutoFormat preset designs, what one element seen in the Preview window will not get changed?

ANSWERS: PAGE 354

202

After working through the tasks in each chapter, you can test your progress and reinforce your learning by answering the questions in the Q&A section. Then check your answers in the Personal Workbook Answers appendix at the back of the book.

Another practical way to reinforce your skills is to do additional exercises on the same skills you just learned without the benefit of the chapter's visual steps. If you struggle with any of these exercises, it's a good idea to refer to the chapter's tasks to be sure you've mastered them.

Working with Tables

CHAPTER 10

EXTRA PRACTICE

1. Create a custom calendar with all of the events happening at work for a given month. Use the BorderArt feature to choose an appropriate outline for the table, given the month you are producing. Post it in the company lounge area.
2. Make a table of household chores for the children. Use the first column for the child's name and list several chores per child in the next column. When complete, merge the cells where the child's name is the same, leaving the chores separated.
3. Make a table for your bowling league with columns for the bowler's name, handicap, date, and score.
4. Create a table that lists all the software that you own. Include the version and serial numbers. You could also list the phone number for technical support.

REAL-WORLD APPLICATIONS

- ✔ In your company's annual report, include a table that compares financial figures for the last three years, broken down into categories.
- ✔ Use a table to make a calendar of events for your organization. Instead of a typical monthly calendar, you use one column for the date and another for the event.
- ✔ Create a table that lists all of the equipment and furnishings in your office. Include manufacturer, date purchased, model number, serial number, and where purchased.
- ✔ Develop a product sheet where a large photo of the product is on the front of the page. On the back, list the features of the product using a table.

Read the list of Real-World Applications to get ideas on how you can use the skills you've just learned in your everyday life. Understanding a process can be simple; knowing how to use that process to make you more productive is the key to successful learning.

Visual Quiz

In this calendar, identify all of the places where cells were merged.

____

____

____

____

____

203

Take the Visual Quiz to see how well you're learning your way around the technology. Learning about computers is often as much about how to find a button or menu as it is about memorizing definitions. Our Visual Quiz helps you find your way.

Acknowledgments

A project this large has so many people involved, lending their expertise and time, that it's truly hard to know where to start. Andy Cummings, first of all, thanks for the call and opportunity to vent some creative juices doing this book. With Katharine Dvorak channeling all the material, all the bits and pieces were successfully assembled. Valerie Perry, my most steady contact, not only exhibited top-notch editing skills to be sure each task was consistent in quality and quantity, but also proved to be a great sounding board to receive feedback on my ideas.

Finally, I would personally like to acknowledge the professionalism and knowledge of Ed Willett and Ed Hanley. Ed Willett not only provided his expertise in writing, but also that of his experience. Finally, Ed Hanley, not only laid the groundwork for this book, but provided his keen excellent technical editing skill, to ensure that accuracy was always paramount.

— *Lee Musick*

Contents

Contents

Contents

Contents

Teach Yourself®
Microsoft® Publisher 2000

PART I

CHAPTER

1 Understanding Publisher 2000 Basics

2 Making Your First Publications

3 Managing Your Files

4 Using Microsoft Publisher Catalog

5 Printing Your Publication

Learning Common Tasks

Using new software is like taking a week-long vacation at a favorite spot. You may return to a favorite retreat simply because you are familiar with the area. The grocery store is just a mile down the road on the left. That favorite restaurant that won't gouge you with high prices is worth the 15-minute taxi ride to a quaint part of the city. You even know where the closest K-Mart is for forgotten items.

This book's first part gets you familiar with the Publisher interface, menus, toolbars, and online help system. Because you have this book as your personal tour guide, your comfort level should start to rise after a few tasks. To start, we even show you several ways to open the program and then build your skill from there.

Publisher is full of goodies for a pretty reasonable price, if you bought it separately from one of the Microsoft Office 2000 suites. If you bought the suite for the three biggies — Word, Excel, and Access — you can be sure that Publisher will soon become a favorite.

If familiarity breeds comfort, Microsoft Publisher 2000 will be among your favorite places to visit when you fire up your computer.

CHAPTER 1

MASTER THESE SKILLS

- Opening and Closing Publisher
- Using Menus
- Using Context Menus
- Using Toolbars
- Getting Help While You Work
- Getting Help from the Office Assistant
- Getting Help Online

Understanding Publisher 2000 Basics

Microsoft Publisher 2000 is a tightly integrated component of the Microsoft Office 2000 suite. So if you are using Microsoft Office, you already have a head start on getting up to speed with Microsoft Publisher. On the other hand, even if you are completely new to Microsoft Publisher, this chapter gives you all of the information you need to get started and hit the ground running.

Microsoft Publisher combines the power of text formatting with graphics to give you the typesetting capabilities that graphic designers use. The nice thing about Publisher, however, is all the wizards and layout help you get when creating your own publications. Sure, you could use Microsoft Word to do layout to an extent, but it doesn't have the flexibility that Publisher has. If you're doing long, technical documents, Word may be the way to go. It's fast, it has styles to make formatting text go quickly, and you can even drop in graphics. But not like Publisher!

If you're ready to kick the tires on this software, this chapter is the place to start. When you buy a new car or rent one while on vacation, you usually check out where all the controls are — lights, turn signals, windshield wipers, power window buttons, and the dozens of buttons on the radio-CD player. Software is no different. You need to know where the menu commands are so you can slide the mouse cursor straight to the command you want. Like the little nondescript pictures on the car's knobs, you have to know what all the button pictures mean and what they do for you.

This chapter helps you become familiar with the basics of Publisher's graphical user interface. You'll learn how to open and close the program, creating a simple publication in the process. Then, you'll be introduced to the way that Publisher puts all of the many tools it contains at your fingertips, through the use of menus and toolbars. Finally, you'll learn how to use the built-in Help system, which not only answers questions you might have, but contains step-by-step instructions for accomplishing practically every task within Publisher, from the most simple to the most complex. So, as they say in the car business, "Are you ready for a test drive?"

Opening and Closing Publisher

Microsoft Publisher, from your computer's point of view, is a series of instructions that are stored on your hard drive, in a number of files. When you open a program, you tell your operating system — Windows 98 for the examples in this book — to read the program off your hard drive and place it into RAM, or random access memory. Remember that whatever information resides in RAM goes away when your computer is turned off, or sometimes even if you experience a power surge or a "brownout." Whatever is on your hard drive is always there and can always be retrieved again. This goes for your program files and the files you create using Publisher or any other program. So, it is important to save the files you create with Publisher to your hard drive before you close Publisher, so you can retrieve them again in your next session.

When you are using Windows 95, 98, or the new Windows 2000, you may have several programs open at once. Because Publisher is cleanly integrated into the Microsoft Office 2000 suite, you may be working simultaneously with Publisher and Word or Excel, or perhaps with another Windows program such as Photoshop or Internet Explorer. In that case, you will want to know how to open Publisher even if you have other applications running as well. That's what the Windows Start button is for.

The first three figures on the facing page show you two ways of opening Publisher, using the Start button or a desktop icon. You also get your first introduction to Publisher's Catalog Wizards for creating publications, which we explore in much greater detail later in this book. The fourth figure shows you how to close Publisher and save any of your work that has not yet been saved.

CROSS-REFERENCE

Learn more about saving your work in Chapter 3.

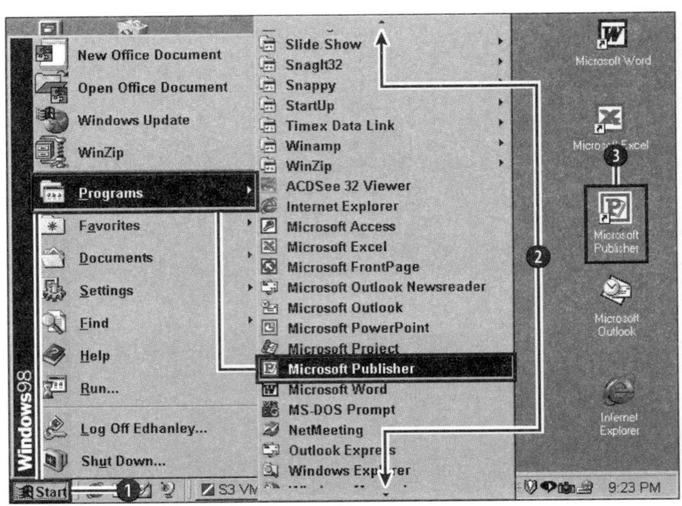

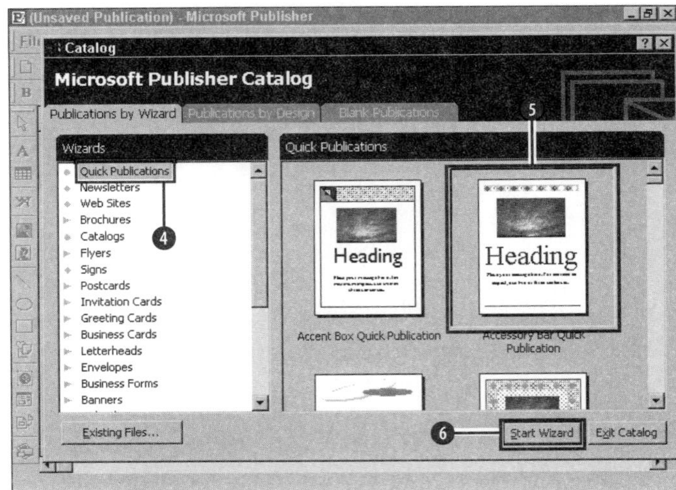

1. *Select Start ➪ Programs ➪ Microsoft Publisher to open Publisher.*
2. *In Windows 98, Publisher may not appear immediately. Scroll through the Programs list with these arrows until it appears.*
3. *Alternatively, single- or double-click the Publisher icon on the desktop.*
4. *The Microsoft Publisher Catalog appears when Publisher opens. Select Quick Publications.*
5. *Click a publication style to select it.*
6. *Click the Start Wizard button. If you are asked for your personal information, cancel this for now.*

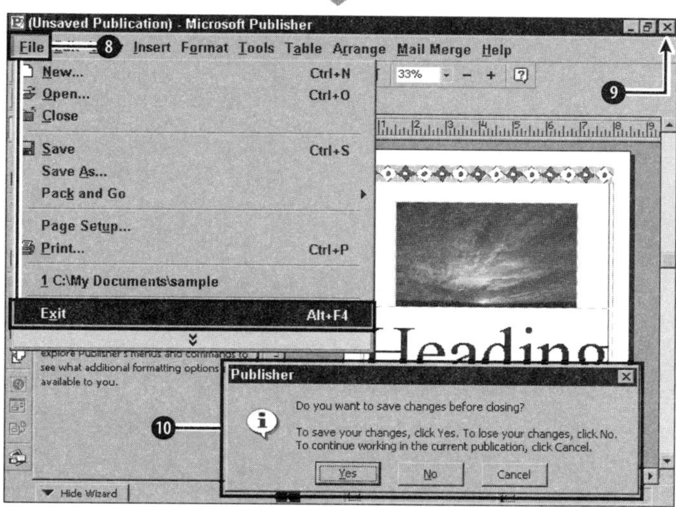

❼ *Click Finish. The wizard creates a Quick Publication in the selected style.*

❽ *To close Publisher, Click File ➪ Exit.*

❾ *You may also close Publisher by clicking the Close (x) icon.*

❿ *If you have made any changes to your document that have not been saved, Publisher gives you a chance to save them before closing.*

TAKE NOTE

MONITORING YOUR SYSTEM RESOURCES

As you become more at ease working with several programs open at once, it's possible to put a strain on your system's resources causing your programs to run more slowly. The System Resource Monitor places an icon in the lower-right corner of your screen that warns you if your system is in danger of becoming overloaded. Place it there by selecting Start ➪ Programs ➪ Accessories ➪ System Tools ➪ Resource Meter.

SWITCHING BETWEEN OPEN PROGRAMS

When you have more than one program open in Windows, you can switch between them by holding the Alt key down and pressing the Tab key. Or, you can simply click the button in the taskbar to bring that program to the forefront.

FIND IT ONLINE

Windows 98 users can increase performance by converting to FAT32. Read about it at **http://www.microsoft.com/windows98/**.

Using Menus

If you are familiar with the other programs in the Microsoft Office suite, you are probably already comfortable with using *menus*. If this is your first experience with them, you will be delighted with the ease of use that menus offer.

Microsoft Publisher is a powerful, multifaceted program that contains a wide variety of tools and functions ready for your use. Such a multiplicity of choices could easily be daunting, but Microsoft has carefully grouped and arranged all of these tools in a logical fashion so that the tools you want to use can easily be found and put into action. Every action that you might want to take within Publisher can be found from a menu. Menus present you with a list of options from which you choose with a simple mouse click. You open a menu to see its options by clicking the menu name on the menu bar, at the top of your screen. Some menu options take you to submenus with more related options. You can recognize these because they are followed by a right-pointing arrow. Other menu options may take you to a dialog box, in which you can make choices by checking off options, clicking "radio buttons," or typing into text boxes. Such menu options can be recognized because they are followed by an ellipsis (. . .).

The best way to learn about the power and facility of Microsoft Publisher is to begin exploring the menus, following where they lead and thinking about what you might do with the capabilities you discover. The most important thing to remember is this: in your explorations you can't do anything wrong, break anything, or cause any damage to your computer or your files. The very worst you might do is accidentally erase the file you're working on. As a matter of fact, while you're exploring Publisher, why not have a "play" publication open to experiment with? All experimental changes you

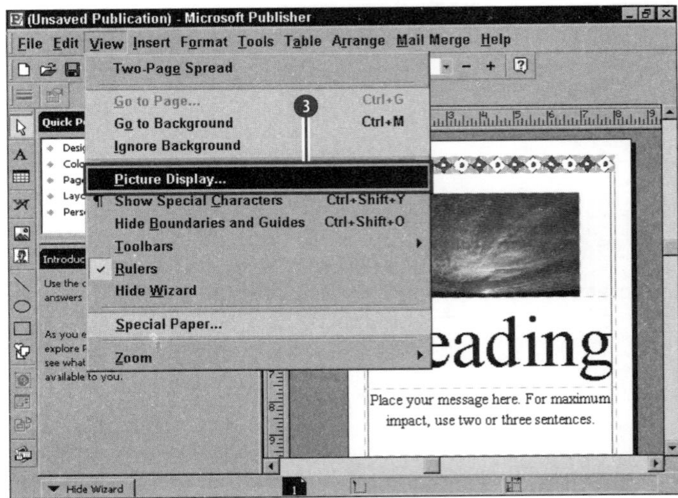

1. Click a menu name on the main menu bar to see the most commonly used options.
2. Click here or hover the cursor to see the rest of the menu options.

▶ Click anywhere outside of the menu to close it without making a selection.

3. This menu option, followed by an ellipsis, leads to a dialog box.

CROSS-REFERENCE

If you have difficulty understanding anything in the menus, check out the Help files, explained later in the chapter.

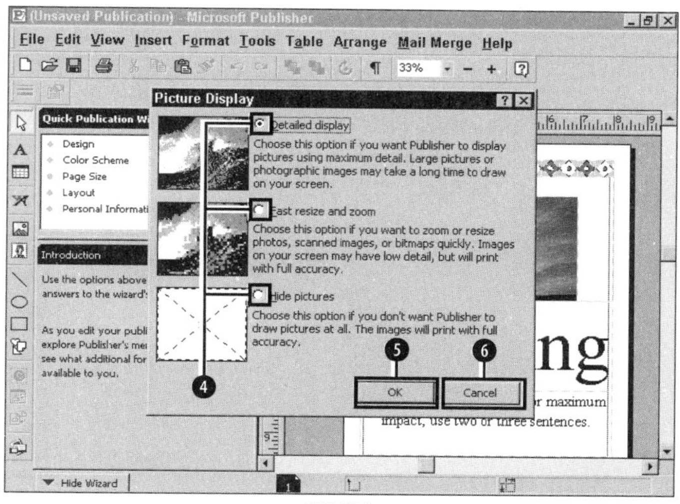

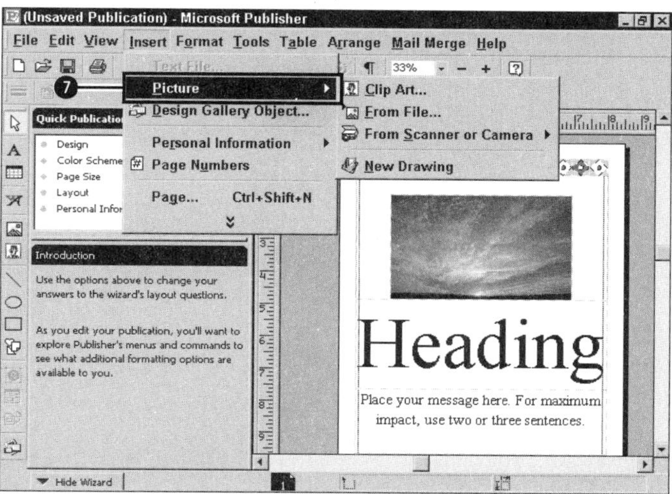

❹ *Select one of these radio buttons to change the way pictures are displayed in your publication while you work.*

❺ *Click OK to apply your selection.*

❻ *Click Cancel to close the dialog box without making any changes.*

❼ *This menu option leads to a submenu.*

▶ *Notice that the submenu has options that lead to further dialog boxes or submenus.*

can make can be undone. Trust me on this one. Then take some time to explore, play, and have fun with the vast capabilities at your fingertips.

TAKE NOTE

EXPLORING MENUS WITHOUT MAKING CHANGES

If you open a menu to view its contents, you can close it without taking any action by hitting Esc on your keyboard or by clicking away from the menu with your mouse.

UNDOING CHANGES TO YOUR PUBLICATION

If you make a change in your document you don't want to keep, you can immediately undo it by hitting Ctrl+Z or clicking the Undo icon on the standard toolbar.

FIND IT ONLINE

For a complete lineup of the Office 2000 products, go to **www.microsoft.com/office/**.

Using Context Menus

While you are using Microsoft Publisher, the program keeps track of what you are doing and where your mouse is on the screen. By doing so, it can offer you menus appropriate to what you are working on at any moment. Click the right mouse button on any object and a *context menu* appears, giving you information about the object or presenting options to do the most common tasks related to that kind of object.

As you work with objects in your publications, such as pictures or text frames, you will frequently use the Cut, Copy, and Paste tools. Occasionally you will delete extraneous objects. Often, you will want to change the appearance of an object in some way, and perhaps change it back if you don't like what you see. You may want to zoom in on the details of an object, or zoom out to see an entire page in perspective. Or you may simply have a question about an object: what are the possibilities for using or changing it in some way? All of these capabilities are presented in context menus, only a mouse right-click away. Using the options available on the context menus is quicker and easier than finding the same options on the menus at the top of your screen. They save you mouse movement, mouse clicks, and most importantly, time. When you develop a facility with context menus, you will find that your work goes much more smoothly and quickly.

You may also right-click the workspace, the toolbars, or the title bar at the top of your screen to see context menus associated with those items. Everything on your screen has some meaning, and context menus give you the immediate options to work with or find out more about each object on your screen.

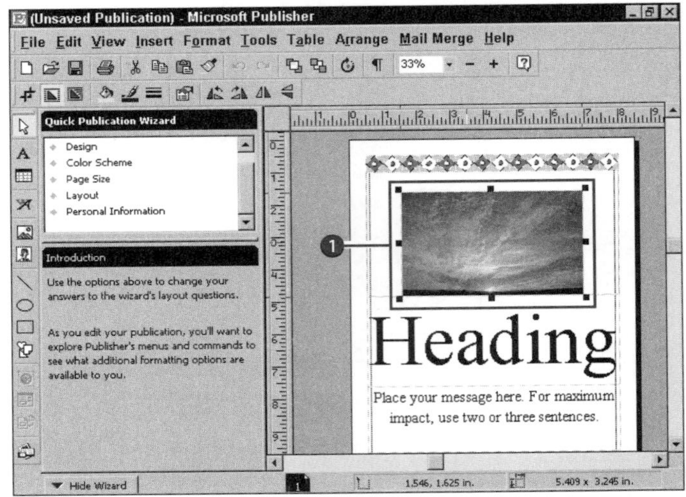

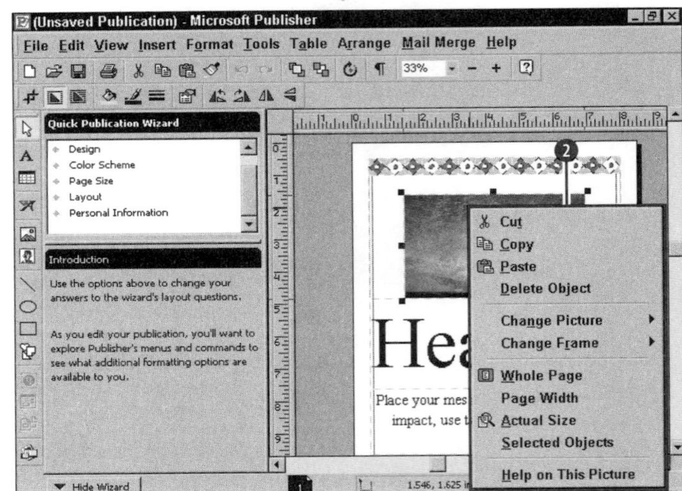

1. Click anywhere within a picture to select it.
2. Right-click within the selected picture to see a Picture context menu.

▶ Hit Esc on your keyboard or left-click outside the menu to close the menu.

CROSS-REFERENCE

See the next section, "Using Toolbars," to learn how menus and toolbars work together.

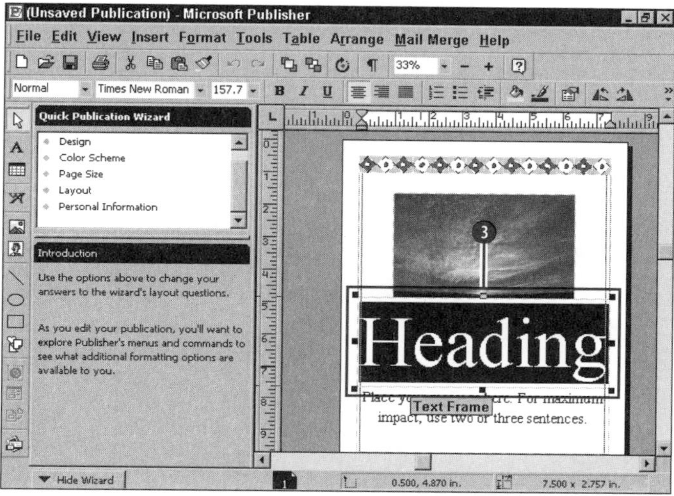

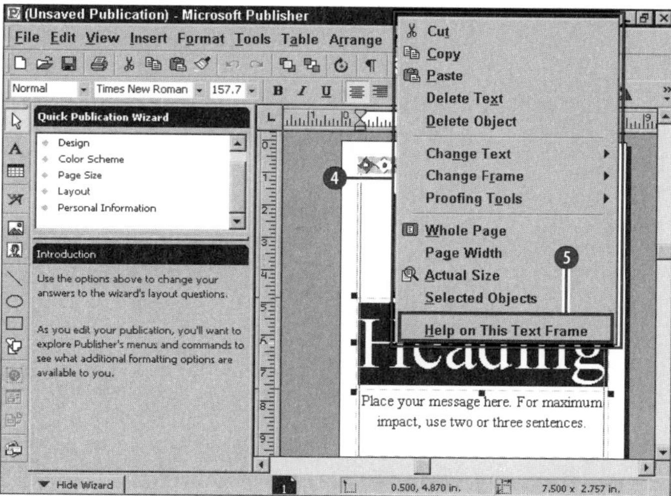

3. *Click within a text frame to select it.*
4. *Right-click within the selected text frame to see a Text context menu. Notice the difference in options.*
5. *Context menus always offer this Help option. Click here to learn more about what you can do with text frames.*

The context menus on the tool bars enable you to turn on or turn off the standard and the formatting toolbars. This leaves room for you to see more of your publication at one time, knowing that you can quickly and easily put the toolbars back into place.

TAKE NOTE

USING HELP IN CONTEXT

The Help option in context menus is particularly useful, because it enables you to explore the help topics that are focused specifically on what you are doing at the moment. You may browse as deeply into a topic as you would like, by clicking hypertext links, yet return directly to your work with a single mouse click, using the Close button in the upper-right corner of your screen, to close the Help screen.

FIND IT ONLINE

You have many mouse alternatives. Explore them at **http://www.synapseadaptive.com/pointing.htm.**

Using Toolbars

I once visited a friend who was building an airplane in a shop behind his house. His shop was clean and organized, and beneath his workbench was a toolbox filled with very specialized tools. Yet on a tool-board above his workbench, neatly arranged in rows, hung all of the tools that he used most frequently. Having them readily at hand, he told me, he was able to get his work done more quickly without having to search through his toolbox each time he did a common task.

Microsoft Publisher, like all of the other programs in the Microsoft Office suite, is organized the same way. At the top of your screen, just below the menu bar, is the *standard toolbar*. Each tool on the toolbar can be reached by going through menus, but the most commonly used tools are represented by icons, so you can always see where they are. A single click activates each one.

The standard toolbar contains common tools grouped by function. For example, the three tools on the far left are used to create a new document, open an existing document, or save the document you are working on. The Print icon is next, followed by a group of tools used to cut, copy, paste, and transfer format characteristics from one object to another. Next are two very important tools: the two curving arrows — Undo and Redo. Click the Undo icon to immediately undo the changes you have just made. The Redo icon puts those changes back.

Explore the other icons on your toolbars. Hold the mouse pointer over each and a *tool tip* appears telling you its function. Click the icon and see what it does. If you don't like what it just did, click the Undo icon (right-curving arrow) to put things back the way they were.

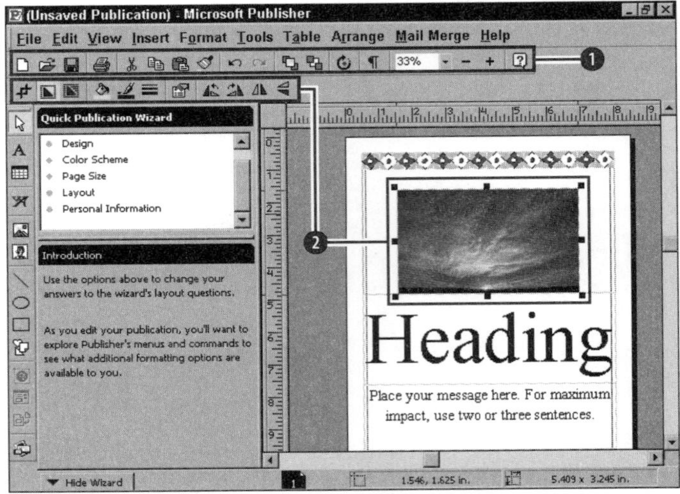

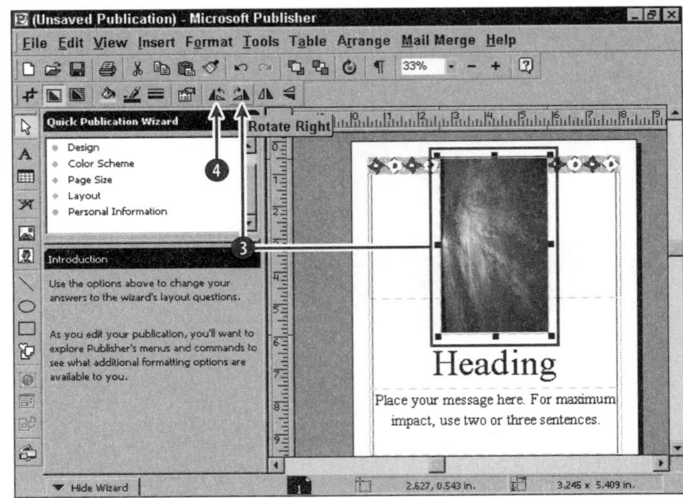

1. *The standard toolbar resides here.*
2. *Click a picture to select it and the picture formatting toolbar appears beneath the standard toolbar.*
3. *Click the Rotate Right icon to rotate the picture 90 degrees to the right.*
4. *Click the Rotate Left icon to return the picture to its original position.*

CROSS-REFERENCE

Learn more about printing your publication in Chapter 5.

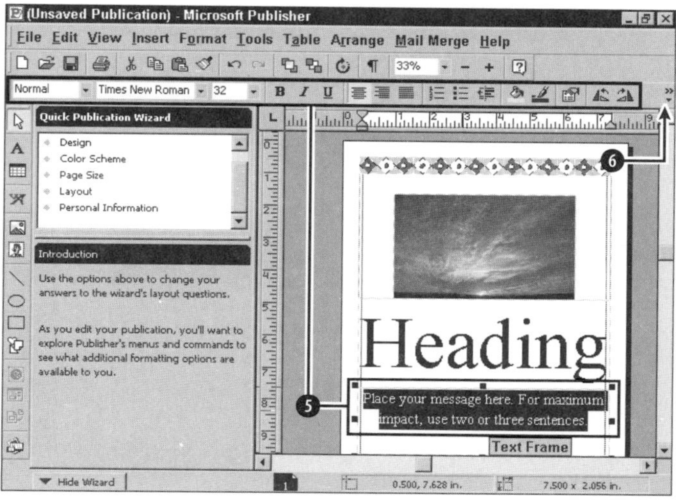

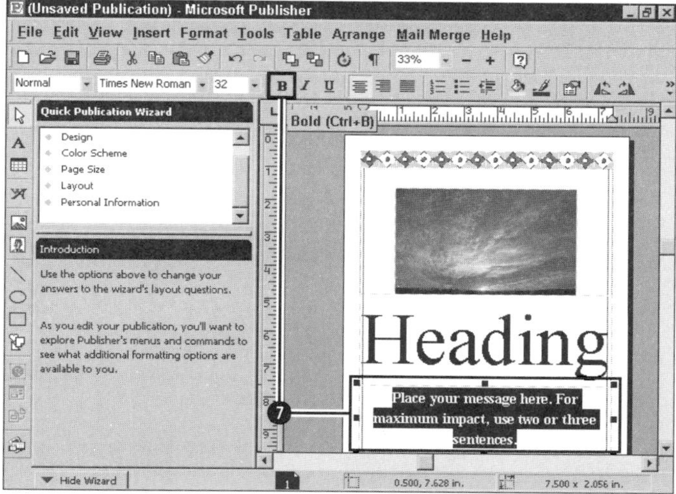

5. *Click a text frame to select it and the text formatting toolbar appears below the standard toolbar.*

6. *Click here to see more text formatting tools.*

7. *Click the Bold tool to bold the selected text.*

▶ *Click the Bold tool again to remove the bold formatting.*

On the left side of your screen is the *objects toolbar.* Each icon places a specific type of object into your publication, such as text or picture frames, WordArt, clip art, drawn objects, and so on.

Certain formatting toolbars appear underneath the standard toolbar only when they are needed. For example, the first two figures on the next page show the *picture formatting toolbar* and how to use it.

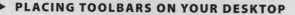

TAKE NOTE

PLACING TOOLBARS ON YOUR DESKTOP

To place toolbars onto your desktop select View ➪ Toolbars. The submenu that appears shows you the toolbars that are available. Place checkmarks by clicking with your mouse on toolbars you would like to see; click to remove checkmarks by toolbars you want to hide.

FIND IT ONLINE

Take a look at all kinds of tools at **http://ourworld.compuserve.com/homepages/faullin/**.

Getting Help While You Work

While you are learning to use Microsoft Publisher, it's good to know that you can easily explore all of the menus and options and discover what they do. But once you get down to business and start putting together a publication, you will probably find yourself with some very specific questions. You might need to know right away how to insert a pull quote into a column of text, how to wrap text around your artwork, or how to make an object in the foreground transparent so the print in the background can show through. When you're using a program with as much capability as Microsoft Publisher, it's expected that you're going to have some questions from time to time, even after you have become quite accomplished at using the program. The software designers at Microsoft have done a good job of anticipating that need, and have built into Microsoft Publisher, and the rest of the Microsoft Office suite, an extensive and thorough Help system. For almost any question you can ask, somewhere in the Help system you can find an answer.

The Help system has been tailored to be user-friendly; it expects you to ask your questions in plain English. If you want information on a specific word, the Help system also enables you to do a keyword search, and returns every topic that contains your keyword. You can also browse the contents of the Help system as a hypertext document. Help acts like a Web browser. When you click an underlined word or phrase, that topic comes up, and the arrows in the upper-left corner enable you to page back and forth between the topics you've read.

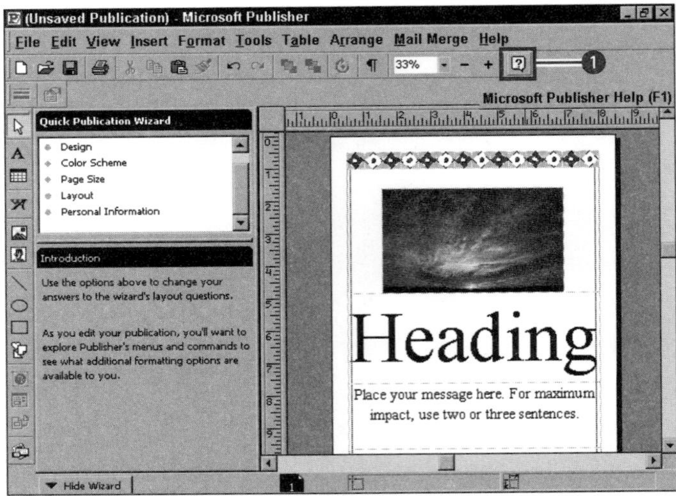

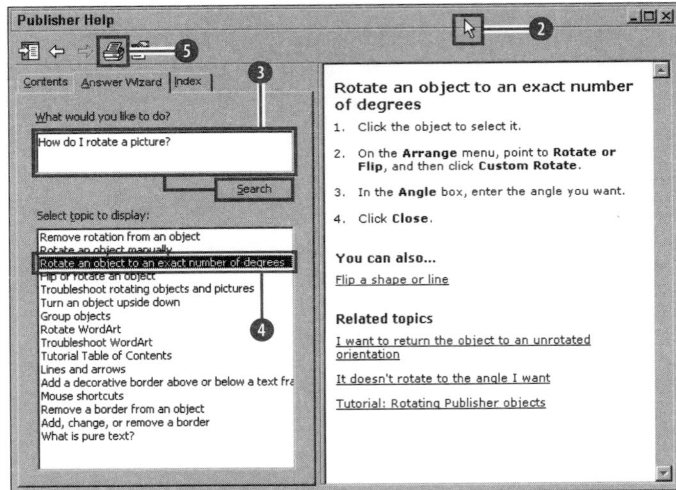

1. *Click the Help icon to open Publisher Help.*
   - *Alternatively, hit F1 on your keyboard to open Help.*
2. *Double-clicking the title bar expands the Help window to full screen.*
3. *Type your question into the Answer Wizard and select Search.*
4. *From the results of your search, select a topic to display.*
5. *Click here to print the topic.*

CROSS-REFERENCE

Learn about the friendlier, over-the-shoulder helper known as the Office Assistant in the next section.

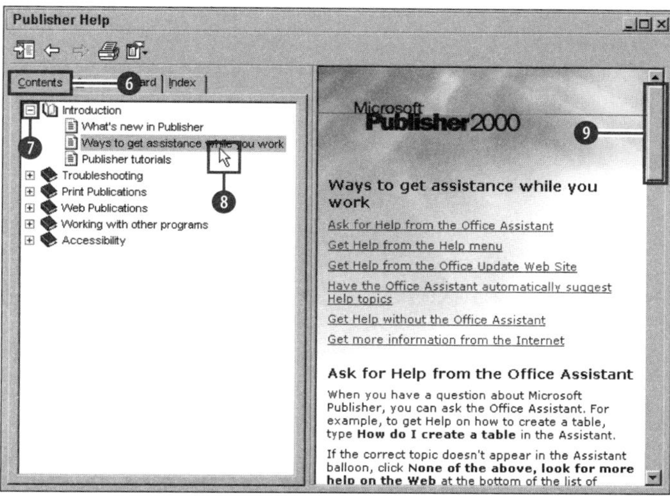

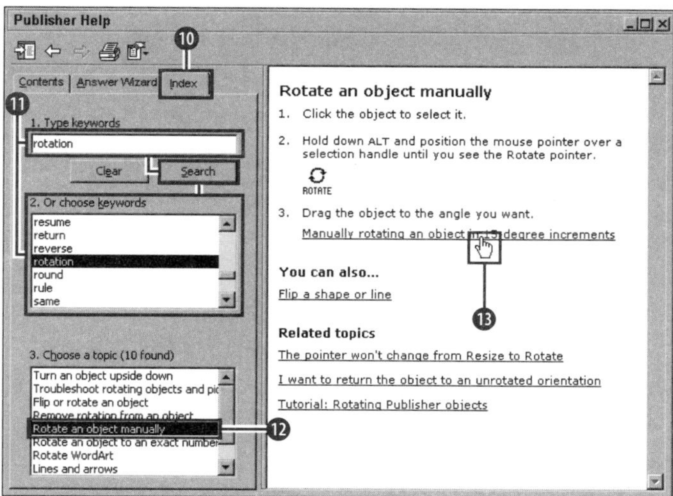

6 *Click the Contents tab.*

7 *Click the plus sign (+) in front of a book to open it. Click the minus sign (-) to close it.*

8 *Select a chapter to read it.*

9 *Click and drag this scroll bar to view the rest of the document.*

▶ *Or, click the scroll bar arrows to move down the screen more slowly.*

10 *Click the Index tab.*

11 *Type in a keyword or choose a keyword from this list, and click Search.*

12 *Choose a topic from the results of your search.*

13 *Click an underlined topic to learn more.*

TAKE NOTE

LETTING HELP GUIDE YOU THROUGH YOUR WORK

You can keep Help open on one half of your screen while you work on your publication in the other half. Click the Show/Hide icon in the top-left corner of the Help screen to see your publication on the left of your screen. To adjust the size of the Help screen, place the mouse on the bar between the Help screen and Publisher until the pointer becomes a double arrow. Click and drag the bar to size the Help screen.

PRINTING HELP TOPICS

If you want hard copy of a Help topic as a reference while you work, click the Print icon in the upper left of the Help screen. The dialog box that comes up enables you to print all or part of the topic you are reading.

FIND IT ONLINE

Get help online from other users by subscribing to the Microsoft Publisher Tips newsgroup at http://www.tipworld.com.

Getting Help from the Office Assistant

This may be hard to believe, but all of the vast resources of the Publisher Help system are available to that silly little paper clip that hangs out on your computer screen. He's Clippy, the Office Assistant, and his job is to keep an eye on what you're doing, guess when you might be having a problem, and offer tips on the best ways to do things. If you have a question, he can answer it. If he starts to get in your way, he'll politely move somewhere else on the screen. He's just that kind of guy — thoughtful, helpful, unobtrusive.

He also has another job, perhaps his most important one. He's helpful, but he's also there to amuse you, and to remind you to lighten up! That's why he occasionally goes into spontaneous antics, scratches his head, or just falls asleep while you work away at your project. Here's a test: right-click the Office Assistant, and from the context menu that appears, select Animate! Watch what happens. Then do it a few more times. If you don't at least get a good chuckle, it may be time for you to take a short break and think for a few moments of the fun things in life.

On the other hand, if the frenetic paper clip is just a bit too frisky for you, fire him and get another Office Assistant. (He won't mind. He's just that kind of guy.) Seven more assistants are available on your computer, and even more out on the Internet, all with different personalities. Chances are very good you'll find an Assistant to suit your own temperament.

The first two figures on the next page show how to begin using the Office Assistant, and how to send him off on a search for information. The third figure shows how the results of your search tie into the Publisher Help system. The last figure shows how to change some options, and how to turn off the Office Assistant so that you can use the Publisher Help system.

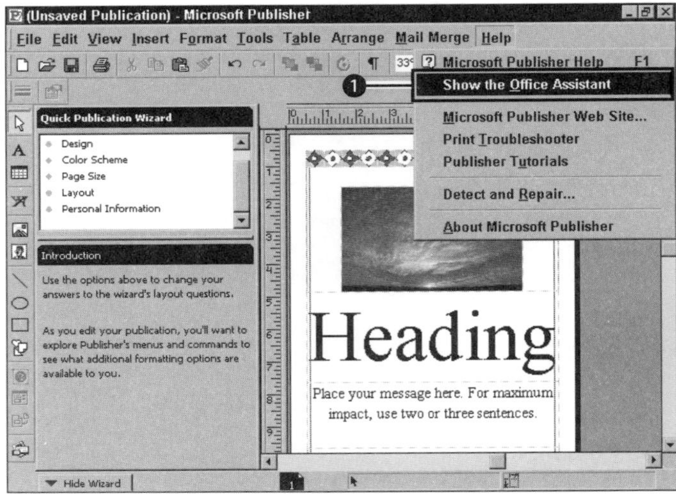

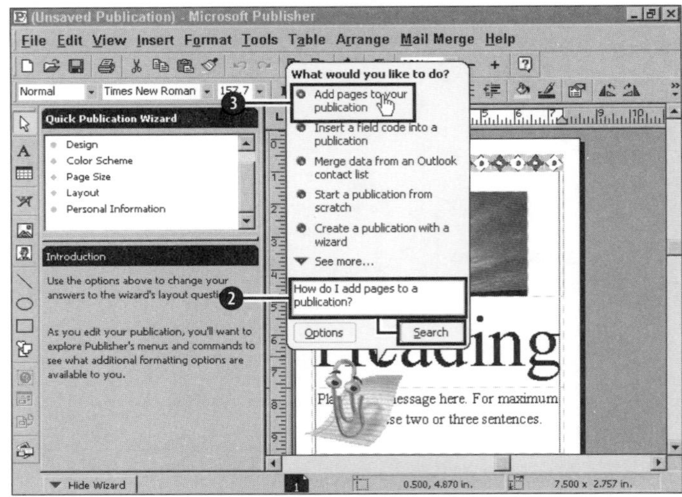

1. *Choose Show the Office Assistant on the Help menu.*
2. *Type your question here and click Search.*
3. *Select a topic results from your search.*

CROSS-REFERENCE

Learn more about the Publisher Help system in "Getting Help While You Work," earlier in this chapter.

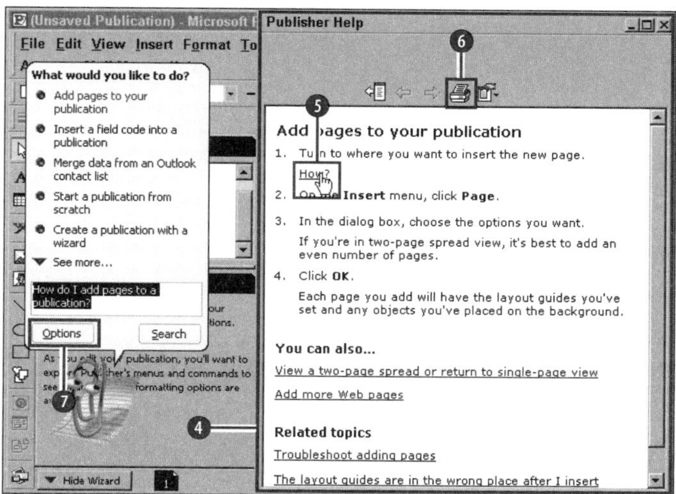

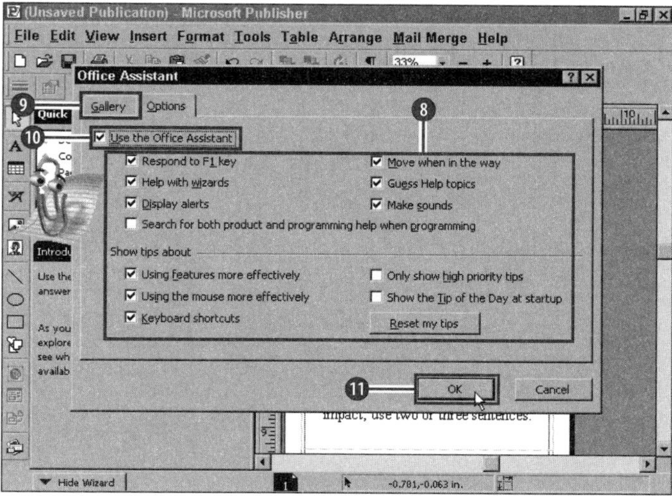

4 *Read the topic you selected.*

5 *Click an underlined topic to learn more.*

6 *Click here to print the topic.*

7 *Click Options to customize the Office Assistant.*

8 *Check or uncheck any of these options to customize how the Office Assistant responds.*

9 *Select the Gallery to choose a new animated Office Assistant.*

10 *Remove this checkmark to enable Microsoft Publisher Help instead of the Office Assistant.*

11 *Click OK to accept your choices.*

TAKE NOTE

HIDING THE OFFICE ASSISTANT

To make the Office Assistant go away, right-click the Assistant and select Hide. To bring the Office Assistant back, click the Help icon or press F1.

GETTING A NEW OFFICE ASSISTANT

Right-click the Assistant and select Choose Assistant. In the Gallery that appears, click Next, and a new Office Assistant introduces himself. Click Next again, until you have met all the Assistants. Click Next or Back to get to the Assistant of your choice, and then click OK to put him to work.

FIND IT ONLINE

Find more Office Assistants, which you can download and install, at http://officeupdate.microsoft.com/index.htm#downloads.

Getting Help Online

The Microsoft Publisher Help system, as you have learned by now, is quite complete. But occasionally you will have questions that can't be answered fully in Help. Access to the Internet makes the full resources of Microsoft's Publisher Web site available to you. There, you can get personal support from Microsoft personnel or communicate with Microsoft on other matters. You can learn about and obtain up-to-the-minute product upgrades, and download useful utilities to enhance your version of Microsoft Publisher. The Microsoft Web site is extensive, but it also contains a search engine to help you find whatever you need with ease.

Learning anything is more fun and effective if you can share the experience with someone else. If you have access to the Internet, you have access to an entire world of others, with a wide range of experience, learning to master Microsoft Publisher just as you are. The Internet gives you an opportunity to join a number of communities where you can both get help and give it to others. There is truth to the aphorism, "to learn something well, teach it to others." As you learn useful tricks with Publisher, sharing what you have learned cements the lesson in your own mind. Soon you will no longer be a beginner, but there will always be beginners who can learn from you while you advance your own skills. The Microsoft Web site hosts a wide range of user groups focused on various products, including Publisher. Be sure to visit the user groups that interest you to find how you can both help and learn at the same time.

The first two screens on the next page show you how to access the Microsoft Publisher Web site from the Help menu. When you get there, be sure to investigate all that's available to you. The second two figures show you how to download the free utilities available to help you get more out of Microsoft Publisher.

CROSS-REFERENCE

Learn how to put up your own helpful Web site in Part V of this book.

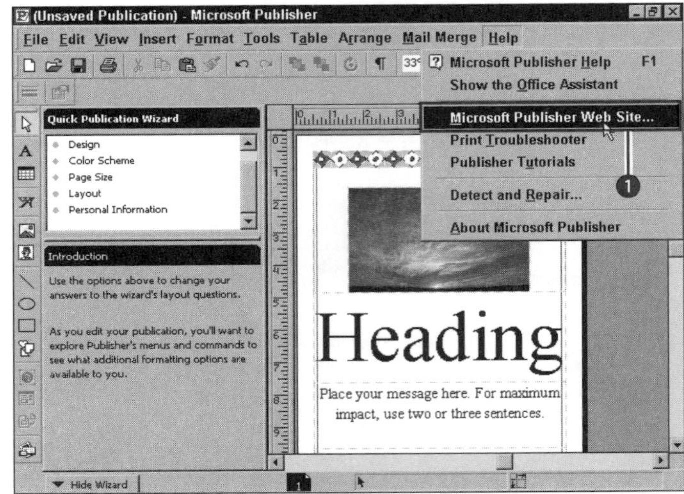

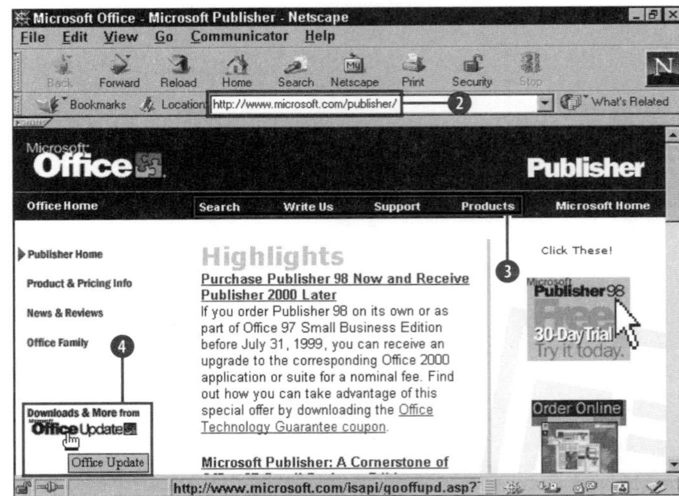

1. *Choose Microsoft Publisher Web Site on the Help menu.*
2. *This is the Microsoft Publisher home page.*
3. *Choose any of these options to search the entire Web site, write to Microsoft, ask for support online, or learn about new products.*
4. *Click Office Update to learn about product upgrades and download free Publisher utilities.*

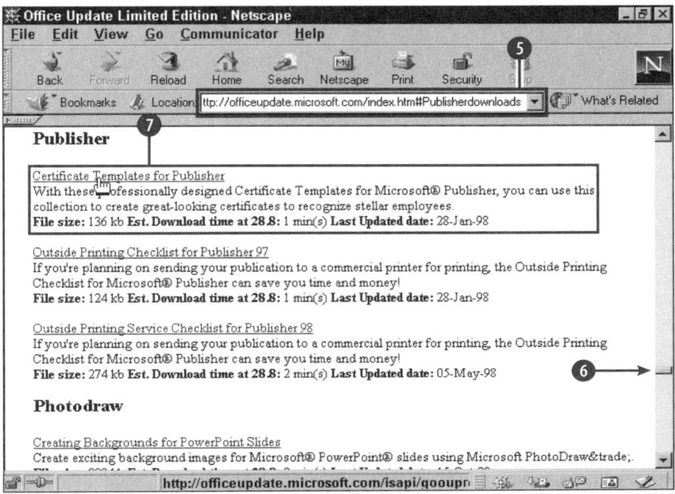

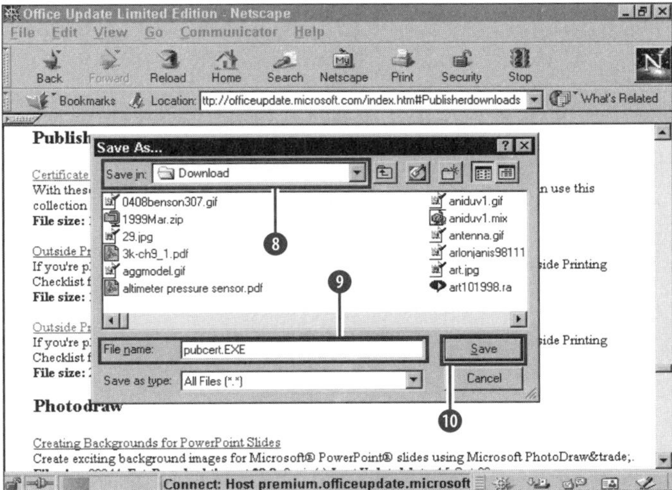

5 *This is the Office Update page.*

6 *Use this slider to scroll down to the Publisher utilities.*

7 *Select a utility to download.*

8 *Select a folder in which to save the utility.*

9 *Accept the file name that automatically appears.*

10 *Click Save to begin downloading.*

▶ *When downloading is complete, you may install the utility by double-clicking its file name in Windows Explorer.*

TAKE NOTE

GETTING CONNECTED TO THE INTERNET

Publisher uses your Internet dial-up connection and your default browser, such as Internet Explorer or Netscape, to automatically dial and connect to Microsoft's Web site when you choose that option. If you don't yet have an Internet service provider, find one in your area by asking your friends who are online or by looking in the Yellow Pages. When you get an account with an ISP, they will give you all the information you need to connect to the Internet and begin using it right away.

FIND IT ONLINE

Find a list of Microsoft sponsored newsgroups you can join, including one for Microsoft Publisher, at **http://support.microsoft.com/support/news/.**

Personal Workbook

Q&A

1. When you have Publisher and another program open at the same time, what are two ways that you can switch between them?

2. What does it mean when a menu option is followed by an ellipsis (...)? An arrow?

3. If you make a mistake in Publisher, what are two ways of undoing the error?

4. Which mouse button do you click to bring up a context menu?

5. How do you bring up the text formatting toolbar? And the picture formatting toolbar?

6. How do you show the Help screen and Microsoft Publisher on your monitor at the same time?

7. Can you use the Help system if the Office Assistant is in use? How do you turn off the Office Assistant?

8. How do you do a keyword search in the Help system?

ANSWERS: PAGE 347

Understanding Publisher 2000 Basics

EXTRA PRACTICE

1. Install the Resource Meter, open Microsoft Word, and then open Microsoft Publisher. Use Ctrl+Alt to switch between them. Open some other programs. How many programs can you have open before your system resources become low?
2. When you open Publisher, select the Business Cards Wizard instead of the Quick Publications Wizard. Select "Plain Paper" and step through the wizard, clicking Next at each step until the card is created. Select each text box on the card to fill in your personal information.
3. Log on to the Microsoft Publisher Web site and navigate to the newsgroup for Microsoft Publisher for Windows. Read some of the questions other users have asked and the answers they have received.

REAL-WORLD APPLICATIONS

- ✔ You are editing your club's newsletter, and just before deadline you have received photos by e-mail from one member, downloaded a text article from another member's Web page, and have artwork from a third member on a diskette. You have Internet Explorer, Outlook Express, Windows Explorer, and Publisher open at the same time. Use the Windows Systems Resource Monitor to ensure all that programs run smoothly.
- ✔ You are going to a job interview for a desktop publishing position and want to refresh your memory on the terminology used in the printing business. You go to Publisher, click Help, and do a keyword search on "glossary." After reading a number of topics, you have not only refreshed your memory but learned much that was new. You face the interview with confidence and knowledge.

Visual Quiz

How did this travel brochure headline get this way? How did we remove the toolbars at the top of the page?

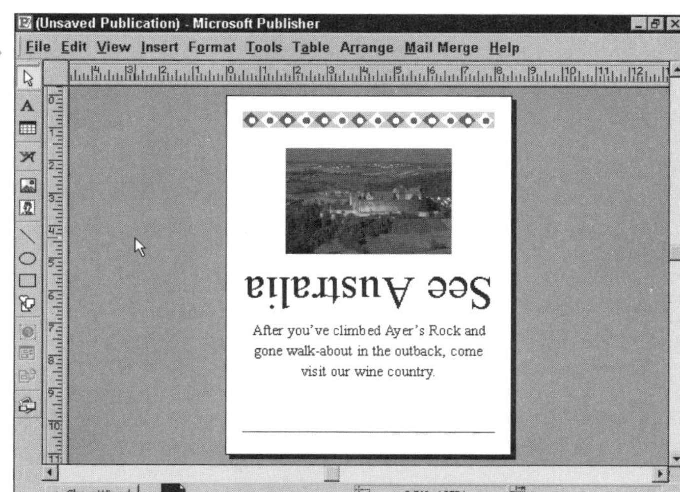

CHAPTER 2

MASTER THESE SKILLS

- Creating a Business Card
- Personalizing Publisher
- Printing Your Business Card
- Creating Your Personal Letterhead
- Printing Personalized Envelopes
- Using Special Paper

Making Your First Publications

You may have heard it said that the most terrifying thing a writer can face is a blank piece of paper. (It's true, by the way.) The folks who designed Publisher would rather that you approach your computer to begin putting your ideas to paper feeling more like a kid in a candy store. That's why, when you start Publisher, you are greeted by the Publisher Catalog Wizards, which lead you step by step through any of a large variety of publications that you might want to create.

You will learn more about the Publisher Catalog and its many options later in this book. Right now, let's just begin to play with its possibilities, do some common tasks, and produce something quite useful at the same time — a business card.

Whether you are going out into the business world, networking with new friends at a seminar, or just meeting someone casually on the street, you only have one chance to make a great first impression. So, it's really useful to have an impressive business card to hand out: a card that conveys your uniqueness, lets people know who you are and what you do, and tells them how to reach you when they need to see you again.

I once met a carpenter who was about to jump off a mountain. He was attaching himself to an arrangement of aluminum tubes and dacron cloth that he was pleased to call a hang-glider. Before he launched, as we were ending our conversation, he handed me his business card. After I watched him circle on the wind, up toward the sun, and disappear over the mountain ridges somewhere toward Lake Tahoe, I was really impressed. "Wow," I thought, "what a great looking business card this guy has!"

In this chapter, you use the Microsoft Publisher Catalog's Publications by Wizard to create some documents you can use to make an excellent first impression, both in person and through the mail. The fun thing about it is discovering how easy it is to do. The exercises in this chapter step you through creating a business card, personalized stationery, and a personalized mailing envelope. You will also learn how to create colorfully designed publications even if you only have a black-and-white printer, such as a laser printer, using colored, preprinted papers from PaperDirect.

Creating a Business Card

Your business card is not only an important part of the first impression you make on someone, it is also a lasting impression that stays on their desk or in their card file, and reminds others of that first meeting. Even when we're feeling lousy, it's an advantage to be able to hand to others a business card that represents the best side of you: the professional and organized you; or the cheerful, colorful, creative you. That business card not only presents you well to others, but sometimes even serves to remind you, yourself, of your own mission — who you are and what you are about.

The elements that make up a good business card are layout and design, color scheme, fonts, and perhaps a logo and a tag line or motto. All of these elements, and the way they combine, provide not only information about you, but a feeling about you as well. Publisher provides you with a wide array of carefully considered card designs to choose from. The wizard lets you choose from a number of coordinated color schemes. When it finishes creating your card, it remains open so you may return to it, to change any of the options you originally chose.

Give some thought to your logo and to your tag line. Your *logo* is an image that represents you to others, so be sure it is one you feel comfortable with. Publisher offers the option to create a logo for you, an option worth exploring. Eventually, you will probably create or scan in the artwork for a more personal logo; the example here shows how to place such a logo onto your card. Your *tag line* is like your mission statement: what is unique about you? What do you have to offer that others may really want?

CROSS-REFERENCE

Learn more about the Microsoft Publisher Catalog and its many options in Chapter 7.

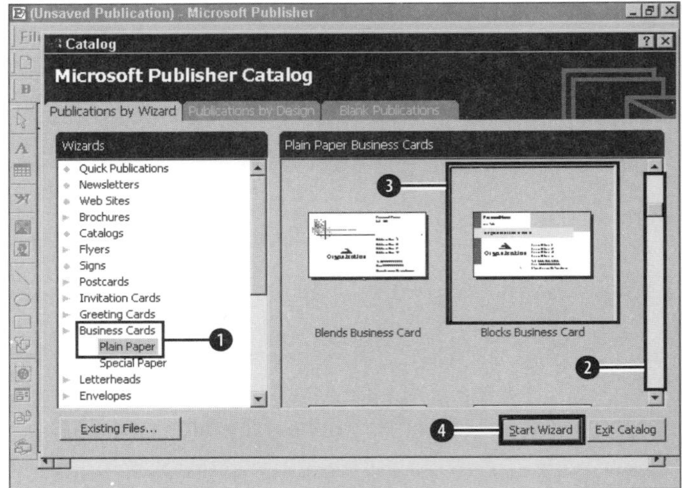

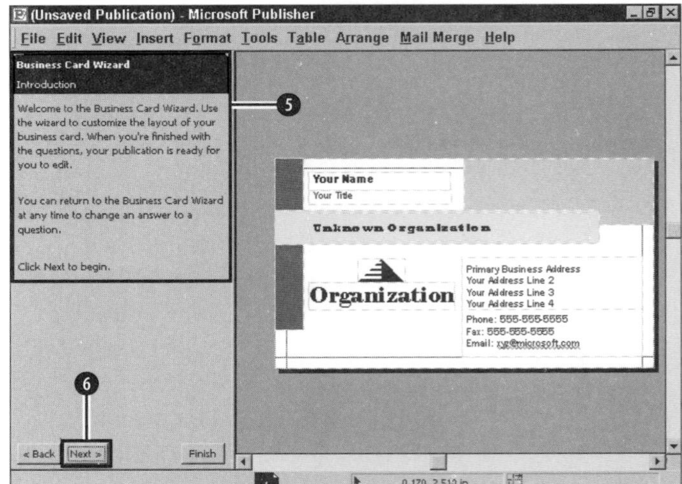

1. *Open Publisher and select Business Cards ⇨ Plain Paper in the Wizards box of Microsoft Publisher Catalog.*
2. *Use this scroll bar to see various designs available to you.*
3. *Select Blocks Business Card.*
4. *Click Start Wizard.*

   If the Personal Information window appears, click Cancel to bypass it for now.
5. *Read the Introduction here.*
6. *Click Next to begin the Wizard.*

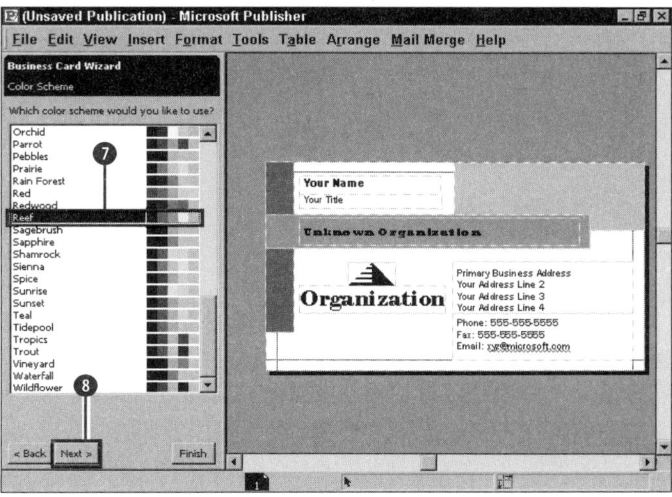

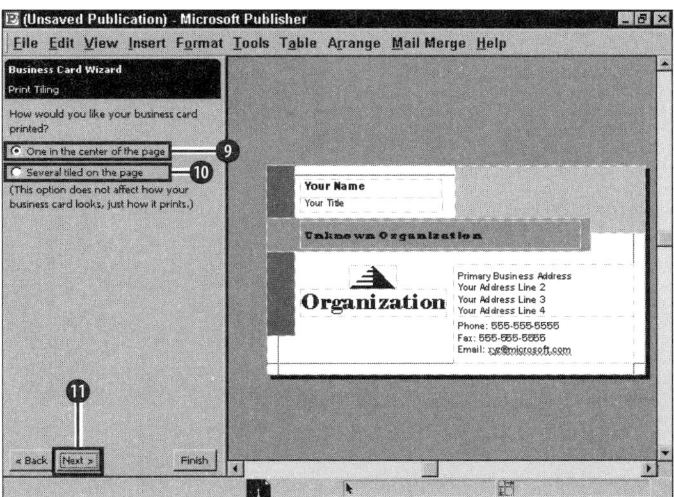

7. *Select a color scheme by clicking its name.*

▶ *Click a number of different color schemes in succession and watch how each changes the appearance and feel of your card.*

8. *Click Next three times. Notice the defaults you accept at each step by doing so.*

9. *In the Print Tiling step, select "One in the center of the page" to print a proof.*

10. *Select "Several tiled on the page" when you are satisfied with your proof and want to print multiple cards on a single page.*

11. *Click Finish to create your card.*

The four figures on the next page step you through the process of creating a business card with the Business Card Wizard. The following task, "Personalizing Publisher," shows you how to add your individual information to your card. Later in this chapter, you will learn how to print your business card.

TAKE NOTE

▶ FINDING THE MICROSOFT PUBLISHER CATALOG

The Catalog appears by default when you start Microsoft Publisher 2000. But if someone has turned off this default setting, you can always open the Catalog by selecting File ➪ New from the main menu bar. To see the Catalog at startup, select Tools ➪ Options, and under the General tab, place a check next to "Use Catalog at startup."

FIND IT ONLINE

Keep your card legible, because it may be added to a database with a scanner. Learn more about this technology at http://www.cardscan.com/.

Personalizing Publisher

You've created a business card, but it is pretty generic. It looks good, but says absolutely nothing about you. It is just the sort of card a secret agent might hand out at a black-tie affair or a cocktail party. At this point you could select each text field in the card and fill in your personal information, one field at a time, but that would be tedious and time-consuming. There is a better way. Tell Microsoft Publisher who you are, and a few things about yourself, your business, or your organization, and Publisher not only remembers all of this information, but inserts it automatically into any future publications you create — wherever you tell it to.

Publisher keeps track of as many as four separate information sets: your Primary Business; your Secondary Business; some Other Organization, such as a club, church or charity; and your Home/Family information. In this exercise, you will learn how to enter all of the relevant information for each data set. Each of these data sets has eight components it keeps track of: your name; your title; the name of your business or organization; your address; your tag line, or motto; your contact information — phone, fax, and e-mail; your graphic logo; and a color scheme of your choosing.

The first two figures on the facing page show you how to use the wizard to enter your personal information into Publisher, which automatically updates that information in your business card. The second two figures show you how to insert a logo into your business card, using either the Logo Creation Wizard or an existing picture file of your own choosing.

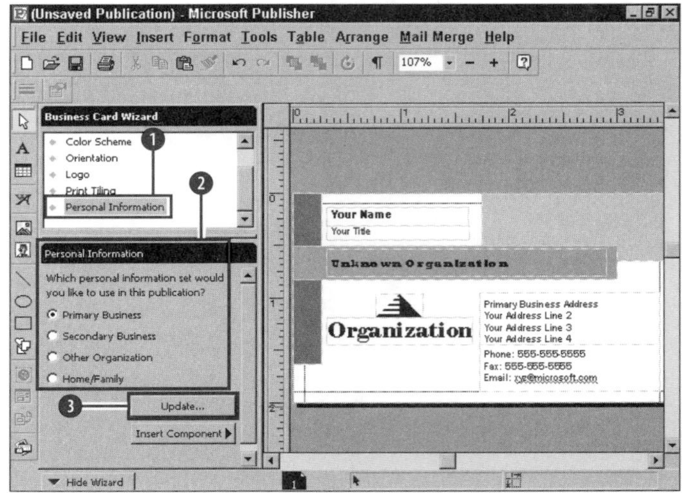

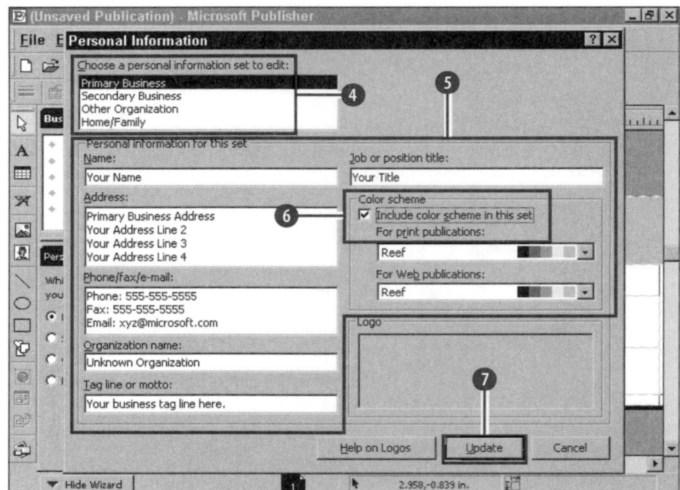

1. *Select Personal Information here.*
2. *Select an information set here to enter personal information, or to update current information previously entered.*
3. *Click Update.*
4. *Select the information set you are editing here.*
5. *Enter your personal information into each of these text boxes. Hit Tab to move between text frames.*
6. *Place a checkmark here to associate a color scheme with this information set.*
7. *Click Update. Your personal information is recorded in Publisher and entered into your business card.*

CROSS-REFERENCE

Learn about moving, sizing, and formatting items of personal information placed into your publications in Chapter 6.

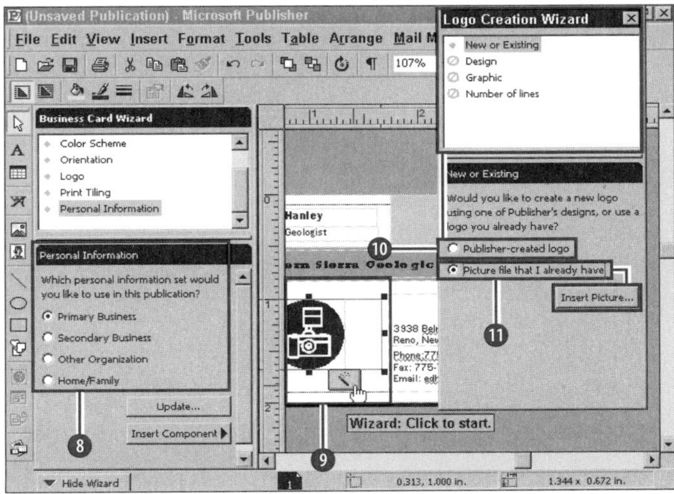

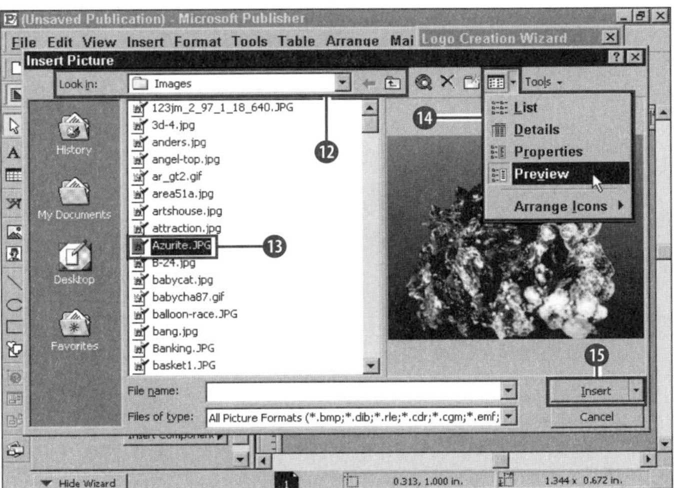

8. *Select another information set here and repeat from Step 2 until all of your personal information is recorded.*
9. *Click anywhere in the logo area, and click the Logo Creation Wizard that appears.*
10. *To let Publisher design your logo, click this button and select from the options.*
11. *To insert your own image, select this button and then click Insert Picture.*
12. *Use these tools to navigate to the folder holding your logo image.*
13. *Select the image's file name here.*
14. *Select Preview under the Views icon to preview your image.*
15. *Click Insert to place the logo onto your card. You may then close the Logo Creation Wizard by clicking its Close icon.*

TAKE NOTE

PLACING PERSONAL INFORMATION INTO A PUBLICATION

When you are working on any publication, the wizard is always there to help. If it is not visible on the left side of the screen, click the Show Wizard button in the lower-left corner to bring it up. Select Personal Information in the wizard's top window, and select one of the four personal information sets in the bottom window. Then, click the Insert Component button and choose from the menu that appears which component you would like to insert. The wizard creates a frame containing that component and places it into your publication.

CHANGING YOUR PERSONAL INFORMATION

You may change any part of your personal information, at any time. Select Personal Information in the Wizard's upper window. Then, select the personal information set you want to update in the lower window and click the Update button.

FIND IT ONLINE

You can find many excellent services online to help you develop a unique logo. Check out, for example, http://eclipse-designs.com/.

Printing Your Business Card

The printed quality of your business card depends on the quality of your computer's printer. A number of inkjet printers that are priced below $200 will print with near-professional results, in black and white or in color. Color laser printers, at reasonable prices, are multiplying upon the scene. Let's face it: you have picked a great time to begin using Publisher 2000, because the printing quality that was once available only at professional copy shops is migrating rapidly onto your own desktop. At least, that is, for small to moderate quantity jobs. When you find yourself needing to make runs of over 500 copies, use a printing professional. You will also be glad that your experience with Publisher 2000 has taught you how to communicate with them in a clear, professional manner.

A standard business card is 2 inches by 3.5 inches, so you can print several cards, as many as ten, on one sheet of paper. Choose the option to print a single card on a sheet if you just want to see a proof. When you are satisfied with your card's printed appearance, choose the option to print multiple copies per sheet.

Your neighborhood copy shop or printer can provide you with an attractive assortment of business card papers from which to choose. Select 80-pound card stock — if your printer can handle it (most can) — to print a card with an impressive feel as well as appearance. Use a good-quality paper cutter to separate your business cards.

Here's a tip: You can pass out different cards to separate groups of friends or associates, and get feedback from them on how they like the design, and the overall effect. When you decide on one card design that you would like to make your standard, take that's card's file to a professional printer and have a large quantity made up.

CROSS-REFERENCE

Learn more about spot color, process color, and using an outside printing service in Chapter 18.

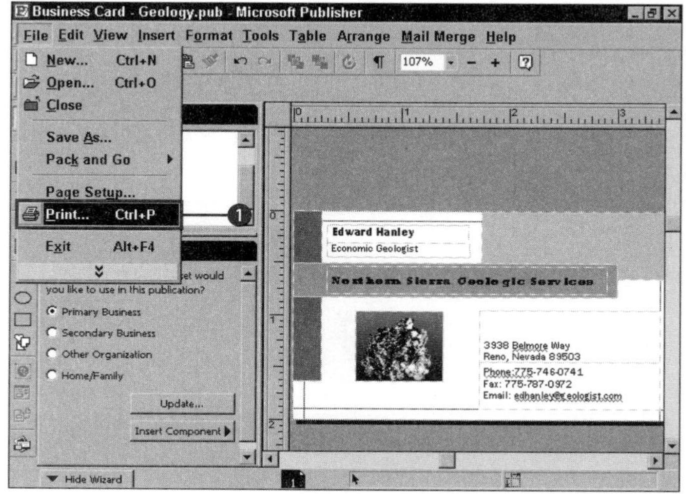

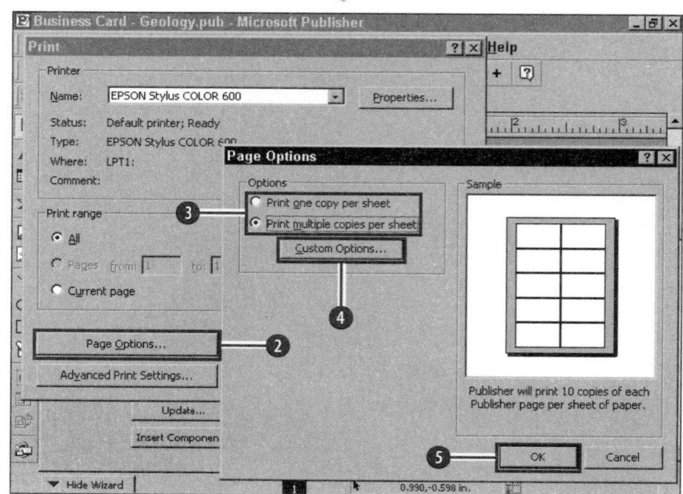

1. Select File ⇨ Print or press Ctrl+P.
2. Click Page Options to see how your cards will be arranged on the page.
3. Select "Print one copy per sheet" to print a single proof. Select "Print multiple copies per sheet" to print ten cards on one page.
4. Select Custom Options to print a different number of cards per page, and specify the space between them.
5. Click OK.

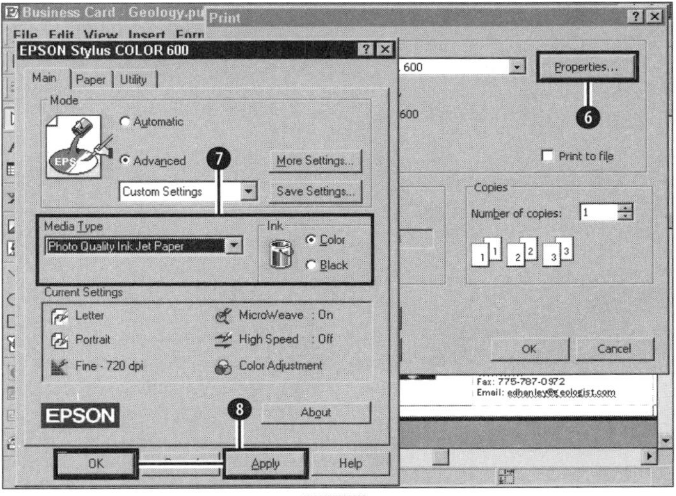

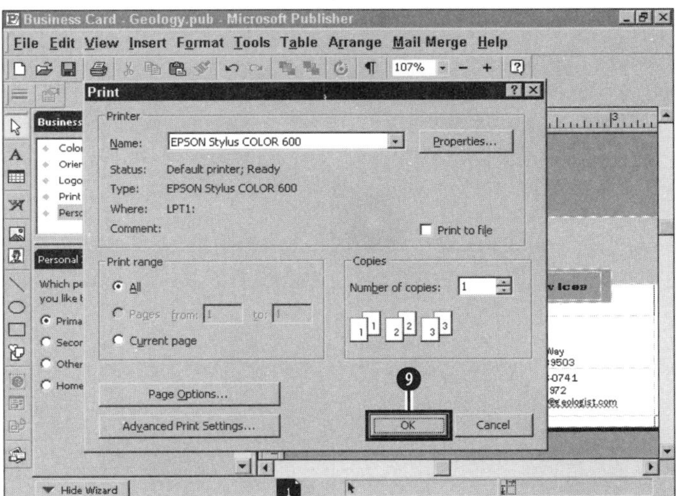

6 *Click the Properties button to set options specific to your printer.*

7 *Pay attention that your printer is set for the type of paper you are using. Decide if you want to print in color or black and white.*

8 *Click Apply. Then click OK.*

9 *Click OK to print your business cards.*

TAKE NOTE

PROFESSIONALLY PRINTED BUSINESS CARDS

If you have a color inkjet printer, you can print very colorful business cards, in millions of colors. You may have noticed, however, that most professionally printed cards use only a few colors. That's because they are printed with *spot color,* which uses only a few selected inks. It is much less expensive than *process color,* which uses cyan, magenta, yellow, and black ink, and requires precise placement of those colors. Consider it the commercial equivalent of what your color printer can do. If you plan to mass produce your business cards, consider using only a few colors and printing them with the spot color process.

FIND IT ONLINE

Get some expert tips on business card design at **http://desktoppub.about.com/msub07.htm?pid=2827&cob=home.**

Creating Your Personal Letterhead

Now that Publisher has your personal information on tap, creating personalized letterhead stationery, using the Publisher Catalog Wizards, is a breeze. Here you create a letterhead that matches your business card from the previous task. In the next task we will let the wizard print an envelope that matches both, giving you a complete, coordinated set of stationery.

Your letterhead, like your business card, makes a statement about you. All of the same design elements — fonts, layout, color and logo — come into play. They combine to create an impact on your correspondents as they open your letters and read your message. The matched styles of business card, letterhead and envelope you are creating in this chapter convey a message of consistency. With practice and experimentation, you can become as creative with the visual impact of your letterheads as you are with the verbal messages of your written word.

Consider, for example, the emotional impact of color. Red represents energy, passion, and impulsivity. On the other hand, green represents calm, firm persistence, and a reliable, comfortable sameness about things. Yellow represents happiness and relaxation, yet it carries a feeling of carefree optimism balanced with a relaxed, focused energy. Blue has a sense of peace and tranquility. Violet mixes red and blue, and suggests a balance between impulsiveness and calm sensitivity, and represents a level of balance and life-acceptance that comes with growth and maturity. Now consider how you might color the tone of your message with the background colors of your letterhead. A green background or border might be appropriate for a letter to a potential financial investor, while a red, yellow, and blue scheme would fit an invitation to your daughter's birthday party.

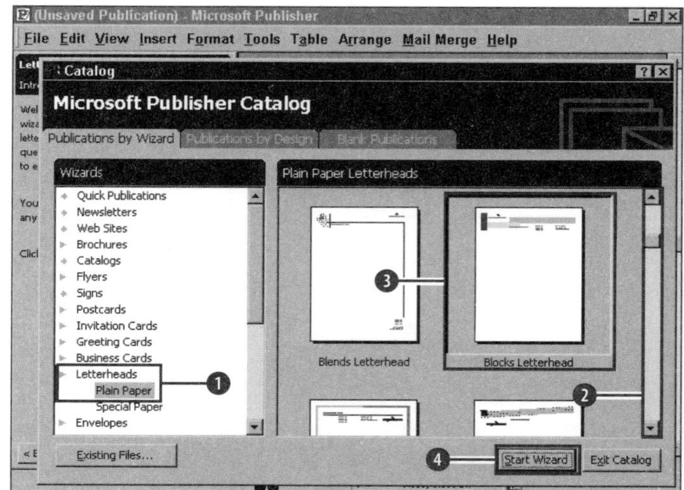

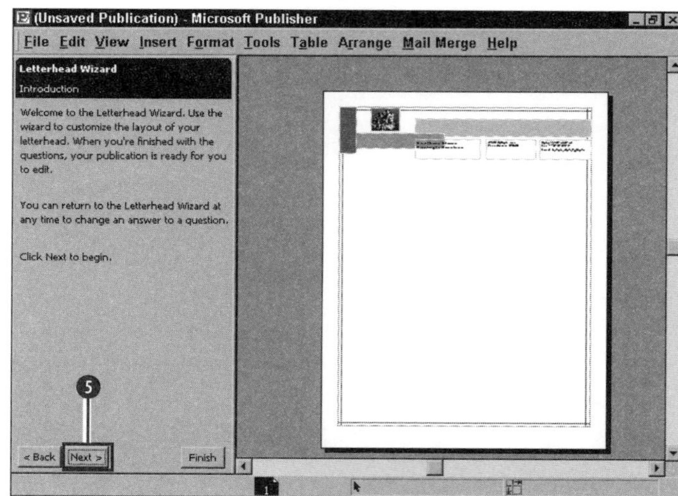

1. *In the Catalog, under Wizards, select Letterheads ⇨ Plain Paper.*
2. *Use this scroll bar to see more design selections.*
3. *Select Blocks Letterhead.*
4. *Click Start Wizard.*
5. *Click Next to begin stepping through the wizard's options.*

▶ *Notice as you proceed that the wizard has remembered all the options you selected when you created your business card.*

CROSS-REFERENCE

Learn the easy way to make consistently coordinated publications in "Using Publications by Design," in Chapter 7.

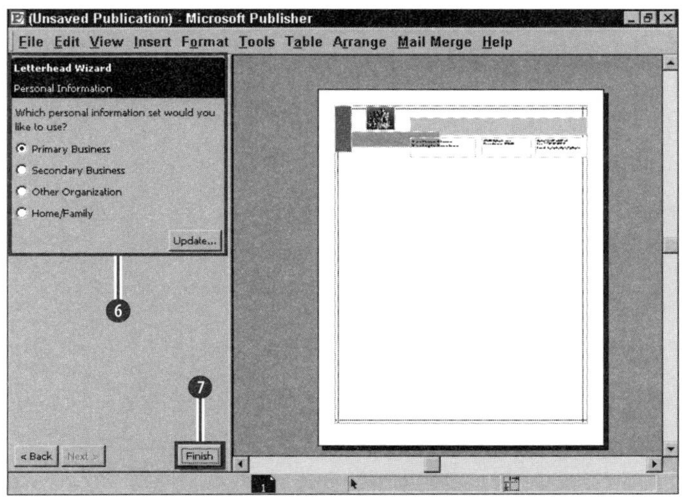

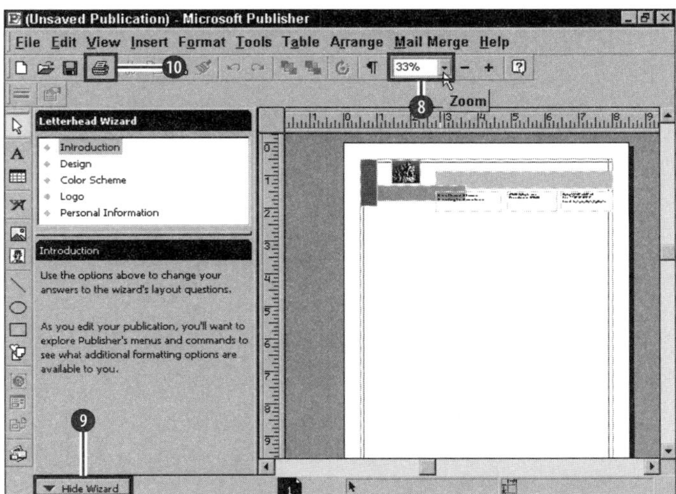

6. *Select the personal information set you would like to appear on your letterhead.*
7. *Click Finish.*
8. *Click the down arrow next to the Zoom text box to select a more readable size, say, 100%.*
9. *Hide the wizard for more viewing room by clicking Hide Wizard.*
10. *Click the Print icon to print your personalized letterhead.*

As you step through the wizard in the following steps, with the Next button, you'll notice a certain consistency, because Publisher has remembered the previous choices that you made while creating your business card.

TAKE NOTE

SAVING YOUR LETTERHEAD

You can save your letterhead in the same way you saved your business card. You may want to save it in the same folder as your business card, in the previous exercise, because it is a design match. Or, you may want to create a separate folder for each type of publication you create.

PRINTING YOUR LETTERHEAD

Select File ➪ Print to open the Print dialog box. In the Copies section of the box, select the number of copies you would like to print and click OK.

FIND IT ONLINE

Get tips on creating and registering an effective name for your business at **http://desktoppub.about.com/library/weekly/aa030199.htm?pid=2827&cob=home.**

Printing Personalized Envelopes

If you're like me, you only open about half the envelopes you receive in the mail. I must admit also to small pangs of guilt as I drop each unopened envelope into the recycling container. I can't help but think of the need that the people who sent me all this mail must have to share some idea or offer with me. But somehow I just don't feel the same need to take the time to read what they have to say. Not unless something on the outside of the envelope really entices me or somehow piques my interest. It comes down to this: in the competition for your correspondents' attention, how do you print up an envelope that "looks interesting" enough to be opened and read? Colorful, well-designed stationery increases the chances your letters will be opened. The good news is that you've already done most of the work toward that goal.

This is the final step in creating your coordinated stationery. You have done most of the work already as you used the Business Card Wizard and the Letterhead Wizard to select a color scheme, create or insert a logo, and personalize Publisher with your contact information. In this exercise you simply enable the Envelope Wizard to use the selections you have already made to create an envelope of the same design.

As you step through the Envelope Wizard, as shown in the next four figures, all you need indicate is the size of the envelope you wish to use. Once the envelope has been created, you must fill in the address before printing the envelope. You may accept the default font and point size, or select from any of Publisher's fonts to further personalize the envelope's appearance.

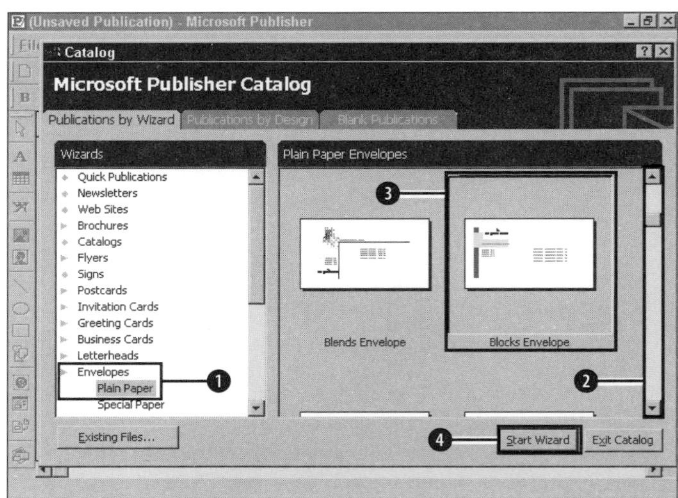

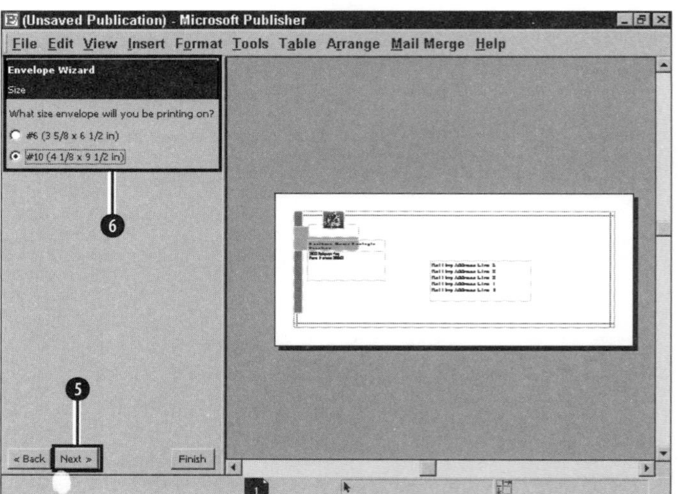

1. *Under the Publications by Wizard tab, select Envelopes ⇨ Plain Paper.*
2. *Use the scroll bar to move down the list.*
3. *Select Blocks Envelope.*
4. *Click Start Wizard.*
5. *Step through the wizard, clicking Next, until you get to the Size option.*
6. *Select the size of your envelope here. We have selected a standard "business" size.*
7. *Click Next, and then Next again.*

CROSS-REFERENCE

Learn how to print customized envelopes and labels of special sizes in "Printing Odd-Sized Publications," in Chapter 5.

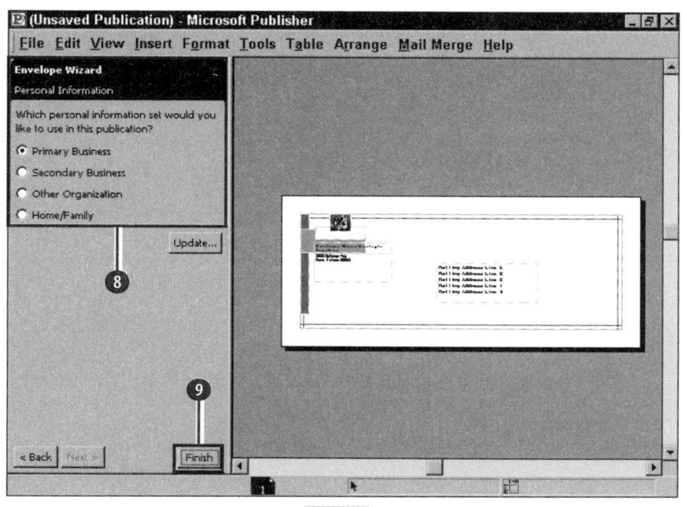

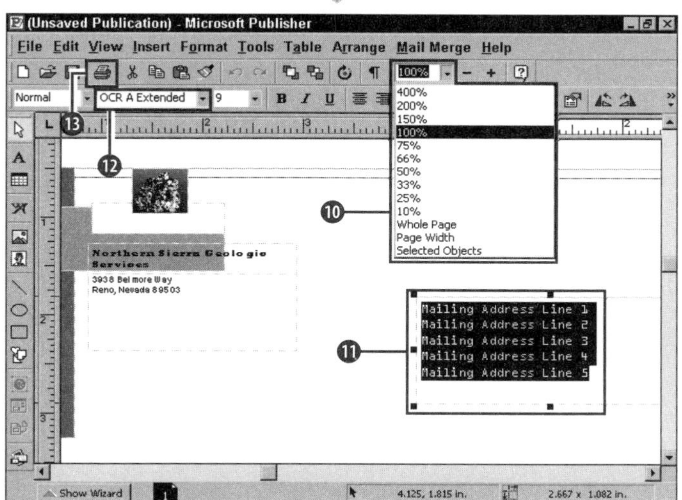

8. *Select the Personal Information set you would like printed on the envelope return address.*
9. *Click Finish.*

▶ *Click the Hide Wizard button in the lower-left corner of the next screen that appears.*

10. *Click the down arrow next to the Zoom window and select an appropriate viewing size.*
11. *Fill in the mailing address.*
12. *Select a font and point size for the mailing address here, if you desire.*
13. *Place an envelope into your printer and click here to print. Be sure to observe the proper orientation of your envelope in the printer.*

TAKE NOTE

OBSERVING ENVELOPE ORIENTATION

The proper way to insert an envelope into your printer is something you have to learn only once. But if you go to a different printer, you may have to learn it all over again. So many different printers, so many different possibilities for feeding envelopes! Here's a trick for discovering how Publisher prints an envelope on any given printer. Place an "X" in pencil in the upper-left corner of a piece of standard paper, and then print your "envelope" on it. Compare the orientation of the printed "envelope" with the way you oriented the paper in the printer. Observe where the printing is relative to your "X", and you can easily see how Publisher will print envelopes on that printer every time.

FIND IT ONLINE

Learn how to make your own special envelopes at **http://www.ghh.com/elf/.**

Using Special Paper

What if you want to print colorful publications, but you can only print in black and white? Laser printers, for example, abound in the workplace. Their reliable, high-speed printing and crisp, professional black output often make them the printer of choice.

The answer is PaperDirect, a company that produces patterned, colored papers, as well as labels and card stock, for practically every kind of publication. Microsoft Publisher has many of PaperDirect's special papers built in, and can display those patterned papers as a background on which to compose your publication. The background itself will not print. You must print onto the paper you would buy from PaperDirect.

There are seven types of special papers in Publisher, which enable you to produce colorfully designed brochures, flyers, business cards, postcards, letterheads, envelopes, and award certificates. The Microsoft Publisher Catalog contains wizards to help you produce each kind of publication with ease. To see these options, open the Catalog by clicking File ➪ New and go down the list of wizards, clicking each one in sequence. Notice that clicking a heading preceded by a gray arrow opens a group of related wizards, which are subcategories of the main heading. Examples of this are the Flyers, Postcards, and Business Cards headings. The subcategories labeled "Special Paper" take you to wizards that use PaperDirect's background. Clicking the Special Paper option lets you review each of the special papers available in that wizard category.

The first two figures on the facing page show you how to produce a business card using Special Paper. The next two figures show you examples of how an award certificate and a trifold brochure would appear when printed on Special Paper from PaperDirect.

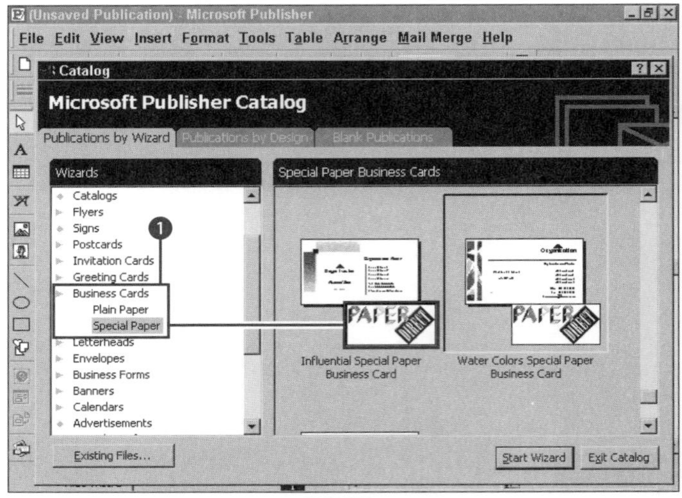

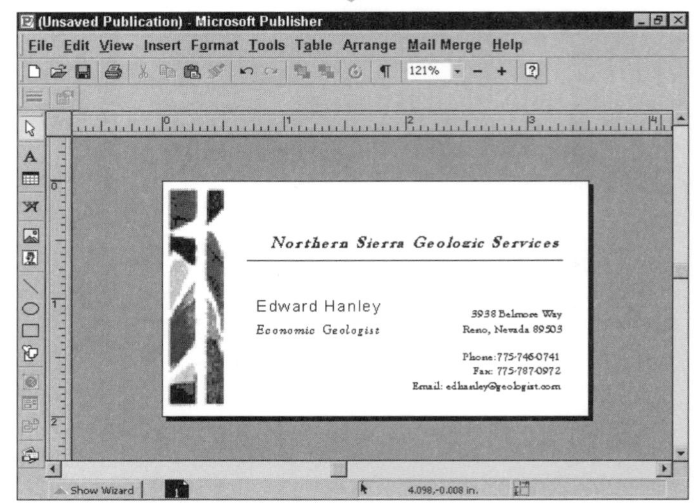

❶ *In the Catalog, select Business Cards ➪ Special Paper. Select a Special Paper and click Start Wizard.*

▶ *Complete your business card just as you did in the first task in this chapter.*

▶ *This business card displays the blend of color along the left side that is preprinted on the Water Colors Special Paper business card stock from PaperDirect.*

CROSS-REFERENCE

Learn another way of making your publications distinctive in "Using Watermarks," in Chapter 12.

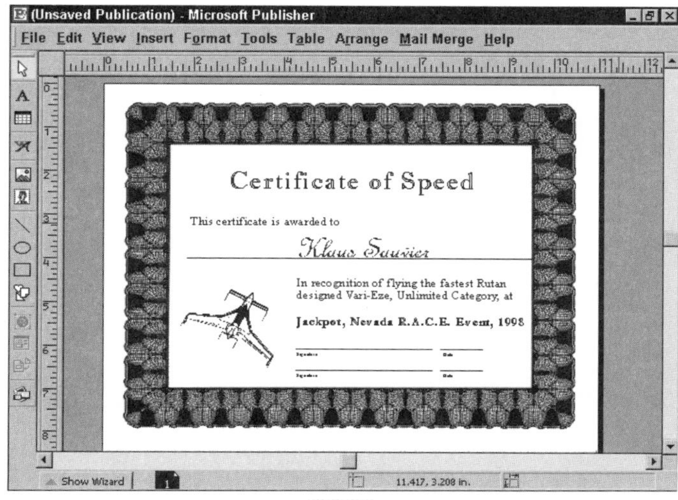

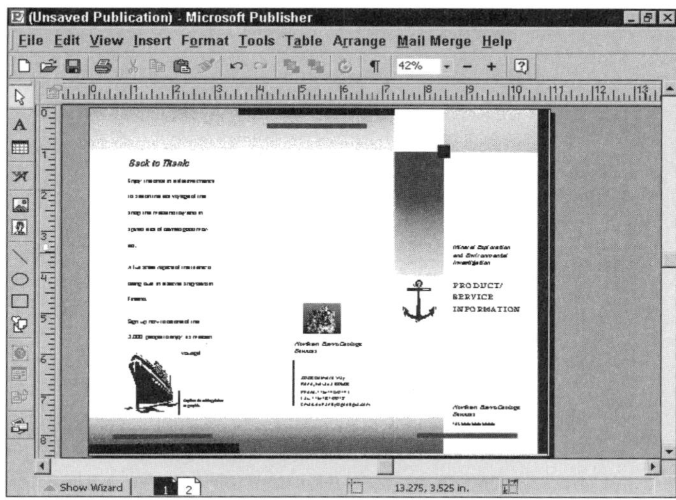

▶ *The frame of this certificate is PaperDirect's Burgundy/Blue Special Paper Certificate.*

▶ *This colorful trifold brochure can be printed on a black-and-white laser printer using PaperDirect's Influential Special Paper Brochure stock.*

TAKE NOTE

▶ VIEWING AND USING THE SPECIAL PAPER AVAILABLE IN PUBLISHER

While the examples in this section have been created by the Catalog Wizards, Publisher has a variety of special papers that you can use to create a document from scratch. To view the designs available to you, select View ➪ Special Paper. In the dialog box that appears, select a Special Paper in the top frame and preview it in the frame below. The name and stock number of each paper is given for ordering purposes. To use a special paper, select it from the list and click OK. To turn off the Special Paper background, Select View ➪ Special Paper, click None, and then click OK.

▶ OBTAINING SPECIAL PAPER FROM PAPER DIRECT

Call PaperDirect at 1-800-A-PAPERS, from the United States or Canada, to order or get a catalog.

FIND IT ONLINE

Visit PaperDirect's Web site at **http://www.paperdirect.com/** to view their catalog, order their products, and see examples of Special Papers.

Personal Workbook

Q&A

1. The Microsoft Publisher Catalog appears each time you start Publisher 2000. How do you turn off this option? How do you turn it back on again?

2. How do you change your personal information in Publisher? Use the Help function to find a second way, not mentioned in this chapter.

3. How do you insert an item of personal information into a publication? Use the Help function to find a second method besides the one mentioned in this chapter.

4. Mention two ways to save your file while you are working. What happens the first time you use either of these methods with a new, unsaved file?

5. How do you print only one business card on a sheet of paper? Why would you want to do this?

6. How do you add a logo to a personal information set?

7. After you have typed in the address on an envelope you are about to print, you decide you would like to print it in a different, larger font. How would you change the font?

8. You have to print up 300 brochures on Special Paper from PaperDirect. Would you print them all on your laser printer, or would you use your office copier? Explain your decision.

ANSWERS: PAGE 348

EXTRA PRACTICE

1. Imagine you are starting a business that you will run as a sideline. Make up information for a Secondary Business and enter it into Publisher. Make your tag line a mission statement about the services you provide. Print up a business card and letterhead stationery for your imaginary business.

2. Print a business card with only four cards per page. Use Page Options ➪ Custom Options to adjust vertical gaps and margins to print four cards. Use Advanced Print Settings ➪ "Crop marks to print marks" to guide precise trimming of the cards.

3. Use Microsoft Paint (Select Start ➪ Programs ➪ Accessories ➪ Paint) to draw a simple logo, and then print a business card using that logo.

REAL-WORLD APPLICATIONS

✔ A stranger shows up at your door and presents a business card that says he works for the power company. He says he needs to inspect some wiring in your home. Knowing how easily anyone can print a professional business card, you ask for a picture ID instead, which service companies normally provide their employees.

✔ You are expecting 90 participants at your Introducing Microsoft Publisher seminar this coming weekend. You would like to present each with a certificate of completion. You use the Awards Certificate Special Paper Wizard to prepare the certificates. Then you call PaperDirect and have 100 sheets of the certificate paper of your choice sent to you overnight, just in time for the seminar.

Visual Quiz

Does the Borders Business Card shown here require Special Paper or not to print in color? How can you tell?

____

____

____

____

____

____

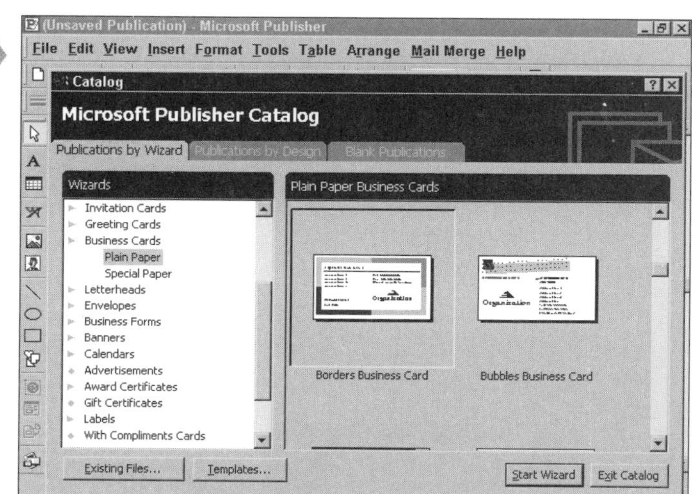

CHAPTER 3

MASTER THESE SKILLS

- Saving Your Publication
- Opening Existing Publications
- Saving Your Publication as a Template
- Creating a Document from a Template
- Managing Your Files with Windows Explorer
- Moving Your Publication to Another Computer
- Sending your Publication Over the Internet

Managing Your Files

Computers are nothing like they used to be when desktop publishing was done on 286 PCs that had a whopping 20 or 30MB hard drive. Today, your Windows machines come with storage for 8 or 10GB (or more in some cases), and that just gives you more places to store, hide, and lose files. That's why it is important to map a file storage plan before you get too far along in your publishing career.

Microsoft Publisher gives you a head start by providing you with folders such as My Documents and My Pictures when it is first installed. You may also find folders such as Favorites and History. You can either choose to accept those storage bins or create locations of your own. File management is a personal preference just like where you hang your coat or which drawer holds the socks. But it behooves you in the long run to stick with a firm, fast rule or two for storing files when you start suffering from file build-up on your hard drive.

As for possible plans, you may want to consider a folder for each client, department, or job type. Within that folder, you may want to store graphics in one folder and text in another folder. For example, make a folder named Smith Accounting and within that folder have two folders named Text and Graphics. Your Microsoft Publisher publication files could stay in Smith while you import from the Text and Graphics folders.

Another Publisher feature that can help you manage your time and storage space is the *template.* By creating a standard layout with key elements that are used repetitively and saving it as a template, you can shave hours off your production time. Take the Smith Accounting TaxTime newsletter. Consider saving your three-column layout with the nameplate, footers, and address area to a template. Once you are ready for another month of tax tidbits from the bean counters, all you need do is open the template and start placing graphics and stories.

Finally, Windows Explorer can get you through the organizational game a lot sooner than you think. It can also help gather the necessary files when you plan on taking your work home with you, but you have better ways to deal with the homework files. Publisher, using Pack and Go, helps you gather all those files outside your publication and assemble them on one handy disk or prepare them for uploading to the Smith Accounting Web site. So, don't fight these features — use them to work more efficiently.

Saving Your Publication

In the computer world, if you're going to use a document again or share it, you have to save it. Saving is just a way of life in computerdom.

Having read the introduction to this chapter religiously and thoroughly, you have all your folders and files perfectly organized. Right? If not, there's no need to shut down Publisher and do the file housekeeping now, especially if you have designed the best layout of your life. You have ways to create the folders on the fly in the Publisher Save dialog box.

What you do need to do, however, is make sure you have enough space on the disk where your files will be stored. Files can be placed on your hard drive, a removable disk such as Zip disks or optical disks, or floppy disks. Remember, because Windows is a multitasking work environment, you don't need to shut down Publisher to see how much space is available on your target storage disk. Launch Windows Explorer or click the My Computer icon on the desktop and check your disk space. In Explorer and My Computer, you'll find the stats on your disks in the status bar when you click the disk drive once to highlight it. For a quick shortcut, you can launch Explorer by right-clicking the Start button and choosing Explore.

The first time you save a file, use the Save As option in the File menu. Don't worry if you click Save; the Save As dialog box appears instead. Thereafter, you can use the Save option unless you want to save the file to a different location from where you first saved it, or you want to rename the file. In that event, use the Save As dialog box to maneuver to a different drive and/or folder, give it a new name, and then save your publication there.

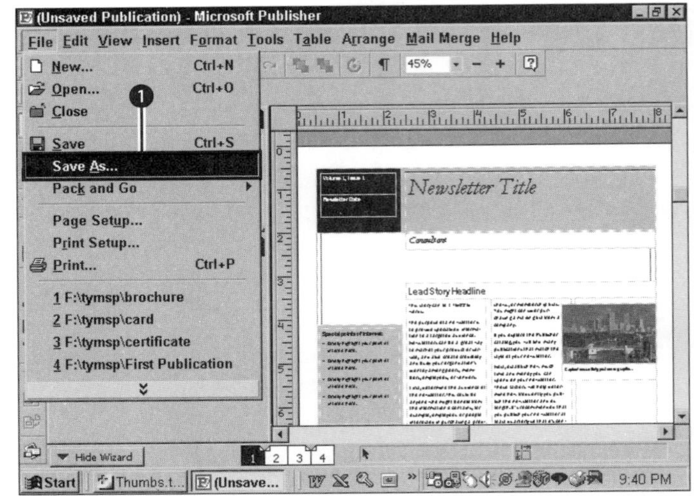

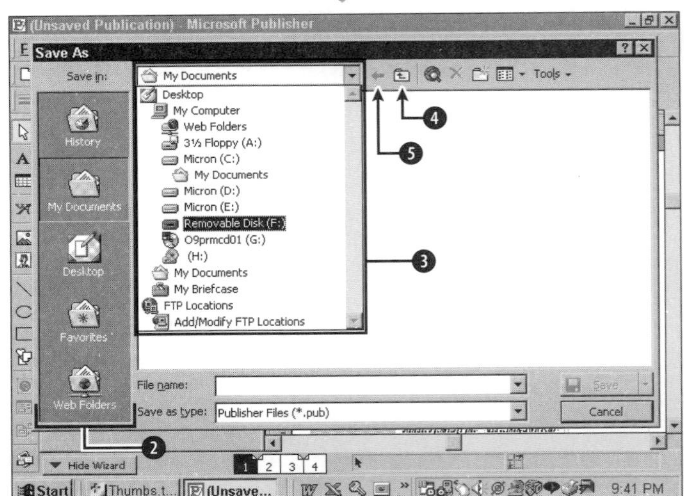

1. *Open the Save As dialog box by clicking File ➪ Save As.*
2. *Choose one of the folders on the left side of the Save As dialog box.*
3. *Alternatively, click the "Save in" drop-down box and choose a drive and folder from the list.*
4. *Use the Up One Level button to move up a folder or drive level.*
5. *Use the Back button to return to your previously selected location.*

CROSS-REFERENCE

See "Saving Your Publication as a Template" later in this chapter for future publications that use the same layout.

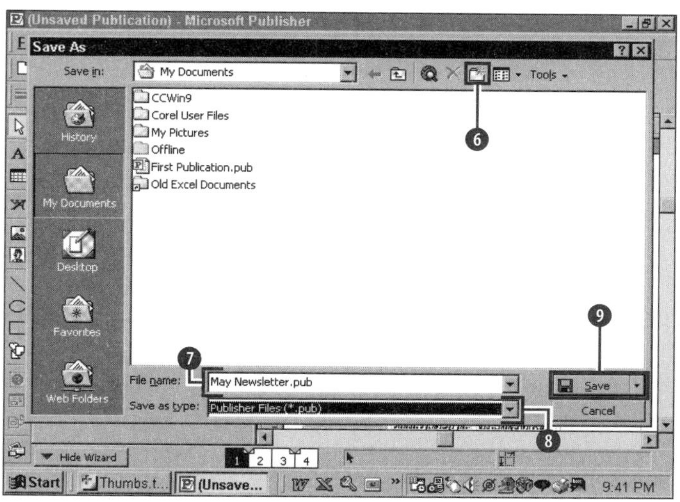

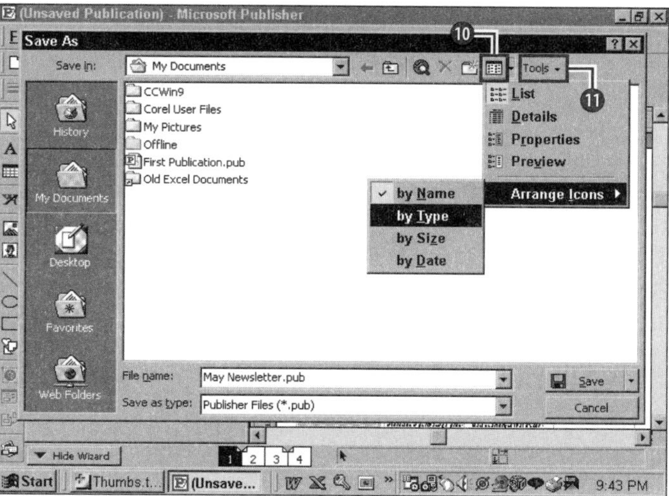

6. *Create a new folder with the Create New Folder button.*
7. *Enter a file name in the File name textbox.*
8. *Select a file format from the "Save as type" drop-down menu.*
9. *Click the Save button.*
10. *Use the Views button to see details such as date and size of files, or arrange the files and folders differently.*
11. *Use the Tools button to map your way to a drive on the network that may not appear in the "Look in" list.*

TAKE NOTE

SAVE OFTEN AND AVOID HEARTACHE

Get into the habit of pressing Ctrl+S or choosing File ➪ Save every so often to commit to disk all the work you complete over a period of time. Nothing is worse than having your computer crash on you after you have been working on a project for hours, never having saved that first time. Once you're in the habit of saving often, you can turn off Publisher's reminder.

SAVE FOR A PREVIOUS PUBLISHER VERSION

In the Save As dialog box, you can change the Save as Type setting to Publisher 98 so that users with an older version of Microsoft Publisher can still open the file.

FIND IT ONLINE

Learn how to run ScanDisk and Disk Defragmenter automatically with Task Scheduler at **http://support.microsoft.com/support/kb/articles/q179/3/06.asp.**

Opening Existing Publications

Now that you've learned to save your publications and figured out a smart way to organize everything, there may come a day when you will have to retrieve that document for revisions. Likewise, someone could have handed you a publication on disk that you have to print on your fancy, 80-page-per-minute laser printer.

Opening a publication in Publisher is much the same as any other Windows program. Those programs list your most recently opened documents in the lower portion of the File menu. Normally, four are listed. If you want to retrieve a publication that you not have opened before, such as the one on your coworker's disk, it is necessary to tell Publisher where the file is located. The steps in this task point the way to opening documents successfully.

Your publications need Microsoft Publisher, and you have to have Microsoft Publisher installed on the computer that is going to open a publication. With few exceptions, other publishing programs won't know how to handle your document should you try to import it into a program such as Adobe PageMaker, Quark Xpress, or Corel Ventura. Though some other publishing programs may offer import filters, they may also mess up the document once it is imported. Then, you may spend more time fixing it than if you had installed Publisher on the computer to begin with. Be safe and use Publisher for any edits.

Another item to watch for is the fonts that are installed on the computer. If you're aware of certain fonts that the publication needs, install those before trying to open a document from another source. Of course, if you have changed your font listing since you last revised or created the publication you are about to open, you need to get your previous fonts installed as well.

If you link graphics to your publication, be sure they are in the proper location for Publisher to find, too.

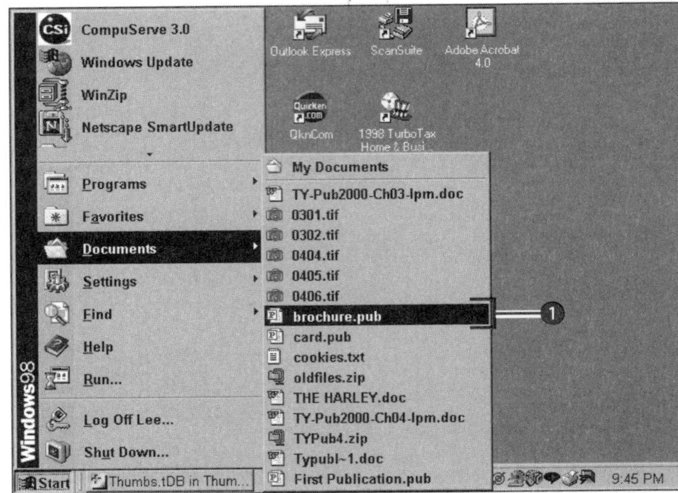

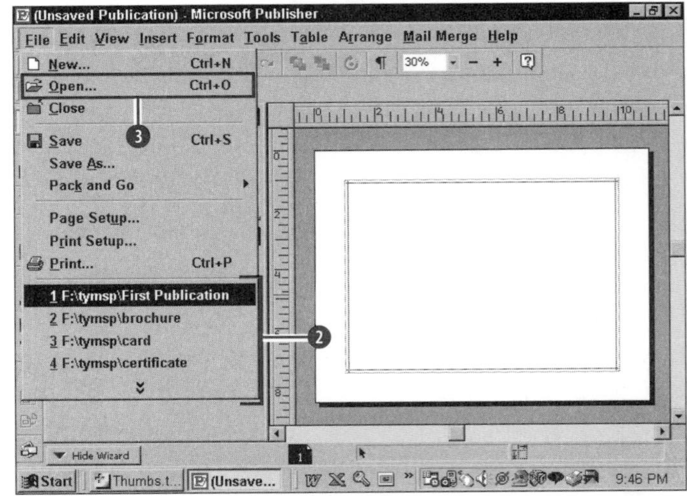

1. Use Start ➪ Documents to open Publisher and your publication.
2. For recent publications, use the File menu and choose from the most recent listing.
3. For publications not listed, click File ➪ Open to select from the Open Publications dialog box.

CROSS-REFERENCE

For more information on linking graphics, see "Using Paste Special to Insert Graphics," in Chapter 11.

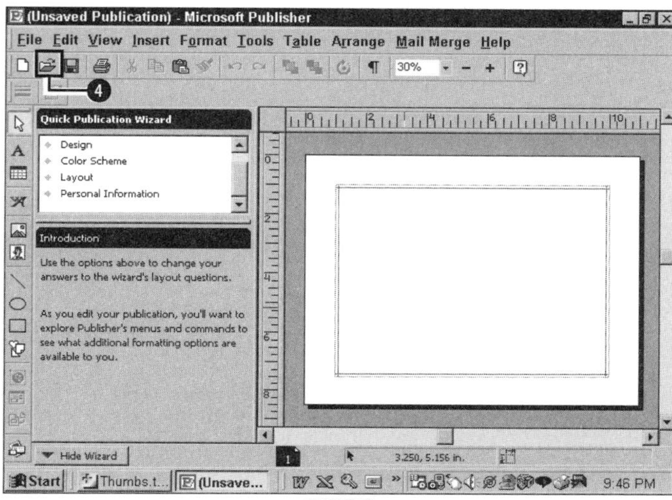

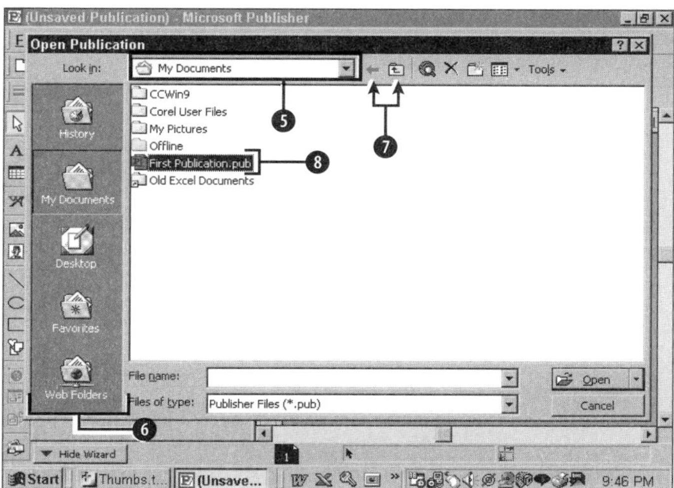

❹ *Or, use the Open icon on the standard toolbar.*

❺ *Choose the drive and directory in the "Look in" drop-down box.*

❻ *Choose a folder from the left side.*

❼ *Use the Back button or Up One Level button in addition to the "Look in" drop-down menu.*

❽ *Choose the publication from the file list and click Open.*

TAKE NOTE

OPENING PUBLISHER QUICKLY WITH A DOCUMENT

Use the Start Menu to open Publisher documents that have been previously opened on your computer. When you click Start ➪ Documents, a list of the most recent files that you have worked on are displayed. Selecting the PUB file opens Publisher and that publication file, as long as you have not moved or erased it.

ACCESSING DOCUMENTS EVEN FASTER

Consider adding a shortcut to your document on the desktop. Clicking it also opens Publisher with your publication loaded and ready to edit. To add a shortcut to the desktop, find the file in Windows Explorer, right-click it, and choose Send To Desktop as Shortcut.

FIND IT ONLINE

For free fonts and information on where to find more fonts, go to **http://desktopPublishing.com/fonts.html.**

Saving Your Publication as a Template

Whenever you have a recurring publication that uses the same elements, you can create a template that you can open and edit for each new project that uses that design. Microsoft Publisher templates let you shave minutes or hours off of a recurring job. Some examples where you may use templates are newsletters, letterhead and envelopes, business forms, annual reports, business cards, and more.

In a way, you are already familiar with Publisher templates. The Microsoft Publisher Catalog is full of examples where the layout is already planned, and all you have to do is provide the variable elements that make the publication your own. For each of the different projects in the catalog, you could create a template just for your business or personal use, and recall it when creating new projects.

Some of the elements that you may want to consider placing on the pages to save as a template are page numbers in the header or footer, newsletter nameplates or banners, graphics and text that appear regularly, page borders, and company name and address information.

When preparing your template, think in terms of multiple pages if your project requires it. For a four-page newsletter, place that Calendar artwork on page 3, the mailing information on the last page, and the publication title on page 1. Set up the page numbers, the volume and date, the number of columns and guidelines, and the name of the publication on the bottom of each page where needed. Some of these items are best suited for the background layer of your publication, but once you have the template opened and ready to start a new project, you can always move elements around before placing them on the background.

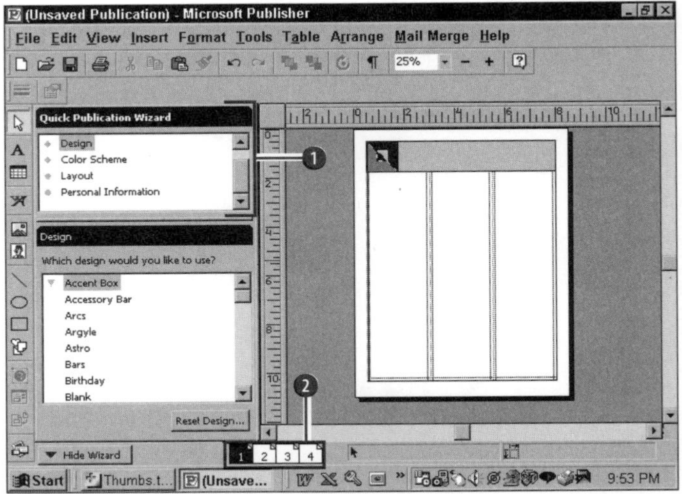

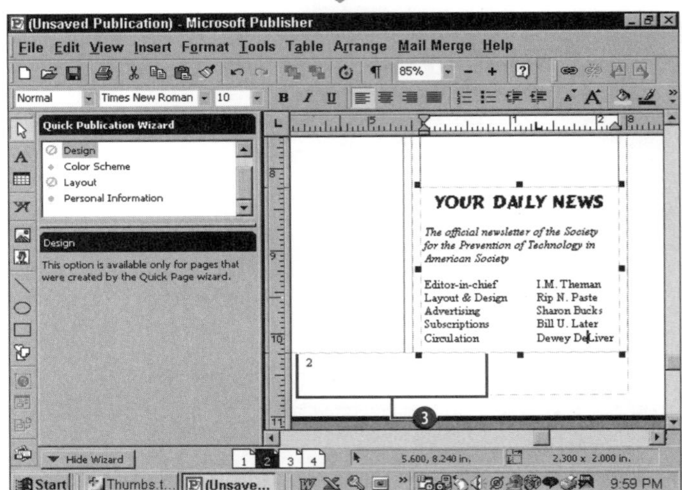

1. You can use the Quick Publication Wizard to add elements to your template.
2. Include the number of pages that the publication will entail.
3. Add recurring elements such as footers, headers, and nameplates.

CROSS-REFERENCE

Placing items on the background in a publication is explained in "Designing a Background," in Chapter 7.

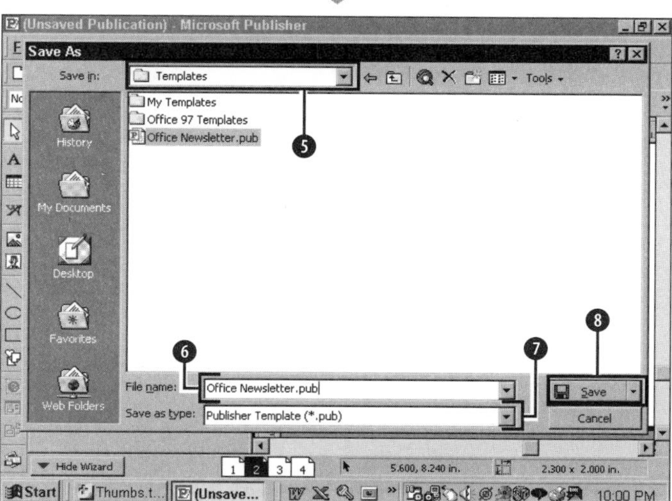

4. Click File ➪ Save As to open the Save As dialog box.
5. Locate the folder where your templates will be stored using the "Look in" drop-down menu.
6. Name your template in the "File name" text box.
7. Change the "Save as type" option to Publisher Template (*.pub).
8. Click Save.

TAKE NOTE

ORGANIZING YOUR TEMPLATES

It is a good idea to save template files in a folder specifically set up for them. You could also arrange them as to the client they will be used for or the type of project they are.

PROTECTING YOUR TEMPLATES

You may want to assign a Read Only designation to the template file. This setting protects them from being overwritten accidentally. To make a file Read Only, use Windows Explorer to find the file on your computer. Right-click the file and choose Properties from the context menu. In the General tab, place a checkmark next to the Read Only attribute in the bottom of the dialog box. Click OK and return to Publisher. Note that the file must be closed when you are changing the attribute.

FIND IT ONLINE

When designing your template, consider using a grid to lay out the elements. Find out more about grid layout at **http://web.nmsu.edu/~brifulle/218/docdes/11.htm.**

Creating a Document from a Template

Once the design work is done on a template, the really hard part is over. Remember, Thomas Edison said something to the effect that genius (and in this case, your designing prowess) is 1 percent inspiration and 99 percent perspiration. Figuring out the color scheme, the fonts to use, and setting the recurring graphics and text should be the most difficult job in publication design. Once you have a winning combination of all these elements, the rest should be cake.

Templates afford you the luxury of not only jump-starting a project, but also give you the ability to hand off a project to an assistant, if you have one. Once styles are in place, someone else can drop in the pictures and text that change from issue to issue, and that person need not have an eye for design. And, once you have given it your stamp of approval or made some minor alterations, it can be whisked off to the printer and duplicated for circulation.

If you have taken the necessary precautions to make your template file read only, trust in the fact that, should you have to do the project next month, the person you assigned to complete the job this month has not altered all your hard work and overwritten the template file. Of course, it is always a good idea to save a copy of the file somewhere else, known only to you, just in case.

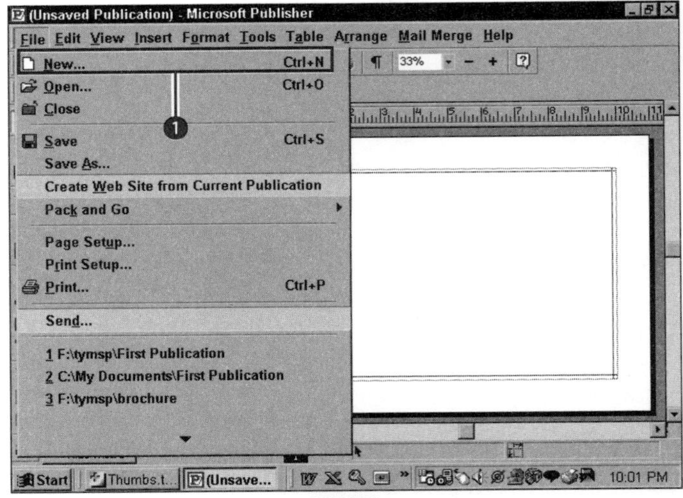

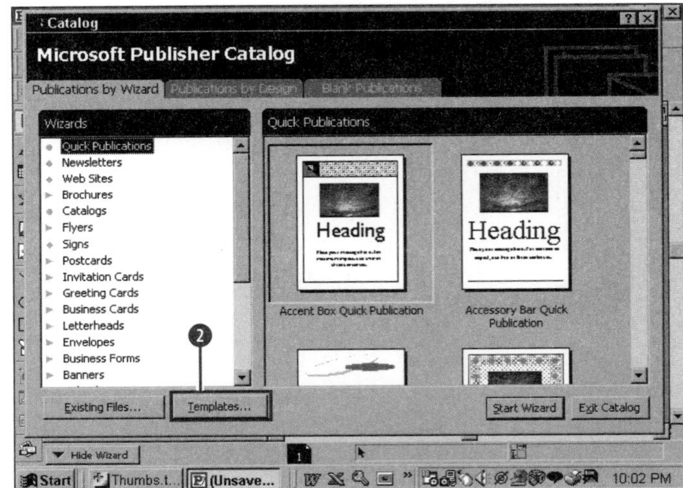

1. To start a document from a template, click File ➪ New.
2. In either the Publications by Wizard or Publications by Design tabs of the Catalog dialog box, choose Templates.

CROSS-REFERENCE

You can include merge codes as part of your template. See Chapters 14 and 15 for details.

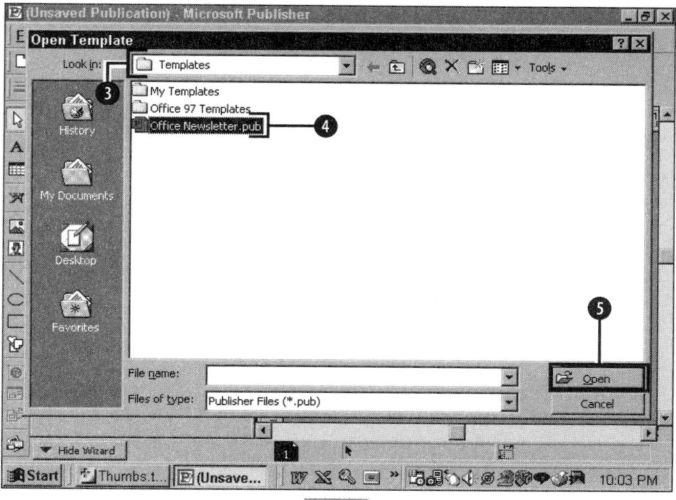

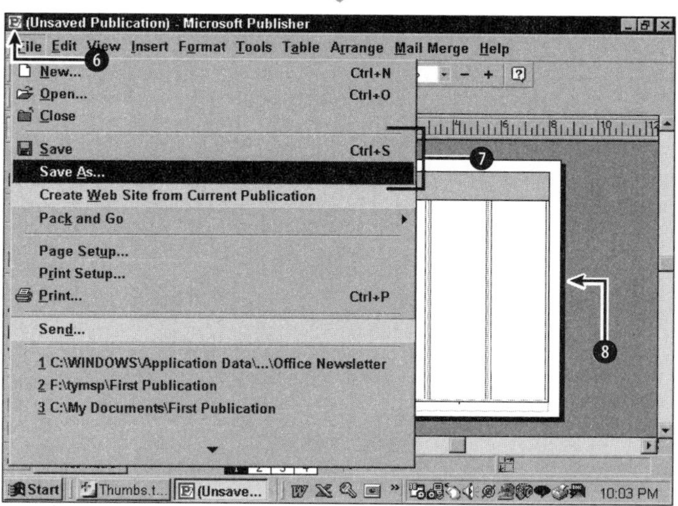

3. *In the Open Template dialog box, use the "Look in" drop-down menu to locate the folder where the template is stored.*
4. *Select the template file name in the list of files.*
5. *Click Open.*
6. *Note that the title bar says this is an unsaved publication.*
7. *Click File ➪ Save or File ➪ Save As to save the new document.*
8. *You can use all of the wizards and tools available to create a new publication.*

TAKE NOTE

MAKING A TEMPLATE FROM A CURRENT PUBLICATION

You don't have to start from scratch to create a template. Take a current publication file and delete all the information that normally changes from publication to publication. Once you have everything on the pages that will be used for the next and subsequent issues, you can save the file as a template (see "Saving Your Publication as a Template," earlier in this chapter).

KEEPING FILES TOGETHER

It is a good idea to store the files that are used in the template in a safe location, possibly in a subfolder from the Template folder. If you ever need to delete a publication from your hard drive to make space for other projects, you'll be sure not to touch the folders where you have stored your templates and the subfolders therein.

INCLUDING PERSONAL INFORMATION

Because you can include the personal and business information that Publisher keeps track of, remember that if you include those fields in your template, they will be updated the next time you change your personal or business information. For more details on incorporating personal or business information in your publication, see Chapter 2.

FIND IT ONLINE

Perhaps your recurring document is in need of an overhaul. Check out http://www.publish.com/ for other design ideas.

Managing Your Files with Windows Explorer

With all the files you will accumulate doing desktop and Web publishing, you'll need a surefire way to copy, move, and delete your collection. Windows 95 and 98 come with a file management utility called Windows Explorer.

When you open Windows Explorer, you'll notice the two large areas. On the left are your drives and folders. On the right are the contents of whatever you select on the left side. That is, if you click a drive letter in the left side, you'll see its contents on the right. Clicking a folder shows you any subfolders and files that are found within it.

Using the two sides in tandem, you can copy, move, and delete files all day by dragging from the right side to the left side or pressing your Del key. You also can use the Ctrl key to help. If you're uncomfortable with using the keyboard in conjunction with the mouse, the buttons below the menu bar will also help.

To copy a file from one folder to another location, select the file and hold down the Ctrl key. To simply move a file, drag from the right side to a folder or drive on the left side while holding the Shift key.

A slicker way to drag files is to use the right mouse button instead of the left. Once you drag with the right button and you reach your destination, let go of the button and choose whether you want to copy or move the files from the pop-up menu.

When you view the listing on the left side, you'll notice plus signs or minus signs next to some drives or folders. Click a plus sign to expand the listing of subfolders; click a minus sign to deflate the listing.

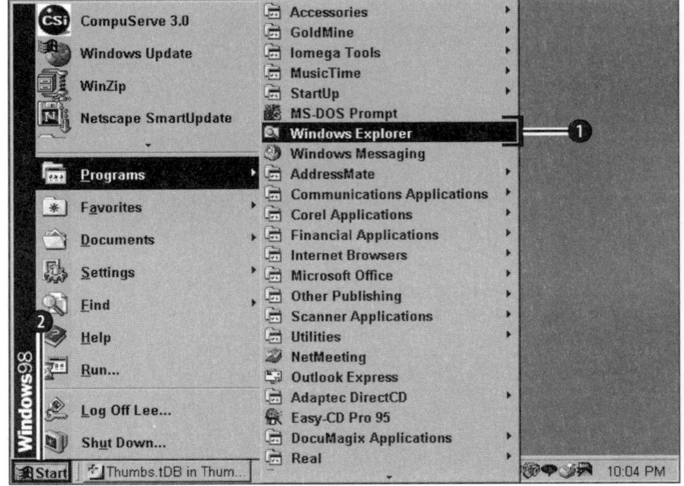

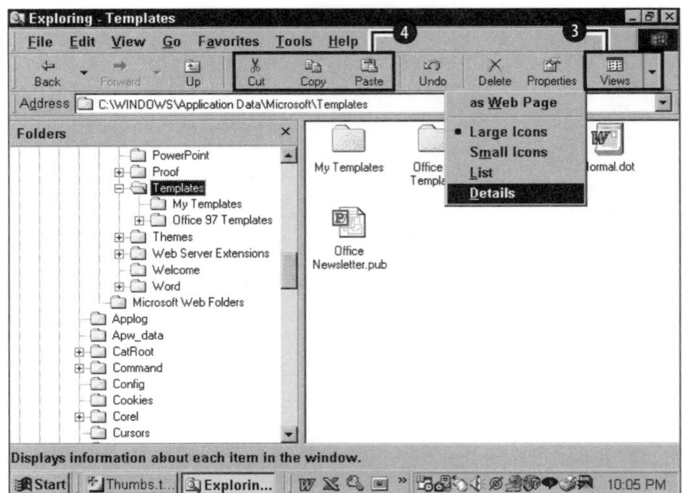

1. *Start Windows Explorer from the Start ➪ Programs menu.*
2. *Or, right-click the Start button and choose Explore.*
3. *Select how you want to view the listing on the right side with the Views button.*
4. *Use the buttons in the standard toolbar to cut, copy, or paste a file.*

CROSS-REFERENCE

For a complete explanation of Windows Explorer, check out *Teach Yourself Windows 98,* by Al Stevens with Brian Underdahl, 1999 (IDG Books Worldwide).

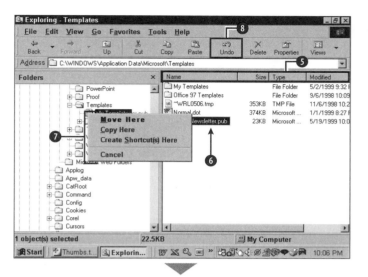

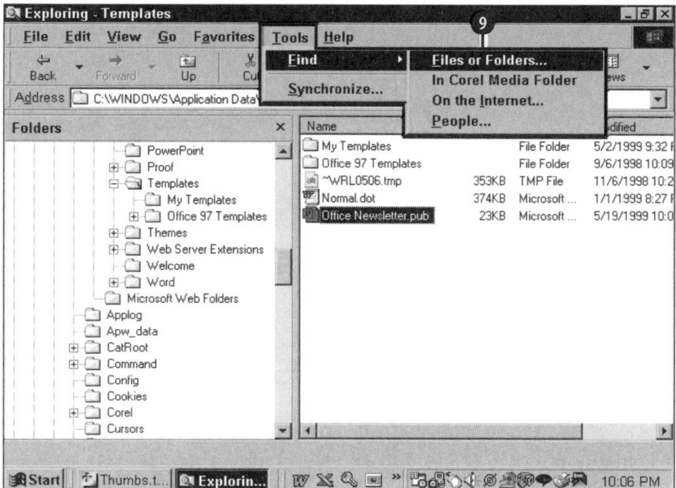

❺ *Click any of the column header blocks to change the sort from ascending to descending.*

❻ *Right-click a file and drag it to a new location.*

❼ *Release the right mouse button and left-click the operation you want.*

❽ *Click the Undo button to return the file to its original location.*

❾ *To locate files, click Tools ➪ Find ➪ Files or Folders. You can enter part of a file name and receive all files that include your criteria.*

TAKE NOTE

CHANGING THE VIEW

You can change the way the right side of the window appears by selecting View from the menu bar and choosing Large Icons, Small Icons, List, or Details. You'll also find a button on the toolbar that lets you change views as fast as a mouse click. Clicking the Views button cycles through the four different views with each click.

GET THE FULL DETAILS ON A FILE

By clicking the Properties button, you can see all that Windows know about a file. Plus, you can change the attributes of a file by clicking the appropriate checkbox. This is yet another place where you can change template files to read only.

FIND IT ONLINE

You'll find some other file-management freeware and shareware at **http://www.download.com.** Check in the Utilities - File and Disk Management section.

Moving Your Publication to Another Computer

By the time you have completed a publication, you may have incorporated a few or many files, placed succinctly in those pages. Some you may have imported; others may be linked. Whichever route you took, you may have reached several different folder locations on your hard drive to acquire them. Remembering the name and location of each file could be impossible. Writing them down as you go would be tedious. Noting the fonts you employed could make you aspirin-dependent.

Built into Publisher is the ideal way to gather up all those files and fonts and pack them into one tidy package for storage.

The Pack and Go feature not only lets you save an entire publication to another location, but it prepares that file for commercial printing. This task shows you how to pack a publication to a disk. You could use a floppy disk, a Zip disk, or some other storage medium. As long as you have a drive letter and/or folder location, you can have all the necessary elements in a portable format to take home, to another computer, or to just archive for safe keeping.

When the process is done, you end up with three files. The PUZ file is the compressed publication. A readme text file instructs the recipient how to decompress the PUZ file. Finally, the unpack.exe file is the small utility that explodes the PUZ file back into its original components on the remote computer.

Using the Pack and Go Wizard takes only a few mouse clicks and some possible patience if you have a lot of data to transfer. And, because Pack and Go writes data over several disks, you can still use those floppies as long as you have enough on hand for those big jobs.

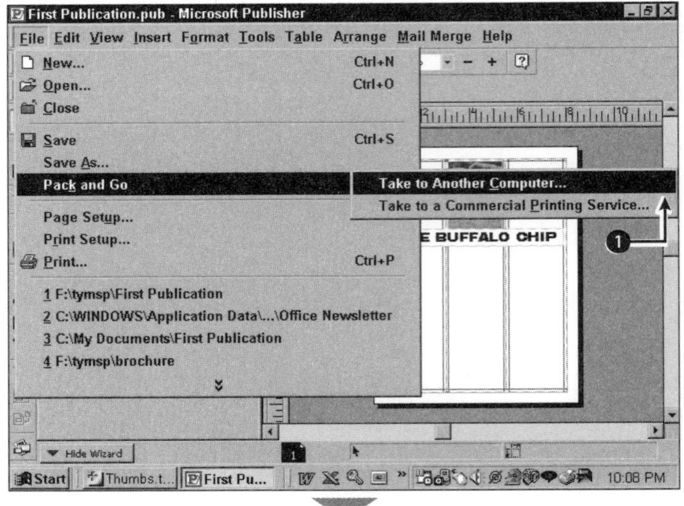

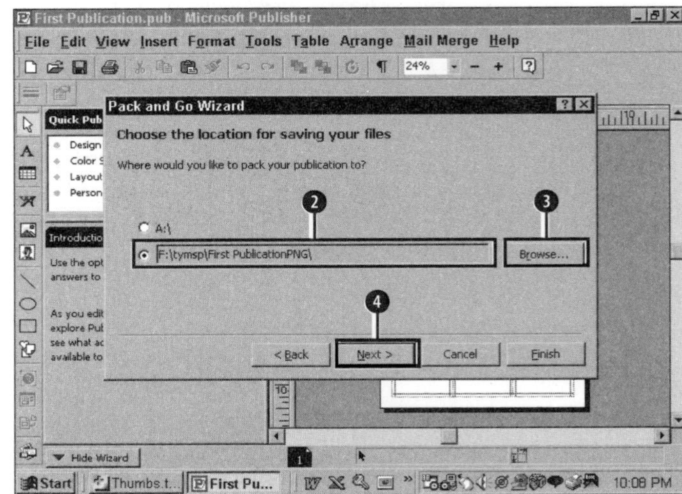

1. *Click File ⇨ Pack and Go ⇨ Take to Another Computer.*
2. *After clicking Next on the introductory dialog box, you choose a location for the file.*
3. *Use the Browse button to navigate to a different drive or folder.*
4. *Click Next.*

CROSS-REFERENCE

For details about using Pack and Go to prepare a publication for commercial printers, see Chapter 18.

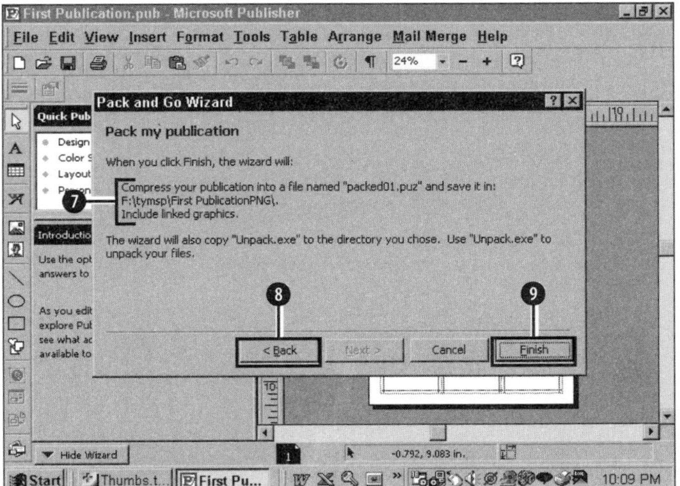

5. *Choose whether to include the fonts and graphics in your file.*
6. *Click Next.*
7. *Double-check the preferences you selected in the dialog box.*
8. *Click the Back button to make changes.*
9. *Click the Finish button to create the Pack and Go file.*

TAKE NOTE

PROTECTING YOUR DISK

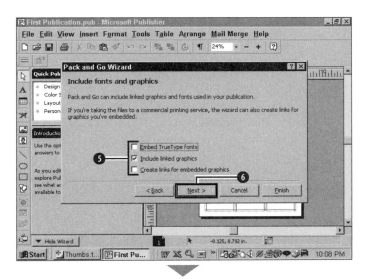

Almost every storage disk — floppy, optical, Zip, what have you — has the ability to be write-protected. Many times it's a simple sliding mechanism on one or both sides of the disk cartridge. Check the documentation that came with your drive to see how you can write-protect your disk.

STORING ON CD OR REWRITABLE CD

The cost of writable CD-ROM drives has decreased dramatically in the last year or so. Consider investing in one of these drives. Writing information to a CD-R will last a long time and the media is very inexpensive. Check into a CD writer that enables you to add to a CD-R progressively. The technical term *packet writing* means that the entire CD-R is not wasted if you only write on a portion of it.

FIND IT ONLINE

To research new hardware for your computer, go to Ziff Davis Publishing and look at the product reviews at http://www.zdnet.com/products.

Sending your Publication Over the Internet

The Internet is booming, no doubt about it. The number of people who use their e-mail address more often than they use the phone is growing phenomenally. Couple that with the number of computers out there, and you can see that the world is getting smaller each week. Plus, with the price of computers falling drastically over the past year or two, you can bet more households will have one or more computers at hand.

Company use of e-mail has tremendous advantages for the users. Being able to send information over the Internet that once had to be faxed, overnighted, or dropped in the mail, is certainly a corporate boon. If you are up on your current events, some phone companies have been proposing adding a surcharge on every e-mail because it traverses the phone lines. This issue is being discussed by Congress at the time of this writing.

Now that you have learned to use Pack and Go in the previous task in order to make your publication portable, don't limit your thinking to handing disks back and forth. The compressed format that your publication has taken on is ideal for sending data anywhere in the world via e-mail. All you need is a dial-up to access the Internet and an e-mail package, neither of which are expensive. You can get an e-mail program called Outlook for nothing. It came with Windows 95 and 98 as a part of Microsoft Explorer.

For those who are not experienced at sending files over the Internet, attached to e-mail, this task is for you. Though the examples and screenshots here are using Netscape Messenger, you may opt to use Microsoft Outlook, Outlook Express, or any number of e-mail programs on the market. Usually the process of attaching files is similar.

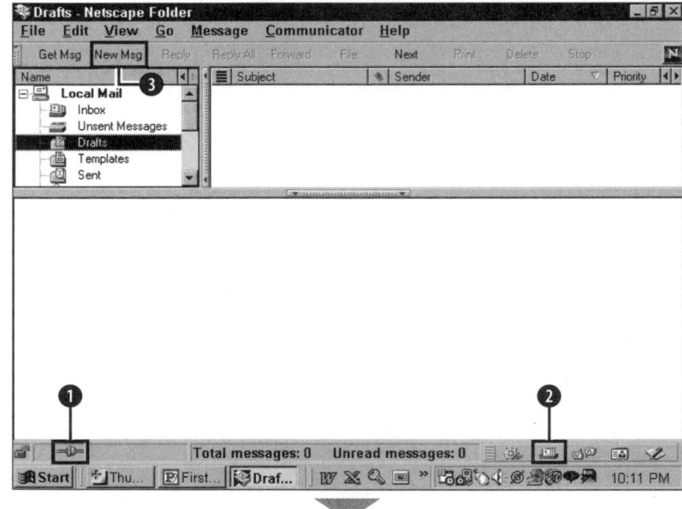

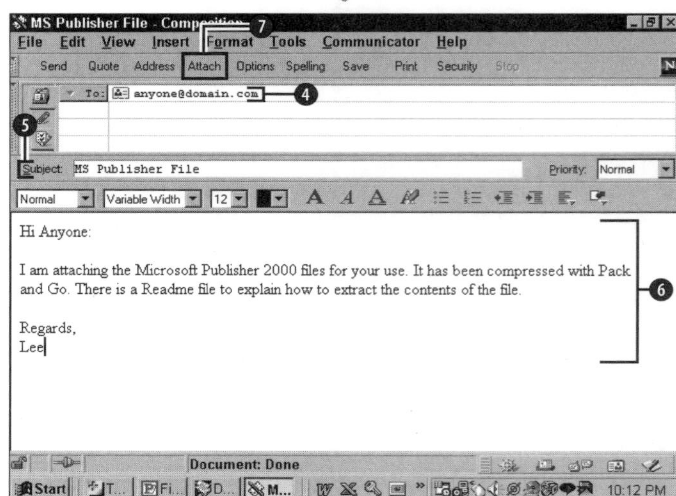

1. *Connect to the Internet.*
2. *Start your e-mail program.*
3. *Begin a new message.*
4. *Enter the address of the recipient.*
5. *Type a subject in the space provided.*
6. *Optionally, send a note along with the file.*
7. *Click the Attach button or select File ⇨ Attach ⇨ File.*

CROSS-REFERENCE

For help in determining possible limitations on e-mail attachments, contact your Internet Service Provider (ISP), network administrator, or Webmaster.

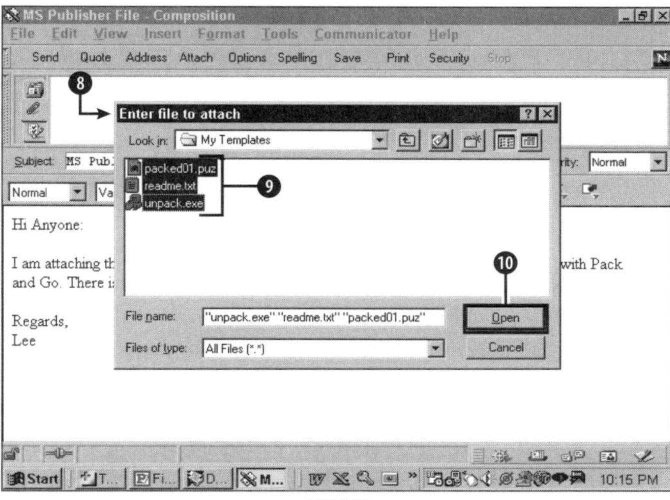

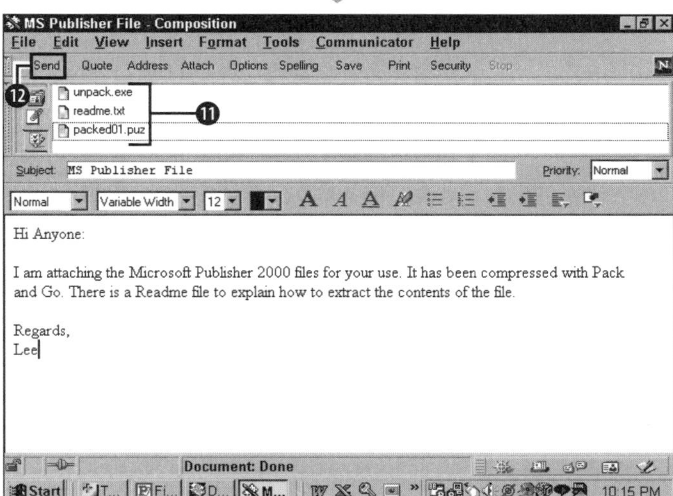

8. *Find the files to send using the "Enter file to attach" dialog box.*
9. *If your e-mail package can send multiple files, you may be able to Shift+click the files and select them all at once.*
10. *Select Open.*
11. *Verify that all files have been attached to your e-mail.*
12. *Click Send.*

TAKE NOTE

SENDING MULTIPLE FILES

Some e-mail packages may only let you send one file per message. Because Pack and Go creates the three files discussed in the previous task, you may have to send them individually (or compress the files into one Zip file). Likewise, some recipients can only receive one file per message even though you can send several. Plan ahead and check with the recipient how he or she would like to receive your files.

CHECKING THE FILE SIZE

Depending on the size of the packed publication, you may want to consider writing the publication to a disk and mailing it traditionally. Two possible reasons for this may be the speed of your connection to the Internet, and there may be a file size restriction on the part of the recipient. Some online services such as American Online and CompuServe have a size limit for files attached to e-mail.

FIND IT ONLINE

For other e-mail software, scan the selections at **http://www.tucows.com.**

Personal Workbook

Q&A

1. How can you save an updated (previously saved) publication without opening a dialog box?

2. How can you find the date and size of a file in the Save As dialog box?

3. If you want to view all Publisher files (*.PUB) together in a folder that also contains graphics and text files, how would you change the file order in the list?

4. For publications that will be updated on a regular basis, what can you create to make subsequent editions quicker and easier to complete?

5. What Microsoft Windows utility may be used to copy, move, and delete files?

6. When using Pack and Go, what three files are created and what are their purpose?

7. What are the three instances when you would want to use Pack and Go?

8. When moving or copying files in Windows Explorer, what key should you press to copy the file?

ANSWERS: PAGE 349

EXTRA PRACTICE

1. Save a current publication to another disk to share with a coworker.
2. Create your own personal letterhead and save it as a template.
3. Write and send a letter to a relative using the personal letterhead template you created in item #2. Save your work.
4. Using Windows Explorer, copy the letter created in item #3 to a new folder under the My Documents folder.
5. Using your e-mail program, send a Pack and Go file to a friend or coworker.
6. After sending the e-mail, use Windows Explorer to delete the Pack and Go files.

REAL-WORLD APPLICATIONS

- ✔ You have Microsoft Publisher installed on your computer at home. So that you don't have to work late into the night or miss an important phone call at home, you save your publication to a Zip disk and finish it at home.
- ✔ To keep track of your expenses, you create a template called Expense Report. Each week, you open the template, fill in the data for hotel, meals, and transportation. You print the report and turn it into the comptroller for reimbursement.
- ✔ Your desktop publishing business boasts eight big clients. In order to organize your files on your hard drive, you make separate folders for each company. Underneath those folders, you create subfolders to hold text files, graphic files, and the publication files, making them easier to find.

Visual Quiz

In this figure, name as many ways as you can to start Microsoft Publisher.

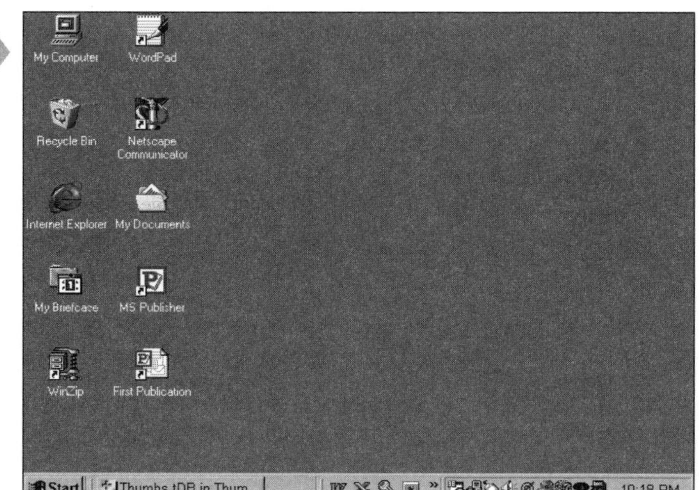

CHAPTER 4

MASTER THESE SKILLS

- Introducing Publications by Wizard
- Modifying Publications with Wizards
- Creating Greeting Cards
- Creating a Flyer
- Creating a Brochure
- Creating a Newsletter

Using Microsoft Publisher Catalog

Have you ever gotten stuck on a project where you just aren't sure where to start, what typefaces to use, or what "look" you're attempting to achieve? Or, your boss or client races into your office and informs you that there's a four-page newsletter that has to be photocopied and mailed before the end of tomorrow. Before you break into a cold sweat or call the babysitter to explain why you'll be late again, consider using the wizards of Publisher 2000 to help you get over the hump of indecision or out of the sticky wicket your employer has placed you in.

Besides the greeting cards, flyers, brochures, and newsletter that are covered in the tasks in this chapter, you can choose from many other items such as business forms, postcards, catalogs, signs, banners, award certificates, menus, and several others. It is good to note that the two fun categories, airplanes and origami, have not left the wizard's book of magic. For those who are unfamiliar with these projects, you can print out patterns of paper airplanes and Japanese folded paper items to keep the kids busy while you continue exploring the rest of this chapter on Publisher 2000 Wizards.

Publications by Wizard is just one of the tabs in the Publisher Catalog. The other two tabs, Publications by Design and Blank Publications, are equally as convenient when creating new publications. The Publications by Design tab carries all of the themed items. That is, all the items that could go together are arranged in categories such as Restaurant Sets, Fund-raiser Sets, and Master Sets. Clicking the various categories opens subcategories below it. These are the different color schemes that are available in each category.

The Blank Publications tab gives you a foot up on page layout. Selecting one of these options gives you correct layout size and orientation to begin your project. The only thing missing is the elements that you will have to place on the page.

This chapter takes you through some of the popular wizards to get you comfortable with the process. But because they are often self-explanatory, you won't find them all covered here. You should also be warned that, depending on the complexity of the final outcome, some wizards do take a bit of time to complete. You may find it an ideal time for a light snack that suits your dietary needs.

Introducing Publications by Wizard

When you first open Microsoft Publisher, as long as you have not chosen otherwise, the Publisher Catalog opens with the Publication by Wizard tab chosen by default. While the Publications by Wizard is arranged by the type of publication you are wanting to create, the next tab over, Publications by Design, is arranged in themes and categories. Selecting one of the options walks you through the same steps — you're just selecting them from a different point of view.

In Publications by Design, you'll notice similarities, as you switch from category to category, in the colors and designs that accent the projects. This gives you an even greater advantage when designing multiple items that all have to have the same look and feel, such as letterhead, envelopes, business cards, brochures, and shipping labels.

Whichever route you choose to start your publication, you notice in the list that some of the items have circle bullets and others have an arrow. Clicking the circle bullets displays everything in that category in the right-hand window. When an arrow appears, a sublist opens when you either click the arrow or double-click the item in the list. Clicking one of the sublist items jumps you to the location in the right-hand window where that project begins.

Wizards take you one step further in providing templates for specialty papers from PaperDirect, a computer paper company that specializes in different paper products for the desktop publisher. With their products and a decent laser and/or ink-jet printer, you have eliminated the need to spend a large chunk of money to have quality printed material available for you or your customer. Another advantage to this printing approach is that you can print small runs to satisfy your immediate needs

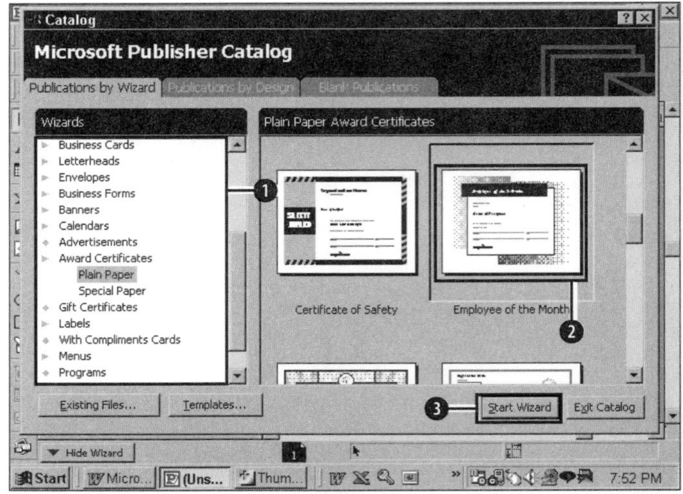

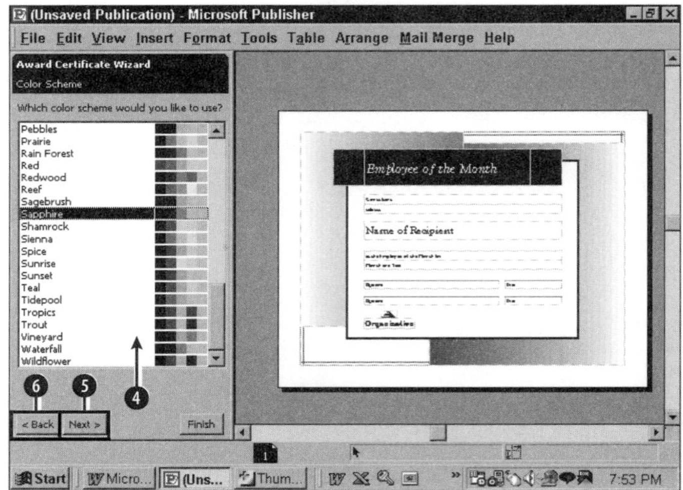

1. Select the type of publication from the left side of the Catalog.
2. Choose the layout from the right side.
3. Click the Start Wizard button.
4. Choose a color scheme.
5. Click the Next button to proceed.
6. Click the Back button to go back and change the design.

CROSS-REFERENCE

If you'd prefer to start with a blank page, see "Starting a Blank Publication" in Chapter 6.

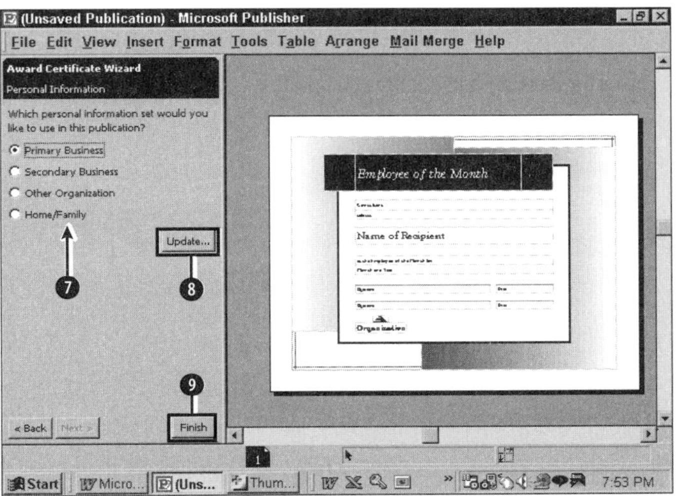

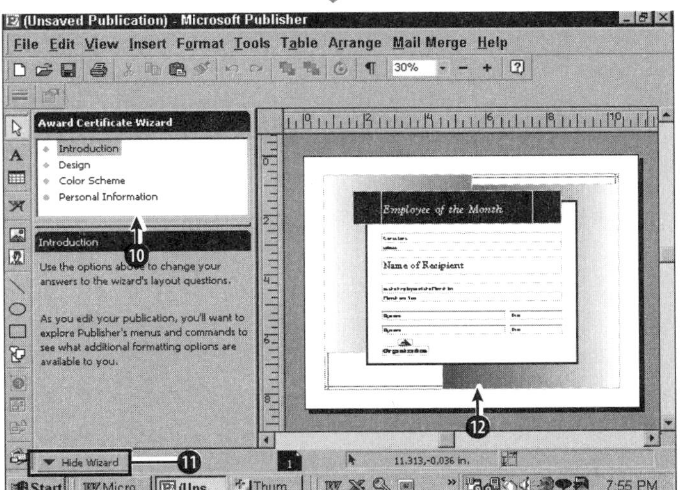

❼ *Click which Personal Information data to use.*

❽ *Click the Update button to make changes to the personal information.*

❾ *Click the Finish button.*

❿ *Change any of the wizard information in the list.*

⓫ *Click Hide Wizard to view more of your project.*

⓬ *Begin customizing the publication.*

with little or no waste. This also affords you the opportunity to make changes should there be an address or phone number change, or a typo. This approach to business stationery can circumvent some embarrassing moments.

TAKE NOTE

HIDING THE CATALOG AT STARTUP

If you would prefer that the Publisher Catalog not be seen when you open Microsoft Publisher, you can turn it off in Tools ➪ Options ➪ General tab ➪ "Use Catalog at startup."

MENUS ARE NOT ACTIVE

While the Publisher Wizard is active, you will not be able to access the program's drop-down menus. If you need to get to them, click Finish on the wizard. You will still be able to use the wizard later to add features or make changes.

FIND IT ONLINE

For help getting design ideas, try Publish RGB at **http://www.publish.com.** Go to the Features Index and scan the makeover articles.

Modifying Publications with Wizards

Once you have a publication on the computer layout table, so to speak, all is not cast in stone. Having used the Publisher Catalog and its many wizards to start your publication, you can return to the wizard to make changes. This sets Microsoft Publisher apart from many other desktop publishing packages.

While you won't be able to turn a greeting card into an award certificate, you can change the layout and design of a publication that you created in a wizard. All it takes is a little sleight of hand and another hand from the Publisher Wizard to transform the look of your project. Then, you can let your boss and coworkers think you spent an entire afternoon making a new design in place of the one that didn't quite come up to par.

Microsoft had some method in their madness when they placed the Wizard window next to the toolbox. A handy button underneath it lets you call it up at will or make it shrink away. When you want to make an alteration, be sure that the wizard is visible and then make your changes from within it.

Some of the things you can change include the design, color scheme, and personal information. . . the same things that you chose from when you created the project at the start. And, all that customization in the text that you made will follow suit. That is, if you entered a recipient name in the award certificate, it stays there when you change the design through the wizard.

Color schemes can set a different tone to a project. Likewise, when you make a change to the color scheme, the design elements remain the same, but take on a new color.

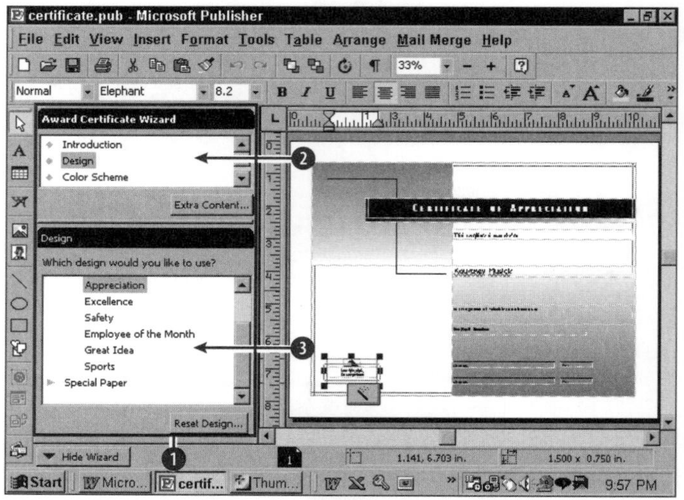

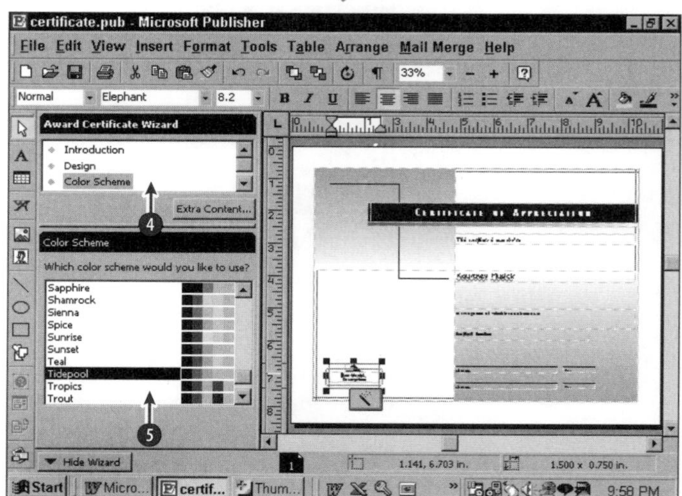

1. *Open the Wizard window, if it is not open already.*
2. *Choose Design in the upper portion of the Wizard window.*
3. *Select a new design from the lower Wizard window.*
4. *Click Color Scheme in the upper Wizard window.*
5. *Choose another color scheme from the lower Wizard window.*

CROSS-REFERENCE

To add elements to your publication, see "Inserting Text Frames and Inserting Picture Frames" in Chapter 6.

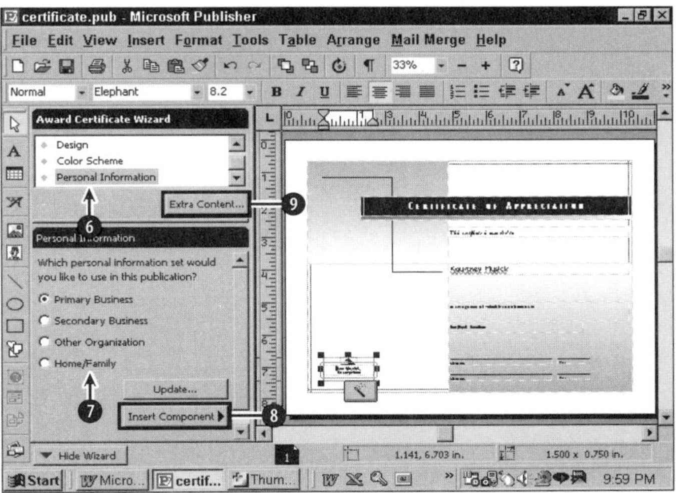

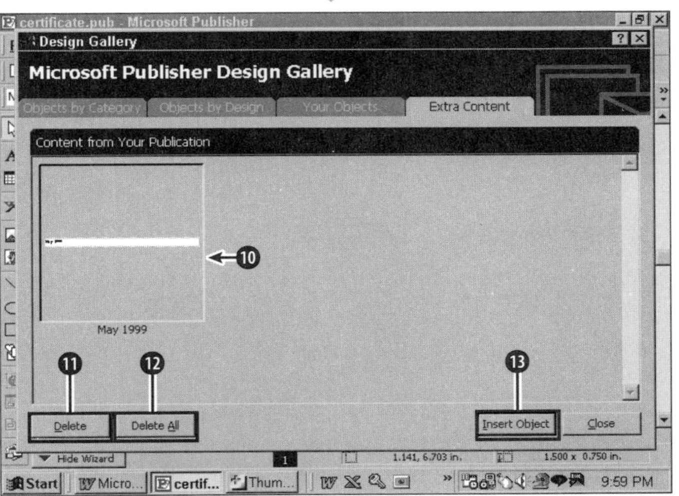

6 *Choose Personal Information in the upper Wizard window.*

7 *Change the information set for the publication, if desired.*

8 *Add other components to the publication from the personal information set, if needed.*

9 *Click the Extra Content button, which only appears if there were items that did not fit in the new design.*

10 *Select an item from the listing.*

11 *Click the Delete button to delete the selected item.*

12 *Click the Delete All button to remove all items.*

13 *Click the Insert Object button to place the item in your publication.*

TAKE NOTE

DISAPPEARING ITEMS ARE NOT LOST

If you change the design after placing some elements on the page, they are not lost. In the Wizard window, you'll see an Extra Content button that, when clicked, shows what had to be removed. You are given the option to delete the element or add it to the design.

DON'T SETTLE FOR EVERYTHING HANDED TO YOU

Even though the designs that are presented in the wizard are ready to run, you can still make changes to the typefaces, logos and other design elements using the menus and tools. Remember that Microsoft Publisher is a popular program and someone could design a project that looks exactly like yours. Take the extra time to put a different twist, typeface, or graphic on your work. That gives it a personal touch.

FIND IT ONLINE

Because color can set a mood, pick the mood you want to achieve. For a discussion of color and its effects, go to http://www.lava.net/~colorcom/.

Creating Greeting Cards

You just about forgot your mother's birthday again. The only problem is it's 1 a.m. and all the stores are closed. There's not enough time to bop into the store before work tomorrow and your mother just can't understand why a card is too much to ask.

Enter the amazing ability of the Publisher 2000 wizards. One of the first things you'll discover is the quantity and quality of the predesigned selections at hand. When you open the Greeting Card category in the Wizard window, you'll find a card to suit just about any occasion. And when you consider that the flexibility of designing each card is almost limitless due to the layout, clipart and messages that the Wizard offers, no one need suspect that you did it all in just a few minutes.

When you have selected the theme of your card, the possible options appear in the right-hand window of the wizard. Don't be fooled into thinking that the way it appears in this window is your only option. Later in the multiple steps to creating your card, there will be options to change the face of the card in one of four other ways. Just so you aren't at a loss when the options appear, here is a rundown of your design alternatives.

- **Juxtaposition:** On the cover, your art and message will be placed next to one another. This gives the card an artsy look.
- **Pattern Pickup:** With the cover message placed in the center of the card, small theme-based icons make up the border around the saying. The centering of text and art give this card a formal and elegant look.

Continued

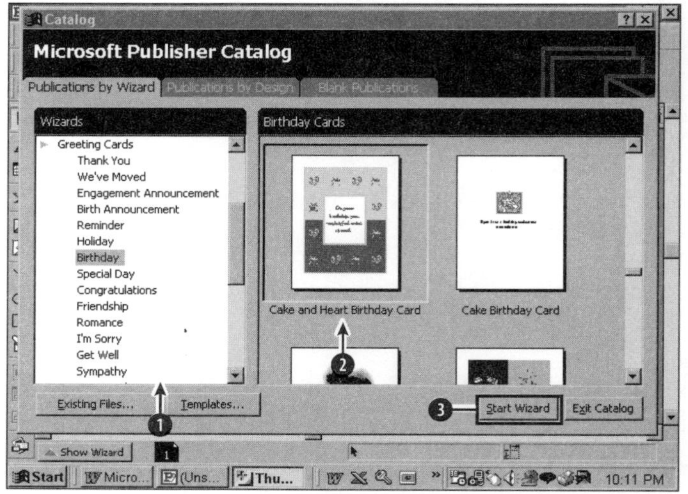

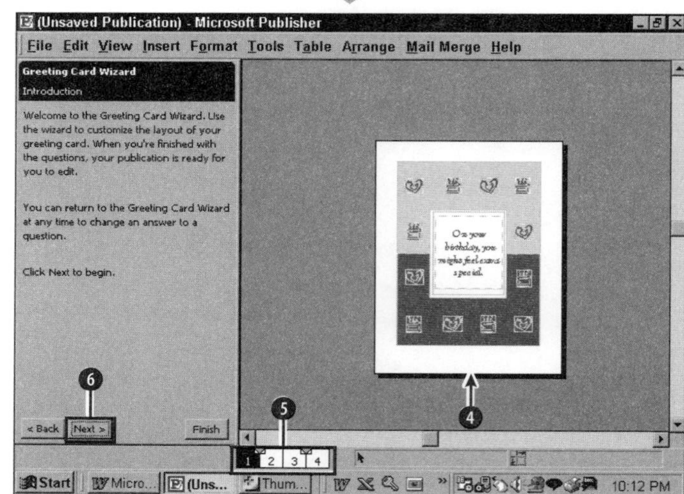

1. *Select the type of greeting card from the Wizard window.*
2. *Choose a style from the right-hand window.*
3. *Click Start Wizard.*
4. *Preview the design.*
5. *Note the number of panels for your card.*
6. *Click Next.*

CROSS-REFERENCE

If your greeting card is announcing your recent move, consider using the Mail Merge option, discussed in Chapters 14 and 15 to personalize each card.

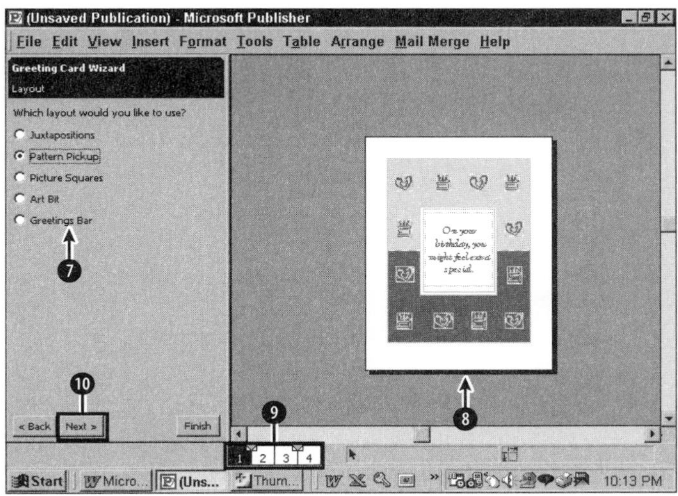

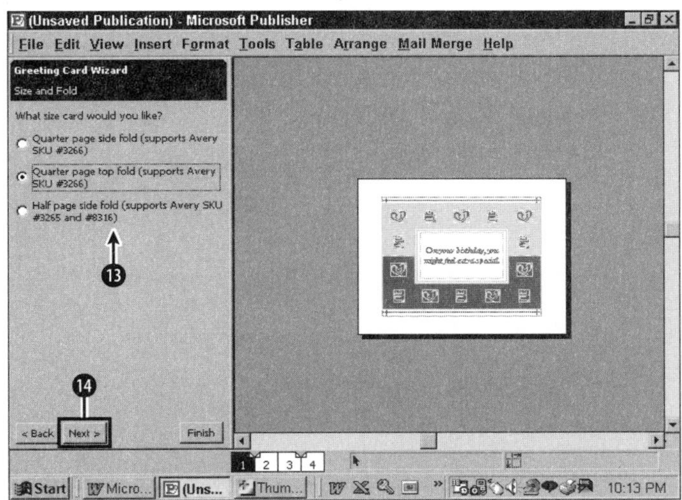

7. *Select a layout from the five options available.*
8. *The Preview window shows the new design.*
9. *Click the Page icons to preview the inside and back.*
10. *Click Next.*
11. *Choose the size of the card.*
12. *Click Next.*

TAKE NOTE

TEST YOUR PRINTING FIRST

Not every monitor is going to display the color used in your greeting card accurately. No matter whether you are printing to an ink-jet or laser printer, you should run a text print first. Try using the draft setting on the ink-jet printer to conserve ink. You should be able to get a good idea of what the final product is going to look like. It also affords you the opportunity to proofread any text you may have entered in the card.

Test printing on a laser printer is recommended, too. Some shades of colors may look fine onscreen, but when they are converted to grayscale, some colors may get washed out or not appear in a laser print at all.

KEEP YOUR PERSONAL INFORMATION UPDATED

Because many of the wizards use the personal information that Microsoft Publisher stores for you, it is wise to double check the information every now and then. In these greeting cards, for example, the back of the card specifies that it is a custom-created card by you.

FIND IT ONLINE

Looking for just the right famous quote to place on your card? Use Bartlett's Familiar Quotations on the Web at www.cc.columbia.edu/acis/bartleby/bartlett.

Creating Greeting Cards

Continued

- **Art Bit:** For a somewhat comic or leisurely look, Art Bit uses a great amount of white space in all four panels of your card. Small graphics are used once, as opposed to duplicated as in the first three options, meaning this card will not only print quickly, but those on an ink-jet budget will appreciate that this card probably uses the least amount of ink.
- **Greetings Bar:** A single, large graphic and text reversed out of a color bar adorn the cover of this card. The outside back cover also uses reverse text in a color bar, which means that this card may eat a lot of ink. The inside message and graphic may offset the outside use of ink, but it's questionable. Use this design for a loud and clear message, destined to be heard.

Once the message and tone of the card are chosen, the wizard asks for paper size and how it will be folded. Although Avery products are mentioned, you can also secure greeting card stock from Labelon Corporation, Hewlett-Packard, Lexmark, and several other vendors. Check with your computer supplies dealer for availability.

Your project is not complete until there's a message on the outside and inside. Publisher offers a wealth of verses for most occasions, but sometimes there's a need for that personal touch. You can always alter the verse once the wizard is done.

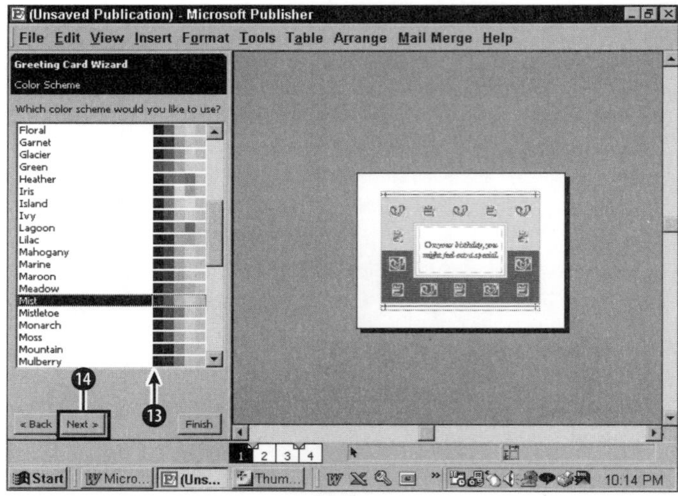

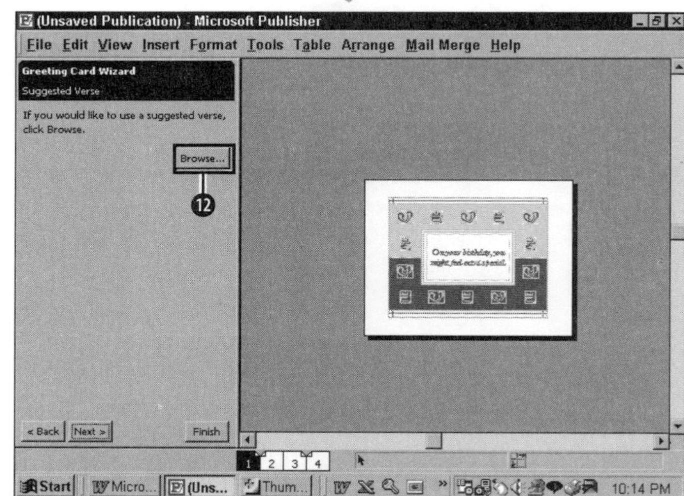

13. *Choose a color scheme for your card.*
14. *Click Next.*
15. *Click the Browse button to choose a different verse in the Suggested Verse dialog box.*

CROSS-REFERENCE

You can change the clip art in your card. See Chapter 11 for ways to bring clip art into your project.

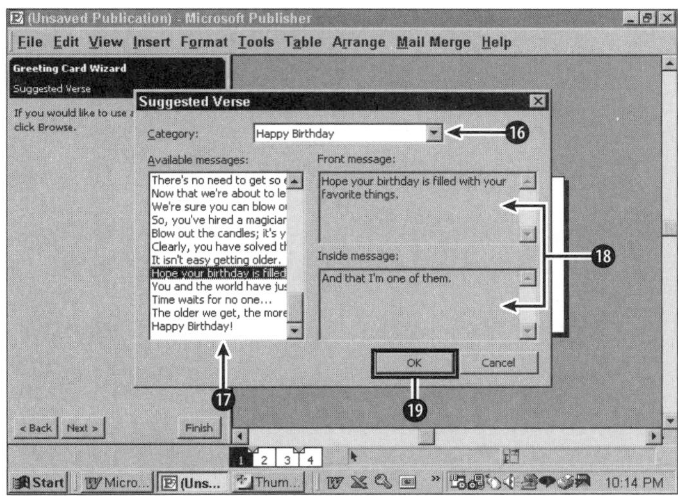

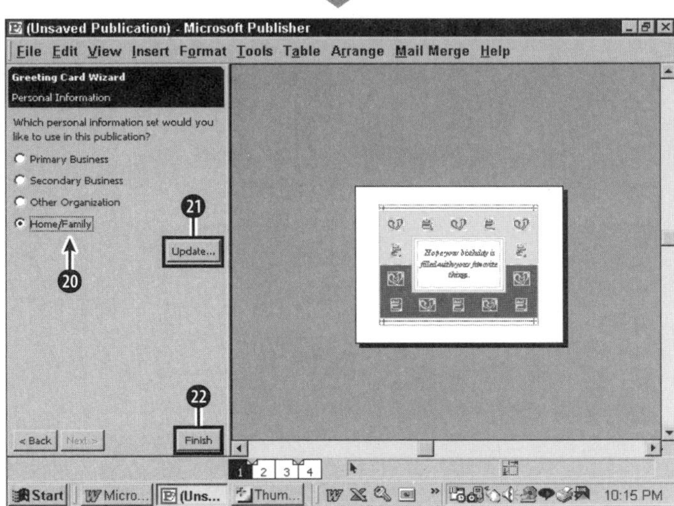

16 *Choose a category from the drop-down menu.*

17 *Click one of the available messages in the list.*

18 *Read the entire front and inside verse for the selection.*

19 *Choose a message and click OK; then, click Next after the dialog box closes.*

20 *Select one of the Personal Information data sets.*

21 *Optionally, click the Update button to change any information.*

22 *Click Finish.*

TAKE NOTE

OBSERVE POSTAL REGULATIONS

Because the U.S. Postal Service places size limitations on mail, check with your local post office to be sure your card meets those requirements. In some cases, you may incur a surcharge for an oversized or undersized piece. If there's not time to get to the post office, you can always go online to find the rates for odd-sized mail pieces. Visit them at **www.usps.gov**.

PLACE YOUR PERSONAL STAMP ON THE BACK

Microsoft Publisher gives you all the tools to create your own logo that suits your personality, avocation, or idiosyncrasy. You'll find all the instructions you need in Chapter 12 to make your hallmark for the back of your cards.

FIND IT ONLINE

Avery-Dennison is the leader in greeting card stock for laser and ink-jet paper. Find the latest offerings at **http://www.avery.com**.

Creating a Flyer

Don't you just hate coming out of the shopping mall and finding some flyer underneath your windshield wiper that tries to tease you into buying a new car at incredible interest rates? Or what about coming home from work and finding a flyer stuck between your flag and mailbox that offers yard service, maid service, or real estate estimates? Don't be too quick to jump to irateness, because you may be guilty of preparing one of those flyers yourself.

Publisher 2000 is loaded with flyer templates that you can conjure with the wizard. From simple black & white to full-fledged color layouts, your flyers can take on the best of them. Plus, you will have avoided a lot of the grunt work in designing it.

Flyer flavors come in several varieties in Publisher, targeted toward specific purposes. Whether you're making a post for the company bulletin board or announcing a special offer to customers in a retail shop, the wizard can handle them all. Specifically, the categories you have to choose from include Information, Special Offer, Sale, Event, Fund-raiser, and Announcement. The last category, Special Paper, enables you to set up one of the various preprinted design flyers if you ordered paper from PaperDirect. And, of course, each of these categories comes with a range of color and art themes.

Among the nifty features in some of the flyers are the tear tabs, as shown in these figures. Many times you will come across this style of flyer in the grocery store, employee bulletin boards at work, or on the college campus. Just to illustrate what a time-saver the Publisher Wizard is, can you imagine laying out this flyer from scratch?

Continued

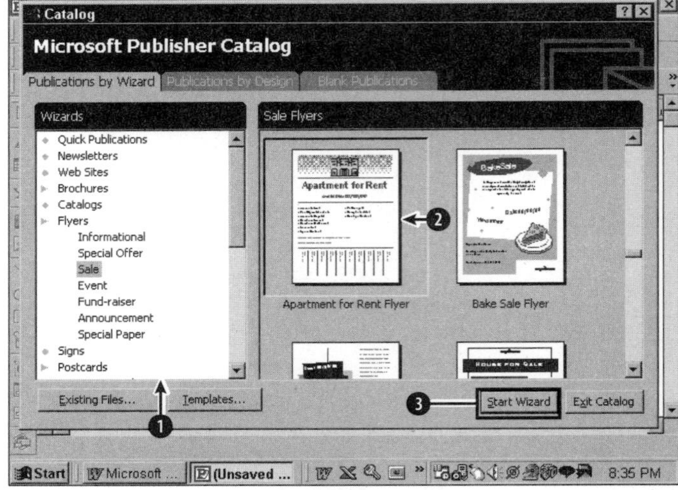

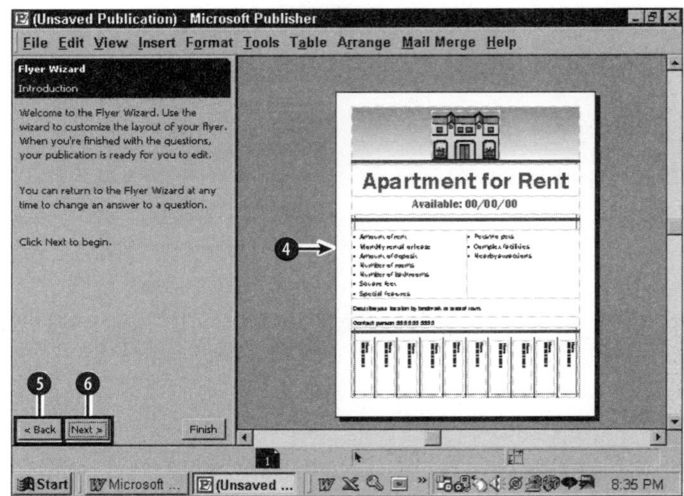

1. *Select the flyer type from the left-hand Wizard window.*
2. *Pick the design from the right-hand Wizard window.*
3. *Click Start Wizard.*
4. *Get a better view of the layout and design in the right-hand Wizard window.*
5. *Click the Back button to choose a different design.*
6. *Or, click Next to continue the wizard.*

CROSS-REFERENCE

To replace any of the clip art found in the wizard designs, use the Clip Gallery as explained in Chapter 11.

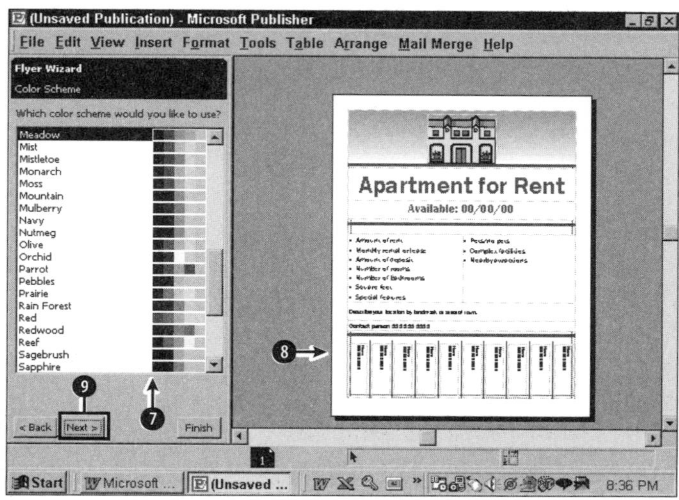

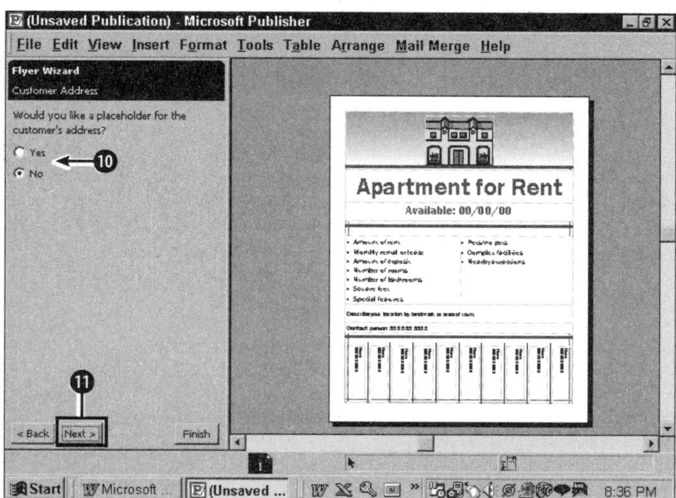

7. *Choose a color scheme from the right-hand window.*
8. *The Preview window shows the color change immediately.*
9. *Click Next to continue.*
10. *Choose whether you will be using a customer address on the flyer.*
11. *Click Next to continue.*

TAKE NOTE

SOME DESIGNS ARE REAL INK OR TONER USERS

When you scan through the different flyer designs in the wizard, be sure to note those designs that take a lot of ink or toner. Some laser printers have a difficult time printing large solid black masses. They can sometimes look dark gray, have streaks in them, or look very uneven. Likewise, ink-jet printers have a tendency to soak the paper if not set properly. This causes the paper to take on a warped look, like a grade school project that used too much glue.

FIND IT ONLINE

For an overview of paper and weight, check out **http://kb.indiana.edu/data/aeou.html** and some of the links off of this page.

Creating a Flyer
Continued

If you dread the idea of preparing reply forms, many of the flyer designs take the grunt work out of it. This brings another thought to mind when choosing a flyer layout. Because you are able to change any of the elements in the flyer once the wizard is done creating it, you can choose a design that includes the elements you want instead of the event, clip art, or concept. For example, if you need an RSVP form for a home party like Tupperware or Mary Kay, go straight for the Tournament flyer design. The heading and large corner graphic are easily changed. The box with the prizes listed can be changed to include what attendees will receive for showing up. The schedule lends itself nicely to announcing what time the demonstration starts, when refreshments will be served, and when orders will be taken. The RSVP form could easily serve as a mini order form, including the name and address of the customer and a short list of items ordered. Lesson learned? Use your imagination and ingenuity to take these projects and customize them for the situation at hand.

The Publisher Wizard even takes care of addressing any of the flyers if you plan on using them as a self-mailing piece. When the wizard asks if you want to create a placeholder for the customer's address, answer yes. A second page is automatically generated, using the Personal Information set you choose as the return address and then places mailing address lines for the customer in the correct location.

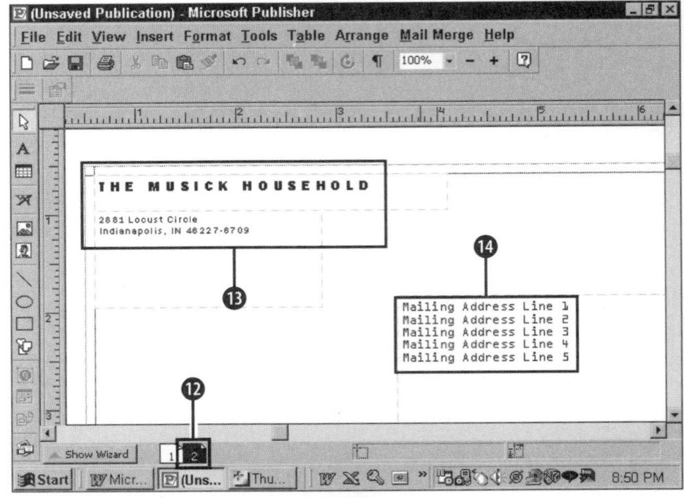

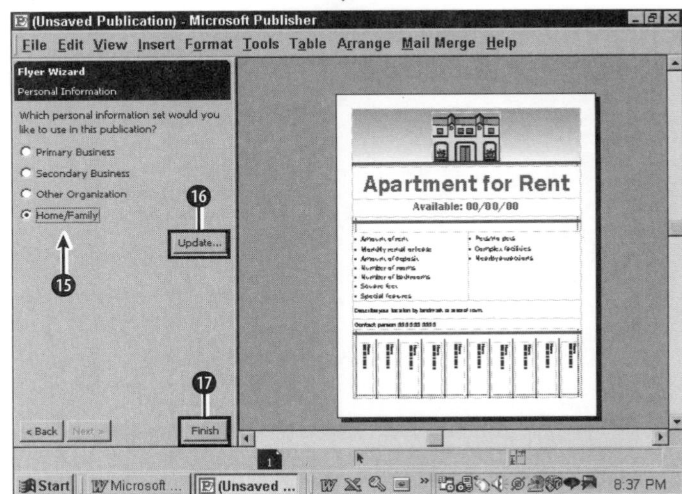

⑫ *If you chose Yes to the customer address, a second page is created.*

⑬ *Though you won't see it up close like this, your return address and organization is placed in the upper-left corner.*

⑭ *Five address lines are placed in the address area.*

⑮ *Select which Personal Information set is used on the flyer.*

⑯ *Click Update to change any personal information.*

⑰ *Click Finish.*

CROSS-REFERENCE

If you choose to include a placeholder for customer addresses, try Publisher Mail Merge, covered in Chapters 14 and 15.

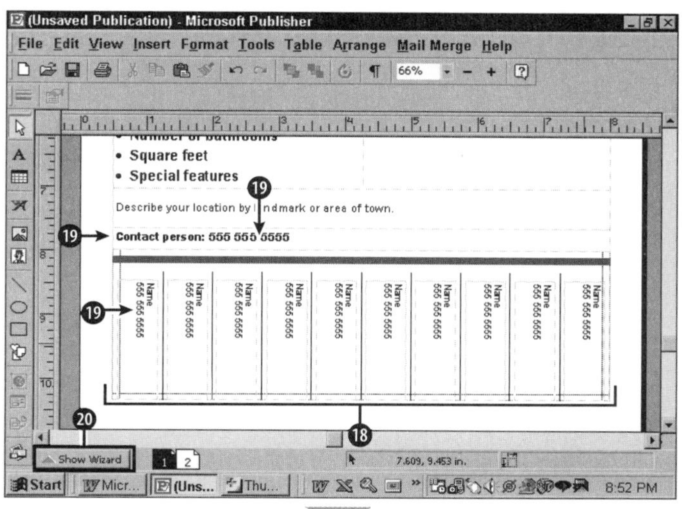

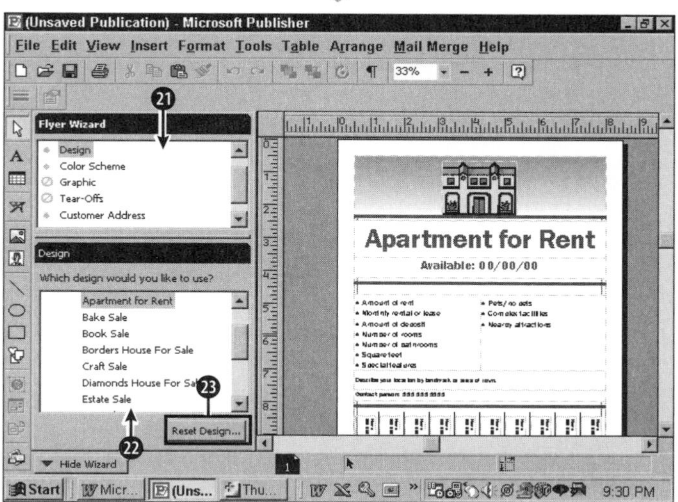

18 *Tear tabs are featured on several flyer designs.*

19 *Edit the information to be included on the flyer.*

20 *Click this button to hide or show the wizard.*

21 *Choose a design element to change, if desired.*

22 *Choose the replacement in the lower window.*

23 *Click the Reset Design button to return to the original settings.*

TAKE NOTE

KEEP IT SIMPLE

If you're unfamiliar with the KISS method of design, listen up. KISS stands for Keep It Sweet and Simple. Of any advice you receive from this book, this is probably the most important. Many designs tend to go way overboard and artists tend to cram a lot of information in a little space. The fewer things a person has to read on a flyer, the more likely it is to get noticed and read.

Follow the same rules that apply toward the first paragraph of a news article. Be sure that your flyer briefly answers the five W's and H: Who, What, When, Where, Why, and How. Of course, some of these won't be applicable, but get as many as you can into your flyer.

CHOOSE PAPER WISELY

If you're planning on mailing your flyer, consider using a heavier paper stock. Regular 20# bond paper, the type you use in most copiers and printers, isn't quite sturdy enough to make it through the postal system. This is not to say that none of your flyers will survive the postal equipment. But, your chances for a trouble-free delivery are greater if you use a sturdier paper stock.

FIND IT ONLINE

To find the latest in home food storage, go to the Tupperware home page at **http://www.tupperware.com.**

Creating a Brochure

Most any corporate environment thrives on brochures. Walk in any bank and you are faced with scores of individual brochures that highlight the programs that are offered. Home equity loans, car loans, certificates of deposit, stock brokerage information, retirement accounts, and many other subjects have their own brochure, spelling out the advantages of this bank's programs over another.

While you're taking note of the number of brochures, you should also notice that they all pretty much look alike. They sometimes carry the same design but vary in color, or the placement of the graphic is the same but the graphic changes with the theme of the piece. This is not by pure accident. In this case, everything the bank releases to the public has the same "look and feel," giving the bank an identity they hope is recognized whenever one of their brochures crosses your path. You don't even have to read it to know where it came from.

It is often true that you only get one chance to make a good impression—true not only for people, but for any publication. Your projects have to win the approval of a majority of people, and your designs have to be comfortable for people to read.

Publisher 2000's Brochure Wizard can help you attain that goal of "similar, yet different" when designing brochures. Considering your ability to change color schemes alone makes Publisher a great design ally.

Designs should be no problem either. The four categories in the Publisher-creates-them-from-scratch wizards give you plenty of ideas. You can choose from informational, price list, event, and fund-raiser brochures to tackle most any project.

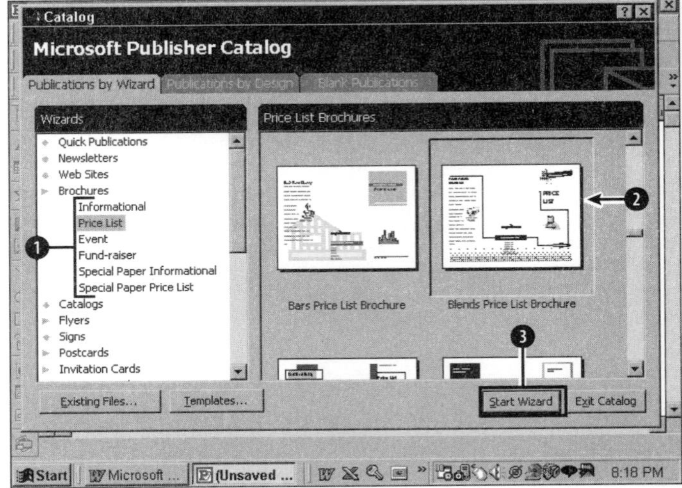

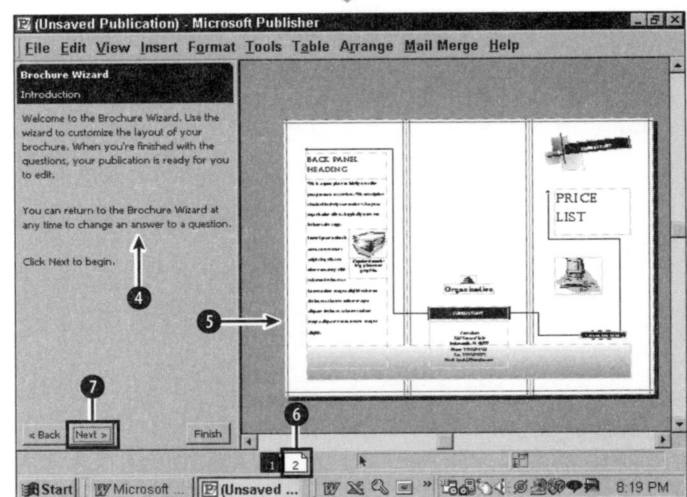

1. Select the type of brochure from the Wizard menu.
2. Choose the design style from the right-hand side of the wizard.
3. Click Start Wizard.
4. Read the specific information about the Brochure Wizard.
5. Preview the design in the window.
6. Click the Page 2 icon to preview the second page.
7. Click Next.

CROSS-REFERENCE

When doing multistyle brochures, consider saving your first design as a template. See "Saving Your Publication as a Template" in Chapter 3.

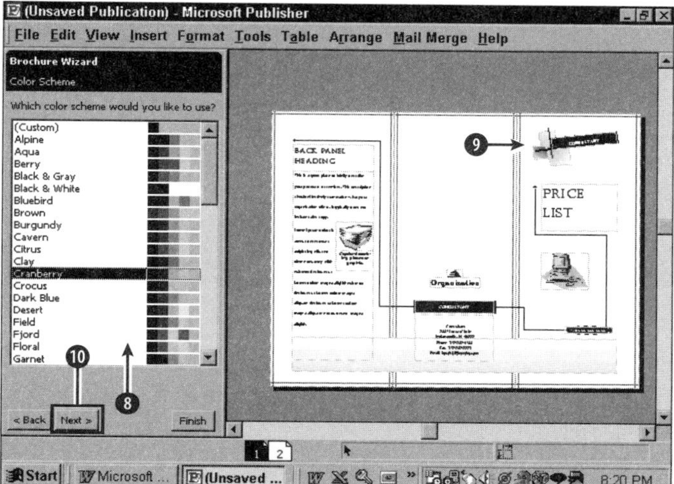

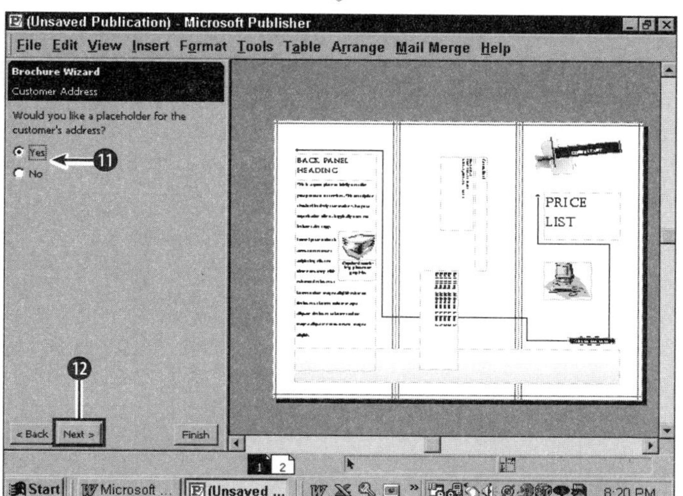

8 *Select the color scheme.*

9 *Preview the color scheme on the page elements.*

10 *Click Next.*

11 *Choose whether or not to include an address area on the brochure.*

12 *Click Next.*

For the PaperDirect templates, you'll find two categories, Informational and Price List, that match up to the preprinted offerings of that company.

Continued

TAKE NOTE

RETURN REPLY FORMS NEED SPACE

When creating a form that an individual is going to be filling out and returning to you, be sure to leave enough space for handwritten responses. Not only should the length of the blanks be adequate, but there should also be enough height for normal handwriting. It's also a good idea to request the information be printed.

CONVERT YOUR BROCHURE TO THE WEB

Several of the brochure designs enable you to create a Web page after the Brochure Wizard has finished. In the wizard's upper menu, there may be a choice labeled "Convert to Web," usually at the bottom of the list. Clicking this item gives you a Create button in the lower half of the Wizard window. Clicking the button starts the Web Wizard.

FIND IT ONLINE

For tips on creating effective brochures, **http://www.gmarketing.com/tactics/weekly_85.html** offers excellent advice and things to ponder.

Creating a Brochure

Continued

Design Tips

- Make a list of the elements that will be included in the folded piece.
- Decide how the brochure will be folded. An accordion fold (like the fans you used to make in grade school) has to be designed differently than the traditionally folded brochure. Accordion-folded brochures may not make the best self-mailers.
- If a tear-off reply section is to be included, be sure to place it so the information that winds up on the opposite side is unimportant. You may have to move elements around once the wizard has finished to accomplish this.
- Will you be mailing the brochure by itself or stuffing it in an envelope? Self-mailing brochures need an address and return address area. If you place the mailing panel on the opposite side of the registration form, you are leaving all of the information presented in the brochure with the individual once the reply form is ripped and sent.
- If you have too much information to place in a letter-sized, folded brochure, consider using legal-size. This gives you two more panels to include in the design. It is better to have a bit of breathing space than to shrink the type size and cram information in. Besides, the cost is not that much more.
- Sometimes when using the Brochure Wizard, the final result may include columns of text that are too close to one another. If so, consider moving the columns further apart or making them smaller before entering your custom text. This way, you won't run the risk of your text being too close to the fold of the brochure.

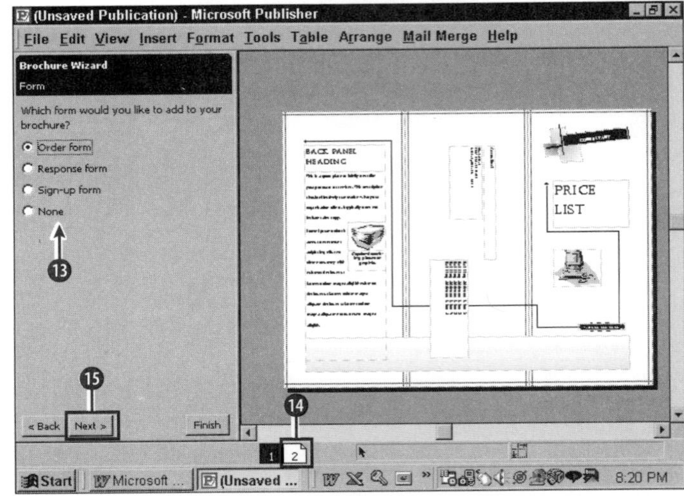

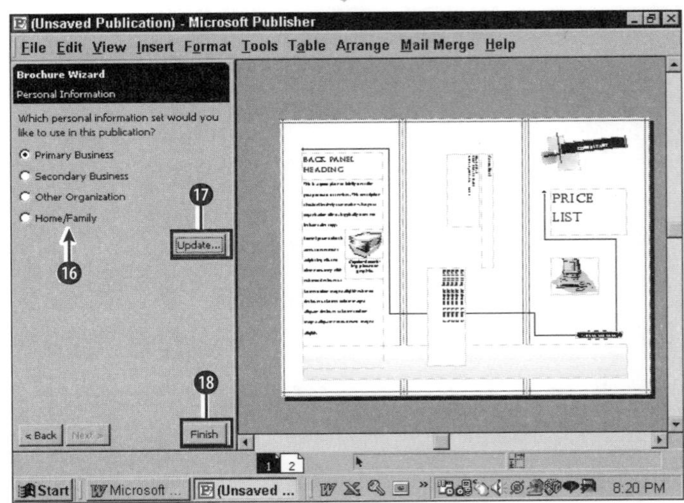

13. *If your brochure includes a form, select the type of form.*
14. *Click the Page icon where the form is located to preview it.*
15. *Click Next.*
16. *Choose the Personal Information set that will be used on the brochure.*
17. *Click Update to make changes to the Personal Information set.*
18. *Click Finish.*

CROSS-REFERENCE

For changing the number of columns or the space between, see "Using the Layout Guides" in Chapter 7.

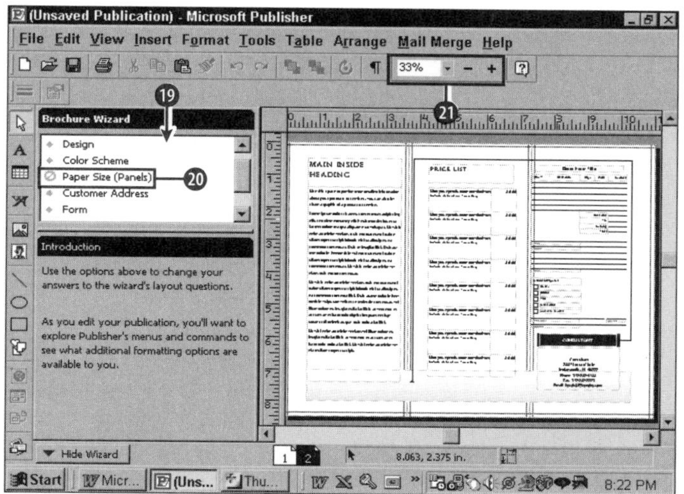

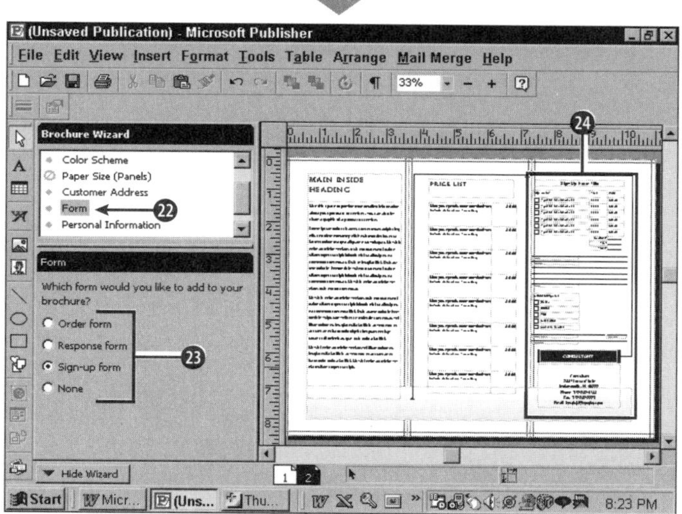

19. *To change individual elements that the wizard created, choose it from the list.*
20. *Note that paper size may not be changed in the wizard. That is done through File ➪ Print Setup.*
21. *Use the Zoom buttons to enlarge or reduce parts of the page.*
22. *Click Form to make changes to the form type.*
23. *Select a new form design.*
24. *Preview the form information and layout.*

TAKE NOTE

LET PUBLISHER ADDRESS YOUR SELFMAILERS

Consider using the Mail Merge features that Publisher 2000 has to offer. That way, when you print the side of your brochure that contains the address area, your return address and customer addresses are applied at the same time. For more information of Publisher's Mail Merge capabilities, see Chapters 14 and 15.

MAKING A DUMMY

Take a blank piece of paper and fold it exactly how your brochure will be folded when complete. Most brochures that use letter-sized pages are folded in thirds or in half. After folding the paper as desired, write some description on each panel to indicate its position or importance. Use terms such as "front cover," "back cover or mailer," "inside panel," and so forth. This helps you visualize the final piece and helps you place elements where they belong.

FIND IT ONLINE

Clip art for the banking industry and other purposes can be found at **http://www2.pcworld.com/fileworld/category/0,1460,graphics+clip%5Fart,00.html.**

Creating a Newsletter

It has long been a secret of public relations firms that newsletters are the greatest tool for keeping a company name in front of its customers. Well, maybe it's a secret that hasn't been real closely held because so many companies produce newsletters. But still, the adage is true. Newsletters inform, entertain, promote, and can give the best PR bang for the dollar.

Newsletters are not only for companies; you can probably think of a dozen newsletters that touch your life on a monthly basis. Childcare providers issue newsletters, as do classroom teachers, little league teams, and nonprofit organizations such as churches and youth groups. Why, it's a safe bet that your bowling league even has a newsletter.

Newsletter editors go through a grueling job hunting for information to fill their page count, typing in the information, scanning CDs and disks for clip art, and then duplicating, folding, and mailing them (unless you're fortunate enough to be able to hand them out).

Microsoft Publisher can't help with the folding and postage, but it can get you through the rough times of designing the layout and providing the clipart. And, if you use the wizard to start your newsletter, you're even closer to making that deadline.

A typical fault of many newsletters is that fledgling editors and designers try to cram as much as they can in the limited amount of space they have to work with. When you scan through the different styles of newsletter templates that the wizard creates, notice the amount of white space that is used on the front pages. This same layout technique is carried through the rest of the pages. Let this be lesson number one: Leaving white space open is not a crime. Unfortunately, many designers even have to battle their boss to keep it.

Continued

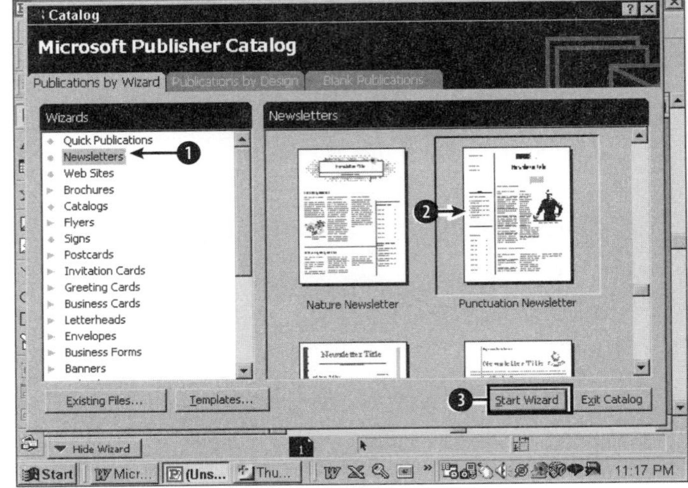

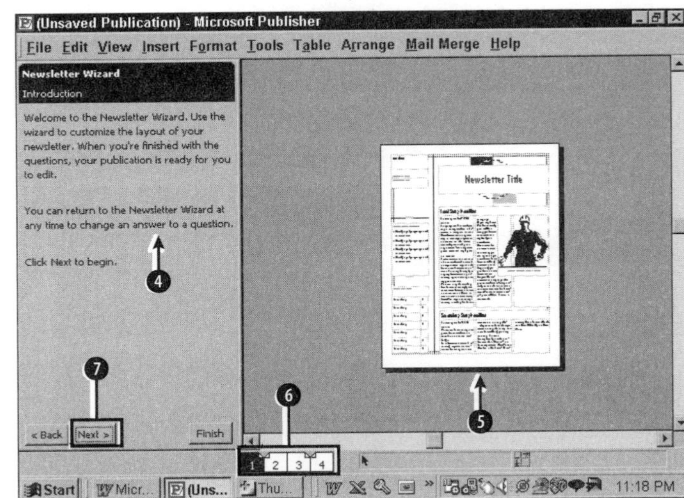

1. Select the Newsletter category.
2. Pick a newsletter style.
3. Click the Start Wizard button.
4. Read the introductory verbiage.
5. View the layout preview.
6. Click the Page icons to view other pages.
7. Click Next.

CROSS-REFERENCE

Converting your publications to HTML is covered in Chapters 16 and 17.

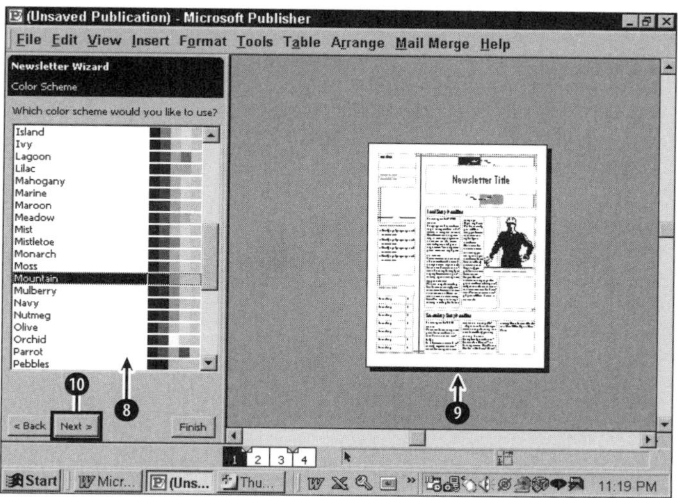

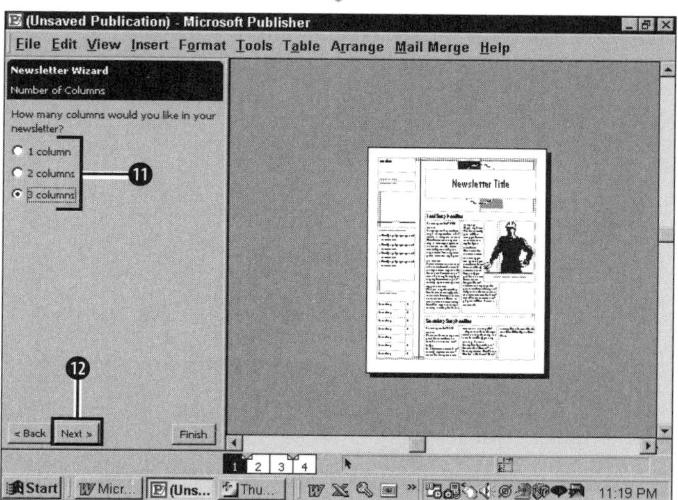

8. *Select a color scheme.*
9. *Preview the changes.*
10. *When satisfied with the color, click Next.*
11. *Choose the number of columns for your text.*
12. *Click Next.*

TAKE NOTE

LIGHTEN UP NEWSLETTER CONTENT

Not all newsletters have to be all news. Try putting in a joke of the month, run a contest for the funniest photo submitted, or use games such as crossword puzzles or word searches to lighten up your publication.

INVITE READER PARTICIPATION

When you encourage letters or comments from your readers, you are indicating that the publication is theirs. You are producing this publication for them. If letters or comments aren't conducive to the publication, offer free classified ads for readers to sell unwanted items.

FIND IT ONLINE

For more information on the family of Adobe Acrobat products, go to **http://www.adobe.com.** The Acrobat reader is free to download from this site.

Creating a Newsletter

Continued

Too much information in small type defeats the purpose of a newsletter. Newsletters are supposed to give readers quality information at a glance. You should be able to scan the headlines quickly, and decide whether an article interests you.

When you decide to read an article, it should be straight to the point, giving most of the pertinent information in the first few paragraphs.

When choosing clip art, be sure it is pertinent to the information in the article and enhances the text. The same goes for pictures. Be sure that they are relative to the topic at hand and not just fluff or filler. Also, be sure they are quality photos and will reproduce well. Faces should be large and visible; contrast should be sharp and clear. If you have any doubt, it is better to leave a picture out than print a bad one. Try using candid shots. If an employee has been selected for an award, get a picture of them working instead of the picture where the boss is handing out a certificate and shaking their hand. This, in the industry, is called the "grip and grin" photo.

While going through the Newsletter Wizard, you will be asked if you want the publication to be single- or double-sided. That is, will you print on both sides of the paper or just one side? Depending on your style selection, the layout of page 2 will possibly change. In the instance pictured in these figures, a column of graphics or short items is maintained on the outside edge of the page. Because page 2 falls on the left side of the inside spread, the graphics column is on the left side. When the layout is changed to a single-sided publication, the column is moved to the right side.

Just because the wizard starts you out with four pages does not mean that is your limit. You can easily add more pages to your newsletter (see Chapter 6.)

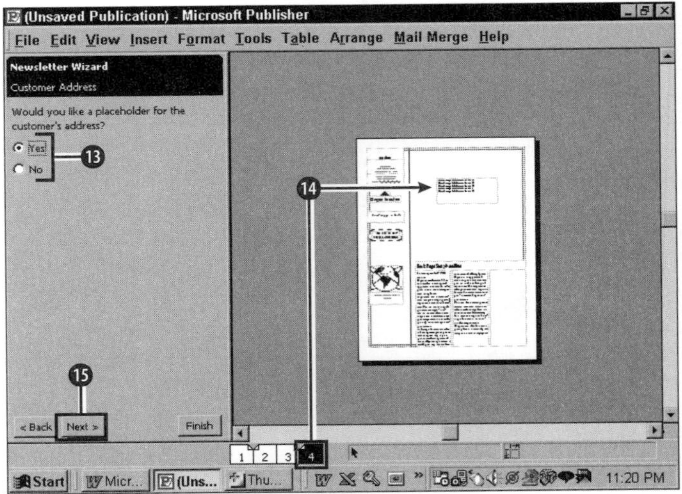

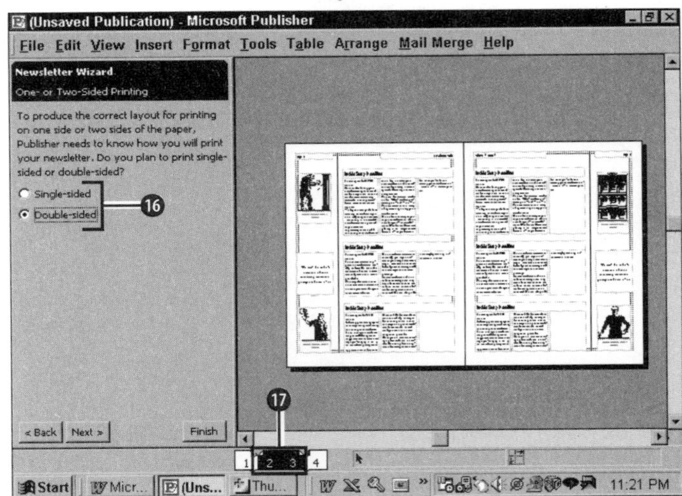

13. *Select whether the newsletter will carry address information for mailing.*
14. *Click the Page 4 icon to preview the address location.*
15. *Click Next.*
16. *Choose whether your newsletter is to be single- or double-sided.*
17. *Click the Page 2 icon to view the effects of your choice.*

▶ *If a double-sided publication is chosen, pages 2 and 3 are visible in the Preview window.*

CROSS-REFERENCE

If you're planning on a commercial printer printing your newsletter, see Chapter 18, "Using a Commercial Printing Service," for those special instructions.

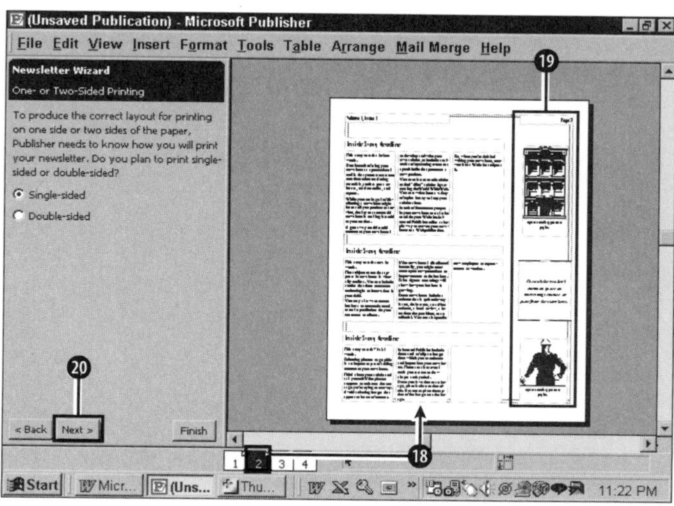

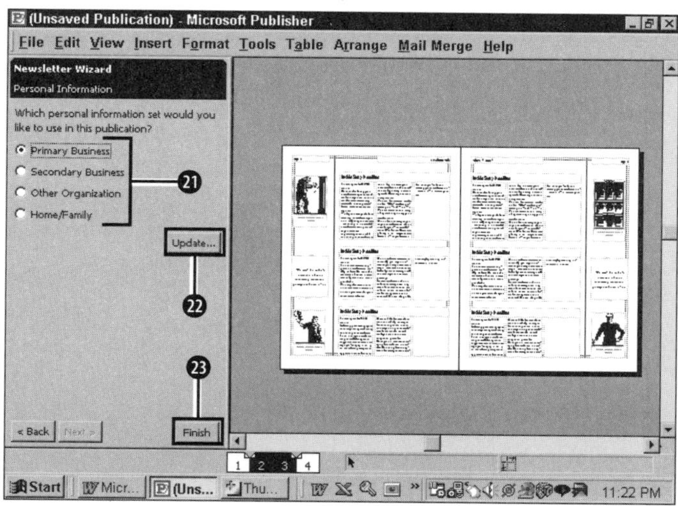

18 *If single-sided is chosen, only page 2 is previewed when the Page icon is selected.*

19 *Graphics that were on the left have been moved to the right side.*

20 *Click Next.*

21 *Choose the Personal Information set that is to be used for the publication.*

22 *Click the Update button to edit the personal information.*

23 *Click Finish.*

TAKE NOTE

CREATE ONLINE NEWSLETTERS

If you have a Web site, why not put your newsletter online? Because Publisher lets you prepare publications and convert them to Web documents, the Internet is just another way that you can circulate your news in a very cost-justifiable way.

If the results from Publisher are less than what you expect, when preparing a Web document, you could consider using Adobe Acrobat to create a portable document, capable of being circulated on diskette, e-mailed, or placed on a Web site for downloading. If your readers have the Acrobat plug-in for their browser, they can also read it online.

Online newsletters have a greater appeal over photocopied or black and white newsletters because color can be included. Acrobat files reproduce the color from your layout program. Readers who have color printers can print their own newsletter in color.

FIND IT ONLINE

Newsletter design and writing tips can be found at **http://www.reasonandrhyme.com/wdfork.html.**

Personal Workbook

Q&A

1. What is the difference between the Publication by Wizard tab and the Publication by Design tab in the Microsoft Publisher Catalog?

2. While the Microsoft Publisher Wizard is active, are the drop-down program menus available?

3. How can you change an awards certificate into a greeting card?

4. When using the wizard, you change from a double-sided publication to a single-sided publication. What could happen and what page could you preview to see if it did?

5. What does KISS stand for?

6. Once you have completed a wizard, how do you clear or close the Wizard window that is left open?

7. When Microsoft Publisher has already been opened and you have closed the Microsoft Publisher Catalog window, how can you open the Catalog window again?

8. What is the difference between the circle and arrow bullet in the list of wizards?

ANSWERS: PAGE 349

EXTRA PRACTICE

1. Use the wizard to create a personal letterhead with your home address and phone number on it. Include your e-mail and Web site addresses, if you have them.
2. Make a greeting card for a coworker, thanking them for something special they did for you. If they did nothing special, make it an invitation to do so (like taking you to lunch).
3. Create a self-mailing brochure that explains what your company does.
4. Create a menu for the week and post it on the refrigerator for your family.
5. Make a set of bookplate labels to stick in your books that people borrow. Be sure to include details on overdue charges and lost book prices.

REAL-WORLD APPLICATIONS

- ✔ You have forgotten your anniversary once again. Using the Gift Certificate Wizard, create a gift certificate for your spouse for some simple act of kindness.
- ✔ All of your old 8mm home movies from your parents have been converted to VHS videotape. Make special face and spine labels to place on the copies that you will give to your brothers and sisters.
- ✔ Your high school class reunion is coming up. Use the wizard to create nametags of all your classmates and their spouses. Hint: Don't forget to finish reading the Mail Merge part of this book before attempting this task.

Visual Quiz

In this figure, explain the steps you would take to change the area in the top right-hand side of the page to a customer address area.

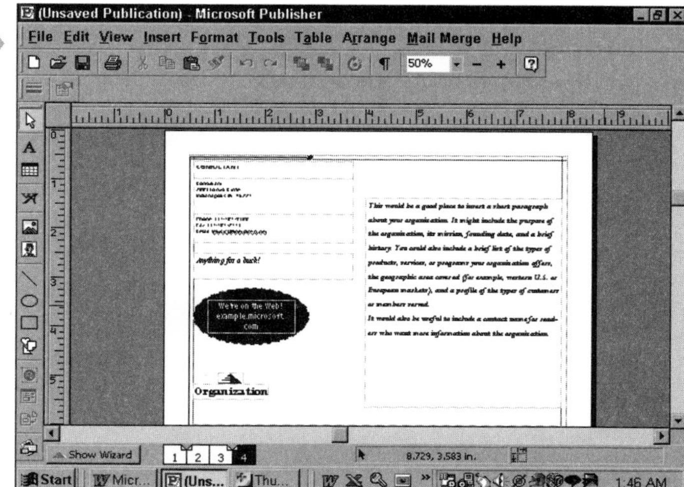

CHAPTER 5

MASTER THESE SKILLS

- Setting Up Your Printer
- Using Advanced Print Settings
- Printing Odd-Sized Publications
- Printing to a File
- Creating a Web Site from Your Publication

Printing Your Publication

When you think of printing from your computer, letter-sized paper streaming into the paper tray would seem to be the norm. Sure, if you're using one of the other programs in the Microsoft Office 2000 suite, 99 percent of the output would be on 8½×11-inch paper. But you're using Publisher 2000, where the possibilities present themselves in quite a different light.

When you couple the capabilities of Microsoft Publisher with the printers available on the market today, your potential for some odd-sized publications increases. In the past, printers handled letter-sized paper and some would let you do legal with a special tray or through a manual paper feed. Nowadays, paper-handling trays and bins let you mix the sheets and even the type of media you print on. Some paper trays can be altered for legal, letter, and envelopes.

Another boon to publishers today is the affordability of printers that print tabloid-sized pages (that's 11×17 inches for those who are just starting out in the business). This capability at a lower price is seen more in the ink-jet arena than laser. Laser printers capable of tabloid output may still be a little pricey for the home office, but certainly not for the small to medium-sized businesses. For example, think about the nice posters that can be generated from these printers.

As always, bear in mind that the larger the surface you have to print on, the more supplies you will consume. And, in some cases, your printing time increases dramatically.

Here are a couple things to keep in mind when you are out shopping for a new printer to ably handle all the new features that Publisher has to offer. Don't just shop for the features in the printer. Shop for the price of the consumables. Many times a manufacturer makes a great printer and sells it at a cheap price. But, when it comes time to buy the supplies, you may be paying more per page in the long run.

Check the variety of consumables. For example, ink-jet printers are now offering permanent inks, photo inks, metallic inks, neon inks, and more. Laser cartridges may come in a standard or high-yield variety.

Try to get a printer that handles a variety of paper weights and sizes. Don't forget envelopes, too.

Setting Up Your Printer

Because there are so many printers on the market, some of the figures in this task may not look exactly like what you'll see on your computer. That's because the various printer drivers for the massive number of printers available look a bit different from one another.

What will look the same, though, is the first printing dialog box you'll see when you invoke the Print command in Microsoft Publisher. It's only in the deeper menus and setups where options start to look different.

Generally, the Print dialog box is where you and the computer tell the printer what is about to be printed, the number of copies that you are expecting, and how the pages that the printer is about to receive will be oriented.

Printers can usually output in two modes: portrait and landscape. *Portrait orientation* is a technical term for straight-up-and-down, the way you wrote all your papers in school. Lines of type run left to right across the shortest width of the paper. Portrait paintings or pictures usually run from top to bottom.

The opposite is *landscape*. Using the painting example again, most landscapes are painted where the longest part of the picture is seen from left to right. If you forget the difference, watch for the little pictures in the dialog box that show the difference.

Publisher, when starting a new document, looks at the default Windows print driver, and the page you see set up is using those default settings. You can change this through the File ➪ Page Setup dialog box and deal with the printer setup when you're ready to print.

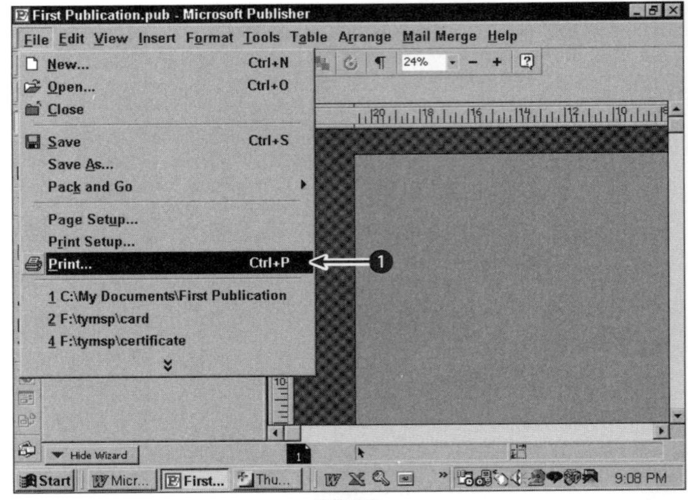

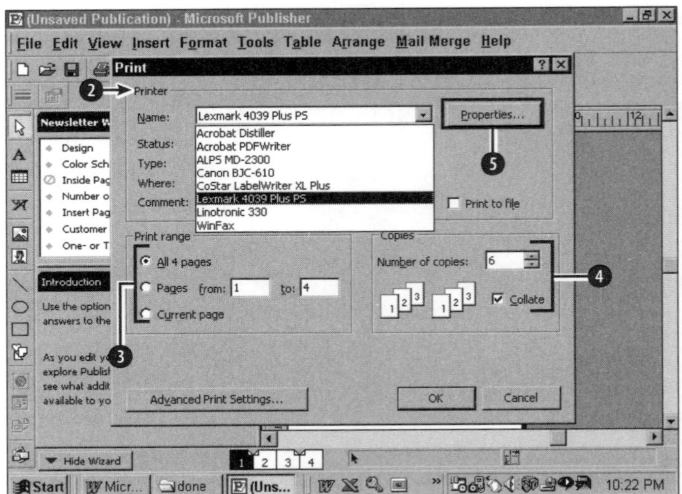

1. Choose File ➪ Print or press Ctrl+P.

▶ If you choose the Print button on the standard toolbar, your publication begins printing immediately. You will not have the chance to set the options.

2. Choose the target printer from the drop-down list.
3. Select what pages you want to print.
4. Select the number of copies and, for multiple page publications, choose whether to collate the pages or not.
5. Click Properties to change the printer settings.

CROSS-REFERENCE

To change the way your page appears on the screen, see "Using Page Setup" in Chapter 6.

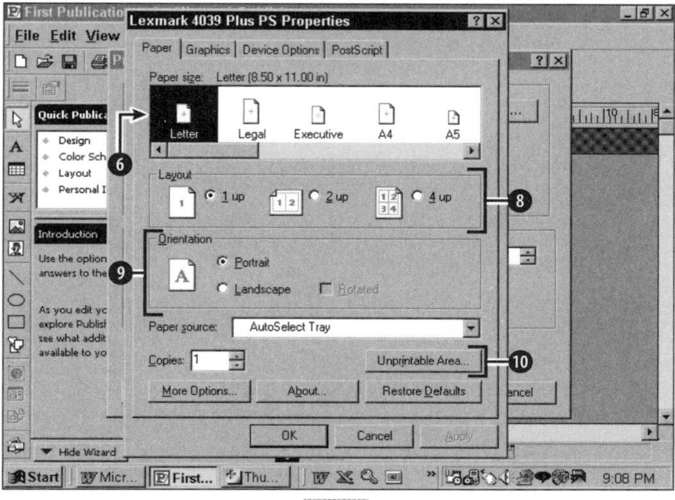

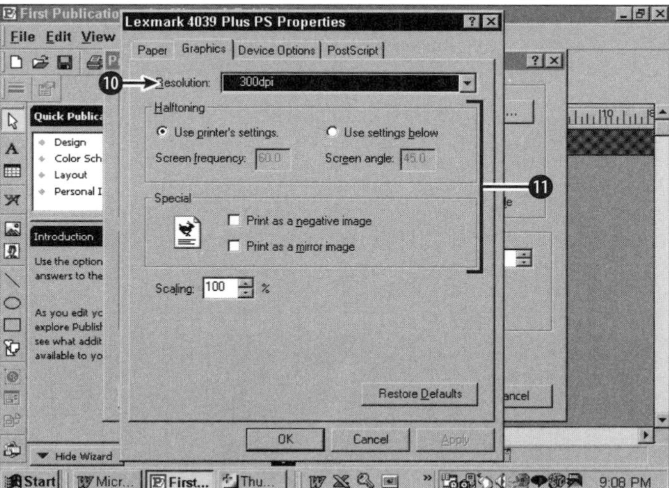

6 *In the Printer Properties dialog box, choose the paper size.*

7 *Choose how many pages will appear on one sheet of paper.*

8 *Indicate portrait or landscape orientation.*

9 *Choose paper source where the paper is loaded in the printer.*

10 *In the Graphics tab, choose the resolution to be printed.*

11 *These settings may be used for commercial printing.*

In addition, you will be indicating how many copies of the publication you want printed, and how they are to be output. When you have a document with multiple pages, you have the option to collate them. That is, if you have a four-page document, request six copies, and check the collate box, Publisher prints pages 1–4, and then starts over again and prints 1–4 again. It continues printing this way until all six copies are printed. With the Collate box unchecked, you get six copies of page 1, six copies of page 2, and so on. If your publication consists of one single page, the checkbox won't even show.

TAKE NOTE

UPGRADE THAT OLD PRINTER

If you have made it thus far in your Windows computing career with an old dot matrix printer, consider investing a couple hundred dollars (or less) to get a nice ink-jet printer. The difference you will see in the color printouts from Publisher will make that investment very worthwhile.

FIND IT ONLINE

To help you pick out a new printer that meets your needs, go to **http://www.zdnet.com/pcmag/pclabs/per/print.html.**

Using Advanced Print Settings

By using the advanced print settings, available from the button at the bottom of the Print dialog box, you'll learn how to change the settings for specific instances. Though many of the options found in the Print Settings dialog box are specifically targeted toward sending your publication to a commercial printer, some can be handy when sending your job to your desktop printer.

Crop marks can be added to show where something will be trimmed down to a final size. Keep in mind if your final size is the same size as what you're actually printing on, crop marks will not show because these are normally placed on the outside edges of the document.

For example, if you're printing a copy to proofread or pass around for others to review and suggest changes, you can print graphics at a lower resolution or hide them entirely. Printer *resolution* is measured in dots per inch (dpi). The higher number of dpi, the more fine and clear the print will be.

You can also indicate the printer resolution in the Device Options tab. Again, for proofing purposes, use a lower resolution to conserve toner or ink and decrease printing time.

Here's a trick: Use the Emulsion Down checkbox on the Device Options tab to create a reverse image of your page. Print overhead transparencies this way so you can mark on the side of the transparency that doesn't have the ink or toner. It's a lot easier to clean off marker or grease pencil for the next presentation.

When you access the Print Settings dialog box, you'll notice many choices grayed out and unavailable. These settings are for preparing your document for a commercial printer.

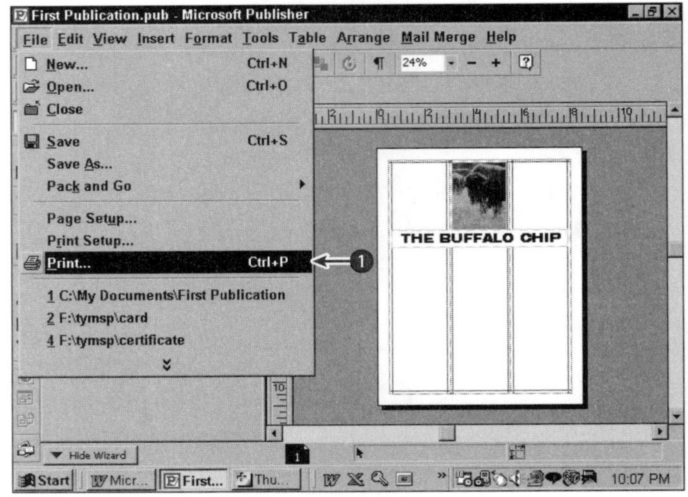

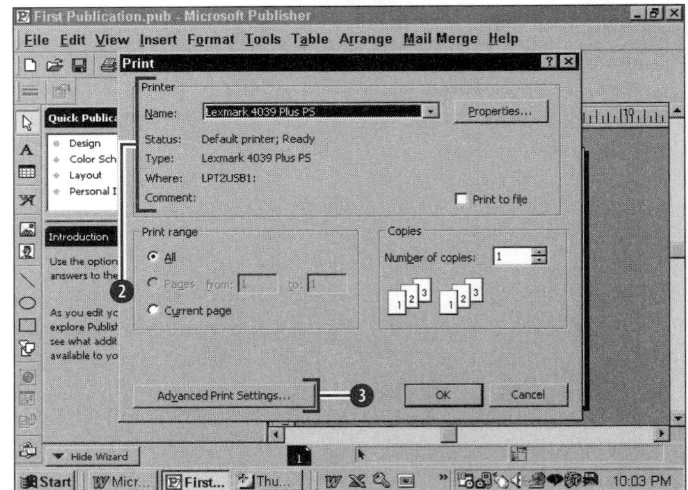

1. Choose File ➪ Print from the menu or press Ctrl+P.

▶ Do not use the Print button on the standard toolbar. This sends your document to the printer immediately.

2. Complete the upper portion of the Print dialog box as explained in the previous task.

3. Click the Advanced Print Settings button.

CROSS-REFERENCE

Preparing your document for commercial printing is covered in Chapter 18.

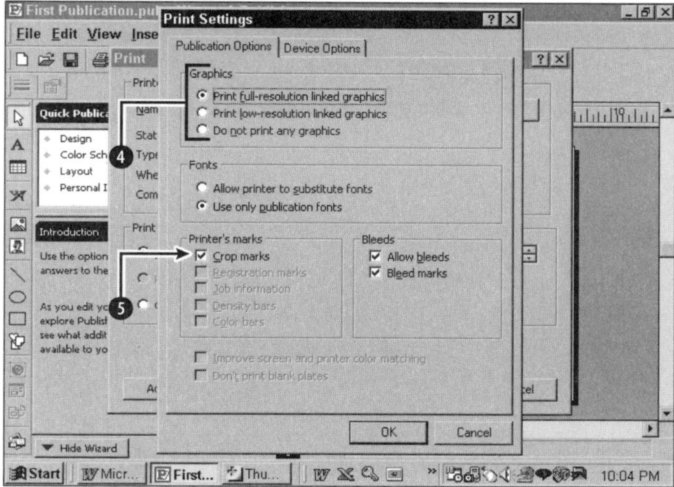

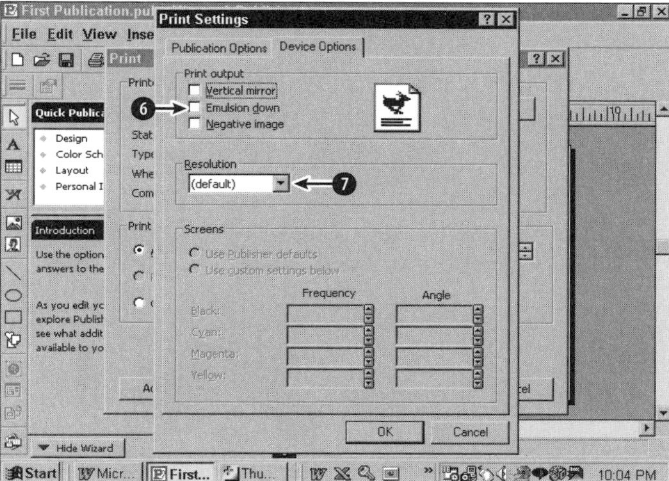

4. *Select the treatment of graphics.*
5. *Turn crop marks off or on.*
6. *Select the Device Options tab.*
7. *Select "Emulsion down" to print a mirror image of your document.*
8. *Change the resolution here, if desired. Otherwise, you should set the resolution in the Printer Properties dialog box.*

TAKE NOTE

DON'T BLEED TO A DESKTOP PRINTER

In the printing world, *bleeds* are where graphics or text is run right up to the edge of the paper. When commercial printing jobs are set up, you normally position and size the graphic to extend off the edge of the paper so when the final job is printed and trimmed, your image will actually be on the trim. It'll do you little good to try to bleed anything on a full page if you are printing to your desktop printer. Most printers have a quarter-inch area all around the paper where it is unable to print. So, bleeding is useless when the printer can't handle it.

However, if you are designing business cards, greeting cards, or anything else that will be trimmed from a normal size page, bleeding is okay because you will be trimming the outside edges from the final printout. It is especially convenient when you are using specialty paper where the sheets are perforated for easy separation.

FIND IT ONLINE

Professional proofreading marks are explained at http://www.eeicom.com/staffing/marks.html.

Printing Odd-Sized Publications

Setting up page size is not the focus of this task; that is covered later in Chapter 6. To whet your appetite, however, Publisher has presets for posters and banners in addition to a custom setting where you specify the length and width of the page. In this task, our focus is how to get those oversized, steroid-popping pages out of your printer.

Your desktop printer, though limited to traditional paper sizes, can give you a large poster or single, small business card. Smaller-sized documents can be printed on standard paper by simply dropping them in the middle of your paper for you to trim out. To print larger posters and banners, however, a process called tiling comes into play.

Tiling is where a large printed piece is divided up into printable pages that can be assembled with a trusty roll of adhesive tape to make one large printed page. Of course, if you are fortunate to have a large-format printer or plotter at your disposal, you can forego the tape and print it all at once.

When you tile print a document, Publisher looks at your printer settings, checks the printer's default paper size, and breaks your large document into multiples of that page size. You might try changing your paper setup to legal size to see if it's a better fit.

Another media that is considered odd-sized is the envelope. Stock #10 and #6 envelopes have presets in Publisher. But, again, you can specify a custom size and Publisher will create it.

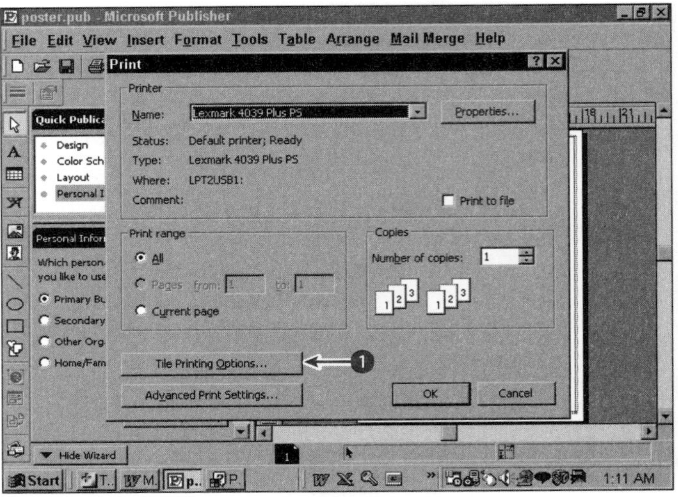

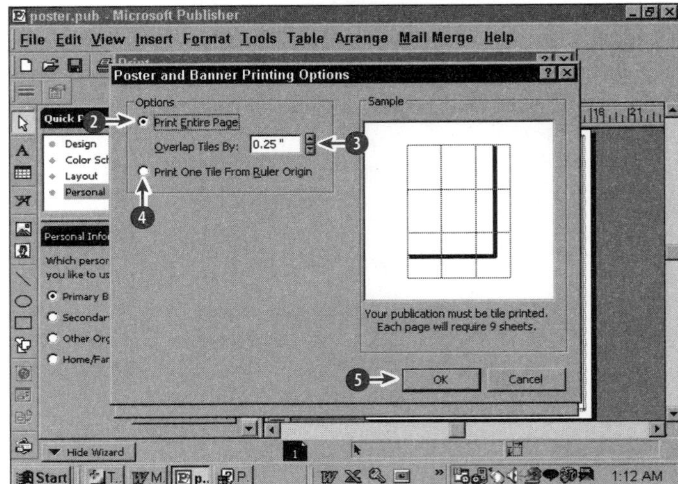

1. For oversized documents, click the Tile Printing Options button.
2. Click Print Entire Page to print entire large print tiled on multiple pages.
3. Specify how much of the image will overlap onto the subsequent pages.
4. Or, click here to print only the first tile in the picture.
5. Click OK to finish printing.

CROSS-REFERENCE

Setting page size is covered in Chapter 6.

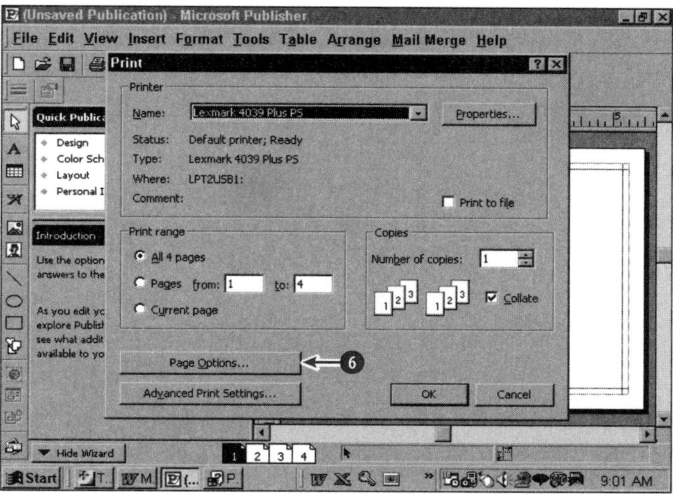

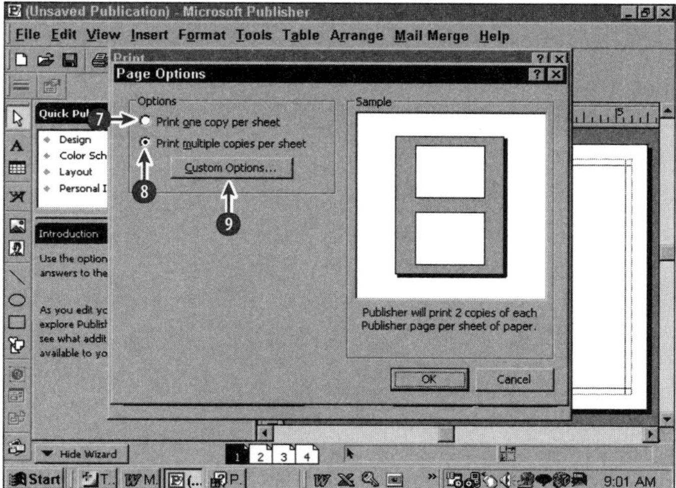

❻ *For smaller-sized documents, click the Page Options button.*

❼ *Choose this to print only one document centered on a page.*

❽ *Click here to print several copies on a page.*

❾ *Custom Options enables you to specify new outside margins and space between the copies.*

TAKE NOTE

SOURCING POSTER PRINTERS

A large-format printer or plotter is a huge expense, usually too much for many businesses. Unless you plan on producing a lot of large documents, consider finding a service bureau. The expense can be well worth it.

Service bureaus may also have additional services to offer. Many offer laminating or dry mounting for framing. Some may reduce the price on multiple copies of the same file.

Look in the Yellow Pages under Service Bureaus, Blueprinters, or Printing to find a business that you can take your files to. Many drafting firms also have these large-format printers to print blueprints and architectural renderings.

PRINTING BANNERS ON DESKTOP PRINTERS

Used to be that dot matrix printers were the only ones that could handle banner paper — a long continuous roll of paper with no perforations. Some ink-jet printers may be set up to use special banner paper. Check your printer manual to see if this is an option for your ink-jet printer model.

FIND IT ONLINE

Hewlett-Packard offers somewhat affordable large-format printers. Check their selection at http://www.hp.com/designjet/.

Printing to a File

Even though Microsoft Publisher gives you the Pack and Go choice for taking a publication to another computer, or preparing the file for a commercial printer, there may be times that a single file would be preferable. Any printer driver provides you with the option to print to a file. You can choose to print only one page or any number of subsequent pages of a multiple-page publication to file. When using Pack and Go, it's an all or nothing proposition.

Printing to a file, to which Windows assigns the .prn file extension, includes all the graphics and fonts necessary to reproduce those pages on a remote printer. You don't have to worry about the same fonts being installed on a remote computer.

Though not as compact as a Pack and Go file, a print file is portable and uneditable in the original application. This ensures that line endings and word spacing is exactly as you had in your original layout. Disadvantages to printing to a file are that you can't edit the file in the original application, and the files tend to be large.

Once you have a print file prepared, you must copy that file to the printer. You have to open a DOS window and issue the following command:

COPY *File name* Lpt1: /B

where *File name* is actually the drive, folder location and file name (*C:\Temp\Prnfile\Document.prn*, for example).

Some shareware programs are made for sending files straight to the printer. One is called Imprint, which lets you accumulate several print files and then send them to the printer of your choice all at once. You have no need to mess with the DOS commands.

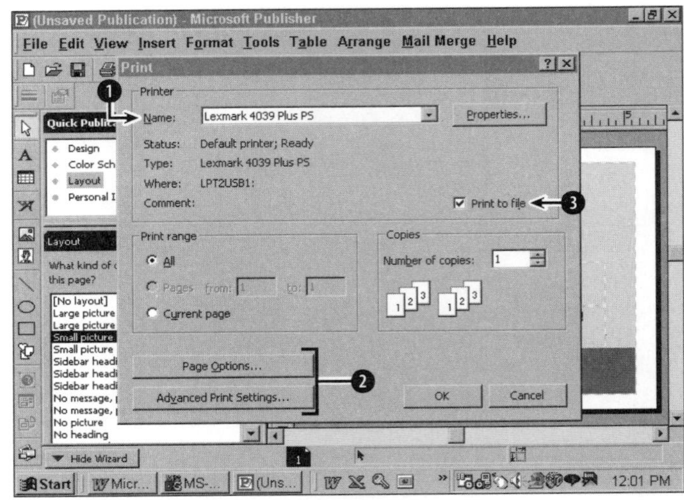

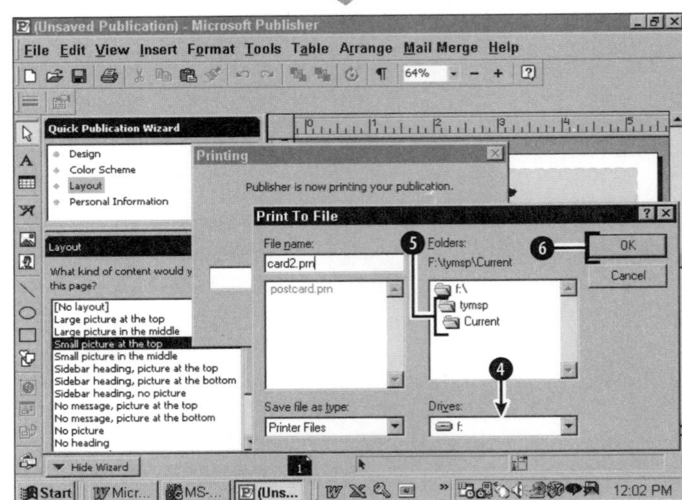

1. *Set printer name.*
2. *Set Page Options and/or Advanced Print Settings.*
3. *Check "Print to file."*
4. *Choose the drive where the file is to be written.*
5. *Choose the folder where the file is to be written.*
6. *Click OK for the file to be written.*

CROSS-REFERENCE

Using advanced print options and printing odd-sized publications were covered earlier in this chapter.

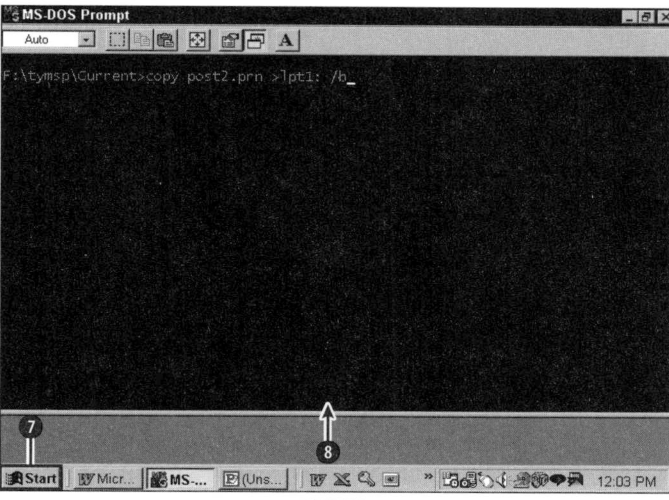

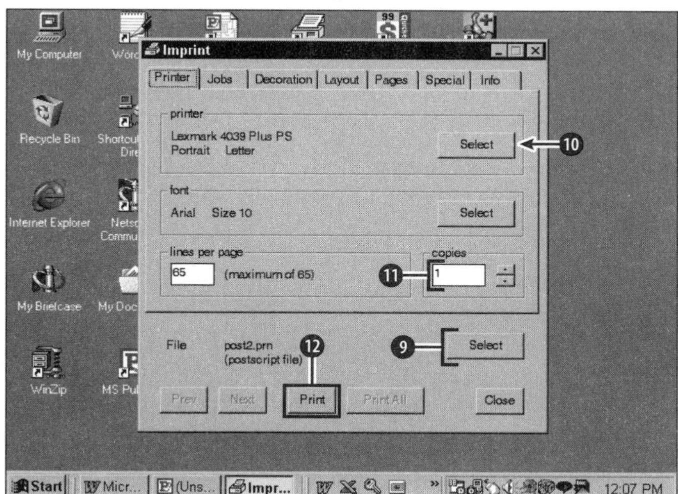

7. *Click Start ⇨ Programs ⇨ MS-DOS Prompt to open DOS window.*
8. *Type the print command at the DOS prompt and press Enter. When typing the print command, be sure to include the drive and subdirectory location of the file.*

▶ *The file is copied to the printer on the port specified.*

9. *Optionally, using software such as Imprint shown here, select a file.*
10. *Select a printer.*
11. *Indicate the number of copies to be printed.*
12. *Click the Print button.*

Remember, everything that you set up in the Print dialog box will be included in the file. If you are printing postcards and choose to print two to a page with crop marks, the crop marks will be on the printout.

TAKE NOTE

▶ COMPRESSING PRINT FILES

WinZip is a shareware program that you can use to compress the print file and possibly fit it onto a diskette or other type media. In some cases, the file may be reduced to half its original size. To find file compression utilities, go to **www.download.com**, and then follow the links to Utilities — File Compression and check out WinZip and other download options.

▶ PRINT USING DRAG AND DROP

You can set up Windows 95 and later versions to drag and drop a print project to a .prn file. To get the instructions, go to **http://support.microsoft.com/support/kb/articles/Q158/0/81.asp**. While this is a viable solution to printing a file via the DOS prompt, Imprint and other programs like it offer you more flexibility.

FIND IT ONLINE

Print utilities such as Imprint may be found at **http://www.download.com**, following the links to Utilities — Printers.

Creating a Web Site from Your Publication

Besides all the printing projects you can do, creating Web pages is also an option. Ideal for business applications, Publisher has the capability to turn your newsletter, annual report, policy handbook, and marketing pieces into very readable Web pages that not only function well on the Web but provide a graphical tie to the original printed pieces, using the same design elements, color choices, and text formatting.

When you have a publication to convert to a Web page (or pages), Publisher furnishes you with another wizard to step you through the process of converting your material to HTML (Hypertext Markup Language) code. (HTML code is the language of the Web.) When activated, the wizard gives you a few choices to make in regards to hyperlinks and design elements. You can either choose to let Publisher handle everything for you, or you can take the responsibility of providing hyperlinks yourself. If your publication contains linked text frames (continued on page "x," for example), take the manual route. If all your stories are in one text frame and have no jumps, you can probably let Publisher do the work for you. The result is not cast in stone. You can go back to your original document and run the wizard again.

For those taking the manual route, Publisher invokes its powerful Design Checker to search out text that has no link back to the home page, empty frames, and graphics or text that may not convert well. When complete, you can make changes to the document, adding hyperlinks, graphics, and/or more text. When you're finished, go back to the File menu and choose Save As Web Page. Notice that the Web Site Wizard is no longer available because you took the manual route.

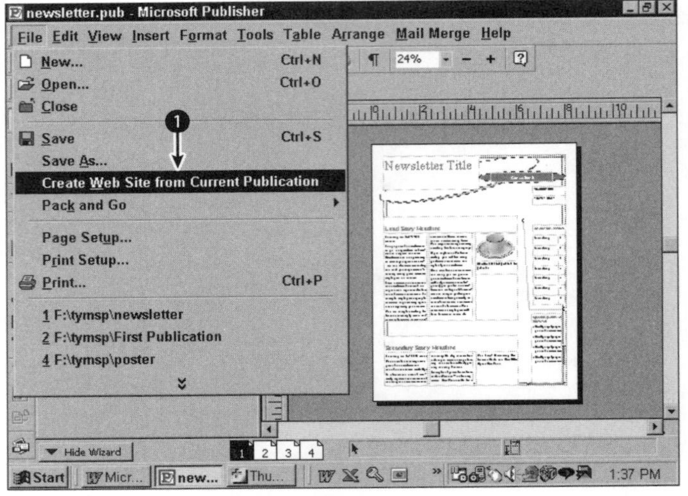

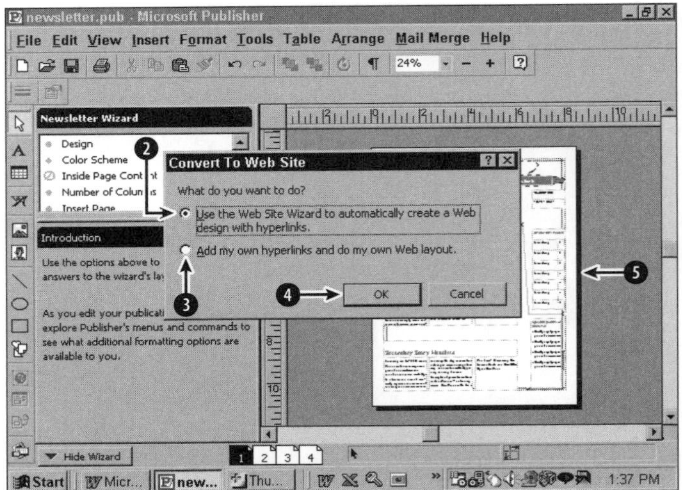

1. Once the publication is complete, select File ⇨ Create Web Site from Current Publication.
2. Choose whether the Web Site Wizard automatically creates the Web pages.
3. Or, whether you will do your own layout after evaluating the publication with Design Checker.
4. Click OK.
5. If you are letting Publisher create the Web layout for you, your Web pages will appear in this window.

CROSS-REFERENCE

To find out how to upload your files to your Internet server, see Chapter 17.

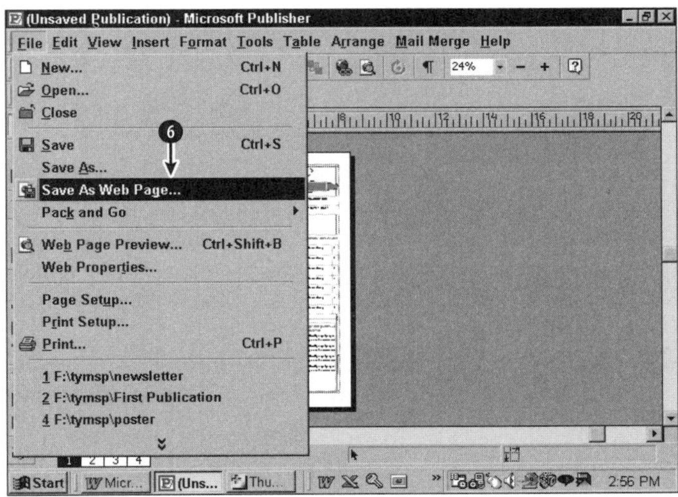

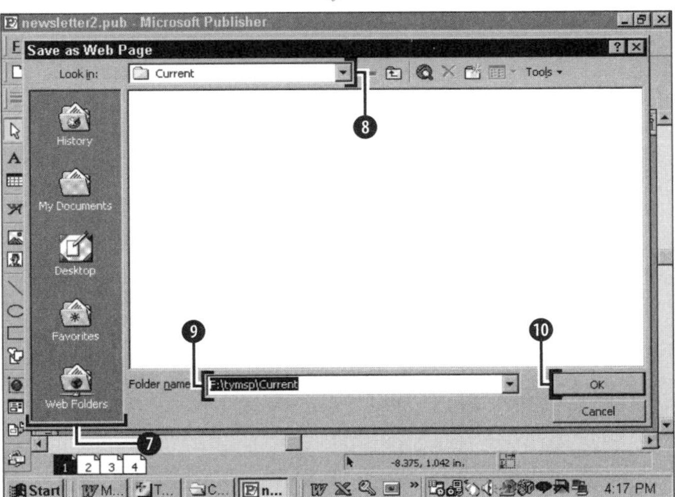

6. After you have finished with your own layout, choose File ➪ Save As Web Page.

▶ This menu option always appears after a document is converted to a Web page or a Web site is created using the wizard.

7. Select a folder to store the HTML and graphics files.

8. Click here to choose an alternate folder location.

9. Confirm drive and folder location.

10. Click OK.

TAKE NOTE

HTML FILES ARE NOT JUST FOR THE INTERNET

HTML files are not used exclusively on the Internet. Because more computers are equipped with browsers, software companies are using the HTML format for help files and readme information. If you want to circulate information electronically and don't want to invest in a program such as Adobe Acrobat to create portable documents, consider using HTML to write the files of your publication. As long as recipients have a browser installed, whoever receives your files will be able to view the documents on their computer, just as you created them.

These files are great for portability, too. When going through the translation, graphic files are reduced in resolution. HTML files are typically not extremely large. That means you can fit a lot on a 3.5-inch diskette.

FIND IT ONLINE

Microsoft has a special Web site for placing any Office 2000 document on a server. Visit **http://www.microsoft.com/office/ork/2000/five/70t2.htm.**

Personal Workbook

Q&A

1. When you are ready to print, why should you not use the Print button on the standard toolbar?

2. What is the keyboard shortcut to print?

3. If you have a multiple-page document and you want to print several copies, what option can you choose to print them so that each set comes out of the printer in page order?

4. Where are two places that you can specify the printing resolution for your document?

5. When printing a long document with many graphics, what can you do to speed up printing and save ink or toner?

6. When printing a large poster-type document that is too large for your printer, what technique do you use to send the document to your printer?

7. What is a Windows .prn file and how can you use it?

8. What is the difference between the File menu options Save As Web Page *and* Create Web Site from Current Publication?

ANSWERS: PAGE 350

EXTRA PRACTICE

1. Create a publication that uses landscape orientation, such as a certificate or a small poster, and print five copies to your printer.
2. Make a banner for the office cubicle wall welcoming a new coworker. Print it and assemble it, and then tack it or tape it to their new workspace.
3. Create a postcard and print two copies on a page. Include crop marks so you know where to trim them out.
4. Create a custom envelope with graphics and personal information such as address and Web site URL. Set up your printer and print several copies.
5. Create a newsletter or brochure in Publisher. Create a print file that you can take to another computer and print the entire file.

REAL-WORLD APPLICATIONS

- ✔ You have to publish a newsletter and circulate it around the office on disk. After completing the design, you publish it to a Web document that includes graphics so you can copy it to diskettes and send them to coworkers. Better yet, you place the files on the company network and use internal e-mail to alert employees that the newest newsletter is located on the company server and they will need their Web browsers to view it.
- ✔ You create a limited edition poster of an event in Publisher and decide to take it to a service bureau and have it printed on a wide-format printer. You print to file so that all the graphics and text will be just as you designed it in the software.

Visual Quiz

When you click the Advanced Print Settings button in the Print dialog box, you get the Print Settings dialog box. In the Publication Options tab, most of the settings are unavailable. Why?

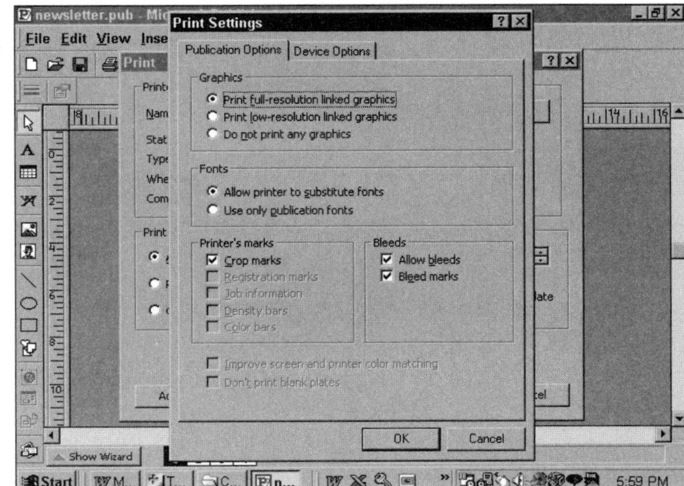

PART II

Designing Your Publication

Basic knowledge can go a long way in a software package. Learning new software is a little like school, where you had to learn the alphabet, how to spell simple words, read simple sentences, and see Spot run several times before you moved on to bigger and better things.

This part lays the foundation for using Publisher throughout the rest of this book. Simple tasks such as drawing frames, using layout guides, and adding pages are something you will most likely do whenever you fire up Microsoft Publisher and start a project. Sure, the wizards are easy to rely on when projects fly at you from all directions, but that is like coloring by the numbers to make a picture. This part hands you your canvas, brushes, and oil paint so you can create from your heart.

Though only two chapters long, this part is mighty on importance. If you feel the need, why not run through these tasks a couple of times. The first run-through will give you the basic techniques; the second time might stir your imagination. You'll soon be thinking, "I know where I can use this!"

MASTER THESE SKILLS

- Setting Publisher Options
- Using Page Setup
- Inserting Text and Picture Frames
- Moving and Sizing Frames
- Changing the View of Your Publication
- Inserting and Deleting Pages
- Moving Between Pages
- Using Design Checker

Creating Building Blocks for Your Publication

By now, you have a good feeling of what Publisher is capable of doing. Also by now, you have played with all the wizards to make greeting cards, business cards, home stationery, and other fun documents. Sure, the wizards are powerful and think of just about everything for you, but trust me, you'll likely get bored with answering the questions, changing the layouts to suit your needs, and tweaking every last element laid before you.

Your experience dictates that the next, maybe timid, step is to begin with a blank page. You are ready to format your page, add pages, drop in the pictures and stories that you have accumulated, and make a design that is uniquely yours.

This chapter starts you on your road to independence from the wizard, and gives you the skills and knowledge you need to boldly enter the realm of designer. Don't worry if your first attempts at layout design aren't quite up to the same precision and eye appeal that the wizards render. It all comes in time. Besides, a little subliminal knowledge that the wizards can give you is an eye for design.

As in everything, start slowly and build on your experience — that's what this chapter is about. Beginning with the basics, you'll see how to make Publisher your personalized software, making choices on the way it operates and interacts with you at the mouse and keyboard.

Follow through this chapter closely, because the rest of the book builds on the concepts and knowledge you learn here. Stepping through these tasks, you'll learn how to set up a page, insert more pages in your document, and prepare to drop elements in frames on those pages. Everything you place on a page is held within a frame. Frames come in several flavors, text and pictures being the most commonly used components of a layout.

Deleting pages also requires a necessary tidbit of knowledge. How to move among those pages, and being able to zoom in to get a closer view or out to see the page layout, is covered here as well.

The final feature of this chapter talks about Publisher's Design Checker tool. While this may be a little premature for those documents you design from scratch, it can tell you things about your wizard documents that you created earlier. Besides, it's nice to run this handy utility during the building process to keep the things that Publisher doesn't like down to a minimum.

Setting Publisher Options

Because you can pick and choose from a lot of settings, here is a brief list of some of their purposes. Some of them are obvious while others are head-scratchers.

- **Start Publication with Page:** If you were laying out this book in Publisher, which you could do, you may want each chapter as a separate document. When you start Chapter 2, you can note where Chapter 1 left off and enter the next page number here.
- **Measurement Units:** Choose Inches, Centimeters, Picas, or Points. Most Americans use inches as their default unless they are in the printing industry and grew up on picas and points.
- **Preview Fonts in Font List:** Check this setting if you want to see what the font looks like. If it takes a while to flip through a large list of fonts, turn this off.
- **Use Catalog at Startup:** If you prefer to start Publisher with a blank page instead of a wizard in the catalog, click this off.
- **Menus Show Recently Used Commands First:** If you hate clicking those double arrows at the bottom of a menu, turn this off and they all show at once.
- **Improve Screen and Printer Color Matching:** Supposedly, this option makes you see on the screen what it will look like when it's printed. Use this if your monitor and printer have Image Color Matching (ICM) profiles.
- **File Locations:** This option sets the default location for publication and picture files. When you open a publication or load a picture, this drive and folder is where the dialog box opens up to.

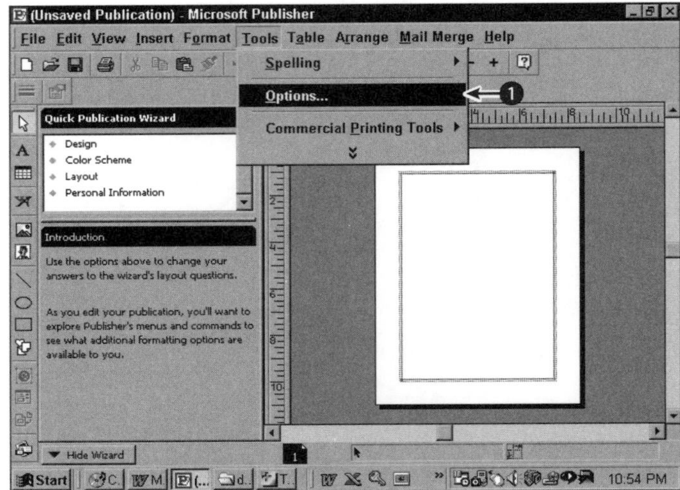

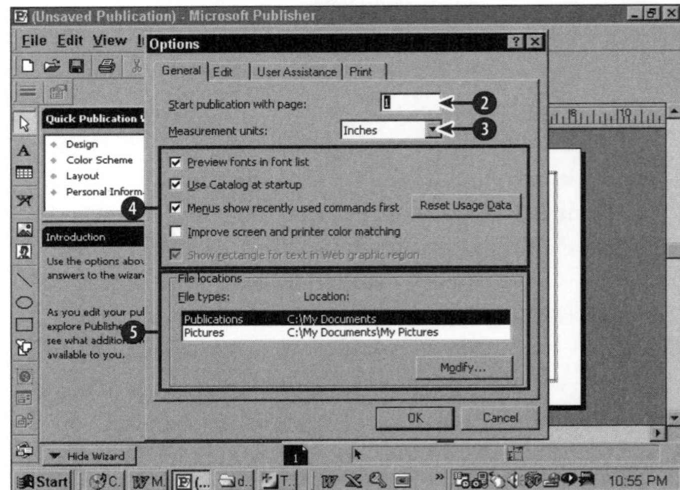

1. *To access the Options dialog box, choose Tools ⇨ Options.*
2. *Set your starting page number.*
3. *Choose your default measurement units. Rulers change to use these units.*
4. *Place a check in these items to turn them on. Uncheck items to turn them off.*
5. *Check the file location defaults. Highlight the one you want to change and click the Modify button.*

CROSS-REFERENCE

Inserting page numbers is covered in Chapter 7.

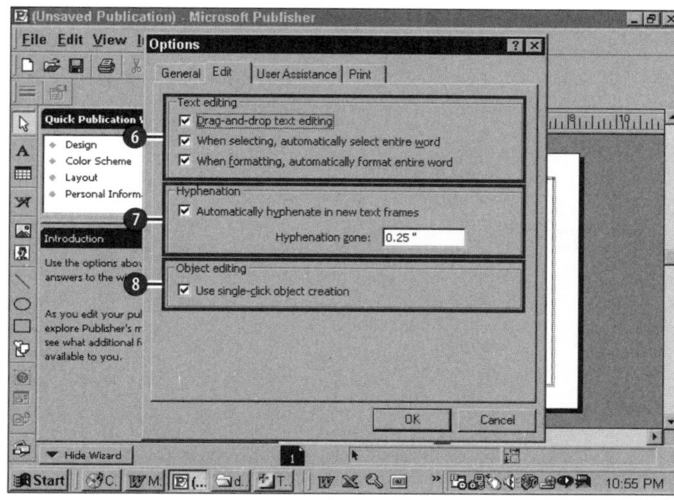

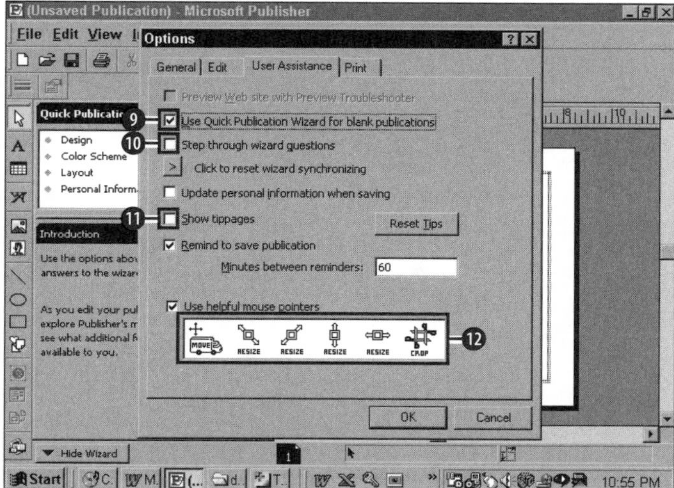

6 *Check the text editing options that you want to make active.*

7 *Uncheck this box to turn off hyphenation. When turned on, change the maximum distance from the right margin for a word to reach before being hyphenated.*

8 *Check here to create an object with a single click after choosing a tool in the toolbar.*

9 *When a new blank document is begun, this option removes the wizard from the window.*

10 *To avoid stepping through the wizard, click here. The wizard creates the document using the default settings.*

11 *Tippages will not show when unchecked.*

12 *Change the mouse cursor appearance. As you click the checkbox, preview the changes in the window.*

- **Drag-and-Drop Text Editing:** This option lets you select some text and drag it to a different location.
- **Single-Click Object Creation:** When you select a tool, this option lets you click once on the page and the frame or graphic will be drawn at a set size. Turn this off to force dragging to create an object.
- **Show Tippages:** If you're tired of Publisher throwing yellow suggestion boxes at you every time you do something, click this off.
- **Remind to Save Publication:** If you need to be reminded, set the number of minutes between reminders.
- **Use Helpful Mouse Cursors:** Turning this option off changes the cursor to a lesser, noncaptioned cursor.

Under the Print tab of the Options dialog box, you'll find a setting to turn off the Print Troubleshooter and some settings for ink-jet printers. When you're designing envelopes, you can also set default printer settings.

TAKE NOTE

WHEN TO SET YOUR OPTIONS

You have two ways to customize Publisher for the way you want to work. Make the settings all at once before you dive headlong into the software, or change them as you go.

CHANGING DEFAULT DIRECTORIES

If you're working on a project for a long period of time, change your default directories for that job. Change them back when complete.

FIND IT ONLINE

To see how picas and points measure up to conventional inches, see **http://itrc.uwaterloo.ca/~engl210e/BookShelf/Recommended/Form/sec_3.htm.**

Using Page Setup

When starting a blank publication, you normally have a finished size in mind, and telling Publisher that size has to be the first order of business.

When you open the Page Setup dialog box, you see a choice of five different categories of possibilities:

- **Normal:** One of the first things you'll notice when this option button is clicked is the page size is already chosen and you can't change it here. A note tells you that this page size is dictated by the printer setup. To change the size, you have to go to File ➪ Print Setup and make your selections from there. The number of page sizes you can select will be dictated by the printer driver, which knows what paper sizes your printer is capable of handling. In the Page Setup dialog box, however, you can still specify whether your document is printed landscape or portrait.
- **Special Fold:** Clicking this option lets you choose from four different folding configurations: Book Fold, Tent Card, Side-Fold Card, and Top-Fold Card. Watch the Preview window to see how the folds affect your layout. When you choose one of these options, Publisher sets the page size to one panel of the final folded piece. When it's time to print, all panels are assembled to print on one page.
- **Special Size:** This option offers choices of standard printed pieces such as business cards, index cards, banners, and posters. A custom setting lets you specify the width and height of the page.
- **Labels:** Clicking the Labels option brings up a list of Avery label style or part numbers. You get a description of the label as well as the individual label

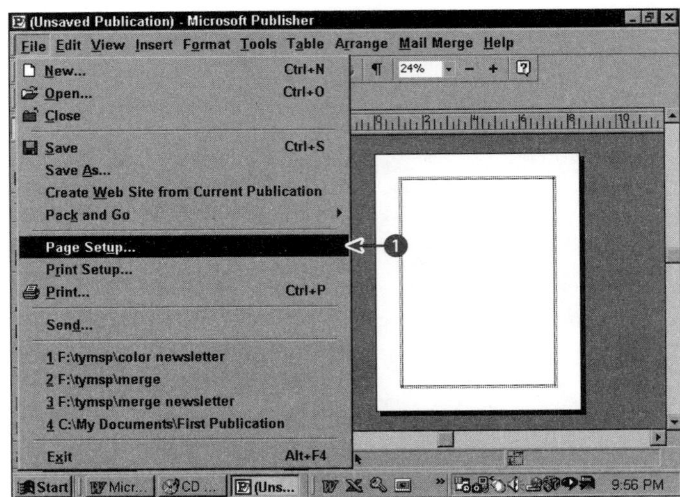

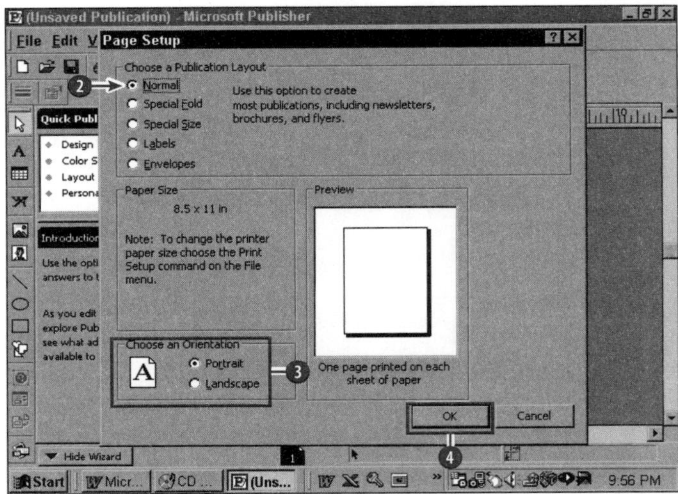

1. Choose File ➪ Page Setup.
2. To select the printer's default page size, choose Normal.
3. Select Portrait or Landscape.
4. Click OK to accept these settings, or . . .

CROSS-REFERENCE

See Chapter 5 on how to set up your printer so the Normal setting reflects that paper size.

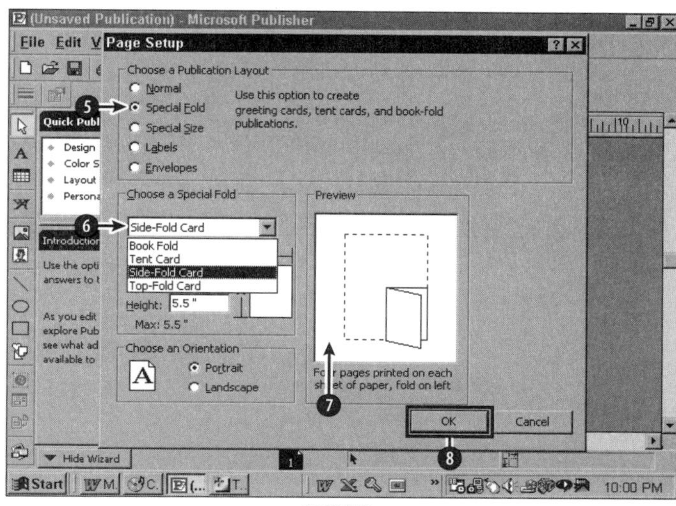

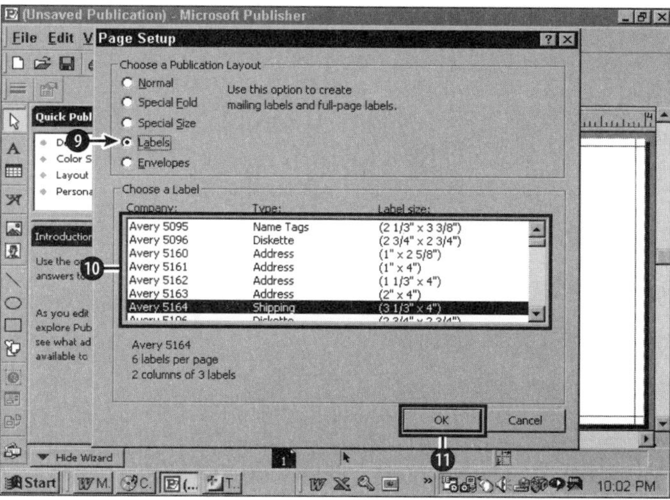

5. *Click Special Fold.*
6. *Choose the fold type from the drop-down list.*
7. *Look at the Preview window to see how the page will fold.*
8. *Click OK to accept these settings, or . . .*
9. *To set up labels, click the Labels button.*
10. *Choose an Avery label from the list.*
11. *Click OK.*

size. Choosing one of these styles presents you with one label to do your layout on. When it's time to print, Publisher replicates your design and drops it on each label on the sheet of labels, if you instruct it to do so using the Page Options in the Print dialog box.

- **Envelopes:** Though only two standard-size envelopes are listed, you do have the options to create a custom-sized page. Choosing the Custom option lets you enter the width and height of the envelope you're designing.

TAKE NOTE

MARGINS ARE SET SEPARATELY

Once you have a page size selected, Publisher assigns a default outside margin. However, if you need to change that, you do that in another menu system. See Chapter 7 for details on margins and layout guides.

FUNNY PAGES ARE LISTED

If you see page sizes such as A4 or B5, they may seem unfamiliar to you. These are the standard paper sizes that are used in Europe and other parts of the world.

FIND IT ONLINE

To learn more about paper sizes, go to **http://gamma.sil.org/lingualinks/library/literacy/vao144/krz1832/vao3925.htm.**

Inserting Text and Picture Frames

Designers sometimes agonize over the exact placement of a picture or the way that type is displayed so that their finished piece is aesthetically pleasing and easy to follow. Publisher gives you total control of the placement of your text and graphics using frames.

Frames serve as containers for any element you place on a page, be it text or graphics. Publisher provides you with two different tools that operate the same to insert text, graphics, clip art, or photos. The only difference is in how you treat the frame once it is drawn.

Photos and other graphics are all loaded into a picture frame. It's a simple process of clicking the tool in the toolbar and drawing a box by dragging your mouse. Once complete, the picture frame is empty, enabling you to find just the right graphic to enhance your publication. Inserting graphics is covered in Chapter 11.

Text frames operate a little differently. After drawing a text frame, you are left with a flashing cursor that lets you type directly within the frame. You can also import word processing files into the frame, but that is covered later in Chapter 8. The other thing you can do to the frame is divide it up into columns and set margins, which is also discussed in Chapter 8. The purpose of this task, however, is to familiarize you with the two tools that create the text frame or picture frame and prepare you for the following tasks and the chapters that explain how to resize the frames, move them around the publication, and drop word processing files or graphics in them.

You may notice some other frame tools in the toolbar: the Table Frame, WordArt Frame, and the Clip Gallery tools. They function pretty much like the Picture Frame tool, except that they open a specialized dialog box that pertains only to those type frames.

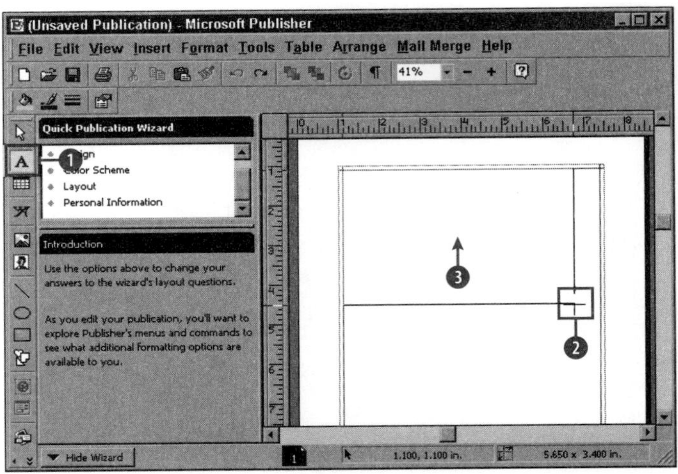

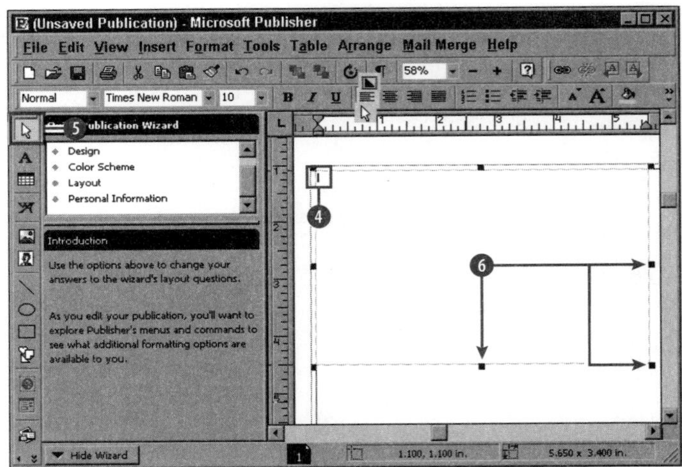

1. *To draw a text frame, click the Text Frame tool.*
2. *Drag inside the page to draw the text frame.*
3. *Or, left-click and a frame will be drawn with the center being where your cursor was placed on the page. This is dependent upon the Single Click Object Creation settings you made in the Options dialog box.*
4. *Once the mouse button is released, a flashing cursor enables you to type text within the frame.*
5. *The Arrow tool is automatically selected once the frame is drawn.*
6. *Handles are positioned around the frame on the corners and in the middle of the top and bottom sides.*

CROSS-REFERENCE

Frames can be filled with color, have borders, and even drop shadows. See Chapter 12 on these procedures.

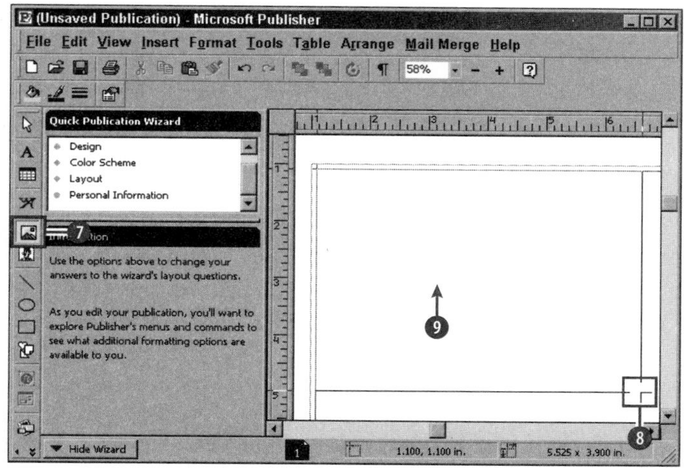

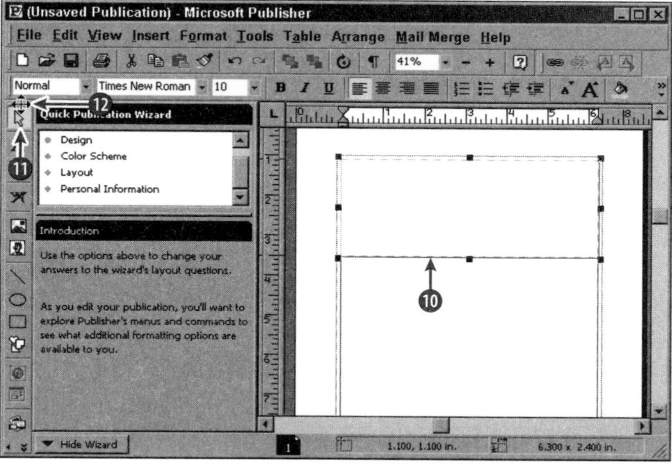

❼ *To draw a Picture Frame, click the Picture Frame Tool in the toolbar.*

❽ *Drag with the mouse to create a frame on the page.*

❾ *Or, left-click and a frame will be drawn with the center being where your cursor was placed on the page.*

▶ *This is dependent upon the Single Click Object Creation settings you made in the Options dialog box.*

❿ *When you release the mouse button, the empty frame is highlighted.*

⓫ *The Pointer tool is automatically chosen.*

⓬ *To have your toolbar closer at hand, place your cursor at the top of the toolbar until the cursor changes to a four-headed arrow.*

▶ *Drag the toolbar into the Document window area for a free-floating toolbox.*

When you finish drawing a WordArt frame, for example, the WordArt Creation window opens and lets you create the artwork that will drop in the frame when you complete it.

TAKE NOTE

FRAMES COME WITH ONLY SQUARE CORNERS

While some publishing programs let you draw shapes of different kinds that will hold text and/or graphics, Publisher is limited to the rectangular shape. You won't be able to insert hearts, starts, or rounded-corner frames to hold your text of graphics.

PICK THE RIGHT FRAME FOR THE JOB

Once a frame has been drawn, you can't convert it to a different type of frame. Text frames can only hold text and graphic frames can only hold graphics. To replace one frame with another type of frame, you have to delete the frame and draw a new one.

FIND IT ONLINE

To get some design ideas for placing your frames, see www.graphic-design.com.

Moving and Sizing Frames

When frames are drawn, you will see eight little black squares on each corner of the frame as well as other ones centered on the top, bottom, and sides of the frame. These little black boxes are called *handles* or, by those who are purists, *control handles*. With these handles, you manipulate the size of the frame by dragging with your mouse.

All object or control handles work the same way. When you position your mouse cursor over a handle, the cursor changes to a Resize cursor, displaying arrows that indicate the direction that the handle may be moved.

In addition to using your mouse button by itself, you can use the Ctrl and Shift keys to change the way the frame behaves when you drag a control handle.

Holding the Shift key releases the frame's lock on maintaining the proportion of the frame outline and therefore its contents as long as you're dragging a corner handle. You can stretch the frame wider or longer. Especially in clip art, photos and other graphics, maintaining proportion is important so your images don't look like they've spent the day in the house of mirrors at the fair, so be careful with the Shift key. The Shift key has no effect on the top, bottom or side handles. Those handles will move independently.

Holding the Ctrl key while dragging a corner handle of the object moves all four corner handles at the same time, either bringing them all in toward the center of the frame or expanding them all equally from the center of the frame. When you use the Ctrl key with the top, bottom, or side handles, the opposite side moves in the opposite direction of your drag. For example, if you drag the bottom center handle down, the top of the frame moves up.

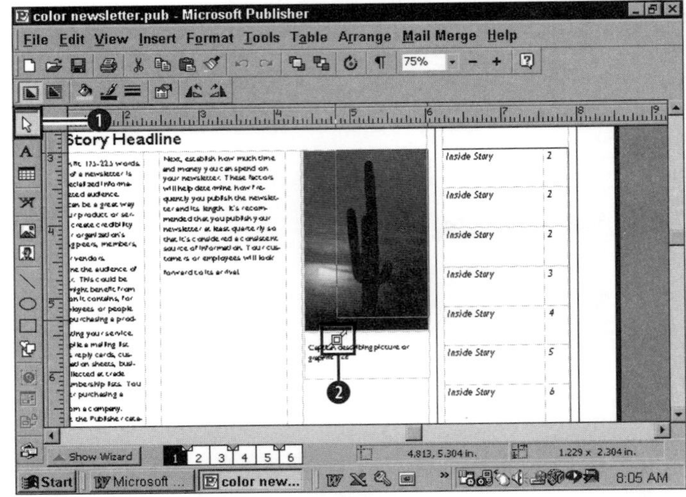

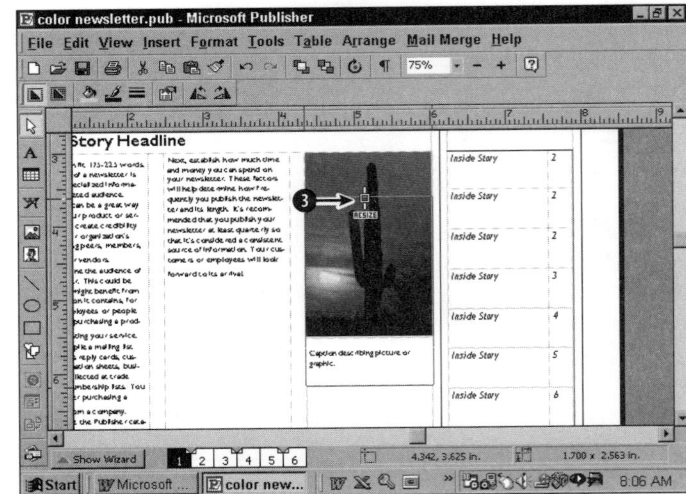

1. *To resize a frame, choose the Pointer tool, if not already selected, and select the object that you want to resize.*
2. *With the cursor on one of the frame handles, drag to enlarge or reduce the frame or group of frames.*
3. *To enlarge or reduce one side, drag the top, bottom, or side handle of the frame.*

CROSS-REFERENCE

To learn how to group objects, see "Grouping and Ungrouping Objects" in Chapter 7.

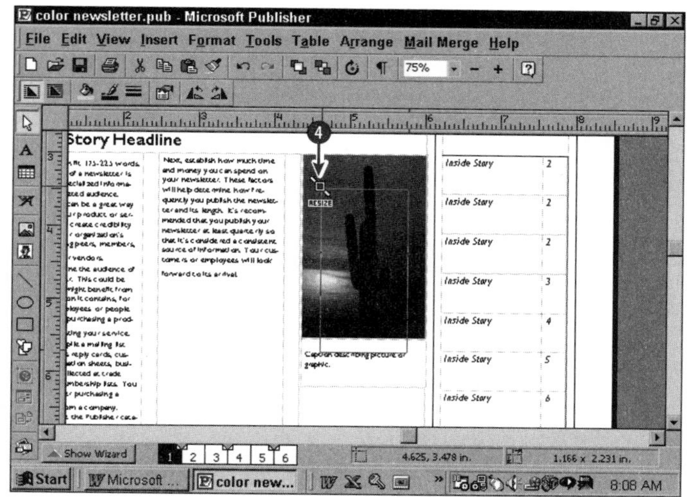

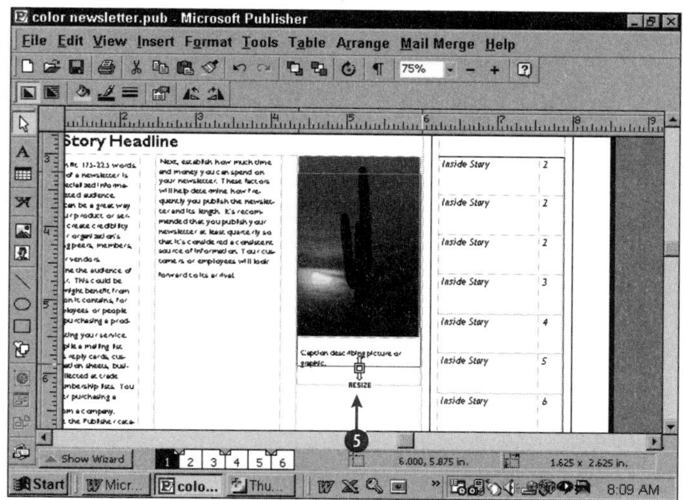

❹ *To enlarge or reduce all four sides at the same time, hold the Ctrl key while you drag one corner of the frame.*

❺ *To enlarge or reduce the sides or top and bottom together, hold the Ctrl key while dragging one of those handles.*

Finally, you can move a frame by placing your cursor in a selected frame and dragging it to a new location on the page. You'll know when your cursor is in the right position to move a frame when it changes to the Move cursor. Once you see it, you can hold down the mouse button and drag the frame.

Holding the Shift key while you drag a frame constrains the frame to moving either up and down or left and right in a straight line. If you hold the Ctrl key while you drag a frame, you duplicate the frame and its contents and end up moving the copy to a new location.

TAKE NOTE

MOVING GROUPED FRAMES

If you have made several frames into a group, when you drag one frame, all are dragged to a new location.

RESIZING GROUPED FRAMES

You can resize a group of frames, reducing any photos or artwork. Text, however, remains the same size with only the margins changing.

FIND IT ONLINE

You can find some tips on Microsoft Publisher at **http://desktoppublishing.com/tipspublisher.html.**

Changing the View of Your Publication

You can maximize and customize the way you see your publication pages or elements with the various zooming features that Publisher has to offer. While other programs offer shortcut keys to zoom in and out of a page, Publisher offers only one — Ctrl+Shift+L — which zooms out to see the entire page. This means you're going to have to know where the menu and button controls are. Starting with the Zoom drop-down in the standard toolbar, you can click the drop-down and pick a preset percentage from the list. Publisher acknowledges your choice and displays the page or two-page spread at that zoom level. If you have an object selected, that object is placed in the middle of the window when you choose a zoom percentage. If nothing is selected, the center of the page will be the center of the zoom level.

Next to the drop-down Zoom list are Minus and Plus buttons. Click these to move up or down to the next zoom preset level. In the list, you'll also find a choice to zoom to the entire page or the width of a page. With an object selected, one additional choice will be available in the list: Selected Objects. Whatever frames you have selected will be displayed at the greatest possible magnification, allowing for everything selected to be viewed in the window.

You can also double-click in the drop-down menu and enter a percentage using your keyboard. You are not tied to the presets that are in the list.

The View menu gives you even more options. View ➪ Zoom repeats the preset magnifications that you'll find in the drop-down menu in the toolbar. In addition, choosing View ➪ Two Page Spread keeps a left and right page together in the window. With this choice unchecked, each page appears individually in the window.

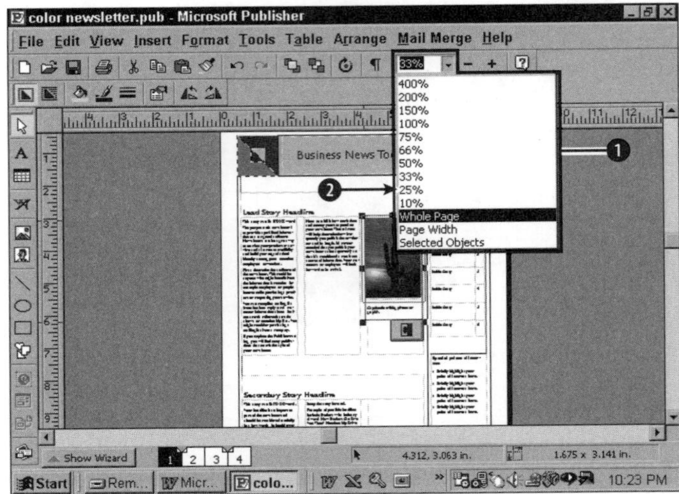

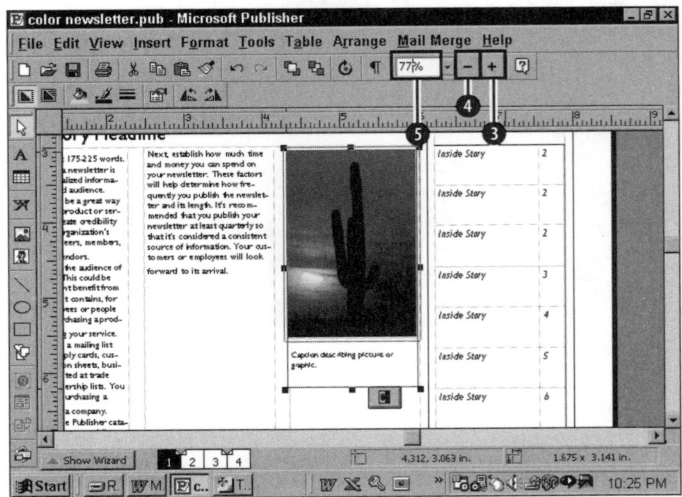

1. Click the Zoom drop-down in the standard toolbar.
2. Click a preset zoom level in the list.
3. Alternatively, use the Plus button to increase one preset zoom level in the list.
4. Or, click the Minus button to drop down one preset zoom level.
5. You can also enter any amount in the drop-down from 10% to 400%.

▶ *Pressing F9 toggles back and forth between actual size and the selected zoom level.*

CROSS-REFERENCE

For more information on Publisher's rulers, see Chapter 7.

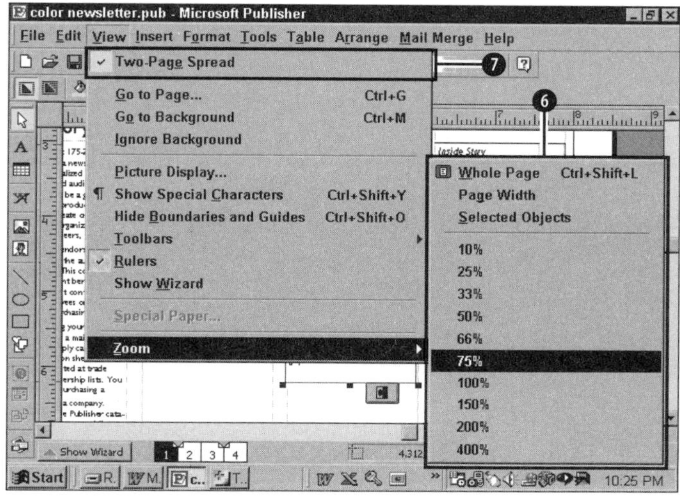

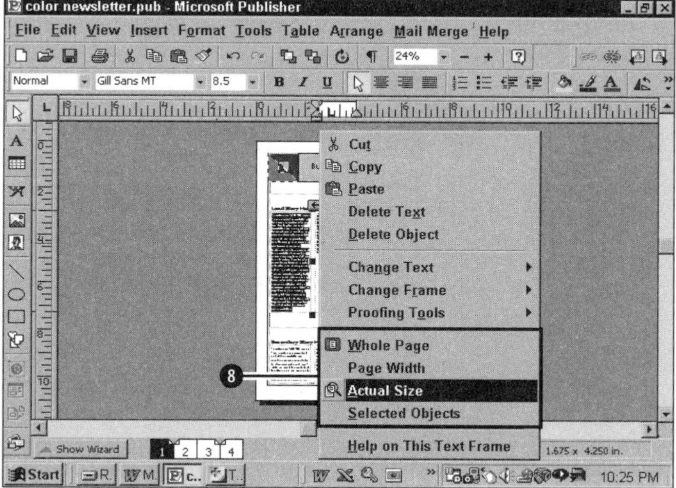

6. *You can also choose View ➪ Zoom and pick a setting from the menu.*
7. *Turn two-page spread views off and on here by clicking to add or remove the checkmark.*
8. *Right-click the mouse button on the page or an object on the page to choose one of the four zoom options in the quick menu.*

For quick and easy zooming, try using the right-click menu. You can view the whole page, zoom in so the width of the page fills the horizontal space of the window, view the actual size of the document (which is the same as 100%), or zoom to the selected objects.

TAKE NOTE

HIDE THE RULERS FOR MORE SCREEN SPACE

If you're working on a computer where the monitor's maximum resolution is 800 × 600 or less, you can hide the rulers to give you more viewing space. Just right-click either of the rulers and click to remove the check next to Rulers. To return the rulers to their place, select View ➪ Rulers. You can also use this menu selection to turn them off.

CHANGE MONITOR SETTINGS

To change the resolution of your monitor, right-click the desktop (not an icon) and choose Properties. Go to the Settings tab and move the Screen Area slider to a higher setting.

FIND IT ONLINE

You can get updated video drivers from your video card manufacturer or try **www.driverguide.com.**

Inserting and Deleting Pages

Publications evolve as you create them. Not only will you be moving items around, placing graphics, and importing text, but you may find the need to add a few pages to fit everything in. Likewise, you may end up with a spare page or two that have to be removed from the document.

Inserting and deleting pages in Publisher are pretty simple tasks, as long as you remember where to go to find the commands.

You can insert new pages before or after a selected page, using either the pull-down menu or the keyboard shortcut Ctrl+Shift+N ("N" for New Page, a nice way to remember it). You can insert up to 999 new pages at a time, but you can do this several times if you want. Just remember that large publications are not only a chore to maneuver from page to page, but the items you place on those pages can also create large publication file sizes.

Whenever you insert new pages, they must be same size and orientation within the publication. Those are the rules; you can't get around it unless you rotate a frame on the page to appear as if it is a different orientation. Keep in mind, however, that your headers and footers will not get rotated.

If you want a publication that can have both landscape and portrait pages, you'll have to create a new publication and change the beginning page number of the second and any subsequent publications.

Now you're thinking that if you can add pages, you can delete them, right? As a matter of fact, you can within limits. Although you can add up to 999 pages in one swoop, deleting those pages is not quite as easy. Publisher lets you delete up to two pages at a time — and that is only if you are working on a two-sided publication. If your publication is single-sided, you can only delete one page at a time.

CROSS-REFERENCE

For more information on linked text frames, see Chapter 8.

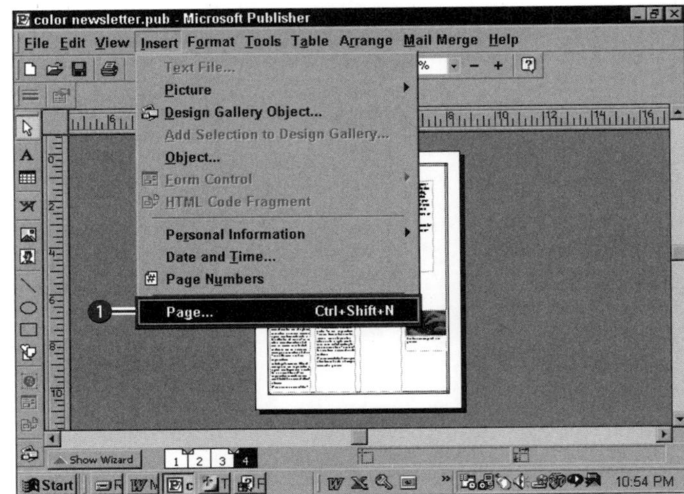

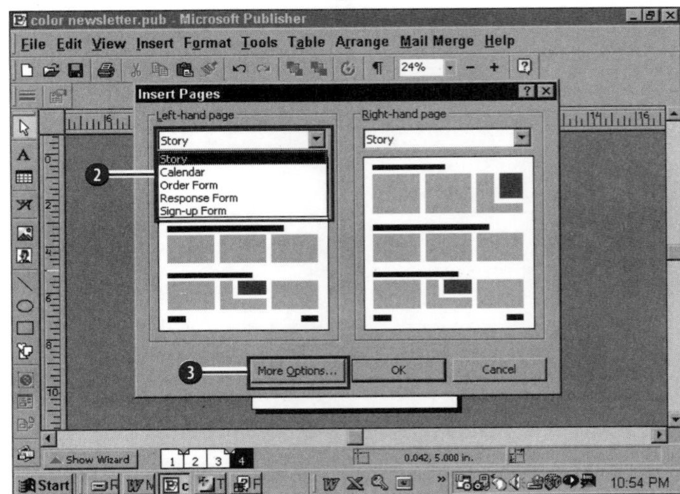

1. *To insert pages, choose Insert ➪ Page or press Ctrl+Shift+N.*
2. *In the Insert Pages dialog box, choose the type of template you want to include on the left page and/or right page.*

▶ *If you have a single-sided publication, only one of the Page Style windows will be open.*

3. *Or, click the More Options button.*

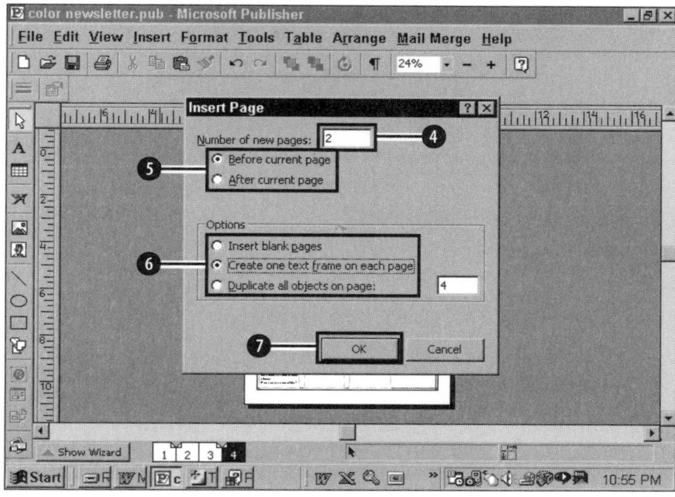

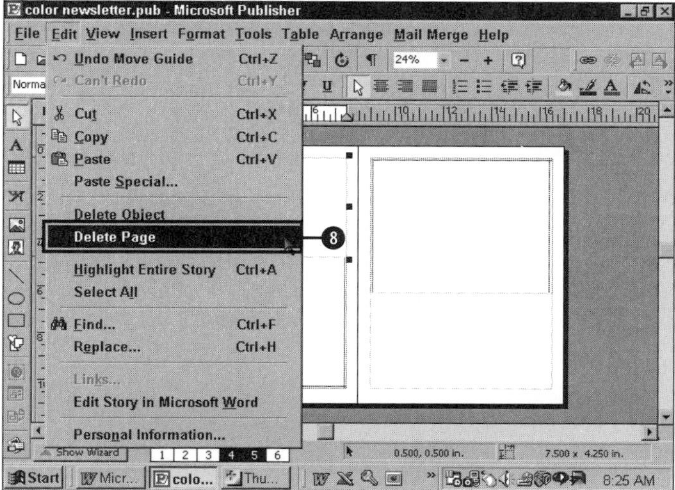

❹ *Type in the number of pages to be inserted, up to 999.*

❺ *Choose whether the new page or pages are to be inserted before or after the currently selected page.*

❻ *Choose whether you want blank pages, pages with one text frame included, or duplicates of the currently selected page or the page indicated.*

❼ *Click OK.*

❽ *To delete pages, choose Edit ➪ Delete Page. If you have a single-page layout, the page is automatically deleted.*

▶ *For double-sided layouts, you are given a dialog box to choose both pages in the spread, the left page only, or the right page only.*

The moral of this little snafu? If you're going to add pages, be conservative and add only what you think you will use. Deleting a half a dozen pages is simple when compared to the time you will have to spend to delete 50 pages.

TAKE NOTE

ADDING PAGES WITH BACKGROUNDS

If you have headers and footers defined, or anything else in the background layer, the background will appear on your inserted pages.

DELETING PAGES WITH ITEMS ON THEM

You can delete pages that are not empty. If they have graphics, which do not appear on the background layer, they will be deleted. Text frames that appear will also be deleted. If those text frames are part of a link, the text will move to the next frame in the link.

FIND IT ONLINE

You can get additional templates for Publisher at www.pcworld.com/software/utility/articles/sep97/1509add_on08.html.

Moving Between Pages

Once you have added all those pages into your document, there has to be an easy way to get from page to page. Publisher gives you plenty of options here.

Panning

You would think that you could use the PgUp and PgDn keys to move forward and backward in your document, one page at a time. However, Publisher uses these keys to let you move up and down on a particular page or spread, a technique called *panning*. If you are zoomed in on the top of a page, pressing the PgDn key moves your page up so you can see the lower portion of the page. Publisher uses what you see in the window as a reference to move the page. When you press PgDn, what you were able to see in the bottom of the window now becomes the top of the window.

Using the Ctrl key with the PgUp and PgDn keys moves you across the page, depending on your zoom level. For a double-sided publication, this process includes both pages. In this case, you are panning across the pages. Again, Publisher moves you one screen at a time instead of a full layout page.

Page Navigation Icons

For moving from page to page in your document, use the Page Navigation icons that you see in the status bar. They are shaped like miniature pages, and you can click the icon of the page you want to view. If more pages exist than will fit in the Page Navigation icons, you'll see arrows on either side indicating that more pages exist in that direction. You can click these arrows to move forward or backward in the number of pages. If you have a

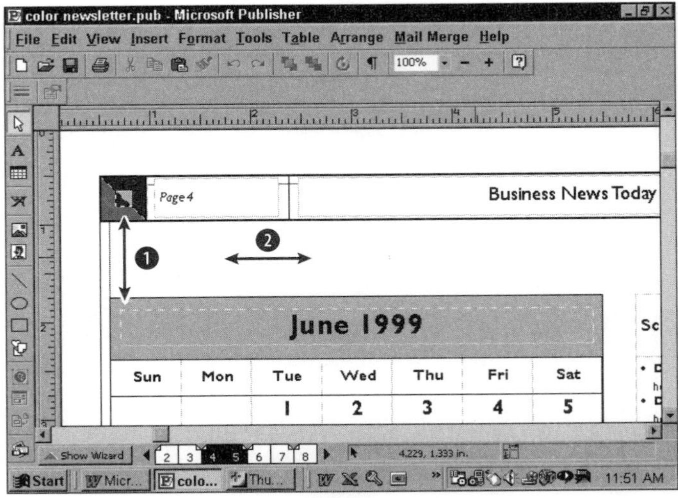

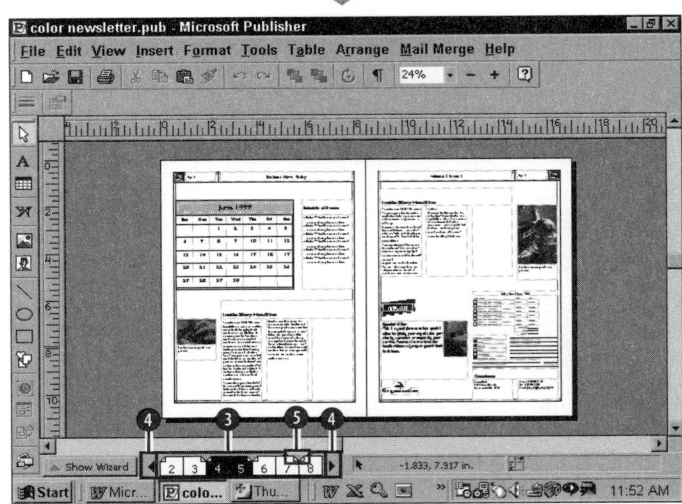

1. When you are zoomed in on a page, you can use the PgUp and PgDn keys to move up and down a screen view.
2. Use Ctrl+Page Up or Ctrl+Page Down to pan across the page, one screen at a time.
3. Click a page in the Page Navigation icons to jump to that page.
4. Use the arrows next to the icons to show more page icons.
5. Page icons have dog-ears to indicate a left or right page.

CROSS-REFERENCE

To learn how to zoom in and out of your pages, see "Changing the View of Your Publication" earlier in this chapter.

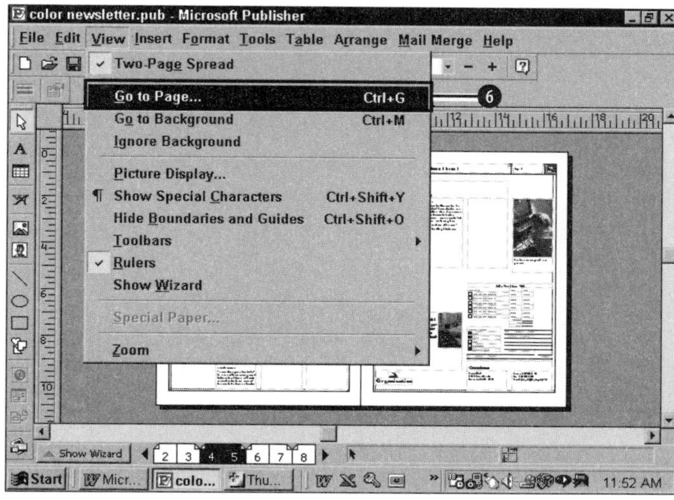

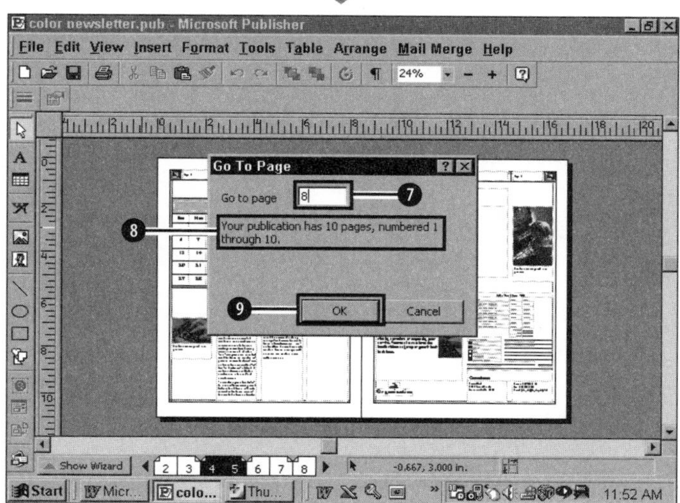

6 *Click View ⇨ Go to Page or press Ctrl+G to get the Go to Page dialog box.*

7 *Type the page number of the page you wish to view.*

8 *Note the total number of pages in your document.*

9 *Click OK.*

double-sided publication, you'll see dog-eared corners indicating whether it is a left- or right-sided page.

Go to Page

Those who know their publication inside and out, or have a cheat sheet that tells them what items are on what page, can use the Go to Page option in the View menu. One handy bit of information that you can find in the Go to Page dialog box is the total number of pages in your document. Typing in the destination page and clicking OK transports you to that page or spread.

TAKE NOTE

RIGHT-CLICK TO ZOOM

Don't forget you can use your right mouse button to access the quick menu. There, you'll see options to zoom to the whole page, actual size, or page width.

REMEMBERING WHERE YOU ARE

The Page Navigation icons are the only things viewable all of the time to let you know what page number you are working on. Use the arrows next to the icons to scroll through the pages. When you find one that is black instead of white, that's what page you're on.

FIND IT ONLINE

Learn a few tips and tricks on using boxes at **http://desktoppub.about.com/library/weekly/aa062697.htm.**

Using Design Checker

If you use some sort of word processor such as Microsoft Word, you may be aware of a handy tool called Spell Checker. Publisher also has the same intelligence built into it. Plus, you aren't just limited to spelling differences — another tool works similarly, called Design Checker. While it's not going to indicate bad choices in color or whether you have the wrong photo placed with a story, it helps you find elements that are not going to sit well with Publisher, at the very most. Here's what Design Checker looks for and analyzes:

- **Empty frames:** Maybe it'll be a subtle reminder of the graphic that you were going to search for and place on the page after everything was finished. Perhaps a story didn't stretch the entire chain of frames you had intended. Whatever the case, Publisher will find them.
- **Covered objects:** If your layering hasn't worked as planned and you have text covering an image, Publisher finds those instances. You can always wrap the text around the image to fix the problem.
- **Text in overflow areas:** The overflow area is an invisible location where Publisher stores any text that doesn't fit into a frame. After you have imported a word processing file, it may not all fit. The remaining text is placed in the overflow area. Of course, if you have linked to another frame and the remaining text fits in it, this error won't appear on any of the frames that the file occupies.
- **Objects in nonprinting region:** Every printer has its limits, with very few being able to print from one edge of the paper to the other. Publisher reads the printer driver and its capabilities and lets you know if you have (or an object you've placed has) overstepped its boundaries.

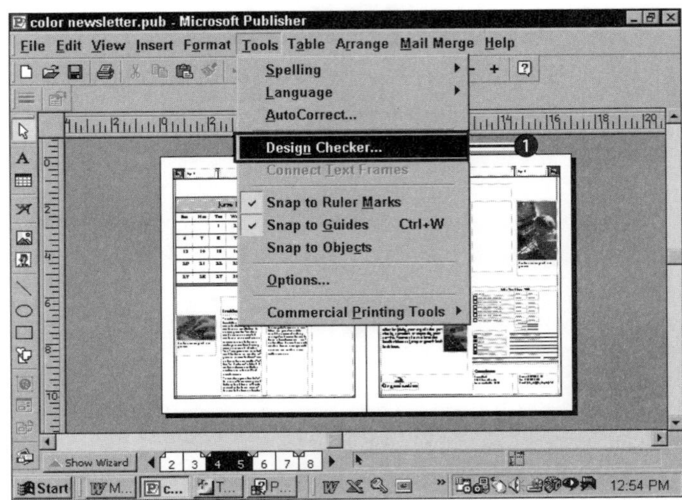

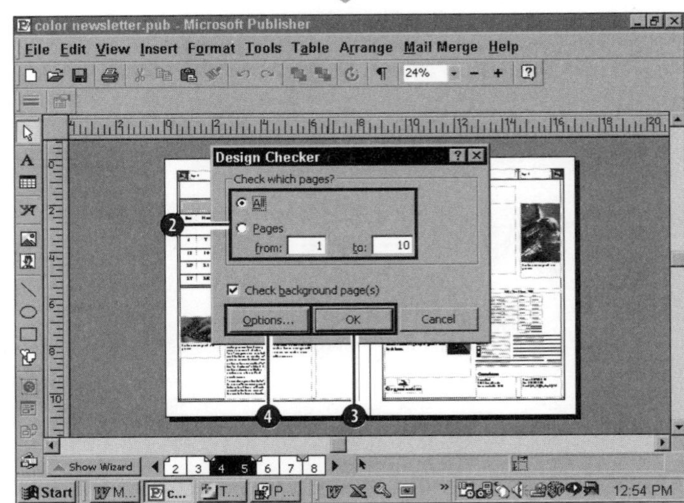

❶ To start Design Checker, choose Tools ➪ Design Checker.

❷ Choose which pages you want checked. You can choose all pages or a range of pages.

❸ Click OK, or . . .

❹ Click the Options button.

CROSS-REFERENCE

When you use Pack and Go for another computer or a commercial printer, Design Checker can be run automatically. Check Chapters 3 and 18 for using Pack and Go.

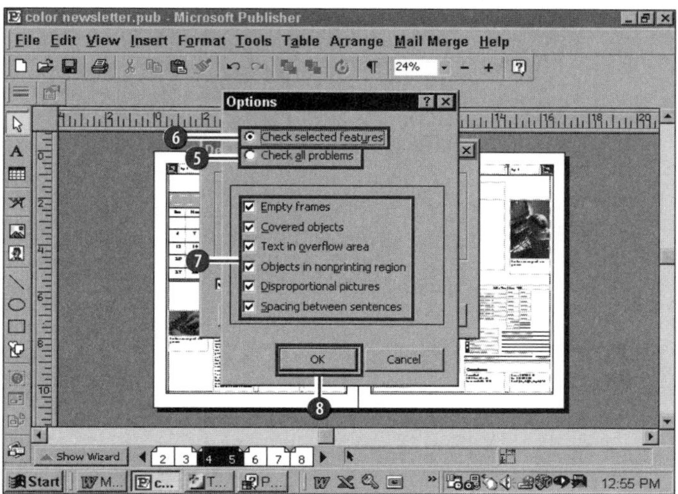

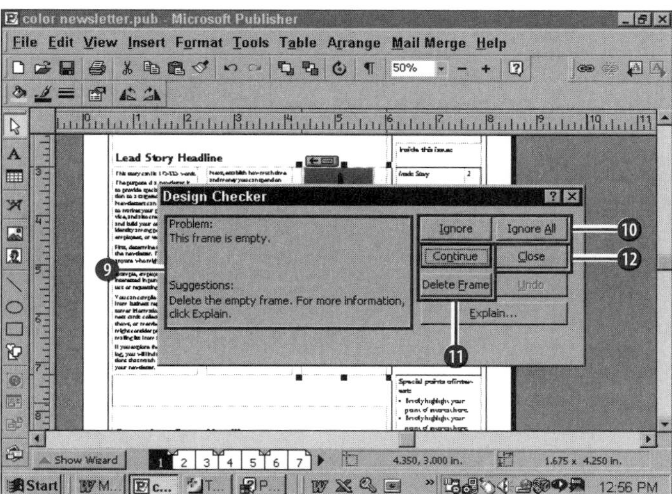

5 *In the Options dialog box, you can specify which elements you want Publisher to check for. Click here to have all items checked, or . . .*

6 *Click "Check selected features."*

7 *Click a check in front of all options in the list to be checked.*

8 *Click OK.*

9 *Read the problem and suggestion.*

10 *Click one of the Ignore buttons to bypass this or all instances of this type of problem.*

11 *Click the suggested fix or Continue to go to the next problem.*

12 *Click Close when finished with Design Checker.*

- **Disproportional pictures:** When you have stretched a photo out of kilter, Publisher knows and tells you about it. If it's intentional, you can always ignore it. If it was accidental and a picture of the boss has been bloated like a bulldog, you have the chance to fix it before anyone is the wiser.
- **Spacing between sentences:** You're a professional, right? Professional typesetters use only one space between sentences. Design Checker finds those double spaces and asks if you want to remove one of them. Typing teachers may have rapped your knuckles if you didn't place two spaces after ending punctuation, but not so any more. Use only one space.

TAKE NOTE

DESIGN CHECKER IS NO SUBSTITUTE

Many people rely on Spell Checker to catch every instance of misspellings. As you know, or will eventually find out, there is no substitute for good proofing skills. Take responsibility for your publication and check it for errors that Design Checker may not be able to find.

FIND IT ONLINE

Beginning designers can get a lot of info and Web links at **http://desktoppub.about.com/library/weekly/aa051799A.htm.**

Personal Workbook

Q&A

1. What measurement units are used predominantly in the United States printing industry?

2. What key do you hold while moving a frame to constrain it to either straight up and down or left and right?

3. How do you change the beginning page number of a publication?

4. Besides the Text and Picture Frame tools, what other frame tools are there in Publisher?

5. What is the maximum number of pages you can add to your document at one time?

6. With a frame highlighted, what happens when you press the Ctrl key while dragging a corner handle?

7. To quickly view your entire page, what keyboard shortcut can you use?

8. When zoomed in on a two-page spread, what key combinations can you use to pan across or up and down a page?

ANSWERS: PAGE 351

EXTRA PRACTICE

1. Instead of using the wizard, go through Page Setup to create a folded greeting card.
2. Create personalized return address labels using Avery 5163 labels.
3. On your greeting card, draw a frame that will hold a family picture. Then, draw another frame that will hold the cover greeting verbiage.
4. Create a four-page newsletter using the wizard. When completed, add two more pages to the newsletter repeating the elements on page 3.
5. In that newsletter, find a picture or graphic that the wizard has inserted. Enlarge the frame from a one-column to a two-column frame.

REAL-WORLD APPLICATIONS

- ✔ You have been working with Microsoft Publisher 2000 for about six months now. You are in the habit of saving your files on a regular basis and want to turn off the automatic reminder. You go into Publisher's Options and deactivate the automatic reminder.
- ✔ When your newsletter is reviewed by your supervisors, they ask you to take the story that is on the top of page 3 and switch it with the article that appears on the bottom of page 3. You use your mouse to drag the articles and graphics on the page to reverse their position.
- ✔ You have just been through several edits on your 18-page booklet. To be sure that all your frames have text or graphics in them, you run Design Checker.

Visual Quiz

Notice the photo highlighted on the right-side page of this spread. What is the quickest and best way to zoom in on this image so that it is centered in the screen?

____

____

____

____

____

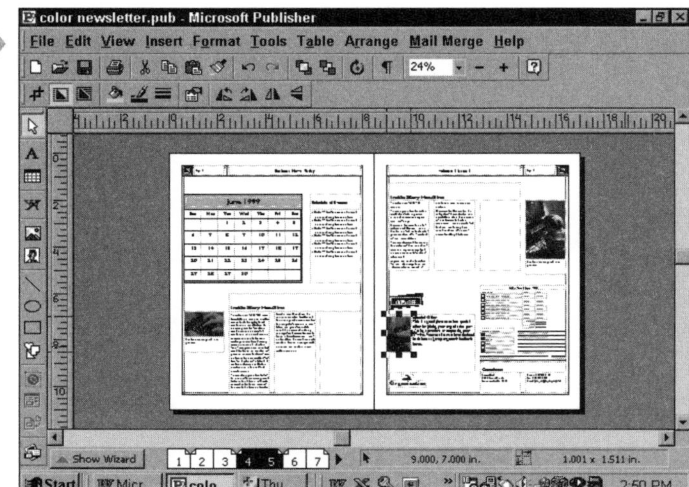

CHAPTER 7

MASTER THESE SKILLS

- Using the Layout Guides
- Designing a Background
- Using Page Numbers in Headers and Footers
- Grouping and Ungrouping Objects
- Using the Rulers
- Using the Snap To Functions
- Using the Measurements Toolbar
- Working with Layers
- Rotating and Flipping Frames and Objects
- Moving Frames Between Pages
- Moving Items to the Background

Arranging Frames and Objects

If this chapter were to be called anything different, it should be the "Essential Tools" chapter. All the tasks you'll find in here will make your layout job go smoothly and easily. In this chapter, you build upon the basics of the chapter before. Now that you know how to add pages, insert frames, and move those frames around a page, these tasks extend upon that knowledge and prepare you for importing text and graphics.

Beginning with placing layout guides on blank pages, you learn to organize your information into columns or grids. Add to that the methods to create a background layer that will hold repeating elements on each page, such as page numbers and graphics. You'll also see how to move objects to the background swiftly.

Layout and design is an intricate and exact science. Though we don't cover design basics, we do give you the tools you'll need to place items accurately on the page. Using the measurement system that comes with Publisher, you learn how to use the rulers and the measurement toolbar to precisely place objects on the page and size them. You can actually instruct Publisher to snap to these guides, giving your layout consistency and accuracy.

In these tasks, you'll discover the handy technique of grouping objects so you can move or alter them, and you discover how to work with layers in Publisher to stack objects on top of one another.

And, for a bit of diversity, you'll see how to rotate and flip frames on your page. When you rotate an object — like a picture, for example — the reader will definitely notice this striking difference from an otherwise straight, up-and-down graphic. Be sure that the graphic is a good one and serves a purpose other than taking up space.

Finally, as you work your way through the tasks in this chapter, bear in mind that you have total control over your layout. Remember to keep your audience in mind while designing and exercise your rights as a designer responsibly. The look and feel of the document can say as much as the content.

Using the Layout Guides

You may think that layout guides are column guides. You would be half right in that assumption. If columns were the only things you could produce with the guides in Publisher, they would probably call them column guides. But, in addition to the vertical columns that you can define with Publisher guides, you can also define horizontal areas, hence the term "layout guides."

Once layout guides are set up, you'll find a bunch of blue and red dashed lines on your page. At the very minimum, you should have guides that define your top, bottom, and side margins. (If you are having headers or footers on your page, be sure to leave a little more space in the top and bottom margin.) Having multiple horizontal and vertical guides to your page gives you a nice grid with which you can design your publication.

Many designers use a grid technique when creating their layouts. Placing text and graphic elements in the grid can give a feeling of organization and balance to a layout. If nothing else, a layout grid gives you a structure. Without that structure, you can place objects on the page in locations you think are visually appealing, only to find out that your eye sees something that just isn't quite right. A grid can help you eliminate the guesswork.

As an example, let's say that you set up a grid with five columns across and four rows down. When you place objects on the page, use a multiple of the columns and rows. A picture could be one column wide by two rows deep. Text could span three columns and run two or three rows deep. The guesswork has been eliminated from what size to make the picture and the body text.

Use white space; it can be an effective tool in design. As a general rule, white space should be kept to the outside of the page border. Having a large chunk of white space in the middle of graphics and text can be distracting.

CROSS-REFERENCE

You can make your frames snap to your guidelines. See "Using the Snap To Functions" later in this chapter.

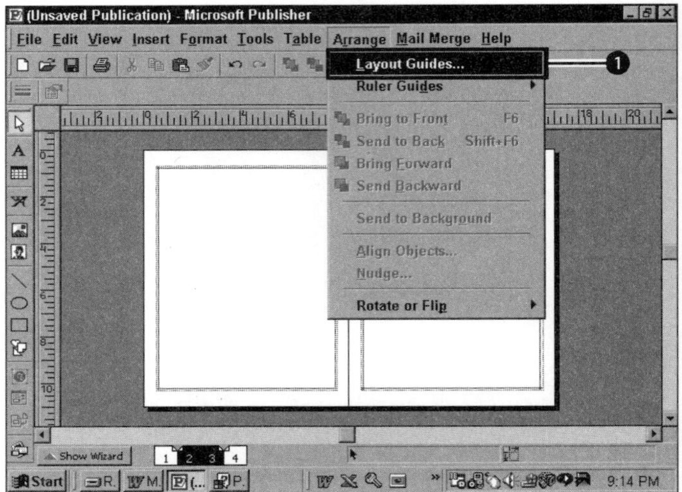

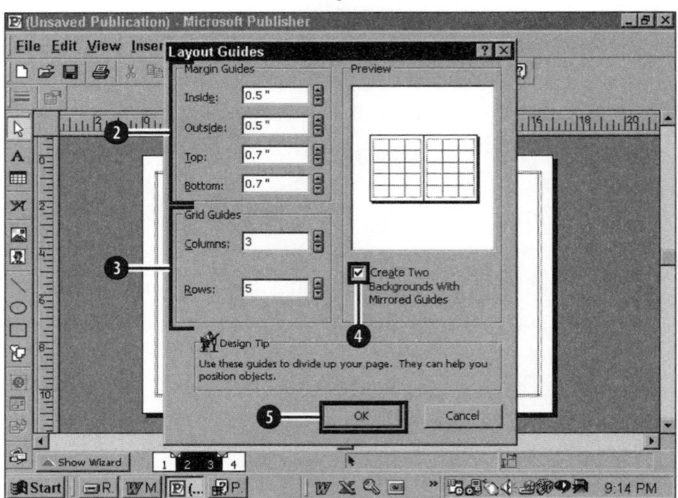

1. *To set up layout guides, choose Arrange ⇨ Layout Guides.*
2. *Set the top, bottom, inside, and outside margins.*
3. *Indicate the number of columns and rows.*
4. *If working on a two-sided document, choose whether to mirror the guides on the opposite page.*
5. *Click OK to set the layout guides on your pages.*

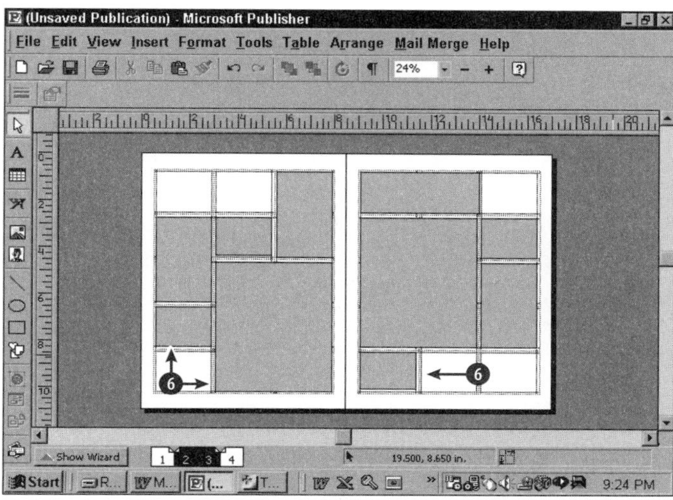

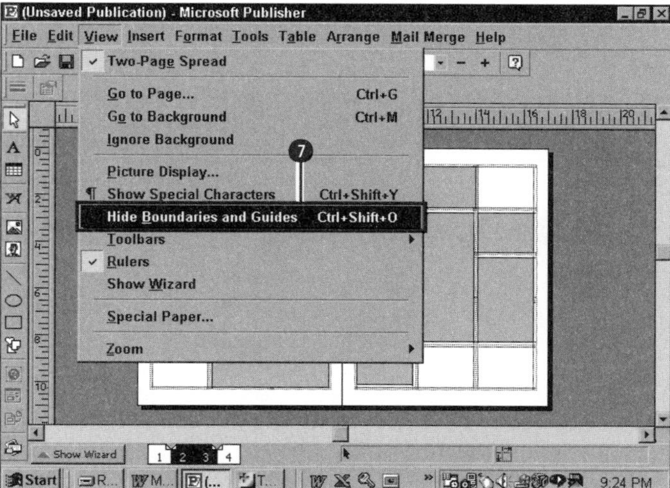

❻ *You can place elements using the columns and rows as guides.*

❼ *To hide the layout guides, choose View ➪ Hide Boundaries and Guides or press Ctrl+Shift+O. This will give you a better idea of your pages as they would be printed.*

Another general rule is don't trap copy. Surrounding text with photos can lessen the message because most people focus on the photos. Try to keep copy to the outside of the layout as well. Many more concepts can be learned when laying out a publication. Why not look into some classes on design or check the Web for design ideas?

TAKE NOTE

LAYOUT GUIDES ARE NOT RULER GUIDES

The "Using the Rulers" section later in this chapter teaches you how to use ruler guides. Don't confuse ruler guides with layout guides. While their function is similar, they do differ.

LAYOUT GUIDES APPEAR ON ALL PAGES

Once you have your guides set up, they will appear on all pages in the document. You can temporarily hide them by choosing View ➪ Hide Boundaries and Guides.

FIND IT ONLINE

To learn more about designing with grids, see **http://designrefresher.i-us.com/juneone.html.**

Designing a Background

Some might call it a template, while others may call them style sheets. In Publisher, however, the background is where you place elements that you want repeated on each page of the document, taking on the appearance of a style sheet or template.

The background is actually the lowest layer of a Publisher document that holds elements that will appear on every page, no matter which pages you are on when you add it to the background. If you're on page 4 and you add a graphic to the background, it will show up on pages 1–3 and any pages after 4.

In the previous task, you already know of one element that gets placed on the background — the layout guides. In order to access these guidelines, you have to activate the background layer, edit your guidelines, and then go back to the other layers.

Why would you access the guidelines? If you remember in the previous task, you were given the option to check a box that indicated you wanted to mirror items on the left side with those on the right and vice versa. Once you have guidelines set up, you can go to the background layer at a later time and move the guidelines around. When you move them on one page, the alteration is mirrored on the opposite page.

Other items that you would place on the background include the headers and footers that will appear on each page. Most of the time, headers and footers include the page numbers, issue volumes and/or dates, and the publication name, but you aren't limited to just those. *Headers* appear in the top margin of the page while *footers* reside in the lower margin area.

Graphics are another thing that may be placed on the background. If you are using a page border, logo, or piece of clip art on a specific part of the page, you can place it on the background to be repeated on each page.

CROSS-REFERENCE

See "Moving Items to the Background" at the end of this chapter.

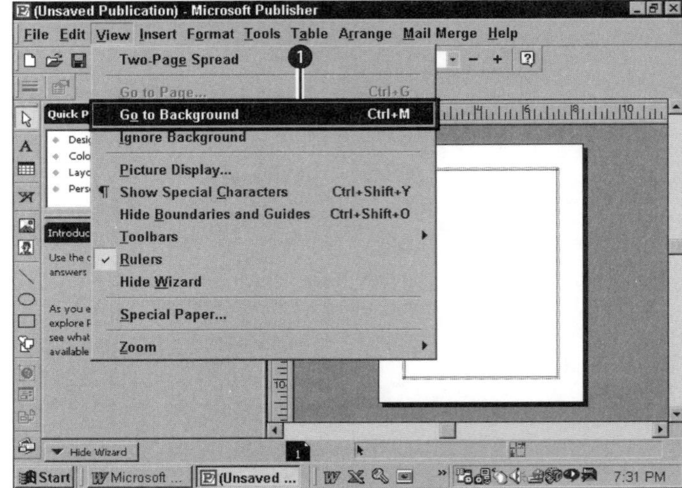

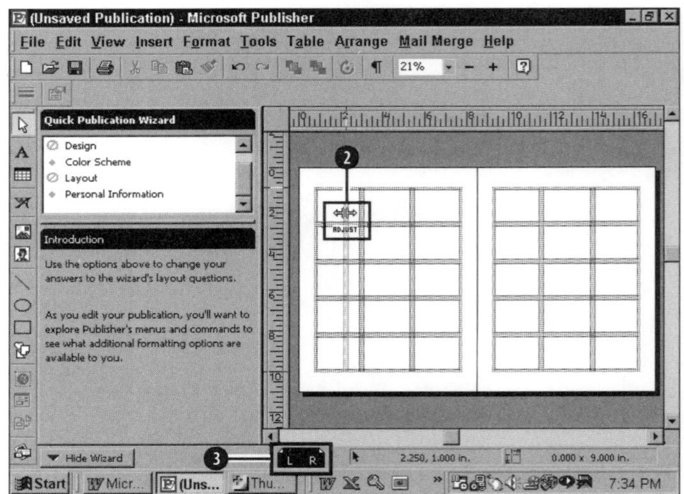

❶ *To place items on the background, choose View ➪ Go to Background or press Ctrl+M.*

❷ *To move layout guides, hold the Shift key while the mouse is over a guide and drag to the desired position.*

▶ *If you checked Create two Backgrounds With Mirrored Guide, changes made on one page will appear on the opposite page.*

❸ *The Page Navigation icons change to L (left) and R (right) to indicate you are on the background layer.*

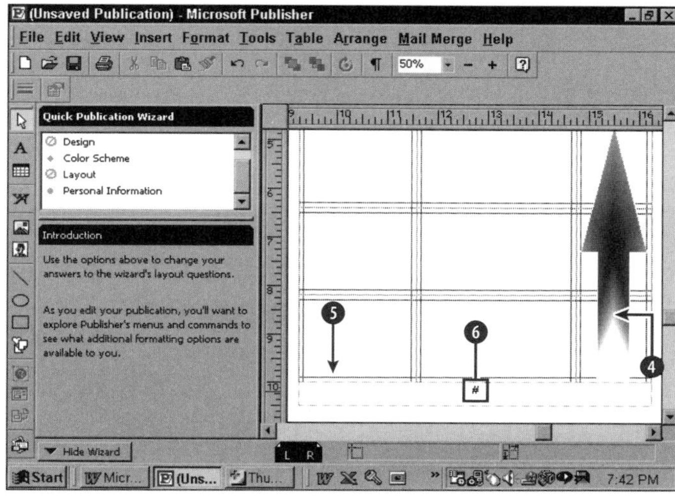

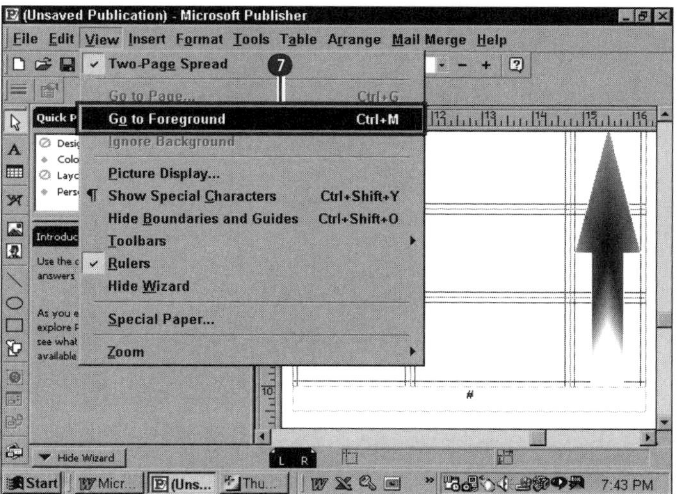

4 *Place any graphics that will repeat on each page.*

5 *Draw text frames to hold the headers and/or footers. Because this is a text frame, you can also add borders, fills, or shadows.*

6 *Insert the repeating text in the frame.*

7 *To quit editing the background layer, choose View ➪ Go to Foreground or press Ctrl+M.*

And, one of the biggest advantages of the background is that while it is not active, you can select, edit, delete, and move the items on the foreground layers without having to worry about accidentally selecting a background element and changing or deleting it.

TAKE NOTE

YOU CAN IGNORE THE BACKGROUND ON CERTAIN PAGES

Even though you have a background defined, you can instruct Publisher to ignore the background on a specific page. For example, you rarely see a page number in a header or footer on the first page of a newsletter. You can instruct Publisher to hide the background on just page 1.

ACCOUNTING FOR HEADERS OR FOOTERS

Don't forget to set larger margins for the top and/or bottom of the page if you're planning on using headers and/or footers.

FIND IT ONLINE

See how one university sets header and footer guidelines at **http://www.uwaterloo.ca/Guidelines/practices.html.**

Using Page Numbers in Headers and Footers

Look at any magazine or book and you're bound to find at least one common element between them. Annual reports have them; newspapers include them. After all, how could you find what you're looking for if it weren't for page numbers?

Sometimes you'll see letters (A, B, C) or Roman numerals (I, II, III), in place of regular Arabic (1, 2, 3) page numbers, but their purpose is still the same. You have to let readers know where they are and where they need to go.

While Publisher lets you add page numbers to any publication, you are limited to Arabic numerals; you won't find any Roman numerals or alphabetic replacements for them. So, settle down and just enjoy the pleasure you can get when you have to add four pages at the front of a hundred-page document. Because, when you add those pages, you won't have to go through eighty pages and change page numbers. Because you placed them using the special Publisher code, Publisher keeps track and does all the renumbering for you.

Typically, page numbers are placed at the top or bottom of a document. Double-sided pages usually will mirror the page number location on the outside corner. Other documents just center the page number in the margin. But, don't let that stop you from using any part of the outside margin. Like the alphabetical thumb index of a dictionary, you can also place your page numbers anywhere on the page.

In addition to the versatility of placing the page numbers in the headers, footers, or outside margins, you can also format the appearance of the page number just as you would any text in Publisher. However, because we haven't quite covered that task yet, you can look ahead to Chapter 9 as long as you promise to come back and finish this chapter.

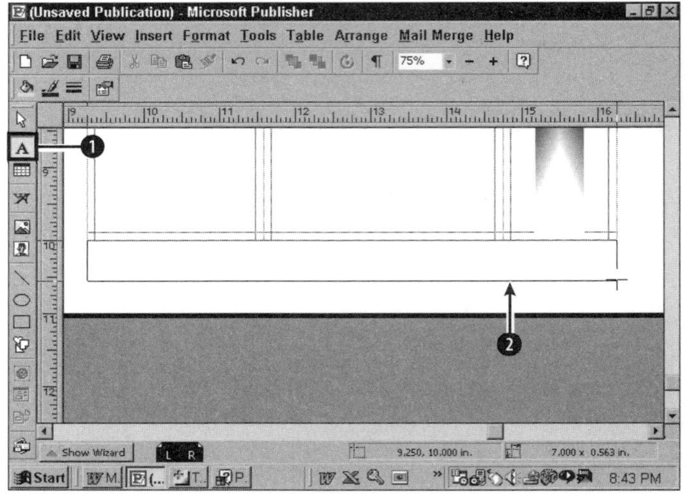

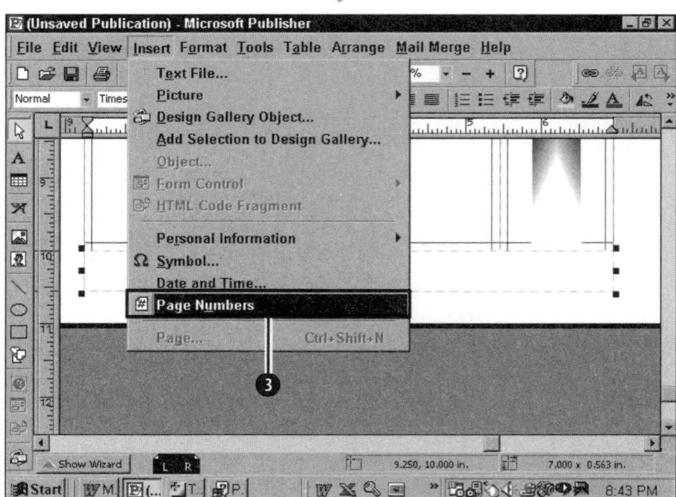

1. *To create a header or footer, switch to the background by pressing Ctrl+M and then select the Text Frame tool.*
2. *Draw a frame at the top or bottom of the page.*
3. *While the flashing cursor is in the frame, choose Insert ➪ Page Numbers.*

CROSS-REFERENCE

Refer back to "Setting Publisher Options" in Chapter 6 to change beginning page numbers of your document.

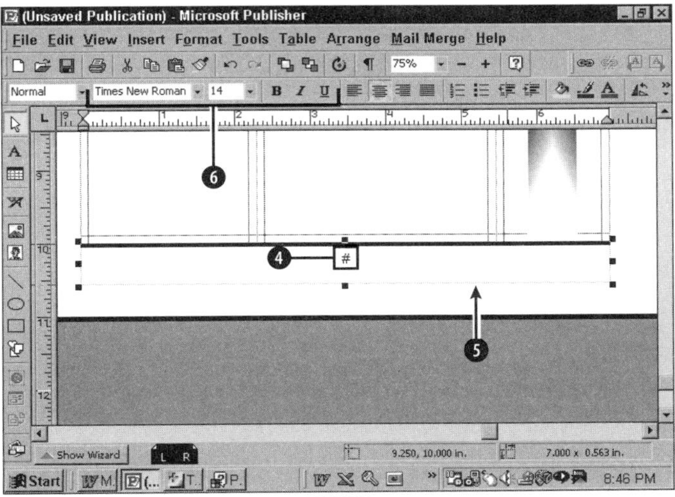

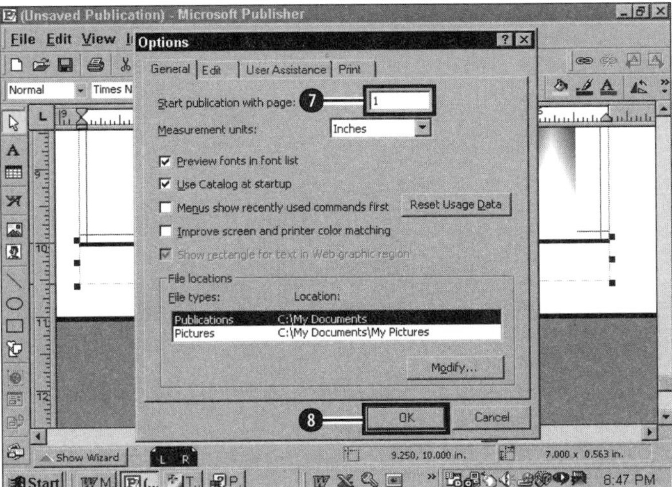

4 Publisher inserts the "#" symbol in the frame to indicate where the page number will be placed.

5 You can format the symbol just as you would any text. The page number takes on the attributes you assign.

6 Likewise, you can format the frame by adding fills, borders, or shadows.

7 To change the beginning page number of the publication, choose Tools ➪ Options and change the setting in the General tab.

8 Click OK to accept this change.

Because Publisher treats the text in a header and footer the same as it does for regular text in the body of the page, it is subject to the same alignment rules as headlines, picture captions, and body copy. You can use any of the text editing techniques to format and place page numbers exactly as you wish.

TAKE NOTE

KEEPING PAGE NUMBERS TO THE OUTSIDE

It is a standard practice among publishers to be sure that page numbers are kept to the center or outside margins so that readers can thumb through a publication and easily find the pagination. Look at how your publication is to be bound and place the page numbers appropriately for convenience.

USING THE BACKGROUND

Don't forget that the background layer is the easiest way to place headers and footers on a page. Even though any other text repeats exactly as it appears, inserting the page number code tells Publisher to keep track of the page and place the appropriate number in the symbol's place.

FIND IT ONLINE

See pagination problems at **http://www.sil.org/lingualinks/library/literacy/vao144/krz1832/krz145/krz509.htm.**

Grouping and Ungrouping Objects

You can exercise tremendous control over the objects you place on your pages. When you have many objects on a page, it becomes very tiresome to move each one individually, especially if you're going to move them to another page.

Publisher's capability to group objects can come in handy for moving several frames of objects together, with the added benefit of the group's formation and alignment staying intact. After you have painstakingly nudged and maneuvered frames to get just the right look, group them together to maintain that design.

Grouping is a relatively easy process. Using the Arrow tool, you select the first items of your group. Then, while holding down the Shift key, you select each of the other objects one at a time. If you accidentally select an object that you didn't want in the group, keep holding the Shift key and click that object again. It will be deselected.

After you select your objects, Publisher adds a little icon that looks like two separated puzzle pieces toward the bottom of the group. You can click the icon and your objects will be grouped. You'll be able to tell if you're successful because the puzzle pieces will lock together. When you ungroup the objects, the puzzle pieces separate indicating the objects are no longer considered as one.

You can also right-click the group and select Group Objects from the pop-up menu. You won't, however, find the menu option to Ungroup Objects here after you have already grouped them.

When you select a group and try to exercise your sizing and scaling prowess, you will actually reduce or enlarge the entire group. All individual frames within the group shrink or grow according to your mouse movements.

In the case of text frames in the group, the margins will move in or expand and the text will reflow to accommodate the margins. Pictures, however, will shrink

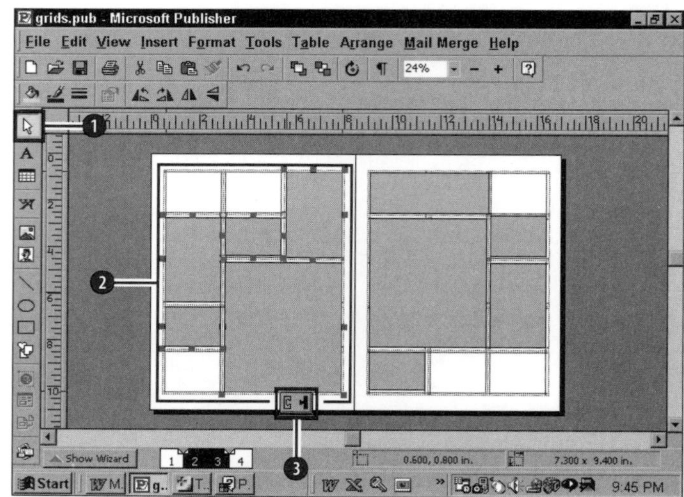

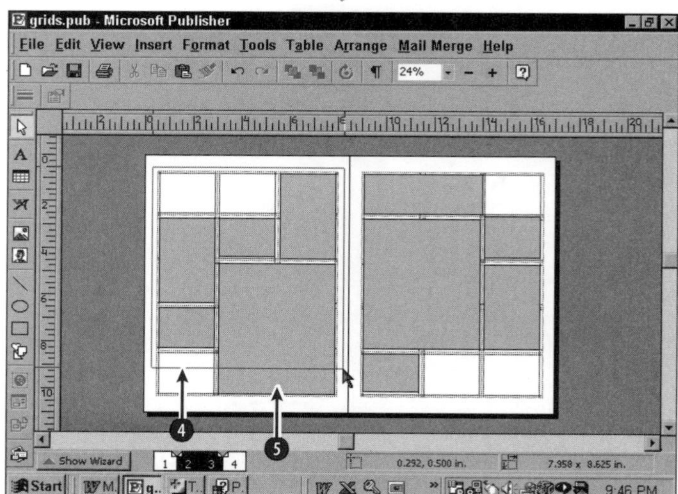

1. *To group objects, select the Arrow tool.*
2. *Hold the Shift key while clicking each item that will be in the group.*
3. *Click the Group icon. (Notice that the puzzle pieces are unjoined.)*
4. *Alternatively, you can drag the mouse cursor around the objects that will be in the group.*
5. *If an object is not totally enclosed in the marquee, it will not become part of the group.*

CROSS-REFERENCE

See "Moving and Sizing Frames" in Chapter 6. **This same technique works with grouped objects.**

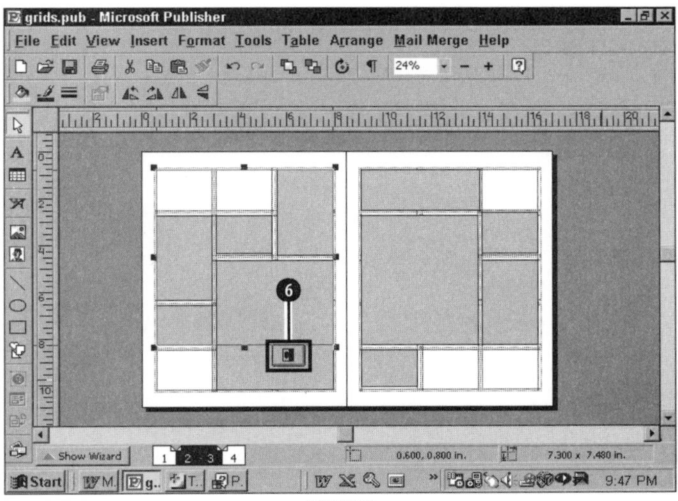

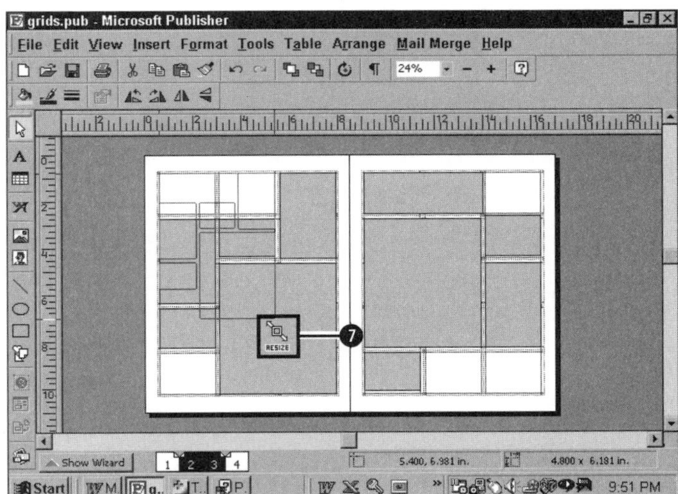

❻ *After clicking the Group icon, the two puzzle pieces are joined indicating a group of objects.*

❼ *By dragging a handle of the group, you can resize all objects in the group. You can also use the Ctrl, Shift, and Alt keys to constrain and rotate the group.*

or enlarge so that what fit into the frame beforehand will still be visible when you're done.

If you have assigned a frame border, the rule line width will not be changed. That is, it won't be enlarged or reduced with the size of the frame. But then, that's how it works whether it's grouped or not.

Finally, to assign fills and borders, you still have to select frames on an individual basis. You can't change those attributes for all the items in the group.

TAKE NOTE

MARQUEE SELECTING INSTEAD OF HOLDING THE SHIFT KEY

You can use the Arrow tool to drag around the objects that you want to group instead of holding the Shift key and clicking the individual items. When you drag around objects, this is known as *marquee selecting*. You have to be sure to surround the objects totally. Merely having the marquee touch part of the object will not select it.

FIND IT ONLINE

Find an e-mail or discussion group for your interests at **http://catalog.com/vivian/interest-group-search.html.**

Using the Rulers

Publisher includes one ruler at the top of the Layout window and one down the left side. You'll notice, as you move your mouse, that corresponding lines move along both rulers indicating the position of your mouse. This feature comes in pretty handy when you have to draw a frame that is a specific size and must start in a specific location.

But that's not all the rulers are good for. You can place green ruler guides on your page by holding the Shift key and dragging down or across from one of the rulers. Ruler guides work just like the layout guides except they only show on the page where you place them. They don't repeat on every page. You can use the ruler guides to help draw or place frames. To remove a ruler guide, hold the Shift key and drag the guide off the page or back to its ruler. You can also use the Shift key to move the ruler guide to a new location.

If the rulers get in your way, you can hide them by either right-clicking either ruler and removing the check next to Rulers, or choose View ➪ Rulers and remove the check from the menu item.

The rulers are not stuck on the side of the Layout window permanently. By dragging them with the mouse, you can bring either or both of them onto the page to get a closer look at the size of an object. Of course, you can also just highlight the object and check the dimensions in the status bar, too.

So that you can move both rulers at the same time, you can start your mouse drag using the box where the two rulers meet at the top of the page. Your cursor changes to a dual-headed arrow indicating the direction the rulers may move.

When holding the Ctrl key while dragging the rulers' corner box, you will not only reposition the rulers on your page, but the zero points will move to wherever the

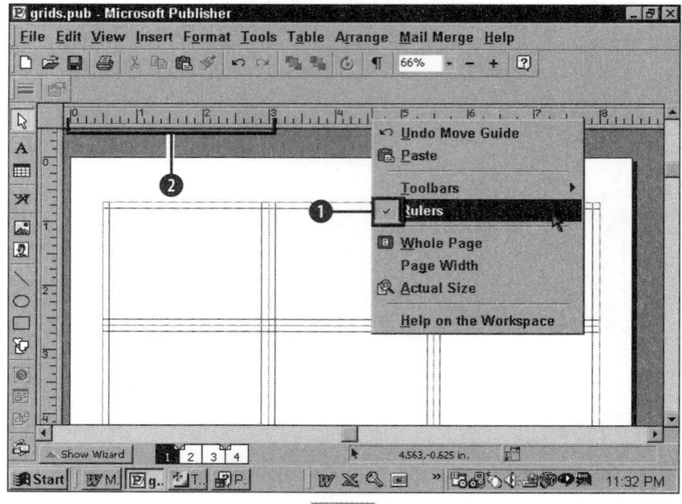

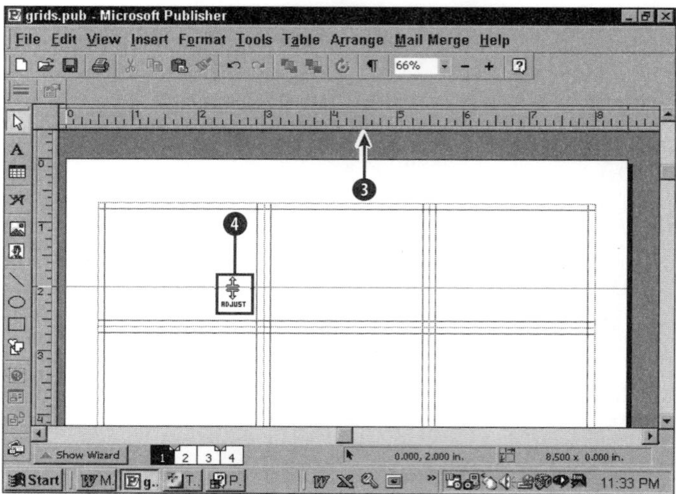

1. *To show or hide the Rulers, right-click either ruler and choose Rulers. A checkmark indicates they are on; no checkmark indicates they are turned off.*
2. *Rulers reflect the units of measure chosen in the Tools ➪ Options dialog box.*
3. *Ruler guides are placed on the page by holding the Shift key while dragging from the ruler.*
4. *Once placed on the page, you can press and hold the Shift key to drag the guide to a new location.*

CROSS-REFERENCE

To ensure exact placement of objects, see the next task, "Using the Snap To Functions."

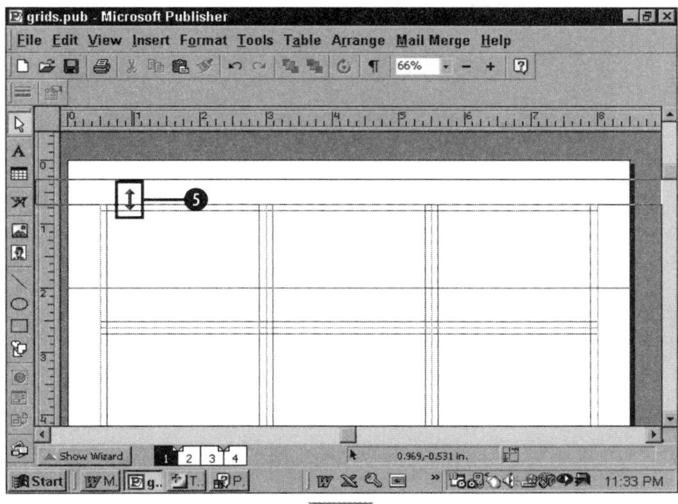

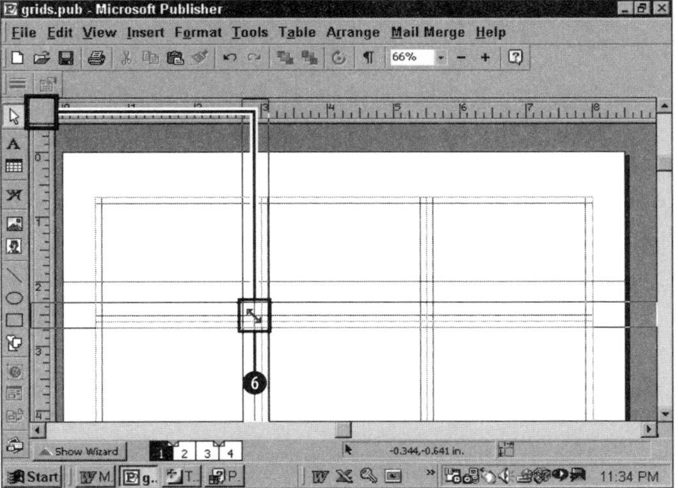

5 *Drag a ruler down from its location to reposition it on the page.*

6 *Drag the ruler junction box to reposition both rulers at the same time.*

rulers intersect. Normally, the zero points indicate the top and left edges of the paper. If you want to keep the rulers in their new location but reset the zero points to the edges of the paper, you can double-click inside the junction box.

You can also change the zero point on a ruler by holding the Shift key and right-clicking the new zero point location.

TAKE NOTE

CHANGING THE UNITS OF MEASURE

You can change the measuring units to inches, centimeters, picas, or points. To do so, choose Tools ➪ Options and, on the General tab, pick a new unit of measurement from the drop-down list. When you change the units, the rulers reflect that change.

FIND IT ONLINE

Need to do some measurement conversions? Go to **http://www.french-property.com/ref/convert.htm.**

Using the Snap To Functions

If you've ever tried to line two very thin objects up to exact precision, you know how difficult it can be. The same frustration could happen in Publisher when you're drawing frames or aligning frames with the layout guides.

Luckily, Publisher has a built-in snapping feature that takes the guesswork out of precision placement. You can instruct Publisher to snap your frame or cursor movement to the nearest guide so that the alignment is exactly on target. When any type of snapping is turned on, objects are sucked to the guides, objects, or markers when they get really close. As most programs with snapping features put it, your cursor is drawn like a magnet to whatever snap features are turned on.

You're already familiar with the layout guides, which were explained in the first task in this chapter. The red and blue horizontal and vertical dotted lines that are created when you define the layout guides can be used for snapping as well as the green ruler guides that you set up on every page.

Objects can also be snapped to the ruler marks. With Snap to Ruler Marks turned on, you can watch your cursor jump from tick mark to tick mark on the ruler. This feature makes an invisible grid on your page and lets you draw frames with extreme accuracy.

The last kind of snap you can activate is Snap to Object. If you're drawing a new frame on your page, you can turn on this feature so the new frame you draw is butted up against an object on the page. Likewise, when you move an object close to another object with this feature turned on, it will be drawn to the border of the stationary object.

When you set the snapping options, you are setting them for Publisher, not just the document that's open at the time. Publisher doesn't save the grid settings with the document.

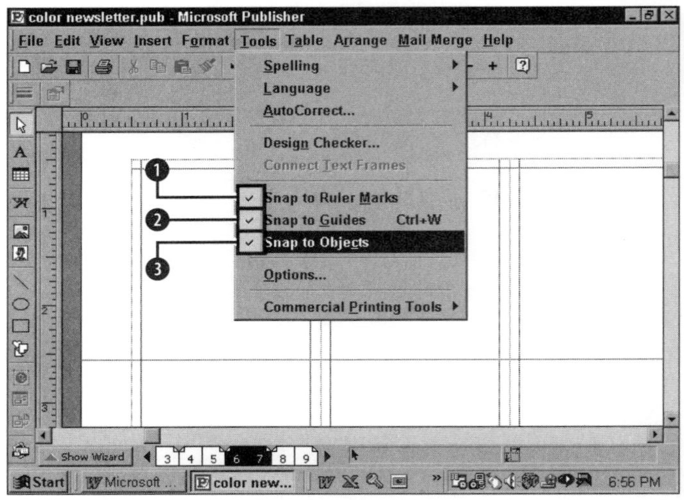

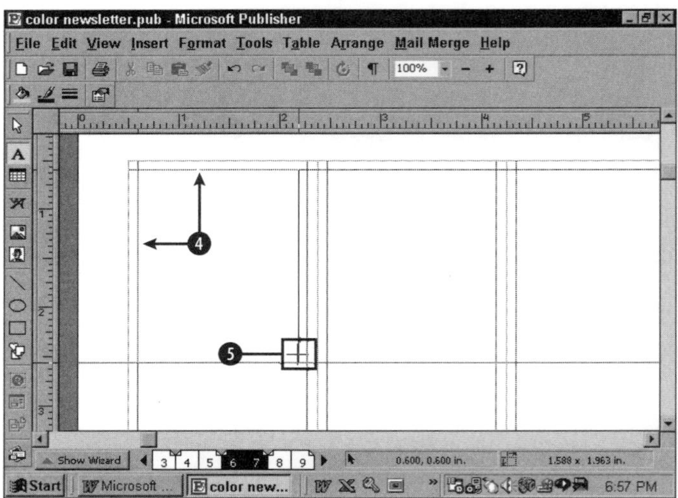

1. *Choose Tools ➪ Snap to Ruler Marks, and/or . . .*
2. *Tools ➪ Snap to Guides (or Ctrl+W) and/or . . .*
3. *Tools ➪ Snap to Objects.*
4. *When snapping to guides, your cursor will be drawn automatically to the layout or ruler guides.*
5. *Notice how the bottom frame border has snapped into place while the cursor is still above it.*

CROSS-REFERENCE

Learn how to wrap text around an object in the task "Flowing Text Around Frames" in Chapter 8.

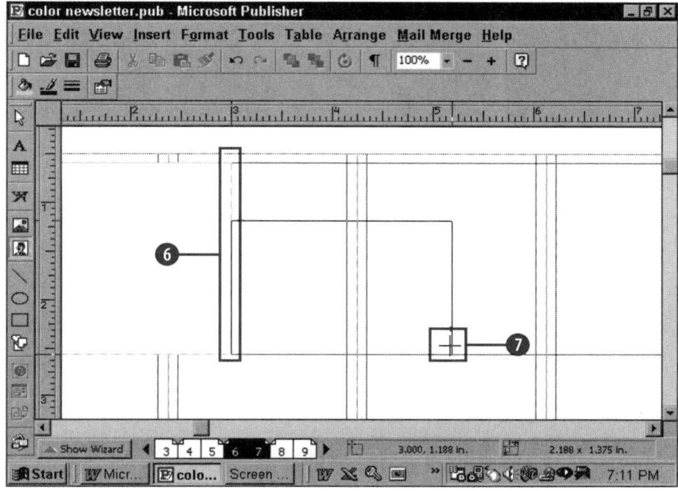

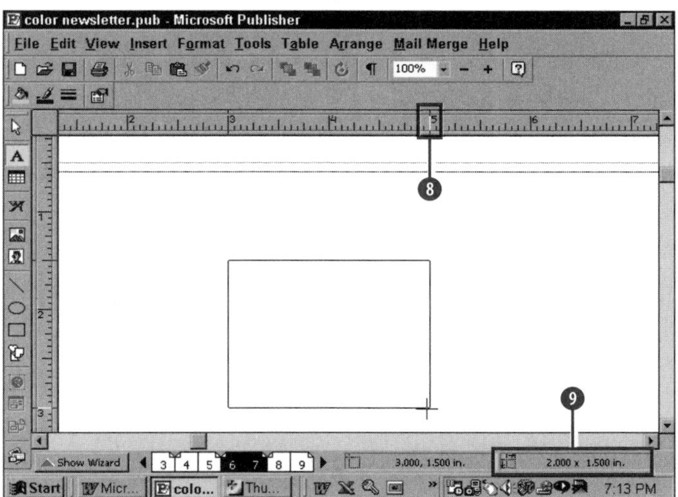

❻ *When Snap to Objects is selected, your cursor will be drawn to the frame border it gets close to.*

❼ *Notice how the frame has snapped to the ruler guide when the cursor is still above it.*

❽ *When Snap to Ruler Marks is active, your cursor snaps to the individual tick marks of the ruler.*

❾ *Drawing a frame to precise measurements is possible. Notice the size of the frame in the status bar.*

Snapping also works with resizing objects. As you drag the handles of an object, they will perform whatever snap you have turned on at the time.

TAKE NOTE

WRESTLING WITH TOO MANY SNAPS

Use caution when turning the Snap To features on and off. You could be causing more work than is necessary. Of the three snap settings, the most used would be Snap to Ruler Marks and Snap to Guides. Sometimes Snap to Objects is turned on for no reason. If you have created your objects with the Snap to Ruler Marks on, your objects will already be on the invisible grid. Any new objects you draw would be on that grid, too. So, you could draw a new object close to the current object and your cursor should automatically snap to the other invisible grid line or ruler mark where current object is sitting.

FIND IT ONLINE

You can make a snapshot of your screen to use in publications. Check out **http://www.screencapture.com.**

Using the Measurements Toolbar

If mousing and dragging isn't your style to get exact measurement of the objects you create, resize or move them, Publisher offers a great tool called the measurement toolbar. In it, you can specify a width and height of a frame, its x-y positions, and its exact rotation in degrees. Granted, you can get some of this information from the status bar, but the measurement toolbar enables you to input the settings directly, avoiding the drag of the mouse.

When you call up this toolbar, notice that it's divided in half. The left half controls the frame while the right half controls text attributes. In this task, we concentrate on the left half of the toolbar. The text side comes later in "Controlling Character and Line Spacing" in Chapter 9.

You're familiar with the terms "height" and "width." However, the other set of measurements that a frame has is its *x* and *y* positions. The *x position* is the distance that the top-left corner of the frame is from the top-left edge of the page. The *y position* is the amount of space from the object's top-left corner to the top edge of the page.

By entering values into the *x* and *y* position text boxes, you can move an object around the page, without ever dragging it with the mouse. Greater control and quicker response is your advantage when using the measurement toolbar to reposition your object.

Likewise, when you enter values in the horizontal and vertical measurements text boxes, you can reduce or enlarge your object at will. Just remember, you don't have the advantage of holding the Alt or Shift keys to constrain the object's proportion. You could end up distorting any pictures inside the frame.

You can enter values in the text boxes just like you do in any dialog box. You can use your tab key to jump to the next text box or use Shift+Tab to go backwards in order. The only thing you have to remember is that the

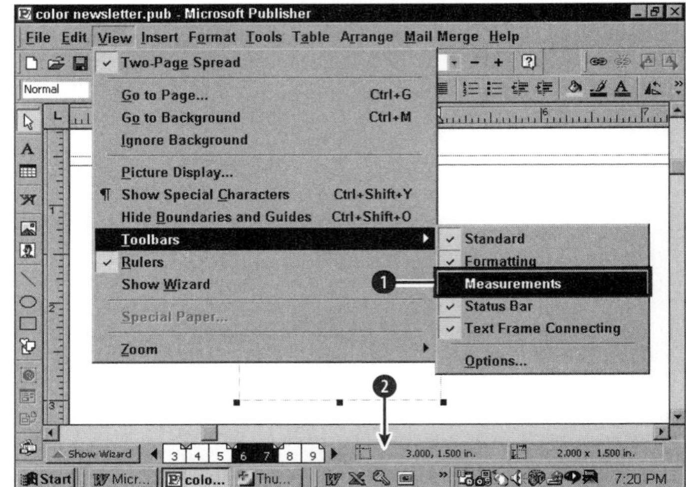

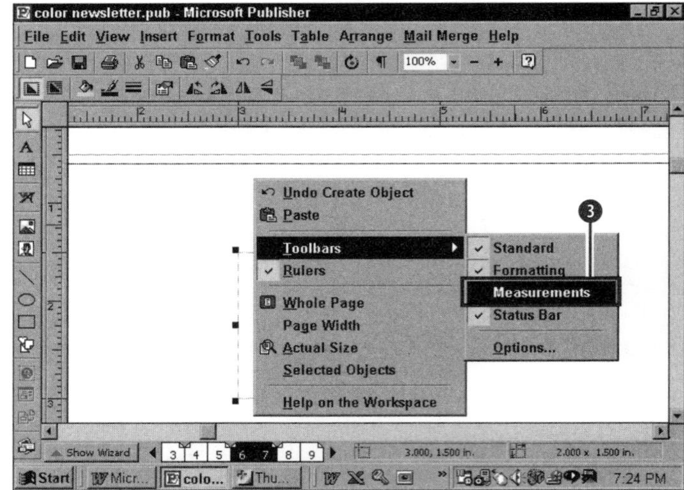

1. *To open the measurements toolbar, choose View ➪ Toolbars ➪ Measurements.*
2. *Or, double-click anywhere on the status bar.*
3. *You can also right-click anywhere on the page background and choose Toolbars ➪ Measurements.*

CROSS-REFERENCE

Measurement units are set the same as the rulers. To change the measurement units, see "Setting Publisher Options" in Chapter 6.

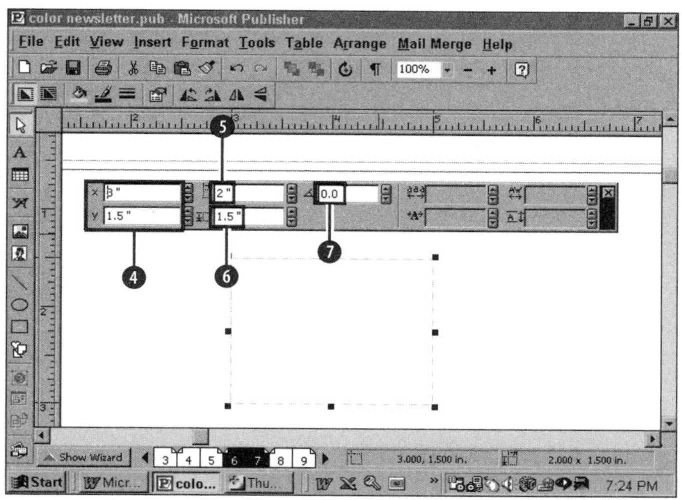

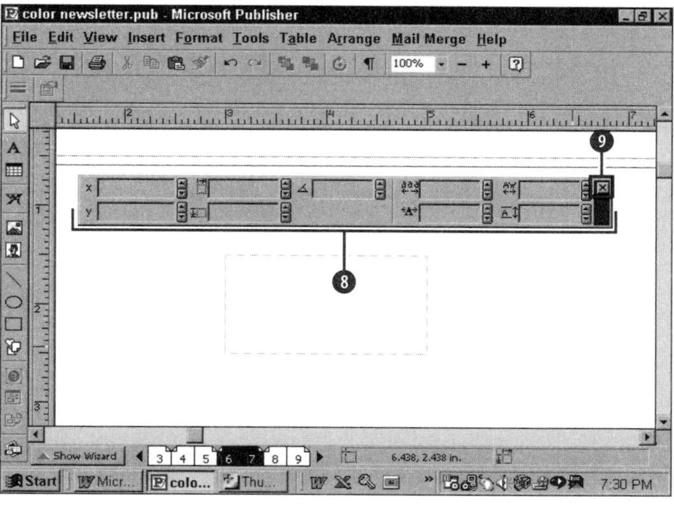

4 *Enter new x and y settings to move the top-left corner of the object.*

5 *Set a new width of the object.*

6 *Set a new height for the object.*

7 *Enter a new rotation in degrees.*

8 *The toolbar shows no settings when nothing is selected.*

9 *Drag on the window bar to move the toolbar to a new location in the window.*

values you enter will not take effect until you use these keys to go to the next setting, or press the Enter key after determining the values.

TAKE NOTE

THIS TOOLBAR DOESN'T RESIZE

Most floating toolbars in Windows programs enable you to drag on a corner to resize it. The measurement toolbar, however, will stay the same size. You can still drag it around in the window using the color bar underneath the Close button.

WHEN YOU CAN'T MAKE CHANGES

If the entire measurement toolbar is grayed out and you have no settings showing, it means nothing is selected. You must have an object or text selected with the Arrow tool before settings are brought into the toolbar.

FIND IT ONLINE

You can use Convert It! to convert units of measure. Check out **http://www.smisoftware.com/Html/ConvertIt/index.htm.**

Working with Layers

Earlier in this chapter, you were introduced to the background layer in Publisher. The items that you placed on the background layer will show on each page of the publication unless you turn them off for a specific page.

The rest of the discussion on layers takes on a different tone. After exiting the background layer, you begin to place objects on the page. Each time you place an object or frame, you essentially create a layer. If you could see the page from its side and the frames were three-dimensional, each item would be ordered with the first one placed on the bottom and each additional item on top of that one. Think of a deck of cards. Whenever you deal the cards, the first one stays on the bottom of the hand (as long as the player doesn't pick them up). Each additional card you place on the table goes on top of the first card. Once the hand is dealt, the player has the option of organizing his or her cards in some order. The elements on your page are no different. You can organize them so some get placed on top of the others.

What matters most when dealing with layered objects is what is on top. The frame that is on top has dominance over the others on the page. Therefore, when you place a frame with more dominance on top of another lesser frame, the contents of the lesser frame can get covered up or, in the case of text, pushed aside.

For a good example of what can happen to text when another frame of text gets placed on top of it, look at a newspaper. A large front-page story can run several columns across, but another story can be dropped on top of it and the text gets pushed around the new frame. This is called *wrapping*—when text moves down or into other columns according to the limitations of those columns.

You have a couple of ways to change the order of the elements on your page. You can use the cut-and-paste

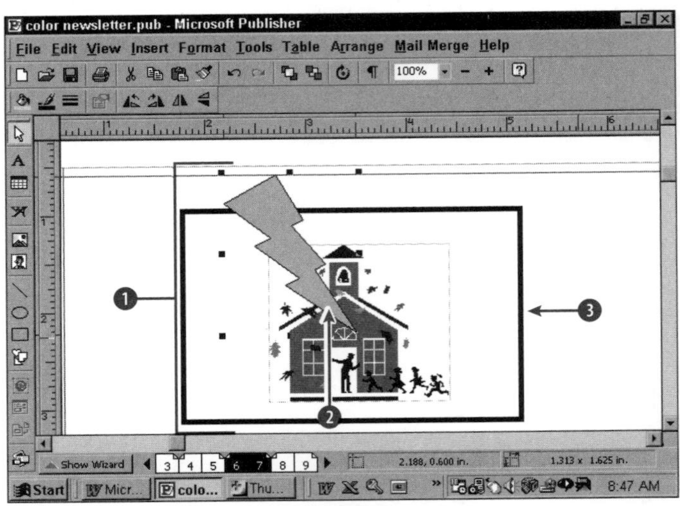

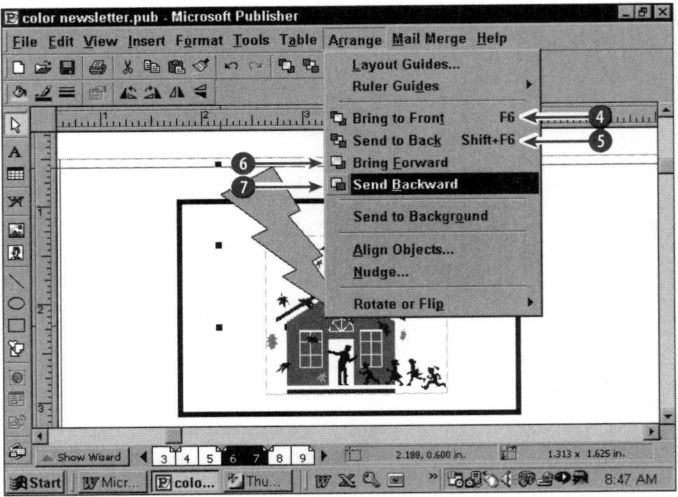

1. *When you have multiple objects overlapping, you have created layers.*
2. *The lightning bolt is the top layer, while the schoolhouse is the middle layer.*
3. *The large frame with the border is on the bottom layer, though it is not really apparent in the figure.*
4. *Choose Arrange ➪ Bring to Front to bring the item to the top.*
5. *Choose Arrange ➪ Send to Back to move the item underneath all the items.*
6. *Choose Arrange ➪ Bring Forward to move the item up one level.*
7. *Choose Arrange ➪ Send Backward to drop the item behind one level.*

CROSS-REFERENCE

Learn how to wrap text around a graphic in the task "Flowing Text Around Frames" in Chapter 8.

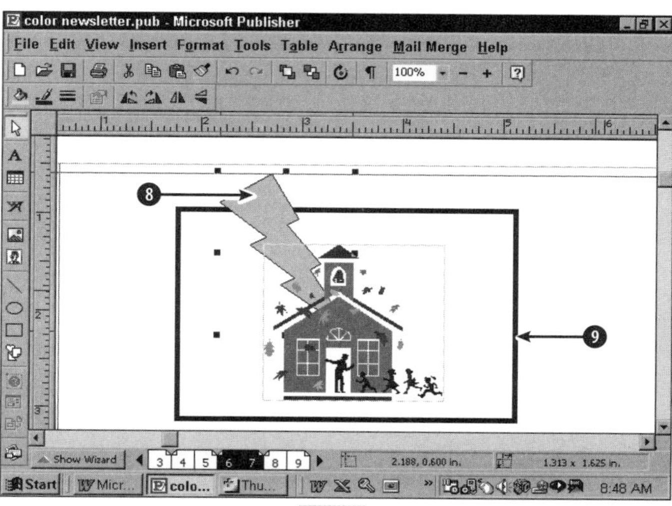

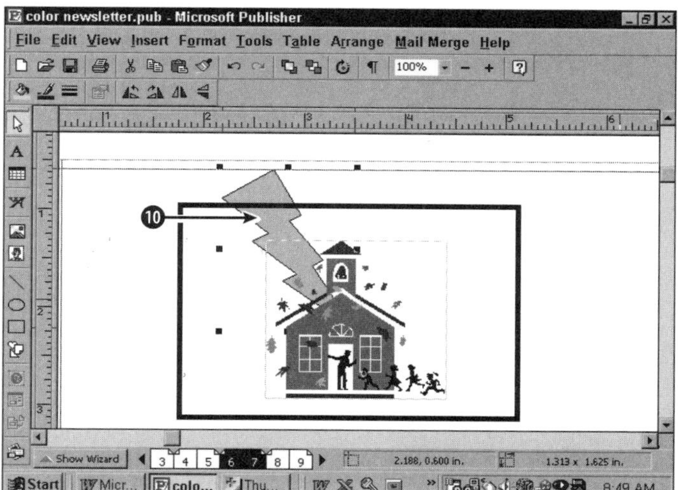

8 *Selecting the lightning bolt and choosing Arrange ➪ Send Backward puts it behind the schoolhouse.*

9 *The frame, however, still remains the lowest of the layers.*

10 *Selecting the lightning bolt and choosing Arrange ➪ Send to Back (or pressing Ctrl+F6) moves it below the frame and the schoolhouse.*

technique. When you cut a frame from a lower layer and paste it on the page, it then becomes the topmost frame. Everything else either gets hidden or has to move around it.

The other way you can control the layer is using the Arrange menu to bring items forward or send them behind objects.

TAKE NOTE

MAKE OBJECTS TRANSPARENT

You can make an object's background transparent so whatever is underneath will show through. For example, if you use WordArt to create a fancy phrase or word, and place it on a colored background or a graphic, you can press Ctrl+T and the white background of the WordArt frame will become transparent.

FIND IT ONLINE

Tiramisu is an Italian layered dessert. Try one of the recipes at **http://italianfood.about.com/library/weekly/ntira.htm.**

Rotating and Flipping Frames and Objects

Frames that hold photos, graphics, or text tend to be a little boring when kept to the rectangular shape. Just for a little diversity, try rotating a frame to add some dramatic intrigue or variation from the boring monotony of traditional layout. Or, use the Flip Horizontal or Flip Vertical buttons to mirror the frame content up and down or left to right. This, however, only works with frames holding graphics.

However, use caution. While rotating a frame can add interest and variety, turning too many frames can lead to a very frustrating and time-consuming layout — and like any special effect, it loses its effectiveness if done to extremes.

Try to keep rotated frames of text at a decent angle for reading. If the reader has to turn the page on its side, the rotation is probably too severe. Also, be sure that graphics that get rotated within the frame still are intelligible.

To give your frame a turn, you use the Alt key while dragging one of the control handles. Just like you learned how to resize a frame, the technique is the same except you rotate instead of reduce or enlarge the frame. After pressing the Alt key, when you see the Rotate cursor, drag any one of the handles to spin your frame around from its center point.

For more conventional angles, you can also turn frames in 90-degree increments. Using the drop-down menu, choose Arrange ➪ Rotate or Flip ➪ Rotate Left or Rotate Right. For a quicker solution, use the standard toolbar. You'll find a couple of buttons that will do the same thing.

In the Arrange ➪ Rotate or Flip menu, there's also a choice for Custom Rotate. If you know the specific degree of rotation that you want to turn a frame, you can enter it in the dialog box provided.

Another method for rotating objects is using your newly discovered measurement toolbar, introduced

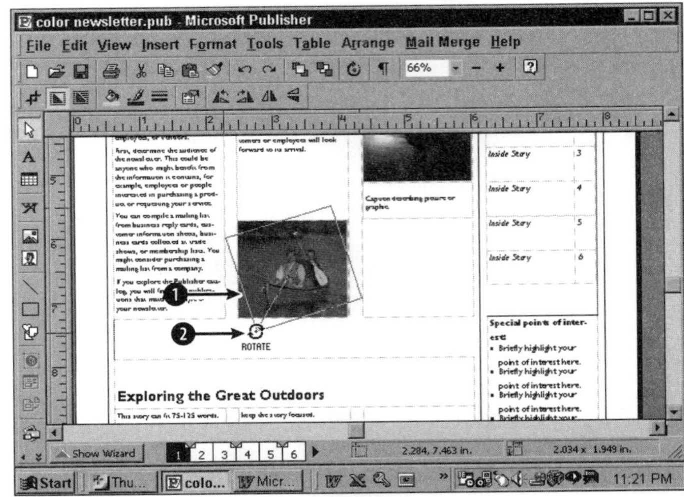

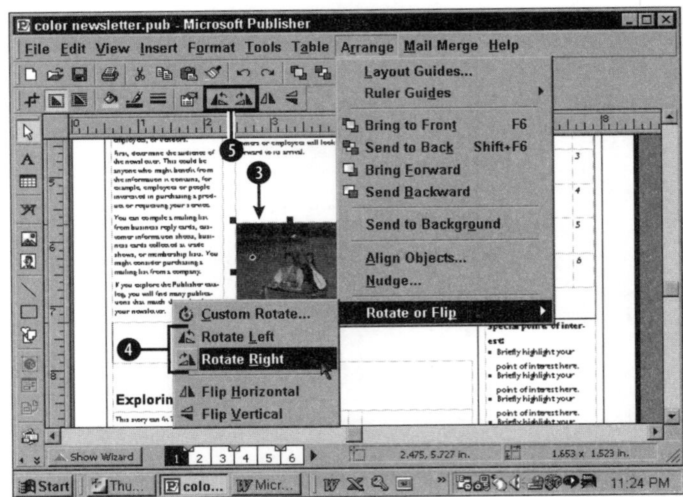

1. *To rotate a frame, hold the Alt key and place your cursor on one of the frame handles.*
2. *Drag the mouse to rotate the frame or group of frames.*

► *Hold the Ctrl and Alt keys to constrain the rotation to 15-degree increments.*

3. *To rotate a frame 90 degrees, select the frame or group of frames.*
4. *Select Arrange ➪ Rotate or Flip ➪ Rotate Left or Rotate Right.*
5. *Or, click the Rotate Left or Rotate Right buttons in the toolbar.*

CROSS-REFERENCE

See "Using the Cropping Tool" in Chapter 11 to see how to crop images. It works with rotated frames as well.

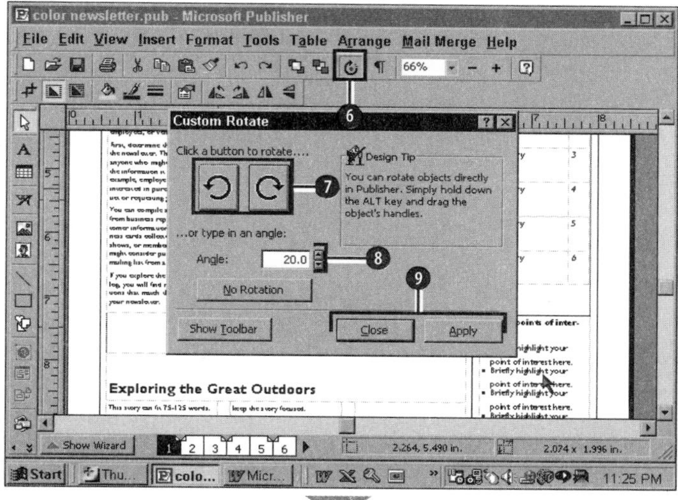

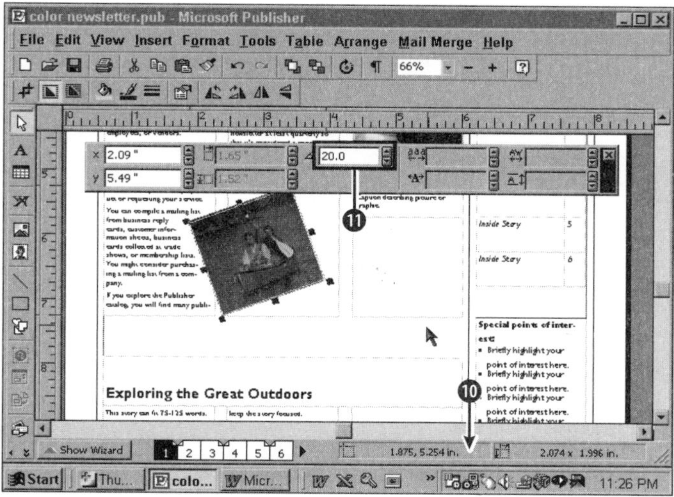

6. *To custom rotate a frame, choose Arrange ➪ Rotate or Flip ➪ Custom Rotate or click the Custom Rotate button on the toolbar.*
7. *Click the Rotate buttons to increase or decrease the rotation by 5 degrees, or . . .*
8. *Enter an amount in the Angle text box.*
9. *Click Apply to preview the rotation and/or Close to close the dialog box.*
10. *To use the measurement toolbar to rotate an object, double-click anywhere in the status bar. Enter a measurement in the rotation text box and press Enter.*
11. *To flip a frame from left to right, click the Flip Horizontal button.*
12. *To flip a frame from top to bottom, click the Flip Vertical button.*

earlier in this chapter. Simply enter a degree of rotation in the text box you'll find on the left-hand side of the toolbar and press Enter. Your frame tilts to whatever degree of rotation you enter.

No matter where you enter your rotation setting, you can use positive or negative numbers. Positive numbers rotate the frame counterclockwise, while negative numbers spin it clockwise.

TAKE NOTE

ROTATING IN 15-DEGREE INCREMENTS

Use the Ctrl key in conjunction with the Alt key to rotate your frame in 15-degree increments. As you drag the handle, the frame jumps every 15 degrees.

TAKING AN OBJECT FULL CIRCLE

Remember that a circle is divided into 360 degrees. If you rotate your object this amount, you won't see any change because you merely rotated it back to its original position. Of course, half of 360 degrees is 180 degrees, and this setting turns your object upside down.

FIND IT ONLINE

To see how rotated objects can impact a design, check the makeovers out at **http://desktoppub.about.com/msubmakeover.htm**.

Moving Frames Between Pages

You can count on changing layouts. It's just a way of life. When it reaches the point that you are asked to move things around from page to page, don't make a fuss. Publisher makes moving things from page to page as easy as placing them there to begin with.

In Chapter 6, you learned how to move frames or objects around on a page. Now it's time to move things within the publication and not just within the same page. You can either use cut and paste or you can use the scratch area.

When cutting and pasting a frame from one page to another, you can either use the menu to choose Edit ➪ Cut or just press Ctrl+X to place a frame in the Windows clipboard. Though you can't see it, Windows maintains a portion of memory that it calls the clipboard. It's a temporary area that is capable of holding only one thing at a time. Once you reach the new page location, select Edit ➪ Paste from the menus or press Ctrl+V. Your frame gets placed on the new page location, having been held in the clipboard, just waiting for the paste command. In fact, it remains on the clipboard until you replace it with something else, so you can paste it again and again in other locations.

The other and less limiting way to move items from page to page, is to take advantage of the Publisher *scratch area.* This is the gray area that surrounds your page layouts. You can place frames and objects on this space and they are held there until you drag them onto a page. No matter which page you flip to, the scratch area remains unchanged. Items you place there are available for any page you choose.

The biggest advantage the scratch area has over the Windows clipboard is the number of items that may be placed there. Remember, the Windows clipboard only

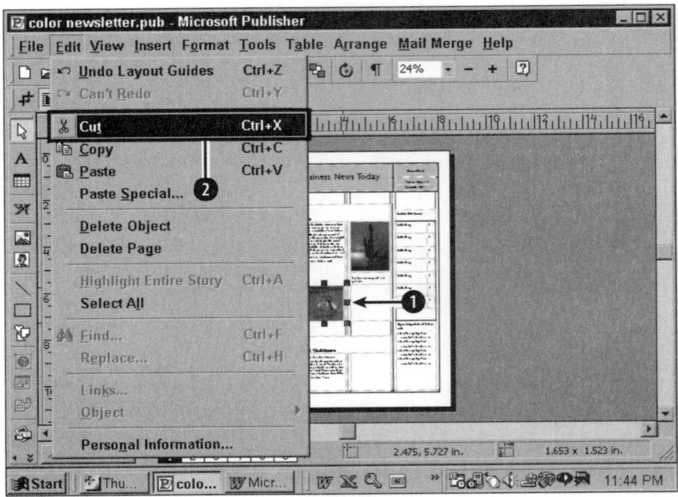

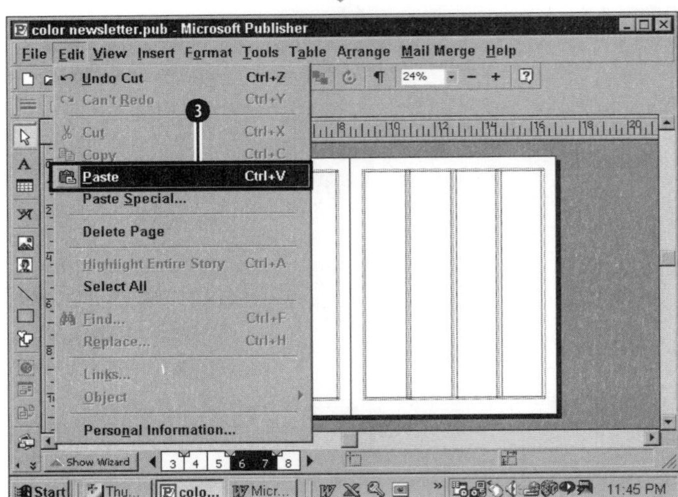

1. *To use the Windows clipboard, select the object to be moved.*
2. *Choose Edit ➪ Cut or press Ctrl+X.*
3. *After moving to the new page location, choose Edit ➪ Paste or press Ctrl+V.*

CROSS-REFERENCE

Review "Grouping and Ungrouping Objects" earlier in this chapter.

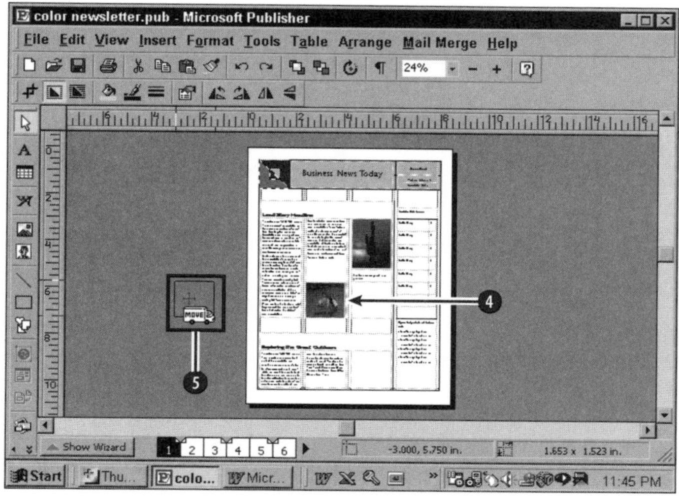

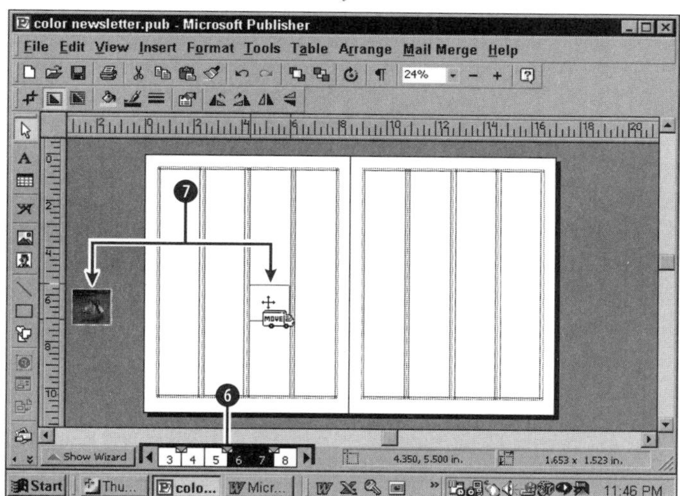

4. *To use the scratch area for moving objects, select the object.*
5. *Drag the object anyplace in the scratch area.*
6. *Go to the new page location.*
7. *Drag the object from the scratch area to the page location.*

holds one item or group of items at a time. But the scratch area can be filled with clip art, stories in frames, or any element that can be placed into a Publisher document.

TAKE NOTE

MOVE OBJECTS IN A GROUP

When you're moving things around in your publication, don't forget that you can group them and move them as a single unit. Not only does this preserve the layout of the frames, but it eliminates duplication of effort. Instead of dragging 15 items individually to the scratch area or committing them to the clipboard, you deal with the one group instead of the individual items.

ITEMS IN THE SCRATCH AREA ARE SAVED

If you're still debating on using the scratch area or the Windows clipboard, consider that items placed in the scratch area are saved with your document. Those in the Windows clipboard are not.

FIND IT ONLINE

Get a jump-start on your design with templates at **http://desktoppublishing.com/templ_mspub.html**.

Moving Items to the Background

Just when you thought you knew everything about the background layer, which you faithfully learned about earlier in this chapter, here's another little feature that you'll be glad to understand.

Activating the background layer and placing objects on it means they will appear on every page of your document unless you tell Publisher to ignore the background on a certain page. However, you don't always have to have the background layer active to add items to it.

Using the procedures in this task, you'll learn to select an object and throw it to the background layer. This process works with any object — be it WordArt, clip art, a photo, or text. Once an object is placed on the background, you need not worry about it being accidentally selected, moved, or deleted.

Although you can add items to the background while the background is not active, you will have to activate the background once the object is placed there to edit or delete it. For example, once you have your pages laid out with the text and graphics in place, you decide that you need a rule line on the top and bottom of the page to dress it up a bit. Once you create the rule line on one of the foreground pages, you can select the object and move it to the background. There's no need to delete the rule lines and redraw them on the background. Moving an item from the background to the foreground is also covered in this task. The procedure is the same, but the menu choice is different.

If you're working with a double-sided publication, be sure that you make changes to both left and right pages if you chose to mirror your background. Otherwise, the change will only show up on the pages that match the side you altered.

It is also possible to hide one or several objects on the background. If you want to hide just an item (or two)

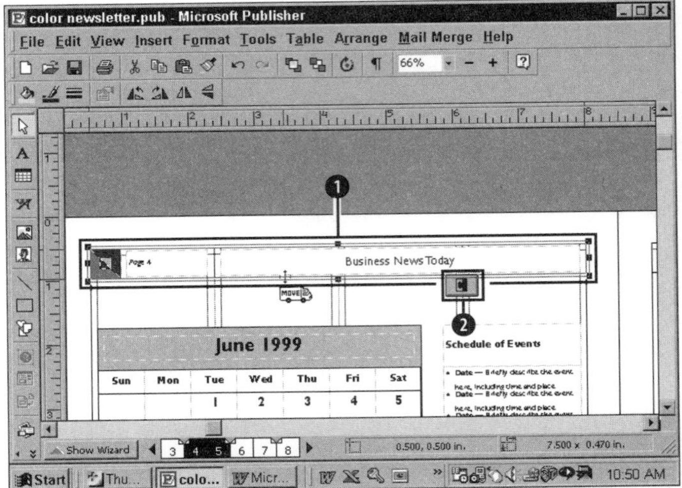

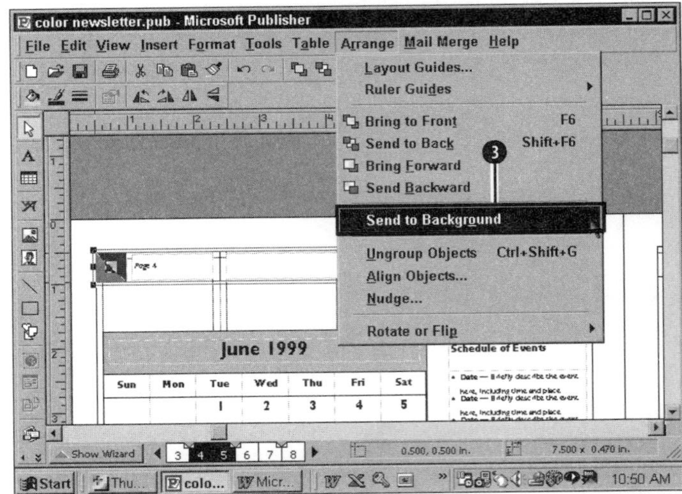

1. Select the object or objects that will be moved to the background.
2. Make a group of them, if you like.
3. Choose Arrange ⇨ Send to Background.

CROSS-REFERENCE

Head back to "Designing a Background" earlier in this chapter for complete details on creating a background.

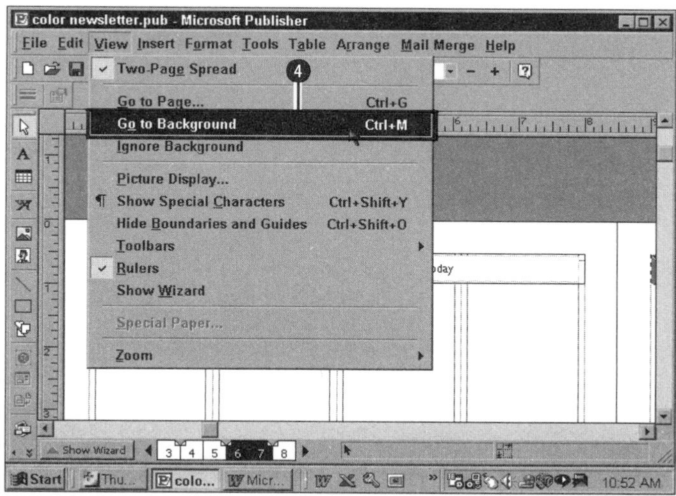

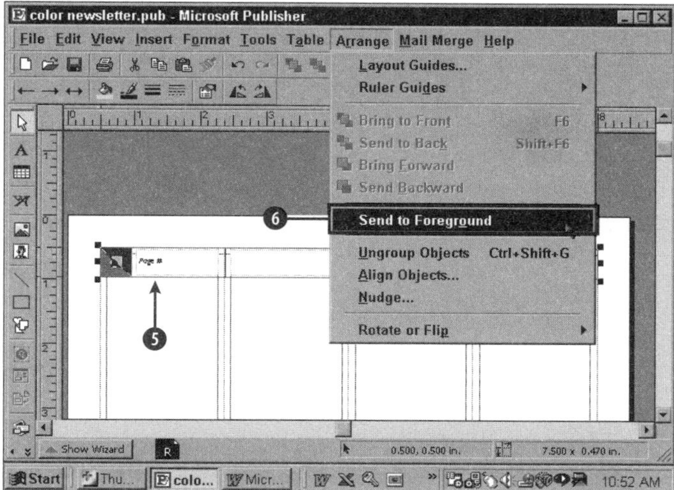

4 *To edit the objects that are now on the background layer, choose View ➪ Go to Background or press Ctrl+M.*

5 *Objects that are on the background layer may be moved to the foreground layer. First, select the object or group of objects.*

6 *Choose Arrange ➪ Send to Foreground.*

that has been placed on the background, you can draw a frame over the top of that item and it will be hidden when you print your document. Just be certain to draw the frame on the foreground layer instead of the background.

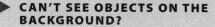

TAKE NOTE

CAN'T SEE OBJECTS ON THE BACKGROUND?

If, for whatever reason, objects on your background are not showing through, be sure that the objects on the foreground layer are transparent. To make an object transparent, you must select the object and then press Ctrl+T. By making the object's fill attribute transparent, you can let the background object become visible through the object that sits on top of it.

FIND IT ONLINE

Stuck with nothing on the page? Get out of the rut at http://www.wcdd.com/dd/editorials/blankpage.html.

Personal Workbook

Q&A

1. What type of guides are usually red and blue?

2. If you cannot select an object or group of objects on the foreground layer, what does that mean?

3. What do you call the information at the top and bottom of a page that can sometimes contain the page numbers or chapter or publication title?

4. When you hold the Shift key and select multiple items, what shortcut key can you use to group the items together?

5. What three things can you snap to?

6. What toolbar comes up when you double-click the status bar that shows an object's dimensions and location on the page?

7. To rotate an object at 15-degree increments, what key combination do you use while you drag one of the object's handles?

8. What do you call the gray area that surrounds your page and what is it used for?

ANSWERS: PAGE 352

Arranging Frames and Objects

EXTRA PRACTICE

1. Create a layout template with four columns and six rows. Save the layout as a template.
2. Using that same template, place headers and footers on it that include page numbers and the document title. Be sure to place these objects on the background layer.
3. Just for the front page, place a ruler guide where the nameplate of the newsletter will be placed. In the case of a book, this could serve as the position of the opening chapter text.
4. Turn on Snap to Guides and draw a text frame on the first page where the main story will be placed.
5. Insert a picture frame in one column of the first page. Be sure that it is in the foreground by bringing it to the front.

REAL-WORLD APPLICATIONS

- ✔ You are creating a book of your poetry. You use the headers and footers to number the pages and include a graphic that serves as your personal logo.
- ✔ The company newsletter must be in accordance with the nature of your business. You create a traditional four-column layout where text is maintained in the inside three columns and you reserve the outside column for pictures and graphics.
- ✔ You've laid out your newsletter. The company owner has just been named Entrepreneur of the Year. You have to move the front-page story to page 2 and add the boss's news to the front page. You group the original front-page story and picture, and then drag it to the scratch area. After inserting the new story, you delete information on page 2 to place the previous page 1 article and photos there.

Visual Quiz

How can you tell that this is the background layer and not the foreground?

____

____

____

____

____

____

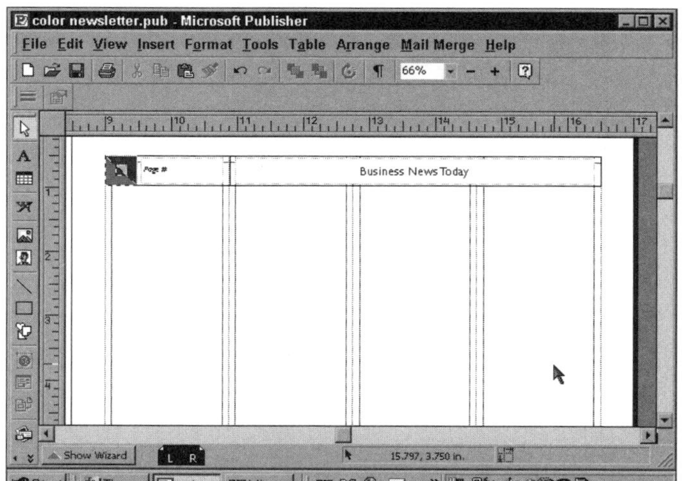

PART III

Putting Text into Your Publication

Here's a challenge: Create a complete publication in Microsoft Publisher without using a single, solitary word. Use no letter in the alphabet, not one numeral, and banish all symbols. What do you have left to communicate with? You get the point. English is a language of written and spoken words. How can you successfully communicate an idea or concept without text?

This part not only shows how you can bring text in from other word-processing applications, but how to format it within Publisher and flow it from page to page. Publisher also comes with some features such as spell checking and text styles that can help ensure accuracy and speed in formatting.

If the simple word is not enough to get your message across, dabble in the selection of fonts and word art to add some zip and pizzazz to your publication. But, as with all things great, use in moderation.

Lastly, though it may not seem to fit with the other two chapters, Publisher's tables can help you organize columns and rows of information within your document. Once you start experimenting with tables, you'll find all sorts of uses for them.

CHAPTER 8

MASTER THESE SKILLS

- Importing Text Files
- Editing a Text File with Microsoft Word
- Fitting a Text File to a Frame
- Connecting Text-File Frames
- Flowing a Text File Between Multiple Frames
- Creating Multiple Columns Within a Frame
- Flowing Text Around a Frame
- Formatting Stories with Tabs, Lists, and Indents
- Spell Checking a Text File
- Using Find or Replace to Make Changes
- Creating and Using Text Styles

Working with Stories

Many of the publications that you will be producing will contain text — sometimes a lot, other times not much. While Publisher is good at displaying your text exactly as you'd like it, the software doesn't equal a good word processing program such as Microsoft Word.

That's why Publisher lets you import text files from other programs such as Microsoft Word, Corel WordPerfect, and even WordPad, the built-in Windows word processing utility. In those programs, you can type away and use their many features to form the words and syntax as you want it.

Another advantage is file sharing. While many of your coworkers may not have Publisher installed on their systems, they will have a word processing program, usually a company standard. Support staff can do the keying in rough layout while you do the formatting in Publisher.

This chapter takes you through all the paces once you have a text file. From importing the file to placing it on the page, you get the ins and outs on formatting the headlines, body text, and subheadings to flow smoothly with your layout.

While you can do some light editing in Publisher, you can open up a text file and actually edit it in Microsoft Word, provided you have that program installed.

Publisher also includes its own spell-checking utility, just to double-check everything before that final print out. Plus, there's a search and replace option for quick text replacement.

Some of the other features covered here include formatting bulleted lists, flowing stories from one page to another, and wrapping text around frames that may include pictures or clip art.

Another nifty feature is the way Publisher puts a jump at the end of a column to tell the reader the article is being continued on another page in the document.

But probably the most important feature to keep your eyes open for is "Creating and Using Text Styles." This great time-saving feature lets you format text and save that formatting as a style to be used later in the document.

If you're afraid that text is all that is going to be covered here, don't worry. In Part IV, you'll learn as much, if not more, about placing graphics in your document. Trust me, we'll leave no stone unturned to make you a top-notch desktop publisher.

Importing Text Files

As indicated in the opening of this chapter, you can enter text into Publisher, but you should probably leave this task to the pro — your word processor. Even though Publisher has many features of a word processor, they aren't as complete as you will find in a program such as Microsoft Word.

Importing text files from your word processor into Publisher has another advantage. You can have someone else do the typing while you concentrate on the layout. Clients can submit stories to you that you can place in frames on Publisher pages. You can also bring in articles from various other sources such as PR firms, administrative assistants, or stringer reporters, or even let mom enter the recipes for her cookbook that you told her you would publish.

Versatility of importing text files is one of Publisher's strengths. Normally, you can tell what type of file you're dealing with by the file extension. That's the three-letter designation that follows the period that follows a file name. It's a carryover from the old DOS days of computing and tells a program what software the file originated from. Following are the types of documents that Publisher can import directly:

- **PUB** — Other Microsoft Publisher files.
- **TXT** — ASCII text files.
- **RTF** — Rich Text Format, a sort of universal word processing file format that preserves much of the formatting from the original word processing software.
- **DOC** — Word 6/95, 97/2000, Word for Macintosh 6/95, Word 2.
- **XLS, XLW** — Excel spreadsheet files with a limit of 128 rows.
- **WPS** — Microsoft Works 3 or 4 for Windows.

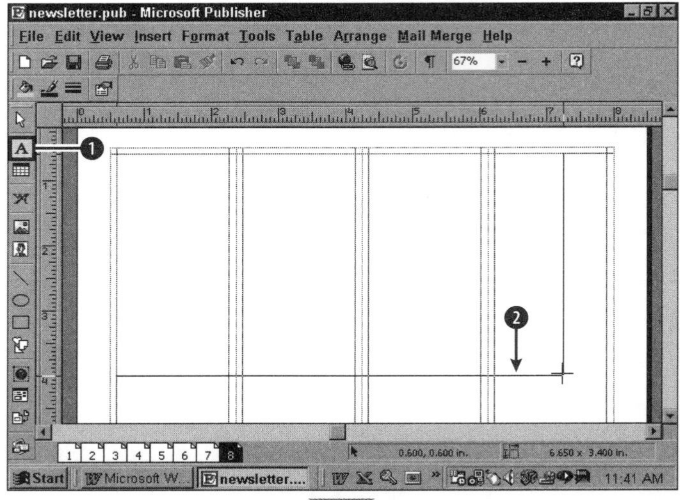

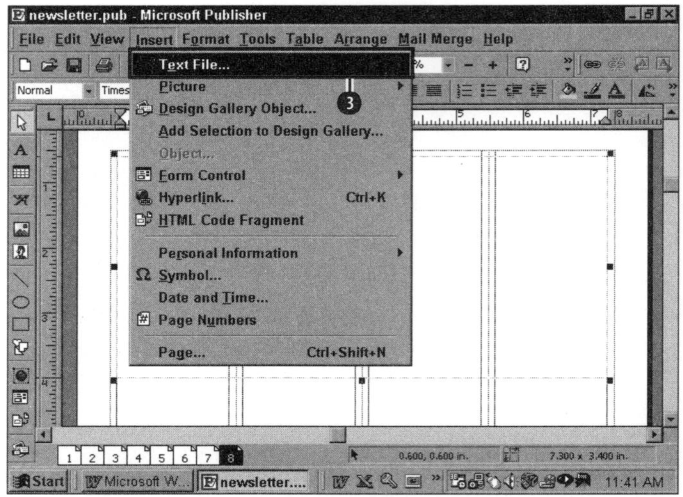

1. *Select the Text Frame tool.*
2. *Draw the text frame where the file will be placed.*
3. *Choose Insert ➪ Text File. You can also right-click at the flashing cursor and choose Change Text ➪ Text File from the menu.*

CROSS-REFERENCE

See "Creating and Using Text Styles" later in this chapter for tips on formatting your text.

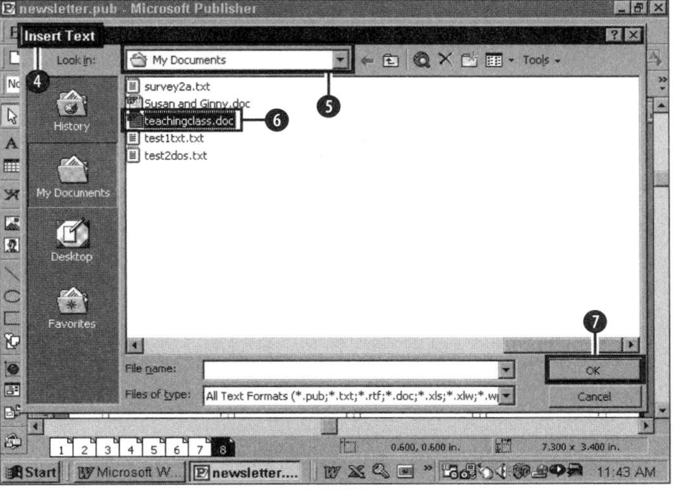

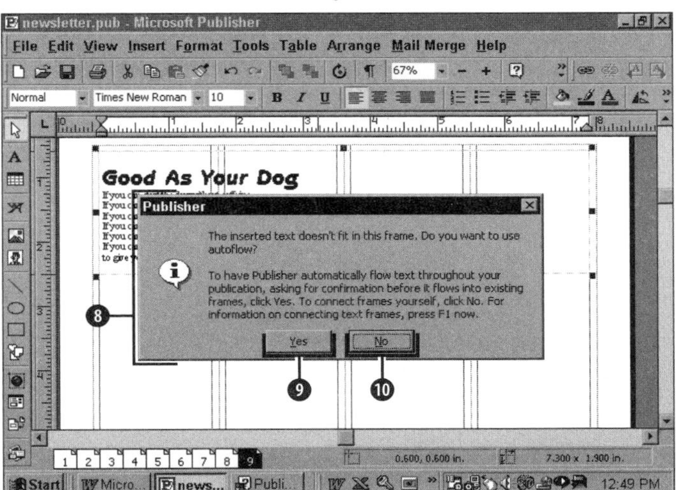

4 *Using the Insert Text dialog box, locate the file you want to import.*

5 *Use the "Look in" drop-down box to locate the drive and/or folder.*

6 *Select the file.*

7 *Click OK to place the text in the frame.*

8 *If the frame is not large enough to hold all the text, Publisher asks if you want to autoflow the file to subsequent pages.*

9 *Choose Yes to have Publisher flow the text.*

10 *Choose No to link the text frames yourself.*

- WPD, DOC — WordPerfect 6, 5.
- WK1, WK3, WK4 — Lotus 1-2-3 spreadsheet files.
- MCW — Word 4.0-5.1 for Macintosh.
- WRI — Windows Write from the earlier days of Windows. This was replaced by WordPad in Windows 95.

If your favorite word processing program is not listed in this group, check your documentation or Help files to see how to export a file to a different file format or use the Save As feature to change the format.

Of course, if all else fails, you can usually cut and paste text from other applications. While this method eliminates a lot of keystrokes, you may have to edit the line endings and eliminate some unneeded formatting.

Depending on how the document was formatted in the word processor package, some of the formatting may be imported and some may not. There isn't enough space here to explain what styles and fonts do get imported and which ones are ignored. Suffice it to say that once the text is placed in Publisher, you are better off formatting it within the publication.

TAKE NOTE

OTHER FILE FORMATS

Depending on the Microsoft software that you have installed on your computer, there may be other file formats that you will be able to import. Microsoft filters tend to work for many of their applications.

FIND IT ONLINE

To find out more about file formats, go to **www.ola.bc.ca/ou/formats/whatare.html.**

Editing a Text File with Microsoft Word

It's only logical that because Publisher is a Microsoft product, Word would be the first choice for a word processing program that Publisher uses to edit the text in your publication. Word is a powerful text editing program that enables you to do much more than Publisher when it comes to adding paragraphs, formatting the look, and doing other word processing tasks.

In order to edit your text in Microsoft Word through Publisher, you must have Microsoft Word installed on your computer. If you purchased Microsoft Publisher 2000 as a separate package and don't have Microsoft Office as well, Word may be unavailable for you to use. If this is the case, you're just out of luck. If you installed Publisher as part of the Microsoft Office 2000 suite of programs, chances are pretty good that you have it on your system already. If not, drop that CD into the CD drive and get busy installing Word!

After inserting text from any word processing file, that text becomes part of your Publisher document. The original word processing file stays intact on your drive as you left it. This means two copies of the file now exist: one in Publisher and the other in its own separate file. The changes you make to the Publisher text do not get made in the original file. While you may think this is a bad thing, consider the possibility that something went wrong with Publisher and the publication you've spent a lot of time on. If your word processing file happens to get corrupted along with the Publisher document, you would be up a creek. At least with the original file sitting safely on your drive, you could always import it again without having to retype it.

It is possible to link your file within Publisher. When you link a file, you place the actual text or spreadsheet within Publisher. When you make changes in your original document, those changes are immediately made

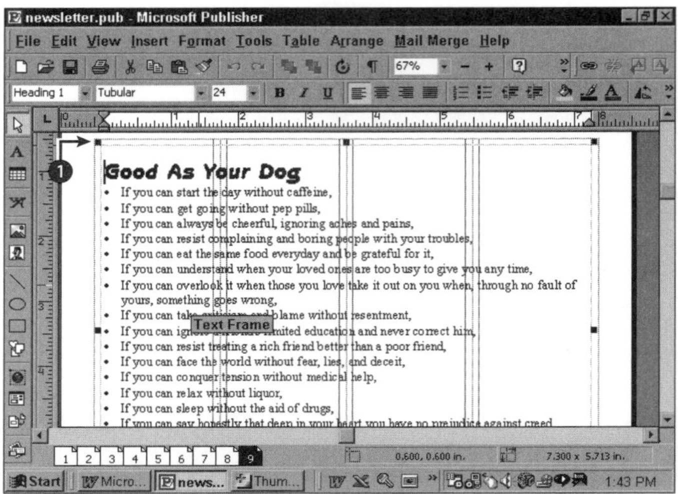

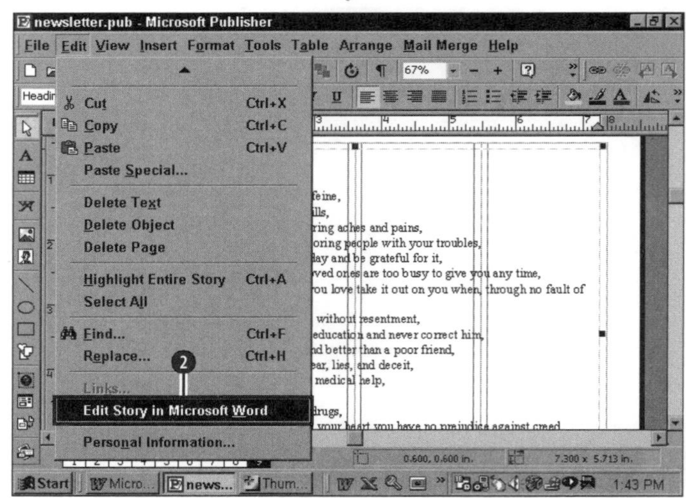

1. Select the frame with the text you want to edit in Word.
2. Choose Edit ⇨ Edit Story in Microsoft Word. (A story is a text file to Publisher.)

CROSS-REFERENCE

To flow text from one frame to another, see "Connecting Text File Frames" later in this chapter.

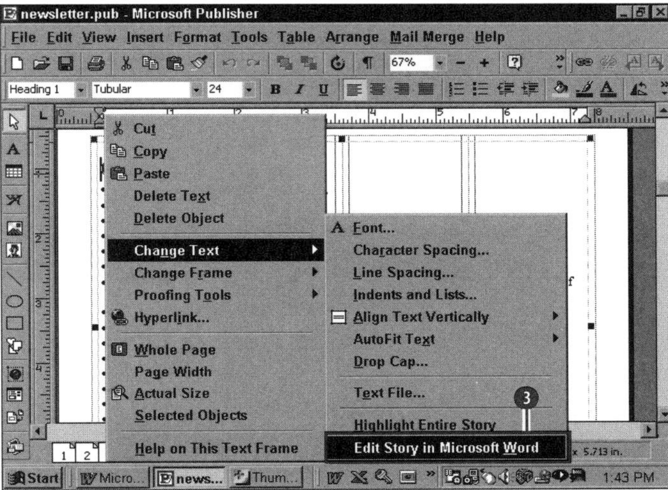

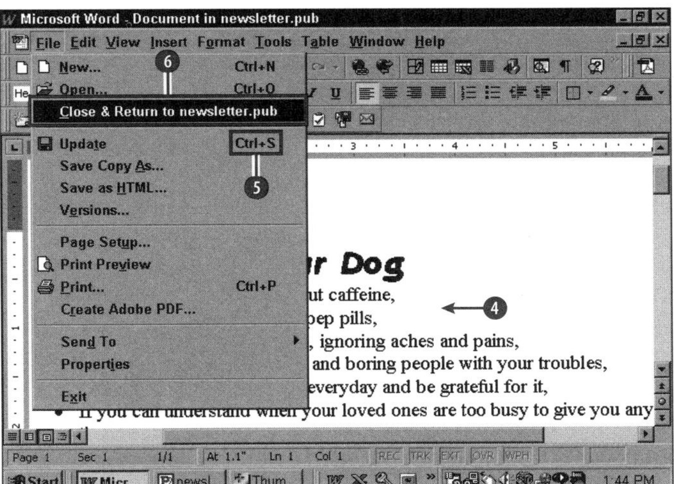

❸ *Or, right-click the frame with the text to be edited and choose Change Text ➪ Edit Story in Microsoft Word from the menu.*

❹ *Make the changes to your document in Word.*

❺ *Choose File ➪ Update to make the changes to your text in Publisher without closing Word. This enables you to preview your edits.*

❻ *When finished editing the text, choose File ➪ Close & Return to *.pub where * is the name of your publication.*

within your Publisher file as well. This feature has some drawbacks, however. First, all of your formatting must be done within the original application. Sometimes that formatting doesn't fit into Publisher frames the way you intend it. To have complete control over the look and formatting, stick to importing text and spreadsheets. Linking is best suited for images and graphics.

TAKE NOTE

SELECTING THE TEXT FILE FOR EDITING

Remember, you don't have to select all of the text in order to edit the text file in Word. All you have to do is have the frame selected. And, you will be editing the entire file including all linked frames, not just the highlighted frame. When you make changes in Word, no matter which linked frame those changes fall in, the alterations will be placed accordingly.

FIND IT ONLINE

See what features Microsoft Word 2000 has to offer at **http://officeupdate.microsoft.com/welcome/word.htm.**

Fitting a Text File to a Frame

If you take a look at the layout of this book, or most any other professionally published piece for that matter, the format is consistent. When you put your publication together, this is what you should aim to do. However, sometimes, you will just have more information than will fit into a frame, or so you think. While you can do many things to avoid having to resort to the AutoFit feature in Publisher, it is there for emergency use.

The AutoFit feature in Publisher takes the text within a frame and shrinks the type size so that all of the text is contained within that frame. This can lead to various frames of text throughout your publication where the font size is totally different. Your reader may not notice it at first, but it's one of those design things where you cock your head and say, "Something's not quite right here, but I can't put my finger on it."

So what are the alternatives? First and foremost, edit your text file to fit the space provided. Chop words, sentences, or entire paragraphs to maintain consistency. It is possible to do this without losing the message.

Or, you can take control of the type size yourself. When Publisher changes the type size, it's done in fractions of the type size. While this works to get all that text into the frame, it can still look funny. When you control the size of the type, you can make it look intentional, with a greater difference than other text in the document. I like to keep type sizes in even increments such as 10, 12, 14, 18, and 24 point. When Publisher makes the changes, you may have 11.5-point type next to 12-point type. That can cause the head to tilt and the mouth to mutter, "Huh?"

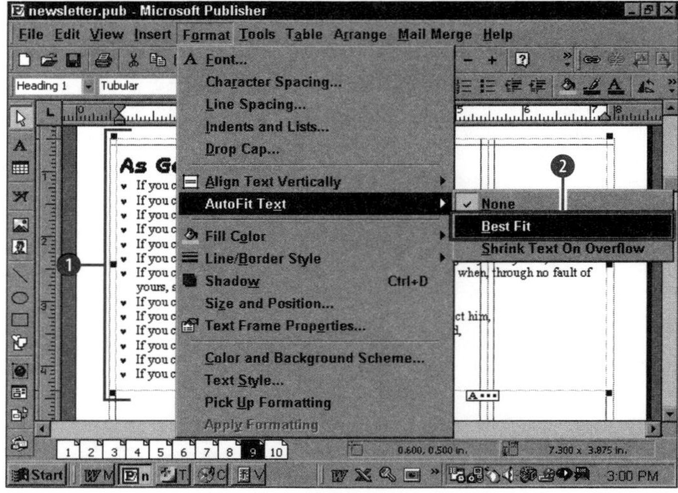

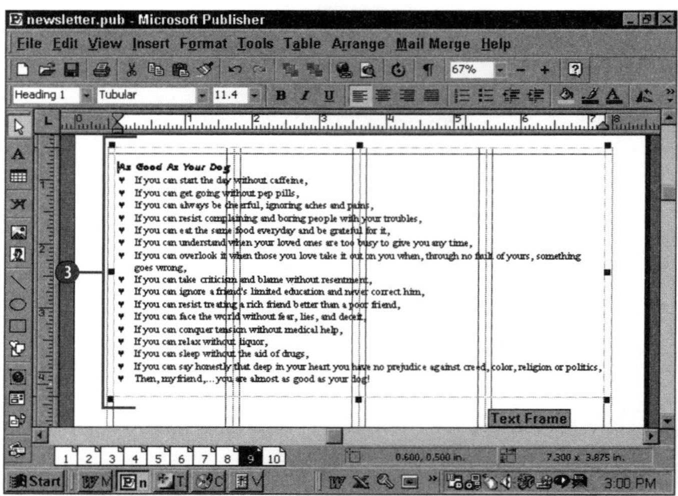

1. Select the frame containing the text that you want to autofit.
2. Choose Format ➪ AutoFit Text ➪ Best Fit.
3. The Best Fit selection reduces the headlines and text to fit within the frame, even after resizing the frame.

CROSS-REFERENCE

Controlling line spacing is covered in Chapter 9.

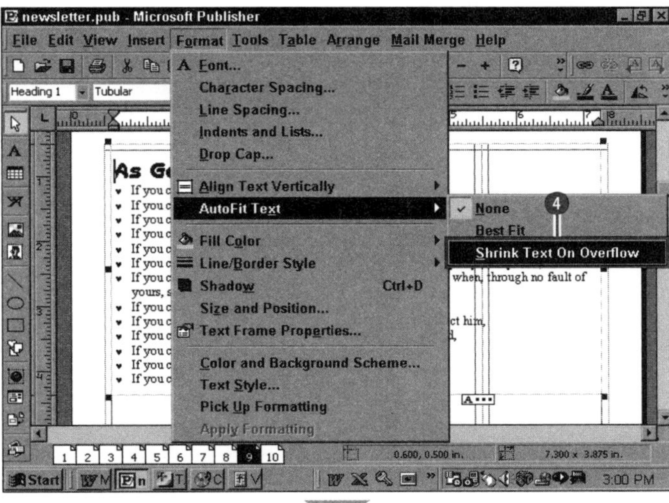

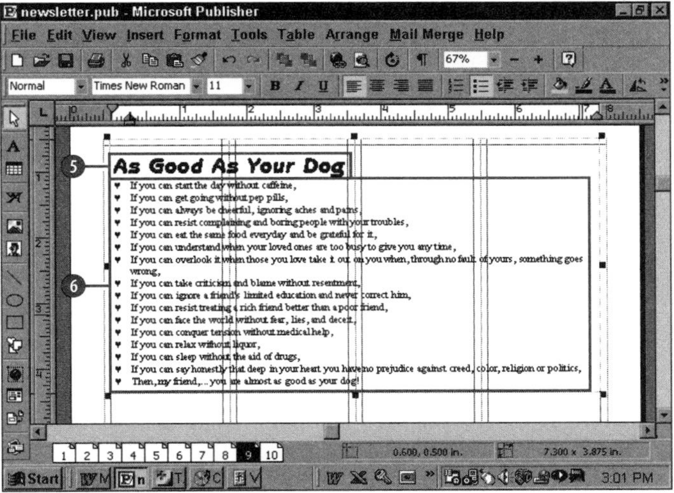

❹ *To have only the text that is at the end of the frame reduced to fit, choose Format ➪ AutoFit Text ➪ Shrink Text On Overflow.*

❺ *Headlines stay the same size as previously formatted.*

❻ *Text that is in the overflow area will be reduced.*

But, if all else fails and you are bent on using the AutoFit feature, you have two choices: Best Fit or Shrink Text On Overflow. Best Fit reduces the entire text file — headlines, subheads, and text — until everything is contained in the frame, even if you should resize it later. Shrink Text On Overflow reduces the type until all text that didn't fit in the frame is now included. Resizing the frame can cause overflow again.

TAKE NOTE

CHANGING LINE SPACING

Leading (pronounced *led-ing,* and rhymes with wedding) is the space between lines of text. In the old days of typewriters, the way to adjust leading was by single, double, or triple spacing lines of type. With the computer, however, you have a lot more control over changing the leading. Publisher calls this control *line spacing.* Be careful, however, because changing this setting can have the same effect as changing the type size. Something just won't look quite right and it may become difficult to read.

FIND IT ONLINE

Get some ideas on editing to fit copy at **http://www.dmgi.com/typog2.html.**

Connecting Text-File Frames

At some time, you'll be faced with text that has to continue on to another page in your document. In the publishing business, this is called a *jump*. You jump the text file from one page to another. Newspapers and magazines are two of the most popular users of this technique. Newsletters, due to their length, seem to try to avoid this and attempt to get the text file all on one page. If it's any longer, some say it doesn't belong in a newsletter because a newsletter should aim for brevity and conciseness.

In Publisher, you can link frames so that text flows into subsequent frames should there be no space left in the previous frame. If you import text into a frame that won't hold all of the copy, a small icon appears on the bottom of the frame. It looks like an "A" with an ellipsis after it. (An *ellipsis* is three periods in a row, meaning something has been left out.)

When you link or chain frames together, Publisher remembers the order in which you linked them. You can flow text onto pages before or after the location of the frame from which the text is flowing. That means that if you begin a text file on page 24 of a magazine, you could continue it several pages before, say on page 18. If there's not enough space on page 18, you can flow more of the text onto page 19, and so on.

And, while you can link text all over a publication of many pages, you can't link from one publication file to another publication file. Publisher is just not capable of this, but then neither are some of the bigger publishing software packages.

Without going into detail here (because we save it for the next task), you can have Publisher insert continued statements in your frame of text that automatically inserts the page location of the continued article. Just be patient.

CROSS-REFERENCE

To brush up on creating text frames, go back to Chapter 6.

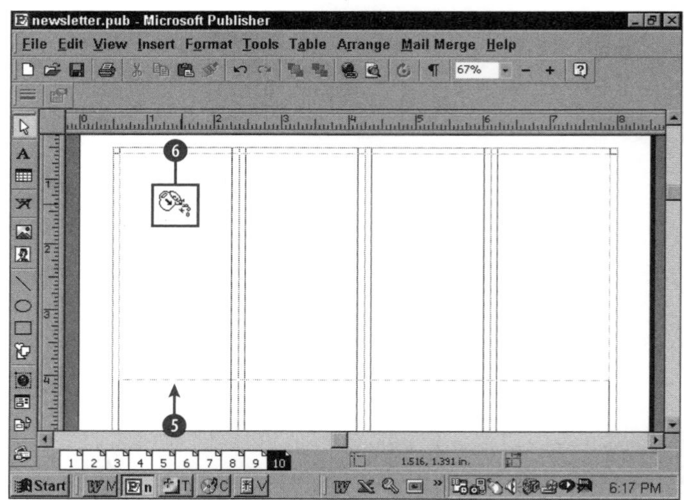

1. *To jump a story (text file) to another location, first draw the frame that will receive the overflow. Then, select the frame from which the text will be continued.*
2. *Notice the icon that indicates that all the text did not fit into the frame.*
3. *Click the Connect Text Frames button.*
4. *Your cursor changes to a cup with a spout and arrow on it.*
5. *Select the frame that will receive the overflow.*
6. *While the cursor is still shaped like the cup, click inside the frame.*

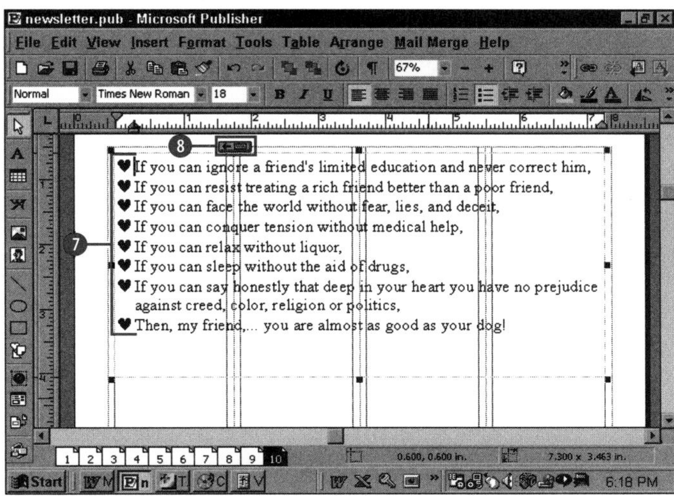

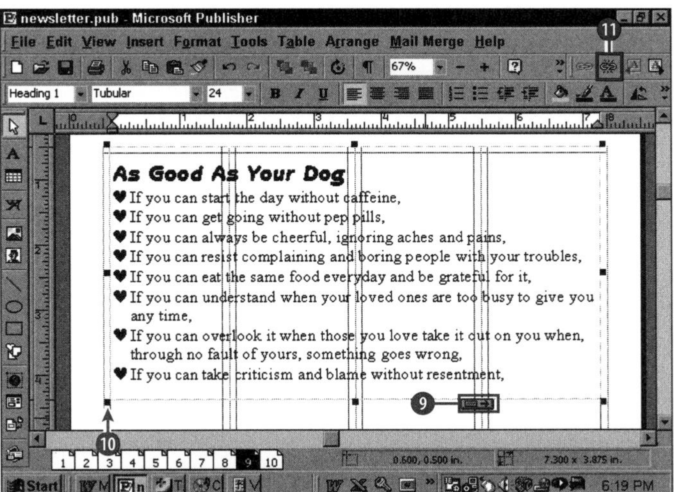

7 *The remaining text is dropped into the frame.*

8 *The icon at the top of the frame indicates the text inside is continued from another location. Click it and you are taken to the location of the previous text.*

9 *The original frame that had spare text now sports an icon that indicates text has been jumped to another location.*

10 *To unlink the frames, select the frame the text was linked from.*

11 *Clicking the Disconnect Text Frames button takes the frame back to its original state as shown in the top-left figure.*

Should you want to break the link between frames, you select the frame that you jumped from and click the "unlink" button. Publisher calls this the Disconnect button, but it looks more like an unlink button.

TAKE NOTE

DON'T LOSE YOUR READERS

Anytime you jump a text file, you run the risk of losing your readers. You start reading an article on page 1 of the newspaper that is continued on page 6. While turning to page 6, you notice a sale ad on the bottom of page 3. After you note the time and location of the sale, you've forgotten where you were heading to begin with. Plus, it's never a good idea to jump a text file to a third location too far away from the second text file location. There, you're really asking for reader disorientation.

FIND IT ONLINE

For some additional info on text frames, go to http://officeupdate.microsoft.com/2000/articles/pbtxtfrm.htm.

Flowing a Text File Between Multiple Frames

Publications can be thought of as road maps. Readers follow along, take in the scenery, and turn a page every now and then. You are going to have to be very sensitive to the needs of your readers. When you jump a text file, or create some sort of detour, be sure the maps are in order by providing a jump phrase — the most common, of course, is "continued on page such-and-such."

Luckily for you, Publisher gives you an automatic way to include, within the linked frames, jump statements. By going into the frame properties, you can specify whether the linked frame has a "Continued on page . . ." or "Continued from page . . ." phrase dropped into the frame automatically. Plus, Publisher even keeps track of the page numbers so you don't have to. Should you insert any number of pages in the middle of your document, either before, after, or in between the pages where the jumped frames reside, the page numbers will change automatically.

Within the frames, the "continued from" phrase will be placed in the top above the first column, if more than one exists. The frame that contains the text that gets continued will have a "continued on" phrase placed in the bottom of the frame at the end of the last column, if there's more than one.

Of course, you're not locked into using Publisher's capabilities for including jump statements. You can insert these manually. I would, however, recommend you create a new frame to hold these. Consider this scenario. You insert your cursor at the end of the line above the last line in a frame. You click the Enter key to start your "continued" statement. When you get to the frame where the text picks up again, the first line gets indented because your text is set up to indent new paragraphs. From here, the text formatting only gets messier. The moral here is to let Publisher do the formatting work for

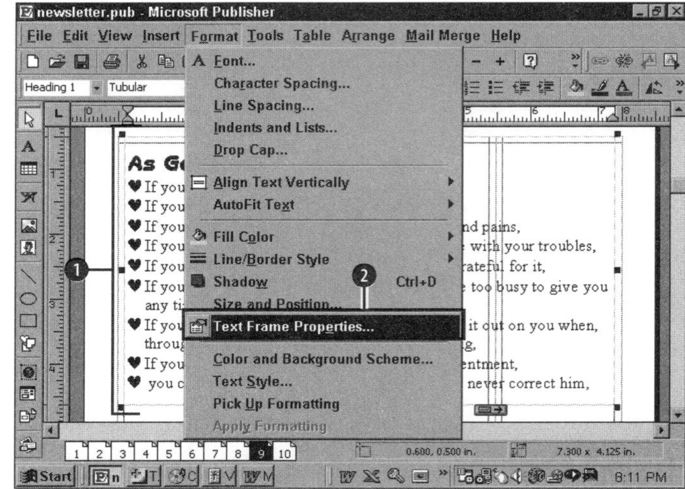

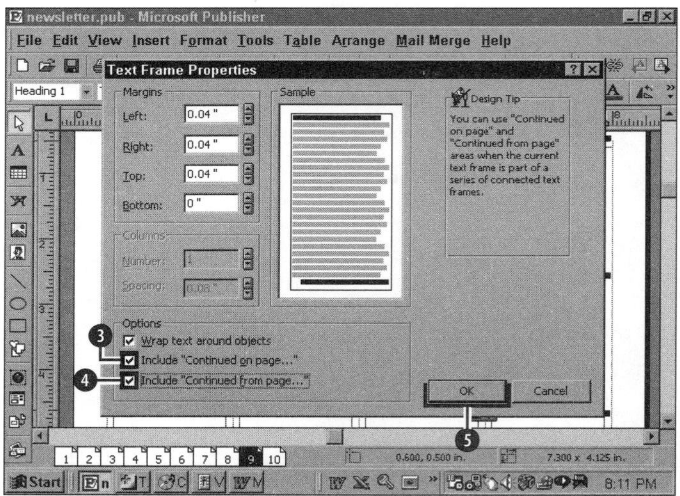

1. *Select the frame that receives the jump statement.*
2. *Choose Format ➪ Text Frame Properties. Or, right-click and choose Change Frame ➪ Text Frame Properties.*
3. *Click the "Include 'Continued on page . . .'" checkbox for frames that have text that is jumped to another frame.*
4. *Click the "Include 'Continued from page . . .'" checkbox for frames that contain the jumped text.*

▶ *Publisher knows the difference between frames and does not insert "continued" in the wrong place.*

5. *Click OK to insert the jump statement.*

CROSS-REFERENCE

See "Creating Multiple Columns Within a Frame" later in this chapter.

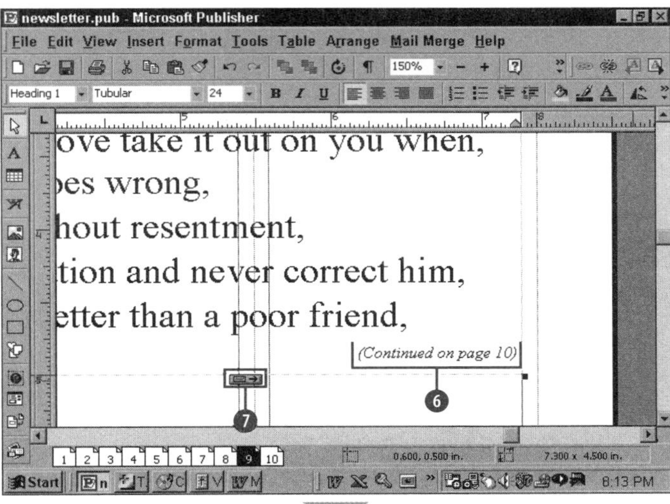

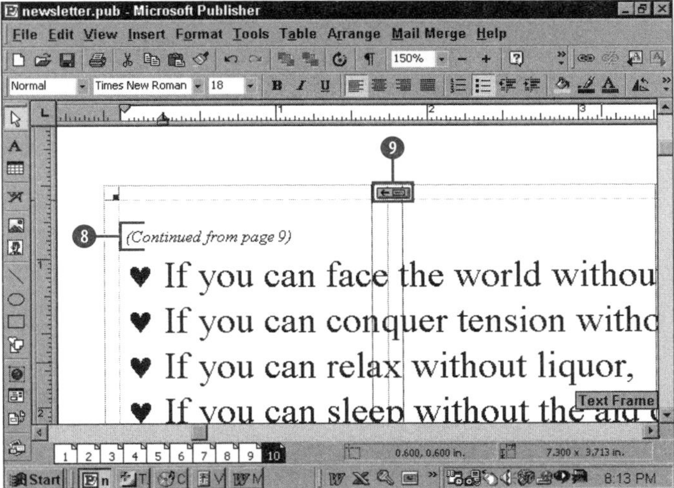

6. *The "Continued on page . . ." statement is inserted in the bottom-right corner of the frame.*
7. *Click the Go to Next Frame icon to move to the frame that contains the jumped text.*
8. *The "Continued from page . . ." statement is inserted in the top-left corner of the frame that contains the jumped text.*
9. *Click the Go to Previous Frame icon to jump to the frame where the text is jumped from.*

you. Resizing frames is a lot less tedious than formatting text to do what you expect it to do.

Don't forget, too, that if you edit the text your "continued" phrase could end up in the next linked frame and you have to go back through the entire fiasco again.

TAKE NOTE

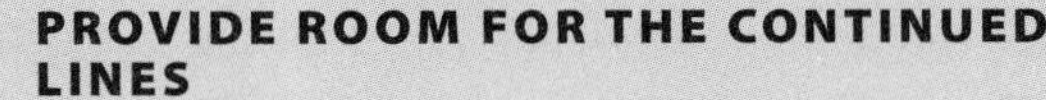

PROVIDE ROOM FOR THE CONTINUED LINES

When you turn on the "continued" statements in Publisher, you have to be sure to provide room. Publisher adds some space above and below the statements that could cause your text flow to be off. Try resizing your frames, if you have room, to provide for the extra space necessary.

FIND IT ONLINE

An excellent source for graphics professionals can be found at **www.graphics-master.com**.

Creating Multiple Columns Within a Frame

So far, you've been drawing frames to hold text or images. Now that you know how to link frames, you're probably sweating profusely about the number of frames that you'll have to draw just to place one text file on a page that has layout guides set up in four columns on the page. While it is possible to draw a frame down one column, import a text file into it, and flow it over to the frames you draw in the rest of the columns, there is an easier way. But then, you guessed that from the title of this task, didn't you?

In the last task, you opened the Text Frame Properties dialog box to have Publisher insert jump phrases. You may have also noticed that this dialog box bears a striking resemblance to the same dialog box you use to set up the layout guides — and, you'd be right.

When you create a frame in Publisher, you can draw it across the entire page without having to draw a frame for each column of text that you want. Each frame has the capability to be divided into columns using the settings in the Frame Properties dialog box. When you create the columns, Publisher defaults to very little space between the columns. You should probably add a little more to the 0.08 inch default. (Layout guides default to 0.2 inches. You would think they would be the same, but they're not.)

Once you have designated how many columns your frame will sport, you can proceed importing text as you learned earlier in this chapter. When you import the text, it automatically flows from the top of the left column and snakes through the columns that you set until it either reaches the end of the text or the end of the last column.

You're not locked in to using the same number of columns as the layout guides underneath the frame. Set the number of columns, and even the spacing between them, to whatever you want.

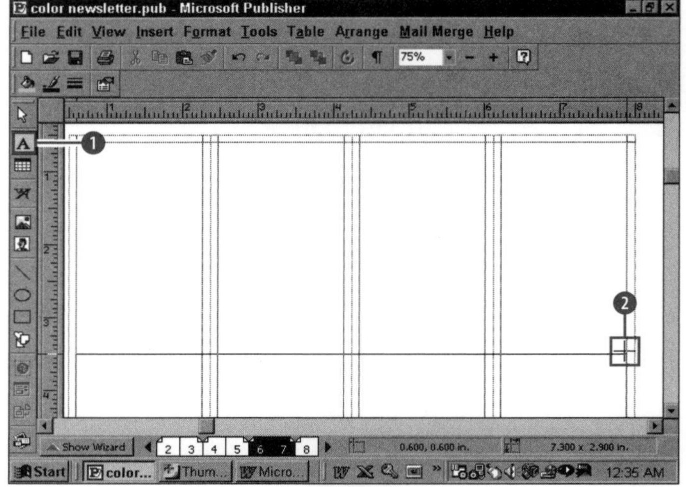

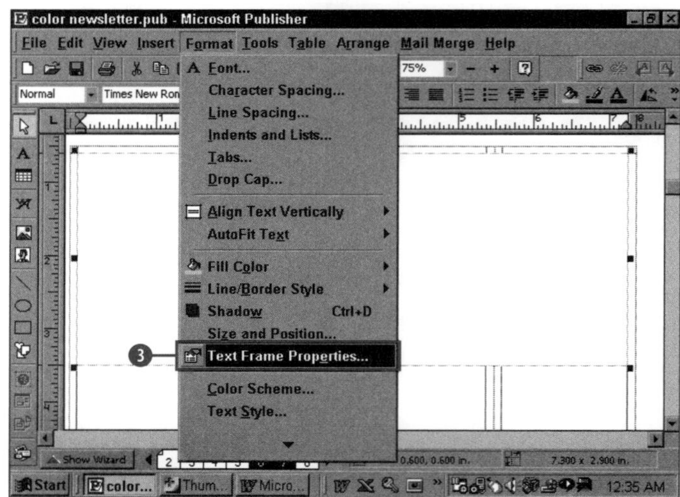

1. *Choose the Text Frame tool.*
2. *Draw the text frame to the width desired.*
3. *With the frame selected, choose Format ➪ Text Frame Properties. Or, right-click the frame and choose Change Frame ➪ Text Frame Properties.*

CROSS-REFERENCE

To review setting up layout guides, see Chapter 7.

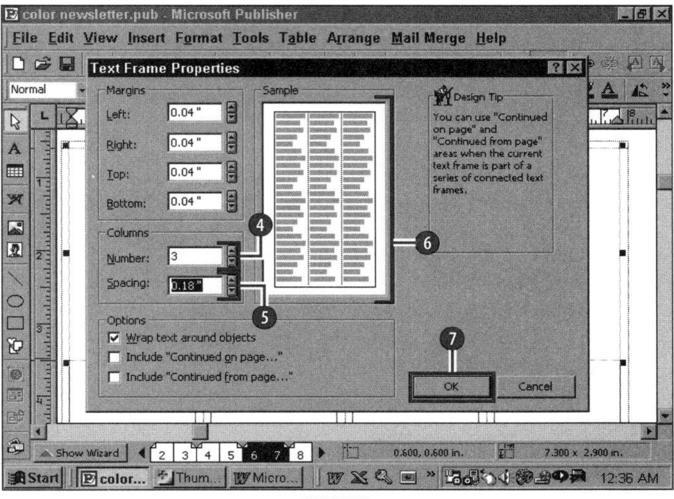

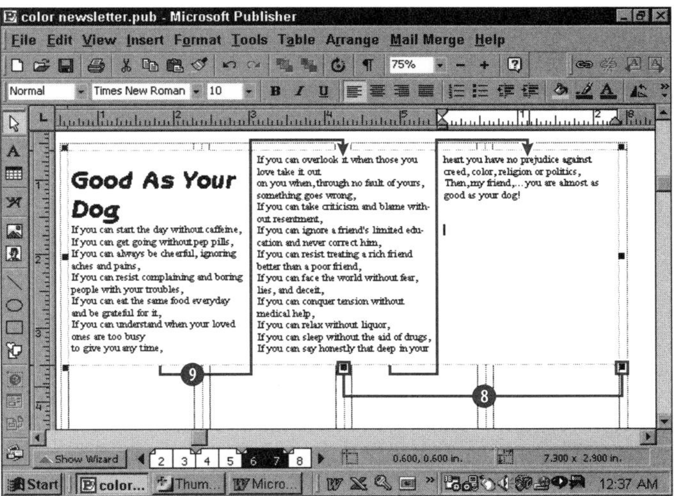

4 *Enter the number of columns for the text frame.*

5 *Indicate the amount of space between the columns.*

6 *The Sample window shows what the layout will look like.*

7 *Click OK to accept the settings for the frame.*

8 *Resizing the frame using the handles maintains three equal columns of text.*

9 *Text flows from the top-left corner of the frame and snakes through the columns until the end of the text or frame is reached.*

After you have set up the columns within your frame, you see gray lines indicating the columns. If you change the spacing between the columns as recommended above, you won't see any change in the gray column guides. The text, however, will be altered to fit within the specification you make.

TAKE NOTE

COLUMNS IN FRAMES MUST BE EVEN

Unlike the layout guides that you specify on the page, the width of columns within frames is immovable. You can't have one column wider than the others if they are set within the frame. To get around this, you will have to draw separate frames when you want columns that are different widths.

COPYING FRAMES

If you copy a frame that has been divided into columns, the newly created frame will also have the designated number of columns as the original.

FIND IT ONLINE

Get tips on column widths and type size at **http://www.netdepot.com/~lmiller/B%26Acolumns1.html**.

Flowing Text Around a Frame

Laying out your publication is like building a jigsaw puzzle. You have all these photos, clip-art images, and text to place on your pages, and you have to make each one fit perfectly and appear as if it really was destined to be just in that one spot.

Depending on the layout style you use, at times you may want to lay an image within your text and have the text flow around that image. Publisher is adept at doing just that. After you place your text, you can insert a picture frame on top of the text. Doing so causes the text to flow around the image frame.

Remember, each time you insert a frame on a page, it's considered to be a layer. These layers could be on top of one another or on opposite corners of the page, never coming in contact. It doesn't matter to Publisher. The program keeps track of the order in which the frames were placed in case they do come in contact. Then, the order determines which item is the uppermost layer.

You can wrap text around a frame that contains either an image or other text. This procedure is pretty easy because text will move out of the way as soon as you draw a frame on top of it.

When you have some clip art, however, you may want to do an *irregular wrap* around the image. This procedure moves the text close to the outline of the image with no regard to the frame border. Text actually goes over the border and gets as close as you tell it to the image.

Why wrap? Because it's a nice effect. When text gets close to the image, it has a very precise artistic look to it. Sometimes square borders and images are a little too structured for the look and feel that you're trying to accomplish. Irregular wrap offers you a handy way to break from this structure.

When text is wrapped around an object, you have to be sure to give the object a little breathing space. You can

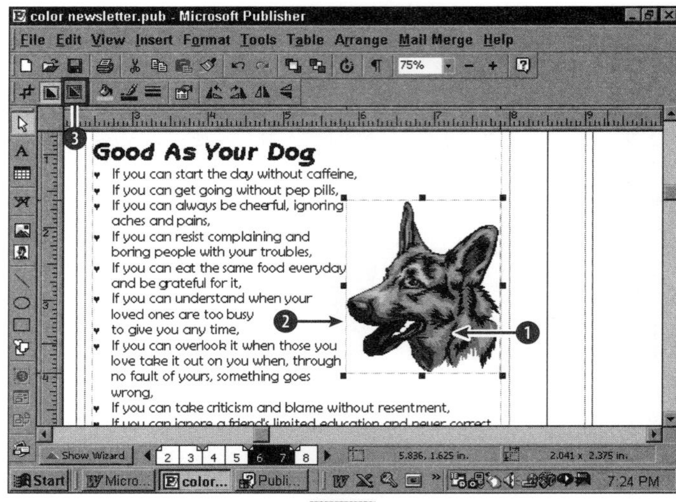

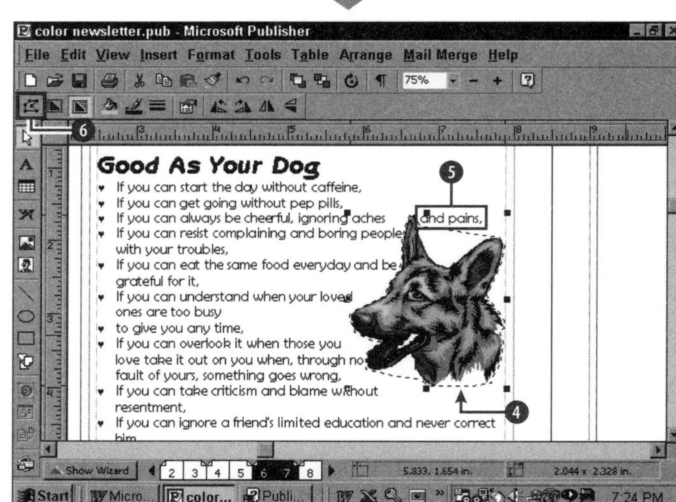

1. *Place your object in a regular frame.*
2. *Text wraps automatically around the frame border.*
3. *Click the Wrap Text to Picture button for an irregular wrap.*
4. *An outline that will not print is placed around the image in the frame.*
5. *Notice the stray text divided by the dog's ear.*
6. *Click the Edit Irregular Wrap button to change the dashed outline.*

CROSS-REFERENCE

Flip back to Chapter 7 for a review of layers.

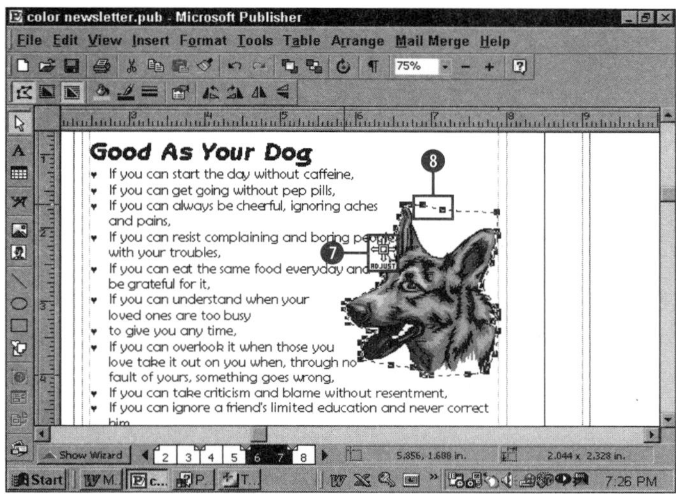

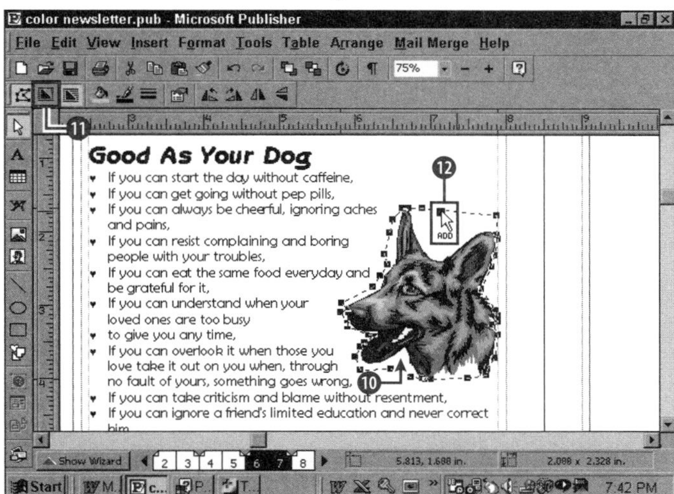

7 *Place your cursor over one of the control points and drag to move it.*

8 *Notice the control points between the dog's ears have been moved to eliminate the stray text.*

9 *Add control points by holding the Ctrl key and clicking the dashed outline. Hold Shift+Ctrl over a control point and click to delete the control point.*

10 *Drag with the cursor inside the outline to move the image and irregular outline.*

11 *To remove an irregular wrap, click the Wrap Text to Frame button.*

think of this as a buffer zone between the text and the image. Publisher lets you dictate how much breathing space to give the image. After all, having text come right up next to an image may reflect poorly on the designer.

TAKE NOTE

DON'T USE THIS TECHNIQUE FOR WEB DOCUMENTS

Publisher won't be able to translate overlapping frames to HTML documents. So, if you plan on placing images on the page so text will wrap around them, you'll have to be sure to place the image and then build the text frames around it, linking the individual frames.

BORDERS PREVENT IRREGULAR WRAPPING

If your frame has a border, you won't be able to create an irregular wrap around your object. Text will wrap to the border.

FIND IT ONLINE

Gather some layout ideas at **www.urban.uiuc.edu/courses/Varkki/pagemaker/layout.html.**

Formatting Stories with Tabs, Lists, and Indents

Publisher can automatically indent text just like your word processor. Plus, you can have bulleted and numbered lists. For spacing things across a page, you can use the default tab settings or set your own.

By default, whenever you hit the Tab key, your text moves half an inch. In the Tabs dialog box, tabs can be set to whatever position you want and avoid the every-half-inch default. As with your word processor, Publisher has four types of tabs:

- **Left** tabs line everything up to the right of the tab. That's the way it worked on the old manual typewriters, and it still performs the same way in your word processor and Publisher.
- **Right** tabs take everything to the left of the tab and shove it against the tab stop.
- **Decimal** tabs are ideal to use to line up all the decimal points down a column of numbers.
- **Center** tabs position the text so that half of each line is on the left side of the tab stop and the rest falls to the right of the stop.

In addition to the different tabs that you can set up for your text, you can also create bulleted and numbered lists with just a few quick mouse clicks. With bulleted lists, small symbols are placed before each paragraph selected — normally a dot that looks like a period on steroids, or any other symbol you pick from the fonts installed on your computer.

When you create numbered lists, Publisher automatically assigns sequential numbers or alpha characters in front of each paragraph so tagged.

The indent settings in Publisher not only let you specify the first line indent like the ones you see in this book, but they also control a paragraph's indentation from the left and right. You can choose any combination

CROSS-REFERENCE

See "Creating and Using Text Styles" later in this chapter.

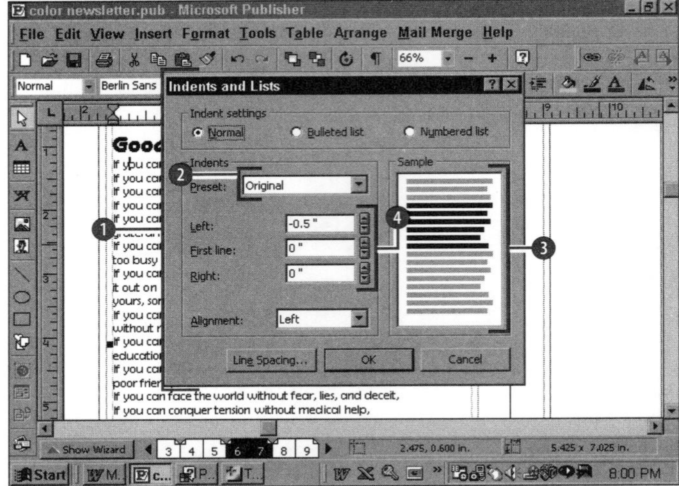

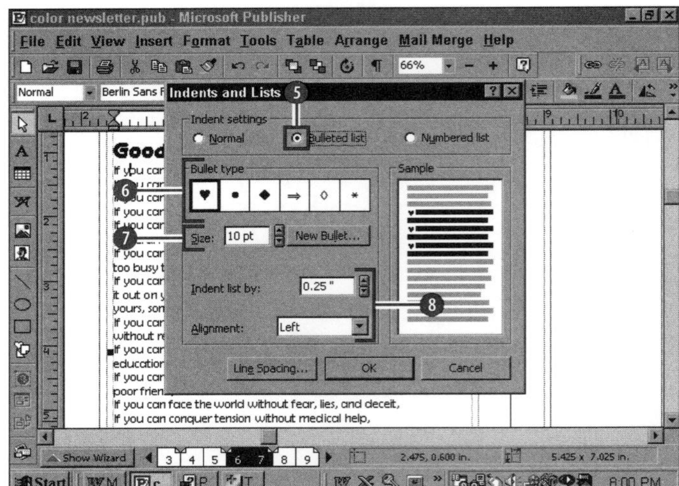

1. *To open the Indents and Lists dialog box, choose Format ⇨ Indents and Lists.*
2. *Choose one of the options from the Preset drop-down.*
3. *The Sample window shows what the formatting will look like.*
4. *For custom settings, insert new measurements in these text boxes.*
5. *To create a bulleted list, choose the "Bulleted list" option button.*
6. *Choose a preset symbol from the list or click the New Bullet button to search for a new symbol.*
7. *Enter the type size of the bullet.*
8. *Set the indent and alignment of the text that will follow the bullet.*

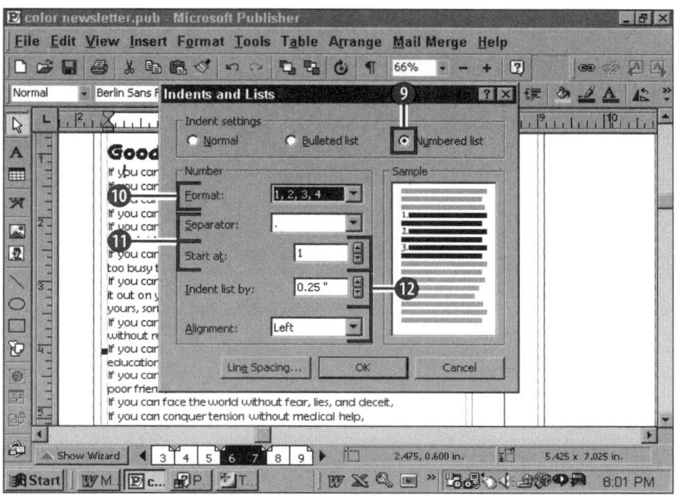

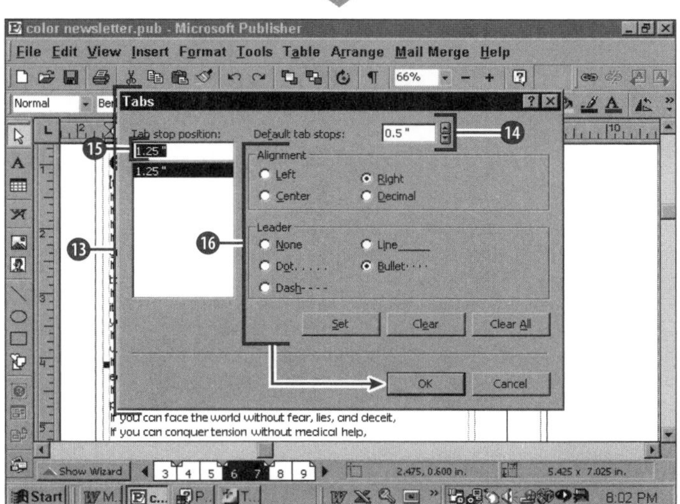

❾ *To create a numbered list, click the "Numbered list" option button.*

❿ *Choose the number or alpha format from the drop-down list.*

⓫ *Choose a separator (the punctuation that will follow the number or letter) and the starting number or letter.*

⓬ *Set the indent and alignment for the text that will follow the number or letter.*

⓭ *To set tabs, choose Format ➪ Tabs.*

⓮ *Change the default tab settings, or …*

⓯ *Type a tab stop measurement into the "Tab stop position" text box.*

⓰ *Choose the alignment and leader character (if any) then click the Set button. When finished setting tabs, click OK.*

of these indents for your text. Normally, text is indented on the left and right when there's a large quote from a speech, book, or other published work.

TAKE NOTE

NEVER USE A TAB TO INDENT A PARAGRAPH

Since the advent of computers and electronic typewriters, users have been able to specify the first line indent measurement of a paragraph, eliminating the need to strike the Tab key. Not only does this save keystrokes, but it lets you make changes to many paragraphs at one time just by changing the indent settings. Otherwise, you would have to go through the entire document and delete the tab manually. You'll discover how to create a style tag to make formatting paragraphs even quicker later in this chapter in the task "Creating and Using Text Styles."

DECIDING ON TABS OR TABLES

If you have columns of information, consider using tables instead of tabs to line up columns of information. You may find it easier and more exact.

FIND IT ONLINE

What's easiest to read? See for yourself at http://www.draytonbird.com/qa/answers/173.asp.

Spell Checking a Text File

So spelling wasn't your best subject in school? If so, you're not alone; many people are terrible spellers. Bad spelling often leads to shoddy grammar, too. For those who are challenged in the spelling arena, there's good news and bad news.

First, the good news — Publisher has a built-in dictionary. You can run Spell Checker to scan your document for misspelled words . . . or at least words that Publisher *thinks* are misspelled (hence the bad news). During spell check, Publisher compares the words in your document to the thousands of words in its dictionary database. When it comes across a word that is not contained in that database, it thinks that word is misspelled. That's where the human brain comes in.

While spell check is a great tool, it is no replacement for careful proofreading. When you check a document for spelling errors, Publisher can only function within its limits. You'll find proper names are usually not recognized, even if they are spelled correctly. Also, homonyms are tricky. *Homonyms* are words that sound alike, but are spelled differently. One common error many people are guilty of is confusing "their," "they're," and "there." Each word may be spelled correctly, but only you will be able to determine whether the correct word is being used in its context. Many other instances will crop up where you have to know the correct spelling because Publisher just won't be much help.

Some of the errors you encounter can be eliminated by adding words to the dictionary as you spell-check a document. Be careful, however, that you aren't adding a word that could prevent another similarly spelled word from being recognized.

Publisher also gives you some controls over the spell-checking process. You can have possible misspelled words highlighted with a red wavy line as you type in

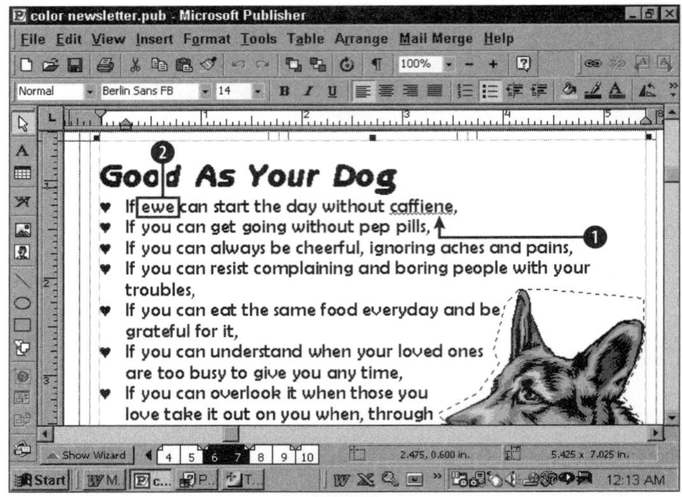

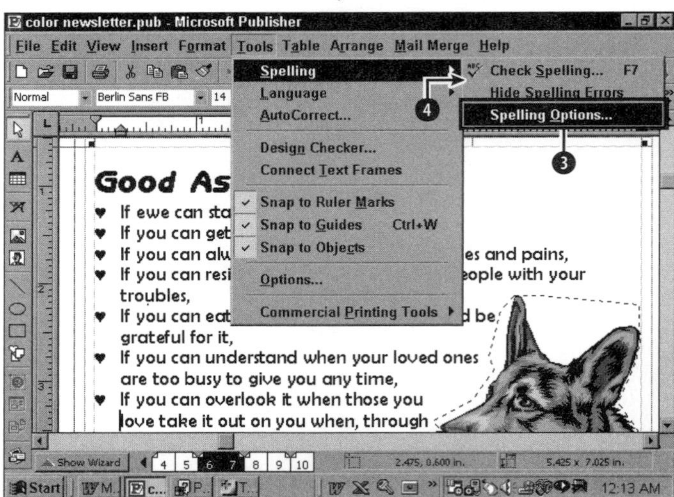

1. If activated, Publisher underlines unidentified words with a red wavy line.
2. Notice, however, that words spelled correctly but used wrongly, are not identified.
3. You can also set spelling options by choosing Tools ➪ Spelling ➪ Spelling Options
4. To start Spell Check, choose Tools ➪ Spelling ➪ Check Spelling or press F7.

CROSS-REFERENCE

Chapter 6 talks about Spell Checker's cousin, Design Checker.

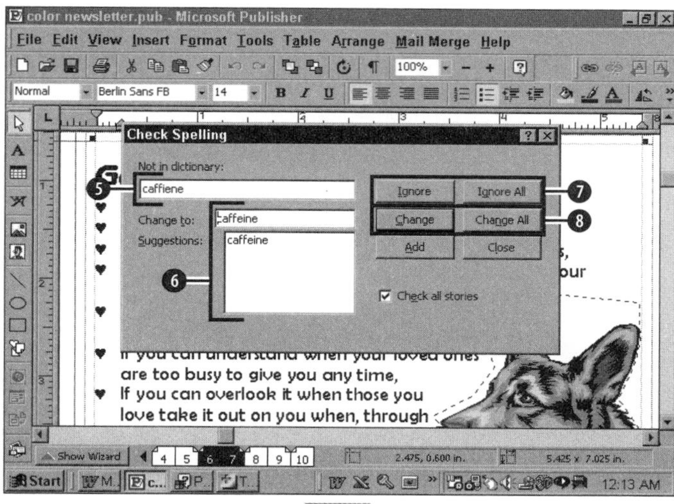

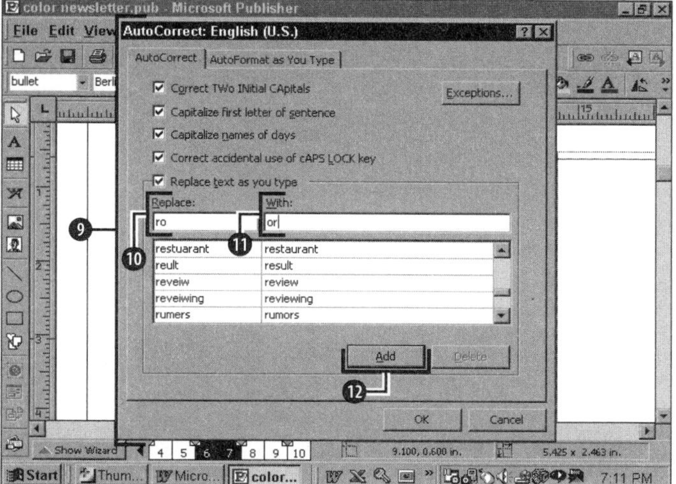

5 *Publisher places the first unrecognized word here. Click the Add button to add the word to the dictionary.*

6 *The best suggestion appears in the "Change to" text box.*

7 *Ignore leaves the word as it appears; Ignore All ignores all occurences.*

8 *Change replaces the word to the one listed in the "Change to" text box. Change All changes all occurences.*

9 *To add a word to the AutoCorrect database, choose Tools ➪ AutoCorrect to view the AutoCorrect dialog box.*

10 *Enter your commonly misspelled word into the Replace text box.*

11 *Enter the correct spelling in the With text box.*

12 *Click the Add button to have Publisher automatically replace the word or phrase.*

Publisher. Words that are repeated can be highlighted, and you can ignore words that appear in all uppercase letters. Choose Tools ➪ Spelling ➪ Spelling Options to set these choices.

When you have the Check Spelling dialog box open, you can opt to change all words as long as you misspelled them all the same way. This is another area where you need to be careful. Blindly changing all words through spell check can actually change words that were spelled correctly to begin with.

TAKE NOTE

USE AUTOCORRECT FOR SOME COMMON TYPOS

Publisher comes with a feature called AutoCorrect that tries to anticipate common errors and correct them as you type. You can add items to the list for automatic correction if you know some of your most common typos. For example, if you always seem to type "teh" for "the", you can add it to the list.

ADD PROPER NAMES TO THE DICTIONARY

If the company you work for or the people you work with are going to be mentioned often in your publications, consider adding them to the dictionary.

FIND IT ONLINE

What are the most common spelling errors in English? See them at http://www.wsu.edu/~brians/errors/errors.html.

Using Find or Replace to Make Changes

When you find yourself suddenly faced with a lot of text changes, consider using Publisher's search and replace features. Case in point — your company has just been acquired by ACME International, or you just changed your official company name to ACME. Every publication you have needs to be redone with the new company name. Or, say you have recurring projects where all you have to do is change a date, committee member name, or event title. These types of changes are tailor-made for search and replace.

When you do a search and replace, you tell Publisher what text to look for and what to replace it with. For example, part number 46782 has been replaced with the new and improved part number 96582. You search for 46782 and replace it with 96582. (At the rate telephone area codes are changing, imagine how helpful search and replace would be.)

You have to be careful, though. Searching for too little information can lead to wrong changes. Because you have the option to replace all occurrences, you can get some changes you hadn't originally planned on. Using the part number example above, if you replaced all 965 area codes with 456, you could be changing the three digits in the part number when you originally wanted only the area codes changed.

Capitalization is another touchy area. When replacing common, lowercase letters, you could change some things that are capitalized. If you were replacing "mark" with "checkmark," you could see where the person's name "Mark" could wind up being "checkmark." So, unless you're 100 percent sure that there is no way something could get altered wrongly, you can use the Replace All option. Otherwise, take the time to go through each occurrence and make the decisions as you go.

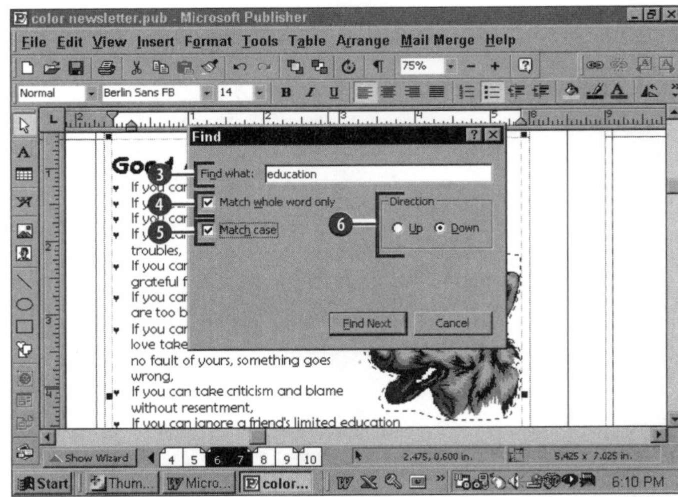

1. To find a word or phrase in a story (text file), select the story's frame.
2. Choose Edit ➪ Find or press Ctrl+F.
3. Enter the word or phrase you're looking for.
4. Place a check in the "Match whole word only" box if you don't want Publisher to find the text within a word.
5. Choose whether Publisher should find the word or phrase without regard to capital letters.
6. Choose to look forward or backward within the story. Click Find Next to search.

CROSS-REFERENCE

To find out more on frames and linked frames see "Connecting Text File Frames" earlier in this chapter.

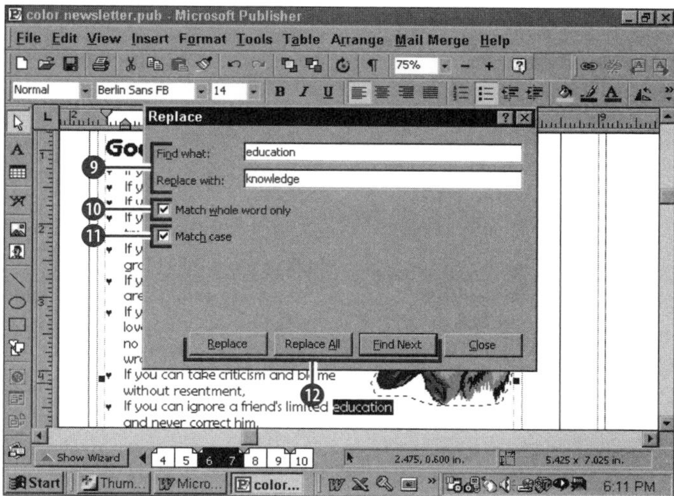

❼ *Select the text frame that will have text replaced.*

❽ *Choose Edit ➪ Replace or press Ctrl+H.*

❾ *In the "Find what" text box, enter the word or phrase that will be replaced. In the "Replace with" text box, enter the text to be inserted.*

❿ *Place a check in the "Match whole word only" checkbox to search and replace the entire word or phrase.*

⓫ *Set your capitalization preference.*

⓬ *Click Find Next to locate the first occurrence.*

What can you find or replace? Words and phrases, letter combinations, numbers, and pretty much any alphanumeric combination you can type. What you can't find and replace are text styles, formatting such as bold or italic, and frame properties such as borders and fills.

TAKE NOTE

WHEN TO USE FIND

Sometimes you just want to know where you used a word or phrase and don't need to replace it with anything. In these cases, just use the Find option in the Edit menu. After filling in the search criteria and clicking the Find button, Publisher takes you to the first occurrence of the word or phrase.

DO ONE TEXT FILE AT A TIME

Publisher can only perform Find or Replace for one frame or text file at a time, including linked frames. You won't be able to do a complete publication with one click. However, when you click the next frame to conduct a Find or Replace, the previous settings are there to eliminate rekeying in the information.

FIND IT ONLINE

If you need to search and replace in general, look into **http://www.searchandreplace.com/search_replace.htm.**

Creating and Using Text Styles

Consider it better than sliced bread, more innovative than indoor plumbing, greater than the Seven Wonders of the World. We're talking about text styles and once you start using them, you'll be in love.

Creating text styles not only saves you time when you're laying out your documents, they give your publication a look of consistency. Once you choose the font, size, alignment, tabs, bullets, numbering, and more, you can roll through a publication, formatting text in record time.

The concept of a text style is simple. You choose a paragraph of text. You create a style name for that paragraph. Taking the time to format the paragraph with all the possibilities that Publisher has to offer pays off when you assign those style settings to future paragraphs. Once a paragraph has been assigned a text style, all that formatting is applied to the paragraph.

When you open the Text Styles dialog box, you'll see a list of the current styles that your publication currently has available. You have the option to delete, rename, or change the settings for the current styles. Plus, you can add styles of your own and program them however you want.

Another very neat feature that Publisher offers is the ability to import styles that you already have set up for other publications. Importing styles saves you time because you don't have to re-create them or remember what the settings were.

Here are a few suggestions when setting up your styles. First, if styles are going to be used close to one another, give them similar names. For example, if you are building a calendar in your newsletter, make styles such as cal head, cal month, cal date, cal event. Because styles are listed in alphabetical order, you won't have far to travel in the styles list to assign new styles to the text.

Second, as a general rule of thumb, stick to two fonts—one serif and one sans serif face. (Many beginning

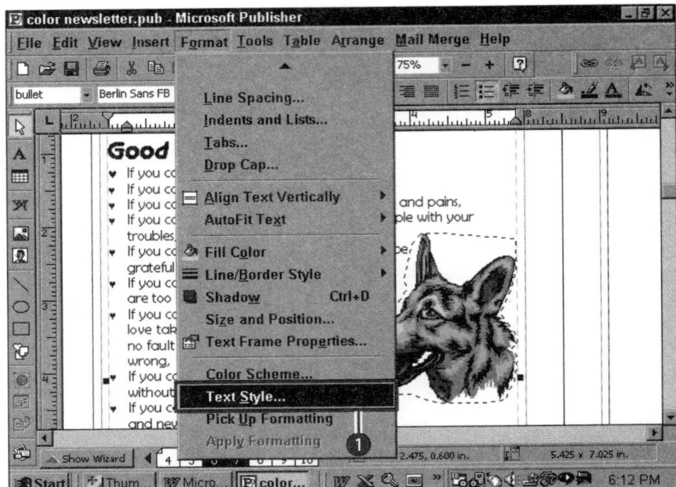

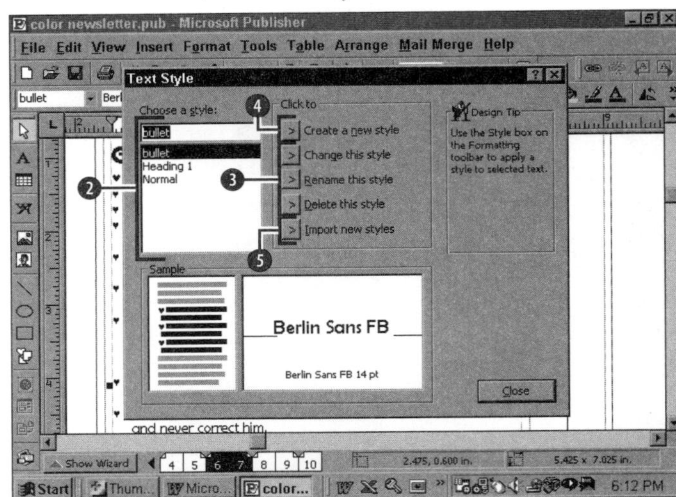

1. *To create a text style, choose Format ⇨ Text Style.*
2. *In the Text Style dialog box, choose a style to edit if you want to change the current one.*
3. *Click the appropriate buttons to change, rename, or delete a text style.*
4. *Click the "Create a new style" button to create a new text style.*
5. *Click the "Import new styles" button to copy styles from another publication into the current one.*

CROSS-REFERENCE

Customizing fonts is covered in Chapter 9.

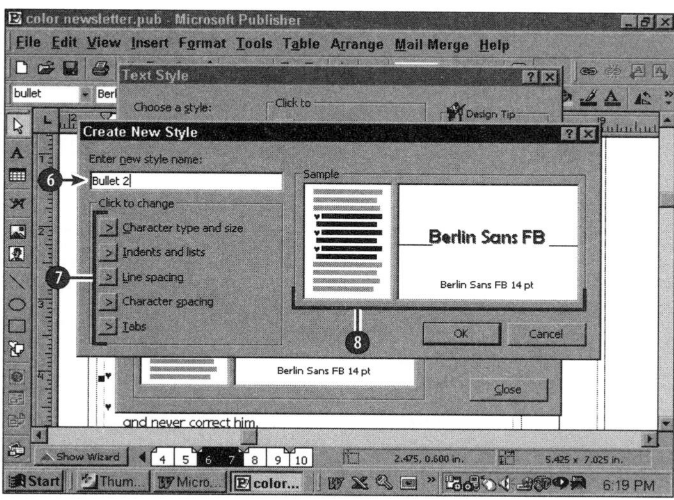

6 *When creating a new style, enter the style name in the text box provided.*

7 *Click each button below the style name to make changes to the character type and size, indents and lists, line spacing, character spacing, or tab settings.*

8 *The Sample window displays what the style alignment, spacing, and type size and style will look like.*

9 *After clicking the "Character type and size" button, the Font dialog box opens.*

10 *Choose the font, style, and type size.*

11 *Choose an underline method and choose a color.*

12 *Click the checkbox next to the effects you desire. The Sample window displays your choices as they are made. Click OK to make the changes.*

publishers have a rambunctious tendency to use every font in their list.) Some experts say that you should try to use a serif face for body copy. Use sans serif faces for headlines and subheads.

Finally, be sure to use decorative, flowery fonts only minimally. They can be very hard to read when you format more than a line or two.

Once you have your styles set up, it's easy to apply those styles to your text. All you do is highlight the text with your cursor and choose a style from the drop-down list in the toolbar.

TAKE NOTE

CREATE ONLY THE STYLES YOU NEED

Try to keep a list of styles for only the ones you use most often. Wading through a long list of styles only slows down your text formatting process.

FIND IT ONLINE

Many of the style tips at **http://ec.hku.hk/writing_turbocharger/formatting/styles.htm** carry over into Publisher.

Personal Workbook

Q&A

1. How can you import a text file if your word processing file format is not among the list of files that Publisher can import?

2. Can you edit a text file in Microsoft Word if it was not created in Word to begin with?

3. When fitting copy to a frame, what are the drawbacks?

4. When do you have to draw separate frames for columns of text instead of assigning a number of columns to the frame?

5. What is the default measurement for tabs in a Publisher document?

6. Once you have wrapped text around a graphic, can you change it back to where it wraps around the frame that holds the graphic? If so, how?

7. What is the major problem you may encounter when you spell check a document?

8. What is the best way to organize your text styles?

ANSWERS: PAGE 353

EXTRA PRACTICE

1. Collect tasteful jokes from the e-mail you receive and assemble them in a word processing file. Edit them in the word processor to remove extra spaces and unwanted characters. Import them into Publisher and make a booklet.
2. Set up four frames on a page and place one joke in each frame. Use the copy-fitting features in Publisher to make them fit.
3. To break up text in long stories, create a frame and divide it up into three or four columns.
4. Insert some clip art appropriate to the stories you are publishing. Make the text wrap around the clip art.
5. To be consistent from page to page, set up text styles for the headlines and body text. You may also want to create a bullet style for your collection of one-liners.

REAL-WORLD APPLICATIONS

✔ Your company newsletter has a very structured look. You create text styles so all headlines have the same font, size, and alignment. Body copy is also on a text style so that the first line of each paragraph is indented half an inch.

✔ You're working on your masters degree and must produce a thesis. You type it into your word processor but use Publisher to assemble it so that you can incorporate graphics much more easily.

✔ You're in charge of creating the rules book for the bantam football league your child plays in. You create text styles for numbering rules and regulations. When it comes time to update it, you do a search and replace of all individuals who have been elected to direct the league.

Visual Quiz

What do the icons on the top and bottom of this frame tell you? What happens when you click them?

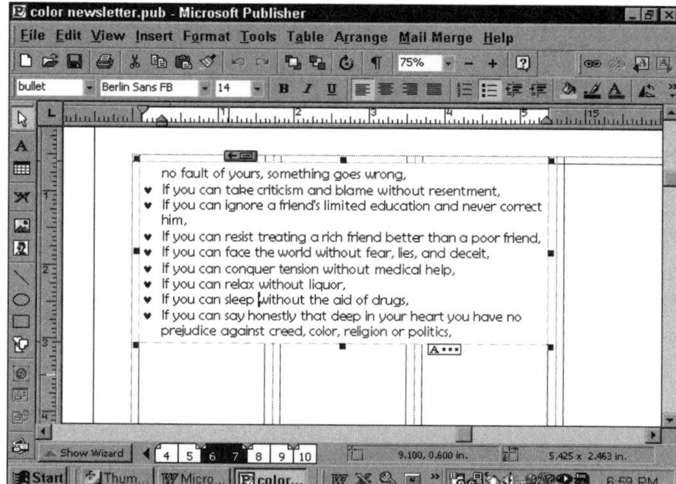

CHAPTER 9

MASTER THESE SKILLS

- Customizing Fonts
- Creating Drop Caps
- Controlling Character and Line Spacing
- Inserting WordArt
- Changing WordArt Special Effects

Using Fonts and WordArt

You might think that you have to add photos and clip art to your publications to get some visual variety to break up the gray blocks of text. While this is a viable option, you can resort to all kinds of typography tricks to make words and letters appear as art.

A significant mistake that many people make is using too many typefaces in a publication. Unless you're sure of what you're doing, or are looking for a fun and crazy look, it's a good idea to stick with one serif and one sans serif typeface. It's typical to use a sans serif typeface for headings and subheadings and a serif typeface for the bulk of the text, referred to by most professionals as body text. As you become more experienced with choosing type, you'll soon see which faces work well together and which ones don't. Take some time and look at successful publications and notice how they use type. You could even do some creative plagiarism and mimic their look and choices.

Besides choosing a different typeface to decorate and enhance a publication (and Microsoft Publisher comes with quite a few fonts), using large initial capital letters at the beginning of paragraphs can also add some flair to your words. There probably aren't many fairy tale books that don't use some sort of decorative letter to begin a story.

Another technique to break up text is line and paragraph spacing. When you come across books and magazines that spread out their paragraphs and increase the amount of spacing between lines, they aren't doing it just to fill pages — they are using this technique to add visual attractiveness and enhance readability.

Finally, Publisher comes with a little side program that is incorporated into it that lets you apply all kinds of special effects on letters, words, and phrases. Twist, turn, bloat, block, flare, outline, shadow, and otherwise distort these elements to actually create a piece of art from otherwise humdrum, boring letters.

As mentioned in several places throughout this book, use these techniques with humility. Too many times beginning publishers will change fonts, add clip art, or use hard-to-read typography just for the sake of using them. A publication that has to maintain a business-like tone or serious note shouldn't incorporate too many, if any, wild and crazy design elements. That type of publication reeks and shouts in a loud booming voice, "Amateur!"

Customizing Fonts

If you're grasping desktop publishing with Microsoft Publisher at a rapid rate, you will soon find yourself in the font monger category. A font monger loves to install scads of fonts on their system and try to use each one of them for one purpose or another. Font mongers have a deep appreciation for the curves and serifs of each letter, much like those who collect works of art from the Old Masters.

Like any collector, your affection can also be an affliction. Too many fonts can bog down even the fastest and largest systems, so be warned to install fonts in moderation. Depending on your system's processor and RAM, the number of fonts that Windows programs have at their disposal can have a direct effect on the performance of that software.

Nowadays, fonts now come in two popular flavors: TrueType and PostScript. Without going into the history of these two types of fonts, suffice it to say that Adobe fathered the PostScript variety of fonts, which were scalable to most any size. Microsoft, not being one to stand still and let font technology rest within one language controlled by Adobe, came up with their own scalable font standard — TrueType.

As a general rule of thumb, if your publication is destined for a commercial printer, it's wise to stick with all PostScript fonts because most imagesetters are based on the PostScript language. For ink-jet and laser printers, TrueType offers a wide variety of inexpensive faces and are handled quite well with these printers.

In addition, fonts can have several styles. Besides the Normal face, you can have Bold, Italic, and Bold Italic. Decorative typefaces usually come in only one variety.

Type is measured in points. There are 12 points to a pica and 6 picas to an inch. That makes an inch equal to 72 points, to give you an idea on the size of type to

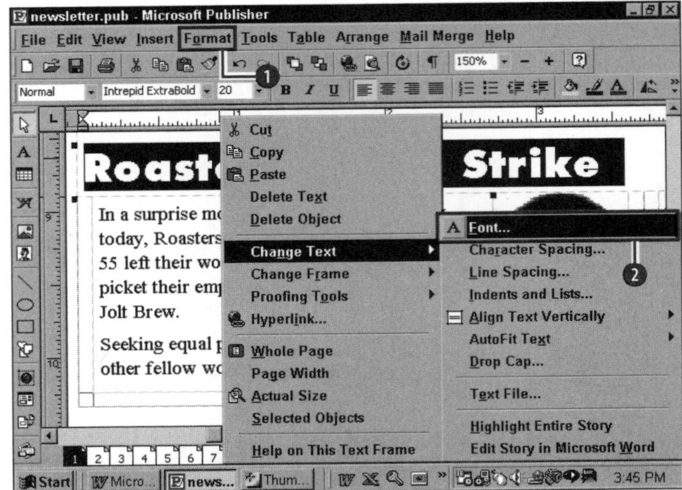

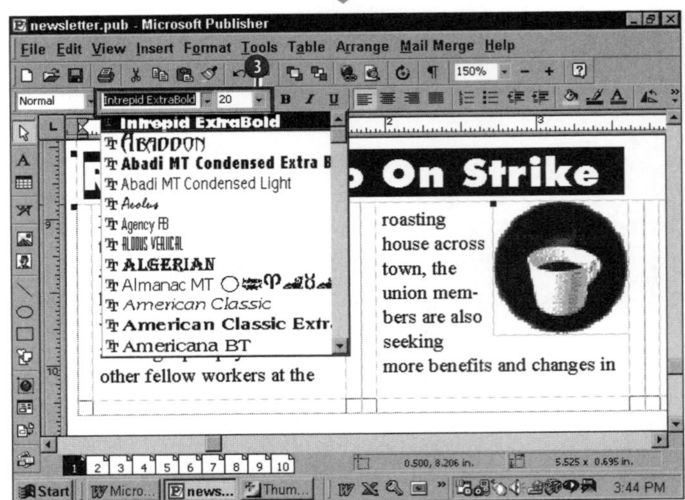

❶ *To change the font of highlighted text, choose Format ➪ Font from the menu.*

❷ *Or, right-click on the highlighted text and choose Change Text ➪ Font to get the dialog box in the lower two figures.*

❸ *Another quick way to change fonts is to choose the font and size from the drop-down menus in the toolbar.*

CROSS-REFERENCE

Save time by creating text styles as shown in Chapter 8.

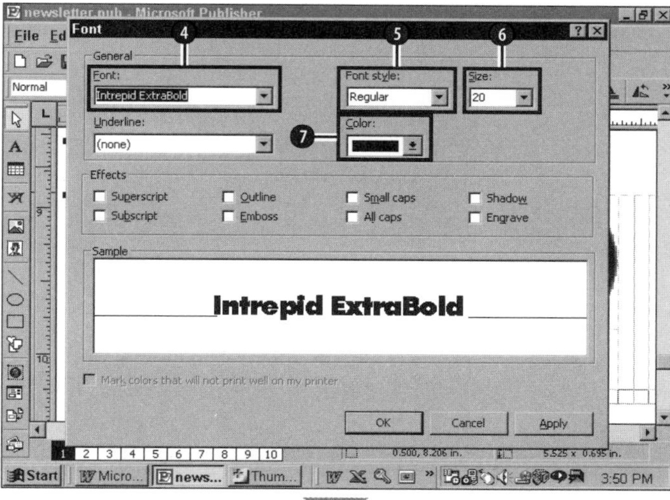

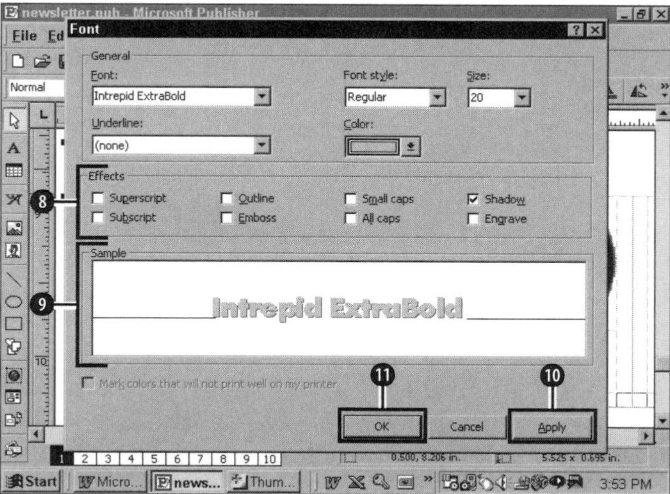

4 *Choose a typeface from the Font drop-down menu.*

5 *Select a style from the "Font style" drop-down menu.*

6 *Pick a size from the Size drop-down menu or click inside the box and enter a value not present in the list.*

7 *Choose the color of the font.*

8 *Optionally, you can choose one of the effects in the Effects list.*

9 *The Sample window lets you preview your creation.*

10 *Click the Apply button to make the changes but keep the Font dialog box open.*

11 *Click OK to apply the changes and close the Font dialog box.*

choose. Further, they are measured from the bottom of a descender to the top of an ascender. The descender is the tail on a "y" or "p." Ascenders are the pieces of a letter that stick up like the flag on the "b" or "d." Whatever fonts you choose, you'll soon get a feel for type. Each font has a personality that can convey friendliness, structure, traditionalism, and other sentiments. Choose your fonts according to the purpose of your publication.

TAKE NOTE

CREATING STYLES WHEN THERE ISN'T ONE

Publisher has the ability to make a font bold or italic when there isn't really that style, as such, within the font. Publisher creates a style on the fly when you choose to boldface or italicize a font. When preparing for a commercial printer, however, you should avoid doing this because the quality of the style will be substandard for imagesetters.

FIND IT ONLINE

Can't pick the right fonts for a projects? Try EsperFonto at http://www.will-harris.com.

Creating Drop Caps

One common way to add some variety to a page that is predominantly text is to make the first letter of a paragraph larger than the rest of the text. Sometimes the next couple of lines of text below it will wrap around the large letter; other times the letter will jut out into the margin. You will see all kinds of variations in many different types of publications.

Drop caps, or initial caps, are not just for fairy tale books. Many publications will use a drop cap to begin a chapter in a book or the start of a new article, or just to break up or dress up the beginning of any text. Drop caps not only drop, but they can also extend up above the rest of the text, in which case they are more accurately called initial caps.

In Microsoft Publisher, the procedure for making an initial cap or drop cap is very simple. The difficult part is knowing what font to use, how many lines to drop it down, and what size the letter should be to offer the best-looking drop cap.

The Drop Cap dialog box in Publisher is divided into two tabs: Drop Cap and Custom Drop Cap. In the Drop Cap tab, Publisher has several different presets to choose from. (Don't forget to use the scroll bar at the bottom of the Available Drop Caps Preview window to see them all.) With several presets to choose from, you can hardly go wrong. However, for the do-it-yourselfers, you can choose the Custom Drop Cap tab and create your own concoction.

Here are some suggestions for creating drop caps:

- ▶ Don't overdo it. Keep the number of lines that the drop cap extends below its original baseline in proportion to the size of the paragraph.
- ▶ Likewise, make the size of the large cap or letters large enough to be construed as a different size

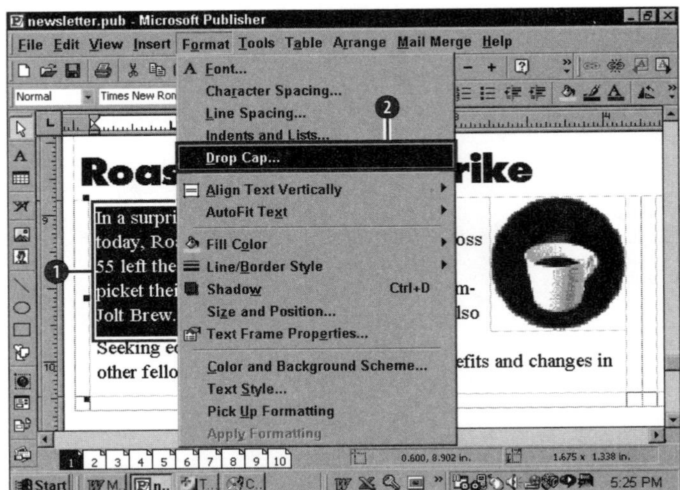

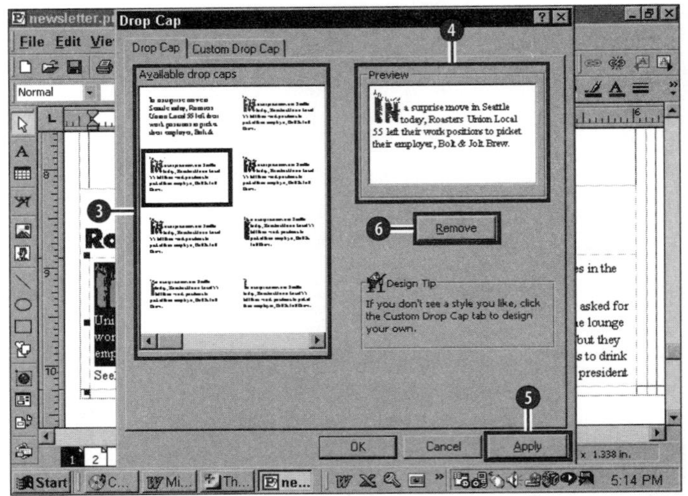

1. *Either highlight the paragraph or just click somewhere inside it to create a drop cap in that paragraph.*
2. *Choose Format ➪ Drop Cap or right-click and choose Change Text ➪ Drop Cap from the quick menu.*
3. *In the Drop Cap tab, choose one of the preset options in the "Available drop caps" window.*
4. *Check the Preview window to see how the settings look.*
5. *Click the Apply button to make the changes and leave the dialog box open. Click OK to apply the changes and close the dialog box.*
6. *Click the Remove button to remove the effect altogether.*

CROSS-REFERENCE

Review how to insert text in a frame in Chapter 6.

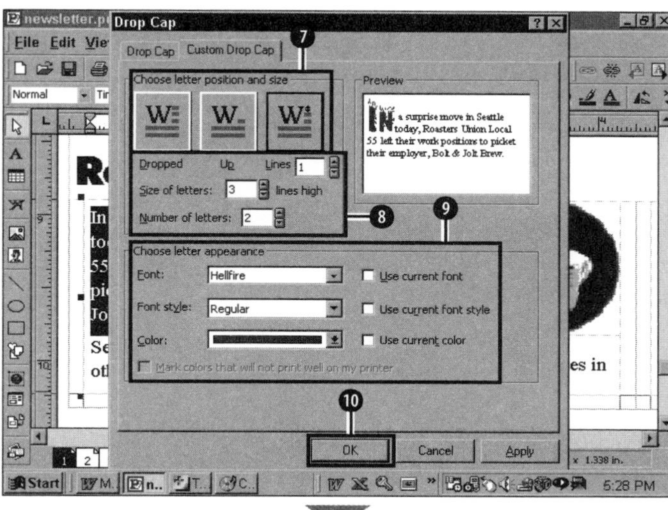

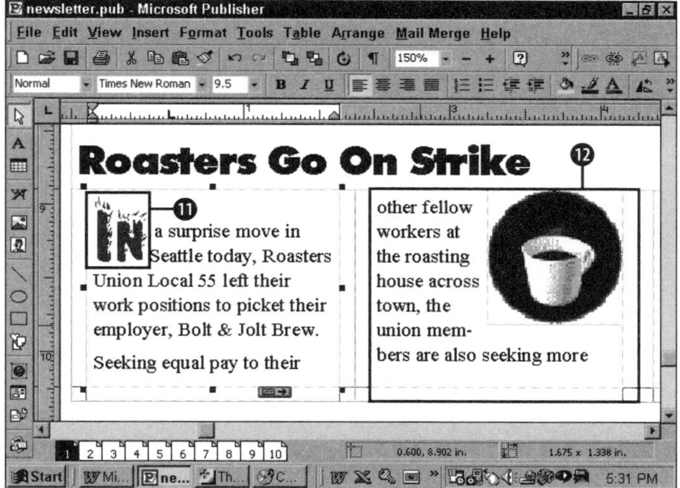

7. *In the Custom Drop Cap tab, choose the style that you want to use.*
8. *Adjust letter size, the number of lines the cap will drop, and the number of letters that will receive the effect.*
9. *Change the font, font style, and color here. Use the checkboxes to keep the same settings as the rest of the paragraph.*
10. *Click OK.*
11. *Drop caps are applied to the chosen paragraph within the frame. The letters do not extend above the frame border.*
12. *The remaining text automatically flows to the next column or linked frame.*

and not just a little bit bigger than the rest of the body text.

- Choose the drop cap wisely. Make it consistent throughout the publication or pertinent to the story.
- Be sure the cap is readable. For extremely flowery and decorative fonts, using only one letter is a good idea so that the reader doesn't have to spend a lot of time deciphering the word.

TAKE NOTE

USE THE PRESETS YOU MADE

Once you create a drop cap, that style is shown as one of the preset options in the Drop Cap tab of the Drop Cap dialog box. You'll see it in a couple of different configurations that you can use.

WATCH PUNCTUATION MARKS

Many times a paragraph will start with a single or double quotation mark. If possible, try rewriting the paragraph to eliminate these marks. They don't make very nice drop caps!

FIND IT ONLINE

For some old-fashioned decorative caps, check out **http://ragnarokpress.com/scriptorium/initials/.**

Controlling Character and Line Spacing

Working with text doesn't just include the typefaces and styles. You can also control the character spacing and the line spacing. For what reasons, you ask? For one thing, fonts may not default to the best character spacing, which is controlled with the font definition file. You may like your letters closer together or further apart. Publisher also has a default formula that it uses to determine the spacing between your lines of text.

Just to get on a professional keel, you should become familiar with some of the terms associated with this task. First, the line spacing for text can also be called *leading* (pronounced led-ding; rhymes with bedding). It stems from the old days of typesetting when small strips of lead were placed between rows of type.

Character spacing includes tracking and kerning. *Tracking* controls the spacing between all characters within the text you have highlighted. For whatever reason, some font definitions render very tight spacing between the characters — with others, the spacing may be too much for your taste. (This, by the way, can be a sure sign of a cheap font.) Then again, you may be looking for an effect that calls for the letters and words to be spread greatly apart.

Kerning lets you scrunch two letters close together because the regular tracking doesn't quite hack it. For example, when you have two letters such as AV or AT, the slant or overhang of one letter makes it appear that there is a space between the two letters when there is not. Highlighting the offending letters and adjusting the space between these characters is called kerning. Some people like to kern so that there is adequate space between the characters, while others like to have the letters kiss, which is where they actually touch slightly. This can be attractive, especially when dealing with serif type.

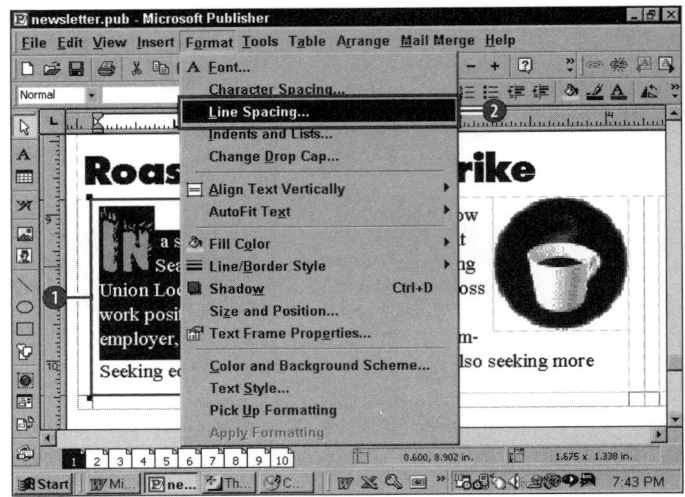

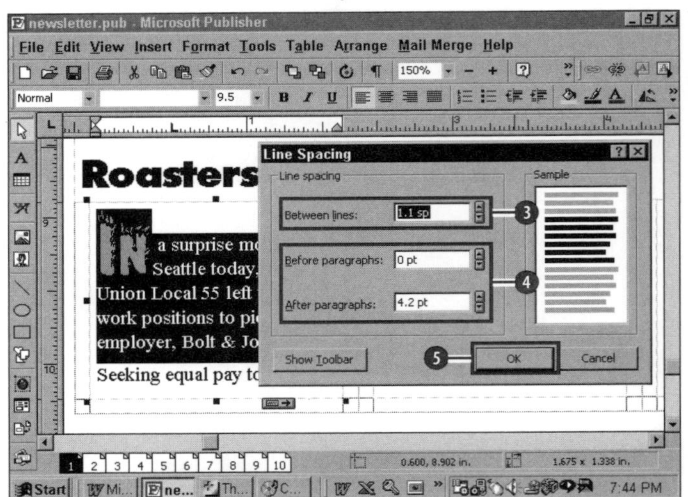

1. Select the text for which you want to change the line spacing.
2. Choose Format ⇨ Line Spacing from the menu or right-click and choose Change Text ⇨ Line Spacing.
3. In the Line Spacing dialog box, increase or decrease the "Between lines" setting. A 1 indicates single spacing, 2 is double spaced, and so on. You can use decimal values.
4. Indicate the amount of space placed before or after the paragraph.
5. Click OK to assign the spacing.

CROSS-REFERENCE

For other ways to fit stories to frames, see Chapter 8.

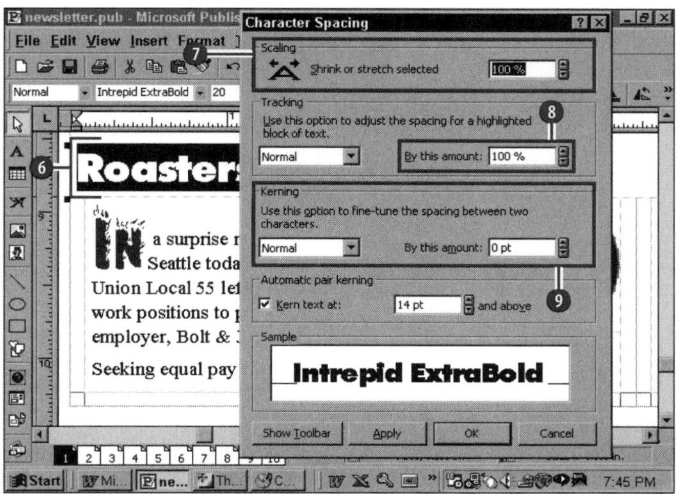

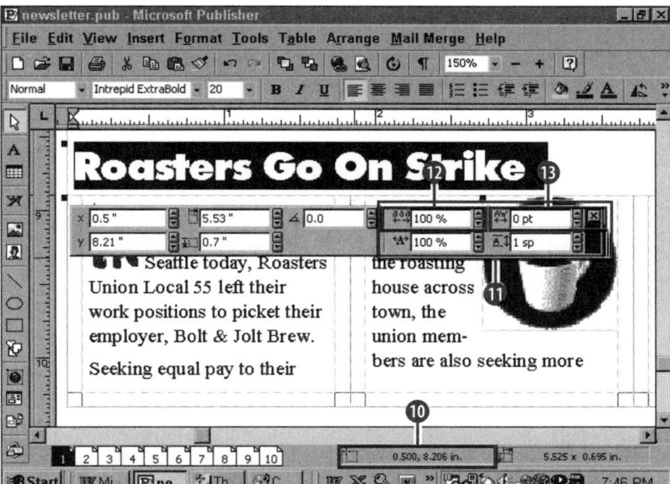

6 *After highlighting the text to change the character spacing, choose Format ➪ Character Spacing.*

7 *Set the amount of stretch in the Scaling text box.*

8 *Change the tracking using preset or enter an amount in the percentage text box.*

9 *After selecting the characters to kern, choose a preset or enter the number of points to move the letters together.*

10 *When you choose the Show Toolbar button, the toolbar appears. Or, you can double-click the status bar to show it.*

11 *The right end of the toolbar controls character and line spacing.*

12 *The top text box on the left controls scaling; the one beneath it controls tracking.*

13 *The top text box on the right controls kerning; the one beneath it controls line spacing.*

Another useful byproduct of adjusting character and line spacing is *copyfitting*. By spreading out the lines of text, you can fill a frame with text that originally came up short. Adjusting the tracking will let you get that last line or two into a frame.

But one of the most common uses for these techniques is as a design element. Type that has had its line spacing spread tremendously can be found quite often in advertisements. Kerning, on the other hand, is not only used in ads, but company logotype where letters are joined to create a corporate logo.

TAKE NOTE

STRETCH ONLY WHEN NECESSARY

The Publisher Character Spacing dialog box includes an option for scaling text. This will stretch words or phrases while maintaining the same character height. Be very careful using this feature if you're sending your document to a commercial printer. Some imagesetters may not interpret the scaling correctly and just place extra space between the letters.

FIND IT ONLINE

For examples of kerning and tracking and its effects, go to **http://www.pbtweb.com/typostyl/letters.htm.**

Inserting WordArt

Microsoft Publisher, like several of the other packages in the Microsoft Office 2000 Suite, gives you a little program that adds special effects to type, called WordArt. Plain words can become a pretty powerful graphic when used imaginatively — yet responsibly.

When you create a WordArt object in your publication, you have to insert it into a frame like your other graphics. The only difference is when you finish drawing the frame, WordArt — another program — opens and enables you to type text, apply special effects like shadows, colors and patterns, and then disappears once you're finished.

Following is a list of the things you can select and do in WordArt, in exactly the order you will find them in the toolbar:

- **Shape:** From curves, circles, waves, and more, the shape that your words take are controlled using this drop-down menu.
- **Font:** Choose a typeface installed on your system. Even after all of the other effects are applied, changing the font will not lose your other settings.
- **Font Size:** To have the phrase fit the frame, you can select the Best Fit option in this drop-down. Otherwise, you can specify the size of the font.
- **Bold:** Makes the text boldfaced.
- **Italic:** Puts a slant on the words.
- **Same Height:** Makes all letters, whether they are uppercase or lowercase, the same height. This can give some pretty interesting results.
- **Flip:** Turns the letters on their side. Depending on the order that you create the effects, this could have different results.
- **Stretch:** Makes the letters and their effects spread out to fill the frame.

CROSS-REFERENCE

For more information on frames, see Chapter 6.

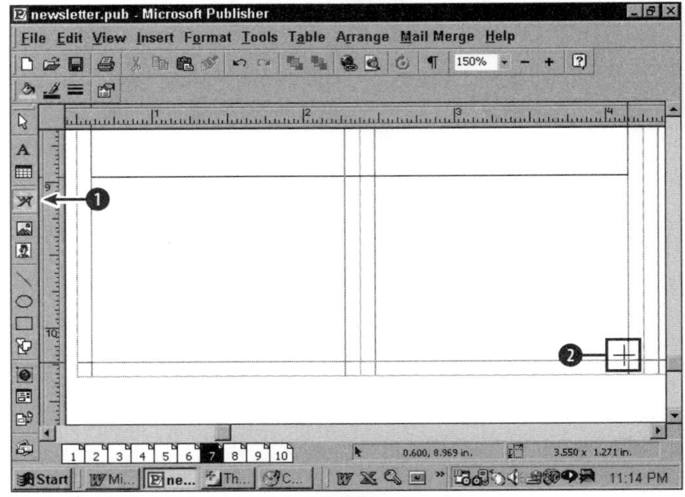

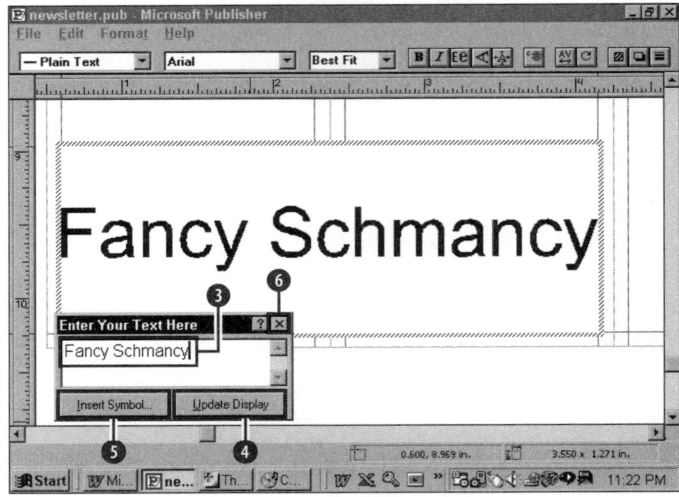

1. *Click the WordArt Frame tool.*
2. *Draw the size of frame to hold the WordArt graphic.*
3. *Enter text in the dialog box.*
4. *Click the Update Display button to show your text.*
5. *To enter a symbol from the chosen font, click the Insert Symbol button and choose the symbol from the dialog box displayed.*
6. *Click the Close button to shut down the Enter Your Text Here dialog box. You can double-click on the text to open this box again to make changes.*

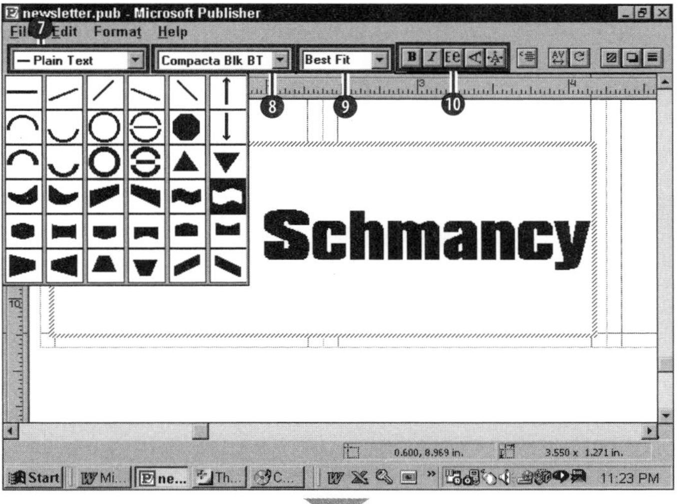

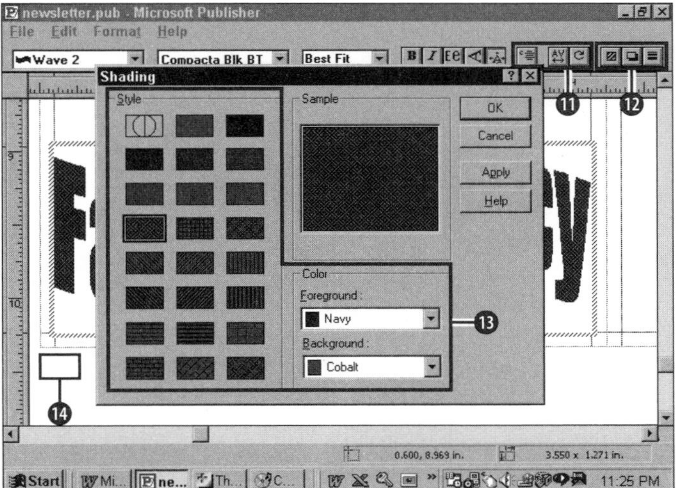

7 *Choose a shape from the drop-down list.*

8 *Choose a font from the drop-down list of typefaces on your system.*

9 *Select a type size or choose Best Fit from the Size drop-down list.*

10 *Click the style buttons to assign those effects. These buttons toggle, so click once to turn them on, and then click again to turn the style off.*

11 *Change the alignment, character spacing or rotation.*

12 *Change the fill, shadow and outline properties.*

13 *In the Shading dialog box, you can pick a pattern and foreground and background color to fill the font with.*

14 *To close the WordArt window, click anywhere on the page outside the frame that contains the WordArt object.*

- **Align:** Offers all of the standard alignment options like center, left, and right, and three different justification settings.
- **Letter Spacing:** Moves the individual characters further apart or closer.
- **Rotate:** Turns the entire phrase within the frame.
- **Fill:** Adjusts the color and fill pattern of the letters.
- **Shadow:** Choose one of eight shadow types and select the color of the shadow.
- **Outline:** Choose the thickness and color of the outline of each character.

Keep in mind that choices in one area may affect your finished art differently. For example, if you have chosen the Best Fit for the type size, you may not see any change in the alignment choice if you have only one line of text.

TAKE NOTE

INSERTING SYMBOLS

You can insert any symbols using the Enter Your Text Here dialog box. Just click on the Insert Symbol button and choose them from the dialog box that opens. You can choose from any of the extended characters of the chosen font.

CHANGING FONTS

If you want to change fonts within the same WordArt object, you can't. Because the font selected is applied to all the letters in the word or phrase, you can't apply more than one face to the letters in one frame.

FIND IT ONLINE

For other WordArt ideas from Microsoft, go to http://www.microsoft.com/HOMEESSENTIALS/howto/WordArt/wordart.asp.

Changing WordArt Special Effects

Once you have the initial WordArt in place, changes are no problem. Making changes is as simple as double-clicking on the WordArt frame. Doing so will call up the WordArt interface again. Once on screen, you can change the font, the wording, or any of the other effects.

While you wouldn't necessarily use these effects for a traditional business-type document, there are some places where these types of headlines and graphics can be fun.

Greeting cards are a great place to utilize these special effects to wish a happy birthday, anniversary, get well, invitation to an open house, and other special events.

WordArt is especially well suited for banners. Stretching the text onto large-format paper and adding festive clip art from the gallery is fun and spreads good will a long way.

Should you choose to use WordArt on your Web page, it gets converted to a GIF image quite nicely.

Flyers and announcements are great places to spice up large headlines to grab attention. Imagine phrases like "Big Sale," "Lost Dog," "Wanted," and others speaking boldly from the top of the page.

Certificates can be dressed up to show recognition for individual accomplishments. Think about using phrases like "Certificate of Appreciation," "Honor Award," and "Excellent Performance" in large decorative letters on the frames certificate.

Calendars are another project where WordArt can be used for the month headings. However, days of the week or the dates themselves may be a bit small to effectively use WordArt, so print a draft copy before proceeding with a large project.

Scan down the list of the projects that you can do with the Publisher Wizard. You'll be thinking of more projects where WordArt will come in handy.

CROSS-REFERENCE

Chapter 4 addresses the Publisher Wizards and how to use them.

1. *After double-clicking on the WordArt object to edit it, you can loosen or tighten the spacing between the character by clicking on this button.*
2. *Choose one of the presets.*
3. *Or, choose Custom and enter a percentage in the text box.*
4. *Click the Rotation button to change curvature or rotate the entire object.*
5. *Enter an amount into the Rotation text box. The effect will take place immediately.*
6. *To increase or decrease the curvature of curved special effects, adjust the percentage in the Slider text box.*

7. *To add or change a drop shadow, click the Shadow button.*
8. *Choose one of the eight presets.*
9. *Pick a color for the shadow from the Shadow Color drop-down menu.*
10. *Outline the text using the Border button.*
11. *Choose a thickness for the rule line by clicking on a setting.*
12. *Click the Color drop-down and select a color for the rule line border. The Auto selection defaults to the same as the fill color.*

Try to avoid using WordArt to accomplish tasks that you can do in the Font dialog box. Remember that there are settings there for applying shadows or outlines, or rendering an embossed or engraved look.

TAKE NOTE

EXPERIMENTATION YIELDS EXCELLENCE

WordArt is unbreakable. Feel free to experiment with all the different options to get just the look you're striving for. Many times the patterns that you can fill the text with won't look that good when you print on a laser printer. Also, some ink-jet printers may not print these effects as clearly as you see on the monitor.

LARGE TEXT IS BEST FOR EFFECTS

When using any special effect on a font, you should be sure that the font is capable of receiving the effect and still maintain legibility. Typically, sans serif fonts are good for WordArt and won't lose their clarity with the various shapes and textures you choose to apply. Also, the bolder or wider the font is, the better these effects will work.

FIND IT ONLINE

You can get additional certificate templates at http://officeupdate.microsoft.com/downloadDetails/pubcert.htm.

Personal Workbook

Q&A

1. What are the two most popular file types of fonts?

2. What point size would you select to make your type one-half inch tall?

3. Besides the number of lines that a drop cap extends down and the size of the letters, what other three elements can you change once the size and position are chosen?

4. What is the difference between tracking and kerning?

5. What is leading and how is it used?

6. How do you open the WordArt interface once you have created a WordArt object?

7. In order to fill the entire frame with the art, what button should you select?

8. If you choose to stretch the WordArt object to fill the frame, what setting has no effect if you are working with a one-line word or phrase?

ANSWERS: PAGE 354

Using Fonts and WordArt

EXTRA PRACTICE

1. Go through a previous publication and change the font on all of the headings or subheadings.
2. Change the font of the body text in your publication and see what effect it has on the flow of different stories from frame to frame or page to page.
3. Create a booklet of your poetry (or your favorite poems if you're not a poet). Start each poem with a drop cap to dress them up a bit. Once you have created a custom drop cap, be sure to choose it from the presets instead of re-creating the style from scratch again.
4. In that same book of poetry, use the line spacing settings to add extra space in front of the stanzas and between the lines in a stanza.

REAL-WORLD APPLICATIONS

- ✔ Your headlines in the newsletter need to be dressed up some. You change the font settings so that a drop shadow is placed behind the letters.
- ✔ The annual report has very few pictures and graphics in it. The bulk of the pages are text. You use drop caps to add a little formality to each page.
- ✔ The bold typeface you selected for the headings in your employee procedure manual has the letters touching. You prefer some space between the letters. Using the Tracking feature in Publisher, you spread out the letters so they no longer touch.
- ✔ Employee notices must be posted on the bulletin board in the break room. To attract more attention, you use WordArt to add some flair and attractiveness to the postings.

Visual Quiz

This headline uses capital and small capital letters. How can you format it by opening only one dialog box one time?

____

____

____

____

____

____

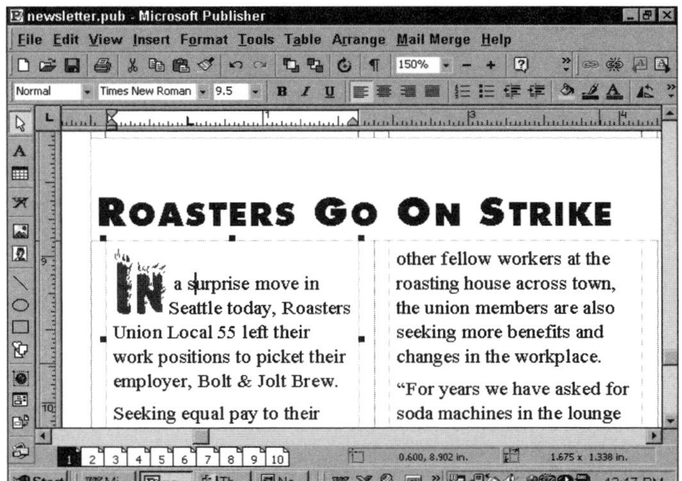

CHAPTER 10

MASTER THESE SKILLS

- Creating a Table
- Inserting and Deleting Rows and Columns
- Merging and Splitting Cells
- Adding Diagonal Lines to Cells
- Resizing Rows and Columns
- Filling Rows and Columns with Repeating Text
- Formatting Cells
- Formatting Your Table with Autoformat

Working with Tables

You may not think of many reasons to use tables in your publications at the moment, but by the time you are finished with this chapter, you'll be thinking of more applications than we have touched on here. When you think of tables, you normally think of columns and rows of figures and data neatly lined up for easy deciphering. But, how much further can you stretch the use of tables for your needs?

At first glance, those familiar with Microsoft Excel or any other spreadsheet programs will see a table and think that they are mini spreadsheets. And, that assumption would be partly correct. Publisher's ability to organize data in rows and columns, while it may appear like a spreadsheet, lacks the mathematical capabilities of those type programs. No, using tables in Publisher is strictly a way to organize information in tidy rows and columns.

Publisher tables aren't all work on your part. There are some autofill features that help shorten the time it takes to enter information.

Plus, unlike many spreadsheet programs, the formatting possibilities are very rich indeed. Not only can you change the typeface and color of fonts within the cells, but you can add background colors and borders to change your table so that it doesn't appear like a table at all.

For quick and effortless formatting, Publisher comes with some preformats that assign these attributes automatically. At the very least, these presets can serve as a springboard for changes you want to make.

Another thing that you can do in a Publisher table that you can't do in many other tables is split them diagonally. This places a slanted line from the top corner to the bottom opposite corner.

Once your table is in place, you can customize the width of the columns and the height of the rows to accommodate even the longest of verbiage. Not only does this enable you to fit more onto a page, but the other columns and rows will adjust automatically.

So, if that whets your appetite and you're ready to belly up to the Publisher table features, read on in this chapter. And don't forget to start thinking about all the different ways you can utilize tables in your documents. After all, if Publisher can set an appetizing table for you, you can fill it with all kinds of tasty tidbits for your readers.

Creating a Table

When you create a table in Publisher, it's just like creating a picture, text, or WordArt frame. There's a button in the toolbar for creating a table frame. Once the frame is drawn, the dialog box that asks for the number of rows and columns comes up automatically.

Clicking in a table frame will not only highlight the frame, but on the top and left sides of the frame, you see the row and column control boxes. These not only indicate the width of a column or height of a row, but they are used to select the entire line of cells.

When Publisher creates a table, it's like many small text frames lined up in the number of rows and columns that you specify. You'll notice the table by the light gray lines that outline each cell. By default, these lines won't print unless you assign them a border. Likewise, the outside border won't print until you specify a border for it.

Because each cell contains a single paragraph, you can move your cursor from cell to cell by using the Tab key to go to the next cell, and Shift+Tab to back up a cell. As you press the Tab key, the cursor moves from left to right. When you reach the end of a row, the cursor starts at the leftmost cell of the next row. Shift+Tab works just the opposite.

Text that you place within a cell automatically wraps within the width of the cell. The row height will automatically change as you add text. The only time that the height will not change is when you have locked the table, something that gets explained later in this chapter under "Merging and Splitting Cells."

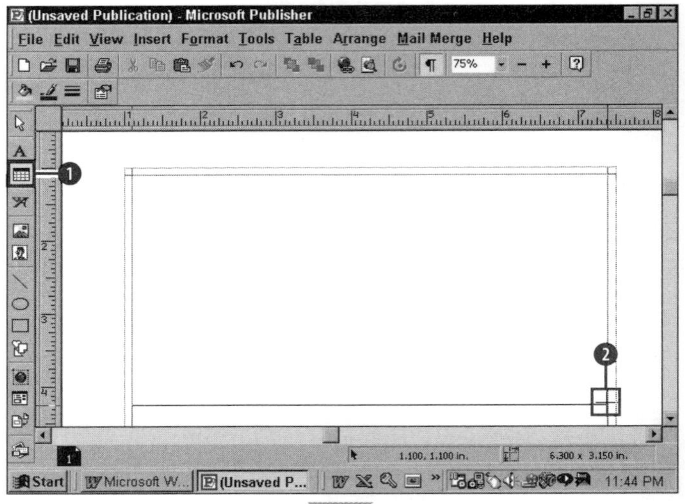

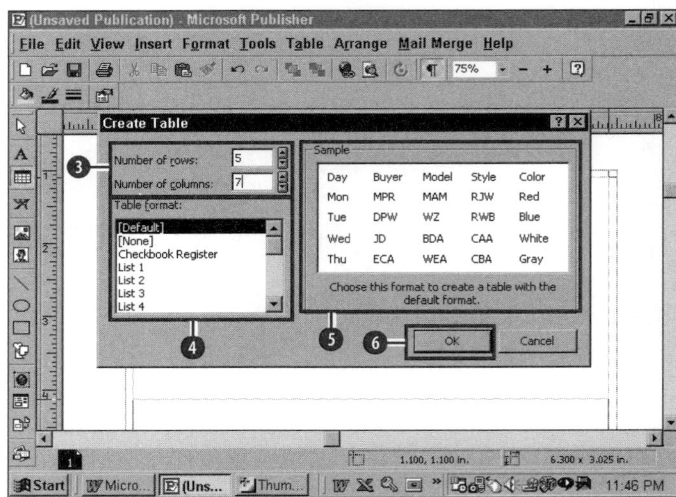

1. *Click the Table Frame tool.*
2. *Draw a frame on the page that will hold the table.*
3. *After the frame is drawn, the Create Table dialog box appears. Indicate the number of rows and columns in the table.*
4. *You can choose a preformat from the "Table format" list.*
5. *The Sample window shows what the preformatted table looks like.*
6. *Click OK to have the table appear in the frame.*

CROSS-REFERENCE

Learn how to create text and picture frames back in Chapter 6.

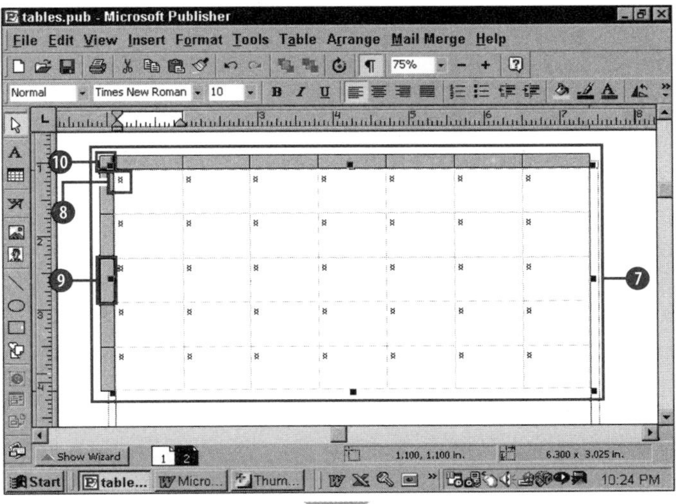

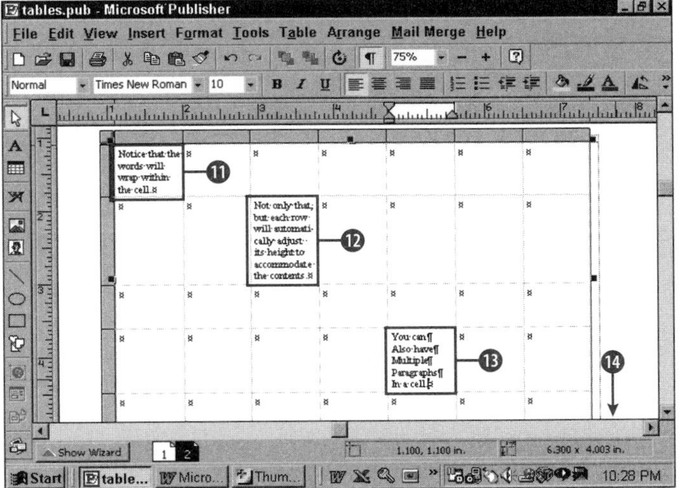

7. *The table is created to fill the frame with the number of rows and columns in Step 3.*
8. *Each cell contains an End of File symbol (choose View ⇨ Show Special Characters to view them).*
9. *To select a row or column, click the buttons at the top of the columns or to the left of the rows.*
10. *This button selects all rows and columns.*
11. *Enter text into the cells. Note that the text will wrap within the cell.*
12. *Also notice that the row expands to accommodate the text in a given cell.*
13. *You can also have multiple paragraphs within a cell.*
14. *Notice that the frame will expand to accommodate the table.*

So, now that you know what tables are and that they can exist in your document, what kinds of things can you do with tables? Probably the most widely used application is making a calendar. You can forgo the wizard and make your own tables with seven columns and about five rows. That should take care of most months.

Organized lists of figures that compare yearly totals, monthly sums, or daily averages are also good applications. Post the swim team events, the swimmers, and their time. Organize a golf tournament and use a table to assemble the foursomes and their tee times. Create a product listing for items that you sell or collect. List your Beanie Babies, their names, birthdays, and value.

How about names and offices for your company or organization? Make one column for a person's name, another for their position in the company, secretary's name, phone extension, and so on. You get the idea — now let's get to it.

TAKE NOTE

USE TABLES IN WEB PAGES

Tables in Publisher will translate to HTML tables when published to a Web page. Don't hesitate to use them.

FIND IT ONLINE

To learn how to accurately and effectively display statistics, check out the resources at **http://ubmail.ubalt.edu/~harsham/statistics/REFSTAT.HTM.**

Inserting and Deleting Rows and Columns

Not everything comes out exactly as planned, so you have to make provisions for change. Publisher does. With just a few clicks of the mouse, you can add rows and columns to your table.

Likewise, deleting rows and columns is just as easy. Another couple of clicks and the highlighted rows and columns will disappear. If you have data in those cells, it will get wasted as well. You can always press Ctrl+Z or choose Edit ➪ Undo to recall the deleted selection back into your table.

Because adding one row or column at a time would be time-consuming, should you have to add several at one time, you can add several rows or columns at once. One way is to drag your mouse over the number of row or column buttons that you want to add. If you want to add more columns or rows than are already in your table, you may have to repeat these steps. When you select Table ➪ Insert Rows or Table ➪ Insert Columns, Publisher will create the number of rows or columns that you highlighted either below or to the right of your selection.

The other option, which gives you greater control, is to place your cursor in a cell. When you go to the Table menu, there is now a selection called Insert Rows or Columns. Selecting this will give you a dialog box where you can indicate the number of rows or columns you want to add and which direction they are to be placed in relation to where cursor is placed.

Choosing Table ➪ Delete Rows and Columns from the menu will give you a dialog box that lets you choose to delete either the row or the column that the cursor resides in.

As you add rows, your frame expands to provide space for them. Adding columns will produce the same results. Be careful, however. As the frame expands, it may expand right out of your margins and off the page.

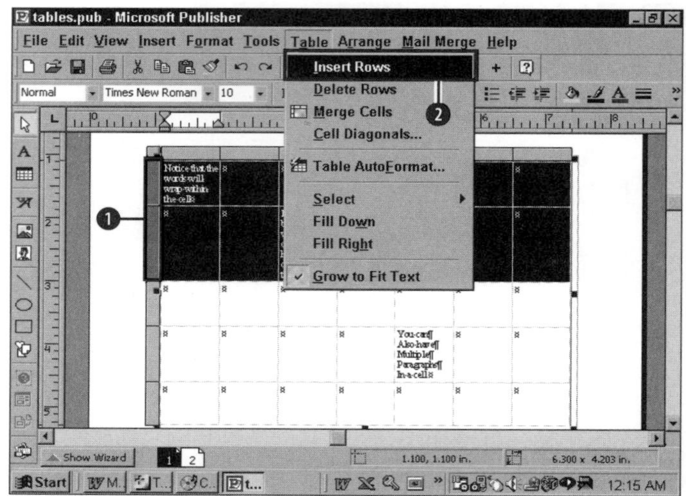

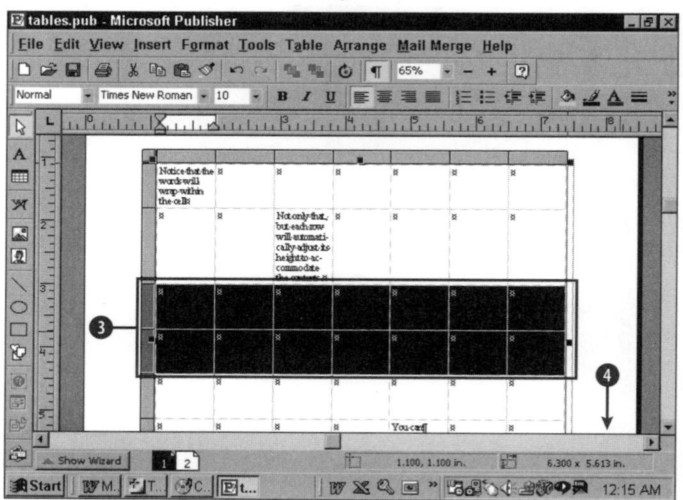

1. To add a couple rows or columns, drag the cursor over the appropriate control buttons.
2. Choose Table ➪ Insert Rows or Insert Columns. The correct menu choice will appear depending on what is highlighted.
3. Blank rows are added below the highlighted selection.
4. The table frame expands to accommodate the added rows or columns.

CROSS-REFERENCE

To refresh your memory on linking text frames, see "Connecting Story Frames" in Chapter 8.

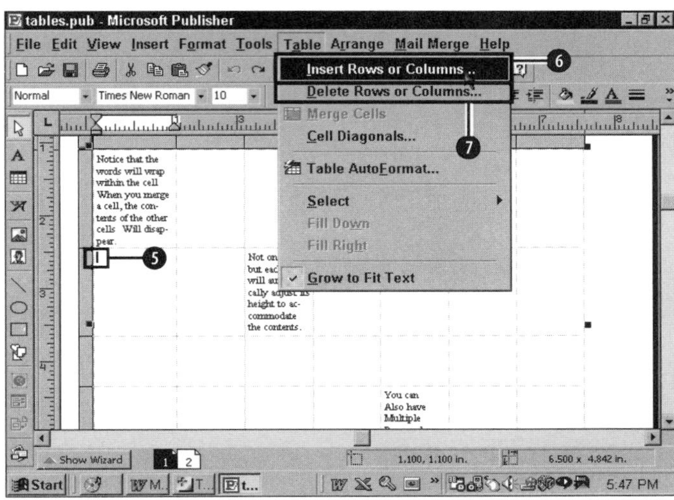

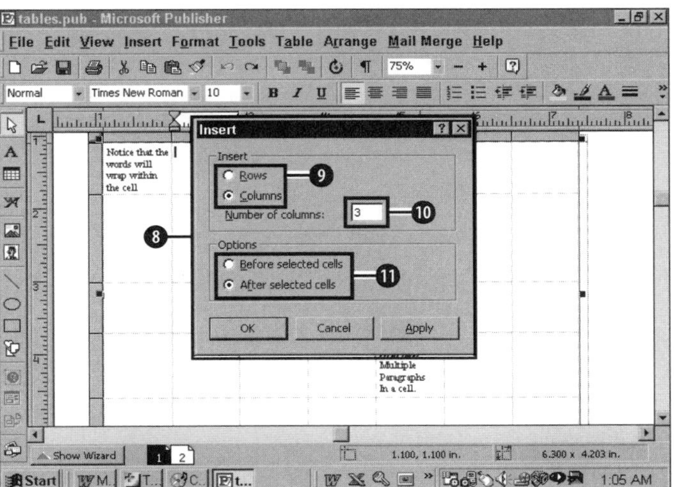

5. *To use the dialog box method to add or delete rows and columns, place your cursor in a cell.*
6. *Choose Table ➪ Insert Rows or Columns to add more rows or columns.*
7. *Choose Table ➪ Delete Rows or Columns to remove rows or columns.*
8. *If you chose to insert rows or columns, the Insert dialog box appears.*
9. *Indicate whether you will be adding rows or columns.*
10. *Enter the number of rows or columns to be added.*
11. *Choose whether to add the rows or columns either before or after the cell where the cursor is placed. Click OK or Apply to add your selection.*

Again, if you don't want to adjust column widths (discussed later in this chapter under "Resizing Rows and Columns"), you can use the Undo command to remove the newly inserted items. Remember that Publisher remembers the last 20 actions. You can undo up to that many things.

TAKE NOTE

LIMITATIONS OF UNDO

As stated above, you can undo up to the last 20 things that Publisher remembers. Although this sounds good at first, you have to remember that procedures are remembered in order. Therefore if you want to undo something you did ten steps ago, you'll loose the nine or so in between that you may want to keep.

TABLES WON'T JUMP PAGES

When creating your tables, plan them to fit on a single page. Unlike text frames that can be linked to different pages, table frames do not enjoy that luxury.

FIND IT ONLINE

For just about any statistic you want to know about children in the U.S., see how tables are used at http://childstats.gov/ac1999/detail.asp.

Merging and Splitting Cells

While rows and columns of cells are useful for organizing data and more, you need a little versatility in formatting. Sure, you can spread columns to adjust for columns that contain more than just a figure or two, but if that's all there were to tables, they'd appear pretty boring.

And, because a lot of tables have headings and such — some having to expand over a couple of columns — Publisher lets you merge cells together. Not just a technique used for column headings, merging cells can also let you eliminate duplicate information in rows. For example, if you have a table of different shirts — their style, color, sizes, and price — why repeat information? Merge the cells that contain the style. You'll end up with a large cell to the left of the smaller cells that describes the rest of the choices in color, size and price.

There's no limit to the table formatting once you start combining cells. Merge cells across an entire row to make a large table heading. Merge just a few cells to make column headings and subheadings. Plus, once the cells are merged, you can format them differently to call attention to them. Fill them with a color, outline them with a border, change the font or type size, or use a combination of all of these. Always keep in mind, though, that tables have a purpose: provide information to the reader in such a way that finding information is simple and easy to understand. Complicated tables are not only a waste of your time to build, but a waste of time for your readers to pore over, searching for information that they may need.

What about pictures? While it is possible to place an image inside a cell or merged cells, it should be considered a workaround. Here's what you do. Once you have all the data (text) in your tables, you lock the table by choosing Table ➪ Grow to Fit Text. You want to be sure

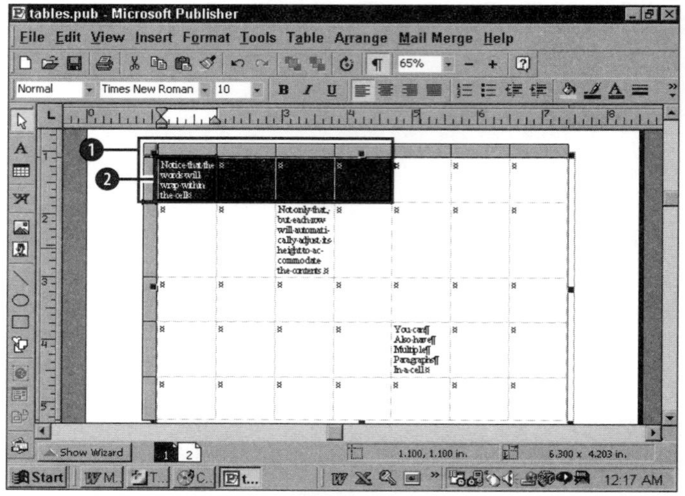

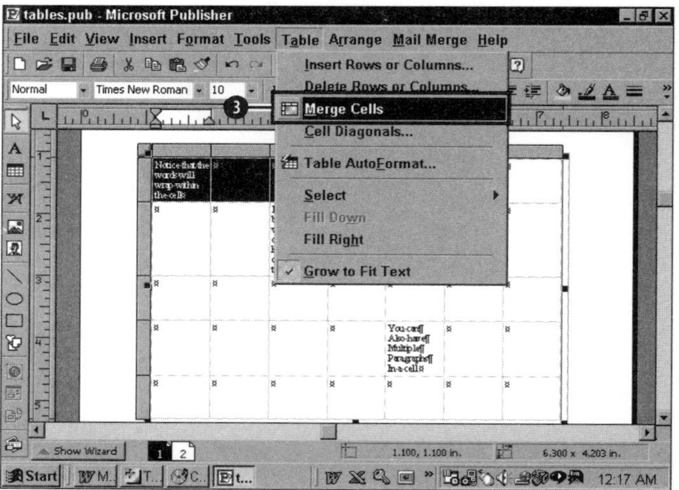

❶ *To merge cells, drag your mouse over the cells that will be merged to select them.*

❷ *The contents of the merged cells will also be merged into one.*

❸ *Once cells are selected, choose Table ➪ Merge Cells.*

CROSS-REFERENCE

Brush up on grouping objects in "Grouping and Ungrouping Objects" in Chapter 7.

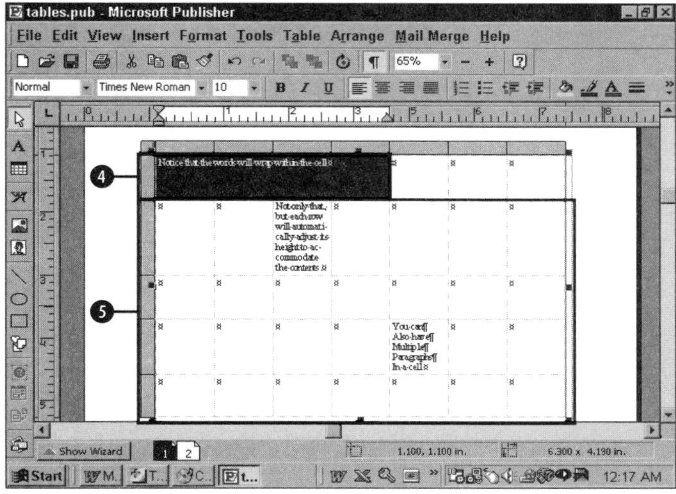

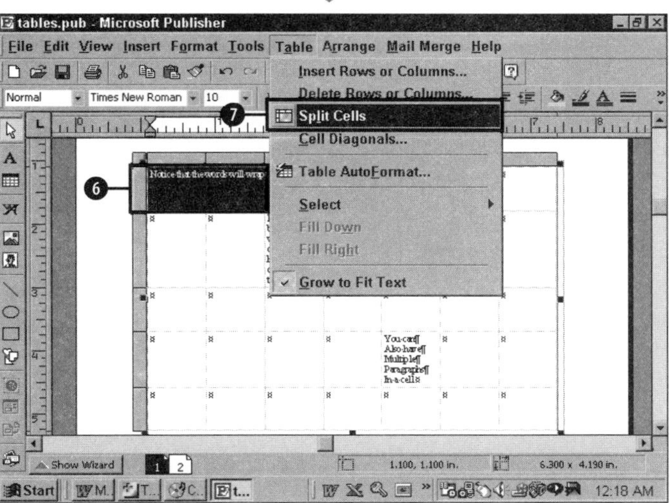

❹ *Cells that were selected will be merged as one.*

❺ *Cells that were not selected, will maintain their column and row position.*

❻ *To split cells, highlight the merged cells as shown here. Or, you can place your cursor someplace in the merged cell.*

❼ *Select Table ➪ Split Cells from the menu. If the previously merged contents were combined with the first cell, all information will remain in the first cell. Text will not split out to its original position in the table.*

that the checkmark is off this setting. This prevents the rows and columns from changing dimensions.

With the table and cells stationary, you can draw a picture frame inside the cell or merged cells and place the image. Though it is not necessary, it's probably a good idea to select all of the image frames and the table frame and group them. That way, you can feel secure when you have to move the group to another location on the page or to another page altogether.

TAKE NOTE

SELECTING CELLS

To select cells to be merged, just drag your mouse over the cells. It doesn't matter whether they're in the same row or column as long as they are connected. Note also that you can merge cells with others that have already been merged. Just drag over the areas you want joined.

FIND IT ONLINE

For a look at how mortgage rates are placed in a table using merged cells, see **http://www.hsh.com/today.html.**

Adding Diagonal Lines to Cells

Merging cells isn't the only feature that Publisher handles when manipulating the cells in tables. Sometimes you just have to split a cell in a way that divides a cell in two. Diagonal lines are excellent for slicing a cell in two.

In Publisher, when you add a diagonal line to a cell, the cell is separated by a line that can either extend from the upper-left to lower-right corner, which Publisher calls Divide Down, or in the opposite way, which is called Divide Up. When the diagonal line is added, you end up with two end of file marks, enabling you to enter text in both compartments. And, while you still have the same flexibility of the row expanding to accommodate the text you enter, it's probably not going to look very attractive with a lot of text in each half. A word or two or some numbers is probably the most ideal use of the diagonal splits. Any excessive amount of text is best left to single or merged cells.

You have probably noticed calendars where the weekends are piggybacked in one square. These types of calendars are targeted toward business use and can come up a little short when scheduling your time off on the weekends. Still, you can use the diagonal splits to drop in those last couple of days in the calendar so as not to waste an entire row that could end up mostly blank.

Other than calendars, you can think of other needs for splitting cells diagonally. When reporting on stock prices, you can diagonally split a cell to indicate the high and low prices. Or, the same thing can be done for temperatures. The high and low for the day can be placed in these formatted cells. You can also use this technique to indicate a suggested retail price versus the sale price. Just about any sport could use split cells to track scoring, errors, fouls, and on and on.

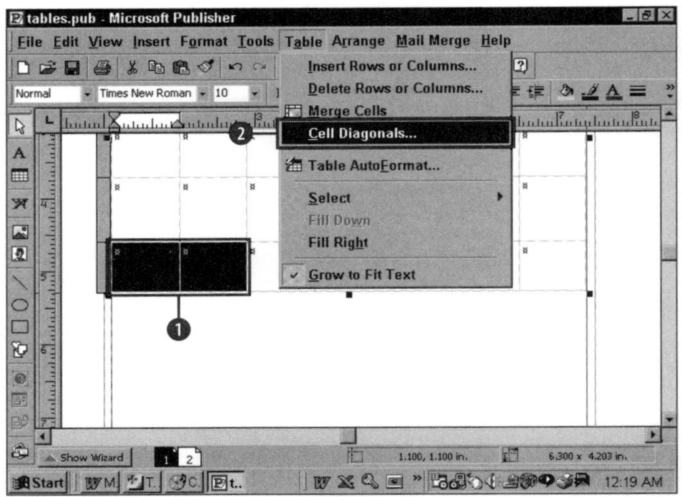

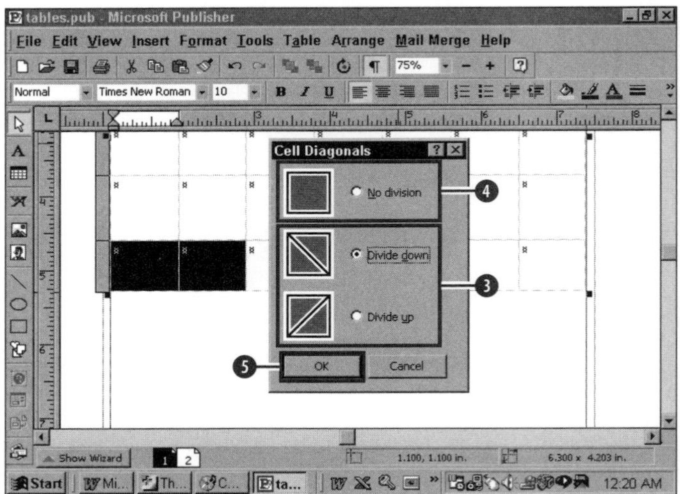

1. To add diagonal lines to a cell, place your cursor in that cell. To select a group of cells, drag the mouse to select them.
2. Choose Table ⇨ Cell Diagonals.
3. In the Cell Diagonals dialog box, choose one of the two diagonal choices.
4. If you are removing the diagonal from the cell, choose the "No division" option.
5. Click OK to assign the diagonal division or remove it.

CROSS-REFERENCE

To review merging cells, back up to the previous task.

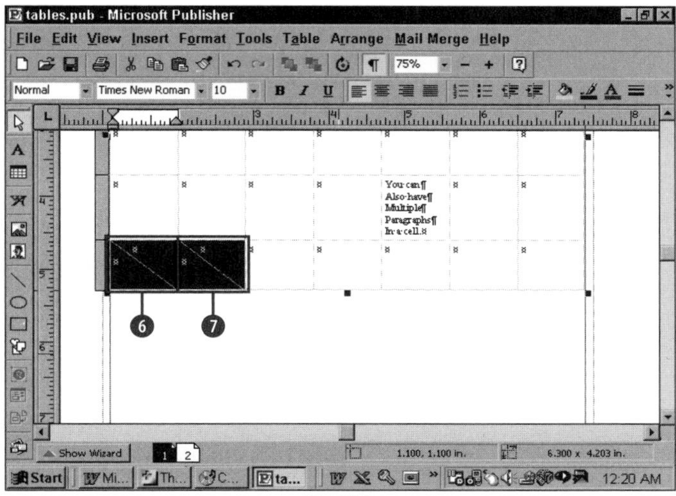

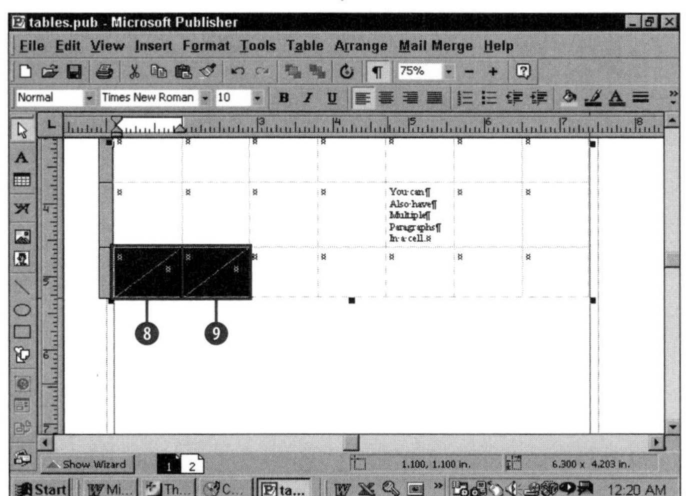

6 *"Divide down" places a diagonal line from the top-left corner to the bottom right.*

7 *End of file marks are placed in each division.*

8 *"Divide up" splits the cell in the opposite direction, with the line running from the bottom-left corner to the top right.*

9 *End of file marks are placed in each division.*

TAKE NOTE

REMOVING DIAGONALS WILL MERGE TEXT

If you need to remove the diagonal split after you have entered information into the splits, there's nothing to fear. The contents of the two divisions will be merged into the single remaining cell once the diagonal split is removed. Reassigning the diagonal split after it has been removed, however will not split the text into its original locations. You'll have to cut and paste the text or rekey the information in.

MERGING AND SPLITTING CELLS

If you merge cells that have diagonal splits, you will lose the diagonal settings and the text will be merged in the single resulting cell. However, once you have merged the cells, you can add a diagonal split. So, you can use these two features in tandem with each other, but just be sure you merge and then assign the diagonal split.

FIND IT ONLINE

The math tables at **http://www.sisweb.com/math/tables.htm** not only show many examples, but they'll help with homework.

Resizing Rows and Columns

If you're the type person who is satisfied with going into a restaurant and closing your eyes to point at something on the menu to eat, you may be happy with the columns and rows that Publisher dishes up when you first create the table. I doubt that's the case, though. You are a publisher who sweats over every project, fidgeting here and tweaking there.

Lucky for you that the width of columns and height of rows aren't cast in stone. As a matter of fact, you have complete control over these facets of your tables. Columns may be sized wider or leaner; rows can be forced to a specific height.

When you draw your table frame and specify the number of columns and rows, Publisher defaults to dividing up these elements within the drawn frame. As mentioned at the outset of this chapter, the frame will expand according to the contents of the cells. When you add columns or rows, you run the risk of the table bloating off of the page. Rather than deleting columns and rows to restrain the frame, you can adjust the width of the columns and height of the rows. Because text automatically wraps within the cell, most of the time this presents no problem.

The buttons at the top of the columns and the left side of the rows are the keys to making these adjustments. You position the cursor on the button border to the right side of a column or the bottom border of the row. When the cursor is in place, it will change to the Adjust cursor. Then, it's just a matter of dragging the border to the new width or height.

When dragging the mouse to resize these rows or columns, you'll notice the rows below or columns to the right will be outlined in a dashed rule line. This indicates that these will move as you make the adjustment. If you don't want these elements to move at all, hold the

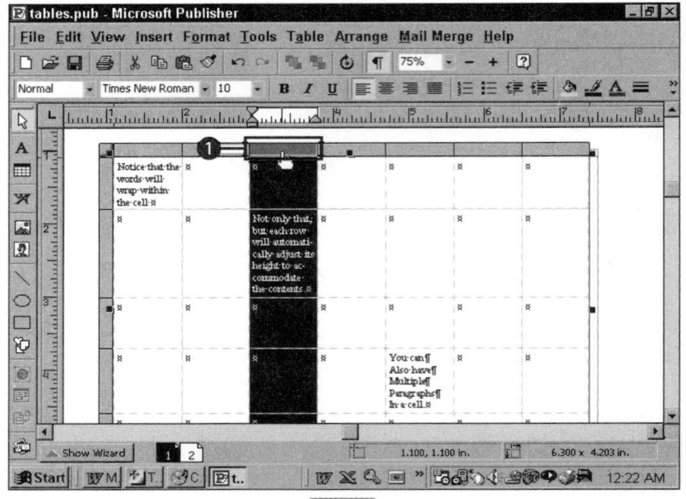

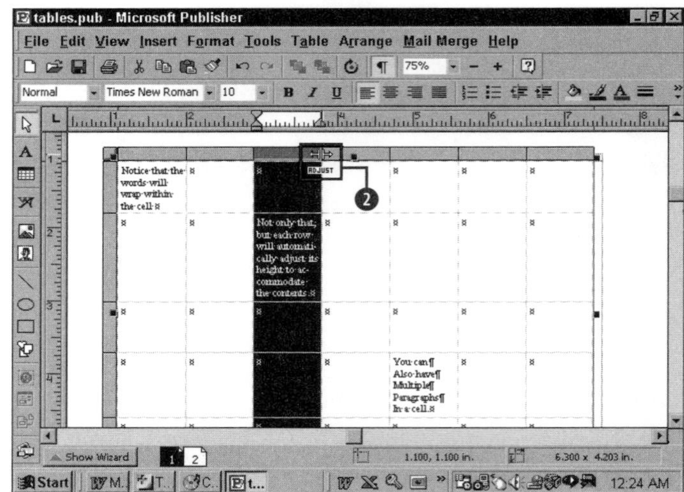

❶ *You can select the column or row to be sized, but it's not really necessary.*

❷ *Place your cursor over the right or bottom border of the button of the column or row you want to resize. Note that the Adjust cursor appears.*

CROSS-REFERENCE

Because dragging the mouse will recognize any guides you have set up, review layout guides in Chapter 7.

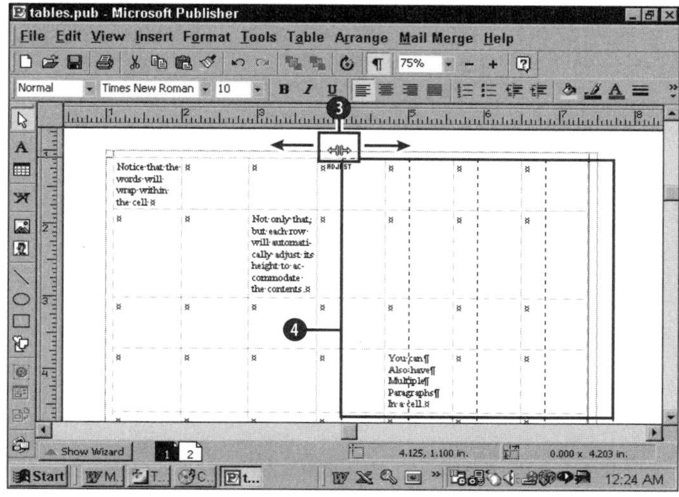

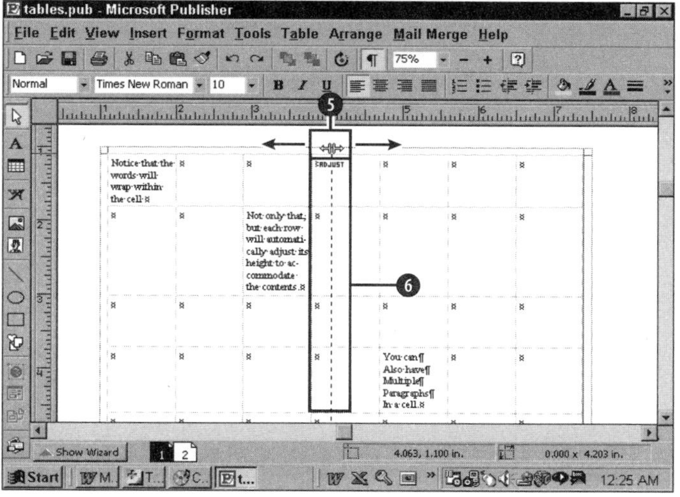

❸ *Drag to expand or shrink the column or row.*

❹ *The remaining columns or rows will be moved to compensate for the new size of the column or row.*

❺ *Holding the Shift key while dragging does not change the position of the remaining columns or rows.*

❻ *Only the column to the right or row below will be affected by the resizing.*

Shift key while you drag. When you Shift+drag, the column or row will be adjusted, but at the cost of the next column or row getting diminished by however much space you drag.

TAKE NOTE

WORK YOUR WAY RIGHT, THEN DOWN

When using the Shift+drag method to resize, you may find it less frustrating to move across the table and adjust the columns and then proceed down to adjust the rows. Of course, it's best to populate the table with all the data, headers, and subheaders. Also, go ahead and merge cells and assign any diagonals that you need before making adjustments.

DON'T FORGET UNDO

Table adjustments may be undone using Ctrl+Z or Edit ➪ Undo. Don't be afraid to experiment adjusting the columns and rows to maximize the page space that a table takes up.

FIND IT ONLINE

See one of the most popular and well-known tables at **http://tqd.advanced.org/2690/ptable/ptable.html.**

Filling Rows and Columns with Repeating Text

Publisher can save you some time when entering in information in your tables. With the autofill feature that's found in the Table menu, you can repeat text across rows and down columns. Though not a feature you may use every day, it can be handy. However, keep reading this task intro to learn another way that may be more useful to you.

When repeating text in the rows and columns, you'll find that is the only thing that Publisher 2000 will do. If you've had some experience with Microsoft Excel, you know that you can autofill a row or column with successive numbers or alpha characters. If you place a 1 in the first cell of a column and autofill down that column, Excel will place successive numbers in the column.

This is not the case with Publisher. When you enter a 1 in the cell and instruct Publisher to Fill Down or Fill Right, you'll get the same character. Not as intelligent and useful as Excel's feature, but it still has possibilities.

The reason I mention Excel and its capabilities is that it is possible to create a table in Excel using that programs advanced handling of numbering and mathematical equations and place it in Publisher. It's just a matter of highlighting the cells in Excel that you want to place in Publisher, selecting Edit ➪ Copy, then going to your table frame in Publisher and choosing Edit ➪ Paste.

When you paste an Excel spreadsheet into Publisher, your formulas are automatically converted to values, so you won't be able to edit those. You can still edit the text as if you typed it into Publisher to begin with. But that's about the only bad news. Your text formatting stays intact. Borders and colors, however, won't make the transition.

So, if you have a lot of tables to produce, you may find Excel an excellent tool to create tables to place into your publication.

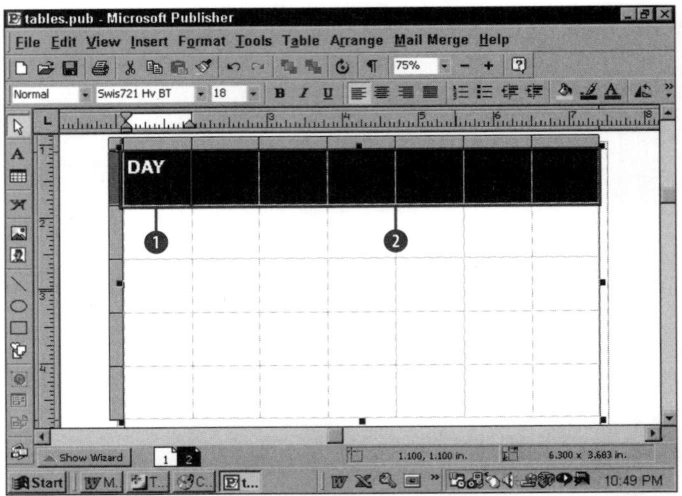

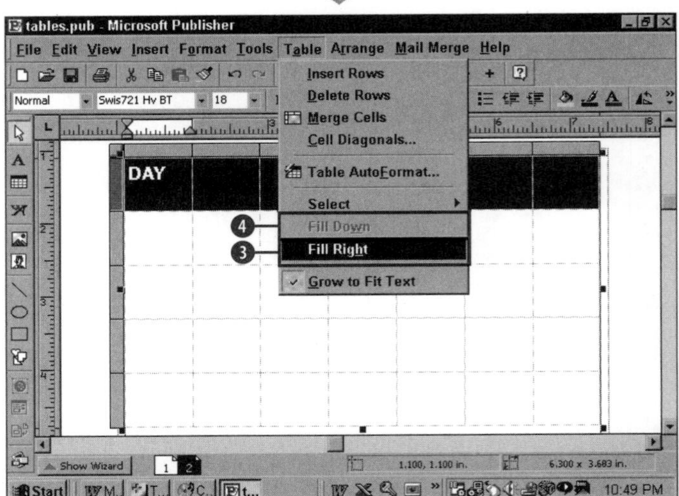

1. *To repeat text across a row, enter the text in the first cell.*
2. *Select the cells that will receive the repeated text.*
3. *Choose Table ➪ Fill Right.*
4. *If a column were being filled, you'd select Table ➪ Fill Down.*

CROSS-REFERENCE

Learn how to create and use text styles in Chapter 8.

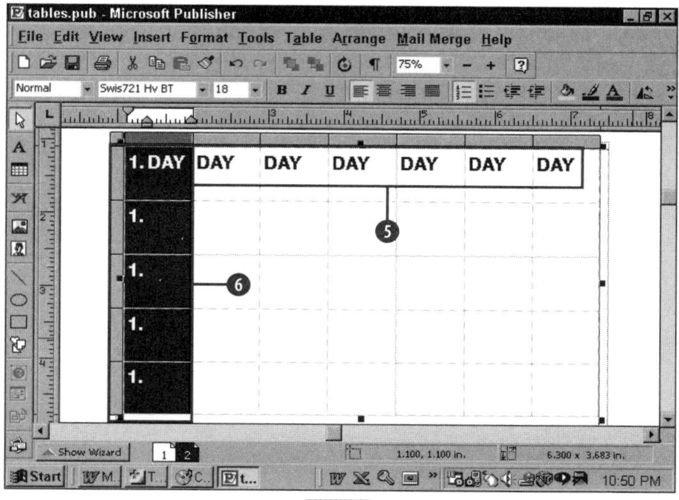

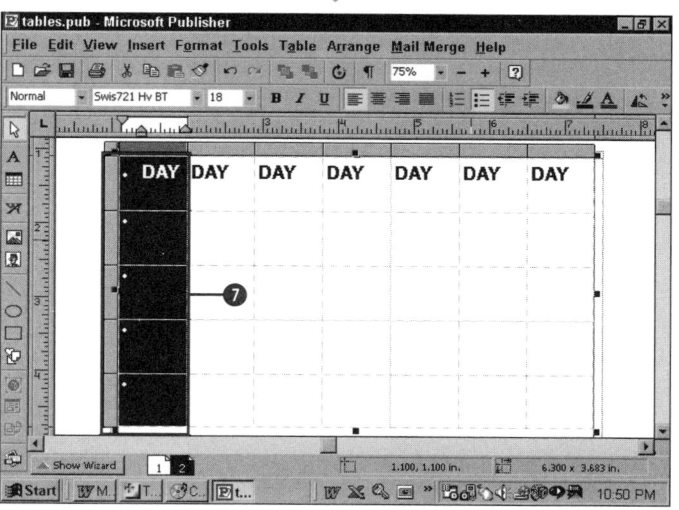

5 *Text will get repeated across the row.*

6 *Text elements within the cells are receptive to text styles and Publisher's numbering.*

7 *Text within the cells may also be formatted with bullets.*

TAKE NOTE

FORMATTING TEXT IN TABLES

Because the text in your table is treated like any other text within the publication, you can use the text styles that you have set up as well as the bullets and autonumbering of text. One caveat to the autonumbering, however, is that the numbering is increased and formatted as such only within the cell, not within the entire table. So if you try to autonumber all the way down a column, each cell will be numbered 1, waiting for you to press Enter to begin a new paragraph within the cell. Then the autonumbering will continue.

WHAT REPEATS AND WHAT DOESN'T

When you use the Fill Down or Fill Right table feature, you'll find that the text formatting that you have assigned to the text being copied will be duplicated. However, any cell background color fill or border formatting will not get duplicated.

FIND IT ONLINE

Find out more about Microsoft Excel at **http://officeupdate.microsoft.com/welcome/excel.htm.**

Formatting Cells

Because table cells are like a group of small text frames, you have some of the formatting capabilities that other text frames have. In particular, you can specify the inside margins, fill color and pattern, and borders. This can add some life to otherwise boring facts and figures. And, by adding some life, you can increase its readability.

You can control the inside spacing of each cell. Especially if you are going to add borders, you need to nudge the text a bit to keep it away from the borders. When you set the margins, you create a buffer space between the text and the edges of the cell. You may find it more efficient to set the borders before setting the spacing. Optically, you may need to add a little more space if you use thicker borders.

Formatting the text in your table also means selecting the right fonts to use. Of course, you want to select a font that coordinates with the rest of the publication. Like a well-dressed model in *GQ*, everything in the publication should meld into one finely designed, spiffy ensemble.

Adding a color background to your cells can also add emphasis. Especially useful for column headers and subheadings, color backgrounds can break up a large table and make it look a lot more organized.

Cells can have borders as well as the entire table. As a matter of fact, the table border is not limited to dull rule lines. You can use any of the decorative borders that you would use on any other frame. When adding one of the BorderArt frames, the table gets reduced to fit within the border inside the frame. Exercise moderation, however, and make the border fit the mood of the publication.

Want to add a drop shadow to the table frame? It's a simple process and can add some dimension to the table, making it appear as if it floats on the page. There's not a lot of choice in shadow configuration. You

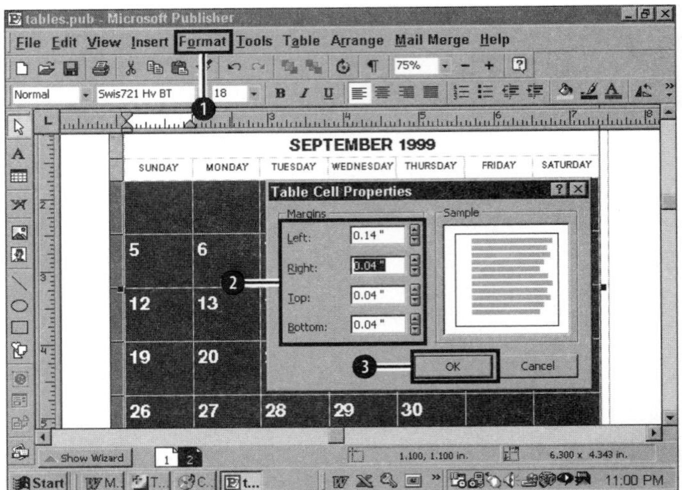

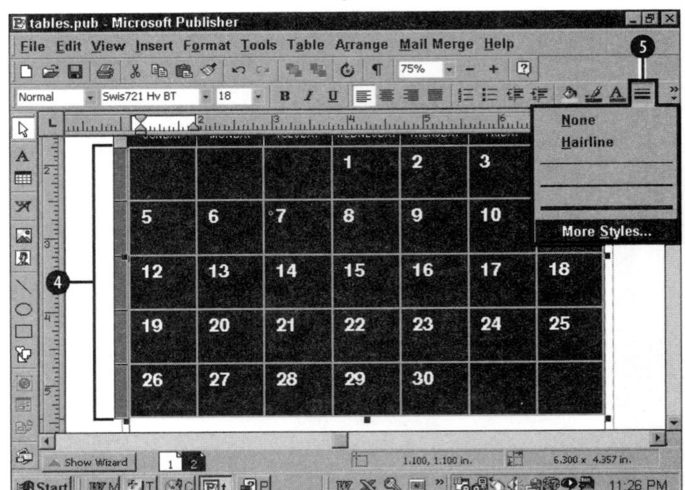

1. *To set the margins within the cells, select the cells for which you want to change the margins and choose Format ⇨ Table Cell Properties.*
2. *Change the individual margins.*
3. *Click OK to add the inside spacing to the cells.*
4. *To set the borders for the cells or the entire table, select the table.*
5. *Choose one of the preset line widths from the Border button on the toolbar, or choose More Styles to open the Border Style dialog box.*

CROSS-REFERENCE

See Chapter 12 to learn of Publisher's fill effects and color options.

either turn it on or leave it off. The default shadow is a typical gray and is set down and to the right of the table frame.

TAKE NOTE

TRY A CONDENSED FONT

Many times a table will contain text that can get pretty long. In order to get the most out of your columns and rows, not to mention the space that the entire table itself takes up, you could try using a condensed font for the table data. Thinner letters means smaller line lengths. Just be sure to use a large enough font to keep the text readable.

USE THE PUBLICATION COLOR SCHEME

Rest assured that you aren't on your own when selecting colors for your table. You can use one of the color schemes that Publisher has to offer or be creative on your own.

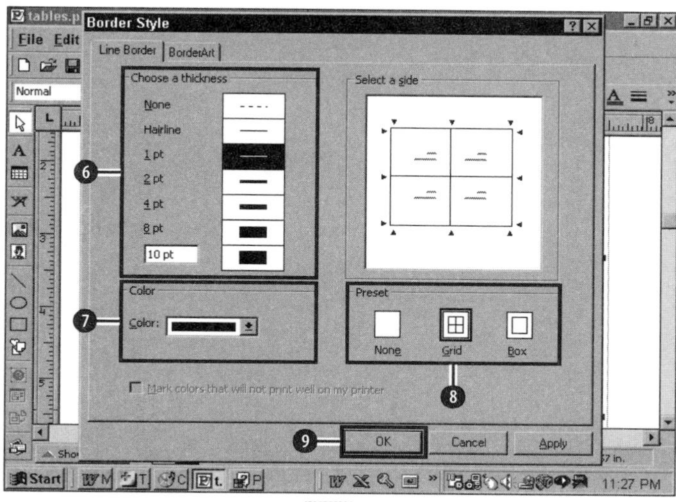

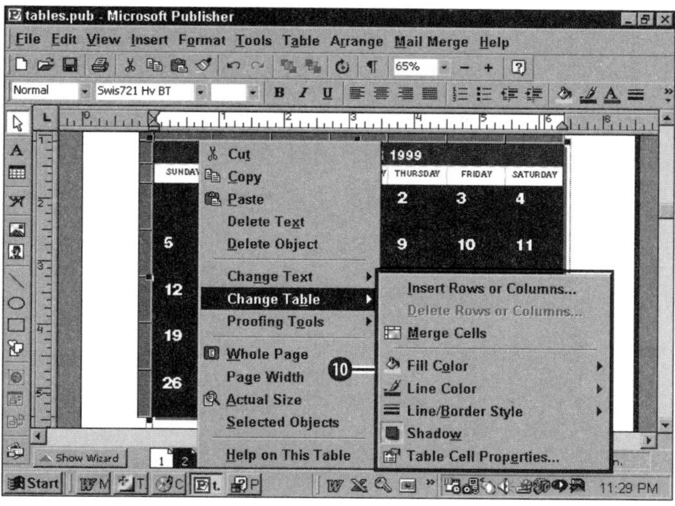

6. *In the Border Style dialog box, choose a line thickness.*
7. *Select a color from the drop-down list or choose one of the two buttons for more color and style options.*
8. *Choose the Preset option for the border. This controls where the border is placed in relation to the cells that you have highlighted.*
9. *Click OK to apply the borders.*
10. *Rather than use the Table and Format menus to reach the different settings available for your table, right-click on the selected cells and choose Change Table.*

▶ *All of the possible formatting options are in this menu.*

FIND IT ONLINE

For an example of a colorful table that uses borders, go to **http://soccer.simplenet.com/ned_but.htm**.

Formatting Your Table with Autoformat

Given that Publisher is so user-friendly and comes with wizards and presets that speed up your work, it only follows that tables are no exception. With over 20 different configurations to choose from, even the design-squeamish can come up with a decent-looking table.

Getting a jump on the format of your table is a good idea. Not only will the borders, colors, and alignment be taken care of, but you save an enormous amount of time. Plus, you aren't locked into the setting. Once the preformat has been established, you can make minor adjustments to the design to make it your very own creation.

The best way to become familiar with the different categories of the predesigned settings is to open the AutoFormat dialog box and scroll through the list. Each selection gives you a color preview. The list takes several configurations into consideration. Text and numerical configurations, and combinations of both, are included. There's even a few ideas on creating a table of contents using — what else — tables.

So, what is included in these designs? Borders and rule lines can be chosen, as well as the color scheme of the entire table. Although the font shown in the preview will not be what you get, you do get the bold, italic, or normal style.

When the dialog box opens, don't forget to click the Options button. The four settings there will let you pick and choose which design elements you want AutoFormat to carry over to your table. Text formatting and alignment, as well as the borders and pattern and shading, can be turned off or on. For example, if you like everything in the preset design except the shading of the cells, take the checkmark off that option. The remaining styles will be assigned as soon as you click OK.

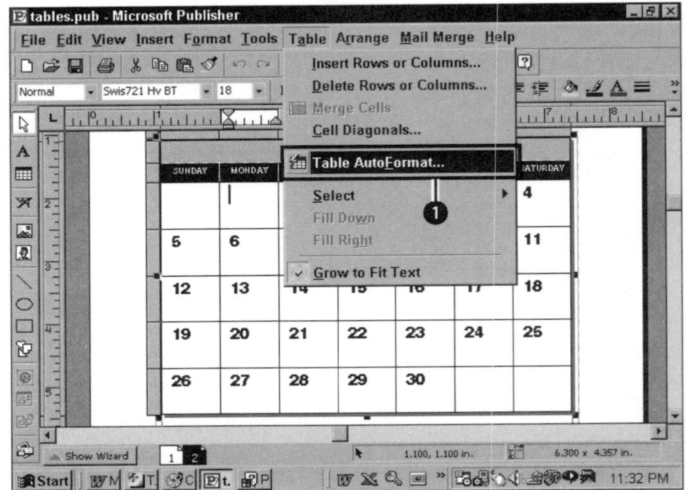

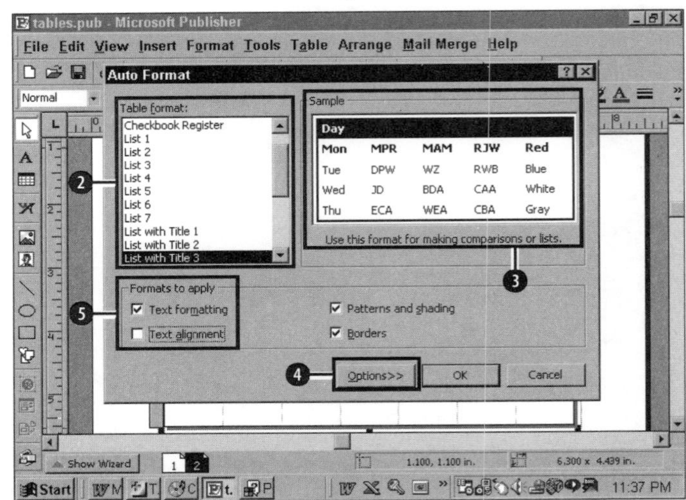

1. With your cursor placed in one of the cells of the table, choose *Table ⇨ Table AutoFormat*.
2. *Select one of the predesigned styles in the "Table format" list.*
3. *Preview the design in the Sample window.*
4. *If the "Formats to apply" section is not visible, click the Options button.*
5. *Choose which formats to apply to your table by placing a check in the options.*

CROSS-REFERENCE

Size your table frame the same as any other frame. Review how in Chapter 6.

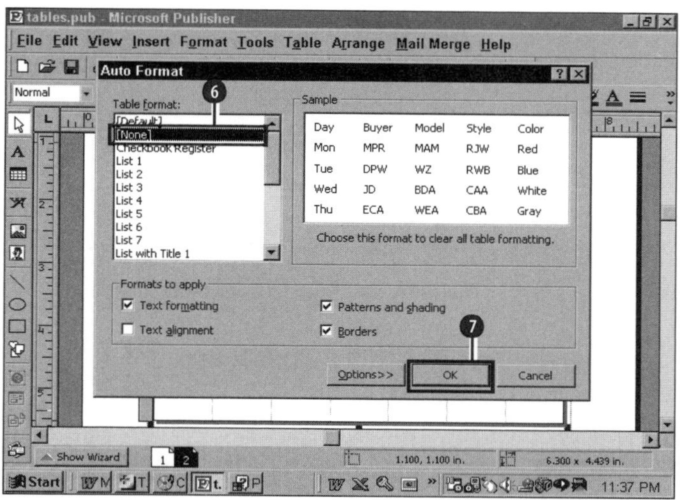

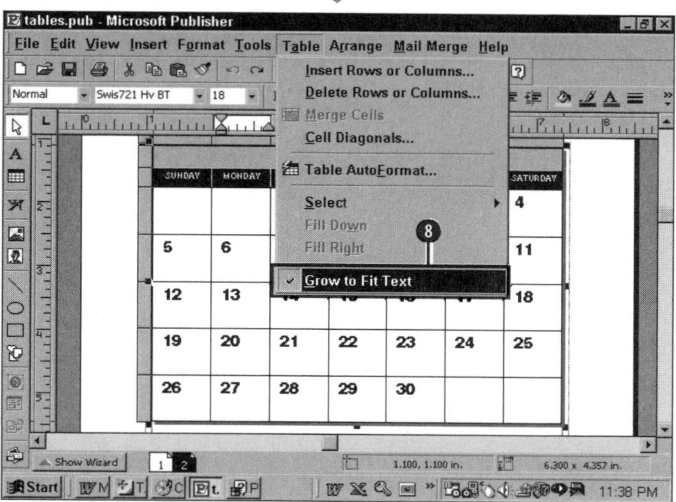

❻ *To remove all formatting from your table, choose the None option in the "Table format" list.*

❼ *Click OK to format your table as you have selected.*

❽ *To lock your table's row and column configuration, select Table ➪ Grow to Fit Text and remove the checkmark.*

Once you have the table the way you want it, it's a good idea to lock the table so that you don't accidentally change the width or height of the cells, and the frame won't automatically expand or reduce. Locking the table takes only a few mouse clicks — choose Table ➪ Grow to Fit Text and remove the checkmark next to the selection.

TAKE NOTE

REMOVING ALL TABLE FORMATTING

If you've gone too far in your table design and want to start over from scratch, you can select the None option in the Table Format listing. This will remove all borders, color, text styles, and alignment. Once applied, you can open the AutoFormat dialog box again and choose a different design.

DON'T FORGET THE DINGBAT FONT

When inserting checkmarks or bullets in columns of your table, don't forget that the Zapf Dingbat or Wingdings font is full of neat symbols to dress up your table.

FIND IT ONLINE

Because Publisher tables translate to HTML, you don't have to do any programming. See **http://www.ccse.net/~harris/designhome/tables.html.**

Personal Workbook

Q&A

1. Tables, like any text or image, have to reside in what type of container?

2. When you add columns or rows to a table, what do you run the risk of having happen to the table?

3. What technique does Publisher offer to accommodate headers and subheads that span across several columns?

4. When you remove a diagonal line from a cell, what happens to the contents of both halves?

5. When you resize columns and rows, what useful Publisher feature can you use to ensure that the borders of columns and rows will be placed in an exact location on the page?

6. To be sure that you are only changing the width of one column or height of one row in addition to the one next to it, what key do you press while dragging the border?

7. What other program in the Microsoft Office Suite can you use to aid you in creating tables in Publisher?

8. When using the Table AutoFormat preset designs, what one element seen in the Preview window will not get changed?

ANSWERS: PAGE 354

Working with Tables

CHAPTER 10

EXTRA PRACTICE

1. Create a custom calendar with all of the events happening at work for a given month. Use the BorderArt feature to choose an appropriate outline for the table, given the month you are producing. Post it in the company lounge area.
2. Make a table of household chores for the children. Use the first column for the child's name and list several chores per child in the next column. When complete, merge the cells where the child's name is the same, leaving the chores separated.
3. Make a table for your bowling league with columns for the bowler's name, handicap, date, and score.
4. Create a table that lists all the software that you own. Include the version and serial numbers. You could also list the phone number for technical support.

REAL-WORLD APPLICATIONS

- ✔ In your company's annual report, include a table that compares financial figures for the last three years, broken down into categories.
- ✔ Use a table to make a calendar of events for your organization. Instead of a typical monthly calendar, you use one column for the date and another for the event.
- ✔ Create a table that lists all of the equipment and furnishings in your office. Include manufacturer, date purchased, model number, serial number, and where purchased.
- ✔ Develop a product sheet where a large photo of the product is on the front of the page. On the back, list the features of the product using a table.

Visual Quiz

In this calendar, identify all of the places where cells were merged.

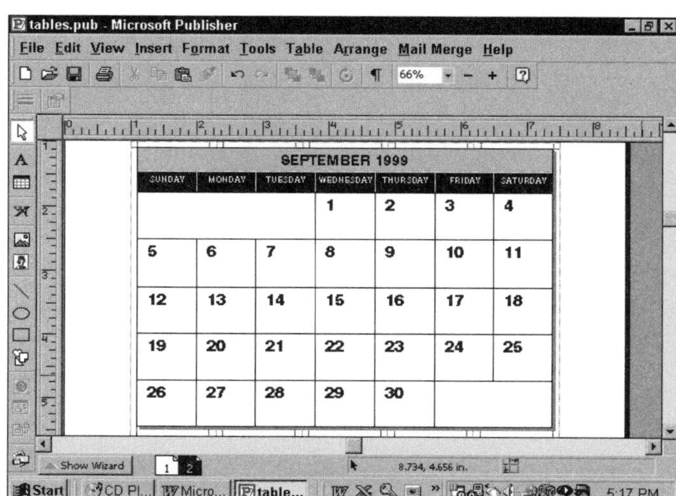

PART IV

Putting Art into Your Publication

A veritable digital museum awaits you in this part. You will explore the many different sources of photos, clip art, and even movies that are placed on the Publisher CD-ROMs. This part unlocks the museum gate and lets you pilfer and ravage thousands of images to include in your document.

Not only are "secret" sources revealed, but you learn how to place these treasures within your publication. You will also discover how to masterfully alter images to suit your needs, even to the extent that the final image is hardly recognizable from its original state.

Of course, CD-ROMs aren't the only source for art. Those who have scanners and digital cameras will see how to use those devices with Publisher and import those prize images.

From manipulation of the images themselves to the alterations of those images on the page itself, this part will have you yearning for larger hard drives to store those graphics to use in untold ways.

CHAPTER 11

MASTER THESE SKILLS

- Importing Pictures with the Picture Frame Tool
- Importing Clip Art from the Clip Gallery
- Adding Images to the Clip Gallery
- Using Clip Gallery Live
- Using Paste Special to Insert Graphics
- Using the Cropping Tool
- Acquiring Images from Scanners and Digital Cameras

Importing Pictures and Clip Art

Microsoft Publisher 2000, as you've seen, is a whiz at handling text — but if all you were interested in were text, you wouldn't need desktop publishing software. Desktop publishing really comes to life with the addition of illustrations: clip art, drawings, diagrams, and photographs. Illustrations have a way of clarifying ideas that, presented solely in words, are hard to understand. They also go a long way toward improving the look of your publication by breaking up all those gray blocks of text!

Most computer users have gathered an extensive collection of images from a variety of sources. Publisher lets you easily import pictures from your hard, floppy, CD-ROM and DVD-ROM drives, and place them where you want and crop them so they look their best. In addition, Publisher itself comes with a large collection of clip art and photographs you're free to use. All these images are carefully organized by category and keyword in the Clip Gallery, where you can find images to illustrate just about any topic quickly and easily. You can also add your own pictures to the Clip Gallery; or, if you can't find exactly what you want, you can add additional images from Clip Gallery Live, Microsoft's image-packed Web site for Clip Gallery users.

You may have a specialized program that you often use to create illustrations, charts, or diagrams. Some of those images may even be dynamic, changing regularly as you receive new information. By using the Paste Special command, you can import those images into your Publisher publication, while retaining the capability to edit them in the application in which they were created. Not only that, you can even link the image in Publisher with the original, so that any changes to the original are automatically reflected in your publication.

Nor are you limited to images that currently exist on your computer. With scanners and digital cameras, it's now easier than ever to capture printed documents, hand-drawn artwork, or photographs in digital format. Publisher lets you add images directly from any scanner or digital camera to your publication, as well.

A picture is worth a thousand words, they say, but pictures and words together are worth even more (this book is a perfect example!). Publisher makes it easy to combine images and text so that both are enhanced, and your message is more clearly communicated than it could be by either alone.

Importing Pictures with the Picture Frame Tool

As you saw in the last part of this book, Publisher organizes content into frames. Text goes into text frames, and pictures go into picture frames (naturally).

A Publisher picture frame is like a real picture frame in that you can place it wherever you want within your publication, just as you can hang a picture in a real picture frame anywhere you want on your wall. Publisher picture frames are also similar to real picture frames in that they don't care what kind of picture is inside them. Whether you've inserted a computer drawing, a scanned image, or something from the Clip Gallery, the frame works the same.

Publisher picture frames are unlike regular picture frames, however, in that the frames themselves can be resized, in the process changing the size of the picture they contain. They can even be shrunk or expanded more in one direction than another. Of course, that tends to distort the picture — but sometimes that's exactly the effect you want.

Publisher picture frames can also be adjusted without changing the size of the picture they contain — just hiding parts of it. This is called "cropping," and it can go a long way toward changing a mediocre picture into a perfect one.

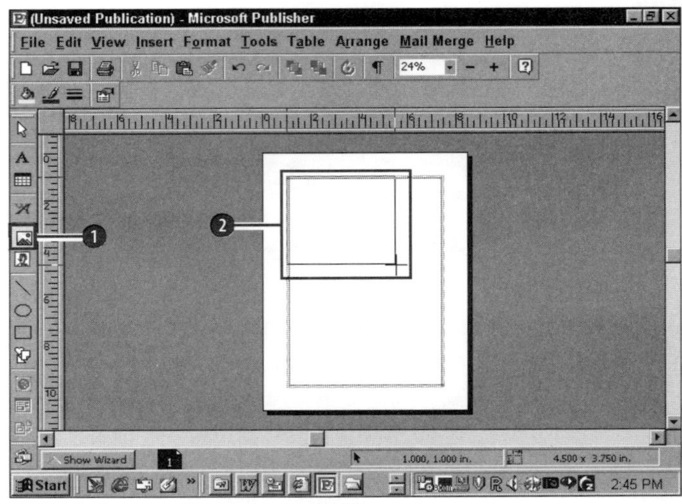

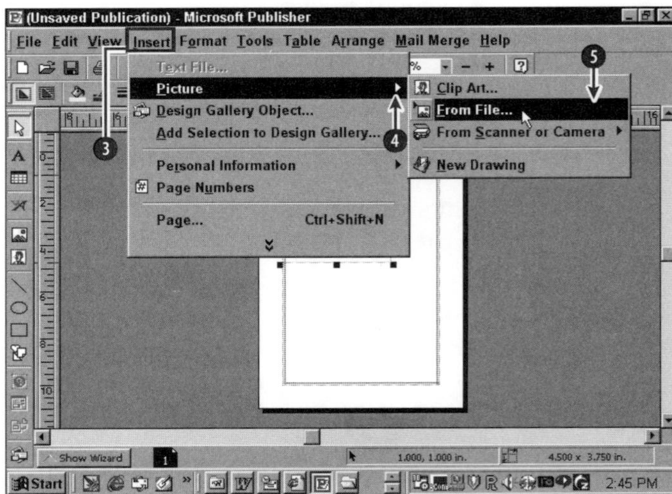

1. *Click the Picture Frame Tool button on the Objects toolbar.*
2. *Draw a frame the height you want and approximately the width you want.*
3. *Choose Insert from the menu bar.*
4. *Choose Picture from the Insert menu.*
5. *From the Picture menu, select the type of picture you want to insert.*

CROSS-REFERENCE

See "Using the Cropping Tool" later in this chapter for more on making the picture fit the frame — and vice versa.

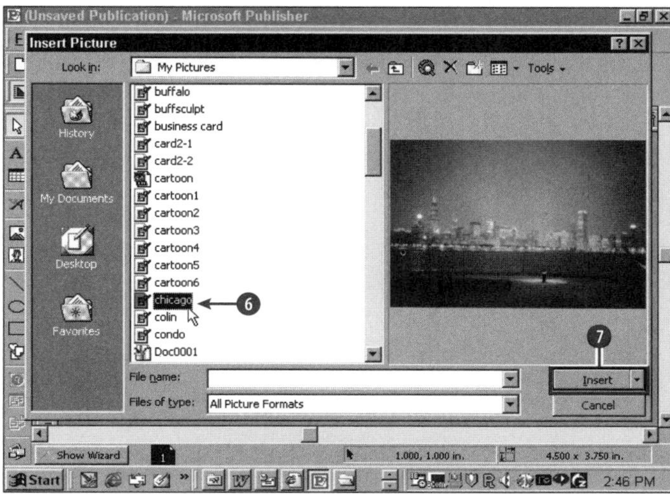

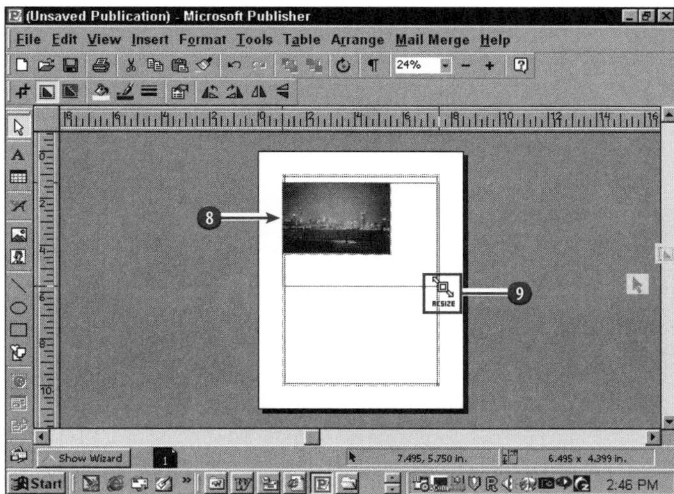

6. *If you choose From File, browse for the file you want to insert. Graphic files are previewed.*
7. *Highlight the file you want to insert and click Insert.*
8. *The image you chose appears in the frame, which adjusts its width automatically.*
9. *Resize the image by using the frame's handles. To change the size without changing the proportions, use a corner handle.*

TAKE NOTE

GRAPHIC FORMATS PUBLISHER CAN IMPORT

Publisher can import pictures created in a variety of formats, including Windows Bitmap (.bmp), CorelDRAW! (.cdr), CGM graphics (.cgm), Windows Enhanced Metafile (.emf), Encapsulated Postscript (.eps), Graphics Interchange Format (CompuServe format) (.gif), Joint Photographic Expert Group (.jpeg or .jpg), Kodak Photo CD and Pro Photo CD (.pcd), PC Paintbrush (.pcx), Macintosh Picture (.pict), Portable Network Graphics (.png), TIFF, Tagged Image File Format (.tif), Windows Metafile (.wmf) and WordPerfect Graphics (.wpg). Occasionally, the first time you try to import one of the less-common formats, you'll be told that feature isn't currently installed and asked if you want to install it. If you say yes, you'll need your Publisher disk.

FRAMES RESIZE AUTOMATICALLY

When you draw a picture frame, and then import a picture, the frame sometimes changes to fit the shape of the picture. Images from the Clip Gallery give you the option of changing the frame to fit the picture or the picture to fit the frame, but images you simply import from somewhere else on your computer automatically change the frame to match their dimensions. Fortunately, the frame only changes in one dimension: width. The picture, no matter what sort it is, is automatically resized to fit the frame's height.

FIND IT ONLINE

Find out more about the various terms used in computer graphics at **http://www.computingcentral.com/topics/graphics/glossary.asp.**

Importing Clip Art from the Clip Gallery

In the last task, you learned how to import a graphic file from a disk on your computer to your Publisher publication. You have several other options for inserting images. One is the Clip Gallery.

Clip Gallery is a separate, built-in program for organizing clip art and other images, including photographs or sound and video clips. You can assign keywords and categories to clips as you see fit.

When you install Publisher, Clip Gallery is also automatically installed, along with a large selection of clip art ready for your use. Later you can add any clip art you may already have to Clip Gallery so you can find it more easily when you work on future publications. You can also add clip art from Microsoft's Clip Gallery Live Web site.

Clip Gallery's greatest asset is its search capabilities. You can look for clips under broad categories, such as Academics or Entertainment, or search out clips from many different categories by entering keywords.

Particularly when time is of the essence, the Clip Gallery is the place to go to find exactly the right art to illustrate your publication.

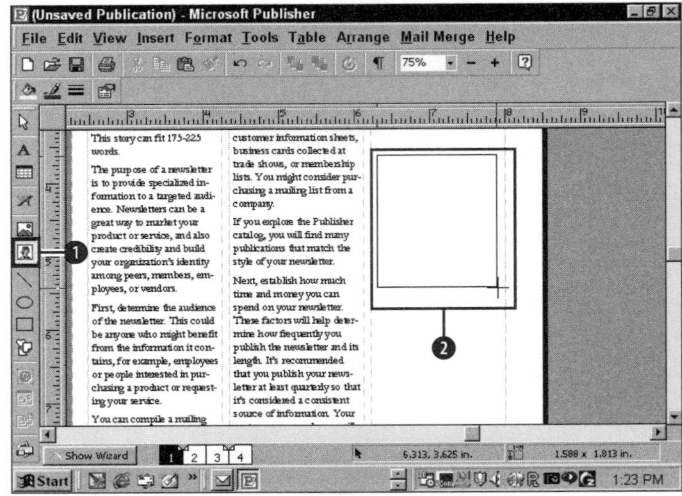

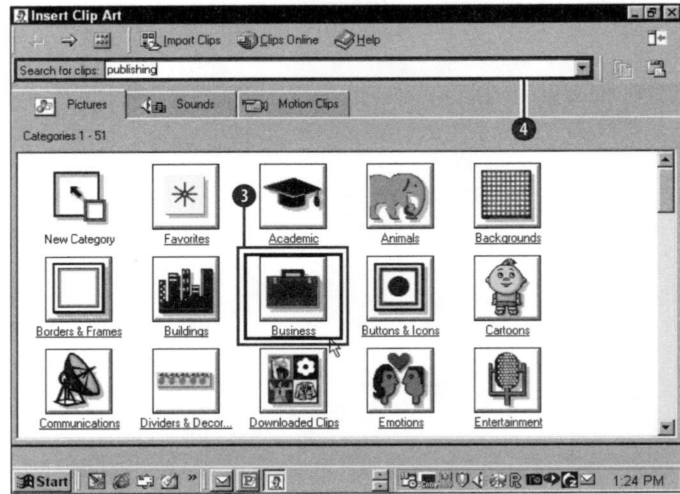

1. *Click the Clip Art tool on the Objects bar.*
2. *Draw a frame where you want to insert clip art. Clip Gallery opens automatically.*
3. *Double-click a category you want to explore.*
4. *Or, enter a keyword (or words) related to the image you want and press Enter.*

CROSS-REFERENCE

For more information on turning Publisher publications into Web sites, see Chapter 16.

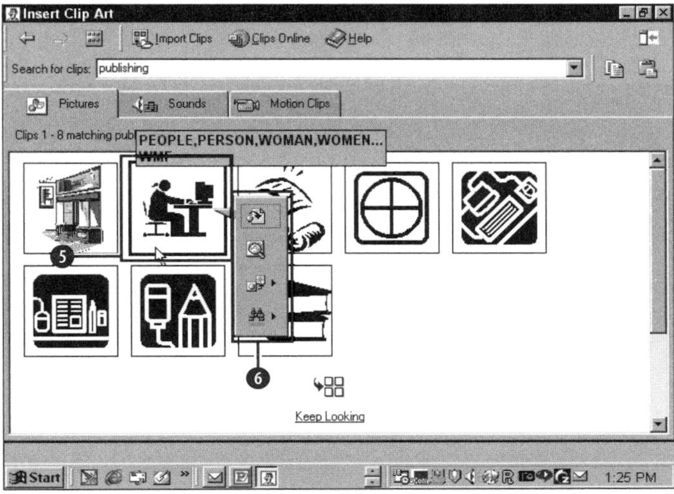

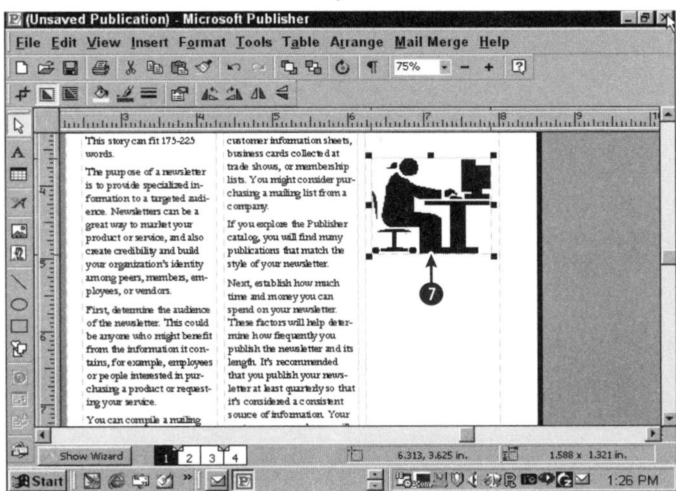

❺ *Click any image to open the submenu. (Pointing at the image shows you some keywords associated with it.)*

❻ *Click one of the four buttons to insert or preview the clip, add it to another category, or find similar clips.*

❼ *Once you click the Insert clip button, the clip is added to your publication.*

TAKE NOTE

INSERTING A CLIP GALLERY MULTIMEDIA FILE

The Clip Gallery includes sounds and motion clips as well as clip art. You won't use these in any publication that's intended for print, but you may use them if you're using Publisher to create a Web page or a document intended for printing online. Inserting a sound or motion clip is the same as inserting clip art. Motion clips appear in your publication as still images — a single frame of the action — while sound clips appear as a Sound icon. If you turn your publication into a Web page, the motion clip plays in a visitor's browser, while the sound clip appears as a link that can be clicked on to make it play.

USING KEYWORDS TO FIND CLIPS

Most clips in the Clip Gallery have more than one keyword assigned to them. The best way to find the ideal clip art for your publication is to enter several fairly specific keywords. Suppose you wanted an image of a laughing man for an article on "The Uses of Humor in Business Presentations." Searching using the keyword "man" brings up several images of laughing men, but you'll have to scroll through many images of nonlaughing men to find them. Using two keywords, "laugh" and "man" brings up every image that has been assigned either keyword; but at the top of the list will be those images that have been assigned both keywords — all of which are images of laughing men.

FIND IT ONLINE

Looking for graphics? Try journeying through The Graphics Ring, beginning at http://www.designheaven.com/GraphicsRing/.

Adding Images to the Clip Gallery

You'd probably already collected a pretty fair collection of graphics long before you installed Publisher 2000 and Clip Gallery. You'd probably also wasted many minutes trying to remember where you'd put, say, that drawing of a butterfly you liked so much. Once you saw how easy it is to find the clip art you want using Clip Gallery, you probably thought, "Wouldn't it be great if I could find all my graphics that easily?'

Well, you can — but it takes a bit of work. Clip Gallery isn't really a collection of clip art, it's an organizational tool. You're not limited to the clips that come with it. You can add any graphics files (or sound files, or motion clips) you have on your computer to Clip Gallery, so that you can find them as easily as you can the clip art that came with it.

First, locate the clips you want to add to the Clip Gallery on your computer (or CD-ROMs, or Zip drives, or wherever else they may be stored). Then, give some thought to how you want to organize those clips — which categories you want to put them in and which keywords you want to assign to them. It will save you time once you begin the actual process of adding them to Clip Gallery.

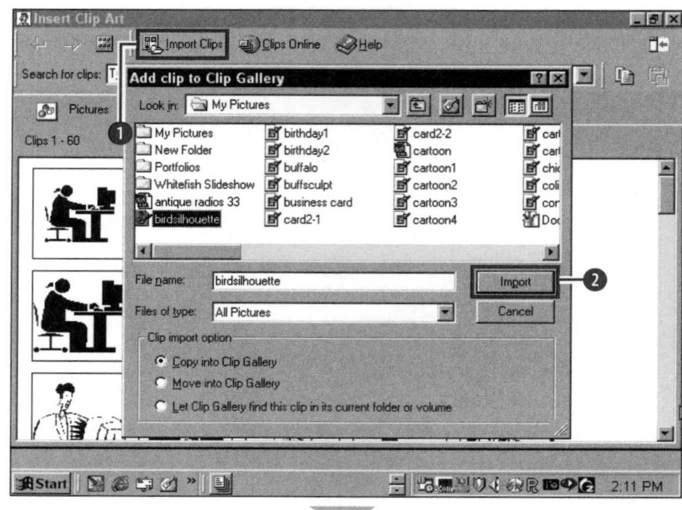

1. *Within Clip Gallery, click Import Clips.*
2. *Find the clip you want to import on your computer and highlight it.*
3. *Choose whether you want the clip copied to the Clip Gallery, moved to the Clip Gallery, or accessed from its current location.*
4. *Click Import.*
5. *Type a brief description of the clip here.*
6. *To preview the clip in a separate window, click Preview.*

CROSS-REFERENCE

Find out more about positioning clip art exactly where you want it in Chapter 12.

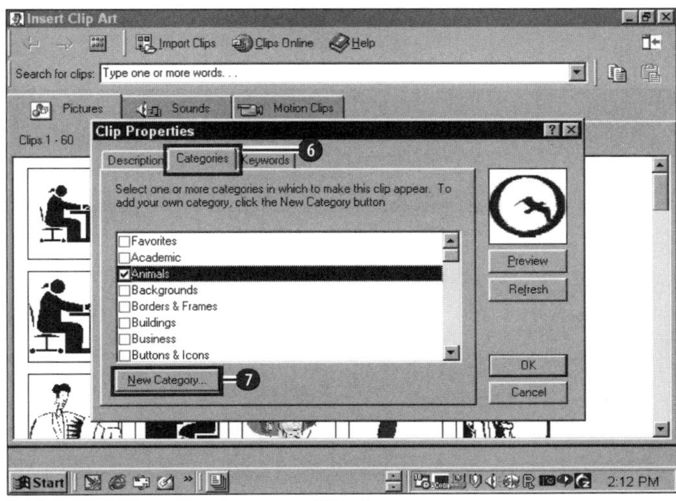

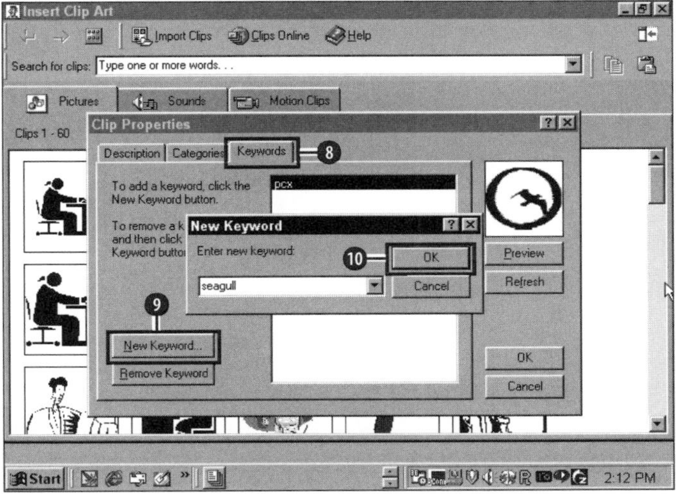

7. *Click the Categories tab.*
8. *Choose which existing categories to include the clip in, or click New Category to create a new one.*
9. *Click the Keywords tab.*
10. *Click the New Keyword button to add keywords to the list.*
11. *Click OK.*

TAKE NOTE

CHOOSING KEYWORDS

Clip Gallery is only as effective as the thought you put into organizing it. In practical terms, that means assigning keywords to images that match the words you're likely to use when you look for that image in the future. Right-click any image in Clip Gallery, choose Clip Properties, and then click the Keywords tab to see the keywords assigned to it. There are usually several, ranging from the general to the specific. For instance, an image of a woman working at her desk with a flask of coffee at hand has a list of keywords ranging from "people" to "vacuum flasks." The more keywords you come up with for each image, the happier you'll be with your Clip Gallery searches.

CHOOSING CATEGORIES

The other way Clip Gallery lets you organize clips is by category. These are broad topics such as "Home & Family," "Nature," and "People." You can assign clips to more than one category. Categories are particularly useful if you have a lot of clips that are closely related. For example, you could have half a dozen slightly different versions of your company logo. Put them all into a new category called "Logos," and you'll always be able to find them in a hurry.

FIND IT ONLINE

Don't think you can organize your clip art because you can't organize your life? Check out http://www.organized-living.com.

Using Clip Gallery Live

One of Microsoft's goals for all of its 2000 series of applications was to enable them to make full use of the Internet. That means you can access Publisher-related information, help, and templates with the click of a button, as well as use Publisher to create Web pages. In addition, you can obtain new clips for your Clip Gallery from the Clip Gallery Live Web site at any time

Microsoft regularly posts new clips to Clip Gallery Live. You can search for clips in Clip Gallery Live very much as you search for clips within Clip Gallery itself, and then download those clips into Clip Gallery for future use. Because Clip Gallery Live is updated regularly, you'll want to go back to it often.

No matter how much clip art you've collected on your computer, the day is sure to come when you can't find exactly what you need among your existing files. That's when you should check out Clip Gallery Live. Chances are, it has what you're looking for — and even if it doesn't today, it may tomorrow.

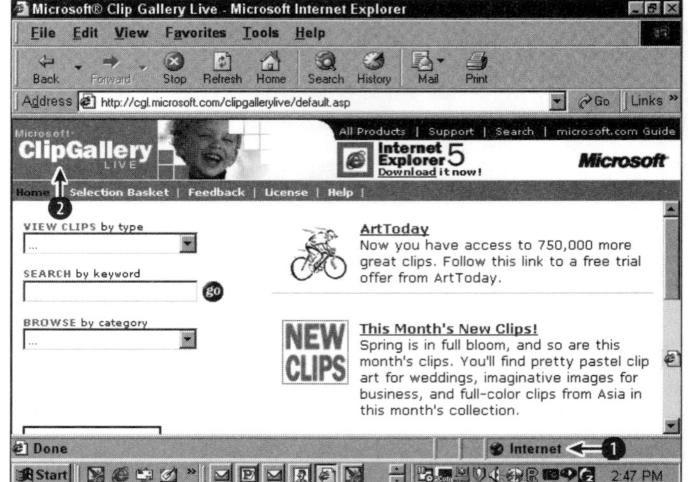

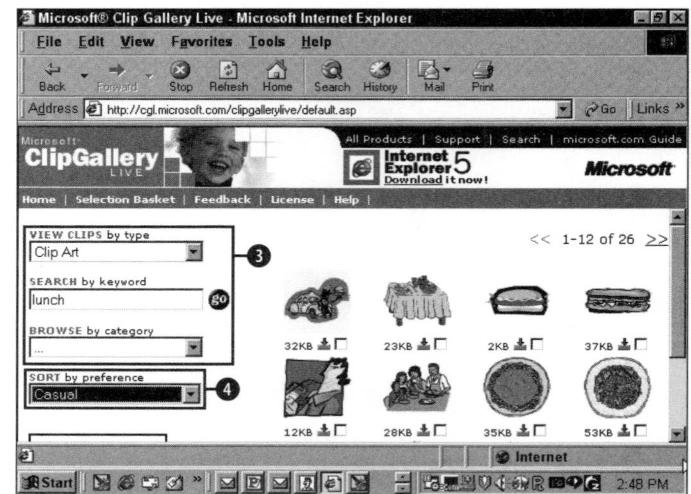

1. *Make sure you're connected to the Internet.*
2. *Within Clip Gallery, click Clips Online. Your browser opens. (Note: You must use Internet Explorer for the following procedure to work properly.) Read and accept the End-User License Agreement to move on to the Clip Gallery Live home page.*
3. *Select the type of clip you're interested in, and then search by keyword or browse by category.*
4. *Related clips are displayed. Choose how you want to sort them.*

CROSS-REFERENCE

Publisher also includes a Design Gallery with useful prebuilt publication elements. See Chapter 13.

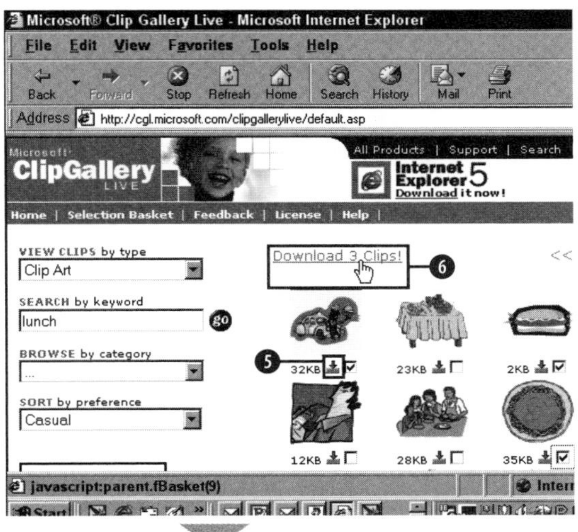

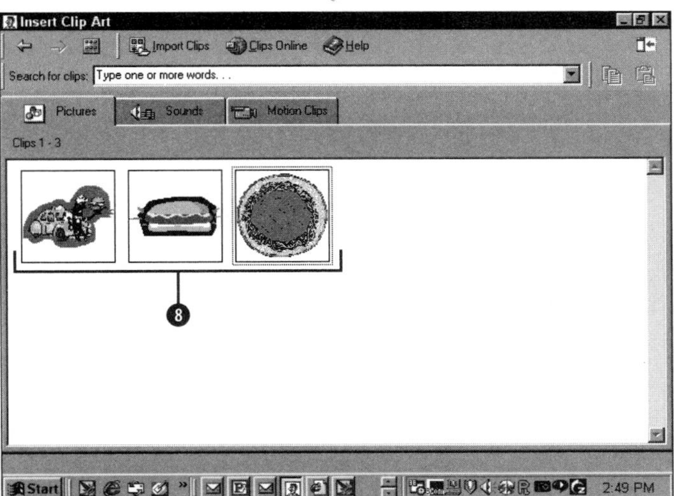

5. *To download a single clip, click the Download Now icon underneath it.*
6. *To download several clips, click the checkboxes beneath them, and then click the Download (x) Clips link that appears.*
7. *Follow the instructions provided.*
8. *The clips appear in Clip Gallery. By default, they're in the Downloaded Clips category.*

- *Right-click them and choose Clip Properties to assign them to other categories or to add keywords to them.*

TAKE NOTE

SEARCHING CLIP GALLERY LIVE

Clip Gallery Live gives you four tools for finding the clips you want. You can view clips by type (clip art, photos, sound, and motion); search by keywords or browse by categories (broad, general topics, such as "flags" or "music"). You can also sort images by any one of a number of criteria, including "black & white," "cartoons" or "abstract." You can combine all of these tools to help you track down the perfect clip. For example, you could look in the Music category for the newest (sort tool) available photograph (type) of a guitar (keyword) player. This ability to narrow your search can help you reduce the number of clips you have to look at as you try to find the perfect one for your publication.

READING THE END-USER LICENSE AGREEMENT

The first time you visit Clip Gallery Live you'll be presented with an End-User License Agreement to read and agree to. You may be tempted to skip reading this, but I'd recommend you take the time to look it over. It spells out exactly how you may legally use the images and other material contained in Clip Gallery Live (and Clip Gallery itself, for that matter). For instance, you can use clip art from the gallery on a Web site, but you can't use it in a TV commercial. Business users of Clip Gallery Live, in particular, should make a point of studying this agreement. It could help you avoid nasty legal surprises down the road.

FIND IT ONLINE

Be sure to visit Microsoft's Publisher Web site at http://www.microsoft.com/publisher/.

Using Paste Special to Insert Graphics

Sometimes the perfect illustration for your publication is one that doesn't exist — which means you have to create it. While Publisher enables you to create drawings using its built-in drawing tools, sometimes you'd prefer to use a different program to create your image, and then place it in your Publisher publication.

One way to do that is to create it, save it in a graphic file format Publisher accepts, and then import it as you would any other picture, using the Picture Frame tool. But if you then find that the picture needs some tweaking, you have to go back to the program you used to create it in, open the picture, fix it, save it again, and import it again — a lot of steps for a minor correction.

Publisher provides a better way to insert graphics created in other programs. The Paste Special command lets you insert a picture you created with another program, and edit the picture, using that program, without leaving Publisher. Some graphics programs also enable you to maintain a link between the graphics program and Publisher so that any changes made to the graphic using the graphics program are automatically reflected in your publication.

Paste Special can save you time and effort if you learn to use it effectively.

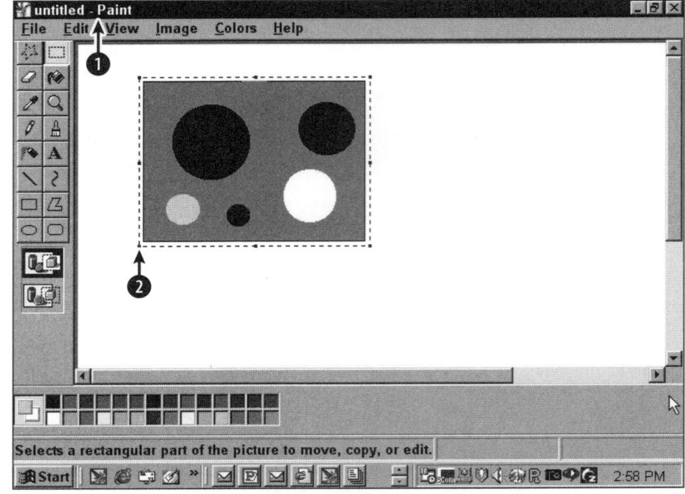

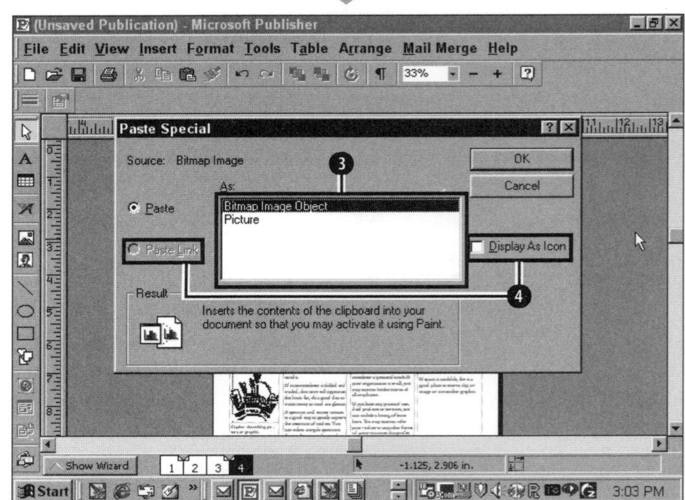

1. *Create the graphic in the program of your choice (this is Microsoft Paint).*
2. *Select the graphic, and then press Ctrl+C to copy it to the clipboard.*

- *Return to Publisher and select Edit ➪ Paste Special.*

3. *Choose the form in which you want to paste it into your publication — as an embedded object or just as a picture.*
4. *Choose whether you want to paste it as a linked object (if possible) or an icon.*
5. *Click OK.*

CROSS-REFERENCE

To learn how to use Publisher's drawing tools to create your own illustrations, see Chapter 12.

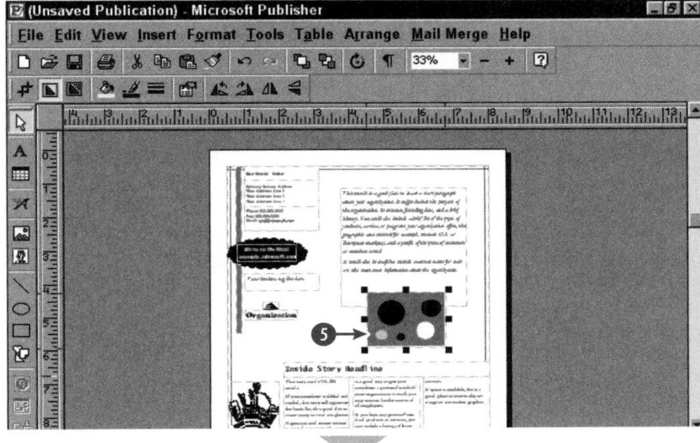

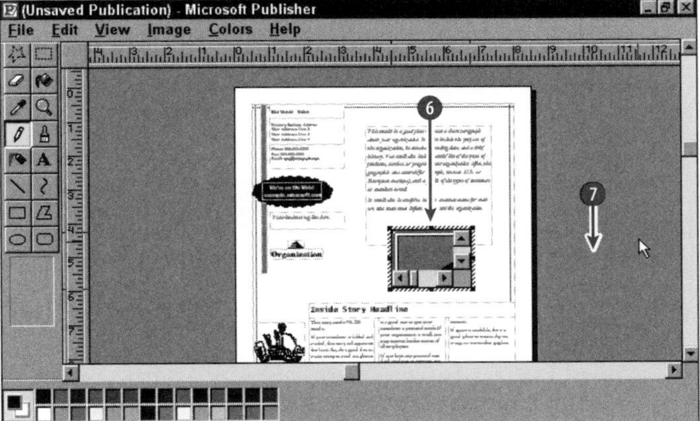

6 *The graphic appears in your publication. Move it or resize it as you see fit.*

7 *If the graphic is an embedded object, double-click it to edit it. Your Publisher controls are temporarily replaced by the controls of the program you created it with.*

8 *Click anywhere outside the graphic to return to Publisher.*

TAKE NOTE

UNDERSTANDING THE DIFFERENCE BETWEEN LINKING AND EMBEDDING

When you use Paste Special, you have different choices to make, depending on what program the object you're pasting into your publication originated in. For some programs, the only option is to simply paste the object into the publication just as you would an object you copied from within that publication. Other programs enable you to embed an object. *Embedded objects* are part of your publication, but are edited using the controls of the program that created them. Changes to the original file are not reflected in the version of the object in your publication. Finally, some programs enable you to insert a linked object. A *linked object* can be changed in either your Publisher publication or its originating program. Any changes are reflected in both programs. Linking is a great way to make sure that many different documents or publications drawing on the same data are equally up-to-date at all times.

SHOWING AN OBJECT AS AN ICON

One option Paste Special gives you is to show the object your pasting only as an icon. Clicking the icon displays the object in the program that originated it. This can be useful for documents that are meant to be viewed and reviewed online.

FIND IT ONLINE

Looking for graphics software (and every other type of software you can imagine)? Check out http://www.tucows.com.

Using the Cropping Tool

In the world of paper and ink, cropping a picture — cutting a bit off — is a problem. What if you don't cut straight? Worse yet, what if you cut off too much? You can't add it back, no matter how skillful you are with glue or tape.

Cropping a photograph in Publisher, by contrast, is easy, safe, and reversible. Although it may look as though you're removing parts of the picture, you're really just hiding it. The entire thing is still there, waiting to be uncovered if you decide your cropping has "come a cropper."

Cropping is important because a cropped picture is often more effective than the original. Look at any newspaper, and you'll see that pictures come in many more sizes than the 4 × 6- or 8 × 10-inch options your local photo store gives you. That's because they've been cropped to emphasize the main subject matter and remove extraneous images. That heart-wrenching photo of a crying child may have originally also shown two laughing kids sharing an ice-cream cone in the background. Cropping the picture made it more effective.

Cropping can also help you fit a picture into a space that's almost, but not quite, the right size. Cropping can turn a rectangular picture into a square one, or vice versa — whatever is necessary to make the picture fit.

Many a mediocre photograph has been rescued with inspired cropping. Learn to use it well, and it can improve your publications, too.

1. *Click the Crop Picture button on the Formatting toolbar.*
2. *Crop one side of your picture by clicking and dragging one of the side handles of the picture frame.*
3. *Crop two sides of your picture at once by clicking and dragging one of the corner handles.*

▶ *Release the mouse button to finish cropping the picture.*

CROSS-REFERENCE

For more information on moving and resizing frames, see Chapter 6.

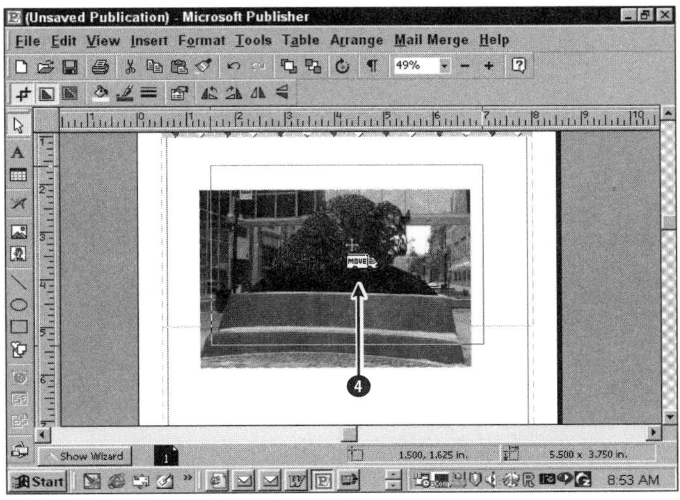

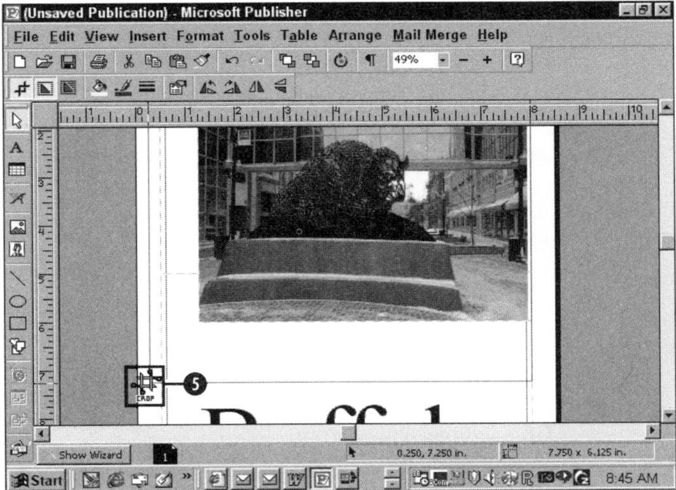

4 *Click anywhere on the cropped picture and drag to adjust its position.*

▶ *To undo cropping right away, click the Undo button.*

5 *If you have already done other things you don't want to undo, undo cropping by activating the Crop Picture tool again, and then clicking the frame handles and dragging them beyond the original edge of the picture.*

TAKE NOTE

CROPPING IS NOT RESIZING

It's important to remember the distinction between cropping and resizing. Although both can be used to make a graphic fit into your publication better, they're not at all the same. When you resize a graphic, the entire graphic remains visible but shrinks or expands to fill the new size of picture frame. (If you use one of the side handles instead of a corner handle to resize it, it may also become distorted, because it changes size in only one dimension.) When you crop a graphic, however, the size of the graphic doesn't change. Parts of it are simply hidden.

MOVING A GRAPHIC

Often, once you've cropped a graphic, you'll find that you need to relocate it slightly within your publication. To move any graphic, move your mouse pointer over it. The pointer changes to a small image of a moving van. Click and drag the image to where you want it to go. (Note that the image doesn't move at first; instead, an empty frame shows you where the image will move to once you release the mouse button.)

FIND IT ONLINE

A good point-form discussion of creating photo essays can be found at **http://the-duke.duq-duke.duq.edu/notes/L11/C010.HTM.**

Acquiring Images from Scanners and Digital Cameras

Using generic photographs in your publications is fine if your publication is on a generic topic. If your publication is about something specific, though — and most publications are — then you're going to want to insert photographs that relate more directly to your subject. Chances are, you're going to want to take that photograph yourself. But how do you turn a standard photographic print into something your computer can insert into a Publisher publication?

The answer is the *scanner,* a marvelous piece of hardware that can convert printed material into a digital file. Good scanners are now quite inexpensive, but even if you don't want to buy your own, you can also get photographs scanned at most photo stores or copy centers. If you do have your own scanner, you can scan photographs directly into your Publisher publication.

If you're using a lot of photographs, an even better choice might be a *digital camera.* Digital cameras function very much like regular cameras, with one big difference: the pictures they take are stored as electronic files, not on film. Most come with a built-in screen that lets you preview the pictures as soon as you take them and immediately delete any that don't turn out. Those you keep you can download into your computer for later use or insert directly into Publisher.

Once you've used a scanner or digital camera to turn your own photos into illustrations for your publication, you'll wonder how you ever got along without them.

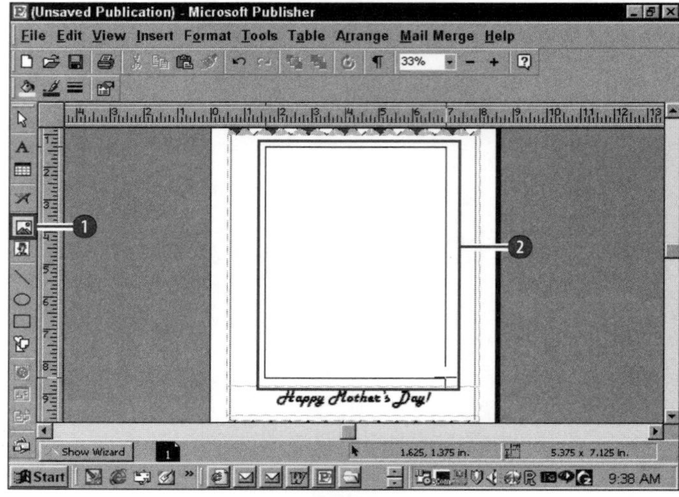

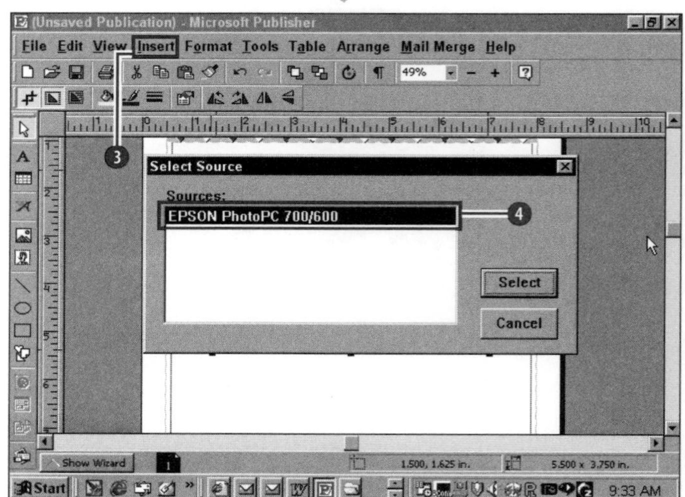

1. *Click the Picture Frame button on the Objects toolbar.*
2. *Draw a frame roughly the size you want the inserted picture to be.*
3. *From the menu bar, choose Insert ⇨ Picture ⇨ From Scanner or Camera ⇨ Select Device.*
4. *From the list of available devices, choose the one you want to acquire a picture from. Click OK.*

CROSS-REFERENCE

For more information on creating publications that might benefit from scanned or digital photographs, see Chapter 4.

- *From the menu bar, choose Insert ➪ Picture ➪ From Scanner or Camera ➪ Acquire Picture.*

5. *The software that came with the device you're using will open. This, for example, is the software for the Epson PC 700 digital camera.*

6. *Use the device software to choose or scan a picture.*

7. *Your picture appears in your publication. Now you can crop, resize it, or reposition it as you desire.*

TAKE NOTE

SELECTING A SCANNER OR DIGITAL CAMERA

Scanners and digital cameras are closely related, and when you're shopping for either one the first thing to look for is resolution, which is expressed in pixels. (One pixel, or "picture element" essentially corresponds to one dot in the final image.) For a scanner, look for 600 × 600 resolution in hardware. (Some scanners boast of higher resolution, but it's usually "interpolated" by software — in other words, the computer creates some of the pixels based on a "best guess" of what they should be.) For digital cameras, the standard resolution of 640 × 480 works fine for online publications, but is low if you're planning to print your pictures. Look for "megapixel" cameras that offer high-resolution modes around twice as high (1,280 × 960).

UNDERSTANDING TWAIN

In order for Publisher to access them, scanners and digital cameras must be "TWAIN compliant." *TWAIN* is simply a protocol for your computer to talk to digital imaging devices. The acronym, believe it or not, stands for "Technology Without An Interesting Name."

FIND IT ONLINE

A good source of information about scanning, and suggestions for making better scans, is http://www.scantips.com/.

Personal Workbook

Q&A

1. How can you import graphic files from elsewhere on your computer into your publication?

2. How can you easily find clip art that's appropriate for your publication?

3. How can you make your own clip art easier to find for future use?

4. How can you use the Internet to expand your collection of clip art?

5. How can you create graphics in another program and insert them into your publication, while still maintaining the ability to use the program you created the graphics in to edit them?

6. What should you try to eliminate from graphics with the cropping tool to make them look better?

7. How can you undo cropping?

8. How can you input images from a scanner or digital camera into your Publisher publication?

ANSWERS: PAGE 355

Importing Pictures and Clip Art

EXTRA PRACTICE

1. Save an image from a Web page onto your computer, and then import it into a Publisher publication.
2. Use Publisher to write a letter to a family member and use Clip Gallery to illustrate it.
3. Go to Clip Gallery Live and try to find the best clip art you can related to the next major holiday.
4. Create a drawing using your favorite graphics program, copy it, and then insert it into a Publisher publication using the Paste Special command. Edit it in Publisher.
5. Find a photograph on the Web or on your computer that you think could be improved by cropping, and experiment to see if you're right.

REAL-WORLD APPLICATIONS

- ✔ You're responsible for creating an employee newsletter. To keep it looking fresh, you use a variety of clip art, and take digital photographs of events around the office that you include in each issue.
- ✔ You're creating a new business, and you need letterhead and a temporary logo, fast. You use Publisher to create the letterhead, and search Clip Gallery Live for an image related to your business that can serve as your logo until you're able to create a permanent one.
- ✔ Your kids are all grown, but you want them to remember your roots. Using Publisher, you create a family history, combining interesting text with old family photographs you scan in. Once it's done, you print out copies for everyone.

Visual Quiz

In this figure of the Clip Gallery, find the places you would click to browse a category of clips, enter keywords to search for clips, add your own art to the Clip Gallery, or look for more clips in Clip Gallery Live.

____

____

____

____

____

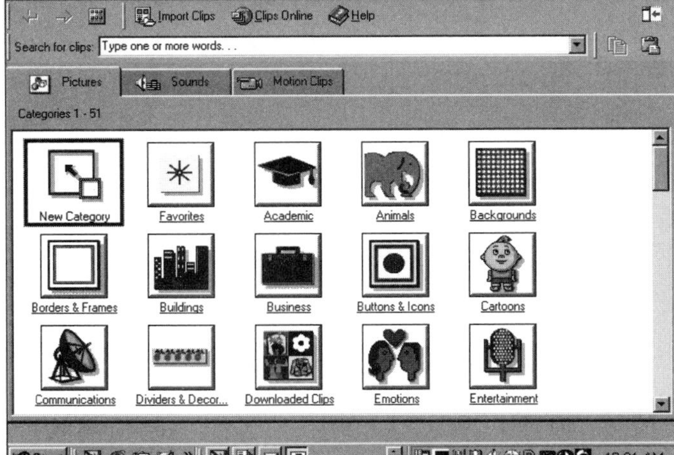

CHAPTER 12

MASTER THESE SKILLS

- Creating a Picture with Microsoft Draw
- Drawing with Lines, Ovals, Boxes, and Shapes
- Changing the Shape of Drawn Objects
- Grouping Objects to Form Complex Shapes
- Drawing Perfect Squares and Circles
- Centering Objects with the Ctrl Key
- Arranging and Aligning Objects
- Formatting Objects with Colors, Fill Effects, and Shadows
- Editing Clip Art with Microsoft Draw
- Changing the Color of an Object
- Choosing a Color Palette

Using Publisher's Drawing Tools

Clip art is very useful, as are digital photographs, but sometimes you need something that's been carefully designed to accomplish a particular illustrative task, something that you can easily adjust as needed. In short, you need a graphic element that you've created yourself.

Now, it's possible that you're a whiz at drawing things freehand. Maybe you can whip out, say, a perfect starburst in a matter of minutes. One way to add a starburst to your publication would be to draw it, color it, scan it into your computer, and import it into your Publisher publication — but in the time it takes you to do that, your compatriot who can't draw a straight line with a ruler may have already drawn two starbursts, a perfect circle, and half a flowchart, and added color and 3-D effects to them. He can do that, despite being artistically challenged, because he's learned to use Publisher's built-in drawing tools.

The main tool is Microsoft Draw, a program that is included with most of Microsoft's Office-related programs, including Word and Excel as well as Publisher. It's designed for creating the kinds of graphic elements that are commonly used in business publications — everything from the aforementioned starbursts and flowcharts to pointers and symbols of various kinds.

Draw objects are *vector-based.* This means they really consist of a series of lines that the computer draws, rather than a collection of pixels such as scanned images. Vectors gives images a big advantage: it means that, like the characters in TrueType fonts, they can be made bigger without losing any sharpness.

The other big advantage Microsoft Draw objects have over the kinds of objects you or an old-fashioned art department might create is that they can be instantly resized, recolored, and reshaped at the click of a mouse. Many shapes can also be given the illusion of three dimensions thanks to clever use of shading and perspective, and other details such as line width and color are also at your command.

Don't spend hours looking for the perfect piece of clip art when you can spend minutes creating it yourself. Use the following tasks to learn how to make the most of this powerful and useful Publisher tool.

Creating a Picture with Microsoft Draw

Creating a picture with Microsoft Draw in Publisher is a bit like using one of those transparent plastic stencils you may have used in a science or computing class to draw diagrams or flowcharts. Like those stencils, Microsoft Draw enables you to create many different preset shapes. Unlike those stencils, it also enables you to change those shapes instantly to a different shape (no erasing required!), change their color, change the thickness and color of the lines they're drawn with, add a shadow, or even add a three-dimensional appearance. You can also group several individually drawn objects together to create a more complex graphic (something I guess you could do with a stencil, but only if all the shapes on it happened to be exactly the right size).

Given that it's such a powerful and useful tool, you could be forgiven for expecting to find a Drawing button in the Object toolbar. However, you won't. To create a graphic using Microsoft Draw, you have to go to the menu bar, as you'll see in the steps outlined on the next page.

In my experience, people tend to go for clip art instead of the drawing tools when they're trying to find some particular graphic element for their publication. That's a shame, because as you'll find out over the next few tasks, Microsoft Draw can create stunning graphics in seconds. It's well worth spending the time to gain expertise in its use.

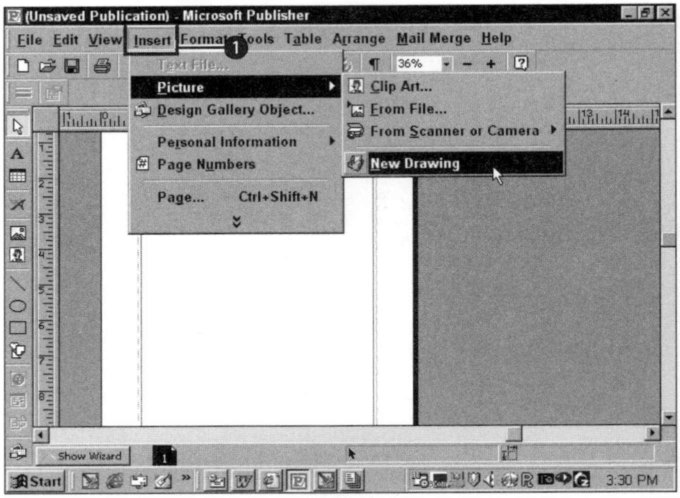

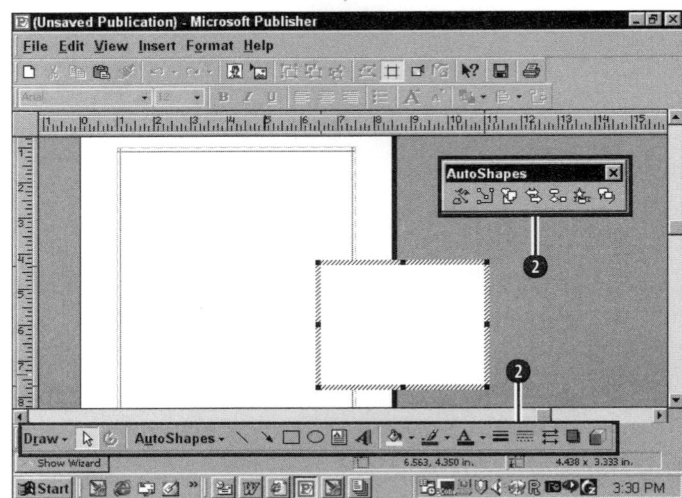

1. Choose Insert ➪ Picture ➪ New Drawing from the menu bar.
2. The floating AutoShapes toolbar appears, as does the Microsoft Draw toolbar.

CROSS-REFERENCE

See "Using Paste Special to Insert Graphics" in the previous chapter for more information on creating graphics in other programs.

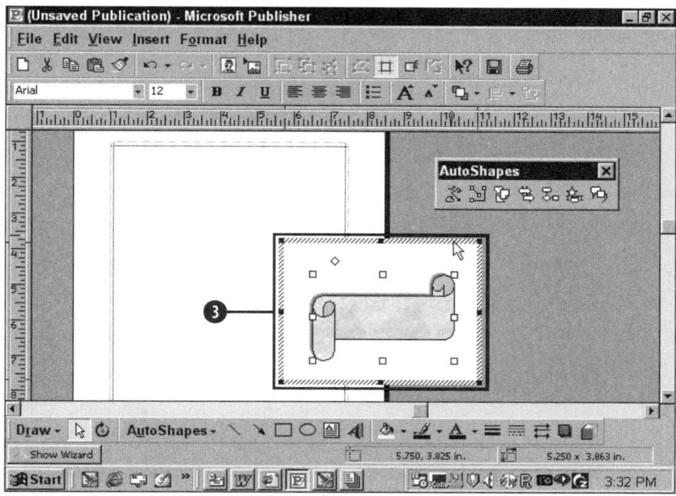

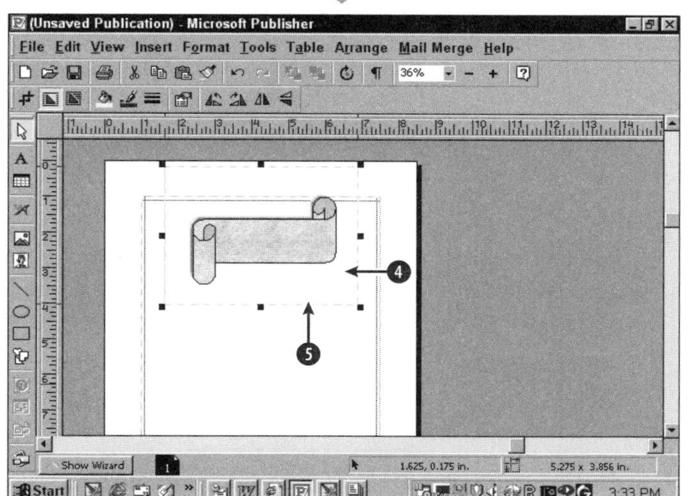

❸ *Create your object inside the Drawing frame. You can resize the frame as necessary.*

❹ *Click anywhere outside the Drawing frame. Your drawing now appears inside a regular picture frame.*

❺ *Position and resize the frame as necessary.*

TAKE NOTE

LOCATING THE DRAWING TOOLBAR

It's easy to overlook the Microsoft Draw tools the first time they appear, because the toolbar isn't where Windows has conditioned you to look for toolbars — at the top of the screen. Instead, it's at the bottom, just above the status bar. Notice that some of its buttons double the ones that appear on the Object toolbar. They're not the same. If you want to be able to apply Draw's various graphics editing tools to a line, box, circle, or shape, you *have* to draw it using the Microsoft Draw tools. Otherwise you'll be limited in how you can change the appearance of the object.

OPENING THE DRAW MENU

Clicking the Draw button at the far left of the Drawing toolbar opens a menu of useful commands (several of which we'll look at in the rest of this chapter).

UNDERSTANDING DRAWING FRAMES

When you create a drawing in Publisher, you work inside a frame that is different from an ordinary picture frame. It's more like what you saw in the last chapter when you created a picture in one program, copied it, and then used Paste Special to insert it into your publication. Essentially, Draw opens its own little window. You work inside that window as you create the drawing. Once you're done, click anywhere outside the window, and the object appears in a standard picture frame.

FIND IT ONLINE

Learn more about the difference between drawing and painting programs at http://graphicdesign.miningco.com/library/weekly/aa042398.htm.

Drawing with Lines, Ovals, Boxes, and Shapes

Microsoft Draw is a powerful drawing program. In fact, it may have more power than you really need. If all you want to do is draw a simple line or two, or maybe a quick box or circle, you may not want to get caught up in the complexities of 3-D effects and all the other options Draw offers. That's all right, you don't have to. Publisher has its own built-in drawing tools that are both simpler and more readily available than Draw.

You can find these tools on the Object toolbar down the left side of the screen. They're the Line tool, the Circle tool, the Rectangle tool, and the Custom Shapes tool.

The Line tool lets you draw lines at any angle, and change the thickness and color of the line. The Circle tool enables you to draw circles or ovals, and change the line, line color, and color fill. The Rectangle tool lets you do the same thing with rectangles. Finally, the Custom Shapes tool provides you with a selection of interesting and useful shapes, ranging from a pentagon to a five-pointed star to a ready-for-Valentine's Day heart.

You wouldn't use a bulldozer to drive a nail, even though, technically, it might work. Instead, you'd reach for a smaller, simpler, and more direct tool: a hammer. The same principle applies to Publisher publications. There's no need to bulldoze a simple straight line with Microsoft Draw when Publisher's own straightforward Line tool as readily at hand.

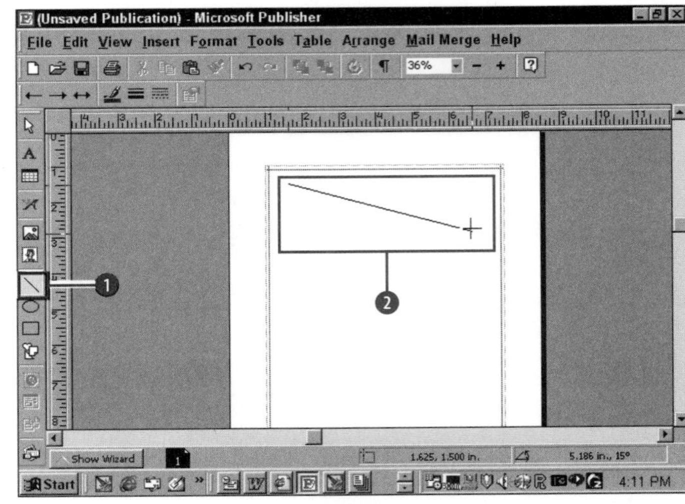

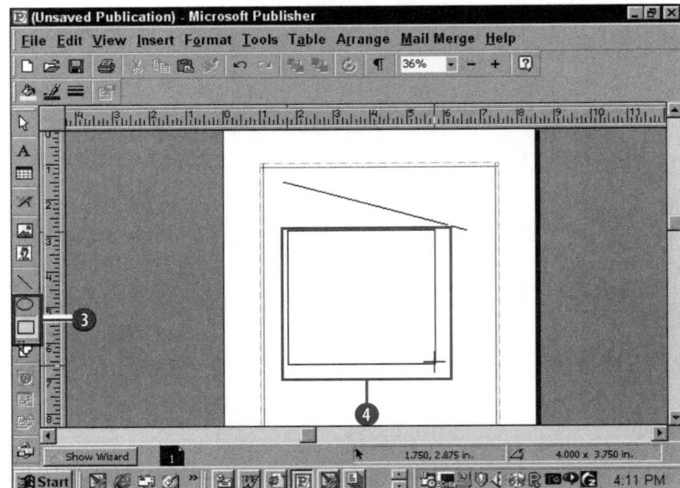

1. *Click the Line tool.*
2. *Click and drag from where you want the line to begin to where you want it to end.*
3. *Click the Rectangle or Circle tool.*
4. *Draw a rectangle or circle by clicking and dragging from where you want one corner of the object's frame to appear to the opposite corner.*

CROSS-REFERENCE

For more information on frames, see Chapter 7.

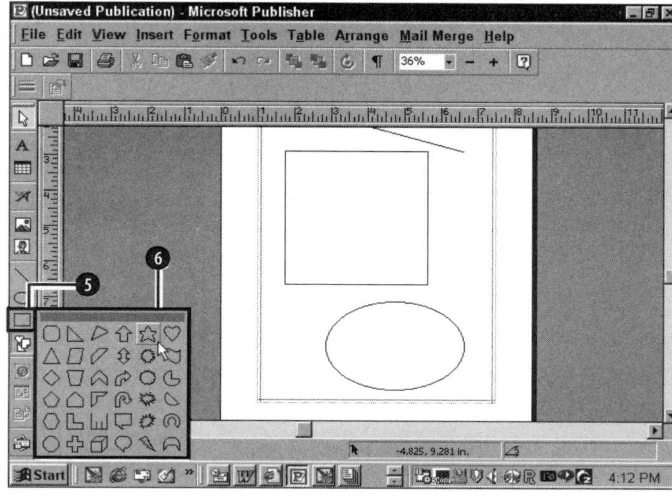

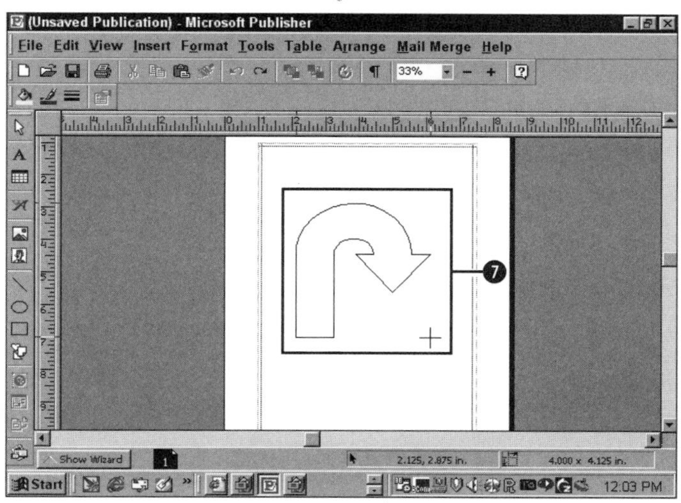

❺ *Click the Custom Shapes tool.*

❻ *Choose the shape you want from the pop-up window.*

❼ *Draw the custom shape just like you drew the rectangle and circle.*

TAKE NOTE

MODIFYING SHAPES AFTER THEY'RE DRAWN

Most shapes appear in Publisher with the usual selection of handles around the outside of the rectangular space they occupy. You can use these handles to resize circles and rectangles. But look closely at most custom shapes and you'll usually see an additional handle, which looks like a gray diamond instead of a black square. You can use this handle to change the appearance of the shape; just place your mouse pointer on it (your pointer changes to two arrows, showing the directions you can move the handle, and the word Adjust appears) and then click and drag. What effect this will have depends on the shape; it's a good idea to experiment to see if maybe you can make the shape fit your needs even better with a little additional fiddling.

MEASURING YOUR OBJECT

If you need to make sure that a graphic is a particular size so that it will, for example, fit a blank space in another document, pay special attention to the object size dimensions listed at the right end of the status bar. This gives you the height and width of the frame the object occupies in whatever your default units of measurement are. In the case of lines, it gives you the length and how much it's angled from horizontal.

FIND IT ONLINE

Interested in learning to draw without using a computer? Visit the online art school at http://www.wetcanvas.com/ArtSchool/.

Changing the Shape of Drawn Objects

If you're like most people — me, for instance — you rarely do anything without having some second thoughts. Should I really have put all my money into potato futures? Should I really have painted the house purple?

In many situations, second thoughts don't do you much good, because it's already too late to change anything. Fortunately, that's not true of things you create using Microsoft Draw. Whether you created a starburst when you really wanted a banner, or a heart when you really needed a star, or simply proportioned something badly, you can act on your second thoughts at once and correct the problem almost instantly. In the case of lines, you can add additional points and angle the line at those points, or even add curved segments between two points.

If you created a shape using Publisher's own Custom Shapes tool instead of Draw's AutoShapes tool, the changes you can make are more limited, but you still aren't stuck with what you created to begin with. You can at least change the proportions.

The ease with which you can change shapes once you create them means that, in Publisher, you can not only act on second thoughts, you can act on third, fourth, fifth, and sixth thoughts as well!

Just remember, sometimes your first thought is your best thought. After all, I understand potato futures are hot right now.

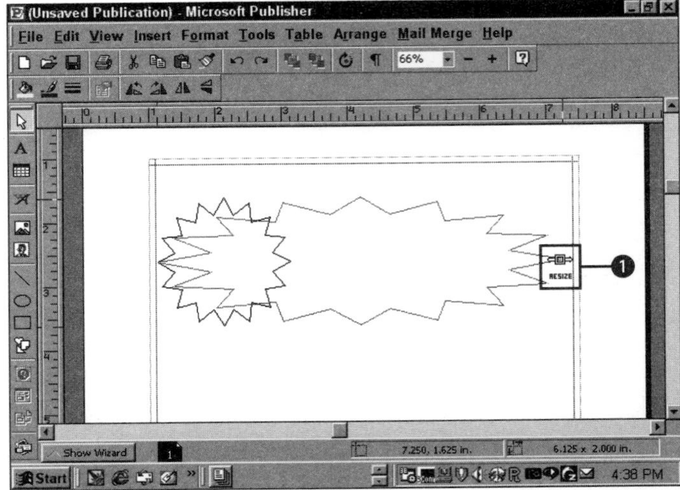

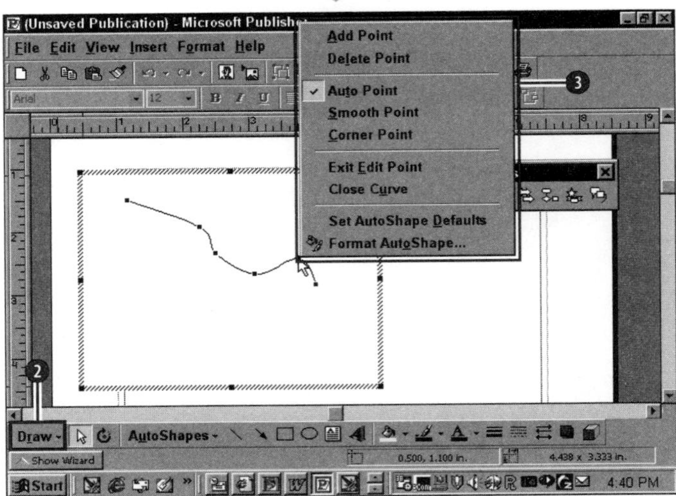

1. To change the proportions of an oval, rectangle, or custom shape drawn using the Object toolbar tools, click and drag one of its handles.

2. To edit a line created using Microsoft Draw, select the line, and then choose Draw ➪ Edit Points.

3. Place your cursor on the line you want to edit, right-click, and choose the command you want from the menu.

CROSS-REFERENCE

You can change more than just an object's shape. See "Formatting Objects with Colors, Fill Effects, and Shadows," later in this chapter.

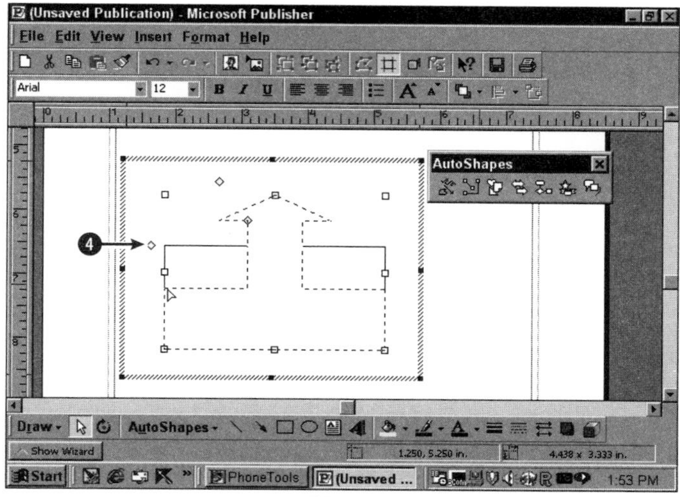

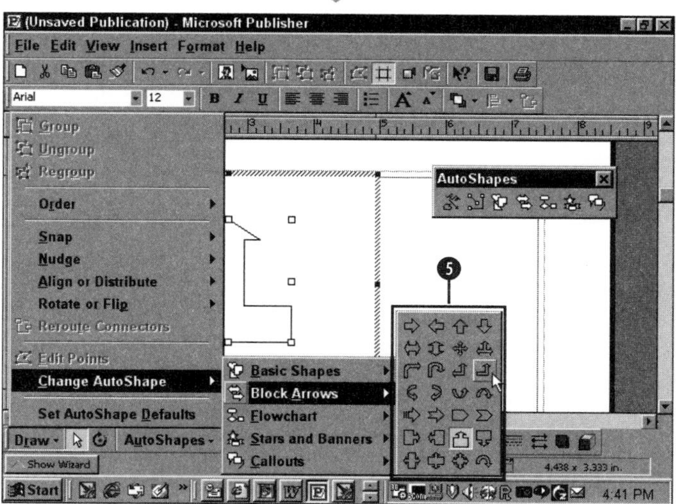

4 *To change the appearance of most AutoShapes and some custom shapes, click and drag on one of the diamond-shaped handles.*

5 *To change an AutoShape from one shape to another, select the shape, choose Draw ⇨ Change AutoShape, and then choose the new shape from the list of those provided.*

TAKE NOTE

CHANGING PROPORTIONS

Once you've created an AutoShape using Draw and then clicked outside the Draw frame, the object appears in a regular picture frame. Objects you create using the Circle tool, Rectangle tool, and Custom Shapes tool from the Object toolbar are automatically placed in picture frames. You can change the proportions of any object in a picture frame by clicking and dragging one of the handles. However, there's still a difference in the way Publisher treats drawings created using the tools from the Object toolbar and those created using Draw. For drawings created using Draw, dragging one of the handles in the middle of one of the frame's edges squashes or elongates the shape, while dragging one of the corner handles simply resizes it without changing its proportions. For drawings created using the tools from the Object toolbar, dragging on the corner handle can resize and change the proportions of the drawing at once. (To resize without changing proportions, hold down the Shift key as you click and drag.)

NOT ALL SHAPES CAN BE CHANGED

Most of the AutoShapes available in Draw can be changed to a different shape easily, as you'll see in this task. The only ones that can't are lines and connectors. In the case of lines, you can edit points to change their shape; in the case of connectors, the only changes you can make are by moving the yellow diamond handles.

FIND IT ONLINE

Find out about other interesting shapes and symbols at http://www.english.unitecnology.ac.nz/resources/units/signs_symbols/international.html.

Grouping Objects to Form Complex Shapes

As you've already seen, Microsoft Publisher, through Microsoft Draw and the tools on its own Object toolbar, enables you to create a number of interesting and useful shapes for use in your publication, and to alter their shapes and sizes to suit your needs even better. Sometimes, however, the available shapes, even when pulled like taffy into a very different shape from what originally appeared, just don't do the job. Sometimes they're simply too simple.

Draw has a solution to that problem: it lets you group several different objects together into one much more complex design. Of course, once you layer objects one over another, some objects are likely to end up in front of others, hiding them; Draw also lets you decide in which order the objects should appear (which should appear to be in front and which further away). You can also ungroup objects at any time and edit them individually.

Once objects are grouped together, they act just like a single object. You can change their size, proportions, line color, fill color, and more, and move and rotate them like a single object.

You can group as many objects as you want, which makes it possible for you to create extremely complex illustrations. Publisher itself, as you saw in Chapter 7, also enables you to group objects, which means you could create a graphic combining a group of Draw objects with lines, shapes, or even text, picture, and WordArt frames created in Publisher.

If you can't find the shapes you need on the Object toolbar or using Draw, try combining shapes. You may be astonished by what Publisher is capable of.

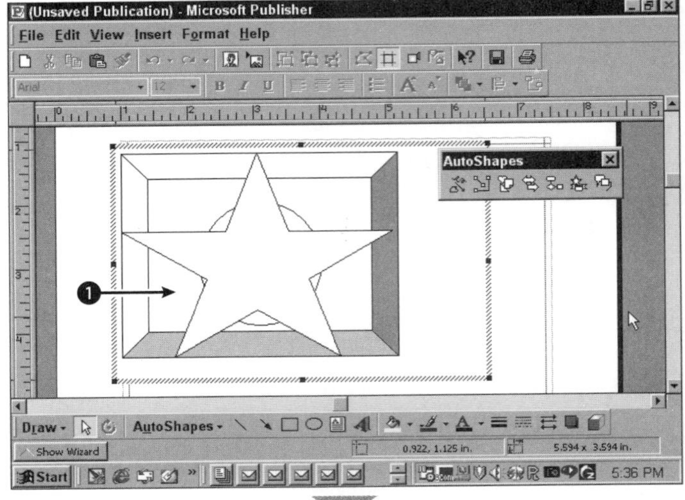

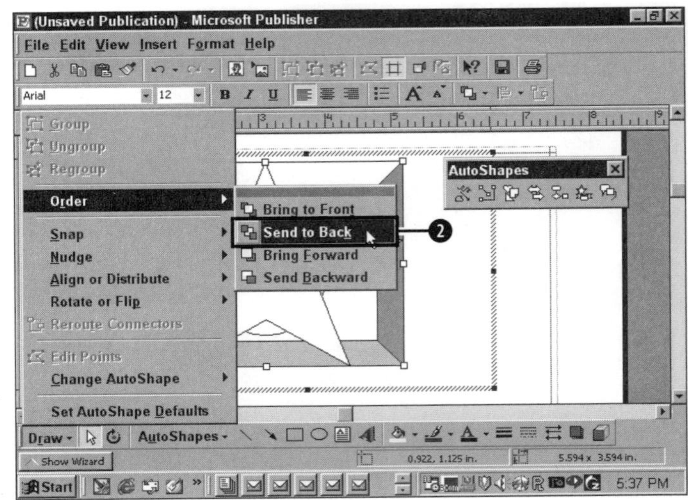

❶ *Draw and position the objects you want to group.*

❷ *To move an object forward or back in the group, select it, and then choose Draw ⇨ Order, and make your selection from the menu provided.*

CROSS-REFERENCE

For more information on grouping objects in Publisher, see Chapter 7.

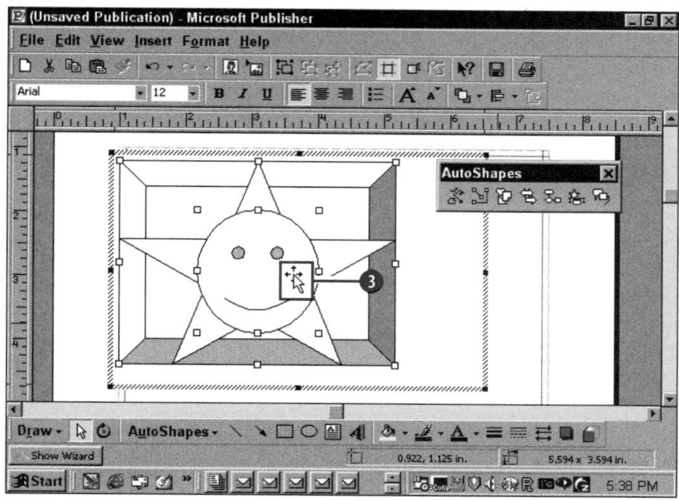

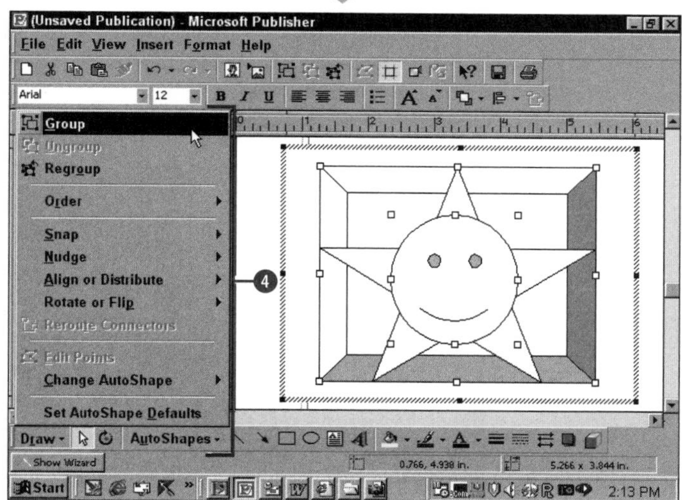

❸ *To group objects, first select them by clicking each one in turn while holding down the Shift key.*

❹ *Once objects are selected, choose Draw ⇨ Group. The group can now be moved or resized as though it was a single object.*

TAKE NOTE

GROUPING, UNGROUPING, AND REGROUPING

Microsoft Draw actually provides you with three different grouping commands on the Draw menu. *Grouping* combines all the selected objects into a single group. (To select more than one object, click each object you want to add to the group in turn while holding down the Shift key.) *Ungrouping* turns the group back into individual items for editing. Once they're edited, choose *Regroup* to reassemble the group you most recently ungrouped. (You can also select them as before and click Group.)

NOT ALL GROUPS ARE CREATED EQUAL

Most graphics you create by grouping several shapes together can be flipped or rotated. However, if you include a bitmap graphic (most clip art and all scanned or digitally photographed images), you won't be able to flip or rotate the group. That's because such a group is made up of two quite different types of graphics. Draw objects, remember, are vector-based — made up of a series of lines. Bitmap images, on the other hand, are made up of a collection of dots. Despite their differences, you can still resize and move a group containing both.

FIND IT ONLINE

More than just drawings come in groups. See **http://www.da.com.au/new/fun/nouns.htm.**

Drawing Perfect Squares and Circles

Do you remember in school having to draw perfect circles or squares? When I was in school, drawing a circle required careful use of a compass, typically a flimsy device made out of cheap metal that had a sharp point on one side and a stub of a pencil on the other. Drawing a perfect circle required sticking the metal point into the paper, and then circling it with the pencil, hoping all the time that the hinge holding the two together didn't shift — which it invariably did. The result was circles that didn't quite close.

Drawing a perfect square was even harder, because all four sides had to be not only exactly the same length, but perfectly parallel. This involved careful use of a protractor to ensure you got perfect right angles at all four corners.

Had we only had Microsoft Publisher in those days, the problem would have been much easier. Publisher provides a very simple method to help you draw perfect squares and circles, based on the same trick I've already mentioned for changing the size of objects without changing their proportions.

To draw a perfect circle in Publisher, using either the Oval tool on the Object toolbar or the Circle tool you can find among the Basic Shapes collection on Microsoft Draw's AutoShapes toolbar, all you have to do is hold down the Shift key as you draw. To draw a perfect square, hold down the Shift key while you draw the shape with either the Rectangle tool on the Object toolbar or the Rectangle tool from Draw's AutoShapes Basic Shapes collection.

Nothing could be simpler — and neither a compass nor a protractor is required.

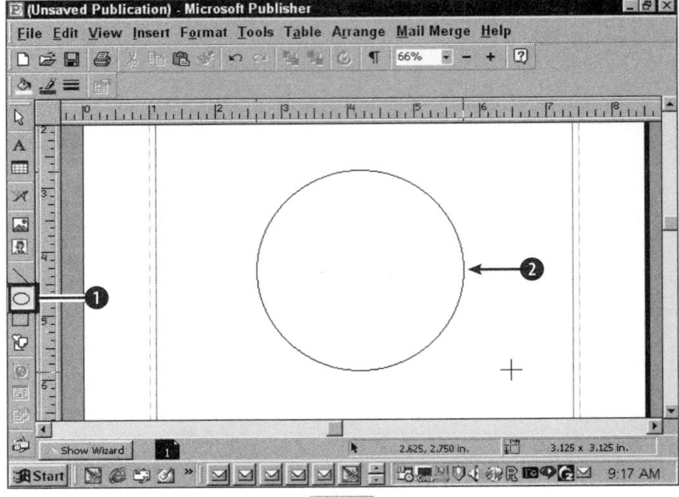

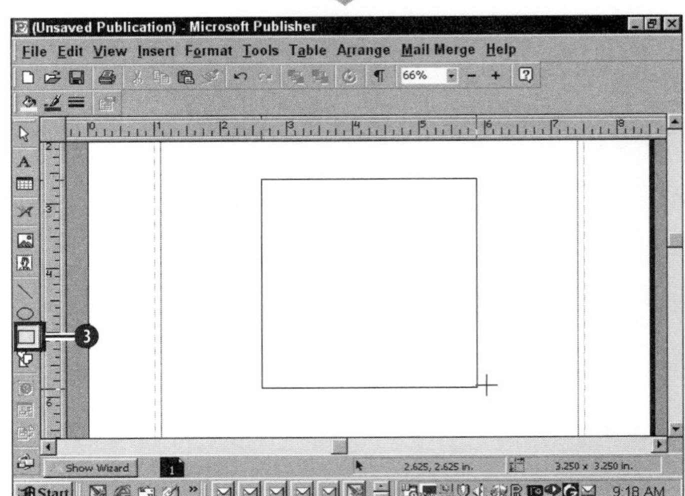

1. *Click the Oval tool on the Object toolbar.*
2. *Hold down the Shift key as you draw the oval to create a perfect circle.*
3. *Click the Rectangle tool on the Object toolbar.*
4. *Hold down the Shift key as you draw the oval to create a perfect square.*

CROSS-REFERENCE

For more information about drawing frames, see Chapter 6.

Using Publisher's Drawing Tools

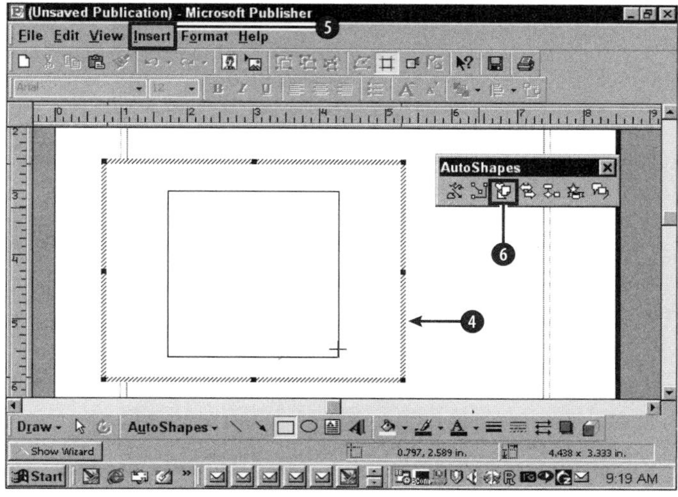

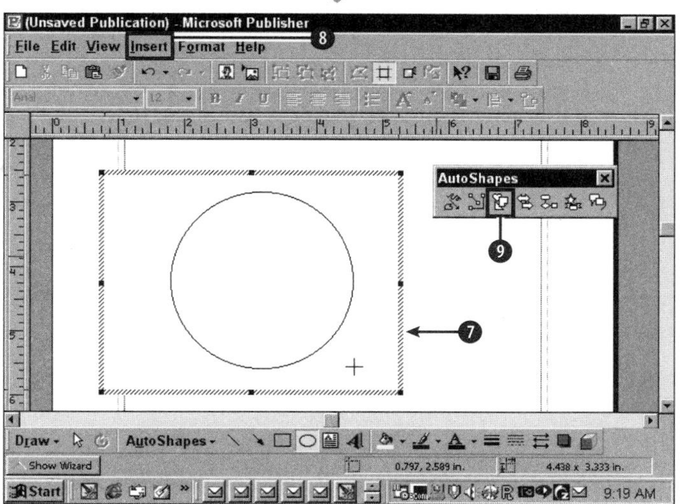

5 *Choose Insert ➪ Picture ➪ New Drawing.*

6 *Click the Basic Shapes button on the AutoShapes toolbar, and then choose Rectangle.*

7 *Hold down the Shift key as you draw the rectangle to create a perfect square.*

8 *Choose Insert ➪ Picture ➪ New Drawing.*

9 *Click the Basic Shapes button on the AutoShapes toolbar, and then choose Oval.*

10 *Hold down the Shift key as you draw the oval to create a perfect circle.*

TAKE NOTE

DRAWING OTHER PERFECT SHAPES

It isn't just circles and squares you can draw perfectly by holding down the Shift key as you draw them. You can do the same with all the other shapes, as well. "Perfect," in this case, means that the resulting shape is equally proportioned in all directions — in other words, the frame it appears in is perfectly square. This gives you perfect pentagons, hexagons, stars, and starbursts, among others.

DRAWING PERFECTLY SQUARE FRAMES

You can use this same technique to draw perfectly square text, WordArt, picture, and object frames, too. Just hold down the Shift key as you click and drag your mouse pointer to draw the frame, whichever type it is, and it forms a perfect square.

RESIZING OBJECTS WHILE HOLDING DOWN THE SHIFT KEY

I've already mentioned it, but it's worth a special reminder: if you're resizing any object, from an inserted photograph to a banner from the Custom Shapes tool to a WordArt frame, holding down the Shift key while you click and drag on one of the corners ensures that the object doesn't get resized more in one direction than another, resulting in distortion.

FIND IT ONLINE

For more about circles and squares, visit Geometry Through Art at **http://forum.swarthmore.edu/~sarah/shapiro/index.html.**

Centering Objects with the Ctrl Key

Ordinarily when you draw an object of any kind in Publisher, it's drawn from the point where you first point and click to the point where you stop dragging and release the mouse button. In other words, if you were drawing a square, your first mouse click would mark, say, the upper-left corner, and your release of the mouse button would mark the bottom-right corner.

Of course that works fine, but it can sometimes make it difficult to position an object. It can be hard to judge exactly where you need to start the drawing in order to make the object fill the space available for it.

The solution is to draw the object from the center out. If you hold down the Ctrl key while you draw the object, your first mouse click, instead of marking one corner, marks its center. As you drag out from the center, you're defining the distance from the center to the outside edge. The object expands in the other direction exactly the same as it is expanding in the direction you're dragging. The result is an object centered on the spot you defined with your first click.

By figuring out where you want the center of an object to be before you start drawing it, and then making your first mouse click at that point, you can create a perfectly positioned object as you draw it, instead of having to reposition it afterward. And it even saves you a bit of work, because you don't have to click and drag as far!

It's a handy little trick to keep in mind as you place objects of any kind in your publication.

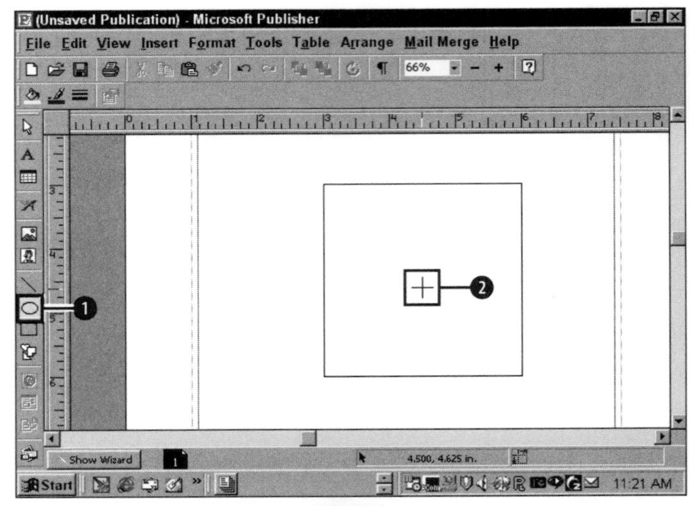

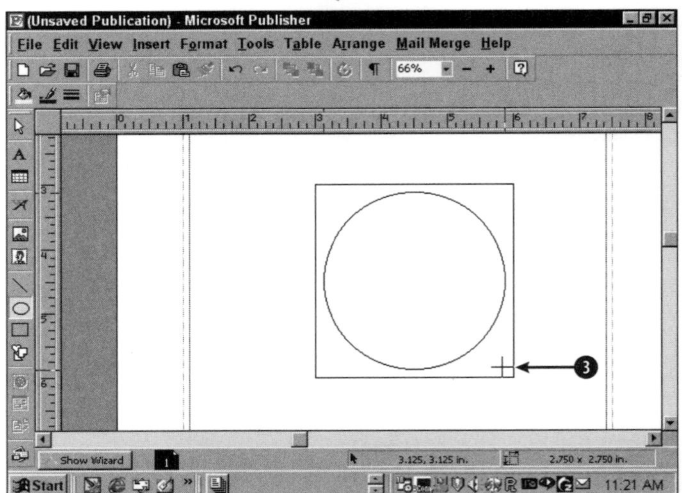

1. *Choose the tool you want to use to draw an object (in this case, the Oval tool).*
2. *Place your mouse pointer where you want the object to be centered.*
3. *While holding down the Ctrl key, click and drag. The object is drawn out in all directions from the place you first clicked.*

CROSS-REFERENCE

For more on positioning objects, see Chapter 7.

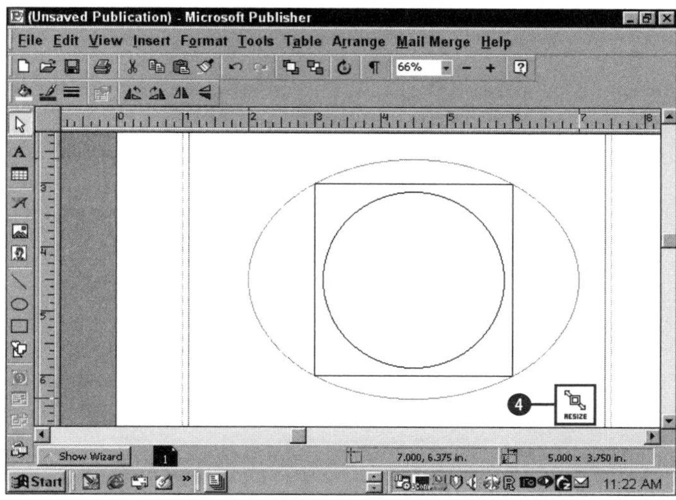

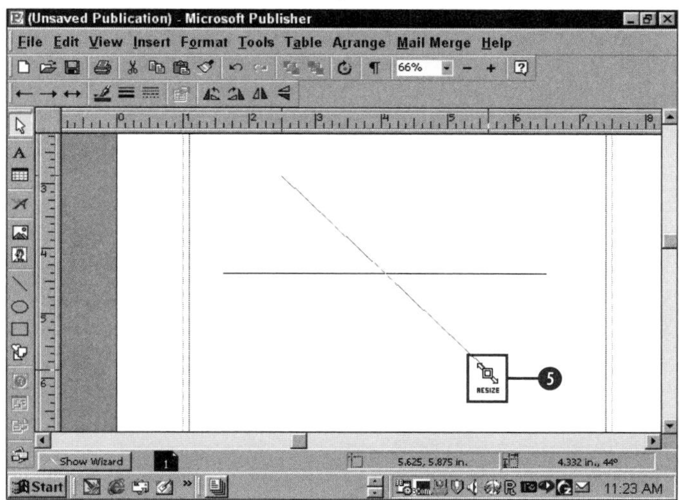

❹ *To resize an object from the center out, hold down the Ctrl key while clicking and dragging one of the handles.*

❺ *To rotate and resize a line around its center, hold down the Ctrl key while clicking and dragging one end.*

TAKE NOTE

USING THE CTRL KEY WHILE RESIZING

The Ctrl key has the same effect on the resizing of an object as it does on the drawing of it. Normally when you resize an object, only the side whose handle you've grabbed (or two intersecting sides, if you've grabbed a corner handle) moves to change the object's size and/or shape. If you hold down the Ctrl key as you resize the object, it resizes around the center; in other words, if you move the right edge of a rectangle in toward the center while holding down the Ctrl key, the left edge moves in automatically at the same time. This enables you to resize objects without changing their relationship to other objects. You can combine the Ctrl and Shift keys to draw perfect squares, circles, and other shapes that are also centered.

USING THE CTRL KEY FOR DRAWING AND RESIZING LINES

The Ctrl key also works with lines. Hold it down, and your first mouse click defines the center of the line; the line is then drawn, not only in the direction you drag but in the exact opposite direction. Holding down the Ctrl key while moving the endpoint of a line that's already been drawn causes the line to rotate around its center. If you don't hold down the Ctrl key, the line rotates around the opposite endpoint.

FIND IT ONLINE

Explore a different kind of center, the center of the Earth, at **http://www.fi.edu/fellows/fellow4/nov98/index.html.**

Arranging and Aligning Objects

In the last task, you learned how to create an object that's centered on a specific point in your publication. That's one good way to make sure an object appears where you want it to, but there are many other ways as well.

Of course, the most basic method is one you're already familiar with — clicking and dragging. Point at any object and your pointer turns into a little moving van; click and drag, and the object obediently moves wherever you take it. You'll use that method more than any other. However, sometimes you need finer control than you may be able to get with your mouse and your own particular level (or lack) of hand-eye coordination. Publisher provides both nudging and alignment controls to help you out. The Nudge control lets you ease an object up, down, left, or right in tiny increments until it's exactly where you want it.

The alignment commands in Publisher let you align objects with any edge of the page or with other objects within a group of selected objects. The alignment commands in Draw let you align objects within the Draw frame, including an option to space three or more objects equidistantly horizontally or vertically.

The Publisher alignment and nudging tools can apply to anything from text boxes to drawings — anything in a frame, in other words. The Draw alignment and nudging tools, as you would expect, work only while Draw is open and only on drawing objects.

All of these controls, however, can help you precisely position objects in relation to other parts of your publication, without requiring you to click and drag each one separately.

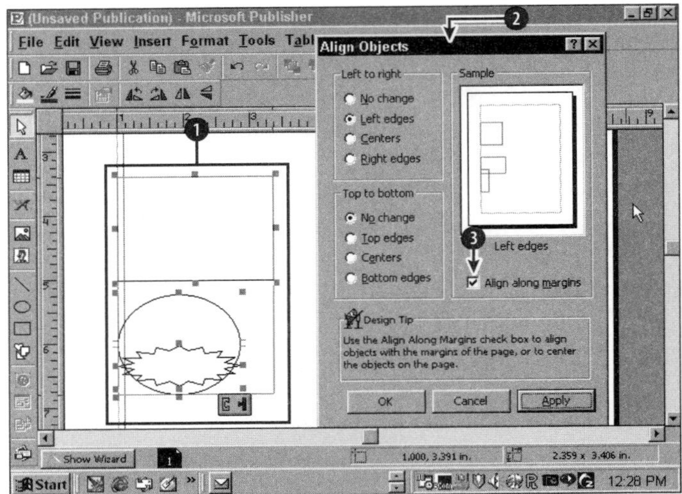

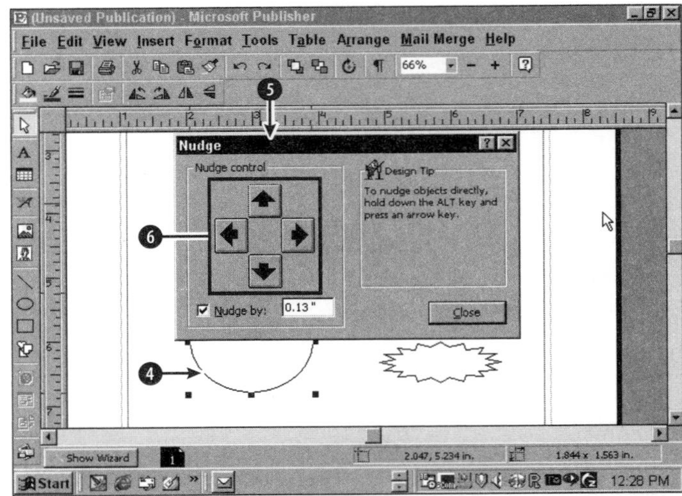

1. Select the objects you want to align.
2. Choose Arrange ➪ Align Objects to display this dialog box.
3. Make your choices from those provided. Click "Align along margins" to align multiple objects with the page margins; otherwise, they align within their own group.
4. Select the objects you want to nudge.
5. Choose Arrange ➪ Nudge to display this window.
6. Use the Nudge controls to move the object in one of four directions. You can specify how big each nudge should be.

CROSS-REFERENCE

For more on moving frames, see Chapter 6.

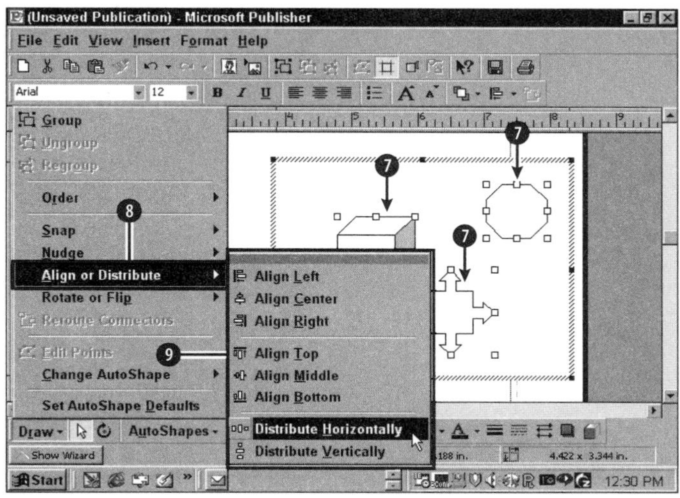

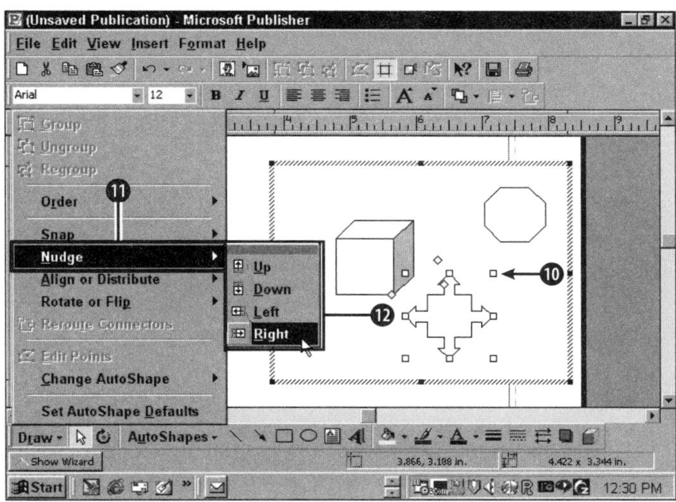

7 *Select the Draw shapes you want to align.*

8 *Choose Draw ➪ Align or Distribute.*

9 *Choose the option you want.*

10 *Select the Draw shapes you want to nudge.*

11 *Choose Draw ➪ Nudge.*

12 *Select the direction you want to nudge the shapes.*

TAKE NOTE

SNAPPING TO A GRID

Both Publisher and Microsoft Draw help you position and align objects by providing you with an invisible grid. If you choose to activate it, the corners of a new frame or selected frame snap to the nearest intersection of the grid, no matter where you originally place it. This enables you to align several objects horizontally or vertically without having to worry about nudging, clicking, dragging, or anything else. In Draw, choose Draw ➪ Snap ➪ To Grid to activate the grid, either before or after you draw an object. In Publisher, make sure Tools ➪ Snap to Ruler Marks is chosen. (The grid in Publisher is defined by the marks on the ruler.) Some people never turn on the grid because they don't like the way it forces them to position objects along strict lines. Others swear by it.

SNAPPING TO OBJECTS

Both Publisher and Draw also enable you to choose to snap to objects instead of a grid. (Choose Draw ➪ Snap ➪ To Shape in Draw and Tools ➪ Snap to Object in Publisher.) With these commands selected, any object you move snaps to any other object as soon as it's close enough.

FIND IT ONLINE

You can find some good basic tips about desktop publishing, including page layout, at http://internetbrothers.com/desktoppub.htm.

Formatting Objects with Colors, Fill Effects, and Shadows

Graphic objects are drawn in Publisher as simple outlines. They're really just a series of interconnected points plotted by the computer, and if you choose to, you can even make the connections between those points invisible so that you can't see the object at all. Of course, that's really boring, so you'll generally want to make those lines visible. In fact, you'll probably also want to change the thickness of those lines, along with their color.

You can also select what appears between the lines. You can fill objects with the color of your choice, or with a variety of textures and patterns. You can even fill any object with a picture you have saved on your computer.

Of course, Publisher really works in two dimensions, but you can give objects an apparent three-dimensional solidity by adding a shadow to them. This makes them look like they're floating slightly above the surface of the page.

You can add even more complex 3-D effects to objects created using Draw. You can turn a simple square, for instance, into what looks like a very solid cube, with each face shaded differently depending on the direction of the light apparently illuminating it — a direction you can also set. You can adjust the apparent depth of the object and even rotate it on two different axes.

If the drawing you've created isn't doing the job because it's just plain boring, don't despair. A little — or a lot — of creative formatting can turn it into a real eye-catcher.

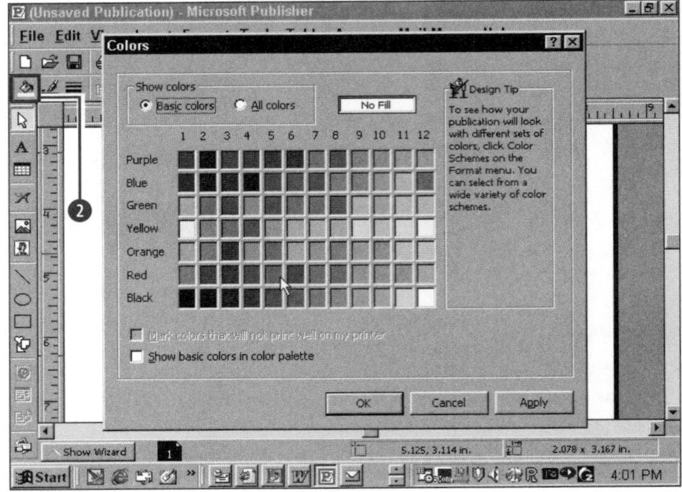

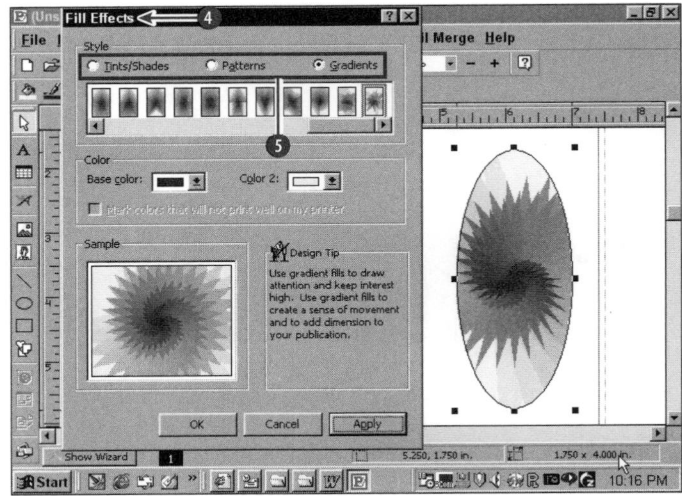

- *Select the object whose fill color you want to change.*
1. *Click the Fill Color button.*
2. *From the pop-up menu, choose a color scheme color or click More Colors and choose a color from this dialog box.*
3. *Click OK to close this box and apply the new fill color.*
4. *To create a fill effect, click the Color Fill button and choose Fill Effects to display this window.*
5. *Select Tint/Shades, Patterns, or Gradients.*
6. *Choose the specific Tint/Shade, Pattern, or Gradient you want by previewing the options in the Sample window.*
7. *Select the color or colors you want to use and click OK.*

CROSS-REFERENCE

For important information about choosing colors for your publication, see Chapter 18.

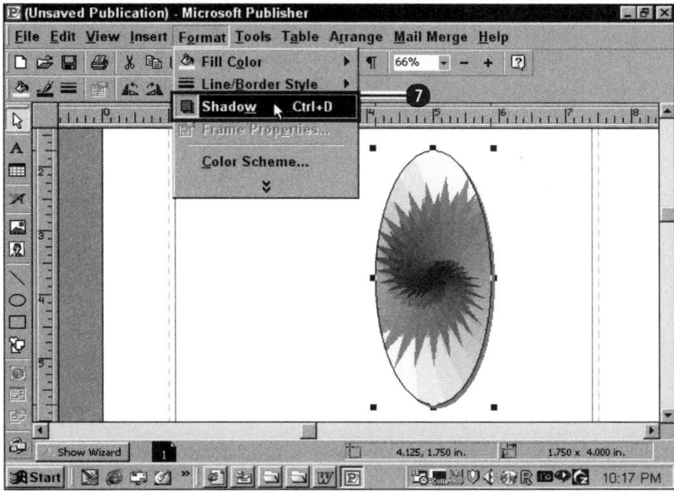

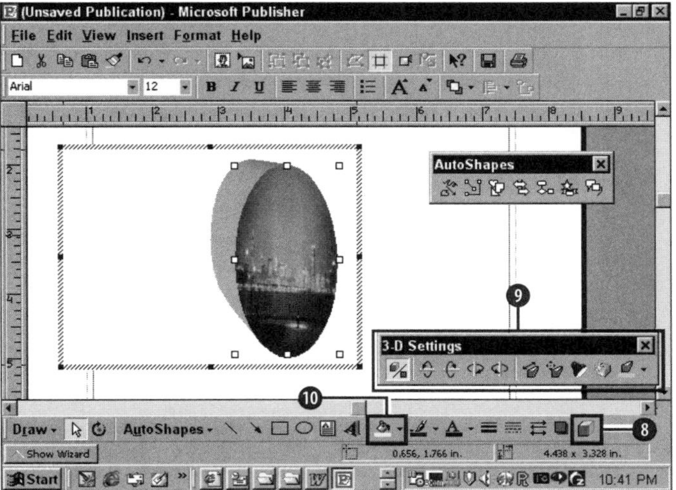

8. *To add a drop shadow to a shape, choose Format, Shadow.*

9. *If you're working with a Draw object, click the 3-D button at the right end of the toolbar to add 3-D effects.*

10. *Click 3-D effects to open the 3-D settings toolbar to fine-tune your 3-D effects.*

11. *Add a fill color or other fill effect, by clicking the down arrow to the right of the Fill Color button on the Drawing toolbar and choosing Fill Effects.*

TAKE NOTE

CHOOSING COLORS

Publisher gives you three different menus you can choose fill colors from. The first, which appears when you click the Fill Color button on the Formatting toolbar in Publisher or the little arrow next to the Fill Color button on the Draw toolbar, is a limited palette of some commonly used colors. If you click the More Colors button below that, you can choose from a larger palette of standard colors. If you still don't see what you want, you have one other choice (accessed by clicking the other tab of the More Colors dialog box in both Publisher and Draw); you can choose any color your computer is capable of displaying — 16.7 million, if you're working in True Color. That should be enough choice to let you find exactly the shade you need!

COLOR SCHEMES

Publisher comes with built-in "color schemes" — groups of colors that work well together. Whenever you click the Fill Color button, the first small group of colors you see are those that are in the current scheme. To choose another scheme, click More Color Schemes. You can also design your own scheme by clicking the Custom tab. Whether you're choosing a preset scheme or designing your own, a Preview screen shows you what the currently selected objects will look like with the new scheme applied.

FIND IT ONLINE

For more information on color and computers, see http://www.alphabet.com/color/.

Editing Clip Art with Microsoft Draw

You've seen how useful Microsoft Draw can be for drawing your own graphics. It can be equally useful for editing existing graphics, both graphic images you've stored on your computer and clip art from the Clip Gallery.

You can't access Microsoft Draw to edit clip art that you've inserted directly into Publisher, however. Remember, Microsoft Draw is really a separate program that creates graphics that are embedded in your publication but aren't really part of it in quite the same way as, say, a circle you draw with the Oval tool from the Object toolbar. Because of that, you have to first open Microsoft Draw, and then insert the clip art into Microsoft Draw. Only then can you edit the clip art in Draw.

Why would you want to edit clip art in Draw? Because Draw provides a few additional tools, such as controls for brightness and contrast, you don't have when editing images in Publisher. In addition, you can combine effects that you add in Draw with those you add in Publisher to achieve different results than you could normally.

For example, the picture you insert into the Draw window is usually smaller than the window. However, when you close the window by clicking outside of it, the picture frame that Publisher creates is the same size as the Draw window. That means there's space surrounding the clip art that's inside the picture frame but not part of the clip art — and you can color that space, add fill effects to it, put a border around it, and more without affecting the clip art itself. It opens up a whole new realm of possibilities for making your clip art as eye-catching as possible.

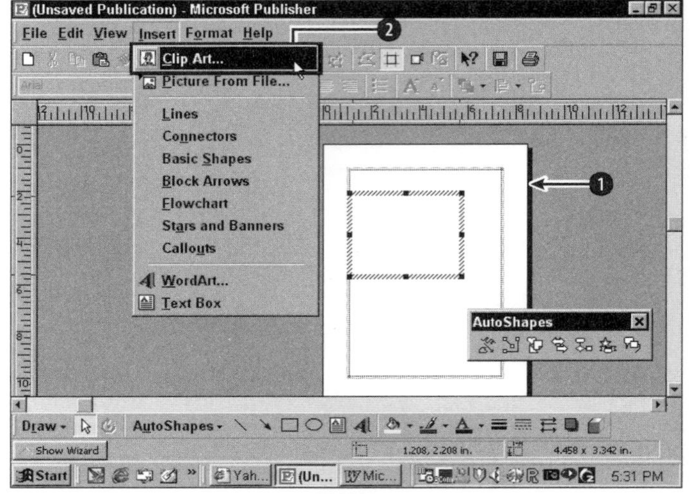

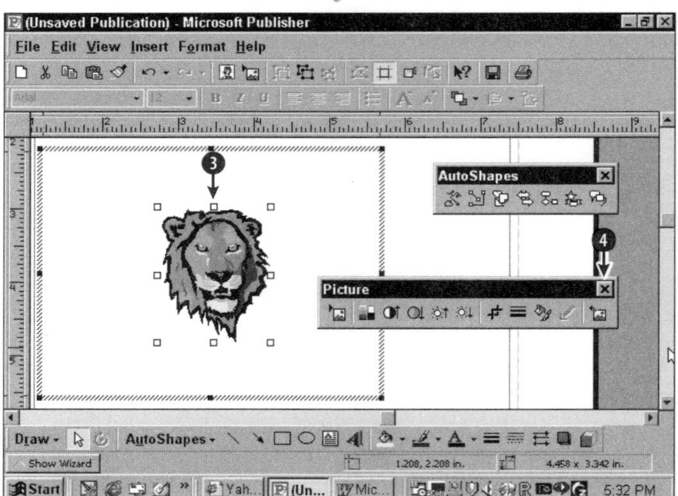

1. *Choose Insert ➪ Picture ➪ Create New Drawing to open a Draw window.*
2. *Choose Insert ➪ Clip Art to insert a picture from the Clip Gallery or Insert ➪ Picture From File to insert a picture from your computer.*
3. *Select the picture you want and insert it.*
4. *If the Picture toolbar isn't visible, make it visible by right-clicking the clip art and choosing Show Picture Toolbar.*

CROSS-REFERENCE

For more on grouping objects, see "Grouping Objects to Form Complex Shapes," earlier in this chapter.

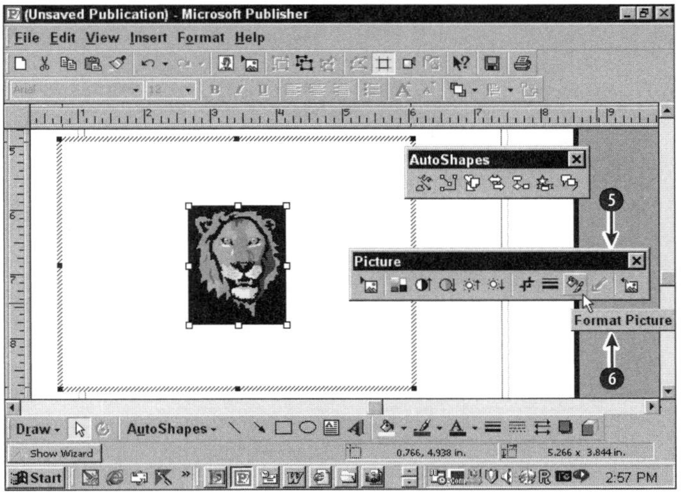

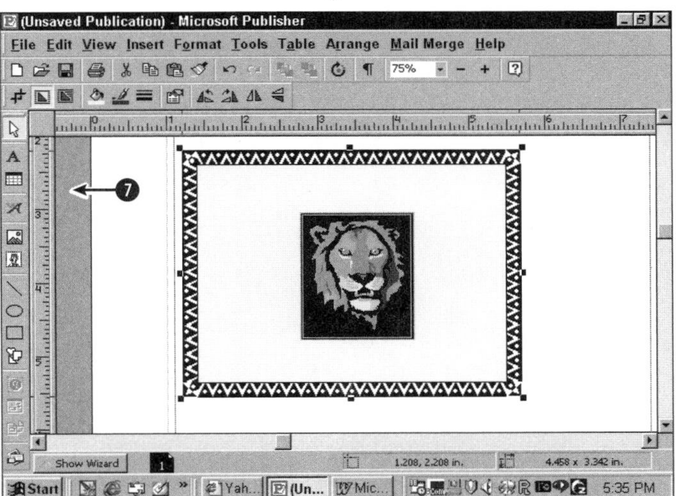

5. *Edit the picture using the tools on the Picture toolbar.*
6. *Click the Format Picture icon to make many of these same adjustments with more precision, and adjust size and position. Using Format Picture, I've added a black fill.*
7. *Click anywhere outside the Draw window to turn it into a regular Publisher picture frame. Use Publisher's own tools to format the part of the picture frame outside the original clip art.*

▶ *I added a yellow fill to the frame using the Fill Color tool on the formatting toolbar, and then chose Format ➪ Line Border Style ➪ More Styles and clicked the BorderArt tab.*

TAKE NOTE

USING IMAGE CONTROL

One of the buttons on the Picture Toolbar in Draw is Image Control. Unlike the others, this doesn't have a direct counterpart in Publisher itself. Image Control offers you four choices: Automatic, Gray Scale, Black and White, and Watermark. *Automatic* sets the colors of the clip art to whatever they were originally. *Gray Scale* creates an image in which the colors are replaced by shades of gray. *Black and white* reduces everything to either black or white, like a pen-and-ink drawing. Finally, *Watermark* fades the image, making it suitable for, for example, printing text over it.

INSERTING MULTIPLE CLIP ART FILES

Just as you created more complex images by combining various shapes earlier in this chapter, so you can create more complex images by combining various pieces of clip art. Once the Draw window is open, you can insert as many pieces of clip art into it as you want, and arrange, align, and group them just as you can AutoShapes.

FIND IT ONLINE

Looking for clip art? Check out Yahoo's list of clip art sites at http://dir.yahoo.com/Computers_and_Internet/Graphics/Clip_Art/.

Changing the Color of an Object

Whether you've inserted art from the Clip Gallery or your computer or drawn your own object using either Publisher's tools or Draw, you may eventually find that the original colors just don't work with everything else in your publication.

Even though, as I've pointed out, you can set the colors of an object as you create it, and you thought you'd picked the perfect color, you may find you misjudged once the publication evolves to its final design. No need to get frustrated or angry, because Publisher makes it easy to change the color of any graphic object: all you have to do is right-click and choose Recolor Object.

Of course, you may not want to completely recolor an object. Many clip art drawings, for instance, consist of several colors. In particular, black is often used to give clip art its definition: most clip art looks a bit like a much higher-quality version of something from a child's coloring book, in which the shape of the drawing was established in black and someone just colored between the lines (although with a great deal more accuracy than most young children achieve).

Changing the black in clip art to a dark version of some overall color tends to leave it looking washed-out and less interesting. You might want it to look like that to achieve a particular effect, but if that's not really what you're after, Publisher gives you the option to leave the black black, even when you change the color of everything else.

Color is a crucial element of your publication, so it's important to realize that Publisher lets you change it so easily.

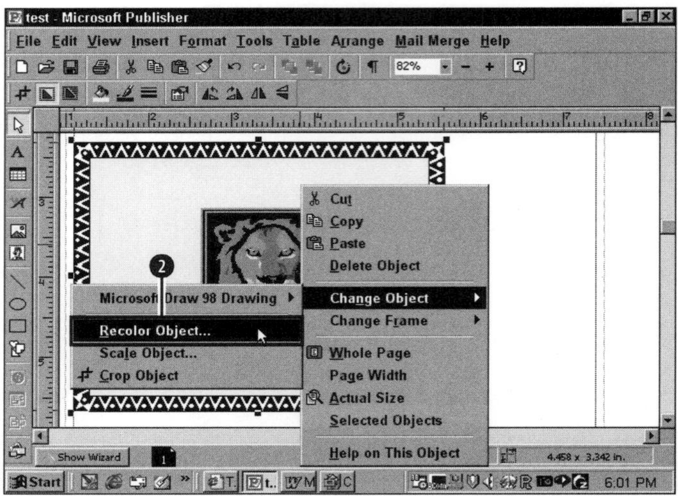

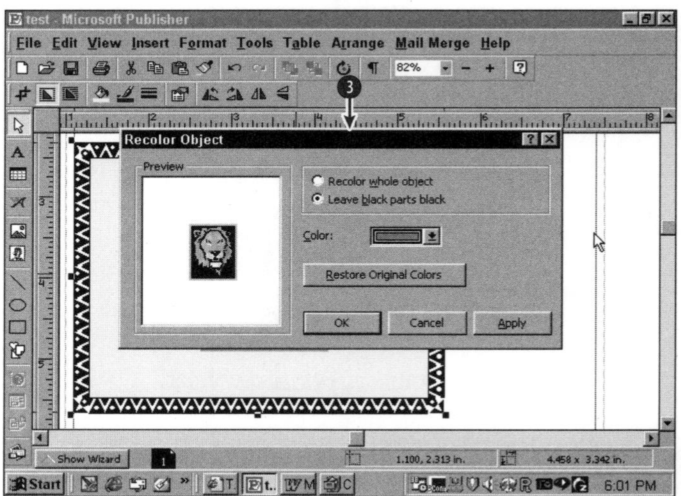

1. *Select the objects you want to recolor, and right-click.*
2. *Choose Change Object ➪ then Recolor Object.*
3. *The Recolor Object dialog box opens.*

CROSS-REFERENCE

For more on coloring objects, see "Formatting Objects with Colors, Fill Effects, and Shadows" earlier in this chapter.

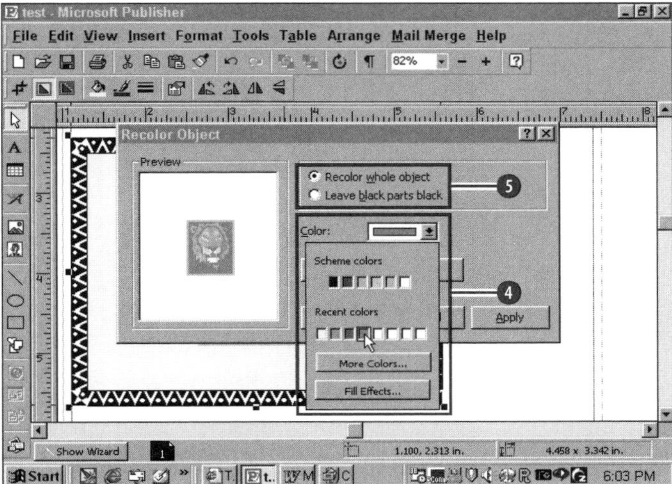

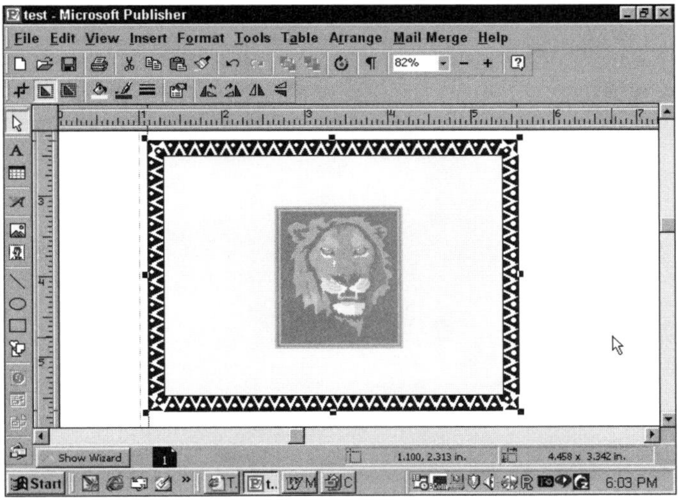

4 *Choose a color.*

5 *Choose whether you want to recolor the whole object or leave the black parts black.*

▶ *Click OK.*

6 *The original object in Publisher is replaced by the recolored one.*

TAKE NOTE

RESTORING ORIGINAL COLORS

Sometimes, after you've changed the color of an object, you may decide you made a mistake and you really need the original colors back again. No need to worry: the Recolor Object dialog box includes a button to "Restore Original Colors." Even if you've saved the document and reopened it, Publisher remembers the colors that originally went with that object, and can bring them back.

USING FILL EFFECTS TO RECOLOR OBJECTS

When you start looking for the color you want to change an object to, you might be surprised to see that you can still open the Fill Effects dialog box. Don't get too excited, though; although you can open that dialog box, patterns and gradients are not available. The only fill effect you can access is Tints and Shades — in other words, lighter and darker versions of the color you've already chosen. You can achieve the same effect by clicking More Colors, and then choosing the All Colors tab, finding the basic color you want to use, and then moving the luminance slider to the right of the color palette up and down.

FIND IT ONLINE

You can find some basic information about color theory at **http://busybrushes.com/Classroom/colorwheel.html**

Choosing a Color Palette

Microsoft Publisher comes with a number of color palettes, but it defaults to its own basic palette. Publisher's color schemes are variations of the basic Publisher color palette. But, you aren't tied to just what comes in the Palette window. The other palettes that you can choose from include the following:

- **CMYK** — This palette lets you mix the four process colors (cyan, magenta, yellow, and black) to closely match the colors you'll get when you send your job to a printing company. Each percentage will be rendered to the individual pieces of film that make up the four-color printing process.
- **HSL** — Mainly targeted toward a finished publication that will be seen on a monitor, the HSL (hue, saturation, and luminosity) color model is best suited for Web publications.
- **Pantone** — Spot colors that cannot be exactly made from mixing percentages from the four-color process, Pantone color models come in two palettes, but the one predominantly used by graphic artists is the Pantone Solid palette. Use this color palette for commercial printing of your publication.
- **RGB** — Like HSL, this color model is best suited for publications that will be displayed onscreen, such as a Web site or electronic document. RGB (red, green, blue) is mixed to make colors that will display exactly the same on your monitor.

Choosing a color from the CMYK, HSL, or RGB palettes is as simple as clicking your mouse cursor in the color picker bar and window. You can also enter values in the text boxes below the Color Model drop-down menu.

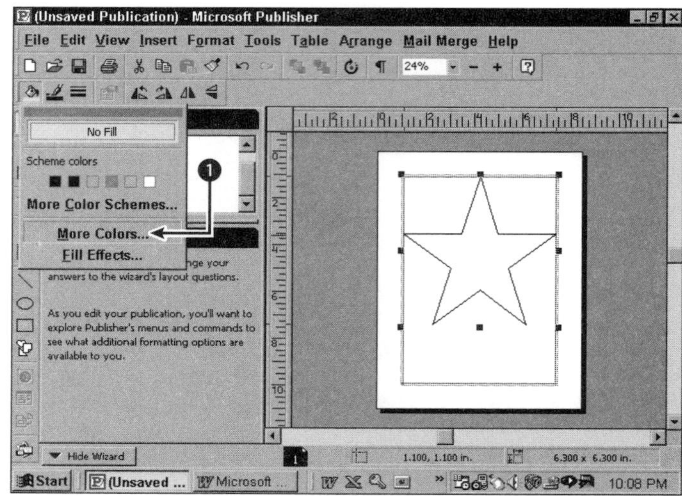

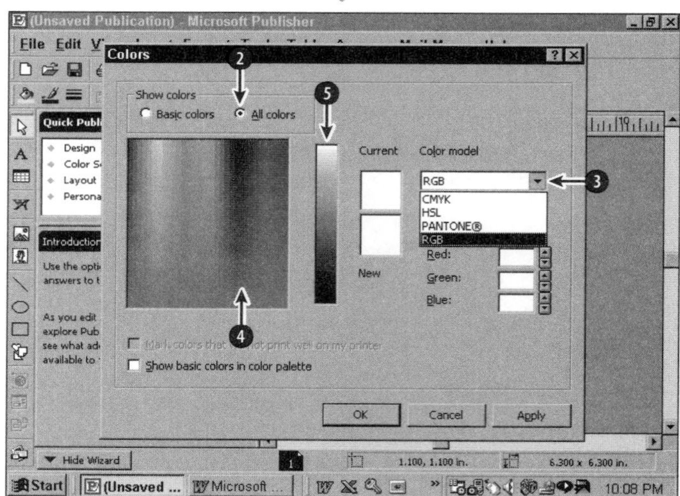

1. With an object selected, click the More Colors option in the Fill Color or Line Color button menus.
2. To access the other color models, choose All Colors.
3. Choose a color model from the drop-down list.
4. For HSL, RGB, and CMYK models, click in the large color window to choose a color.
5. Use the slider to pick a shade of that color.

CROSS-REFERENCE

See Chapter 18 for how to prepare your document for a commercial printer.

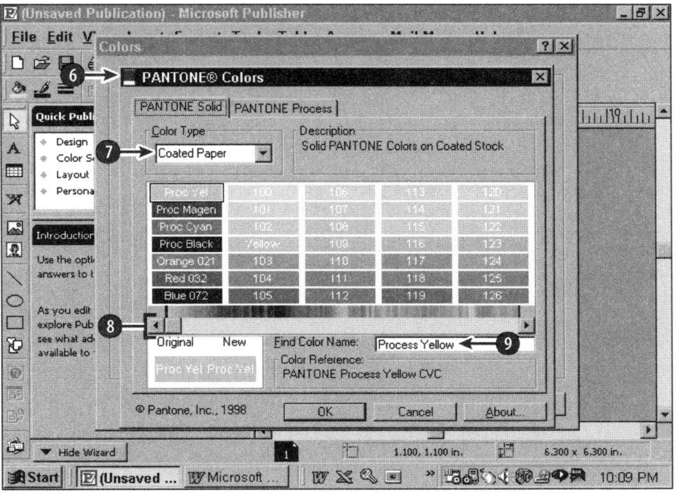

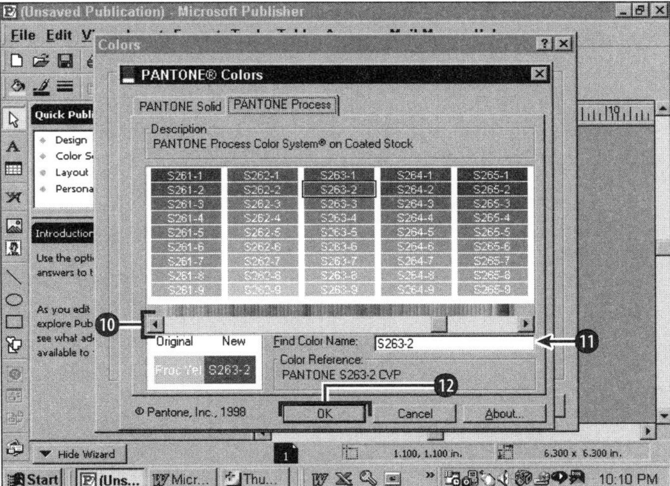

Pantone color selection is done a bit differently. Usually, you have a PMS (Pantone Matching System) color swatch book at hand that shows you the exact color to be reproduced on the press. Use the number on the swatch that you want to look up the PMS color in the Pantone Colors dialog box.

Another option you have in the Pantone Colors dialog box is to choose the type of stock that your print job will be printed on. You can choose coated or uncoated stock.

A third choice in this drop-down is to Convert to Process. Should you not want to pay the extra price for a fifth color on your printed piece, you can choose this option in the drop-down and Publisher will assign a CMYK equivalent to the object that is receiving the color.

6 *If you choose Pantone , the Pantone Colors dialog box opens.*

7 *Choose whether the color is for coated stock, uncoated stock, or if it is to be converted to CMYK.*

8 *Pick a range of color, and then pick a color from the window above it.*

9 *You can also enter a PMS color number or name here. Press Enter to retrieve it.*

10 *For Pantone Process colors, use the slider to reach a general color then pick a color from the window above it.*

11 *Or, you can enter a number in the Find Color Name text box and press Enter.*

12 *Click OK to assign the color to the selected object.*

TAKE NOTE

SPECIAL PANTONE INKS ARE MISSING

Most publishing programs, including Microsoft Publisher, do not include some of the Pantone metallic inks in their palettes. The main reason is that most desktop printers are unable to print metallic inks or interpret the command to print them. So, if you're wanting a metallic ink, choose a color close to the metallic ink and tell your printer to substitute the metallic for the one indicated in the layout.

FIND IT ONLINE

At **http://www.undu.com/DN971201/00000019.htm** you can learn more about the HLS and RGB color models.

Personal Workbook

Q&A

1. How do you open Microsoft Draw so you can draw your own illustrations for your publication?

2. How can you draw basic shapes using Publisher's own Object toolbar?

3. How can you change the shape of an object you've drawn?

4. How can you create more complex shapes from simple ones?

5. How can you draw a perfect circle or square?

6. How can you add colors, fill effects, and shadows to objects?

7. How can you edit clip art in Microsoft Draw?

8. How can you change the color of an object?

ANSWERS: PAGE 356

Using Publisher's Drawing Tools

CHAPTER 12

EXTRA PRACTICE

1. Create a newspaper advertisement for some coming event using starbursts and other AutoShapes from Microsoft Draw.
2. Draw an oval frame around a text box using the tools on Publisher's Object toolbar.
3. Create a logo for your business by combining several Microsoft Draw shapes into one.
4. Make a page of clip art look like all the images are hung on the wall of a real gallery. Use the arranging and aligning objects functions to ensure they're all placed where they should be.
5. Create a 3-D version of the logo you created in the third exercise.

REAL-WORLD APPLICATIONS

- ✔ You're responsible for your company's Web site. To give it a new, exciting look that lifts it off the page, you make all the boxes and buttons for the page yourself in Microsoft Draw, using 3-D effects.
- ✔ You're working on an important publication and you can't find any clip art that illustrates it properly — but it looks so dull without clip art that you can't leave it without any. You use Microsoft Draw to create your own art, a diagram that does exactly what you want and makes the accompanying text both clearer and less boring.
- ✔ You want to create a publication that features text over a faint image. You recolor the image using Publisher, making it a faint shade of purple that shows through the text perfectly without making the text illegible.

Visual Quiz

In this figure of Microsoft Draw, find the controls you would click to add 3-D effects, apply a shadow, change the fill color, change the shape to a different AutoShape, and add a new AutoShape.

____

____

____

____

____

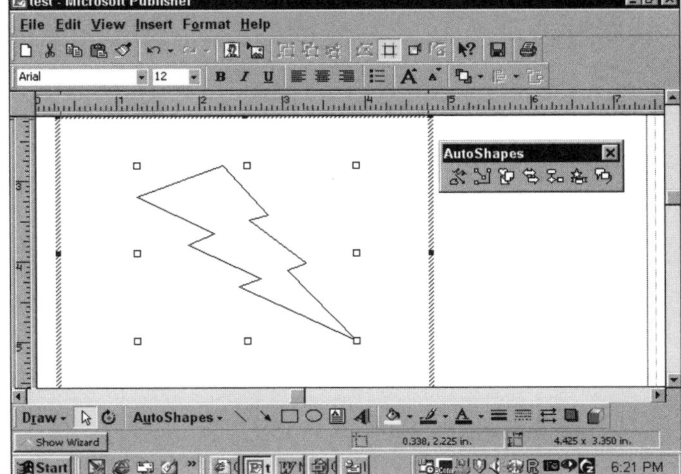

CHAPTER 13

MASTER THESE SKILLS

- **Selecting Objects by Category**
- **Selecting Objects by Design**
- **Modifying Design Objects**
- **Building Your Own Design Gallery**

Using Publisher's Design Gallery

There's no use in reinventing the wheel, goes the old saying, and that's certainly true when it comes to creating design elements for publications. Over the years, hundreds of thousands of newsletter heads, tables of contents, coupons, and advertisements have been created. Many of them are very similar to each other. Good design is good design, and when you need to have it, there's no shame in basing your design on something that's already been created.

You could do that by browsing through magazines, finding designs you like, and then re-creating them in Publisher using its various drawing and text tools. You may want to do that anyway, but you have an easier method to get predesigned elements for your publication. That's because Publisher, recognizing how much time and energy you can save by using predesigned elements, has gathered together a number of excellent, useful designs in its Design Gallery, a catalog of elements that you can use as is or modify to suit your own needs.

Many of the elements are part of consistent design sets, groups of related designs that can help give your publication a unity of design that make it look professional — which is particularly helpful if you're not a designer yourself, but you don't want the people reading your publication to realize it.

You can search the gallery by design sets, or you can search it by category — i.e., "coupons" or "attention getters." Previews show you exactly what you'll get if you choose to insert that item into your publication, and if you do insert it, a wizard is available to take you step by step through modifying it to suit your needs exactly.

And if, perchance, you are a first-rate designer in your own right, no worries: you can save your own designs in the Design Gallery so they're readily available for you to use in future publications.

The Design Gallery is a powerful tool in your ongoing effort to create the most attractive, effective, and professional-looking publications you can. Use it wisely and your publications will stand out from the crowd — and because the goal of all publications is to communicate effectively, that's exactly the effect you need to achieve.

Selecting Objects by Category

I love art galleries, but I have to say that some galleries are better than others. In some, there seems to be no rhyme or reason to the way the paintings are displayed. Abstract paintings are cheek-by-jowl with Baroque religious works, and paintings of saints rub shoulders with paintings of cars. The result of such a mish-mash is that even if the gallery has the world's finest collection of Monets, you probably won't be able to find them.

Most galleries, of course, take much greater pains to catalog and organize their collections, so that you can stroll from a room of medieval religious icons through a hallway filled with paintings from the first flowering of the Renaissance to a room full of Old Masters, and always know where you are and what you can expect to see.

The Design Gallery that comes with Publisher is one of the latter sorts of galleries, well organized and easily accessible. Best of all, there's no admission charge and no lines — and you can take the artwork off the walls and use it for your own purposes without setting off alarms or bringing the wrath of the curator down on your head.

One way in which Publisher organizes work is by category. This would be the equivalent of an art gallery organizing its collection by subject matter: religious art in one room, book illustrations in another, editorial cartoons in a third. In the Design Gallery, the categories include such things as boxes, advertisements, and "attention getters."

If you have a need for a specific type of element, this is the best way to approach the Design Gallery. It's not the only way to approach it, however; we'll look at browsing by design in the task following this one.

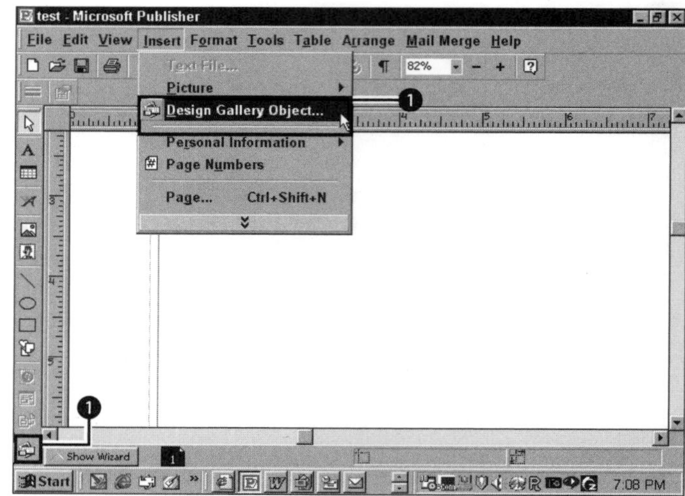

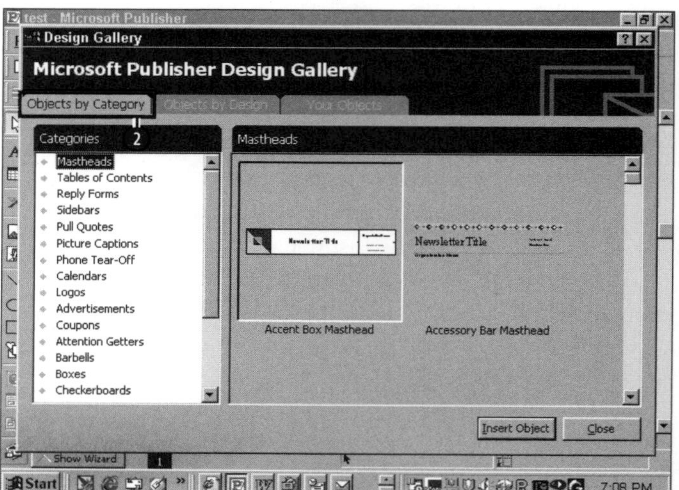

❶ *Choose Insert ➪ Design Gallery Object (or click the Design Gallery button at the bottom of the Object toolbar).*

❷ *The Design Gallery opens. Make sure the Objects by Category tab is selected.*

CROSS-REFERENCE

See Chapter 4 for information about another useful collection of preset designs.

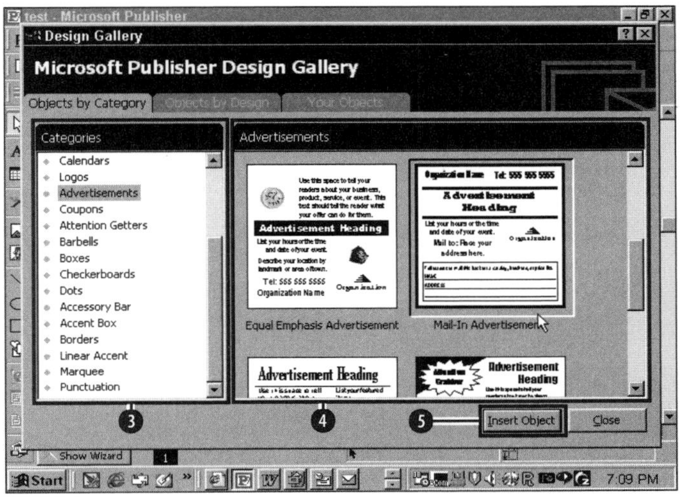

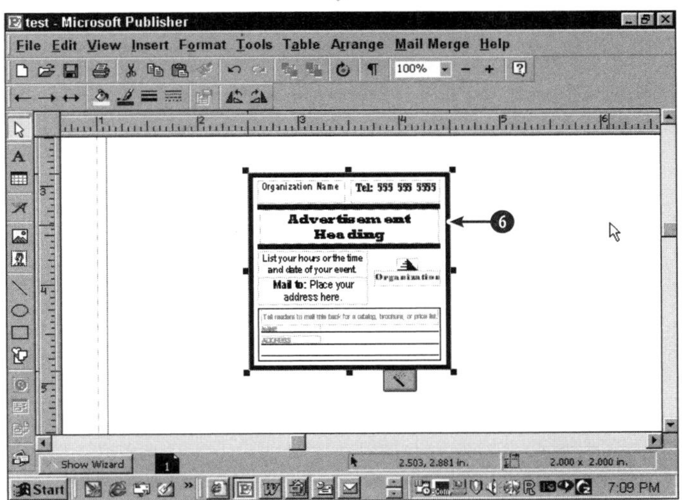

3 *Select the category you want to browse from the list at left.*

4 *Select the item you want to insert by scrolling through the previews at right.*

5 *Click Insert Object.*

6 *The object you selected is inserted into your publication.*

TAKE NOTE

FINDING WHAT YOU NEED

It's important to remember, as you browse through the Design Gallery, that just because you don't see exactly what you need doesn't mean that it's not there in embryonic form. The Design Gallery objects look so finished and final that you can sometimes forget that any Design Gallery object can be edited. Most of them, in fact, have to be, because they contain generic text. We'll look at how you modify Design Gallery objects later on in this chapter, but for now, just remember that the objects you see aren't necessarily ends in themselves, but may also serve as springboards for your own imagination and design skills.

PREVIEWING OBJECTS

Some of the names of the categories in the Design Gallery might seem a bit obscure to you, if you don't have a background in publishing. "Masthead," for instance. But if you aren't sure exactly what a category is, you'll soon figure it out; click it, and all the items in that category are previewed at right. Be sure to scroll down so you're sure you're seeing them all.

FIND IT ONLINE

See samples of what you can create with Publisher at http://www.microsoft.com/office/98/Publisher/Gallery/.

Selecting Objects by Design

Continuing our art gallery metaphor, there's another way to organize art — by style. In this type of gallery, all the Dadaist paintings would be in one room, all the impressionist paintings in another, and all the surrealist paintings in a third.

Publisher's Design Gallery also enables you to browse its contents by style — more specifically by *design sets,* which are collections of items that share common design elements, such as certain colors and shapes. The Kid Stuff design set, for example, uses blue and orange, the same fun font throughout, and a repeating image of a handprint that looks like it was made by a kid who'd dipped a hand in paint.

By using elements that all belong to the same design set, you can ensure that your publication has a unity of design throughout, which, in turn, makes it look like it *was* designed, and not simply thrown together using whatever fonts, clip art, and other graphic elements you happened to have lying around the computer.

Unity of design within a publication is important because the goal of any publication is to communicate — and a basic element of effective communication is to convince the person you're trying to communicate with that what you're saying is worth listening to. A well-designed publication sends the unspoken message that whomever has created it knows what he or she is doing and therefore is worth paying attention to. A poorly designed publication, on the other hand, screams "amateur," and makes whatever information appears in the publication, no matter how well thought out, suspect.

Design sets can help you send the vital subliminal message that you deserve to be listened to, and put your publication one step further along the road to the successful communication of your message.

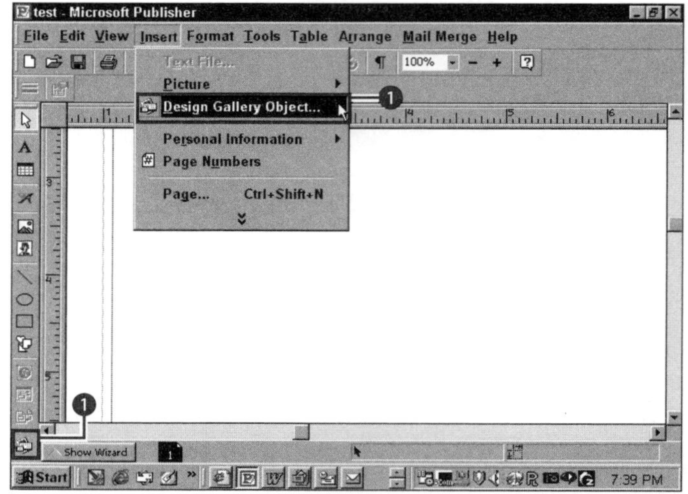

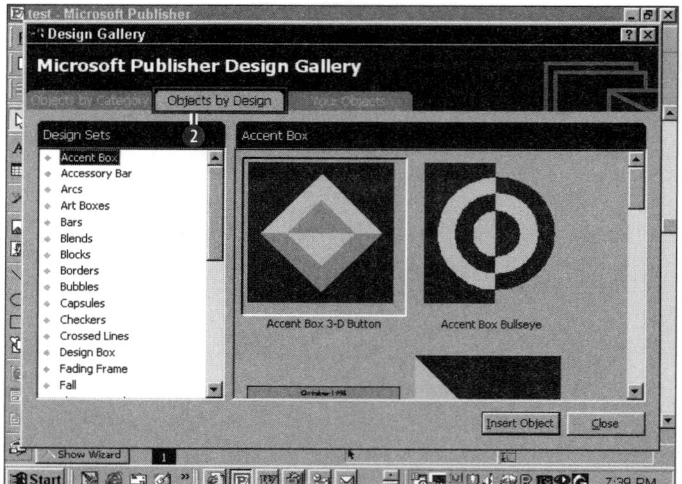

❶ Choose Insert ⇨ Design Gallery Object (or click the Design Gallery button at the bottom of the Object toolbar).

❷ The Design Gallery opens. Make sure the Objects by Design tab is selected.

CROSS-REFERENCE

For more information on drawing your own graphic elements, see Chapter 12.

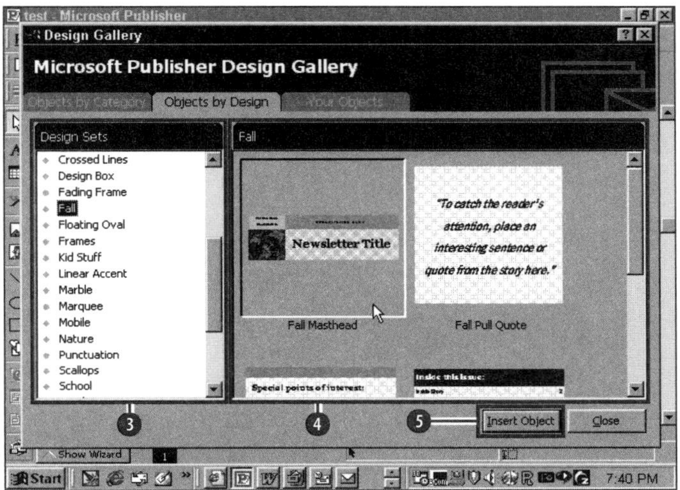

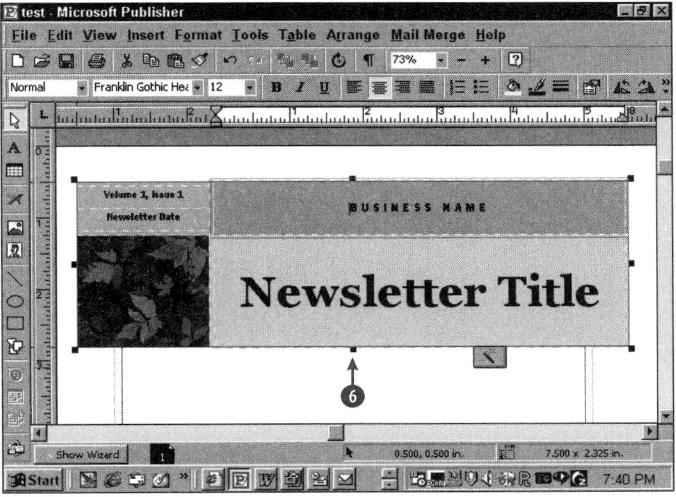

3. *Select the category you want to browse from the list at left.*
4. *Select the item you want to insert by scrolling through the previews at right.*
5. *Click Insert Object.*
6. *The object you selected is inserted into your publication.*

TAKE NOTE

CHOOSING A DESIGN SET

Something you'll quickly realize as you browse through design sets is that they don't all contain the same objects. Some contain calendars; others contain newsletter mastheads; some contain both, while others contain neither. Before committing yourself to using a particular design set, you need to look through the contents of the design set closely to be sure that all the objects you need for your publication are in there. If they aren't, you need to search through the other design sets to see if you can find one that's complementary — that does contain the elements you need. If you still can't find what you need, you should consider a different design set.

CREATING MISSING ELEMENTS

You may find a design set that contains almost everything you need, but is missing one or two items. The other option to switching designs completely is to commit yourself to creating the missing elements in the same style. It's quite possible, but it does require that you feel very confident of your ability to use all of Publisher's tools effectively.

FIND IT ONLINE

Visit an online art gallery at **http://sunsite.doc.ic.ac.uk/wm/**.

Modifying Design Objects

As noted in the last task, sometimes you can't find exactly what you need, even in a design set that's otherwise ideal. Other times, when you're searching through the Design Gallery by category, you may find the right category of items but nothing that looks exactly like what you need.

In either case, there's no need to despair: the objects in the Design Gallery aren't immutable. They're really made of standard Publisher elements — text frames, WordArt frames, picture frames — grouped together. That means they can be ungrouped and edited just like design elements you might invent on your own.

You can change the text, change the colors, remove graphic elements, add new ones, whatever you like. Design Gallery elements, then, are really just suggestions — excellent suggestions, and suggestions you might do well to follow, but suggestions just the same. You're not required to use them as they are.

This flexibility means that even if you're very confident in your ability to use Publisher's tools to create publications from scratch, it's worth your while to thoroughly investigate what's available in the Design Gallery. If you see something that you like some aspects of, but not others, you can insert it and then modify it as you see fit. You can remove the parts you don't like, keep the parts you do like, and in the process create your own Design Gallery object that you can add back to the Design Gallery for future use (more on that in the next task).

Where I live, you can rent artworks from a local branch of the city library to hang on your walls for a month — but you have to take them back in the same condition as you took them out. Publisher's Design Gallery, by contrast, not only encourages you take artwork out of it, it encourages you to repaint it to suit yourself.

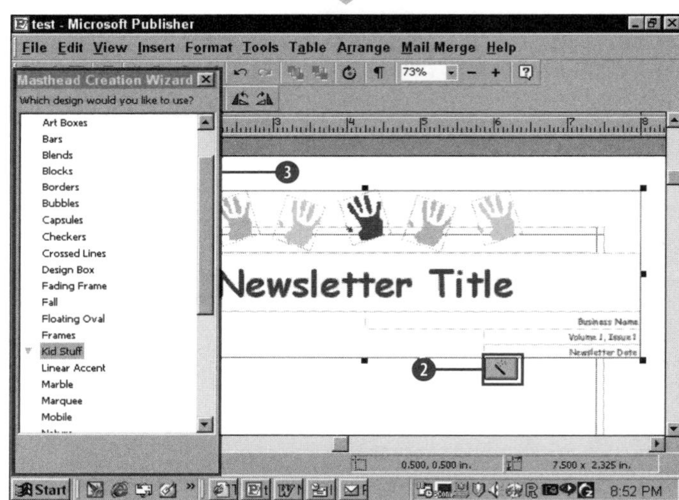

1. *Insert a Design Gallery object as usual.*
2. *Click the Wizard button to open the Object Wizard.*
3. *Choose the design you would like to change the current option to.*

CROSS-REFERENCE

For more information on grouping and ungrouping frames, see Chapter 7.

4 *Select or highlight the element of the design object you would like to change.*

5 *Edit that element as you would normally.*

By modifying Design Gallery elements, you can make your publication uniquely your own while still taking advantage of the professional design expertise represented in the Gallery's objects.

TAKE NOTE

USING THE DESIGN GALLERY WIZARDS

Each Design Gallery object has a button at the bottom, where the Group/UnGroup button normally appears, which activates a wizard. Unlike most wizards, this doesn't take you step by step through the process of changing elements of the object; instead, it opens a new method of browsing the Gallery, listing all the design sets that contain the type of element you've inserted (for example, a newsletter masthead). You can instantly change the object you inserted to the same sort of object from a different masthead by clicking the name of another design set.

UNGROUPING DESIGN GALLERY OBJECTS

As noted, a Wizard button replaces the Group/Ungroup button you would normally expect to see on a Design Gallery Object. You can still ungroup the object, though; just choose Arrange ⇨ Ungroup Objects (or press Ctrl+Shift+G). Note that once you ungroup an object, the wizard will no longer be able to change it for you.

FIND IT ONLINE

View the winners of an interesting international design competition at http://www.worldinc.com/idra/.

Building Your Own Design Gallery

By this point, you've had extensive experience using all of Publisher's many desktop design tools. You may feel that you don't really need to draw on the preset designs Publisher has included in the Design Gallery; you feel quite capable of designing your own.

The great thing about creating your own designs, of course, is that they're exactly what you want — by definition, they meet the particular needs of your publication. As well, they'll give you a great deal of creative satisfaction and a unique sense of ownership over the finished work.

That said, there's no need to work any harder than you absolutely have to. If you create a newsletter every month, for example, there's no good reason why you should have to build the masthead all over again for each issue. Nor does Publisher expect you to. Instead, it enables you to save it into the Design Gallery, where it's just as accessible to you for future issues as the designs already included there.

If you make a point of saving all your best design elements as you create them, you'll soon have your own "design set" in the Design Gallery that will enable you to create future publications much more easily.

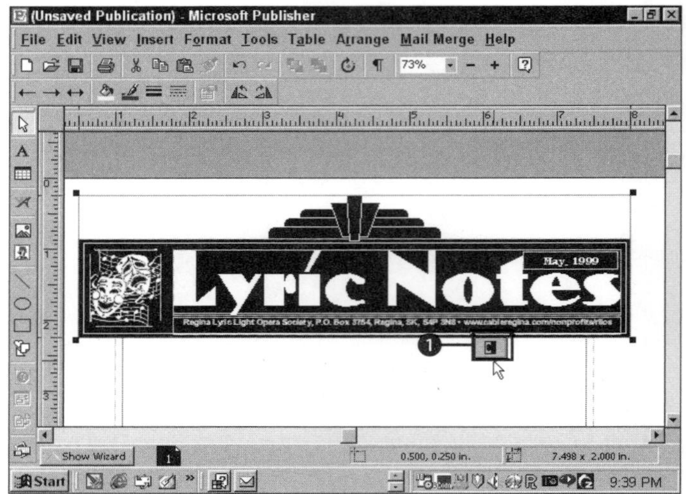

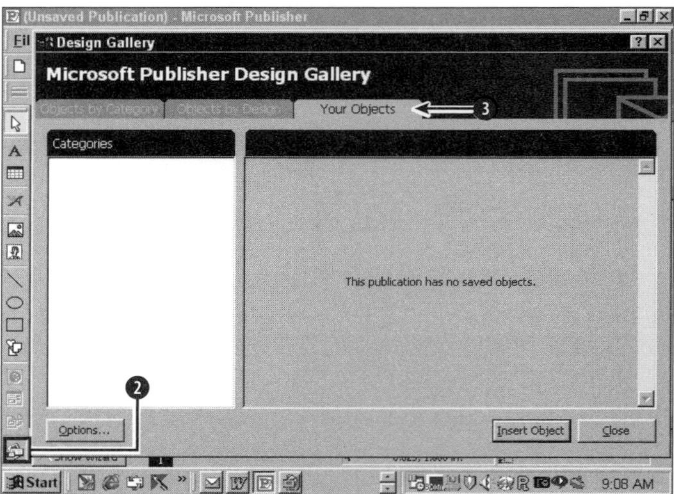

❶ *Group together the individual elements that make up the object you want to save.*

❷ *Click the Design Gallery button on the Object toolbar.*

❸ *Choose the Your Objects tab.*

CROSS-REFERENCE

For more information on saving Publisher files, see Chapter 2.

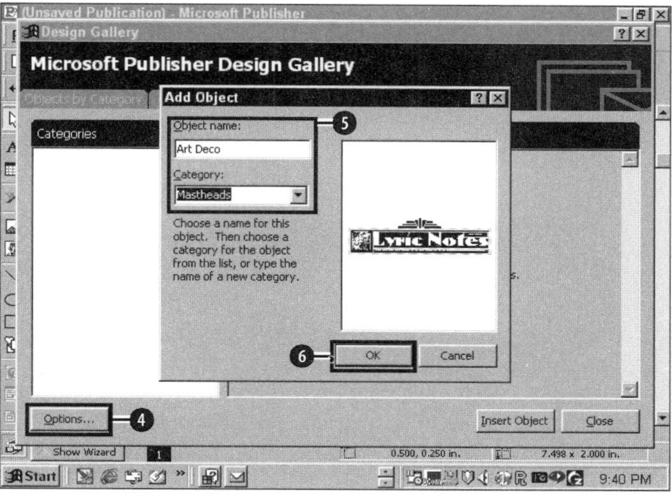

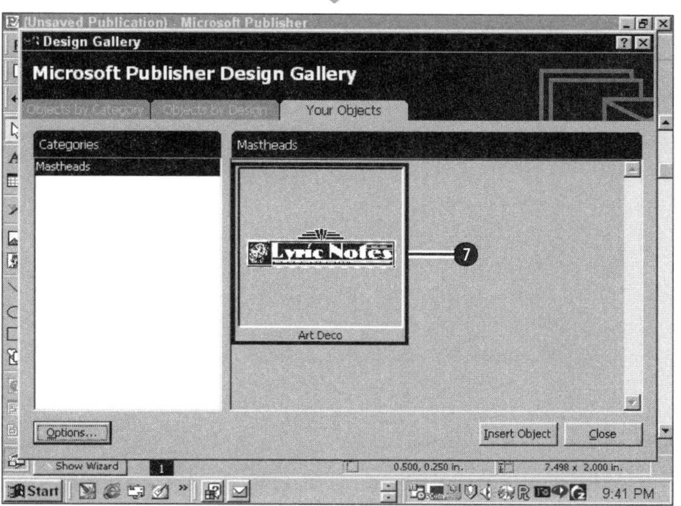

4. *Click the Options button.*
- *Choose Add Selection to Design Gallery.*

5. *Enter a name for the object and select (or create) a category for it.*
6. *Click OK.*
7. *The object is added to the Design Gallery.*

TAKE NOTE

NAMING CATEGORIES FOR YOUR DESIGN OBJECTS

Whenever you save an object you've designed to the Design Gallery, you're asked to place it in a category. Unfortunately, Publisher doesn't let you place it in any of the categories that already exist with the Gallery. Instead, you have to create your own categories. I can think of two good ways to do this. One option is to create categories that are at least comparable to those the Design Gallery already uses; for instance, "Mastheads," "Advertisements," "Attention-Getters." Because that's consistent with the rest of the Design Gallery, it may make it easier for you to remember what's in each category in the future. Another option would be to save objects in terms of the subject matter of the publications they were created for, i.e., "July Garage Sale" or "Drama Club." You may come up with a different method of organization that suits your tastes better.

IMPORTING DESIGN OBJECTS FROM ANOTHER PUBLICATION

Unlike the standard Design Gallery objects, the objects you add to the Design Gallery are saved as part of your current publication. In other words, they won't appear in the Design Gallery if you start a new publication and look under the Your Objects tab in the Design Gallery. That doesn't mean you can't use design objects from one publication in another, however. Go to Your Objects, click Options, and then choose Browse. This lets you locate the Publisher file that contains the design objects you want, and import them into the Your Objects section of the Design Gallery for your current publication.

FIND IT ONLINE

Learn how to develop your personal creativity at http://uniquorn.simplenet.com/creativ.htm.

Personal Workbook

Q&A

1. How do you browse the Design Gallery for specific categories of objects?

   ____

   ____

   ____

2. How can you find several different design objects that all share the same style?

   ____

   ____

   ____

3. How can you change a design object to an entirely different style?

   ____

   ____

   ____

4. How can you edit the text in a design object?

   ____

   ____

   ____

5. How can you change the graphics in a design object?

   ____

   ____

   ____

6. How can you turn a group of separate elements in a publication into a single design object?

   ____

   ____

   ____

7. How can you import design objects from another publication?

   ____

   ____

   ____

8. How can you organize your own design objects so you can find them again?

   ____

   ____

   ____

ANSWERS: PAGE 357

Using Publisher's Design Gallery

EXTRA PRACTICE

1. Create a sample newsletter using design elements you find by browsing the Design Gallery by category.
2. Create a sample newsletter using design elements that all belong to the same design set in the Design Gallery.
3. Find the newsletter masthead in the Summer design set and insert it into a publication. Now, change the text and picture to completely alter the masthead's appearance.
4. Save the altered masthead in the Design Gallery under a new name.
5. Open a new publication and import the masthead you redesigned into its Design Gallery, and then insert it into the new publication.

REAL-WORLD APPLICATIONS

✔ You operate a small business with a small advertising budget. The newspaper charges extra for building advertisements. Using the design objects in the Advertisements category of the Design Gallery, you're able to give them camera-ready ads that change every week.

✔ You're the publicity director for an amateur theater group, responsible for preparing programs for all their shows. By saving design elements all the programs have in common to the Design Gallery, you're able to cut the time it takes to prepare a program in half.

Visual Quiz

In this figure of the Design Gallery, locate the Fall design set, the Fall Masthead design object, and the button you would click to insert the Fall Masthead into the current publication.

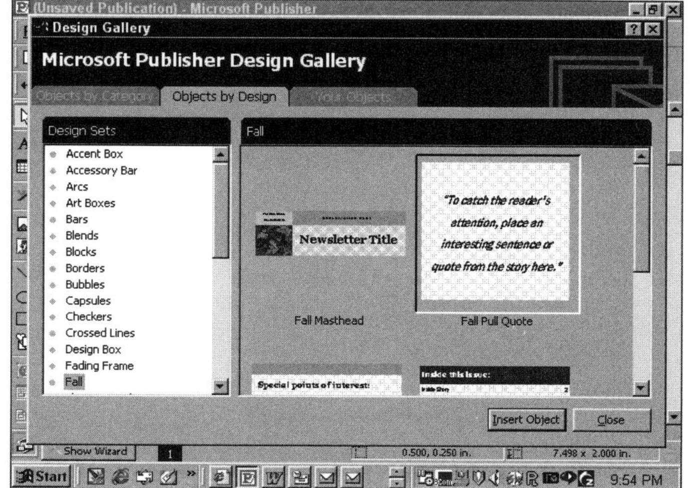

PART V

Presenting Your Publication to the Public

Congratulations! You've made it to the final part of the book. You've mastered text formatting; you've amassed a great wealth of images and art. And now, you are about to experience the culmination of all that hard work.

While you may think some of these chapters and tasks are of little use to you now, rest assured that you may be called upon one day to merge a database with a publication, post a Web site, or send your job to a commercial printer. Those tasks and more are explained within this part.

Many people feel that creating and posting a Web site requires more advanced knowledge. Nothing could be further than the truth. With a little help from Publisher and your Internet Service Provider (ISP), you can have a Web site operational in less than a few hours.

Nothing, however, can compete with the warm glow that befalls you when you hold a printed color document in your hands that you have taken from that wisp of gray matter in your head to a finished, professionally printed piece. Take a moment and bask in your glory!

CHAPTER 14

MASTER THESE SKILLS

- Creating a Publisher Address List
- Adding and Deleting Fields in the Address List
- Editing Your Address List
- Using Your Outlook Contacts as an Address List
- Importing an Address List from Other Sources
- Filtering and Sorting the Address List

Using Mail Merge

In earlier chapters, hints have been dropped about Mail Merge. If you haven't understood fully what Mail Merge is, here is an overview.

In order to use Mail Merge, you have to have two major components: a document and a database. By now you should be well aware of what a document is. You may, however, be clueless as to what a database is.

In brief, a *database* is a collection of records that are made up of *fields*. Each field holds a specific piece of information that, when combined with the rest of the fields, tells you a lot of information about a given thing. For example, an address book is a database. The fields in that database could include a person's first name, last name, address, city, state, ZIP code, phone number, e-mail address, and more. You could even go so far as recording the person's age, weight, favorite color, hobbies, and so on. Each person that you enter information for is called a *record*. It's not necessary to fill in all the fields in a record, but an efficient database will contain completed fields.

When you have a database of names and addresses, you can insert a special merge field code in a document that will extract the content of the field you specify. This doesn't have to be done in Publisher exclusively; Microsoft Word, for example, has a Mail Merge feature, too. Mail Merge in a desktop publishing (DTP) program, however, is a rare bird. Even many of the high-end DTP packages do not provide this feature.

In order to use Mail Merge in Publisher, you have to have a list of names and addresses. The great thing about Publisher is that you don't have to create them in the program itself, although you can. You can reach out to several different places and bring that data into Publisher so that your mail merge can be accomplished with little data entry on your part.

In this chapter, we explore the source of your mail merge data and the way you can recall some of the records in your database by using filters. Also, you can sort the database through Publisher so you can alphabetize things such as last names or cities, or sort on the ZIP code to satisfy mailing requirements. In the next chapter, we learn how to put this data to work.

Creating a Publisher Address List

Names and addresses are what business is all about. Just think about all the advertisements you receive in the mail each day — probably five or six just from credit card companies because of your excellent credit history. Corporate America thrives on mail, and sometimes consumers gag on it.

Mailing lists are bought and sold. Your demographic information is stored all over the country. Data about homeownership, hobbies, magazine subscriptions, mail order companies, and so on makes a lot of money for businesses that sell your address to prospective advertisers and direct mail houses. Enough already — you get the point.

When you begin to build your database of names and addresses to include in the Publisher address list, you should keep many things in mind because database purists love consistency. You will save yourself a lot of editing later if you set down guidelines when building your list. Will you include a period after abbreviations such as "Mr." and "Mrs."? Will "Post Office Box" be spelled out or simply entered as "PO Box"? Will you use ZIP plus four or stick with the standard five-digit ZIP? These questions and more will enter your head as you enter the data. It's much better to think it out ahead of time.

While you're entering information into the New Address List dialog box, a few shortcuts may make your data entry go faster:

- Press Tab or Enter to jump your cursor to the next field.
- Use the hot keys to access the buttons you see. (Hot keys are activated by holding down the Alt key and pressing the underlined letter of the button label.)

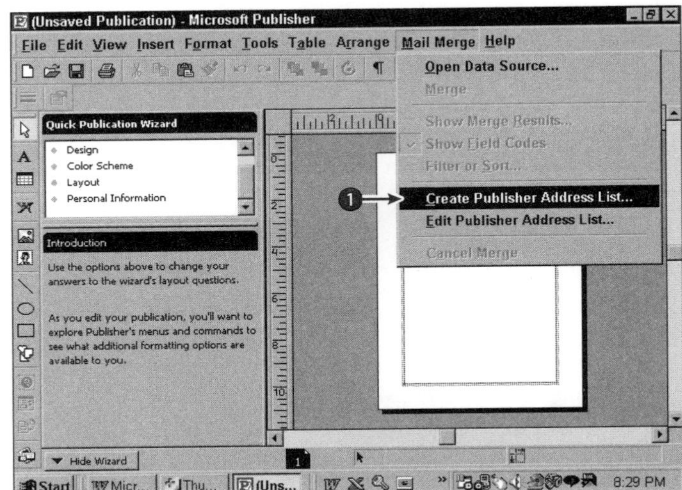

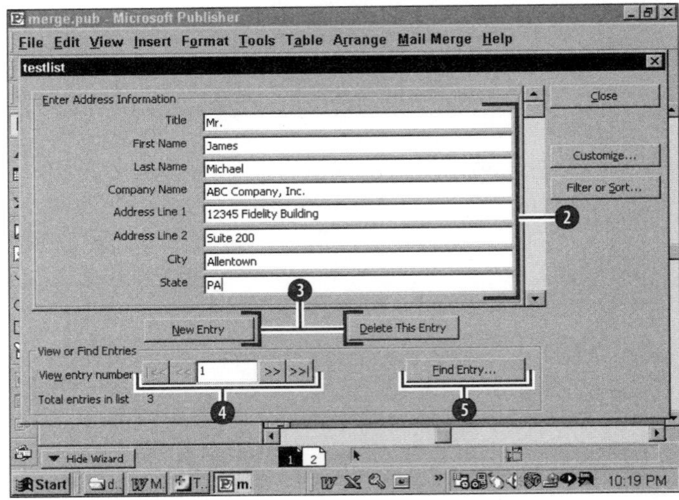

1. *From the Mail Merge menu, select Create Publisher Address List.*
2. *Type the data for each record. Use Tab or Shift+Tab to move between fields.*
3. *Click the New Entry button to create a new record or click the Delete This Entry button to remove the current record.*
4. *Use the "View entry number" buttons to scroll through the records or enter a number in the text box.*
5. *Click Find Entry to search for specific text in the record.*

CROSS-REFERENCE

To add or delete fields in the address list, see the next task.

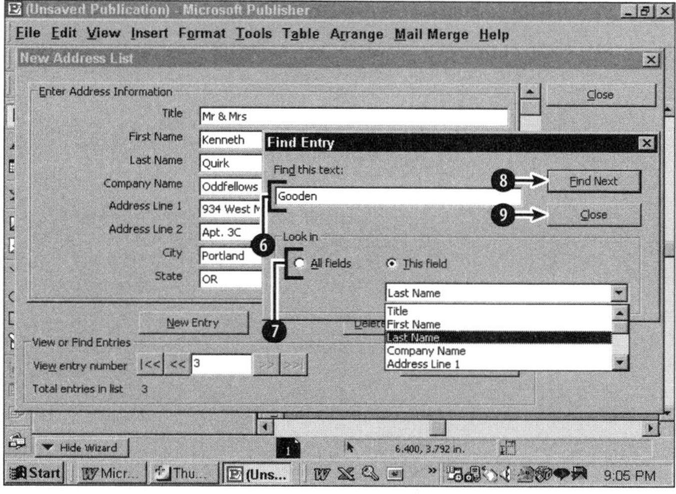

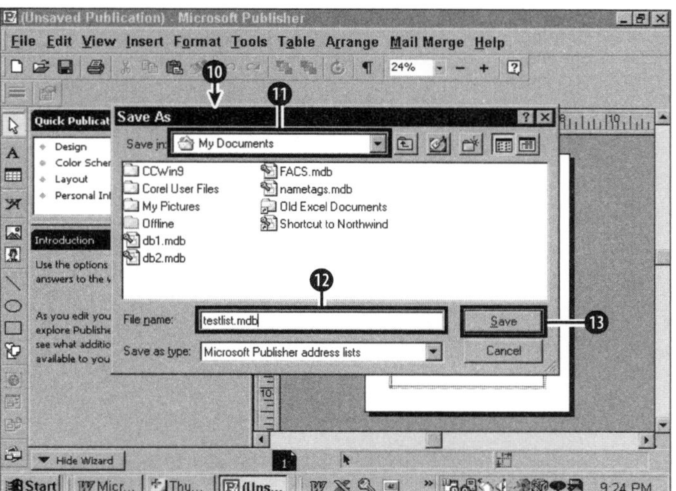

6. *Enter the search text.*
7. *Choose whether to look in all fields or choose a file from the drop-down list.*
8. *Click Find Next to retrieve the record.*
9. *Select Close to close the Find Entry dialog box.*
10. *After closing the New Address list dialog box, the Save As dialog box appears.*
11. *Choose a drive and folder to store your database.*
12. *Name the file.*
13. *Click Save.*

- Remove fields from your list if you don't need them.
- Use your address list in other Office 2000 applications; it's stored as an Access 2000 database, which makes this possible.

TAKE NOTE

PREPARE DATA THE POSTAL WAY

The address readers at the U.S. Postal Service really prefer a certain style. It makes their automated equipment hum with joy and it also makes your mail reach its destination more accurately. For example, the Post Office prefers no punctuation in the address and, ideally, all uppercase letters are sheer bliss. That's great for the Post Office, you say, but my boss doesn't like the correspondence to look that way. In that case, strike a compromise and leave out the punctuation and use upper and lowercase letters.

USE MAIL MERGE FOR LABELS

You can create a database of book titles you have in your personal library and make bookplates for the inside covers, or use Mail Merge to make a 3×5-inch card catalog of the titles.

FIND IT ONLINE

To find out more about Microsoft Access 2000 go to **http://officeupdate.microsoft.com/welcome/access.htm.**

Adding and Deleting Fields in the Address List

After the brief tour through entering your data in the address list in the previous task, you may have found that the fields that Publisher provides aren't adequate for your needs. For example, you may want to enter a URL for the company Web site, or a spouse's name, or other information to store with the record.

This task takes you through the steps of not only adding new fields to the Publisher address list, but also how to delete the fields you don't need.

Publisher gives you a good head start on the database by giving you all the vital fields the way they should be given to you. The whole purpose of a database is to break down a record into its smallest common denominator. That means instead of having a field called "name," you split it up into "first name" and "last name." This lets you alphabetize your list by a person's last name. Also, many people make the mistake of having one field for the city, state, and ZIP code. That is another faux pas, because then you can't filter records out into people who live in the same state or do a ZIP code presort for the Post Office.

If you've made any of the above mistakes, don't be afraid to can all the fields and start from scratch. You can make this database anything you want. If you're in the manufacturing business, you may want a database of the products you sell, their price, shipping weight, and box quantity. Using the example in the previous task, you could make a database of all your books, including titles, author, and date published. Your possibilities are pretty much endless.

As you add and delete fields in your database, keep in mind that you can reorganize the order in which the fields appear in the Address List dialog box. Move the fields around to match the order in which you key in the

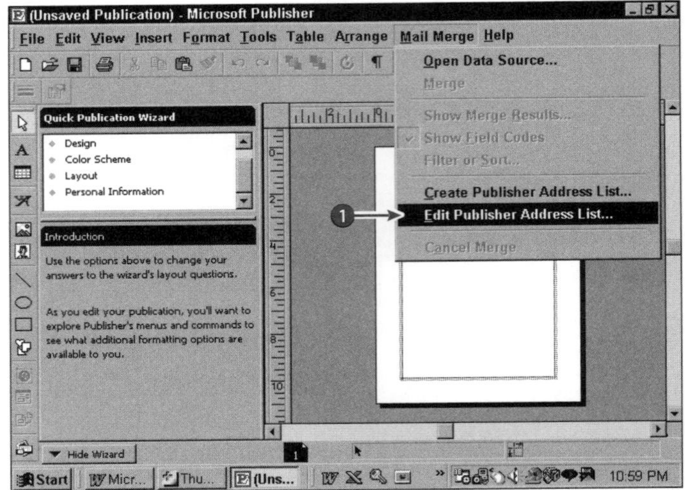

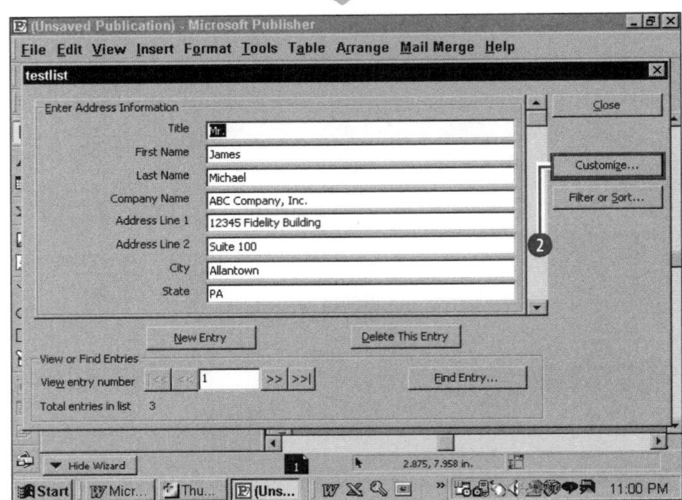

1. From the Mail Merge menu, select Edit Publisher Address List.

▶ Use the Open Address List dialog box to find your address list.

2. Click the Customize button.

CROSS-REFERENCE

See "Editing Your Address List" later in this chapter to learn about changing the data in your database.

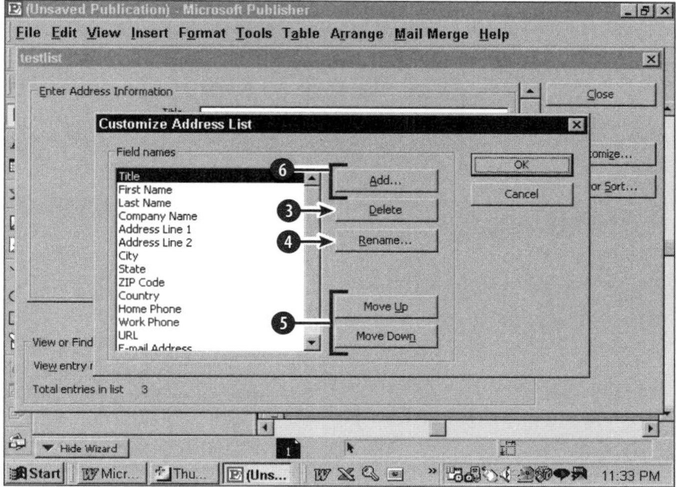

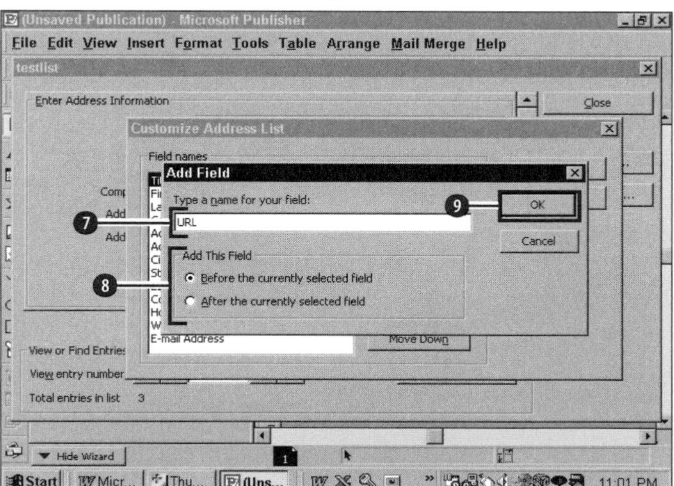

3. *Click the Delete button to remove a field.*
4. *Click the Rename button to rename a field.*
5. *Use the Move Up and Move Down buttons to change the order of the fields.*
6. *Click the Add button to insert a new field.*
7. *Insert a name for the new field in the text box.*
8. *Choose whether this field is to be added in front of or behind the currently selected field highlighted in your list.*
9. *Click OK to add the field.*
- *Click OK to close the Customize Address List dialog box.*

data. If you are handed a list with the last name placed in front of the first name, you can swap the fields so when you read down your original list, you don't have to worry about getting data out of order. Once the data is entered, you can go back and customize the list order to better suit your needs. The data remains intact in the appropriate field.

TAKE NOTE

DELETING FIELDS DELETES DATA

If you decide to edit your address list after you have entered data, any fields you delete will also delete the data that you have entered. However, if you decide to add a field, the data in your current fields remains where it is.

FIND IT ONLINE

ZIP code information can be confirmed at **http://www.usps.gov/ncsc/.**

Editing Your Address List

Because the Publisher address list is an actual, bona fide Access 2000 database, you are free to add records, delete records, and edit records whenever the need arises. And, at the rate that all of the telephone area codes are changing, keeping a database up-to-date is not easy task. Unfortunately, the Publisher address list has no way to globally update records with a search and replace. However, if you familiarize yourself with Access, you can make global changes there without affecting the way that Publisher reads and uses the data.

If you prefer not to buddy up with Access, the tools in Publisher will help you somewhat in making changes. Plus, if your database is bursting at the seams and you have to find specific records, a few tools can help you find the correct record to make changes in a split second. (If you haven't noticed, the address list database is rather quick. It doesn't take a lot of time to find records or edit them. You can thank the Access file structure for that.)

For finding records, a simple dialog box enables you to key in text to search for in all the fields, or just the one you specify.

When you click the Delete This Entry button, the entire record will be eliminated, never to return again unless you reenter the data.

The New Entry button takes you to the end of the database and presents you with a blank record, ready for your input.

All the while, you can keep track of the number of entries in the database by looking at the total sitting at the bottom of the dialog box, diligently keeping track of every record you enter.

This task takes no design talent or even an eye for what looks good. Fast typing skill may come in handy for entering new records, but that's about it.

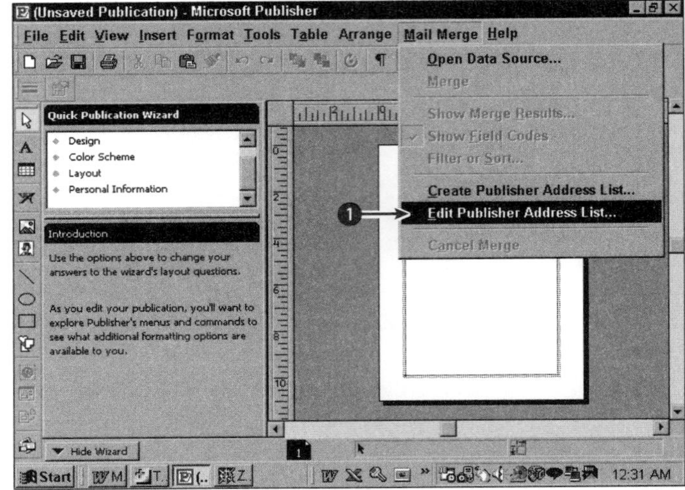

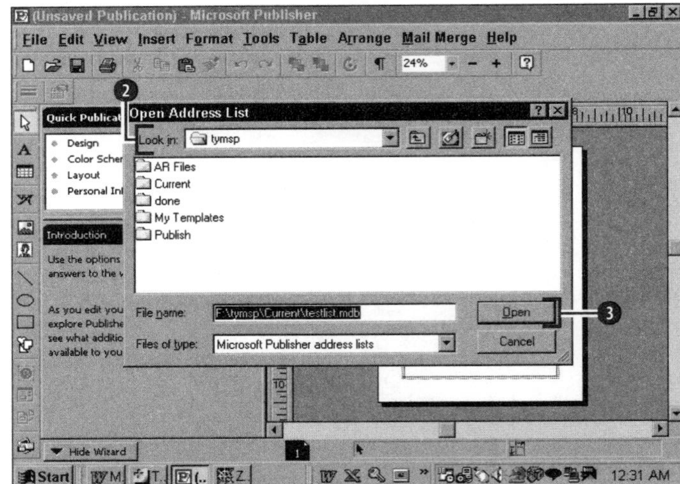

1. Select Edit Publisher Address List from the Mail Merge drop-down menu.
2. Use the Look In drop-down list to find the drive and folder where the file is located.
3. Click Open.

CROSS-REFERENCE

Many wizards provide for customer contact information to be created. Chapter 4 explains how to use the wizards.

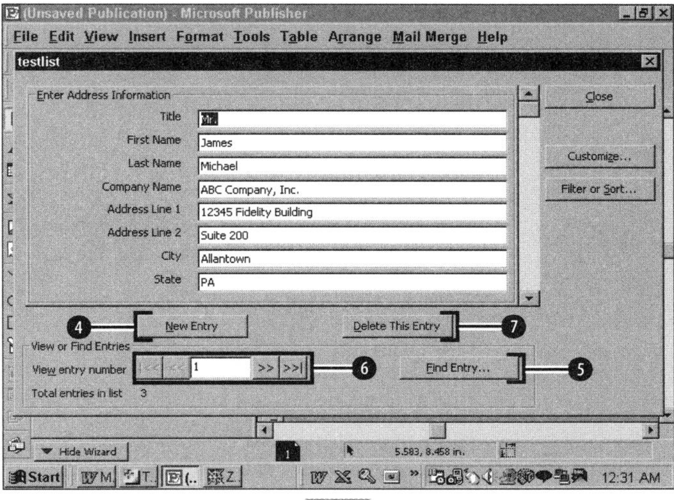

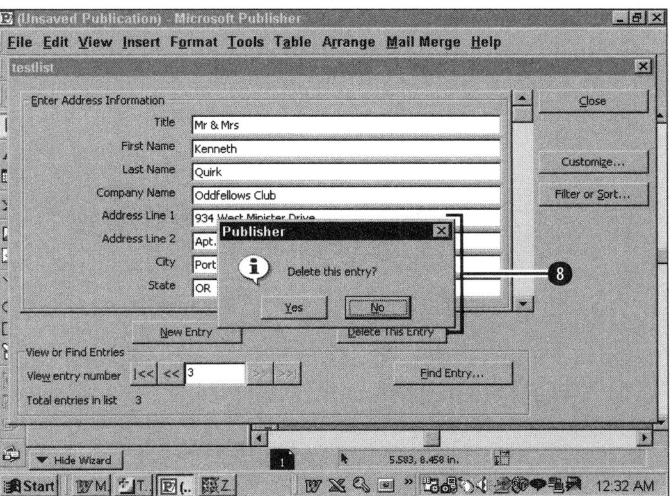

4. *Click the New Entry button to add a new record.*
5. *Use the Find Entry button to locate a record to edit.*
6. *Alternatively, use the "View entry number" arrows to locate a record.*
7. *Click the Delete This Entry button to remove a record.*
8. *A warning box asks if you are sure that you want to delete this record. Answer Yes to complete the deletion. Answering No keeps the record intact.*

TAKE NOTE

DELETING ENTRIES

Although it's been mentioned before, it bears repeating. In the Publisher address list, record deletions take effect immediately. You won't be able to cancel the operation in any way. It's the same story with editing records. Once you have made a change to a field and moved to another field or record, you can't reverse the operation unless you retype it. You can, however, press Ctrl+Z to undo an edit in a field as long as you have not moved your cursor out of that field.

FIND IT ONLINE

Standard address abbreviations approved by the Post Office are at http://www.usps.gov/ncsc/. Click the link to Official Abbreviations.

Using Your Outlook Contacts as an Address List

These days, it's hard to keep track of e-mail, contact information, a calendar schedule, and a to do list. You, however, may be fortunate to have a handy application in your repertoire of software if you are using Microsoft Office 2000. Inside that bundle of programs, you'll find Outlook 2000.

Most people use Outlook as an Internet e-mail package, keeping track of their e-mail addresses and messages. Outlook, however, is more than an e-mail package for the Internet — you can also use it as your e-mail software for the local area network in your office. And there's more. Outlook could serve as your personal information manager (PIM) because it includes a calendar for scheduling, a to do list, and a place for notes. You not only can keep track of your contacts, their addresses (both home and business), a slew of telephone numbers, and e-mail addresses, but spouse's name, manager's name, Web address, birthday, anniversary, and a lot more.

Outlook also gives you the ability to group individuals by common interests in a distribution list. When you use Outlook as the merge file for Publisher, you will be able to separate out the group or groups of contacts that you wish to use.

Publisher isn't the only Office application that can use Outlook as a merge file. Word is capable of pulling in data from Outlook as well. While the process is a bit different, the technique and outcome are the same. This means that because your contact data is capable of being used in several places, the importance of correct information and its appearance should take top priority. Be consistent when you enter the data.

While we can't really get into explaining the workings of Outlook in this book, we can tell you how to use

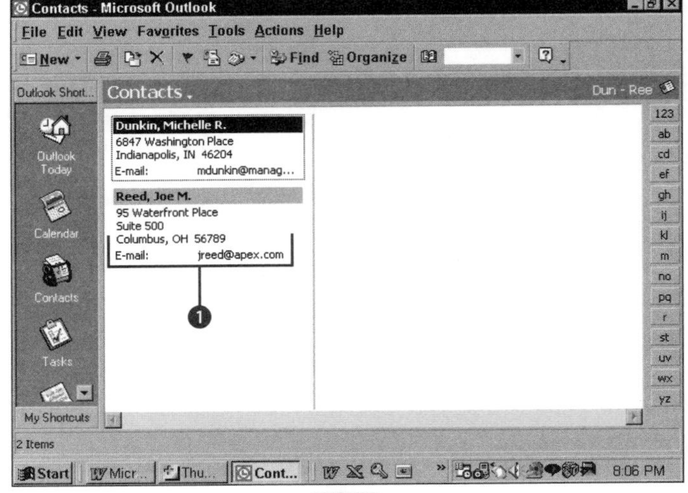

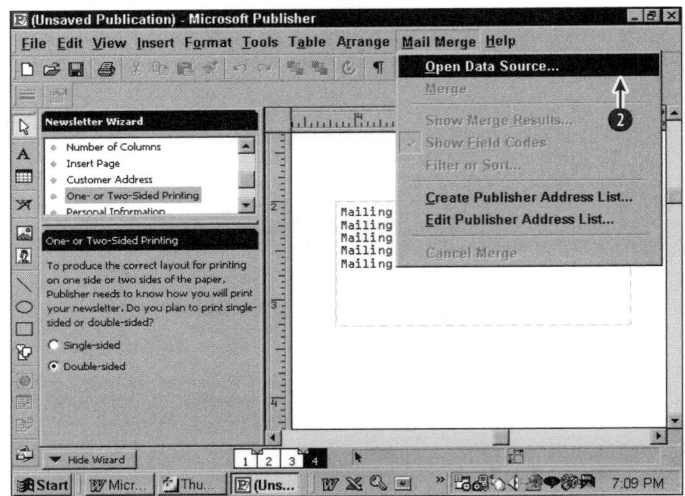

1. *Enter data into Outlook.*
2. *Choose Open Data Source from the Mail Merge menu.*

CROSS-REFERENCE

To preview your Outlook data in Publisher see Chapter 15.

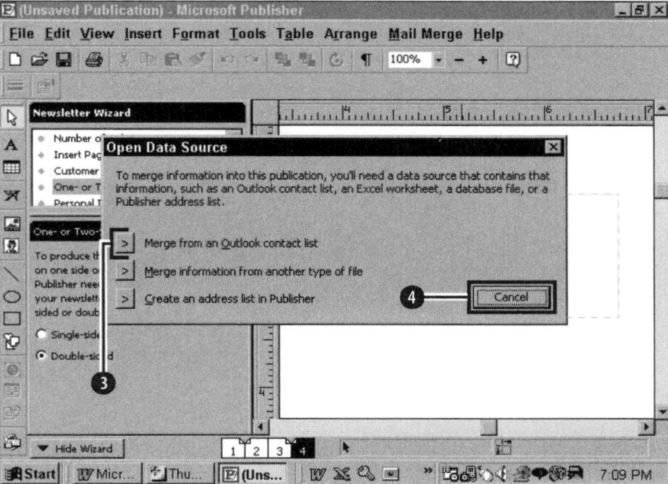

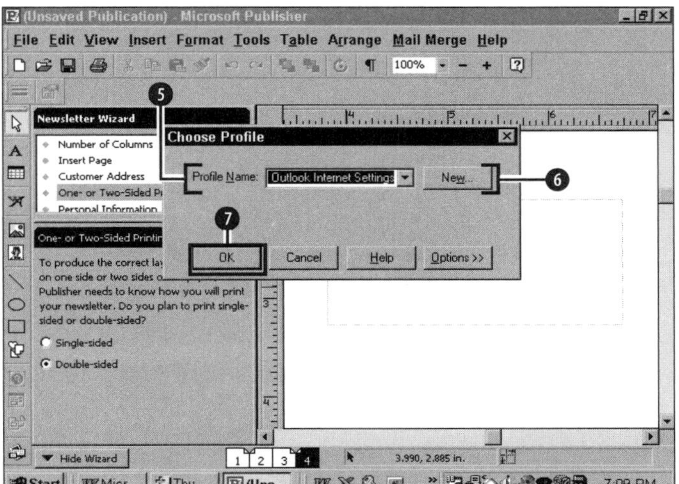

3. Select "Merge from an Outlook contact list."
4. Or, click Cancel to discontinue the operation.
5. Choose your Outlook Profile Name.
6. To search for another Profile that is not in the list, click the New button.
7. Click OK to make the link between your publication and the Outlook contact list.

Outlook as the data source when you want to merge with a publication created in Publisher.

Once you set up a merge to a publication, the link to the data file is saved with the publication. The next time you open the document, the data file is available for use through the Mail Merge menu.

TAKE NOTE

KEEP OUTLOOK CLOSED DURING MERGE

Be careful. You cannot have Outlook open at the same time as Publisher. If you try to open Outlook while Publisher is open, Outlook gives you an error message that the data is in use. The same is true when the situation is reversed. Publisher can't open the data file if Outlook is open.

CLOSING A MERGE LINK

When you want to sever the link between the data file and the publication, choose Cancel Merge from the Mail Merge menu.

FIND IT ONLINE

More info on Outlook and its features can be found at **http://officeupdate.microsoft.com/welcome/outlook.htm.**

Importing an Address List from Other Sources

For years, dBase was the king of database file formats. Paradox moved into the limelight as well. Microsoft's own Access format, of course, is supported as well as the standard ASCII delimited files. Suffice it to say that there aren't too many database files that you won't be able to bring into Publisher. Of course, you may end up having to import it into another database program such as Access to convert it, but where databases are concerned, you don't have near the translation problems as you do in publishing programs.

The following table presents the official database formats that are available directly through Publisher 2000:

DATABASE FORMATS AVAILABLE IN PUBLISHER 2000

Format	Function
MDB	Microsoft Publisher address list (as you learned to create earlier in this chapter)
MDB	Microsoft Access files (all versions up to and including Access 2000)
DOC	Microsoft Word address lists (tables or merge data documents)
WDB	Microsoft Works database files (DOS version 3 as well as Windows versions 2.0–4.x)
XLS	Microsoft Excel spreadsheets (versions 3, 4, 5, 7, and 8)
DB	FoxPro Paradox database files (2.0, 2.5 and 2.6)
TXT, CSV, TAB, ASC	ASCII text files that may be delimited with commas, quotation marks, or other characters (fixed field width files will not work).
DBF	dBase files (which include s versions III, IV, and 5)

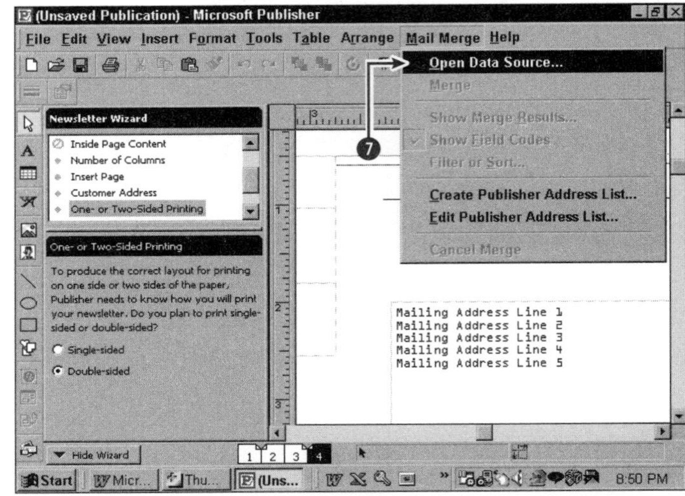

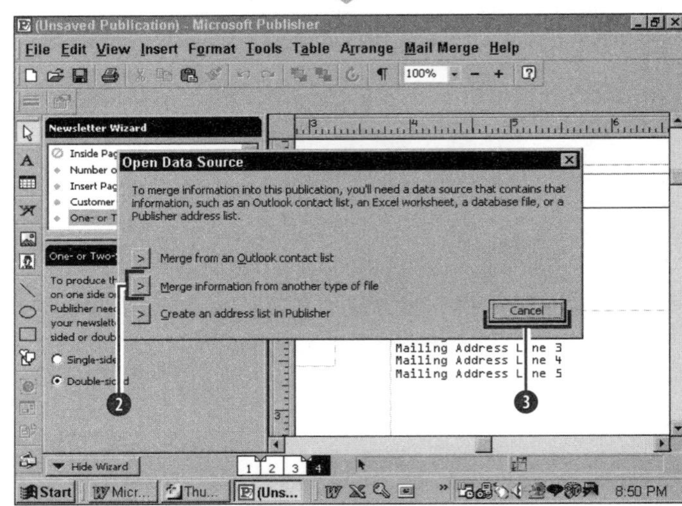

❶ *Choose Open Data Source from the Mail Merge menu.*

❷ *Select "Merge information from another type file."*

❸ *Click Cancel to abort the operation.*

CROSS-REFERENCE

To learn how to insert the field codes in your publication, read "Inserting Field Codes into your Publication" in Chapter 15.

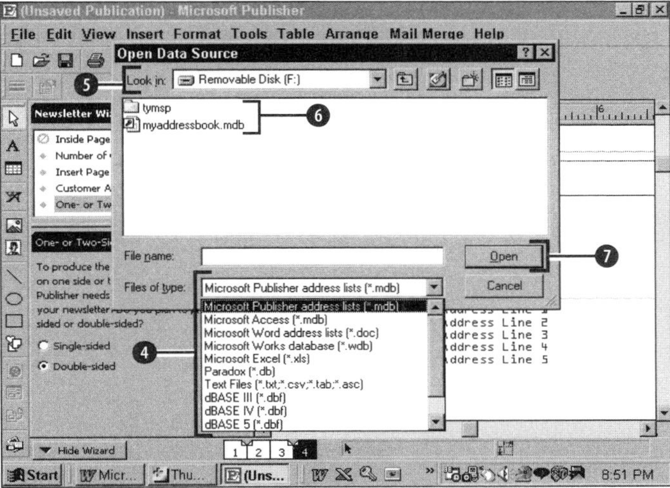

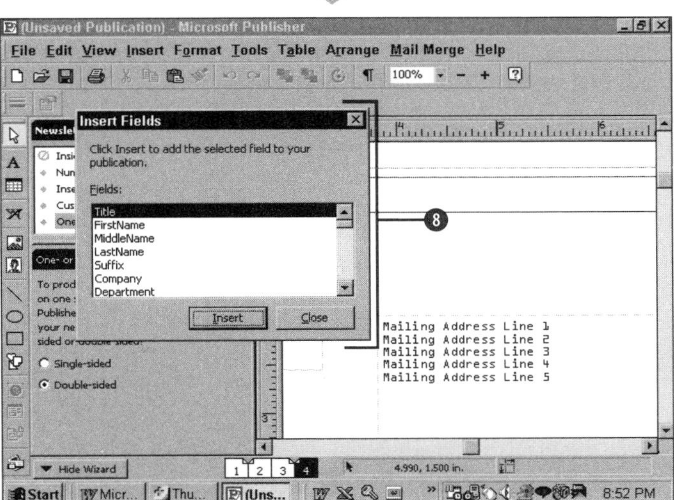

4. *Select the file format.*
5. *Go to the drive and folder where the file is located.*
6. *Select the file.*
7. *Click Open.*
8. *The Insert Fields dialog box opens to enable you to place the database fields into your publication.*

As previously stated in this chapter, if you're going to be working with databases a lot, it would be a good idea to learn Microsoft Access. The time you invest will be well worth it, not only in using the software itself but in understanding databases and their file structures.

TAKE NOTE

BE SURE TO HAVE FIELD NAMES

If you receive a file from someone else in one of the ASCII versions, be sure that they give you a list of the fields in the order they appear in the file. Imagine the confusion if there were three fields for telephone numbers and you don't know which is the fax, office or home number. Also, have them tell you how the file is delimited. Some programmers use tabs, while other prefer commas and quotes.

WATCH OUT FOR PROPRIETARY FILE FORMATS

If your data is coming from another personal information manager (PIM), the file format may not be quite what you expect. Many of these programs use a file format that cannot be imported directly because they are in nonstandard format. Many PIMs do, however, have export utilities to make the file usable in Publisher.

FIND IT ONLINE

You can take classes online to learn about Access at http://www.zdu.com (for a fee).

Filtering and Sorting the Address List

You won't always want everything in your database merged with Publisher. And at certain times your merged pieces must be in just the right order. For example, large mailings can be sorted by ZIP code to save postage.

Any database program lets you sort records by a number of fields. In Publisher, the filtering and sorting capabilities can go three levels deep. Plus, you can combine them to filter and sort at the same time. Using the previous example, you can sort by ZIP code and filter out everything except those addresses that are in a certain state.

In the Filter portion of the Filter and Sorting dialog box, you can specify up to three conditions that a record must reach in order to be included in the final listing. Each of these conditions ties together with either "AND" or "OR," which are referred to as *Boolean operators*. Use these guys carefully, especially "AND." When you use "AND" as an operator, you are telling the software that each record must satisfy both conditions. If you ask for records where the state equals "IN" and "OH," you would have no records returned because the state field would only contain one or the other.

Also, choose your comparison phrase carefully. When you ask for something to be equal to or not equal to a field in the database, the compare to match has to be exact.

The other comparison terms, "Is less than" and "Is greater than," are good to use with numbers and dates. You could use them with regular text to get anything starting with a specific letter or phrase, but that may get a little tricky. Experiment and preview the results. If they aren't what you expected, start over again.

CROSS-REFERENCE

Test your queries by using the Preview options discussed in Chapter 15 under "Viewing the Merge Results."

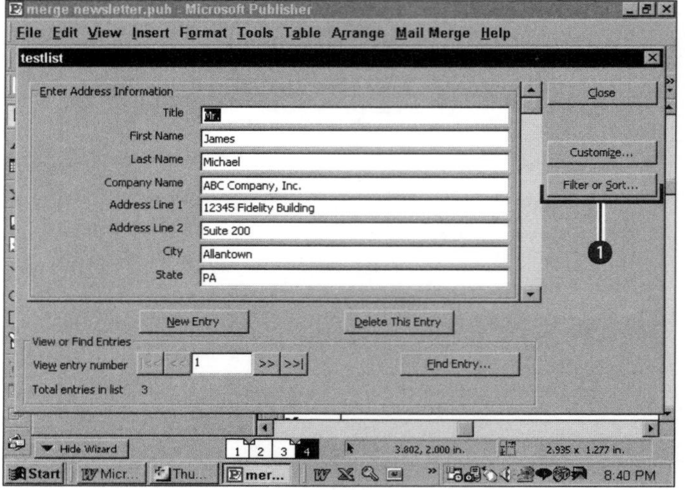

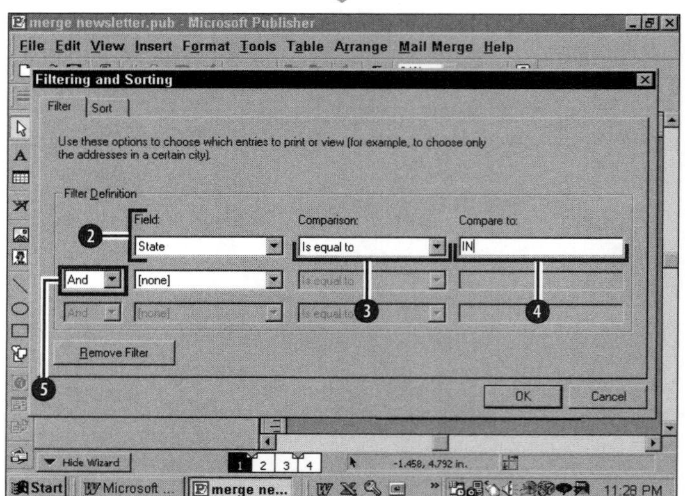

1. From the Mail Merge menu, select Edit Publisher Address List. Then, click the Filter or Sort button.

▶ Optionally, if you have a data source already open, you can choose Mail Merge ➪ Filter or Sort to manipulate any data source file.

2. To filter records, select the field name that will be filtered.
3. Select how the data is going to be compared.
4. Enter the criteria the data in the field should match.
5. Optionally, choose a Boolean operator and repeat Steps 2–4 on the second line.

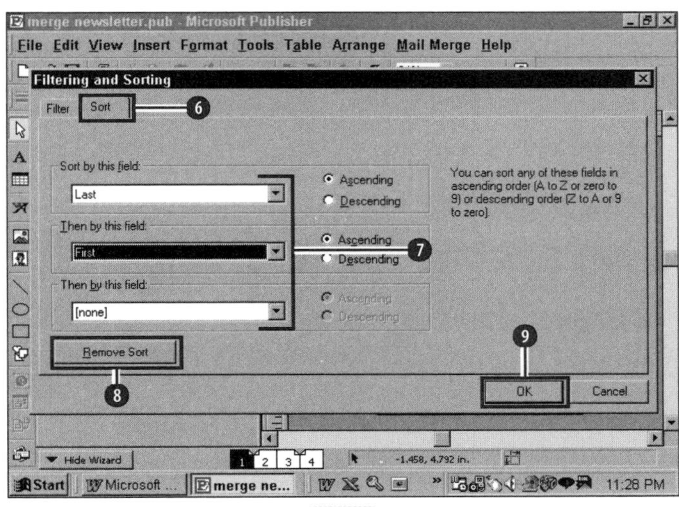

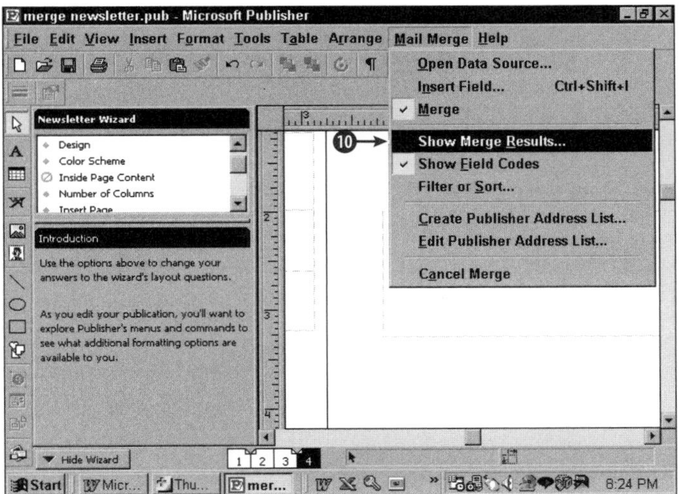

6. *To sort the output, click the Sort tab.*
7. *Choose up to three fields that the records will be sorted on.*
8. *To reset all the fields back to none, click Remove Sort.*
9. *Click OK.*
10. *To preview the records generated, choose Show Merge Results from the Mail Merge menu.*

▶ *For steps on viewing your results, see Chapter 15.*

TAKE NOTE

ENTER DATA CAREFULLY

When you specify a filter criteria, it is very important that the data in your records are consistent. If you apply a filter for all the records that have "McDonald" as a last name, the filter will exclude "Mcdonald" because the "d" is not capitalized. Likewise, "IN" is not the same as "In."

FILTER AND SORT ORDER

If you remember in math, anything within parentheses was calculated before the rest of the equation. The same holds true for these qualifiers, except Publisher will look at them in the order they appear. So, in the Sort area, the first field will be sorted, and then the second, and lastly the third. In the Filter area, the criteria is not as critical if you are only using OR as the Boolean. But when you use it in conjunction with AND, the order you place the criteria will be considered.

FIND IT ONLINE

To understand Boolean operators and how they work, visit **http://itd.umd.edu/psycinfo/help/boolean.htm.**

Personal Workbook

Q&A

1. Can you only create one Publisher address list?

2. So you can make the Publisher address list more streamlined for entering data, what should you do to the fields?

3. Name two ways that you can find records in your Publisher address list.

4. What other types of database files can you use to mail merge in Publisher? Name at least three.

5. What is the name of the Microsoft software program that helps you keep track of contacts, dates, and e-mail addresses?

6. What other special abilities or features does the program in question 5 have?

7. What is the function of a Boolean operator when filtering a database?

8. What are your two choices for sorting a field?

ANSWERS: PAGE 358

Using Mail Merge

EXTRA PRACTICE

1. Create a Publisher address list that consists of the following fields: first name, last name, street 1, street 2, city, state, ZIP, and home phone. Save the file and input data for five family members
2. Open the address list that you created above and add a field for work phone number and birthday. Then, go through the database and add the data for your five records.
3. Get a database from a friend or coworker in a file format that Publisher is capable of importing. Open the data and sort the records by two of the fields.
4. Create a publication in Publisher and attach a data file to it for mail merging. Cancel the merge and attach another database file.

REAL-WORLD APPLICATIONS

✔ You are in charge of a mailing list of addresses all over the country. You only have postage to send to three states at a time. You use the filter capabilities of Publisher to extract only those records that match those three states.

✔ After receiving the vacation requests of the employees in your company, you create a database of the employee names and the dates they have requested off. Using Publisher's sorting capabilities, you make two lists: one arranged alphabetically by employee name and the other by the date that personnel will be missing work.

✔ You use Microsoft Outlook as your e-mail program of choice. You enter in all known data in the Contacts file so that you can use it for mail merging in Publisher.

Visual Quiz

You have 32 Smiths and 44 Jones in your database. How many records will be returned from this filter setting and why? What can you change to ensure you get all of the Smiths and Jones?

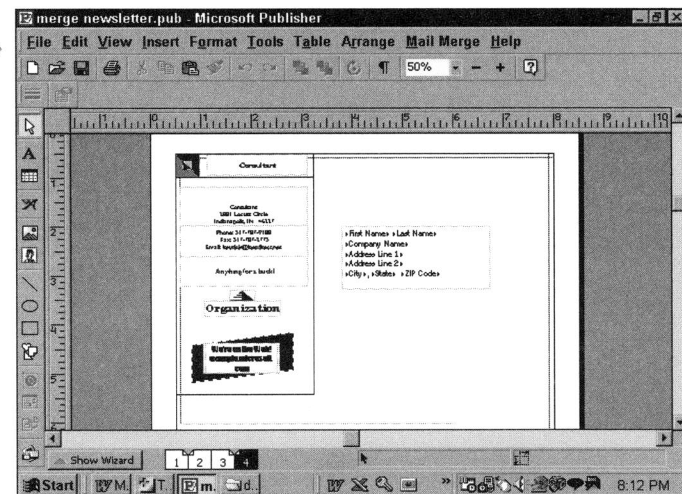

CHAPTER 15

MASTER THESE SKILLS

- Inserting Field Codes Into Your Publication
- Merging Your Publication with Your Address List
- Viewing the Merge Results
- Printing Your Merged Publication

Linking Address List Fields to Your Publication

Hopefully any mystery has dissolved regarding database files, how to alert Publisher that they're on your computer, and how you intend to use them for a mail merge of some sort. As with everything, it may take some trial and error and extended practice to get exactly the result you want, but it will be well worth it in the long run. Trust me on this one. You will soon be able to wow your boss and coworkers, and go home to excitedly tell your family that you are master of your database and mail merge.

Of course, you still have to overcome one slight technicality — this chapter. Yes, you know how to find or create a database and tell Publisher that it is about to be merged with your data, but now you have to tell Publisher what to do with the data.

This is the part of the symphony where you are the conductor. Publisher has practiced its part and the database has been rehearsed. The score has been arranged through the filters and sorts that you composed. Now, the audience — your printer — will receive the fruits of that labor.

This chapter explains how to insert the merge codes so Publisher knows exactly what field of information you want to extract from the database and where to place it. You get to hear the breathless hush of the audience while it waits for the first movement.

Your preparation is complete when you next begin to physically merge the database and publication. With a wave of the baton or a few mouse clicks and keystrokes, your data appears in the publication.

Previewing your data as it flows on the page sends sweet music through your very being.

And when that hush is pierced by the first notes meticulously played, you'll smile with contentment because you are now one of the old masters in the mail-merge symphony. Your printer hums along and produces your masterpiece.

So, maybe I have embellished things a bit and you now have an urge for Beethoven's 5th or the 1812 Overture, but one thing's certain. You'll be singing the Hallelujah Chorus when it all works as you planned.

Inserting Field Codes Into Your Publication

There's really no trick to placing field codes in your publication. As a matter of fact, if you used one of the wizards that asks if you want to place contact information in the document, much of your work for a mail merge is done for you. Placeholders for the name and address are placed nicely in a conspicuous and logical mailing area. You even have the option to include the data in your personal information as a return address. If you didn't choose a wizard that affords you this luxury, don't sweat it. Inserting merge fields is neither time-consuming nor intrusive to your soul.

For one thing, when you insert fields in Publisher, you'll want to include any spaces and punctuation between the fields that is not already included in the database. For example, after inserting the first name, press the spacebar before inserting the last name. When you preview your data, as explained later in this chapter, take a look at the sample data. You may not have to include some punctuation because the database you inherited from the old stodgy secretary that can't seem to leave the typewriter behind has included the comma after the city data that was keyed in. In the case of pricing, you may or may not have to include the dollar sign in front of the price. All prices may have been entered with it, or the database converted it to a currency field.

Once you have the first line of fields formatted and you are ready to begin a new line, press Enter when you're ready — just because you lay down a new field doesn't mean that Publisher knows you want a new line.

When you see the Field List on your screen, you can double-click the fields to insert them. It's not necessary to click the Insert button each time. After a field is inserted, your cursor defaults to the end of that field, preparing you to press the spacebar, enter some form of punctuation, or press the Enter key to begin a new line.

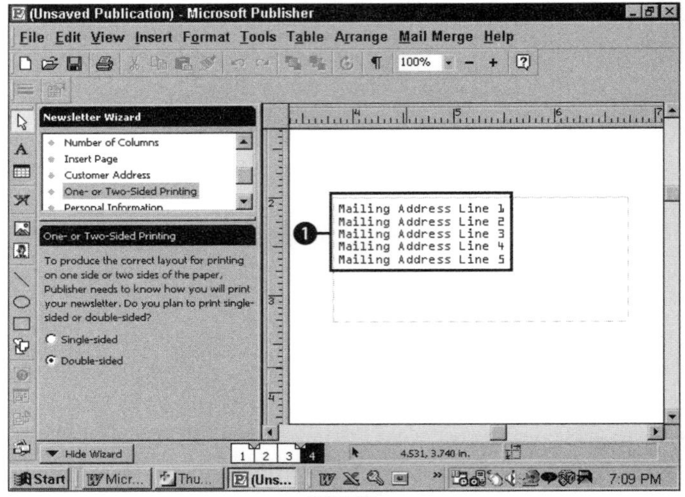

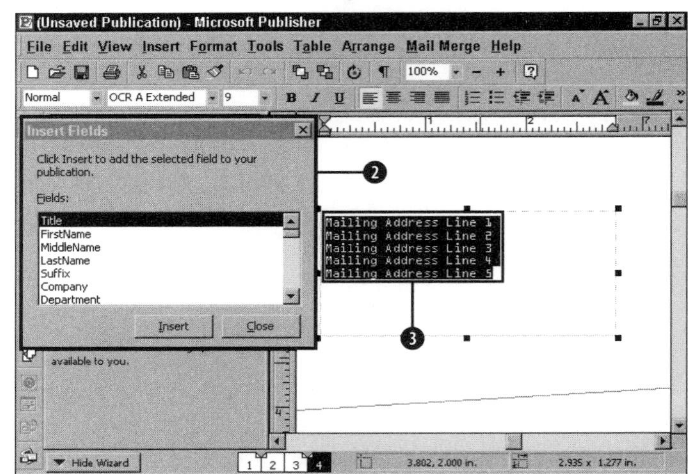

❶ *If you used a wizard to ask for customer information, Publisher displays five mailing address lines.*

❷ *After making your database connection as explained in Chapter 14, your Insert Fields dialog box appears.*

❸ *Delete the placeholder text that Publisher inserted, or create a text frame with your cursor placed in it.*

CROSS-REFERENCE

Chapter 4 covers wizards and inserting customer information placeholders.

Linking Address List Fields to Your Publication

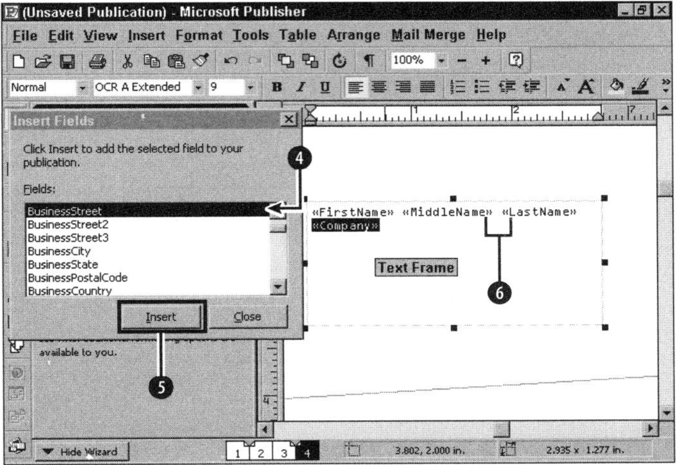

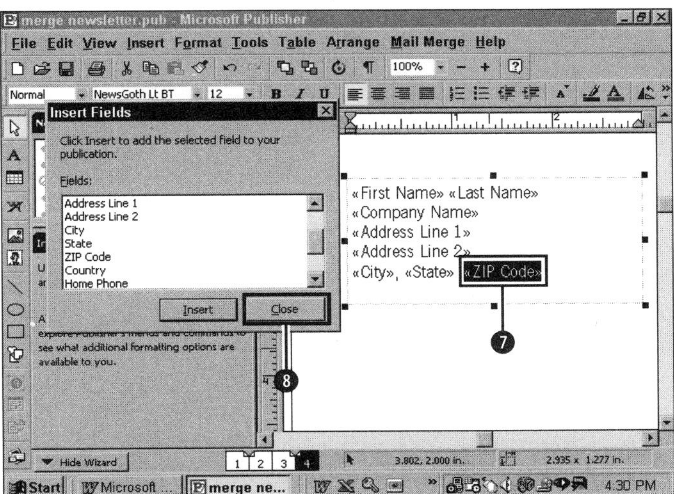

4. *Find the field you want to insert in the publication and highlight it.*
5. *Click the Insert button.*
- *Or, you can double-click the field name and forgo the Insert button.*
6. *Insert spaces or punctuation as needed between the fields.*
7. *Highlight a field and press the Delete key to remove a field.*
8. *When finished with the Insert Fields dialog box, click the Close button.*

This isn't rocket science, by any means. Once you get the hang of it, you'll have one hand on the mouse and the other on the keyboard, laying fields down with precision and speed.

TAKE NOTE

INSERTING COMBINED DATA AS ONE FIELD

In Outlook, you'll find a field named Business Address. Inserting this field inserts the street address, city, state and ZIP code all at one time. Some other databases may give you this chance, too, but Outlook is a good example because you may already have it installed on your computer. Of course, you can still enter the fields one at a time, because they show up in the list, too.

FIND IT ONLINE

To play some classical music on your computer while you begin your composition, log on to **http://midiworld.com/cmc/index.htm.**

Merging Your Publication with Your Address List

You might consider this task to be the miracle to all your hard work thus far. The database has been put in shape with all the data consistently entered with the correct spelling and punctuation where needed. You have specified the filter requirements and sorted the data to suit your needs. The merge fields have been carefully placed on the pages of your publication. You close the Insert Fields dialog box and find nothing except the field names on the page.

Two things you should notice: no data from the database appears on the page, and the font really needs some help. Now is an ideal time to make a change to the font that will be used to address your document. Publisher defaults to inserting the address placeholders in an OCR (optical character recognition) font that bears a strong resemblance to the unintelligible numbering scheme on the bottom of your checks. While that works for banks and probably the post office, it does nothing to enhance your publication's design. Change it now. Quick.

Once the font is changed, you'll be glad because the data from the database takes on the font characteristics that you have given the field names. And, in the words of Martha Stewart, that's a good thing.

What if no data shows up? If you find yourself scratching your head and perhaps swearing under your breath, don't feel alone. Most people would think that the minute the Insert Fields dialog box is closed, the merge ought to take place. But if you stop to think about it, you really need to keep the publication this way until you are ready to preview and print the merged information. This gives you time to do some last minute editing, print a draft copy for passing up the ladder for approvals, or even experiment with the color scheme or design.

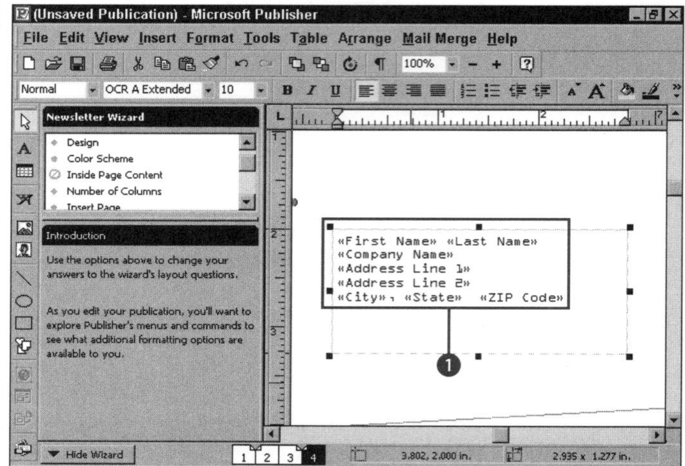

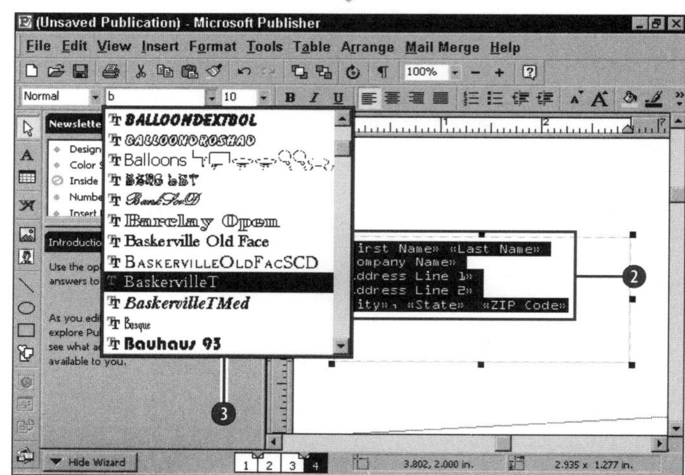

❶ *Merge Fields defaults to a tacky font.*

❷ *To change the font, highlight the fields, treating them exactly like text.*

❸ *Choose a font from the drop-down Font menu.*

CROSS-REFERENCE

Text formatting is covered in Chapter 9.

Linking Address List Fields to Your Publication

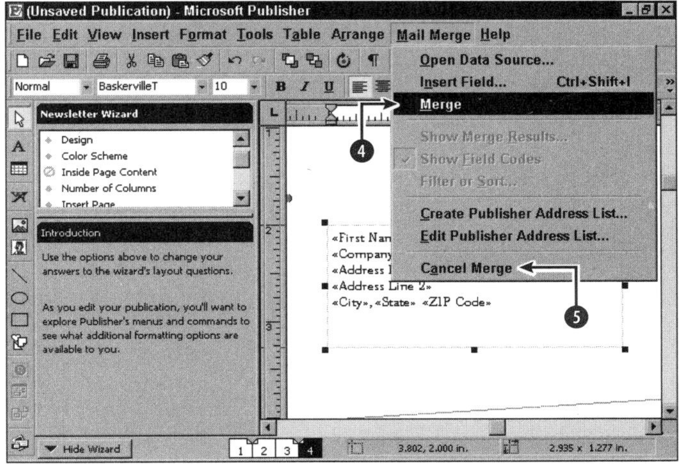

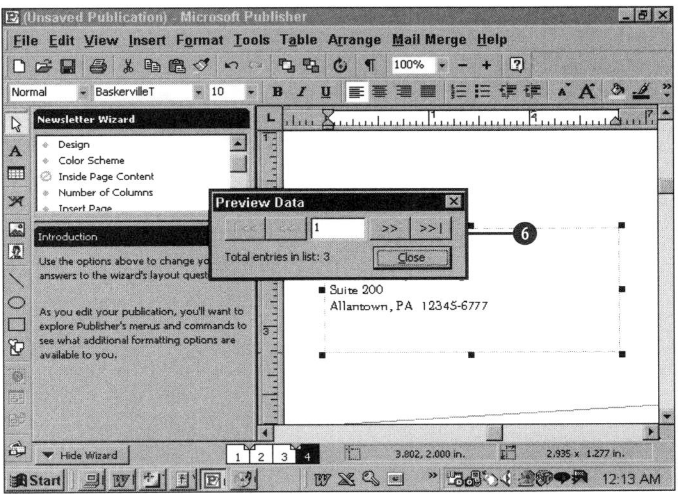

4. *To complete the merge, choose Mail Merge ➪ Merge.*
5. *To remove the link with the data source, click Cancel Merge.*
6. *When the merge is complete, the Preview Data dialog box appears.*

▶ *Viewing the merged data is covered in the next task.*

To complete the merge, you have to tell Publisher to do the deed. Selecting Merge from the Mail Merge menu cinches the job, but don't get in such a hurry. If another staff member is editing the data, you aren't jeopardizing the data integrity. They have full ownership of the data.

TAKE NOTE

PLACE DATA ANYWHERE

You can place those merge fields anywhere in the publication — not just in the address area. Think in terms of the way a merge is accomplished in a word processing program. You can insert variable information from the database anywhere in the document.

Just think of all those direct mail pieces you receive in the mail for credit cards, sweepstakes entries, or resort condominium offers. Each of them appears as though they typed that letter or entry especially for you. Wrong! You are part of a database that is being merged during the printing.

FIND IT ONLINE

To get a look at all the fonts on your systems, try using FontLister available at http://www.theill.com/fl.

Viewing the Merge Results

If you're like most Windows users, half a ream of paper will have passed through your printer before you remember how to cancel the print job. And, at the speed you have to react to cancel a print job these days, it wouldn't hurt to have consumed at least a half pot of coffee so the caffeine has you on the edge and endowed you with lightning-fast reflexes.

Let's review all the reasons why you should preview your merge and review your data.

I'm not suggesting that you read every record as it will appear on your publication, but when your eyes get accustomed to glaring at the names and addresses, you will notice little discrepancies between records. Maybe you accidentally added a period after the state abbreviation or had a name or two entered in all caps. These are the types of things you're looking for.

Check to be sure your Sort and Filter features are working as you expect. Check alphabetizing or ZIP code order. Also, watch for any stray records that made it through the filters. For example, if you filter out a particular state, all the ZIP codes should be very similar, maybe starting with the same digit.

Look for any overruns. That's what I call it when an address line is too long for the text box that it's confined in. Not that it will matter much when it's delivered, but you've spent this much time on the project learning to mail merge, you may as well stop and resize the text box so every address fits exactly in the layout you specified.

While you're scanning through the records, notice the wonderful job that Publisher does when assembling the text. When you have two-line addresses where there's a line for a street number and a second line for a suite number or building, both appear. But, when the second line is null (that's database lingo for empty), Publisher

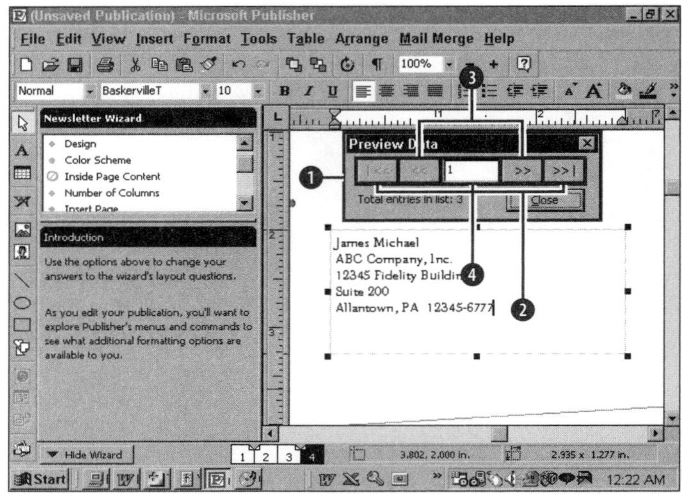

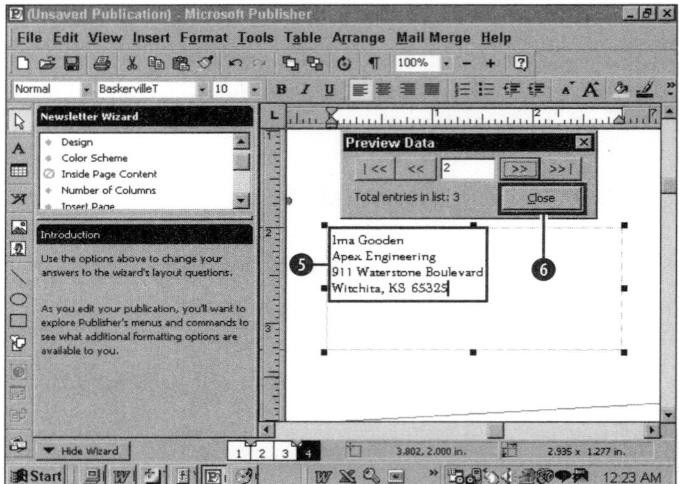

1. *Once the merge is complete, the Preview Data dialog box appears.*
2. *These buttons take you to the first or last record.*
3. *These buttons take you to the previous or next record.*
4. *If you know the record number you want to preview, you can enter it in the text box.*
5. *Notice that a second street address line was not available in this record. The city, state, ZIP line was moved up.*
6. *When finished with the Preview Data dialog box, click Close.*

CROSS-REFERENCE

Resizing and moving text frames is covered in Chapter 6.

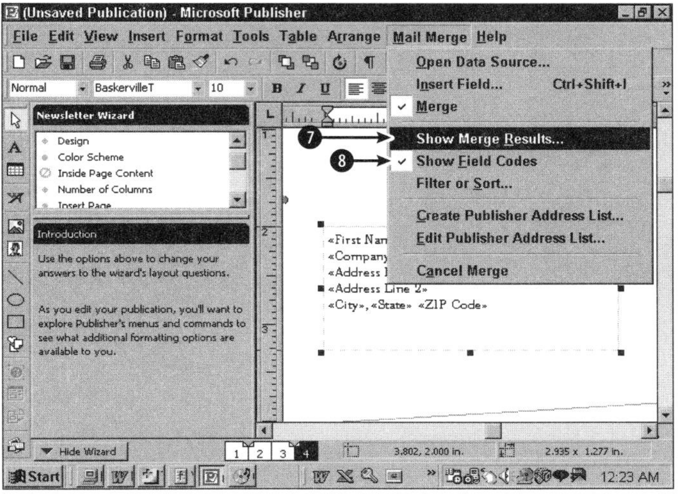

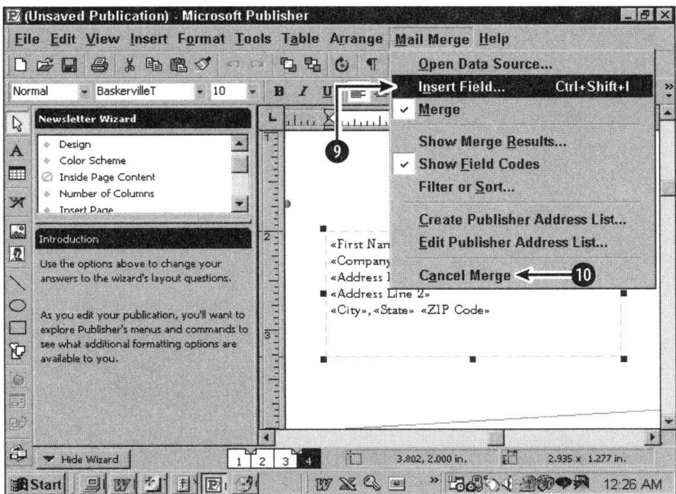

7. *Once the Preview Data dialog box is closed, you can click Mail Merge ➪ Show Merge Results to recall it.*

8. *Instead of clicking Close on the Preview Data dialog box, you can choose Mail Merge ➪ Show Field Codes.*

9. *Anytime you want to add a field to the publication, choose Mail Merge ➪ Insert Field.*

10. *Click Cancel Merge to separate the data file from the publication.*

shoves the city, state and ZIP line up so no gaps occur. And you didn't even have to pay extra for it!

This task, though short on instruction, is long on usability and advice that will come in very handy. In other words, you get the benefit of learning from the mistakes commonly made by others.

TAKE NOTE

PICK A READABLE FONT

When it comes to addresses, the post office is serious about its business. Avoid using flowery, decorative type for addresses. Not only are some of them very difficult to read through the postal machinery, but the letter carrier may go blind trying to find the right person or company, given some of the fonts on the market today.

FIND IT ONLINE

For some new fonts on your system, try **http://www.jumbo.com/pages/mm/fonts/index.htp.**

Printing Your Merged Publication

You think you're now ready to merge all that data to your publication and then to your printer? Obviously you have scoured your data for changes to make. You have refined your layout and design elements to perfection. Yes, I'd say you're ready to print, almost.

But, before you send massive amounts of data and pages to your printer, give your printer a checkup. Here are some things to check if you're printing a lot of copies.

Do you have enough paper on hand to complete the job? By checking, you can save yourself from doing the one-minute mile to the supply closet.

Is your printer up to the task? Massive numbers of imprints are not quite what the manufacturer of your $200 ink-jet printer had in mind when they made that little printer.

Do you have the time? Can you sit there in case of a paper jam or you run out of ink or toner?

And while we're talking about imaging supplies, how's your stockpile? Or, in some cases, how's the limit on your charge card if you need to go out and buy some more to polish off a really long print job? It's important, when you're printing long jobs, that you have a spare toner cartridge around just in case yours goes empty or, heaven forbid, the drum goes bad.

One nice thing about Publisher is that you can specify what records to print in the Print dialog box. Or, you can just go back into the Filter and Sort options and request just the records that didn't print when the printer pooped out on you. You'll see that instruction in the steps presented with the accompanying figures.

And, it's wise to warn you here, before you start printing a multipage document, you are faced with an all or nothing proposition. That is, you cannot specify to print all of page 1, and then all of page 2 and so on. You have to print the entire set of pages, merged with your database.

CROSS-REFERENCE

See "Printing to a File" in Chapter 5.

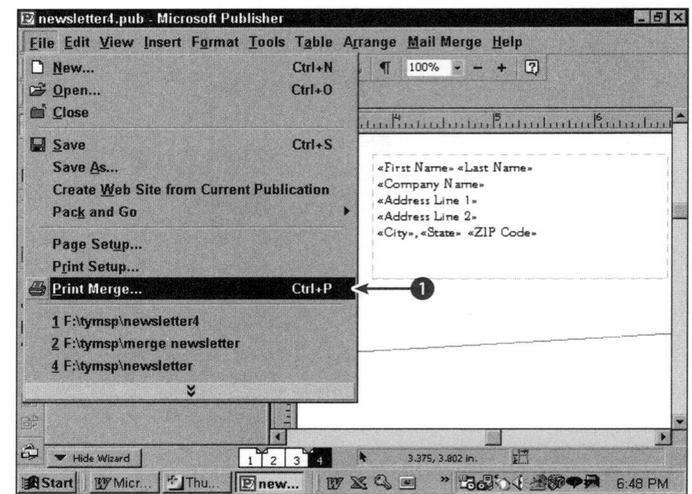

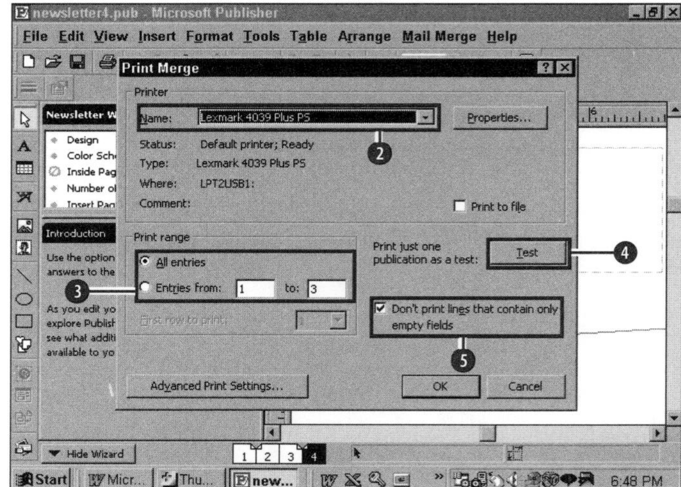

1. *Choose File ⇨ Print Merge or press Ctrl+P.*
2. *Choose a printer and set printer properties. Also set Advanced Print Settings if you want to ignore graphics or print them at a lower resolution.*
3. *Choose print range of the records to be merged.*
4. *To print a test using the first record, click Test.*
5. *Check here for Publisher to skip the fields that are empty.*

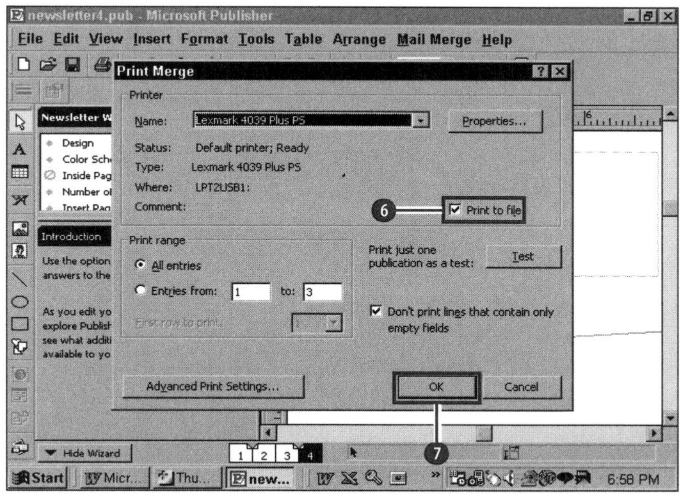

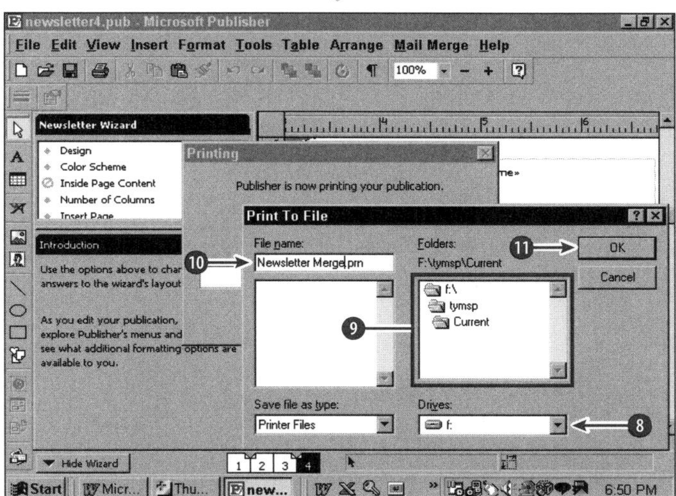

6. *To make a file to print on another computer, check "Print to file."*
7. *Click OK.*
8. *Choose a drive to store the file.*
9. *Choose a folder for the file.*
10. *Name the file.*
11. *Click OK.*

TAKE NOTE

PRINTING TO A FILE

One thing you'll notice in the Print dialog box is the option to print to file. If you have a large enough disk storage system, conceivably, you can merge everything to a PRN print file and use a larger, faster printer in the office. Try printing to the hard drive that has the most open disk space and then copy or move your file to the removable disk. Not only will the job print faster, but you'll be able to see how large the PRN file is and judge whether you have a disk large enough to hold it. Remember, you don't have to have the software or fonts installed on a remote computer when you print to file.

FIND IT ONLINE

Iomega offers an inexpensive 250MB Zip drive for those large print files. Check out **www.iomega.com**.

Personal Workbook

Q&A

1. What must you remember to enter between field codes unless they are included in the data in your database?

2. How does Publisher know when to begin a new line when you are entering field codes in your publication?

3. What menu commands can you use to alternate between seeing the data in your layout and seeing the field codes?

4. In order to change the font that your data appears in once the document is printed, what must you do?

5. What are the four arrow buttons and what are they used for in the Preview Data dialog box?

6. Besides using the arrow buttons to preview your data in the Preview Data dialog box, what else can you do?

7. When printing to a file, where is the best place to put the PRN file and why?

8. How can you print just one page of your multipage merged publication?

ANSWERS: PAGE 290

EXTRA PRACTICE

1. Create a two-sided postcard using the wizard. Use mail merge to address them as they print.
2. Begin a brochure from scratch. Include an address area for mailing. In your database of names, filter out only prospective customers or customers who have not contacted you in the last year.
3. Create a database of your parts inventory. Include the part number, description, and price. Print small labels to attach to the products. Create larger labels to place on shelves where the product is stocked.
4. You have several accounts that are 90 days past due in payment. Create a database with all the information that would be included in a delinquent letter and use the data to incorporate the information in the body of the letter.

REAL-WORLD APPLICATIONS

- ✔ After you receive a database from the IS department, you mail merge it with a publication and use the Preview option to scan through the records to be sure that all the data is input correctly and consistently.
- ✔ A birthday party is being planned for your son or daughter. You use Publisher's wizard to create the invitations and then use the Mail Merge feature to address the envelopes.
- ✔ You just hired a new group of salespeople. You use Mail Merge to make temporary business cards for all of them in one printing.

Visual Quiz

This is the address area of a four-page newsletter. How can you add a custom message in the black diagonal box based on the customer whose address appears during the mail merge?

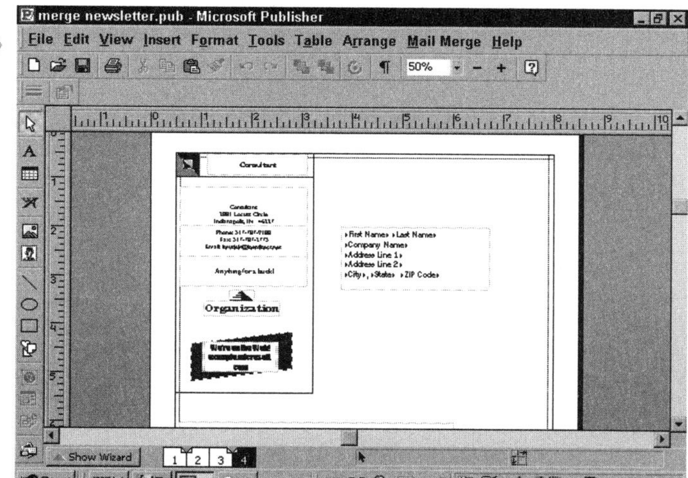

CHAPTER 16

MASTER THESE SKILLS

- Using the Web Site Wizard
- Connecting Web Elements with Hyperlinks
- Inserting Hyperlinks with the Hot Spot Tool
- Linking to JPEG Files
- Inserting Inline Graphics and Animated GIFs
- Getting Feedback with Forms

Creating a Web Site

Back in the old days of college, the professors used to have a saying, "publish or perish," which meant, if you want to keep your teaching position at Purdue (my alma mater) or many other universities, you had to write insightful books and articles that could be published in your professional circle of periodicals. Rarely, if at all, did those written pieces get in the mainstream magazines that normal, nonacademic people read.

The same, it seems, holds true for corporate America. Having your own Web site lends credibility to your business, so the psychology works. Now this concept has trickled down to the actual users of the Internet (that would be you and me), where anyone can have a Web site somewhere in cyberspace. I have a site and, with the help of Microsoft Publisher 2000, you can too. It's easy.

Starting out, you'll see how the Publisher Web Site Wizard can give you a jump start on preparing pages for you to upload to your Internet server, where your Web pages will reside. You'll find the wizard handy, but it doesn't provide you with the rest of the knowledge to add pages and links on your own.

The rest of the tasks step you through the different types of links, what you can link to, what you can link from, and how to insert graphics that have different functions on the Web versus on your computer without the benefit of a browser. Finally, you'll be introduced to creating forms on the Web. Forms are very handy items for collecting data from your visitors.

Just so you don't break out in a cold sweat worrying about learning HTML (that programming language of the Web), we don't much of that here. As a matter of fact, we cover the easiest stuff, so relax. You'll have to go elsewhere if you want to dive into HTML programming.

And a final note: Microsoft Publisher is not the best tool for editing Web sites. If you are the lucky owner of the Microsoft Office 2000 Professional Suite of applications, you have the best way to get into Web site publishing — Microsoft FrontPage 2000. So, if you get hooked on creating Web sites, you're going to have to advance up to FrontPage.

Using the Web Site Wizard

Now you have no excuse not to get your Web site up and running. Microsoft Publisher affords you the opportunity to create Web pages at a quick click or two of the mouse buttons via the Web Site Wizard. With 45 different design themes, you can get a running start on a personal or company Web site.

To give you some indication of the choices in store for you, here's a rundown of the items that you'll be asked for and what you might be able to do with them.

Additional Pages

When you reach the part where you are asked to insert different types of pages, you might consider including these pages, even if you have no intention of using them as they are intended. Remember, use the templates to build a page and then change it. It sure beats creating one from scratch to match the rest of them.

- **Story** — The Story page is a headline, a graphic, and a lot of room to place text. This is an ideal template for telling the purpose of your site, giving details of the company and its mission, or just telling a bit about yourself. The graphic could be a picture of yourself, the company building, or the company president.
- **Calendar** — At first glance, this might be self-explanatory. However, a calendar is only a table. Remove the text and use the table as a large graphic element, dropping images inside the cells. You could also remove the table and insert a map to your location with the text below being turn-by-turn driving directions.

Continued

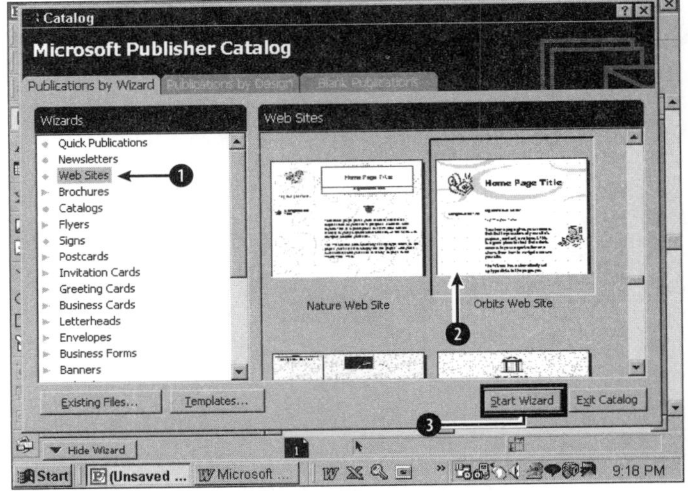

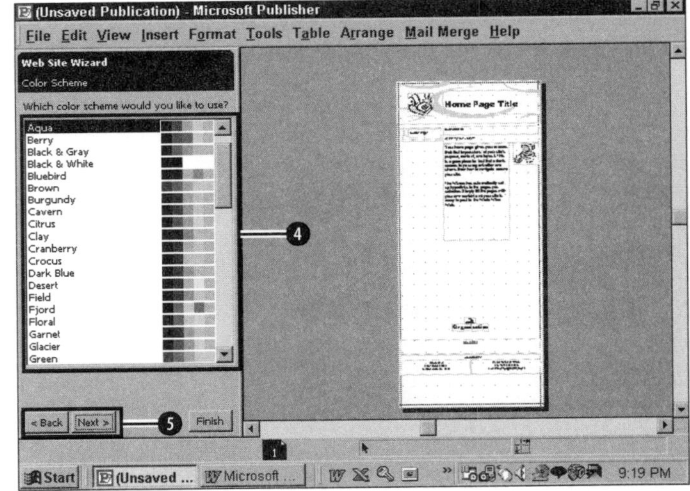

1. *Choose Web Sites from the wizard.*
- ▶ *If you just started Publisher, the wizard should be running. If not, click File ⇨ New.*
2. *Click a design.*
3. *Click the Start Wizard button.*
- ▶ *After the introduction to the wizard, click the Next button.*
4. *Choose a color scheme.*
5. *Click the Next button.*

CROSS-REFERENCE

To view information from the forms you post on your site, see "Getting Feedback with Forms" later in this chapter.

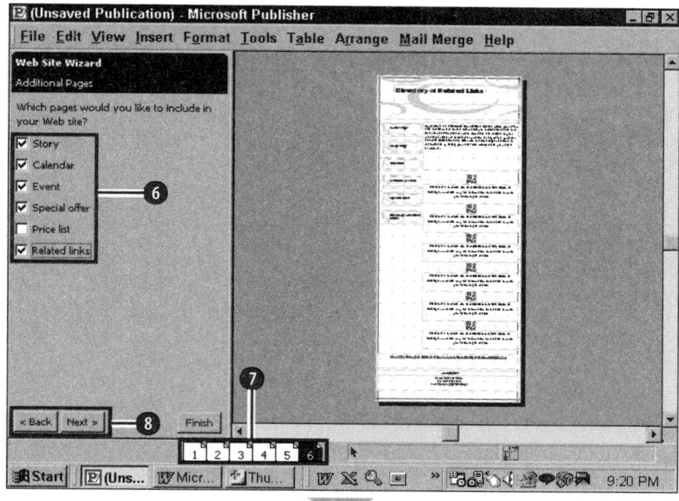

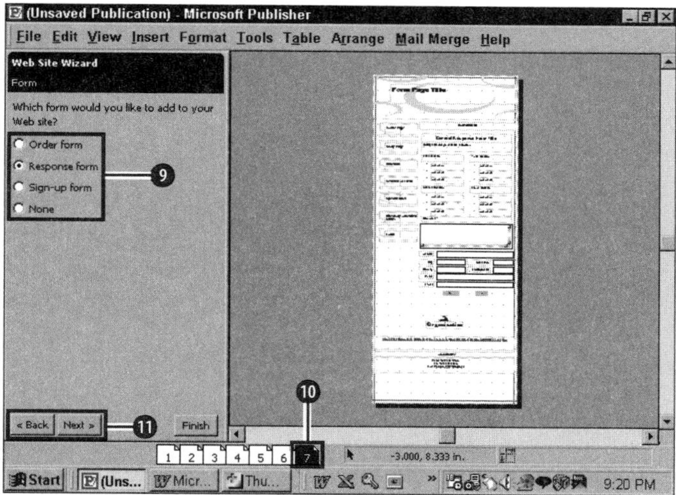

6. *Choose the items you want included in the Web site.*
7. *A new page is created for each item you select.*
8. *Click the Next button.*
9. *Select the form you want to include, or choose None.*
10. *A new page is created to hold the form.*
11. *Click the Next button.*

- **Event** — No one said you have to put on a dog and pony show. Use the Event layout for a special spread of employee recognition. The winner can go at the top and the three smaller images could be the runners-up. You could also feature coworkers, your family, pets, favorite hobbies, and more.
- **Special Offer** — Again, this could be used for recognizing an individual in the company, or show off some of the work you've done. Place a graphic on the page, explain the job or task, and use a quote from the customer that indicates excellence. You can still use this layout for special sales or new products that your company has just released.

TAKE NOTE

INSERTING WEB PAGES

If you find you need more than one form on your site, open the wizard, if it is closed, and click Insert Page in the upper portion of the Wizard window. In the lower portion of the Wizard windows, click the Insert Page button and choose the page type you want to insert. Likewise, you can choose Insert ➪ Page from the menu or press Ctrl+Shift+N.

FIND IT ONLINE

If you've created a Web site but don't have a clue how to get it on the Internet, find some help at **http://www.folksonline.com.**

Using the Web Site Wizard

continued

- **Price List** — What's a price list? It's just a large table that you replace the text in. Think about using this as a telephone directory for the staff, or the different departments or office and branch locations in a large company. When you use it for this purpose, why not add the hours of operation and maybe eliminate some phone calls?
- **Related Links** — This page is excellent for including hyperlinks to favorite or similar sites. However, if you have expanded your company Web site to include a section on each department, use this page as the link to those departments. The graphic above each description could be a link and the text could explain those departments and their purpose. Then, use the wizard once more to make a separate set of Web pages for those departments. This page of links hooks them all together to make one large site.

Forms

You have three options for forms. While they suit their purpose very well, you may be able to alter them for a specific purpose.

- **Order Form** — People don't have to buy things from you to use the order form. Little League moms can post a form such as this to collect the player's shirt sizes for the team uniform. You can also use a form such as this to find out how much fund-raising candy a child sold or is wanting to sell. They fill in the amount and their name and you have it on record.

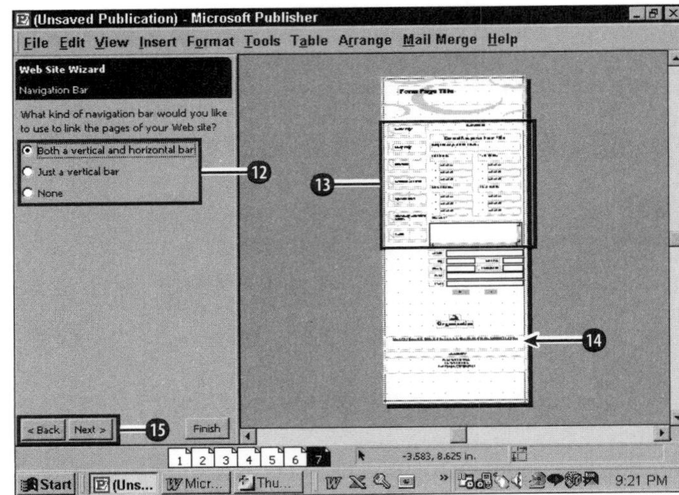

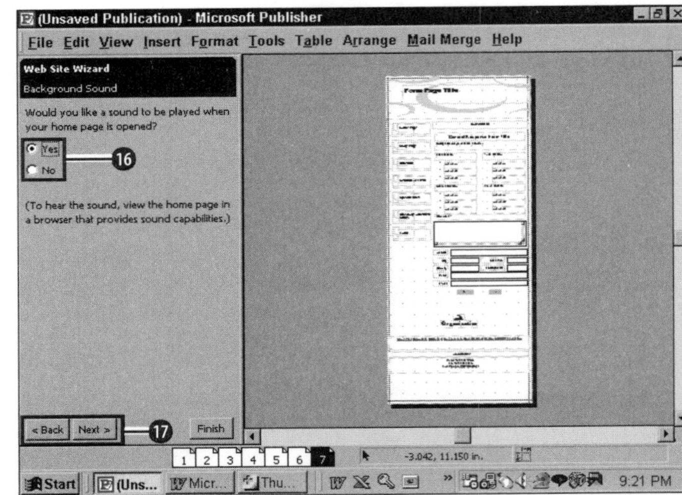

12. *Choose where the navigation links will be located. For a one-page Web site, click None.*
13. *Vertical links appear on the left side of the pages.*
14. *Horizontal links appear on the bottom of the pages.*
15. *Click the Next button.*
16. *Choose whether a sound plays when a visitor accesses your home page.*
    - *The sound files are set according to the style you create. It is possible to change the sound later. It is also possible to add sound to each page in your site using the Wizard window.*
17. *Click the Next button.*

CROSS-REFERENCE

For more information on adding or deleting pages, see "Inserting and Deleting Pages" in Chapter 6.

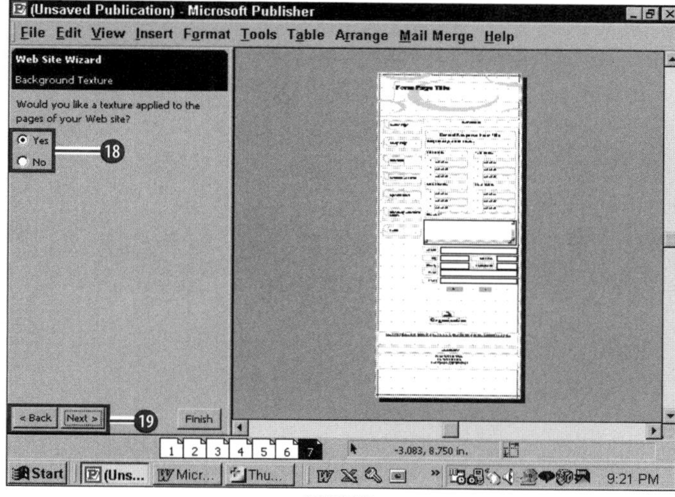

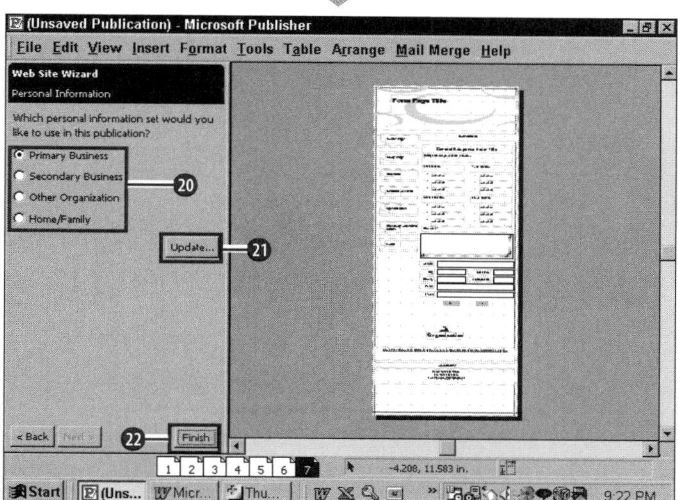

⑱ *Choose whether a graphic background appears on your pages.*

⑲ *Click the Next button.*

⑳ *Choose the Personal Information set to appear on your Web pages.*

㉑ *Optionally, click the Update button to change any information.*

㉒ *Click the Finish button.*

- **Response Form** — Couldn't you see a teacher using this form for multiple choice tests? It's also a good tool to test people on how much of your site they visited and if they appreciated the information presented.
- **Sign-up Form** — Besides being a nice short sign-up form, you could use this as an order form if your product line is pretty short. Otherwise, you could think of this form, without pricing in it, for committee volunteering, bowling league interests, an RSVP for family reunions, or a nonprofit organization's solicitation for donations.

Navigation Bars

When you have Publisher include the navigation bars for you, they appear on the left side of each page as a graphic, at the bottom of the page as text only, or in both places.

TAKE NOTE

INCLUDING TEXT NAVIGATION LINKS

Because the navigation links at the bottom don't take that much space, you might consider including both text and graphics. Some visitors may have graphics turned off on their browsers. In that case, they will still be able to navigate your site without the help of the graphics down the side.

FIND IT ONLINE

More Web beginner info can be found at **http://www.webnovice.com.**

Connecting Web Elements with Hyperlinks

The whole concept behind the Web is linking. You link to things in your own site, and maybe even link to some outside sites that are either of interest to you or to your visitors.

Simply put, a *hyperlink* is something you click and it transports you to another location or causes some other type of action. Hyperlinks come in two visible formats: text and graphic. You can make any word or group of words a hyperlink, or a graphic can serve as a hyperlink. In the next task, you'll learn how to make just a portion of your graphic a link using the Hot Spot tool.

These are the five most common uses of hyperlinks:

- **Links within a page** — You can use hyperlinks to speed your visitor to another part of the Web page they are on.
- **Links within your Web site** — If you have multiple Web pages, your visitor has to have a way to get to each of them. These types of links switch your visitor over to one of those pages on your site. If you completed the Web Site Wizard in the previous task, the navigation links are carrying out this function.
- **Links outside your Web site** — Sharing like knowledge over the Internet is a wonderful thing. By creating a page of links, as was your option in the Web Wizard, you can point your visitors to other sites that may interest them and have some relevance to you or your site. Of course, you can place these exterior links anywhere in your Web site and not just on the Links page.
- **E-mail links** — If you're looking for some personal feedback or wanting to give your visitors an easy way to contact you, you can make a hyperlink that opens an e-mail composition window, complete with your e-mail address in the address text box.

CROSS-REFERENCE

See "Creating a Web Site from Your Publication" in Chapter 5.

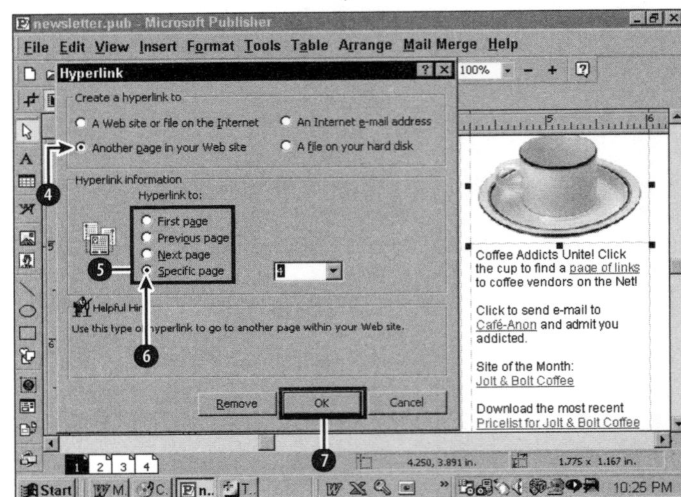

- *Highlight the text or picture that will serve as the hyperlink. Press Ctrl+K, or choose Insert ⇨ Hyperlink.*

1. *Click here to link to a site or file on the Web, outside your Web pages.*
2. *Enter the Web address. If it is saved in your Favorites folder, click the Favorites button and choose it from the list.*
3. *Click OK to assign the hyperlink.*
4. *Click the "Another page in your Web site" box to link to a different page in your site.*
5. *Choose the page from the list of options.*
6. *To jump several pages, use the Specific page radio button. Pick a page from the drop-down menu.*
7. *Click OK to assign the hyperlink.*

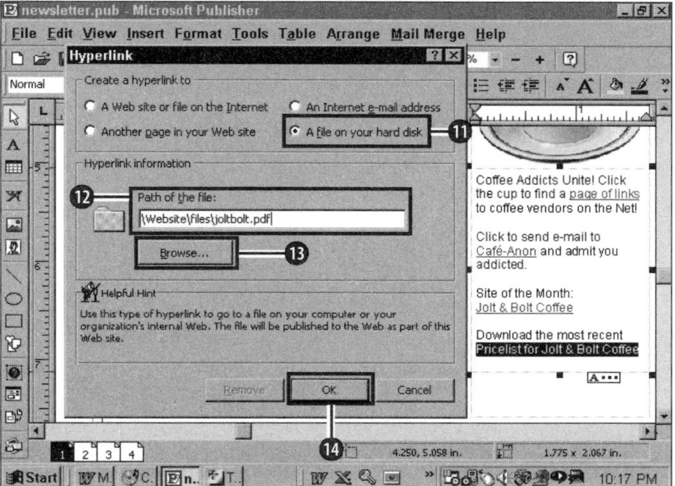

8. *Choose the "An Internet e-mail address" radio button to create a hyperlink to an e-mail address.*
9. *Type in the e-mail address of the individual to receive the e-mail.*
10. *Click OK to assign the hyperlink.*
11. *Click the "A file on your hard disk" radio button to link a file on your server that may be downloaded.*
12. *Insert the location of the file's drive (if on a network server) and/or folder.*
13. *Or, use the Browse button to find the file on your computer.*
14. *Click OK to assign the hyperlink.*

- **File download links** — If you want to make files available for others to download from your site, you can place a file on your server and when someone clicks this link, they will be prompted as to where, on their computer, to store a file.

TAKE NOTE

CHECK EXTERNAL LINKS REGULARLY

If you're going to include links to external sites on your Web pages, be sure to check them on a regular basis. Many times, links get outdated because Web pages change and Web sites close. A dead site link is a bad reflection on your site. It shows that you don't update your Web site and therefore, visitors may think your site has nothing new. So, why should they return in the near future? Make changes and keep people coming back.

FIND IT ONLINE

If you are a bit inexperienced with the Web and how it works, check out http://www.gactr.uga.edu/exploring/index.html.

Inserting Hyperlinks with the Hot Spot Tool

As hinted in the previous task, you have other ways to insert hyperlinks on a Web page. No doubt, you have visited sites where a huge graphic appears on the home page with what looks like text links placed hither and yon over the top of the graphic. Truth be known, those phrases are not actual text in the Web's eyes — they are part of the graphic.

So how do you create several hyperlinks on top of one large graphic? You use the Hot Spot tool, which Publisher provides. Once you import a large graphic and assign the hyperlink areas, you have created an image map, as it is called by Webmasters.

Of course, the graphic doesn't necessarily need to fill up the entire screen. Many sites make their navigation bar one large graphic and assign hot spots to sections of it. The graphic can occupy most any place on the page, but many use the left side or top of the page so that browser windows with different sizes will show them.

Using the Hot Spot tool, you can draw rectangular shapes around portions of an image and assign a hyperlink to that area. For layout purposes, the rectangle area will not show once your page with the graphic is on the Web, but when your visitor's cursor passes anywhere within that area, they will see the little hand that indicates a hyperlink.

Luckily and intentionally, Publisher keeps the hot spot outline visible during layout so you can always find it, go back to resize it, or change the hyperlink. Of course, you can also delete it altogether.

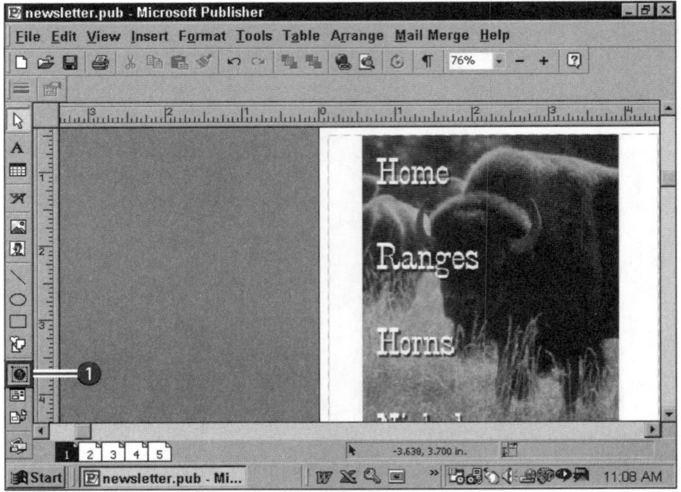

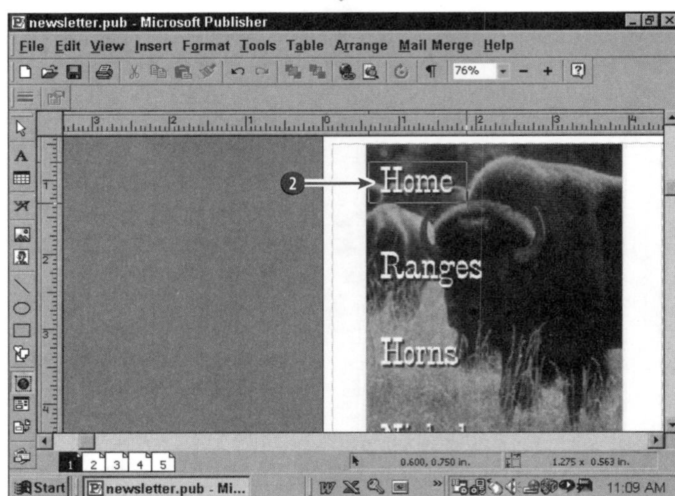

1. *Click the Hot Spot tool button in the toolbar.*
2. *Drag to form a rectangle around the area where the link is to be placed.*

CROSS-REFERENCE

Freshen up on importing images back in Chapter 11.

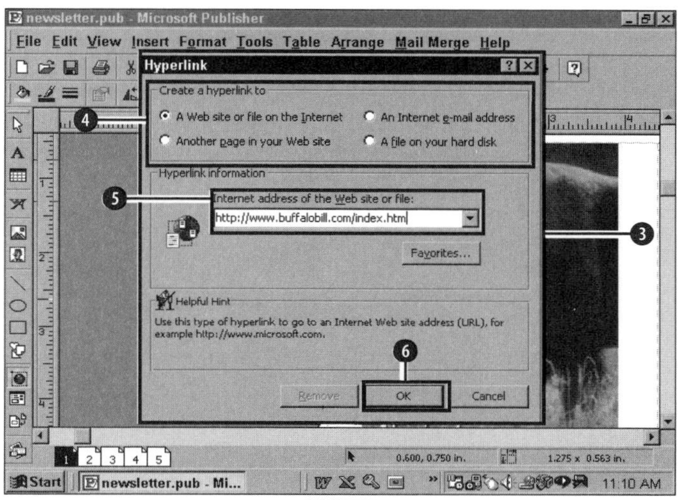

3 *When you release the mouse button, the Hyperlink dialog box appears.*

4 *Choose the function of the hot spot hyperlink.*

5 *Enter the hyperlink information in the text box.*

6 *Click OK to assign the link to the hot spot defined.*

7 *Once the hot spot is in place, you can use the handles to resize the rectangle.*

8 *The rectangle may also be moved to a different spot. This moves the hyperlink as well.*

9 *When you hover your mouse over the hot spot, you see the hyperlink address.*

▶ *To edit the hyperlink, press Ctrl+K or right-click and choose Hyperlink while the hot spot is highlighted.*

TAKE NOTE

WATCH THE SIZE OF LARGE GRAPHICS

You must be careful when designing a large graphic that will be used as an image map. Large images that choke modems and take a long time to download to the browser window may create a hostile visitor. Many people don't want to wait very long for a page to load, or they may think their system is hung up because it takes awhile for the graphic to appear. If you're going to use a large graphic in this manner, you have ways to reduce the file size without losing clarity. Consult any number of books that teach you specifically how to create graphics for the Web.

BREAK UP THE IMAGE

You may find pages on the Internet where frames appear before a large graphic does. Inside those frames, which are actually tables, is a portion of the large image. This is accomplished through several software packages and should be considered. As the images in the cells load, they keep people interested because something appears while they wait.

FIND IT ONLINE

To explore other ways to make image maps, check out **http://www.personal.psu.edu/users/k/x/kxs156/tut1.htm.**

Linking to JPEG Files

If you have ever run across a Web page that is loaded with pictures, you usually have time to walk the dog or wash the car while they load. This is not a good idea when you are developing your Web pages.

Smart Webmasters use small versions of larger pictures, called *thumbnails,* which serve as hyperlinks to a page that will display the entire picture. By providing a page of thumbnail images, you are not only saving your visitor a lot of download time, but you are giving them a choice of which pictures they want to see in full view.

If you don't feel like creating a page for each large JPEG (JPG) file, you can make the hyperlink straight to the larger JPEG file. (JPEG files are one of the more popular file formats for images on the Internet.) The image file opens up in the browser window without the benefit of riding in on an HTML page. The only problem is that visitors will have no navigation options other than the Back button on their browsers. At least if you place the full image on a page, you can include the navigation bar you have set up.

Programs such as Microsoft PhotoDraw 2000 offer an easy way to save a large image as a thumbnail, automatically reducing the image in size and resolution. Check the Help files in your graphics program to see if there's a quick way to generate a thumbnail. If not, you can reduce the image size and save it as a new file.

If you post a lot of images on your Web site, you should look into some other books or Web sites that deal with optimizing your images for the Web. Things that they will cover are the best resolution, the color palettes, file format, and image size. All of these have a bearing on how well you can display Web images.

CROSS-REFERENCE

To review how to insert tables and fill them with text and graphics, go back to Chapter 10.

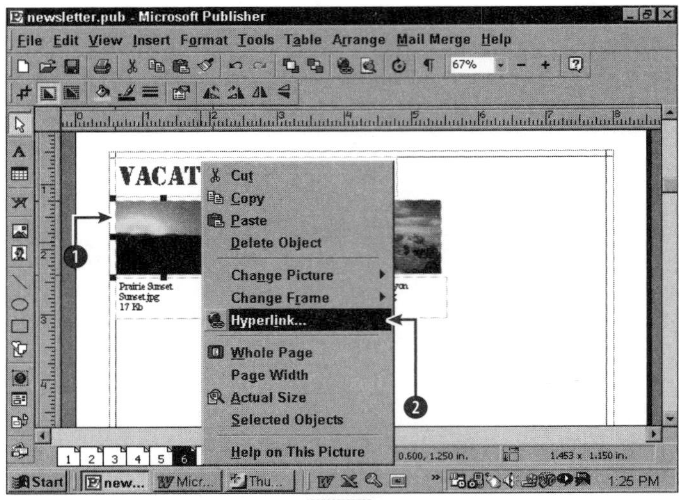

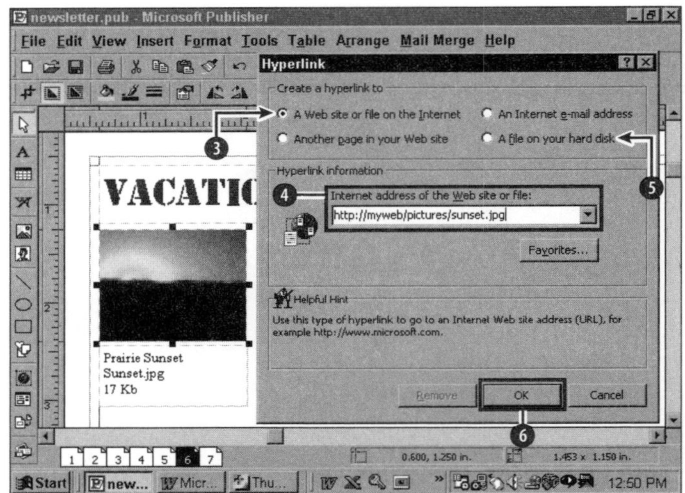

1. *Select a thumbnail or phrase to attach the hyperlink to.*
2. *Right-click and choose Hyperlink from the pop-up menu. Or, press Ctrl+K.*
3. *In the Hyperlink dialog box, choose "A Web site or file on the Internet" if the file or page is not on your Web site.*
4. *Type in the Web address where the file or page is located.*
5. *If you just want the picture to display in the browser, choose "A file on your hard disk" and fill in the folder location.*
6. *Click OK to assign the hyperlink.*

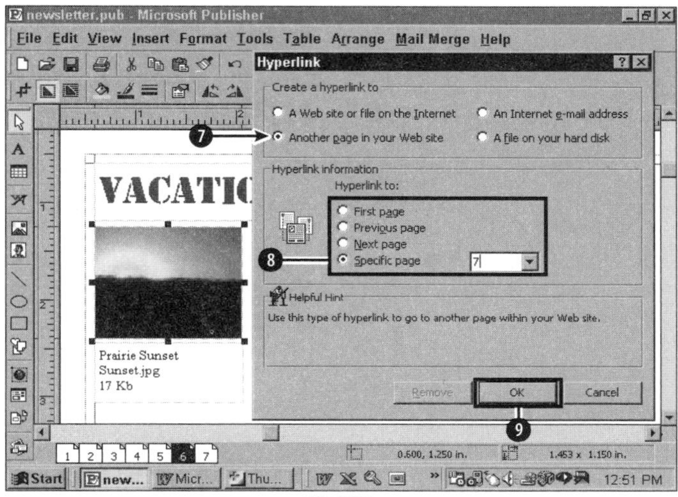

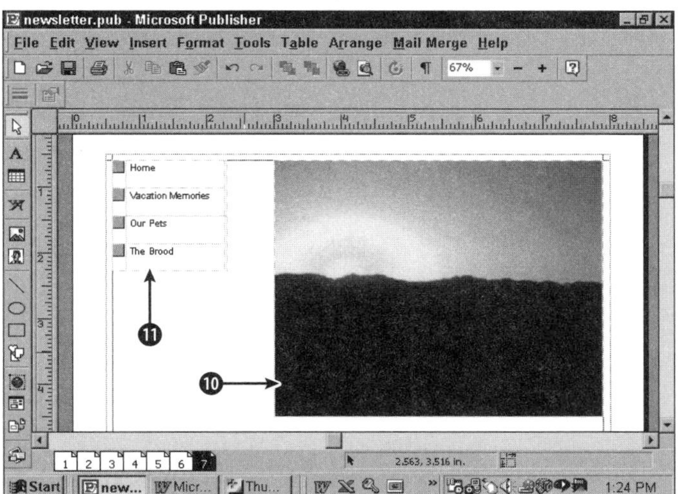

7. *If the picture resides on your Web site, click "Another page in your Web site."*
8. *Choose the page location.*
9. *Click OK to assign the hyperlink.*
10. *If the picture is on a page in your Web site, be sure the picture is placed on the page.*
11. *Optionally, you can insert a navigation bar on this page, too.*

TAKE NOTE

USING IMAGE INFORMATION ON THUMBNAILS

Consider placing captions underneath thumbnails, not only to describe the picture visually, but to include the file name and file size as well. This gives visitors the option to bypass some of the larger images if their time is short.

MAKE FILE NAMES SIMILAR

If you have to generate your own thumbnails, set up a file naming convention that ties the large file to the small one. For example, both files could be called the same thing, except the thumbnail file could begin with "sm" for small. Not only does this alert you to the purpose of the file, but they will all be grouped together in the folder making them easier to find and import on your thumbnail page.

FIND IT ONLINE

Xoom.com has a lot of pictures that you can use for free. Be sure to follow the guidelines, though.

Inserting Inline Graphics and Animated GIFs

Up to this point, pictures have stood on their own and been placed outside the text area. Inline graphics actually get placed with the text. You won't find any definitions of inline graphics in the Publisher Help files, but this task will show you how to place graphics among your paragraphs so they flow with your text.

While many inline graphics are static, the Web lets you use animated GIFs — small movies or cartoons, so to speak, that are created in the graphics interchange format. When you load an animated GIF into your browser, you are actually opening one file that contains several images within it. As the picture loads, you see each image in succession. If you remember those little flip books that came in the boxes of Cracker Jacks when you were a kid, animated GIFs work just like that. As you flipped the pages in the little book, the individual pictures on the page gave the illusion of some motion. As the GIFs load, you get that same type effect.

Creating animated GIFs is relatively simple. All you need is a software program to create the individual GIFs and assemble them in one file. A number of shareware programs are available on the Internet that will do this. Download one and give it a try.

But, before you waltz off to the Web, consider using the Motion Clips that you have available in the Gallery. They are excellent specimens of animated GIFs and can be used with little difficulty. You can also find entire Web sites dedicated to animated GIFs. Use your favorite search engine and use "animated GIFs" as your keywords to search on.

The reason why inline graphics and animated GIFs are put together in this task is that they are placed the same. Those GIFs can be inline graphics just as easily as the static clip art images.

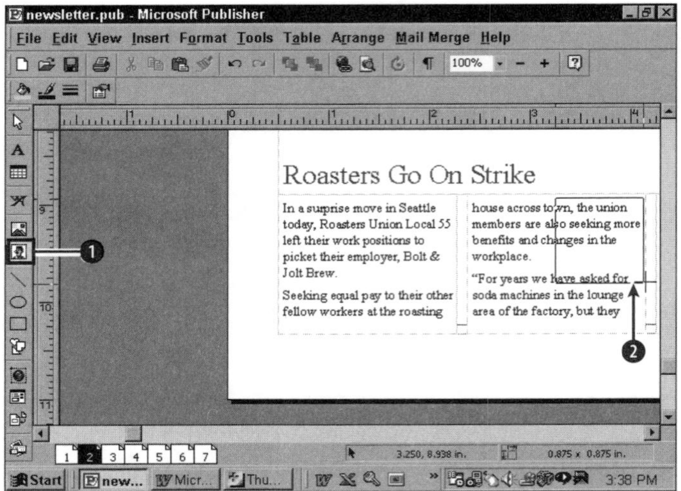

1. Click the Clip Gallery tool in the toolbar.
2. Draw a frame where the inline graphic or animated GIF is to be placed.
3. In the Insert Clip Art Gallery dialog box, select the Motion Clips tab for animated GIFs.
4. Click a category.

CROSS-REFERENCE

Chapter 11 has more details on working with the Microsoft Clip Gallery and clip art.

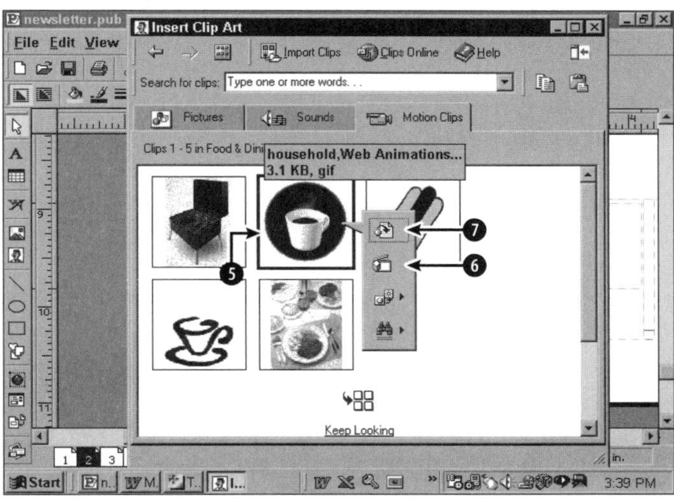

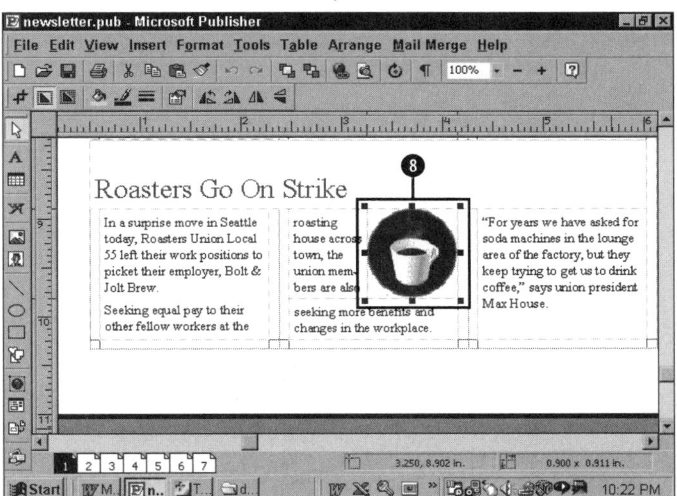

5 *Choose an image.*

6 *Click the Play Clip button to preview the animation.*

7 *Click Insert Clip to place the animated GIF in the frame that you drew.*

8 *Once placed, you can use the handles to resize the graphic. You can also move the graphic to a different location.*

TAKE NOTE

WATCH FILE SIZE

When creating an animated GIF, you can get carried away with wanting the animation as realistic as possible. The only way to do that is to use quite a few stills that, when merged together into an animated GIF, will cause the file size to be quite large. Word to the wise: keep the GIFs small and quick to download.

BEWARE COPYRIGHT MATERIAL

Many sites on the Web offer free use of animated GIFs. However, some have stipulations that they are for noncommercial use only. That means, if your Web site is in the business of making money, you're probably not supposed to use them. When in doubt, contact the site administrator and get clearance. It's also a nice touch to note where the animation comes from, and include either the creator or the site where it was secured.

FIND IT ONLINE

You can get a nifty GIF animation shareware package from **www.mindworks.com**.

Getting Feedback with Forms

Using your Web site to solicit information from your visitors is nothing new on the Net. If you think about all the locations where you have to register just to get into the information you need, forms are pretty much a way of life.

Microsoft Publisher comes with three types of forms that are available through the wizard or the Design Gallery. If you use the wizard to create your site, as explained earlier in this chapter, you know that a Response Form, Order Form, and Sign-Up Form are just a few clicks away. If, on the other hand, you have specific information that you can only get through a custom form, this task is what you need.

Forms are made of elements. You'll notice a striking resemblance between the form elements and the elements you find in most software dialog boxes. They server the same purpose — they gather information from the user and submit it. Your Web forms can contain the any of the following elements that Publisher provides:

- **Check boxes** — Use check boxes when multiple choices are involved. Users can click more than one in the group. Responses are returned as Yes or No, indicating whether an item was checked or not.
- **Option buttons** — When you want only one response from a list of several choices, use option (also called radio) buttons. When you view your responses, these will also have a Yes or No associated with them, telling you which item in the group was checked.

Continued

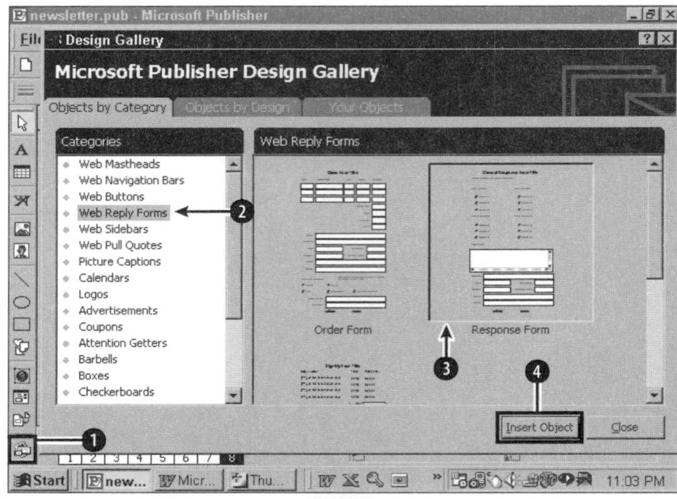

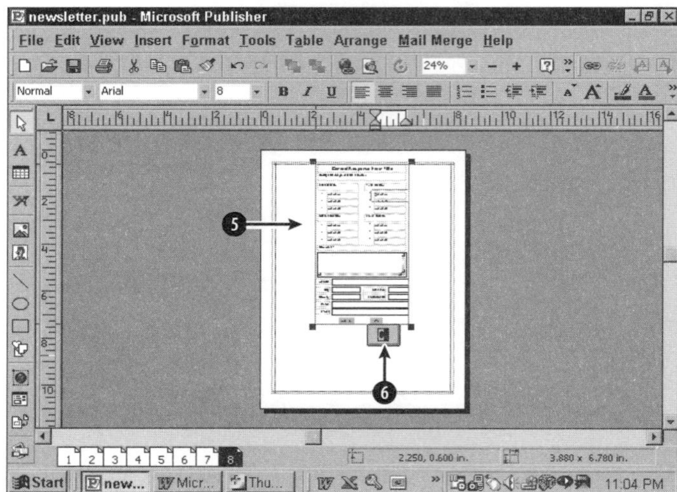

1. *To insert a prefab form, click the Design Gallery Object button in the toolbar.*
2. *Click Web Reply Forms.*
3. *Choose the type of form you want to start with.*
4. *Click Insert Object button.*
5. *Position the grouped form on the page.*
6. *Click the Unlock button to separate the pieces of the form.*

CROSS-REFERENCE

See "Using the Web Site Wizard" earlier in the chapter on creating forms using the wizard.

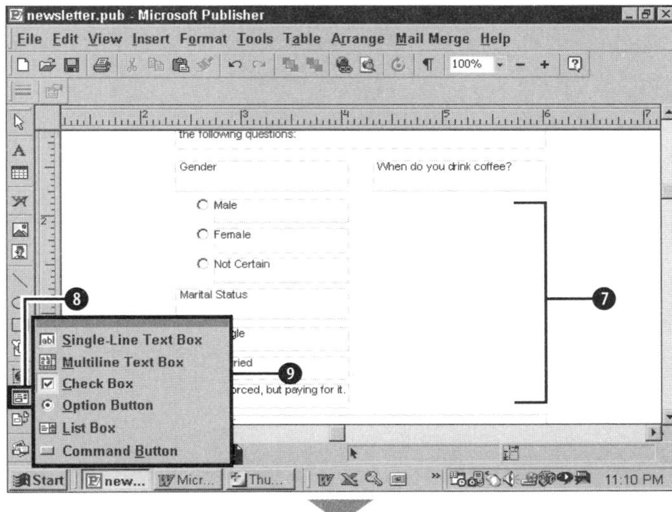

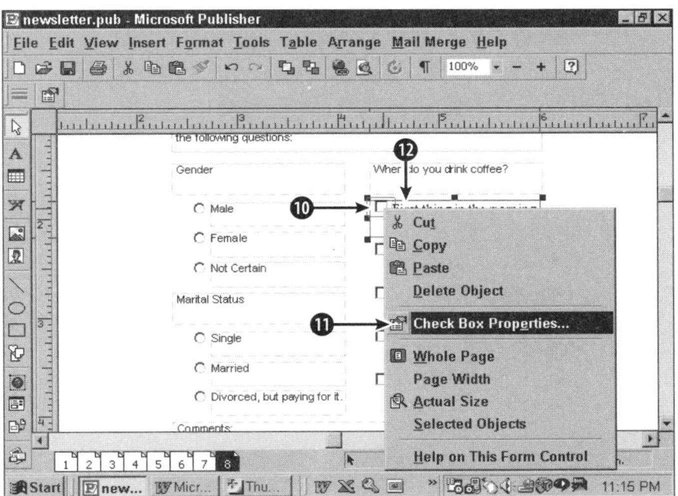

7. *Delete the unwanted form elements.*
8. *Click the Form Control button in the toolbar.*
9. *Choose the type of form element to place in the form and draw a frame with the cursor provided.*
10. *Once the form element frame is drawn, right-click the element.*
11. *Choose the Check Box Properties option for the chosen element. This menu item changes depending on the element you drew.*
12. *Optionally, you can double-click the form element.*

- **List boxes** — Set choices that you determine can be placed in a list box. Users can click one or more of the selections. When you have a lot of choices, the list box makes better use of space than a group of option buttons. The values for the items in the list box can be called the same as what you labeled them on your Web page. In the case of long phrases, you may want just a word that tips you off to the value.

TAKE NOTE

GETTING A HEAD START ON FORMS

Custom forms don't have to start out from scratch. You can use the Design Gallery to insert one of the three forms that has many of the components that you need in your form. Then, delete the elements that you don't need and insert the new ones for the specific information you're looking for.

BE BRIEF

Unless your Web site is aimed at a specific audience where the visitors don't mind taking a lot of time to answer questions and fill in your form, keep your form brief and to the point. You usually receive more responses if it takes only a minute or two to complete your form.

FIND IT ONLINE

To help find an ISP that is FrontPage 98 compatible, go to **http://microsoft.saltmine.com/frontpage/wpp/list/.**

Getting Feedback with Forms

continued

- ▶ **Single Line text box** — Very common element for users to enter information such as name, address, and other words or phrases. You can specify how many characters can be entered. For example, if you are asking for a ZIP code, the default 255 characters is a bit lengthy. Change the maximum to 10 in case someone enters their entire ZIP plus the dash.
- ▶ **Multiline text box** — For an essay, or at least a paragraph or two, use the multiline text box. Users can type away inside it and use their Enter key to add a new line.
- ▶ **Submit button** — When the form is complete, users click the Submit button, which causes an action on the server. The information could be e-mailed to you or stored on the server for you to retrieve later.
- ▶ **Reset button** — In polite Web company, a Reset button enables your user to change his or her mind and start over from scratch. It erases all the checks and text in the form. Once the Submit button is clicked, however, the form is emptied of its data and the user can't go back and change anything.

When you add a form element on your page, you have to assign it a label and value. The label tells what the element is and the value tells what data was returned from your Web visitors. For example, if you have a group of option buttons that give different age ranges, you can use the same wording for the label as you do for the button. If the text next to a button is labeled 15-25, you can label the button 15-25. The value, in the case of option buttons and check boxes, is either Yes or No. They are either clicked on or off.

CROSS-REFERENCE

Once complete, you may want to see what your form looks like. Check out "Previewing Your Web Site" in the next chapter.

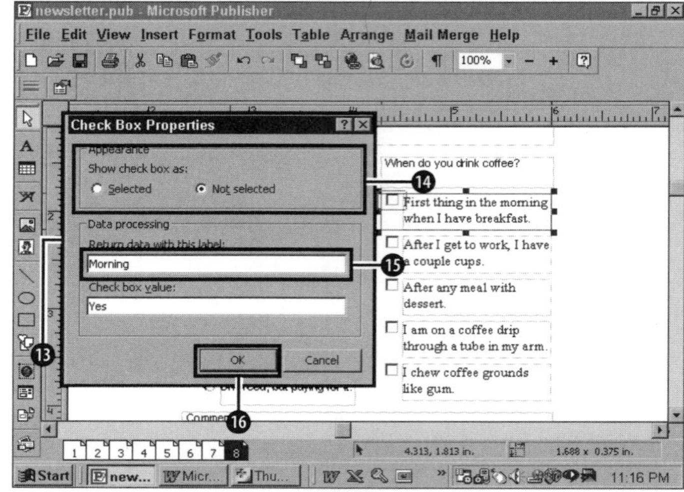

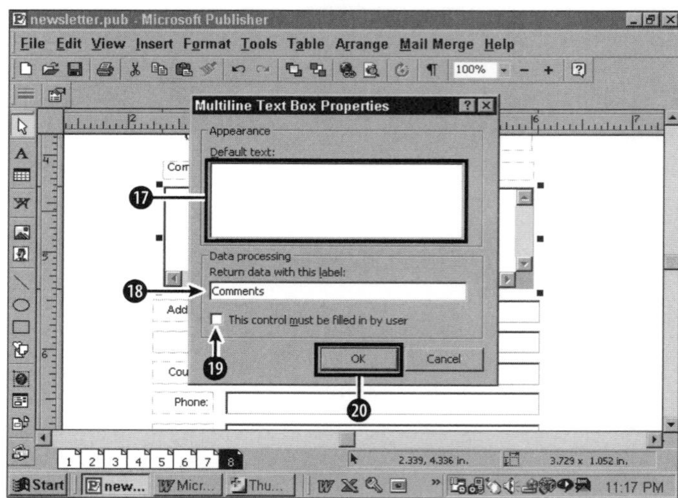

⓭ *The Check Box Properties box appears for your chosen element.*

⓮ *For Check Box elements, choose whether it will appear on the Web page as already selected or not.*

⓯ *Enter the label to identify the data and the value that will be returned when selected.*

⓰ *Click OK to assign the label and value.*

⓱ *For multiline text boxes, insert any text you want to appear when the form is presented to the visitor.*

⓲ *Assign a label to the element.*

⓳ *Check whether this element is required to be filled out.*

⓴ *Click OK to complete the Multiline Text Box.*

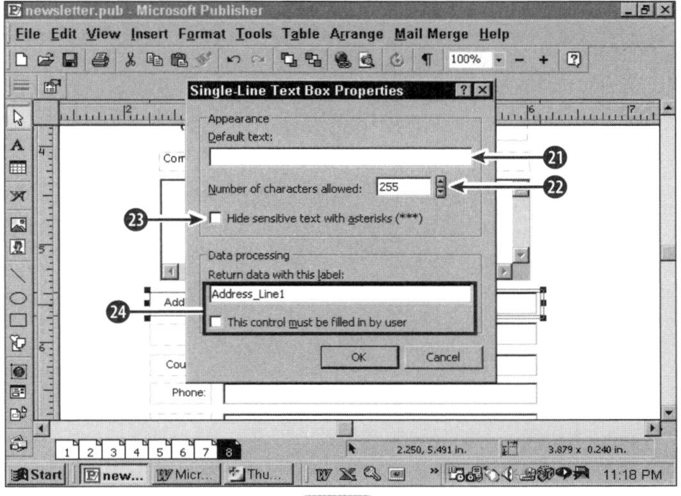

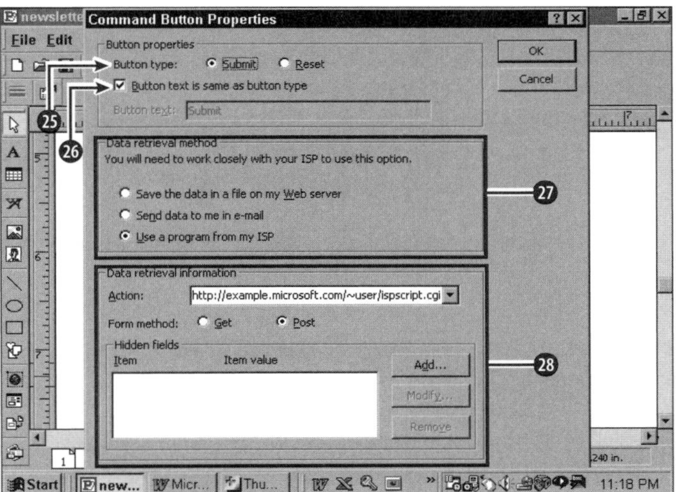

21. *For single-line text boxes, type in the default text that will appear.*
22. *Indicate the maximum number of characters a visitor may enter.*
23. *Check this box if something such as a password is solicited.*
24. *Assign a label for the field and indicate whether it is required.*
25. *When inserting a command button, indicate whether it is a Submit or Reset button.*
26. *Uncheck this check box to make your own label appear on the button.*
27. *Choose the type of action the button will perform.*
28. *Complete this information depending on the action to be performed. This area changes based on which radio button you select.*

If you're getting the impression that you are creating the user-friendly front-end for a database, you're right. That's what forms do — collect data.

Once the form is complete, you have to find a way to receive the data. This is where your Internet service provider (ISP) comes into play. If your ISP has Microsoft FrontPage Extensions installed, you can receive your form data via e-mail. Or, you can save the data in a file and retrieve it at your leisure. If your ISP doesn't have the FrontPage Extensions installed, they can instruct you about CGI scripts that can process your data the way you want. In the Command Button Properties of the Submit button, you indicate where the CGI scripting files are located so the server knows how to process your form data.

TAKE NOTE

LIMIT THE CHARACTERS

For those elements where you can specify the field length, do it. Fewer characters make your file size smaller and keep people from entering their life story in the blanks.

FIND IT ONLINE

If you need information on CGI and Web resources relating to CGI scripting, try **http://www.cgi-resources.com.**

Personal Workbook

Q&A

1. What are the two most common ways that a hyperlink appears on a Web site?

 ____

 ____

 ____

2. Hyperlinks can do other things besides take you to a different location on the Internet. Name two of them.

 ____

 ____

 ____

3. What is another term for a large graphic that has several hyperlinks embedded in it?

 ____

 ____

 ____

4. What are small copies of larger pictures called and what is their purpose on a Web page?

 ____

 ____

 ____

5. What are animated GIFs called in the Clip Art Gallery?

 ____

 ____

 ____

6. What is the difference between check boxes and options buttons?

 ____

 ____

 ____

7. Why should you limit the number of characters in a single-line text box?

 ____

 ____

 ____

8. In order for forms to be e-mailed to you or someone else, what Microsoft product must be installed on the Internet server where your Web site resides?

 ____

 ____

 ____

ANSWERS: PAGE 359

EXTRA PRACTICE

1. Start with a Web site you designed using the Web Site Wizard. Then, add pages that are specific to your needs.
2. Starting with a blank page, build a two-page Web site from scratch. You can make it either a funny site or a personal site.
3. Create your personal Web site that showcases your favorite hobbies or activities. Find other sites on the Internet and provide links to them on your site.
4. Build a simple form for your Web site that asks whether the visitor found your site useful, entertaining, or boring.
5. Build a form on your links page that asks for other Web sites that you can add to your links page. Have the form e-mailed to you, if possible.

REAL-WORLD APPLICATIONS

✔ You are building a Web site for your company. You have informational brochures available, both printed and electronic. You build a form asking for name, address, and e-mail address. Then, you ask whether they would prefer to receive the information by U.S. mail or via their e-mail address.

✔ You collect TY Beanie Babies and want to buy ones that are no longer available. You create a form for people to tell you that they have the babies you want and what the price is. You include fields for their phone number and e-mail address.

✔ On your personal Web site, you include pictures of all your pets in different situations. You build a page of thumbnail pictures so that visitors can choose which pictures they want to see in full.

Visual Quiz

This image shows five visible hyperlinks in the page. Can you name them all?

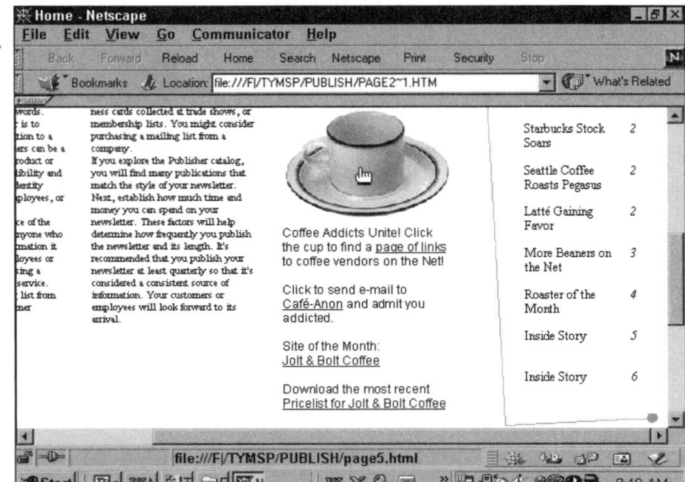

CHAPTER 17

MASTER THESE SKILLS

- Changing Background Textures and Color Schemes
- Changing Web Site Properties
- Inserting HTML Code Fragments
- Changing the Size and Width of Your Web Page
- Previewing Your Web Site
- Putting Your Web Site onto a Web Server

Changing the Appearance of Your Web Site

You have built a Web site. You're darned proud of it and invite everyone to go see it. You have animated GIFs, forms for users to fill out, and it reeks of quality information. You think you're done and are ready to sit back and relax. Right?

Wrong! The quickest death a Web site can have is to remain static. The beauty of the ever-evolving Web is also your challenge. As the Web changes, so should your site. Keep your site updated and current. Add things, and delete things. Change the design to give your visitors the feeling that all of this is current.

One way to make your Web site appear current is to include a date on the home page that indicates when the site was last updated. This tells your visitors right away that you work on your site constantly, or at least continuously. Even if you add one page or a picture on a page deep within your site, change the date.

Why not set out a maintenance plan? Once a month — or more frequently — visit and evaluate your Web site as if you were a visitor. You should also check all external links to be sure those sites are still up and running. Visitors who try using those links and find that many are dead will think poorly of your site.

Another thing you should do is read and reread your text. Because the Web is still mostly a reading medium, such as a newspaper or magazine, make every effort to check for spelling and grammar errors. Many visitors are turned off by these goofs, and many get the impression that you, as Webmaster, are not the knowledgeable expert that you may purport to be via your Web site. If your language skills aren't very good, ask for help from a friend or coworker.

Through Microsoft Publisher, you can add background sounds or animated GIFs that change your site page from static, boring, read-only to exciting and interesting. Just don't overdo it.

If you're ready to meet this challenge, this chapter is for you. Through these tasks you will smooth the rough spots in your site, refine the ones that are already good, and give your site the attention that it and your visitors deserve.

Toward the end of the chapter, you learn how to preview your site on your own computer and then upload the entire Web site to your Internet server. In other words, this is payday for all your hard work.

Changing Background Textures and Color Schemes

Back when the Internet and World Wide Web was used mainly by the government and academic population, the background color of a Web page was a static, boring gray. It served its purpose. Black text displayed nicely on it and hyperlinks were easy to find.

Nowadays, the competition is stiff on the Web. Web designers try to outdo one another to have the best-looking site. Sometimes they succeed in posting a beautiful site that has graphics and text neatly arranged on the page. All of it is very readable and easily understood. Other times, the color of the text is such a clash with the background color or graphics that you can barely read what is there. Other times, you close your browser because your eyes hurt from the strain.

While they are certainly nice to look at, the background on your Web site may be a hog. It can also distract from the text and pictures that you are displaying.

Backgrounds can be controlled with either a graphic or a color. When a site uses a graphic, you will notice that it appears seamless underneath the entire page. That's because the elements are usually tiled, where the graphic begins in the upper-left corner of your browser window and gets repeated to the right and underneath the first one. When you use a graphic for your background, be sure that it is a small file. It makes the page load more quickly and visitors don't have to wait long because the background is the first thing to load in a browser window.

Instead of a tiled graphic, you may opt for a solid color. Color can appear not as distracting as a graphic as long as what is placed on top in the way of text and other graphics is still readable.

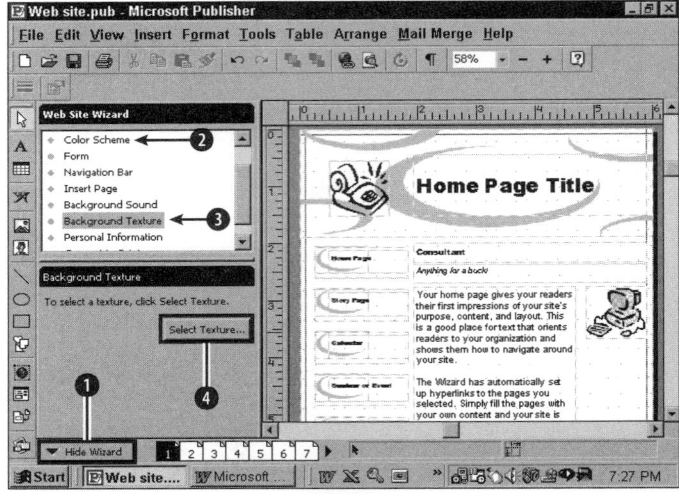

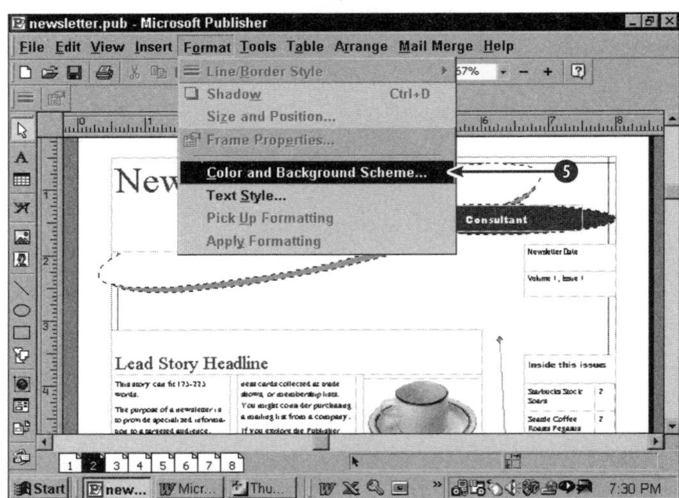

1. If you designed your site in the Web Wizard, show the Wizard, if it is not showing already.
2. Click Color Scheme in the upper window and pick a new scheme in the lower window.
3. Choose Background Texture in the upper window.
4. Click the Select Texture button. The dialog box in the lower-left figure appears.
5. If you began your publication from scratch, click Format ➪ Color and Background Scheme.

CROSS-REFERENCE

See "Using the Web Site Wizard" in Chapter 16.

Changing the Appearance of Your Web Site

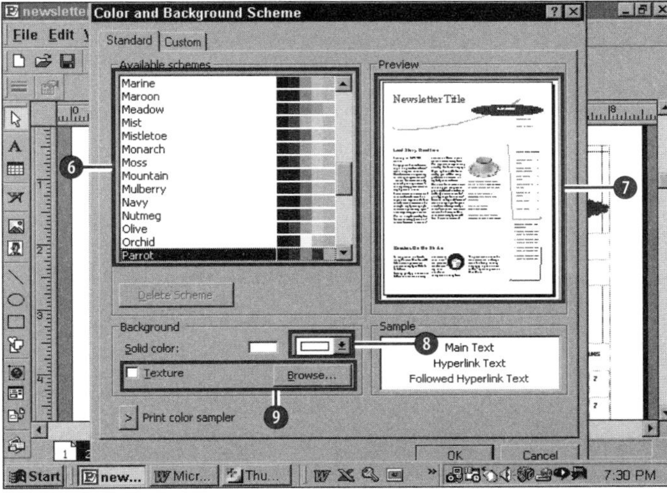

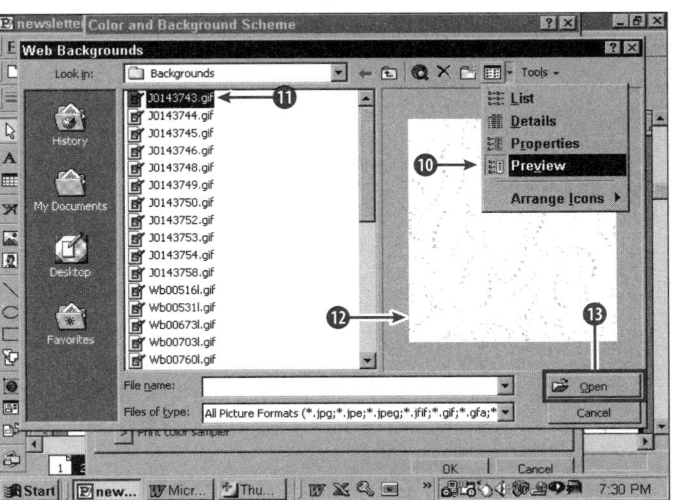

6 *Choose a new Color Scheme here.*

7 *Preview the changes here.*

8 *Select a solid color background using the drop-down menu.*

9 *Click the Texture checkbox for a graphic background and then click Browse.*

10 *If the Preview is not on, select Preview from the Views drop-down button.*

11 *Choose a file on the left side.*

12 *Preview it on the right side.*

13 *After you find the one you want, click Open.*

Truth be known, you may be inserting background graphics and colors for nothing. Netscape and Microsoft Internet Explorer both offer the user options to turn off or ignore coloring schemes in favor of the ones the user can set in these browsers.

TAKE NOTE

USE THE PREVIEW

When you are looking at possible backgrounds, use the Preview option in the Web Backgrounds dialog box. It will save you a lot of time. Otherwise, you have to load a background, and then preview it in the Publication window. If you don't like that one, you have several mouse clicks to go through before you can even look for a new one. Publisher doesn't default to this view, so watch for the instructions in the steps.

FILES COME IN DIFFERENT SIZES AND SHAPES

When you preview the background files, you'll notice that they come in all shapes and sizes. Some files need to be larger so they can tile correctly. When these graphics are loaded and tiled on your Web page, they give you different effects.

FIND IT ONLINE

If Publisher doesn't have enough backgrounds to choose from, try the ones at http://www.grsites.com/textures.

Changing Web Site Properties

When you use Yahoo!, Alta Vista, Excite, or some other Web search engine, did you ever wonder how those Web sites got categorized or even listed? It's really a simple process. Code is placed in the header of the HTML file that defines the Web page. Large search engines scan the Web finding these pages and collecting the information in the code. The terms are interpreted and classified along with the Web site address and added to the huge database of sites that are stored on these massive Web servers.

In Publisher, you can enter the code that the search engines are looking for and thereby increase the chances that your site will be listed in those search engines when someone enters the keywords that you define. And, because you can enter these keywords at the top of every page in your site, your chances of getting listed in several places are increased as long as you use different keywords.

The controls for these keywords and more can be accessed through Microsoft Publisher's Web Properties. The description area enables you to insert a couple of sentences describing the content of the page. Some search engines pick up this description and include it in the listing it generates.

Among the other items that you can control in these settings is which browsers your site is best suited for. As browsers such as Microsoft Internet Explorer and Netscape Navigator have progressed, their capabilities of interpreting the content of your site, especially multimedia elements, have increased. Be cautious, however. Some Web "netizens" are very lax in upgrading their browsers once they get comfortable with one. Many users who have older computers haven't bothered to download any upgrades, and their browser is the one that came on the computer.

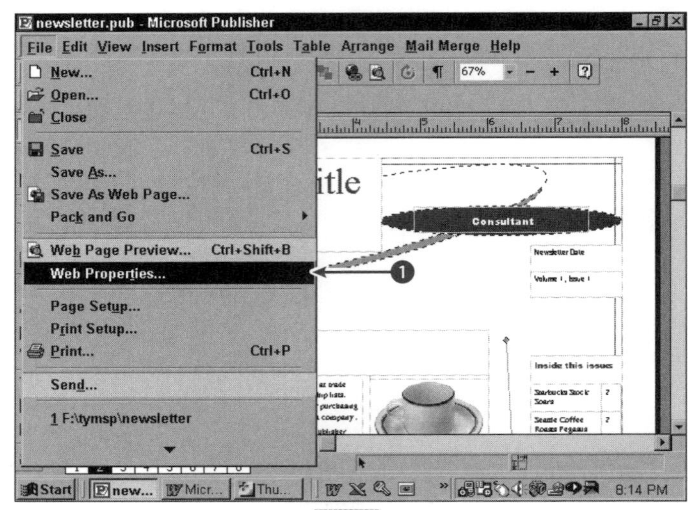

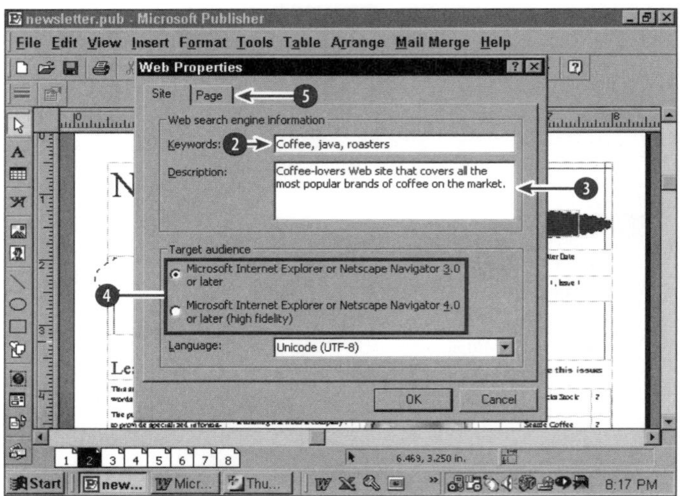

1. Choose File ➪ Web Properties to change the properties of the page currently displayed.
2. Enter keywords here.
3. Enter a few sentences to describe what is on the page in the Description area.
4. Choose the user browser type you are targeting.
5. Click the Page tab.

CROSS-REFERENCE

See "Using Clip Gallery Live" in Chapter 11.

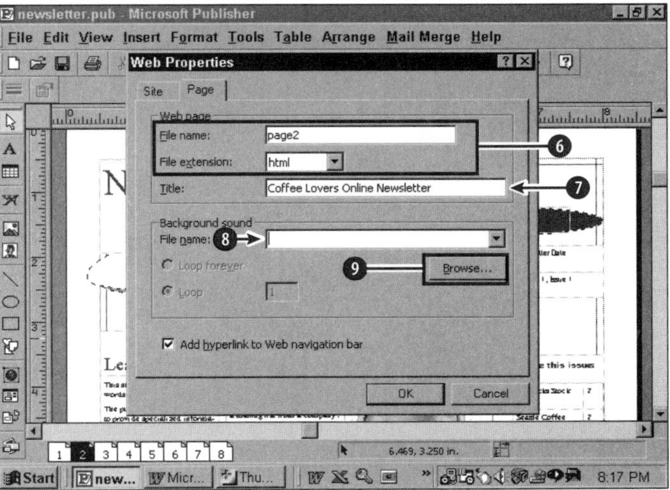

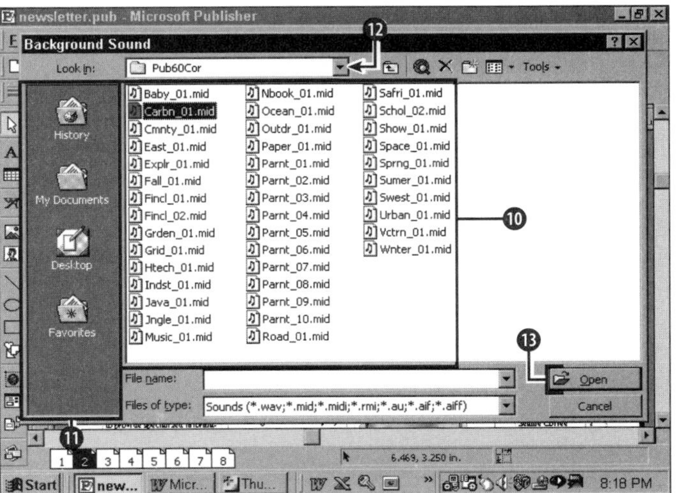

6. *Change or keep the file name and choose an extension.*
7. *Enter the page title. This is what appears on the title bar of the Web browser.*
8. *Type the name of the sound file to play when the page opens. Leave it blank for no sound.*
9. *Click the Browse button to find a sound file.*
10. *Choose a sound file from the list.*
11. *Use the folders to locate a different sound file on your computer.*
12. *Or, use the "Look in" drop-down menu to find another location.*
13. *Click Open to insert the sound file. Then click OK to close the Properties box.*

In the Web Properties, you can have a sound file play when the page first loads. Not only can you assign this on the home page, but on every page within your site. Try to keep the sound files small, because larger ones do take a while to download.

TAKE NOTE

CONSIDERING SOUND FILES

If you're thinking strongly about including a sound file on your site that plays automatically when someone accesses that page, choose carefully and think about the settings. A short sound file is not obtrusive if it plays once and really is short. To loop a sound file can grate on even the most patient person's soul.

CHOOSING KEYWORDS

When you are entering the keywords for the Web page, be sure to separate them with commas. Try to think of every form of the word, including singular and plural. When possible, use similar words even if they aren't included on the Web page itself.

FIND IT ONLINE

To submit your site to Yahoo! for searching, go to http://docs.yahoo.com/info/suggest/.

Inserting HTML Code Fragments

This is as close to HTML programming as it gets in Microsoft Publisher. True to form, Publisher tries to get you through an entire Web publishing experience without making you learn one bit of HTML code. But, for those of you who have to push the limit, this task is for you.

Why and where would you need to insert HTML code fragments? First of all, you'll find a lot of ActiveX and Java applets that you are free to use on your site. This is one way to incorporate those. And, while Java and ActiveX will be the most likely candidates for this procedure, you can use it on VBScript and standard HTML as well.

Java is a programming language that enables you to have animated marquees of text running across your page. They can take on the form of other small animations as well. Java applets can run chat rooms or create charts and graphs. They run in their own little world, and some take a little time to download.

ActiveX is like Java to a point. Microsoft invented ActiveX to compete with Java. You will find ActiveX components that do the same things as Java applets. For a while, ActiveX would only run in Microsoft Internet Explorer, but newer versions of Netscape run them as well.

VBScript (Visual Basic Script) is another programming language that can do several things on the Web. Many of the shopping sites on the Web use a form of VBScript to enable you to do tasks as specialized as adding items to a virtual shopping cart or configuring a computer.

Standard HTML is the basic language of the Web. When you convert your Publisher documents into Web pages, this is the language that the browser can read to display your page.

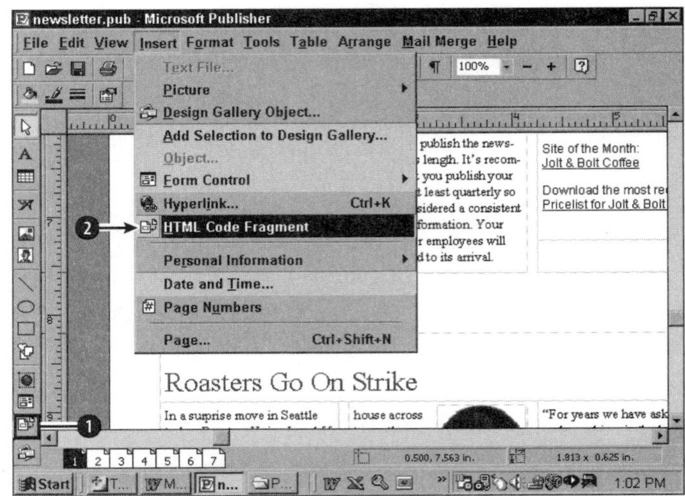

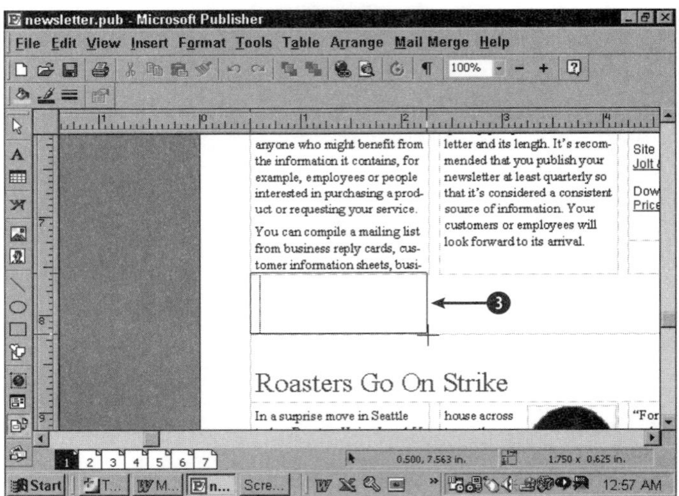

1. *Click the HTML Code Fragments button in the toolbar.*
2. *Or choose Insert ➪ HTML Code Fragment from the menu.*
3. *With the resulting cursor, draw a frame where the result of the code is to be placed.*

CROSS-REFERENCE

To learn how to preview your site in a browser, see "Previewing Your Web Site" later in this chapter.

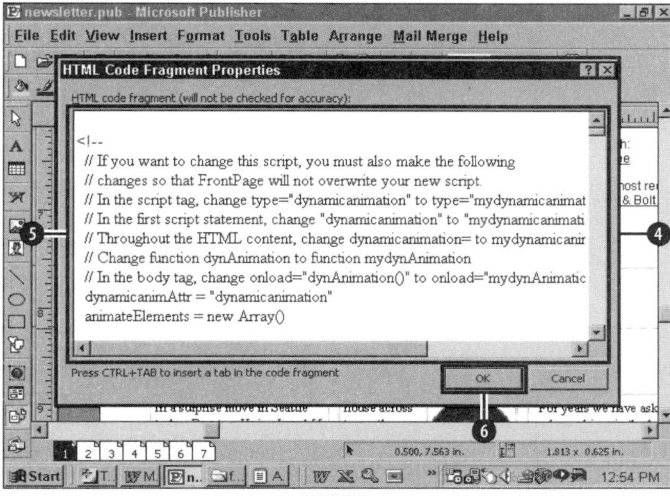

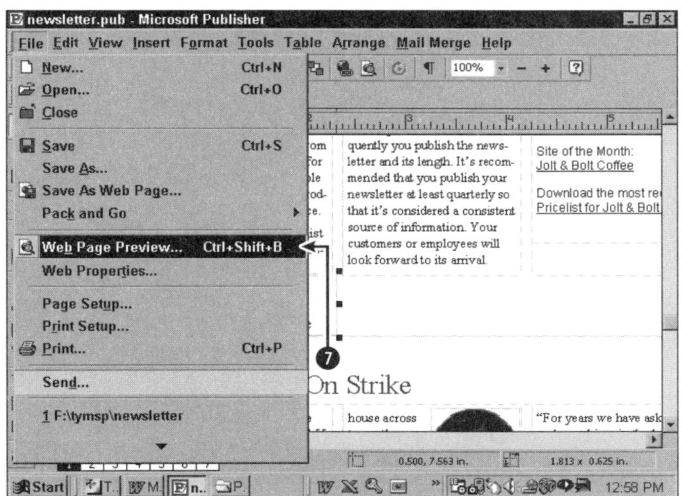

4. *Once the frame is drawn, the HTML Code Fragment Properties dialog box appears.*
5. *Type or paste in the HTML code.*
6. *Click OK to close the dialog box.*
7. *To preview your HTML code in a browser, choose File ➪ Web Page Preview or press Ctrl+Shift+B.*

When you insert an HTML code fragment in Publisher, you won't see anything of any importance that is intelligible. Only when you preview the page in a browser will the code be invoked.

A couple of factors may prevent Publisher from reading your code: You can't surround your code fragment with BorderArt, and you can't place the code fragment on top of anything else on the page. This causes the programming to fail.

TAKE NOTE

CHECKING BROWSER CAPABILITY

Be sure that your browser is capable of the elements that you insert into the HTML code fragment. Otherwise, you will get an error or broken logo displayed where the fragment would be.

USING CUT AND PASTE

If you find a Java applet or ActiveX element that you want to use on your site, remember that these are all ASCII text files. Open them in WordPad or some other ASCII editor and copy the text to the clipboard. When you open the HTML Code Fragments dialog box, simply paste the code in the space provided.

FIND IT ONLINE

For more information on Java applets or a place to download some free ones, try The Java Centre at **http://www.java.co.uk.**

Changing the Size and Width of Your Web Page

Using the Web Wizard creates a default page size of 6" × 14". For some users, that is no problem; for others, it may be too long. In a browser window that is set to 640 × 480 resolution, that's three or four clicks to get down to the bottom of your Web page.

Some purists insist that each Web page should be self-contained. That is, nobody should have to scroll down more than one mouse click, if at all. Realistically, you could have more items on your page that just can't get separated, so your visitors are just going to have to scroll. It all boils down to your personal taste. And if you get some complaints about the length of your pages, you can always change it later.

You may recall that the default page size for the Publisher Wizard is 6 inches wide. Through the page setup properties, however, you can change this. A 6-inch wide page is ideal for VGA (640 × 480) displays. If you feel your visitors are going to be on SVGA (usually 800 × 600 or larger) displays, you'll find another standard setting to make your pages 7.5 inches wide with a default length of 14 inches.

If neither one of those settings suits you, a third option lets you define a new length and width for your page. They call this the custom setting.

When you convert printed publications to Web documents, your task is going to be a bit larger if you plan on having a page where there is not horizontal scrolling. You may want to consider redoing the layout on a custom page setting, and then saving it as a Web document.

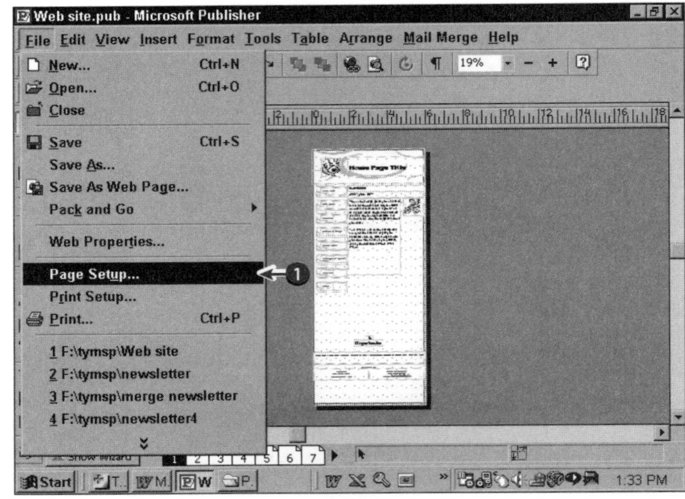

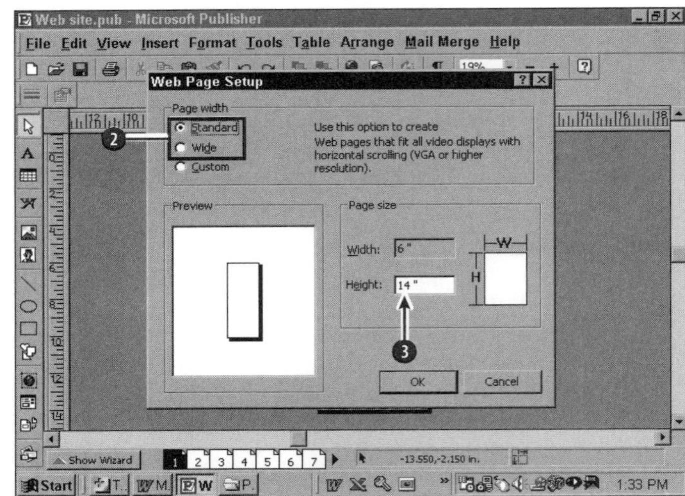

1. Click File ➪ Page Setup.
2. In the Web Page Setup dialog box, choose Standard or Wide for Publisher's presets.
3. On either Standard or Wide, you can change the height of the page but not the width.

CROSS-REFERENCE

For setting custom page size for a printed document, see Chapter 6, "Using Page Setup."

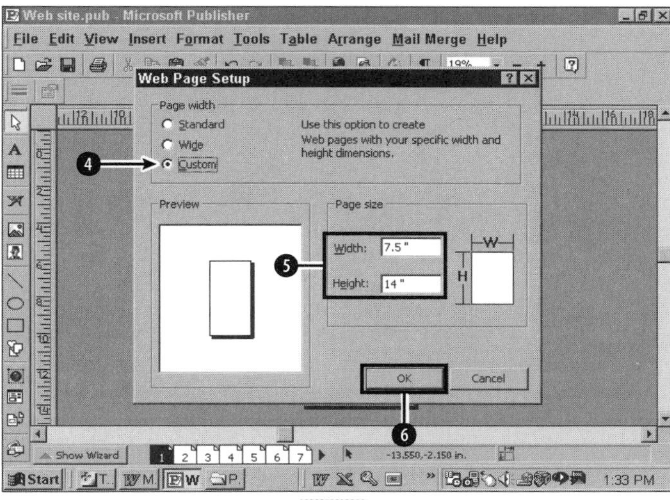

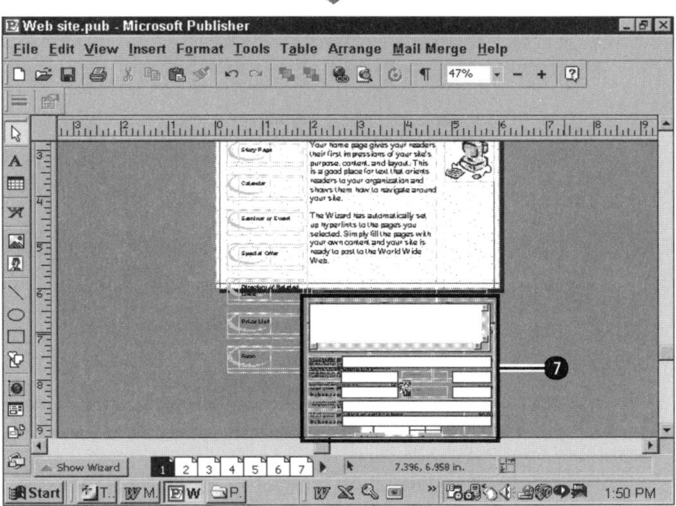

4 *Or, you can select Custom.*

5 *These settings enable you to set Width and Height.*

6 *Click OK.*

7 *By changing size before you move elements on the page, all elements that do not fall into the width or height will drop into the scratch area.*

▶ *If you aren't happy with the new page size, you can select Edit ⇨ Undo to return to your previous settings.*

▶ *Even though items drop into the scratch area, they are still selectable and movable.*

TAKE NOTE

MOVE ITEMS ON THE PAGE BEFORE CHANGING IT

If you're planning on shortening a long page that already has items on it, move them on your longer Web pages using the rulers as a guide for where to place them. You can also add pages, if needed to keep articles in order. When you shorten a longer page, all the items that were placed in the area that got chopped off will stay in the scratch area. If you have multiple pages, you could have several items stacked on top of one another. To make matters worse, they may not have been grouped together, meaning a lot of small components will have to be separated out and moved separately.

CHOOSING TARGET RESOLUTION

A few years ago, most Webmasters would target their pages toward the 640 × 480 resolution masses because most people surfing the Net fell into that category — laptop users especially. Now, more Webmasters are designing for the 800 × 600 monitors because many notebook computers fit in that display arena. But, it's your decision.

FIND IT ONLINE

Change any application window to a specific resolution. Size-O-Matic is available at http://www.pythoness.com/SizeOMatic/.

Previewing Your Web Site

Everybody who excels has some guiding force behind them, and the magic behind success is practice. You know that Mom always told you that practice makes perfect, and it's true in most anything you do. However, you can poke and prod Microsoft Publisher options for a month of Sundays — massaging elements, refining text, and gathering the right graphics. But, until you load your site to the Web and launch it for the entire world to see, it does little good just sitting on your computer.

To give your site a test drive, you should try previewing it in a couple browsers. If you have only one browser on your computer, it may be worthwhile to get the other major browser. That means Netscape users should have Microsoft Internet Explorer and vice versa. If possible, try to round up version 3 or 4. By using earlier versions, you are ensuring that you won't leave out all those people who are a little behind the times. If you have the hard drive space, it is possible to have several versions of both browsers loaded on your computer.

When you run a preview of a multiple-page Web site, you have the option of viewing just the current page showing in your window or the entire site. Don't be shy about previewing your whole site, because it takes no time at all to load in your browser window because you don't have to deal with dial-up connection speeds. Besides, it gives you a chance to test those internal hyperlinks before going live.

If you run into any trouble previewing your site, be sure to consult the Publisher Help file. You'll find quite a few troubleshooting tips and ideas in there that may not have occurred to you. The troubleshooter is available by clicking Help ➪ Web Preview Troubleshooter.

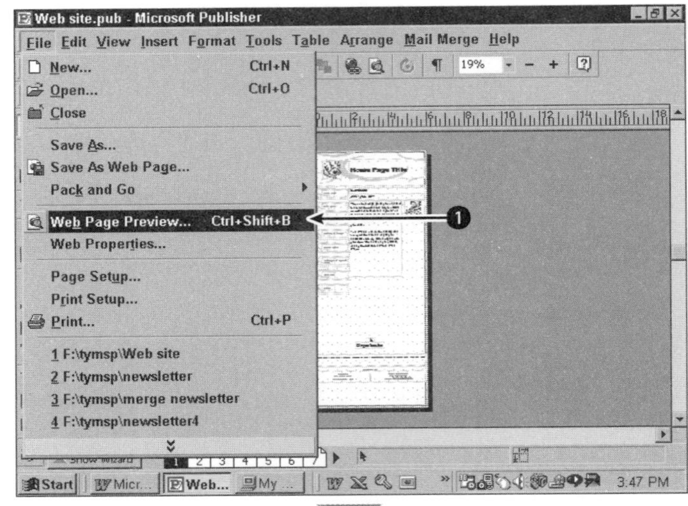

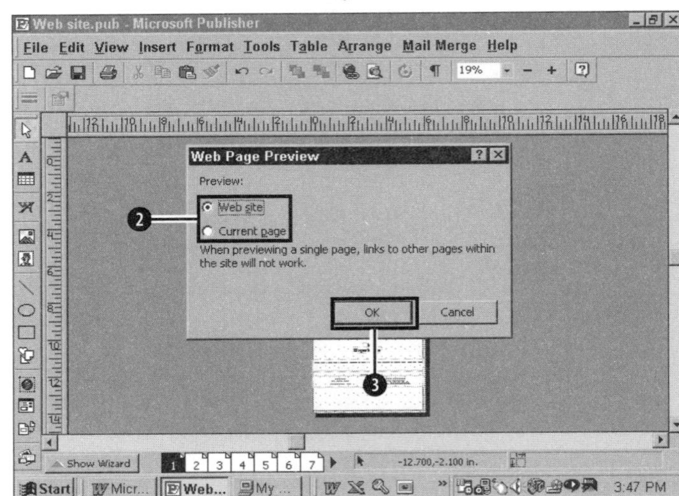

1. Choose File ➪ Web Page Preview or press Ctrl+Shift+B.
2. Choose whether to preview the entire site or just the current page.
3. Click OK.

CROSS-REFERENCE

Before previewing, you may want to run through Design Checker. Its capabilities and uses are found in Chapter 6.

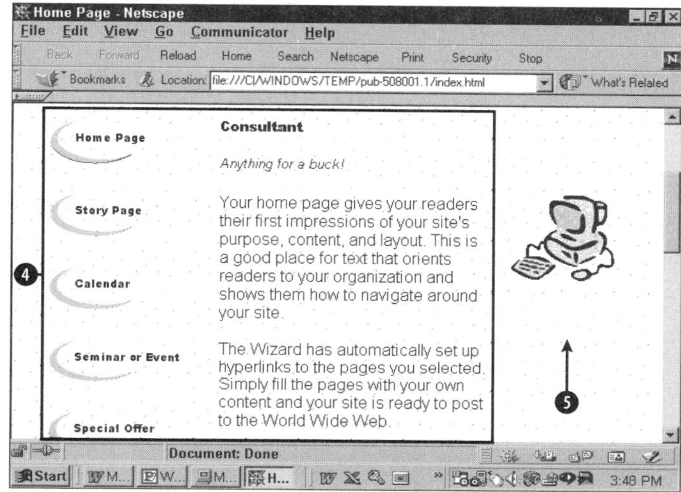

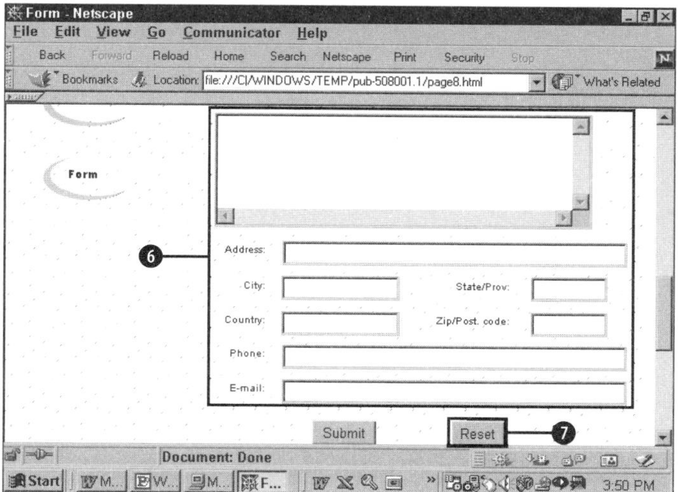

4. *Check all hyperlinks in the navigation bars.*
5. *Listen for any background sounds that were attached to the pages.*
6. *You can enter information into the forms to check them, but clicking the Submit button will do no good because you aren't on a live server.*
7. *The Reset button can be tested, however.*

TAKE NOTE

SETTING YOUR DEFAULT BROWSER

Microsoft Publisher uses your default browser to preview the Webs site you're working on. As a general rule, the last Internet browser you install will be your default. Microsoft Internet Explorer provides a way to redefine itself as the default browser, but Netscape does not.

TEST YOUR SITE IN PREVIEW

Preview is an excellent time to test all your hyperlinks. If you have your Internet connection open, external hyperlinks will be available to test as well; as will e-mail links.

PREVIEWING CHANGES

While your browser window is open and you are previewing your site, any changes you make in Publisher will not be reflected in the browser window automatically. You have to close the browser and start the preview in Publisher again.

FIND IT ONLINE

BrowserMaster is a shareware program that lets you preview your Web pages at different resolutions. Find it at **http://www.vasile.com/racecar/stampware/**.

Putting Your Web Site onto a Web Server

Because your arrangement with your Internet service provider (ISP) may be unique, there's no possible way this task can cover every scenario of putting your Web site on the Web. It is all dependent upon whether or not your ISP has FrontPage server extensions installed on their Web server, or if they use some other type of procedure for uploading your files to your Internet site. The good news, however, is Microsoft Publisher has provided numerous ways that should satisfy most ISP requirements. The first thing you have to do is publish your Web pages to a folder. Doing so gathers all the files necessary into one location for easy uploading. Then, you can use one of the procedures below to, in the words of Jean-Luc Picard of *Star Trek*, "Make it so, number one."

Creating a Web Folder

First, create a Web folder that will store all your files as a gathering place before moving on to the Internet server. Click File ➪ Save as Web Page and then choose or create a folder to hold the pages. If Publisher comes across a problem with your pages, you will be notified through this process. Fix the problems and do this procedure again. And, don't forget where you put the folder and the subsequent files.

Uploading Files via FTP

Once the Web folder has possession of your files, you can use an FTP (file transfer protocol) program and an Internet connection to copy the files to the location on the server where your ISP has designated your site to reside. Again, get the FTP location from your ISP after they have set your site up. Luckily, Publisher has this ability built into it. You can specify the FTP location on

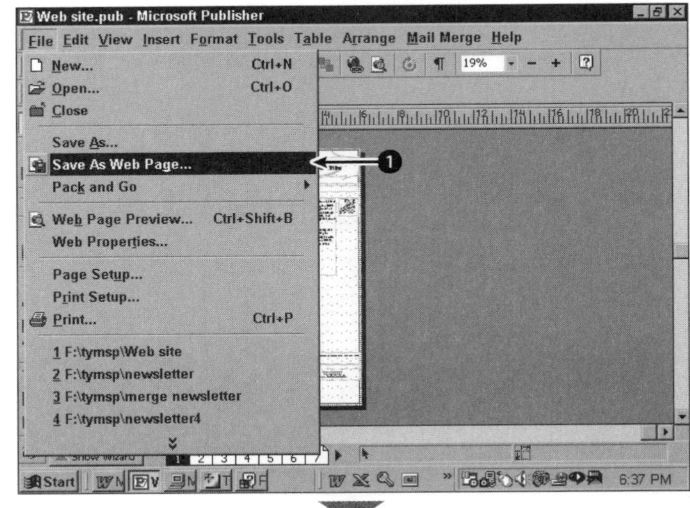

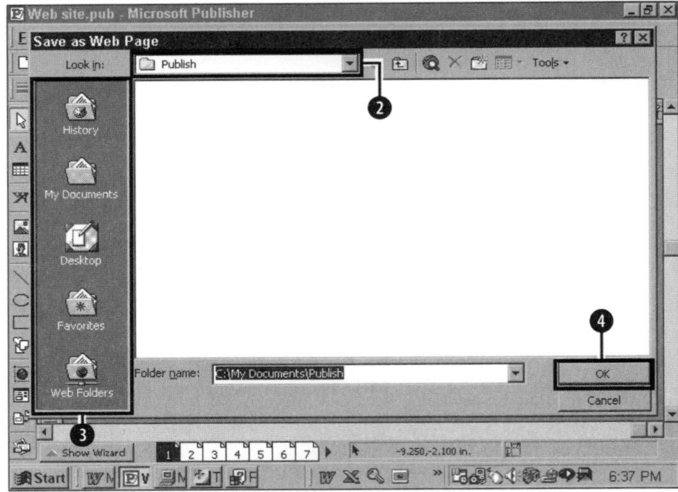

❶ To publish to the Web, click File ➪ Save As Web Page.

❷ Choose a location to store the files using the "Look in" drop-down menu.

❸ Or, you can use the folders in the Places list.

❹ Click OK to save the files.

CROSS-REFERENCE

You can view the files that Publisher created using Windows Explorer. See Chapter 3 on how to find and manage the files.

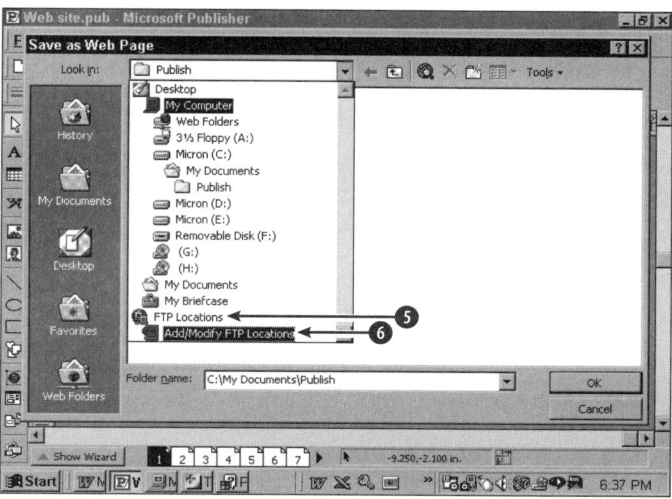

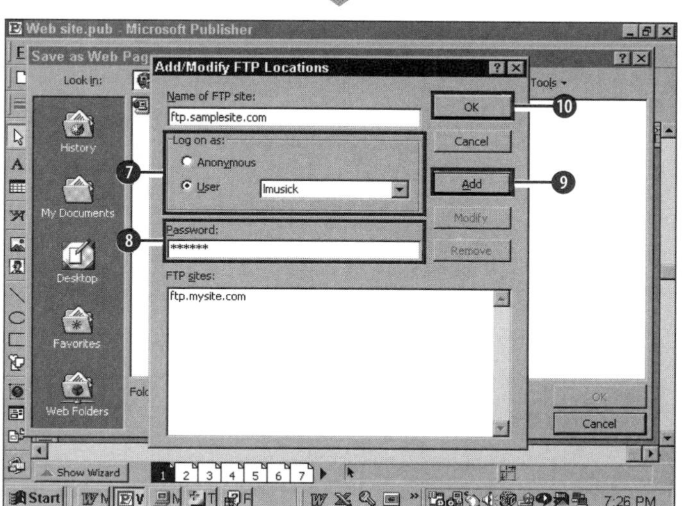

5 *To FTP your files, click the "Look in" drop-down menu and choose FTP locations.*

6 *Click Add/Modify FTP Locations to create a new server location or modify an existing one.*

7 *Type in the name of the FTP site to receive the file. Your ISP can give you this.*

8 *Select your logon information and enter username and password, if needed.*

9 *Click Add to save this information for later use.*

10 *Click OK.*

the Web, enter your login and password, if necessary, and upload the entire site in a few clicks of the mouse button. Publisher also remember all this information for later uploads.

You can set up the FTP location ahead of time. If you choose File ⇨ Open, and then click the "Look in" drop-down menu, you'll find FTP Locations at the bottom of the list with a choice to Add/Modify FTP Locations underneath it.

Continued

TAKE NOTE

CHANGING WHAT'S ALREADY UPLOADED

If you find you need to add pages or alter the ones that are on your Web site, all you have to do is make the corrections in Publisher, save the files to your Web folder, and upload the whole thing again, overwriting the files that are currently on the server.

WHERE TO FIND WEB PUBLISHING WIZARD

The Microsoft Web Publishing Wizard is part of Internet Explorer and could have been installed when you loaded that program. To check, click Start ⇨ Programs ⇨ Internet Explorer and see if it is in that group of programs. Optionally, it could be in Start ⇨ Programs ⇨ Microsoft Web Publishing. Another location it may be hiding is Start ⇨ Programs ⇨ Accessories ⇨ Internet Tools. If you can't find it in your menu system anywhere, Windows 98 users can open Control Panel and click Add/Remove Programs. Under the Windows Setup tab, highlight the Internet Tools choice and then click Details. Place a check by Web Publishing Wizard and click OK.

FIND IT ONLINE

Wanna exchange info or questions about Publisher 2000? Check the newsgroups listed at http://officeupdate.microsoft.com/newsgroups/newsPublisher.htm.

Putting Your Web Site onto a Web Server *Continued*

Creating a Network Location

Have you noticed that many software companies are using HTML for the Readme and Help files? It makes sense, really. Considering that most Windows computers have an Internet browser already installed, the size of the files are pretty compact and the hyperlink capability makes it easy to jump around the file. Businesses are doing the same thing. Employee manuals, procedures, and other internal business publications are finding a home in HTML on intranets. Should you find that this procedure makes sense for you, you can lay out these types of documents in Publisher and upload them to your company's network server. Space could be designated as an employee digest with all of the interoffice memos, manuals, announcements, and so on being available to the employees whenever needed.

When you Save as Web Page, as described earlier in this task, everyone on the network can view your documents using the browser that is installed on their computer. A network administrator should be able to help you set this up.

Web Publishing Wizard

The final way, and probably the easiest way, for you to upload your Web site is with the Web Publishing Wizard. This separate program takes the files that you have in your Web-published folder and uploads them to the Internet address that you specify. This program works like an FTP program, only more easily. It steps you through the procedure. The advantage of this technique is that it works with several known ISPs such as AOL, CompuServe, and more. Check to see if your ISP is in the list under the Advanced button. If not, you can still use the Wizard's FTP method or, if your ISP has

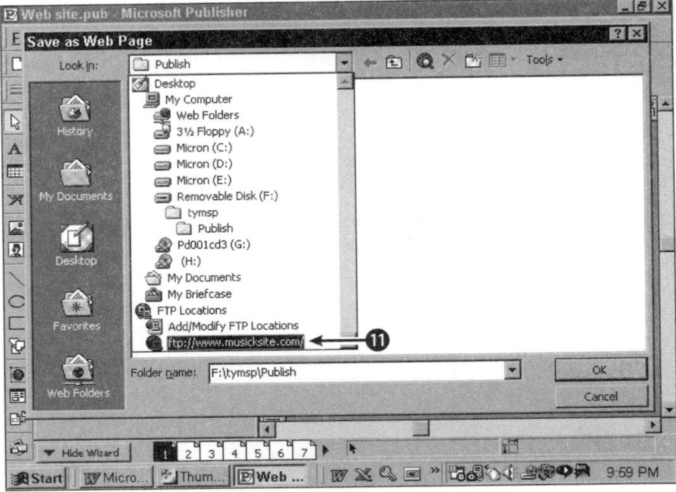

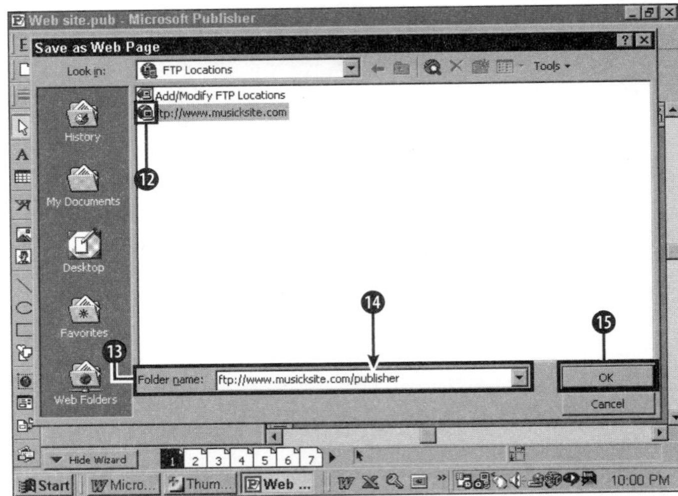

11. *Once your FTP site has been set up, you select it from the "Look in" drop-down list.*
12. *Or, you can choose the FTP Locations option and click the selection in the window.*
13. *Once selected, the address appears in the "Folder name" text box.*
14. *Enter the rest of the FTP address, which your ISP provided. This usually includes a forward slash (/) and a folder name or more.*
15. *Click OK to begin uploading your files.*

CROSS-REFERENCE

Existing publications can be converted to Web pages. See Chapter 5 for procedures.

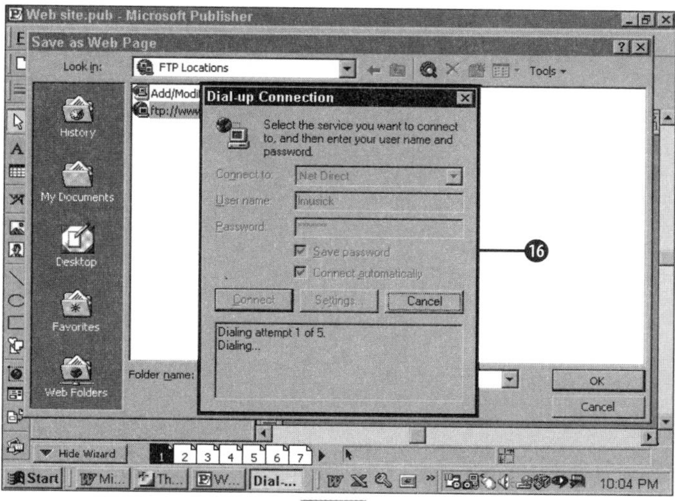

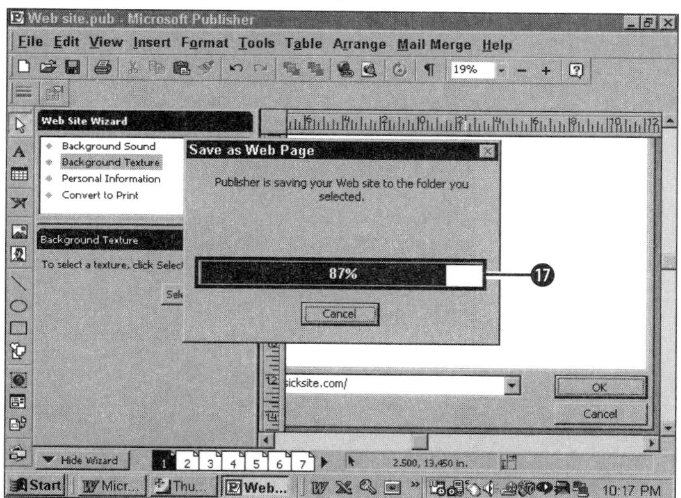

⑯ *After you click OK, your Dial-up Connection dialog box will open if you haven't already made your connection to the Internet.*

⑰ *After clicking OK, you'll see a progress bar showing the estimated percentage of upload completion.*

FrontPage server extensions installed, you can use the FrontPage Extended Web choice. You'll find the Web Publishing Wizard by choosing Start ➪ Programs ➪ Internet Tools ➪ Web Publishing Wizard.

If you're creating a personal Web site and don't have a lot of money to spend, several companies provide a couple of megabytes of space on their server for your site. Geocities, Angelfire, and others give you a home on the Web, and some are even FrontPage-capable. The disadvantage to these sites is that you don't have your own domain name like **www.mysite.com**.

TAKE NOTE

USING CURRENT FTP SOFTWARE

There's no hard and fast rule that you have to use Publisher to FTP your files to your server. If you have current experience with using an FTP software program such as WS_FTP, you can continue to use it to upload your Web files from Publisher. In this instance, you would go ahead and publish your Web site to a folder location and then contact the FTP server using your software. You then copy all the files in the published folder to the directory you want on the server, and you're done.

FIND IT ONLINE

To add a new Places folder on the Open and Save dialog boxes, check **http://officeupdate.microsoft.com/2000/downloadDetails/PlaceBar.htm**.

Personal Workbook

Q&A

1. What are two ways you can change the background color or texture of your Web pages?

____

____

____

2. When you change or add a background to your Web site, what is the single most important thing to consider regarding your visitors?

____

____

____

3. What purpose do keywords serve when they are assigned to your Web page?

____

____

____

4. How can you place Java or ActiveX components into your Web page?

____

____

5. What is the keyboard shortcut for previewing your Web site in your system's default browser?

____

____

____

6. What are the two standard widths that Publisher provides for Web pages?

____

____

____

7. Before shortening a Web page, what should you do?

____

____

____

8. Name two ways that you can upload your Web pages to an Internet server?

____

____

____

ANSWERS: PAGE 360

Changing the Appearance of Your Web Site

CHAPTER 17

EXTRA PRACTICE

1. Use the wizard to change the color scheme and background of your Web pages. See what kinds of moods you can create.
2. Add a short sound clip to your home page. Ensure that it plays only once.
3. Find a Java applet on the Internet and place it on your Web page.
4. After running the Web Wizard to create your Web site, alter the page size so that you can print it on letter-sized paper.
5. Find an ISP that provides free Web sites. Create a Web site on your favorite hobby. Upload it to the site.

REAL-WORLD APPLICATIONS

- ✔ Your company just enacted a new policy on Internet and e-mail use when at work. Create a publication in Publisher that details the procedures for monitoring and consequences for abuse. Upload it to the company's network server for all employees to access. Send an interoffice memo to alert the employees to the file location.
- ✔ The background and color scheme that Publisher created for your Web pages is too distracting. You want a plain white background and subdued colors. You go into Web Page Properties and make the changes.
- ✔ You just opened an AOL account. Instead of using the FTP procedure, you use the Web Publishing Wizard to upload your Web pages to the server.

Visual Quiz

This computer is set up for 640 × 480 resolution. Notice that the visitor has to scroll from left to right to see the entire page width. What can you do to your Publisher document to eliminate scrolling left to right?

____

____

____

____

____

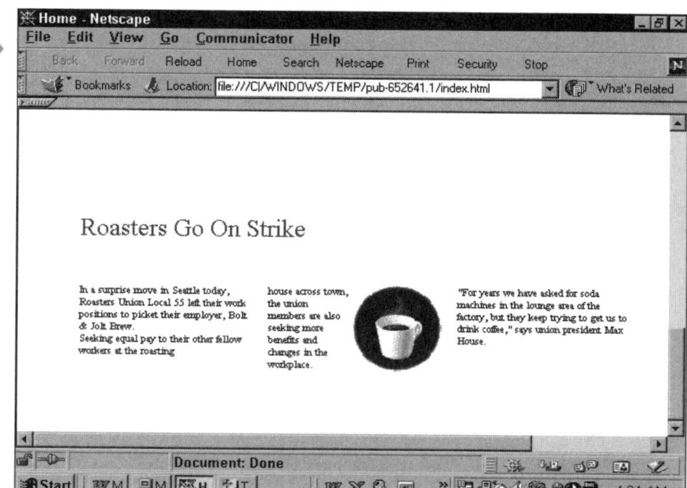

CHAPTER 18

MASTER THESE SKILLS

- Setting Color Printing Options
- Using Commercial Printer Drivers
- Setting Color Trapping Preferences
- Embedding Fonts
- Managing Links to Graphic Objects
- Using Pack and Go for Commercial Printing

Using a Commercial Printing Service

Printing to the printer attached to your computer can be gratifying when you finally see the payoff for the hard work you invested while sitting at the computer. Some jobs take hours, while others can take days.

Those using Microsoft Publisher 2000 in a business environment can certainly run simple black and white jobs to a high-quality laser printer and take their finished product to the copy room for duplication, or even to an outside service such as Kinko's. But for those jobs that took half your lifeblood, only the best output will do. And that means a commercial printer should be contacted who will take your Publisher files and print exactly what you intended when you designed the piece.

You have a several reasons for choosing a commercial printer. Most companies are not equipped to print large volumes of color output. Although many large corporations are equipped with high-speed color copiers, there reaches a point when having a job put on the printing press makes more economical sense.

Another reason for commercial output may be size-related. Large-format publications are difficult to produce on standard office copiers, and quite prohibitive on large-format color copiers.

Multiple-page documents that have to go through some sort of binding and trimming process are also best left to the professionals.

So, you ask, what is the printing process all about? In a normal procedure, you create a publication in Publisher. Once everything is proofed and you have all the appropriate authorizations to print, you create a file from Publisher, which the printer uses to produce film. That file contains all the information necessary to translate your document — text, fonts, graphics, and all — to an imagesetter. An *imagesetter* uses a photographic process to make a negative image of each page, which the printer places over a light-sensitive metal plate. This plate gets installed on the printing press and your piece gets printed.

And, if you are printing in four-color, there are four plates for every page: cyan, magenta, yellow and black (CMYK). These four inks are applied so that, when laid on top of one another, they render a complete color page.

That is a simple explanation of four-color process printing. Some other items come into play, such as spot color, which your printer will be glad to explain to you.

Setting Color Printing Options

You may know that you'll be sending your publication to film, but you have to start the process by telling Microsoft Publisher that the final destination is going to be film and a printing press. The first two figures show you how to accomplish this. Do these steps before you do anything else. If you don't, you'll not be able to access the settings in the Advanced Print Settings dialog box.

A lot of what you'll be doing in this task is dependent upon your service bureau's or printer's equipment. Many makes and models of imagesetters are on the market, not to mention some legacy models that still serve their owners well. Before you make any setting changes here, be sure to contact your commercial printer or service bureau to see what equipment they have and what settings they prefer.

To make some sense of all these terms and settings in the Advanced Print Settings dialog box, here's a brief rundown.

- **Graphics:** Print them at full resolution. To do less would make the pictures and clip art fuzzy.
- **Fonts:** Keep control of your fonts by embedding them and not allowing the equipment to substitute. Otherwise, you may end up with funny word and line spacing.
- **Printer's marks:** Unless the equipment attaches these marks automatically, keep these items checked. They let the people who strip up the film (preparing them for the printing plates, known as *registering*) align everything.
- **Bleeds:** Large or bound print jobs usually get printed on larger sheets of paper. After drying and/or binding, the finished pieces are trimmed so that bleeds reach the end of a trimmed edge.

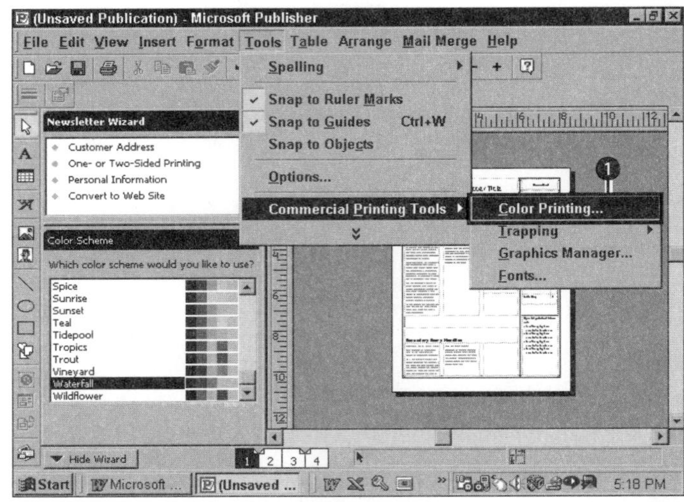

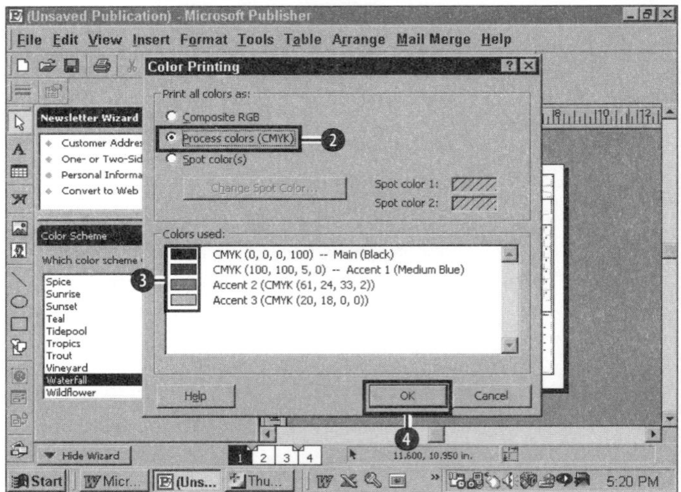

1. Choose Tools ⇨ Commercial Printing Tools ⇨ Color Printing.
2. Click "Process colors (CMYK)."
3. Note that the colors that you have included in your color scheme are shown with the percentage amount of CMYK ink they will be printed as.
4. Click OK.

CROSS-REFERENCE

Chapter 5 explains more about the advanced print settings in the Print dialog box.

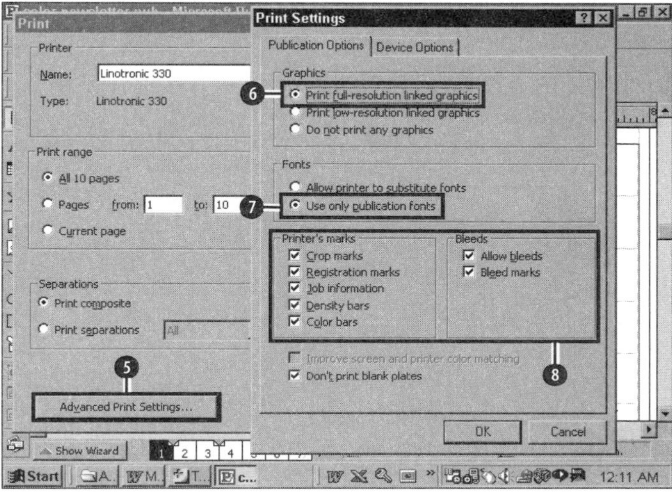

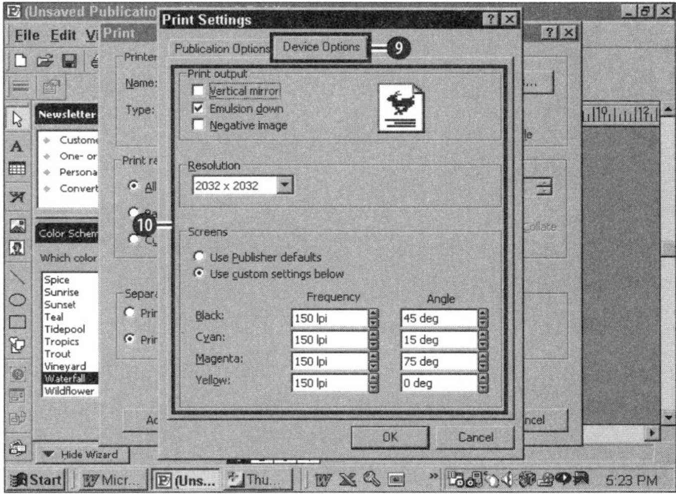

5. *Click the Advanced Print Settings button after opening the Print dialog box (Ctrl+P).*
6. *Print graphics at full resolution.*
7. *Use only publication fonts.*
8. *Set "Printer's marks" and Bleeds settings accordingly.*
9. *Click the Device Options tab.*
10. *Change all settings to specifications prescribed by your commercial printer.*

- **Printing Blank Plates:** Sometimes, there won't be four pieces of film for every page. Don't waste the film; keep this item checked.
- **Print Output:** Follow the instructions of your printer here. Depending on the press, film may have to be set up differently.
- **Resolution:** The naked eye can't see a difference in printing text above 1,270 dpi. Most color photos will do well at this setting, too. Follow the printer's instructions here, too.
- **Screens:** If you look at CMYK printing closely, you'll see that it's made up of dots of different ink. You can see this process in the color Sunday comics pages, which run at a coarser lines per inch (lpi) setting. Many magazines run at 150 lpi or higher for better-quality color. Use your printer's specifications here or leave the default 100 lpi alone.

TAKE NOTE

WEB DOCUMENTS DON'T CONVERT

If you already have a publication converted for the Web, you'll find the Color Printing option missing from the Tools ⇨ Commercial Printing menu. Wait to convert a publication for the Web until after you have film run. Or, just save your document under a new name so you can come back to it.

FIND IT ONLINE

Even though some of it is Mac-slanted, you can find tips on printing to files for your commercial printer at http://www3.teleplex.net/jr/.

Using Commercial Printer Drivers

Commercial printer drivers differ from the traditional desktop printer drivers. High-quality output comes from very specialized machinery. The ability to print as exactly as possible is the strength of large imagesetters. That's why it's always important to install the correct printer driver that your commercial printer recommends.

Though you may not see it in a printout from your desktop printer, the media you are printing on can shift ever so slightly, making it nearly impossible to register. You can see this sometimes in some color newspapers — a bit of yellow or cyan will halo around the other colors. And when you are working with four-color separations, you must have each piece of film lined perfectly on top of one another or your printed piece will be off-register. Imagesetters have their own way of handling paper or film, just like your desktop printer. Laser printers can have multiple paper drawers to draw sheets from in addition to whatever manual feeds that are available. Some imagesetters use large sheets of film, while others may use rolls. The printer driver you choose must match the imagesetter.

The function of the printer driver is to tell the output device — be it imagesetter, laser, or ink jet — what size the media should be, how to place the document data on that media, and what resolution to produce that data in. This is why it's important to use the proper printer driver when preparing a document for imagesetter output.

An exception exists, however. Some service bureaus or printing houses will want your file in an encapsulated PostScript (EPS) format. Their equipment may be better suited to take a composite file (where all the colors are still together rather than separated into individual CMYK pieces of film) to do all the separating and trapping according to its own abilities.

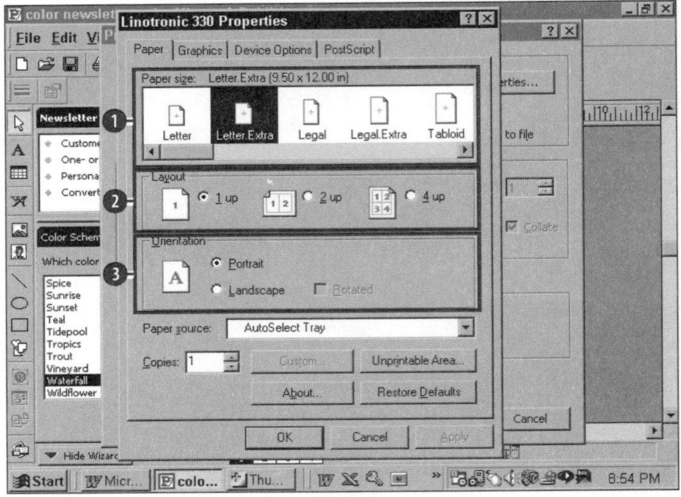

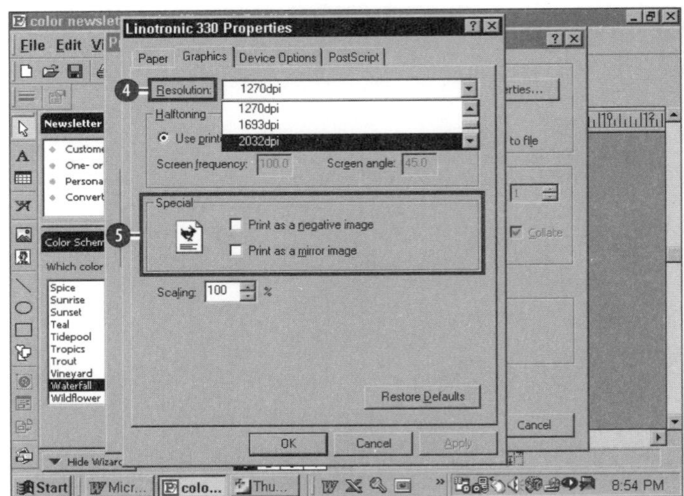

1. In the Printer Properties dialog box, choose the paper size that the service bureau has instructed you to choose.
2. Indicate the layout.
3. Choose the orientation.
4. In the Graphics tab, pick the resolution that you and the printer have agreed upon.
5. The Special settings can be controlled either here or in Publisher's Advanced Print Settings. Do not repeat the settings; it may give inaccurate results.

CROSS-REFERENCE

To brush up on printing to a file, see Chapter 5.

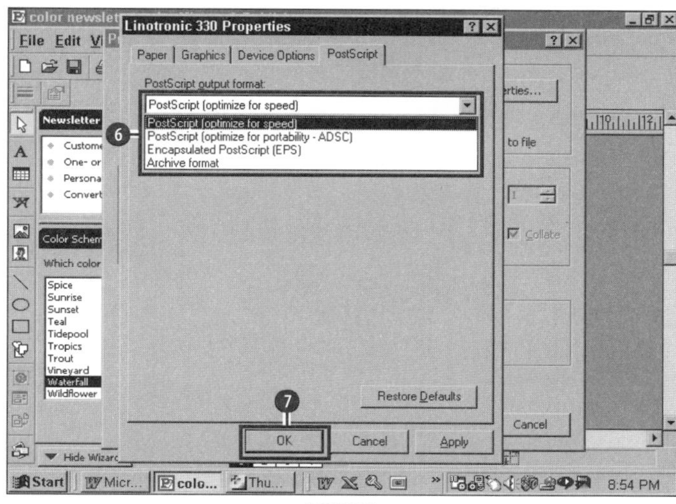

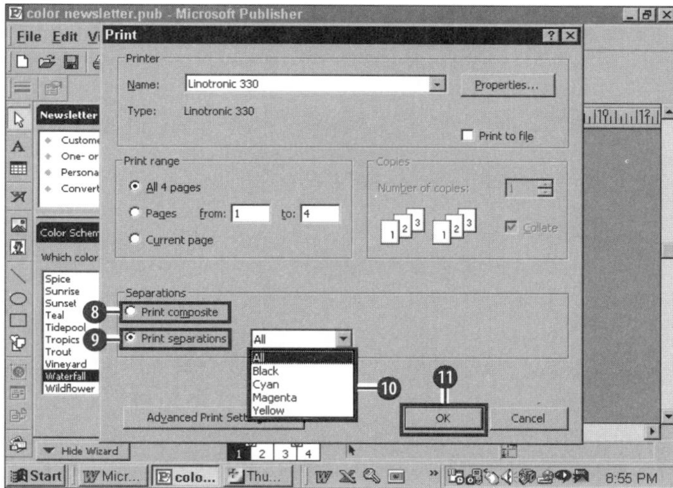

6 *In the PostScript tab, pick the file format that your service bureau has instructed you to use.*

7 *Click OK.*

8 *Choose whether to print a composite page for the service bureau to trap and separate.*

9 *Or, choose "Print separations."*

10 *You can choose to include all four pieces of film in one file, or you can make a file for just one of the four colors.*

11 *Click OK to open the Save dialog box, where you will name your file and the drive it will be saved to.*

TAKE NOTE

PREPARING FOR FILE SIZES

When you create print or EPS files for an imagesetter, the file sizes can be large. When you consider that you are including all the graphics and fonts necessary to create a high-resolution duplicate of a page or publication, the file size for a single page can be more than a 3.5-inch floppy disk can hold. Be sure to have some sort of high-capacity storage disk such as a Zip or optical disk available to submit to the printer.

DOING ONE PAGE AT A TIME

When writing your files, unless the printer asks you to do otherwise, consider writing a single page or couple of pages to an individual file. This keeps the file size down and makes it easier on your computer to write. It also makes it easier on the service bureau if any elements cause problems with the imagesetter. Your entire file may not run because of one graphic.

FIND IT ONLINE

Find service bureaus that accept Publisher files at **http://microsoft.saltmine.com/publisher/pspp/list/UserSearchCriteria.asp.**

Setting Color Trapping Preferences

When printing presses roll and ink gets applied to paper, you can be sure that there may be some play in the system. That is, even the best of printers needs help to be sure that when colors butt up to one another, there's no trace of space in between. This is where trapping comes in. *Trapping* is the point at which colors that get printed next to one another overlap slightly to compensate for the variables in the press, ink, and paper. Publisher gives you two options for trapping your job. You can set trapping for the entire publication or you can trap individual items.

When you accept Publisher's defaults and trap an entire publication, each place where color meets color is evaluated and automatically trapped. That's not a bad route for you to take when starting out. Let the software do its thing and make the decisions for you.

Control freaks (and I mean that in the most complimentary way), however, may want to pick and choose how items are treated on the press. Purists have plenty of opportunity to specify how individual objects are trapped. Typically, here are the trapping options available:

- **Overprint:** The selected item is printed over the top of the color beneath it. This can cause some untrue colors. For example, if you print yellow on top of blue, you may end up with something green.
- **Knockout:** The color underneath is removed only where the item that is to be printed would be. If you knock out the blue background, the yellow type would stay yellow.
- **Custom:** Enables you to specify whether you want an item choked or spread in relation to the underlying color. You can specify the thickness that this overlap will be.

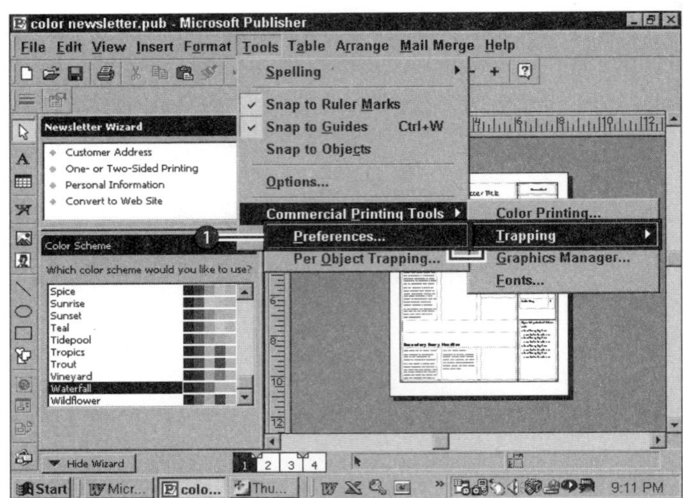

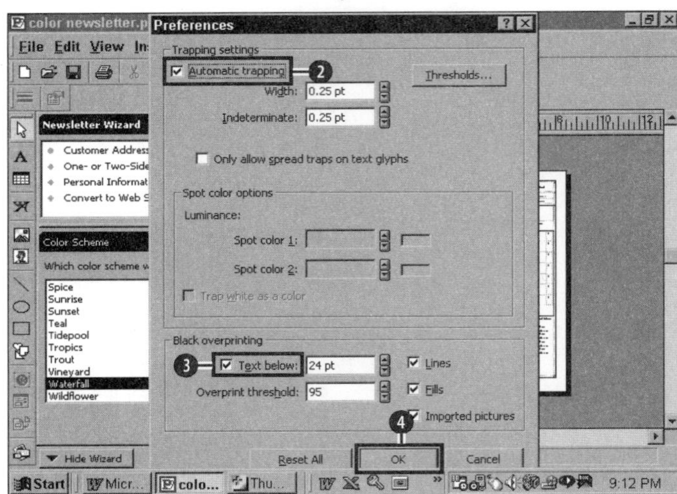

1. *For overall trapping preferences, choose Tools ➪ Commercial Printing Tools ➪ Trapping ➪ Preferences.*
2. *To have Publisher automatically trap your color, click "Automatic trapping."*
3. *Set the text size for overprinting. The default settings usually suffice.*
4. *Click OK.*

CROSS-REFERENCE

To apply a color behind text, go back to Chapter 12 for a review.

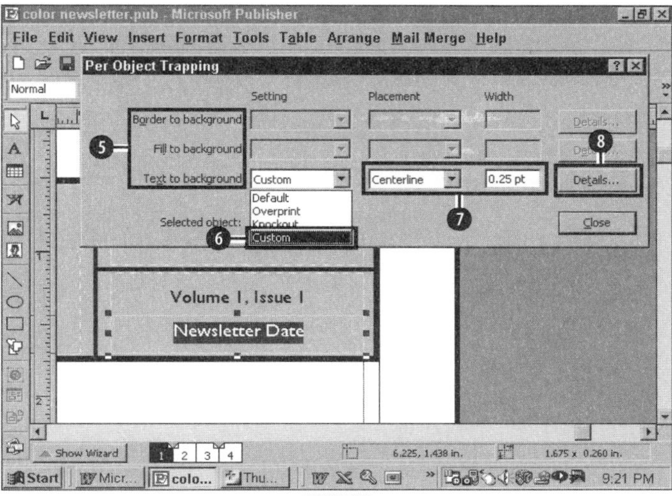

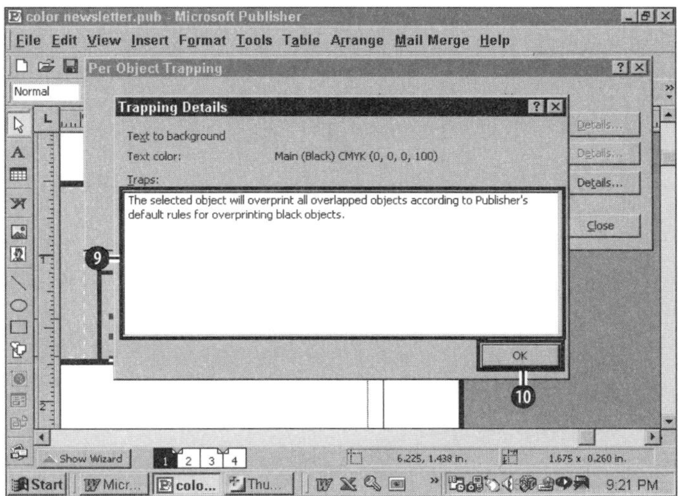

- *Repeat Step 1 after selecting an object, but select Per Object Trapping to trap a specific object with the background.*

5 *Depending on the type of object you choose, one of the Setting options will be active.*

6 *Click Setting and choose trapping setting.*

7 *Choose the placement of the trapping and the width.*

8 *Click Details.*

9 *The Trapping Details dialog box tells you what will be trapped and how it will be done.*

10 *Click OK to exit the Trapping Details dialog box, and then Close to accept the settings in the Per Object Trapping dialog box.*

- **Choking:** the underlying color is brought over the top of the item that is printed on top of it (for example, big guy is choking the little guy).
- **Spreading:** the item on top of the underlying color is thickened slightly to cover the top of the underlying color (for example, little guy is expanding on top of the big guy).
- **Centerline:** Both the item and the background are expanded a bit from where the two butt together.

If you're inexperienced with these types of settings, you should consult your printer to see which works best for each particular printing job. Many times, the type of trapping to be done is dependent upon the paper you're printing on and the type of press that will be doing the printing.

TAKE NOTE

LEAVE IT TO THE EXPERTS

Most service bureaus will trap your output when it is written to film. Their software is more sophisticated than what Publisher offers. Why not turn off the trapping and leave this to the experts?

FIND IT ONLINE

For a complete discussion on trapping, visit **http://www.technology.ewu.edu/tech360/DPTRAP1.html.**

Embedding Fonts

Chances are, you may be using fonts and your service bureau has no clue where they came from. It seems like every time you install a program, a gaggle of fonts are placed in your system for all programs to use. Microsoft does its fair share of this standard industry procedure, along with many other software vendors. God and your Win.ini know how many fonts you may have.

Publisher, when writing a print file, picks out only the fonts you have used in your publication and places the font definition files within the print file if you instruct it to do so. This is called *font embedding*. Unless you're sure that the service bureau you're using to output your film has all the fonts in your publication, this is probably a good idea.

In the steps on the opposite page, you'll see a choice to embed fonts when you save your publication. To me, this is a useless setting. Embedding your fonts in your publication only serves to enlarge your file. Plus, if your reason for embedding the fonts is to make the document portable, you can always use Pack and Go to take your publication to another computer and embed the fonts at that time.

What may be a nice feature, though, is to embed a subset of your fonts. *Subset font embedding* stores only the character(s) of the font you have used. For example, if you have used a decorative large cap at the front of a few paragraphs, only those letters in that font are embedded in your file, making the overall file somewhat smaller.

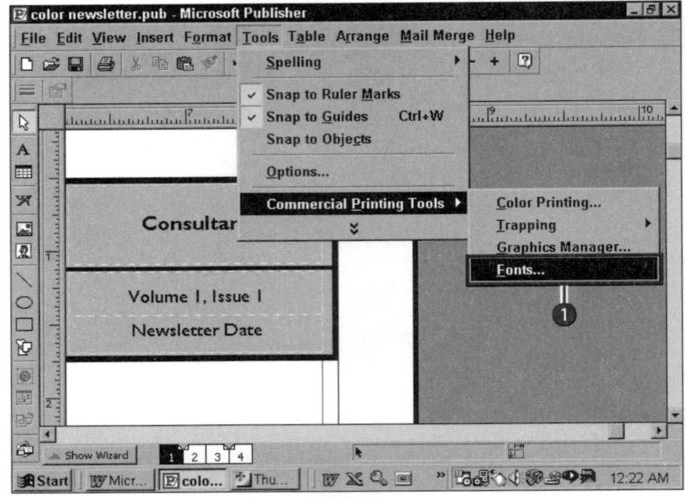

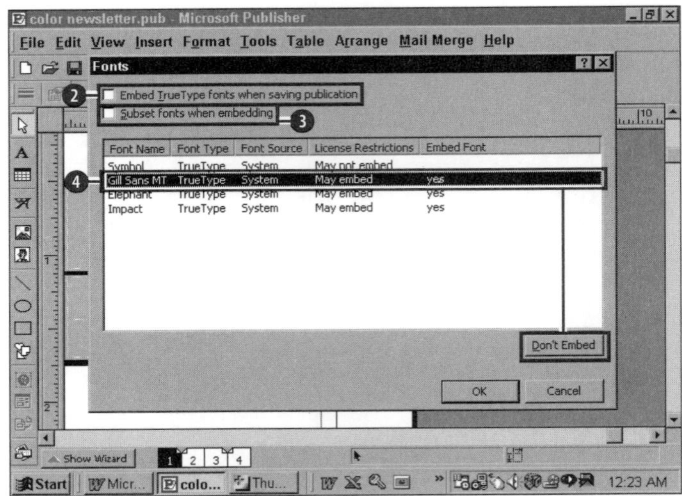

1. *Click Tools ➪ Commercial Printing Tools ➪ Fonts.*
2. *Click whether you want to embed TrueType fonts in your saved publication.*
3. *Click if you want a subset of your fonts embedded.*
4. *Highlight an embedded font and click Don't Embed to prevent it from being embedded.*

▶ *If a font is not embedded and you want it to be, this button says Embed when that font is highlighted.*

CROSS-REFERENCE

See Chapter 5 for more information on advanced print settings.

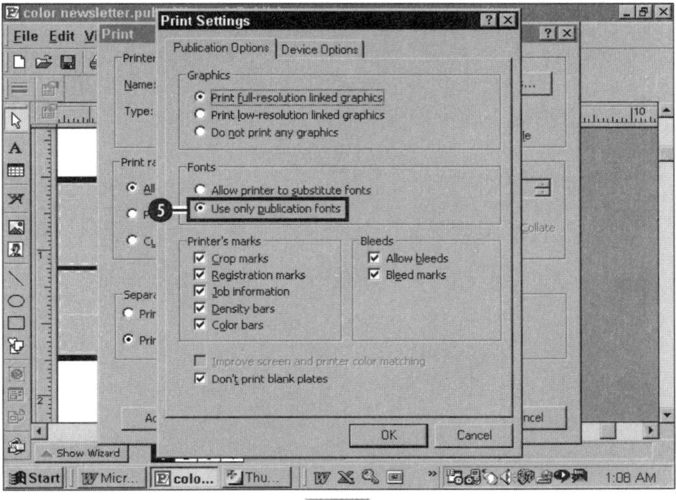

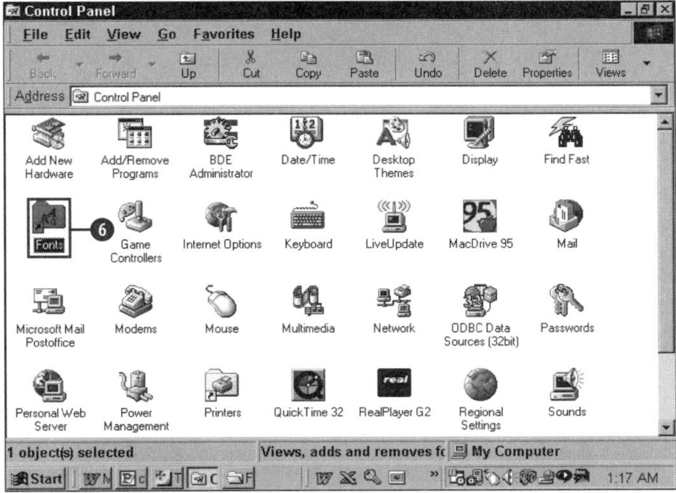

5 *To prevent font substitution, open the Advanced Print Settings dialog box and click here.*

6 *For a list of the TrueType fonts in your system, open the Control Panel and double-click Fonts.*

In the Fonts dialog box, you may notice that some fonts may not be embedded. Within the font definition file, code exists that tells Windows and Microsoft Publisher that the font is protected by copyright and/or trademark laws and cannot be shared, not even with your service bureau. Your only options at this point are to switch the font in your publication or check with the service bureau to see if they have the font in question. If they don't have the font, and don't wish to purchase the font, your only legal option is to switch to a font that may be embedded.

It's also a good idea to turn off font substitution in the advanced print settings. Otherwise, if someone opens your publication without the proper fonts installed, other fonts are substituted automatically.

TAKE NOTE

STICK WITH TRUETYPE FONTS

While you may have PostScript fonts installed, Microsoft Publisher recommends that you stick with TrueType fonts when preparing for commercial printing. Publisher will not embed PostScript fonts, so your service bureau must have them installed when they open your publication.

TRAPPING POSTSCRIPT FONTS

Unless you're running Windows NT or 2000 and have Adobe Type Manager installed, Publisher will not trap PostScript Type I fonts.

FIND IT ONLINE

If you feel you don't have enough fonts installed, you can find more at **http://www.1001freefonts.com.**

Managing Links to Graphic Objects

When you import graphics into Publisher, you can choose to either link them to the original file or embed them in the publication. Both of these procedures have pros and cons.

Embedding a graphic means it becomes part of your publication file. You lose control of making any changes to it unless you reimport the file and replace the old one. When you embed a graphic, especially large color photos, your file starts to bloat, making it stretch beyond what you may have intended. On the upside, embedding ensures that your graphic stays with your publication. On the downside, if you take your publication to a commercial printer, they will not be able to access the individual picture to make changes that may enhance the way it prints.

Linking a graphic doesn't place the file in your publication; rather, it tells Publisher where the file is stored on your drive and merely points to the file. A lower-resolution graphic is created and placed in the picture frame. If you edit the graphic file, the next time you open your Publisher document, the updated image is already placed on the page, but you may have to go into Graphics Manager to update the link so your low-resolution file is also updated.

Should you choose to link a file, you have to be certain that the file doesn't get moved or accidentally deleted from your system, or Publisher can't retrieve it until you go in to the Graphics Manager and relocate the file — thereby refreshing the link. Linking files keeps the images separate from the publication, yet still enables you to view them in the picture frame.

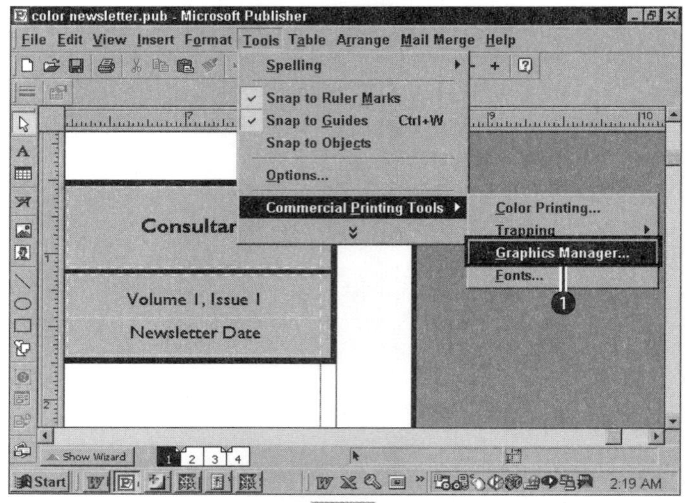

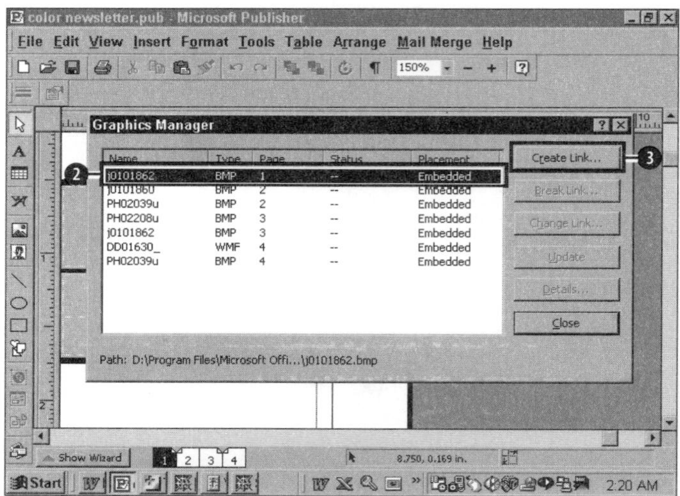

1. Choose Tools ⇨ Commercial Printing Tools ⇨ Graphics Manager.
2. Click the name of a graphic in your publication.
3. If it is embedded, click Create Link to make it a linked graphic.

CROSS-REFERENCE

To use Pack and Go to prepare your file for a commercial printer, see the next task.

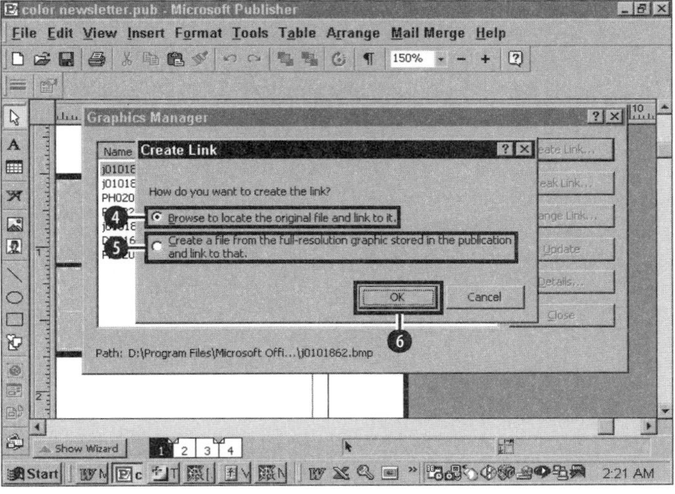

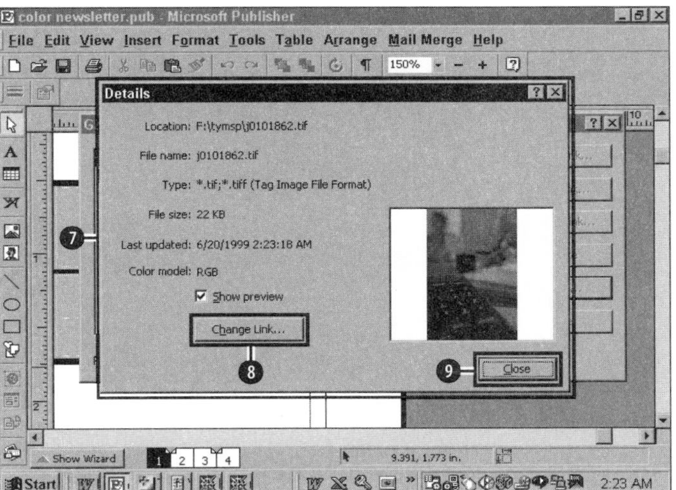

4 *Click this button to find the original file on your drive and create a link to it.*

5 *Click this button to make a copy of the high-resolution file that is currently embedded and store it in a different place on your computer.*

6 *Click OK.*

7 *Once the image is linked, click Details in the Graphics Manager dialog box to retrieve the graphic's data.*

8 *To change the link to this graphic, click the Change Link button.*

9 *Click Close and proceed making changes to the rest of the graphics in the list.*

▶ *Click the Close button to close the Graphics Manager dialog box.*

These two choices that you have in the Graphics Manager are different from an OLE (object linking and embedding) object. The files you see listed here are only those that you or the Publisher Wizard imported using Insert ➪ Picture ➪ Clip Art, From File, or From Scanner or Camera. The items you won't see here are the ones that you brought in via Insert ➪ Picture ➪ New Drawing or Insert ➪ Object.

Using Graphics Manager, you can change whether an image is embedded or linked. If you decide to break a link, you are given the choice to embed the high-resolution graphic or embedding a lower-resolution image. Embedding a low-resolution graphic comes in handy when you are converting a print publication to a Web document. There's no need to embed a high-resolution image when the Web can't display it at that resolution.

TAKE NOTE

LINK FILES FOR COMMERCIAL PRINTING

So that your printer or service bureau can access your images, always link your files if they are to be commercially printed. Also, be forewarned: if you embed a CMYK separated TIF file, the original separations are not maintained.

FIND IT ONLINE

To learn more about the different graphic file formats, go to **http://www.dcs.ed.ac.uk/~mxr/gfx/.**

Using Pack and Go for Commercial Printing

Earlier, in Chapter 3, you used Publisher's Pack and Go feature to suitcase all the files of a publication together so you could take them to another computer. The Pack and Go for commercial printing service works somewhat the same, except there are a few other things that it does as well.

After you start up Pack and Go for commercial printing service, you still choose a file location and what you want to include in the file, but at the end Publisher asks what you want to print and give to the service bureau or commercial printer.

The first choice you have is to make a composite printout of all the pages. *Composite* is simply all colors printed on one page. This lets the commercial printer compare what you think they should receive from your files to what they actually do receive. I have yet to send a job to the print shop where they didn't insist on laser prints of the pages, so be prepared.

The second choice you have is to print actual separations of the pages. Publisher prints one page for each of the four process colors: cyan, magenta, yellow, and black. These printouts are helpful for making sure the file and all the graphics in it are separating into the four colors as they should. If they aren't, you need to go back and check the offending element to see what the problem is.

While printing the separations, you may get a message from Publisher that the page size you're printing on is too small to show the printer's marks. That's normal if your document is letter-sized and the paper you're printing on is letter-sized. The printer's marks always fall outside the image area of the page.

So, now you're ready to copy the Pack and Go files to a Zip disk or some other media. Then, take the disk and your printouts to your commercial printer.

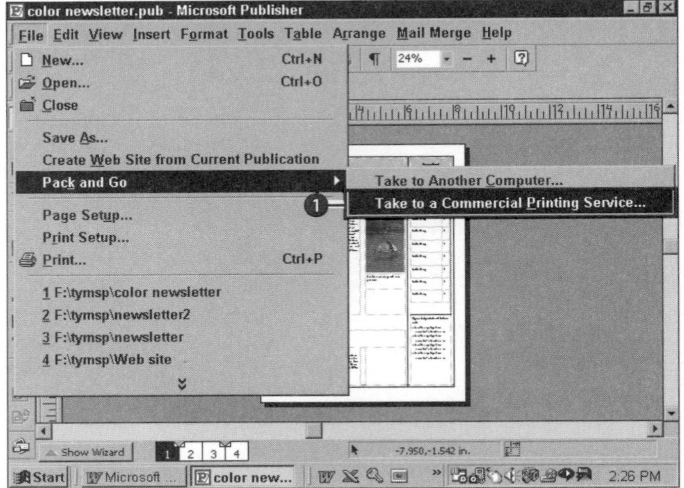

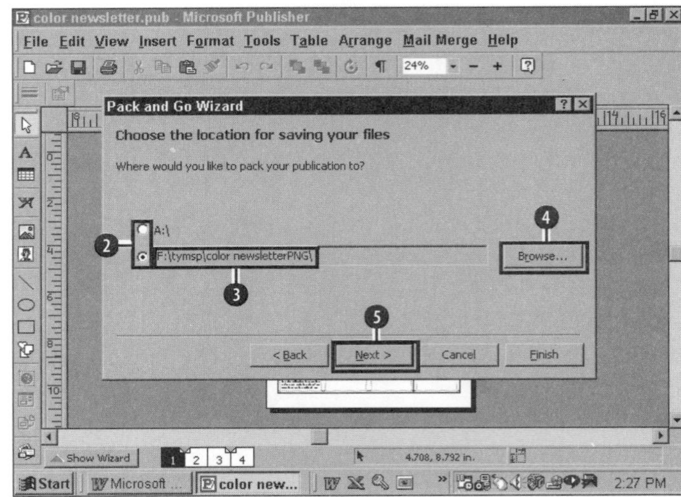

1. Choose File ⇨ Pack and Go ⇨ Take to a Commercial Printing Service.
2. After clicking Next on the opening screen, choose a drive location for the files to be taken to the printer.
3. If this folder does not exist, you will need to make one. The wizard does not make folders on the fly.
4. Use Browse to locate a folder or choose a drive and create a folder in the dialog box.
5. Click Next.

CROSS-REFERENCE

For other ways to print your publication to your desktop printer, see Chapter 5.

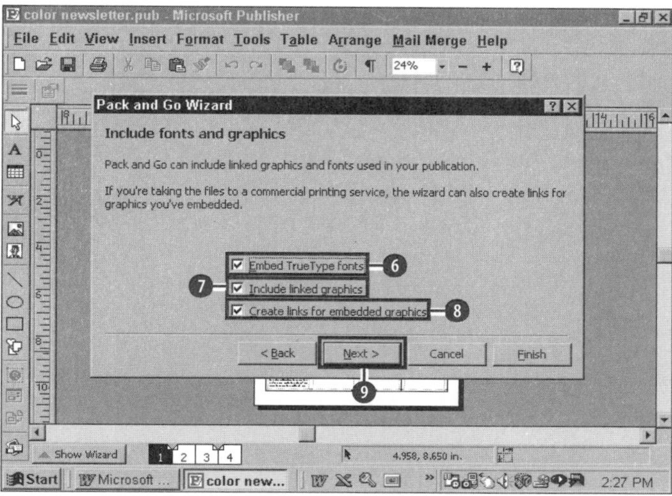

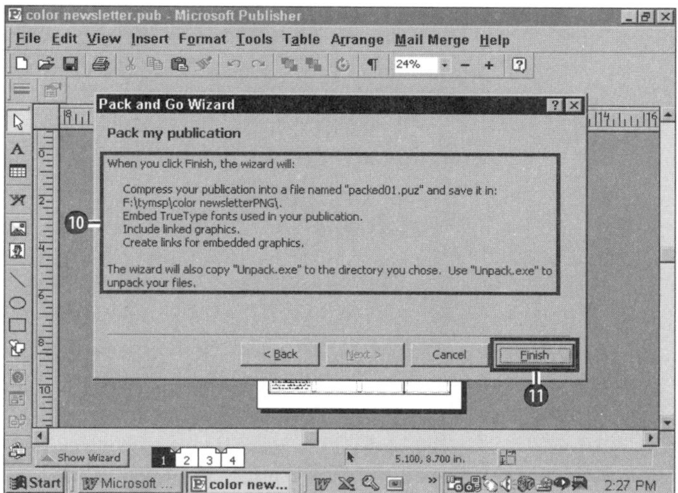

6. *Check whether you want to embed the TrueType fonts that are allowable.*
7. *Check to include the linked graphics.*
8. *Check to create links for the embedded graphics.*
9. *Click Next.*
10. *In the summary screen, review your settings.*
11. *Click Finish.*

TAKE NOTE

INSIST ON A "PRESS OK"

When the color job you finish is being put on the press, printers should let you be present to do a press approval. Do it! Go look at the first pages that come off the press. Even if they are running your job at 2:00 A.M., be there! It's better to pull the job for color corrections than for it be totally printed, folded, and/or bound only to be wrong.

GET COLOR PROOFS OR MATCHPRINTS

Most four-color printers will furnish you a color proof or *matchprint* so you can see how the film came out and get a good idea of the colors that will be printed. Because the color you see on the monitor can vary from the actually printed piece, color proofs let you go back and make corrections before the job ever hits the printing presses.

FIND IT ONLINE

Read about digital printing directly from your files, without film or plates, at http://www.agfahome.com/roadmaps/knowhow/dp/basics.html.

Personal Workbook

Q&A

1. What must you do first in the Commercial Printing Tools menu before you can print four-color separations? Hint: You will not be able to apply printer's marks unless you do this first.

2. Where can you change the lines per inch of your film?

3. What are two different ways that you can send your print job to a service bureau?

4. What imagesetting or prepress process uses choking and spreading?

5. Can you embed any font in your publication? Why or why not?

6. What are crop marks and how are they used?

7. Should you link or embed graphics when they are being sent to a service bureau or film output? Why?

8. What is the difference between the two Pack and Go procedures: Take to Another Computer and Take to a Commercial Printing Service?

ANSWERS: PAGE 361

EXTRA PRACTICE

1. Make a color brochure in Publisher. Use the wizard, if you like. Customize the headlines and insert some photos from the Clip Gallery. Print composite pages and then print the separations for the first page.
2. Using the brochure created above, go into the Graphics Manager and be sure that all your images are linked.
3. Using the same brochure, check the publication's fonts. Which ones are used? Can they all be embedded?
4. In the same brochure, place some text on a color background. Create a custom trap for the text so that the background color is knocked out.

REAL-WORLD APPLICATIONS

✔ You are in charge of preparing a marketing brochure for a new line of products that your company manufactures. The brochure will be 11" × 17" and folded down to 8½" × 11". You lay out the job in Publisher and make print files to give to the service bureau.

✔ In order to announce your company moving into a new building across town, you create a postcard using four-color art and photos. You use fonts that your service bureau doesn't have. Because they may be embedded in the file with the job, you include them in your print file.

Visual Quiz

Looking at this newsletter inside the spread. Do you need to use bleed marks?

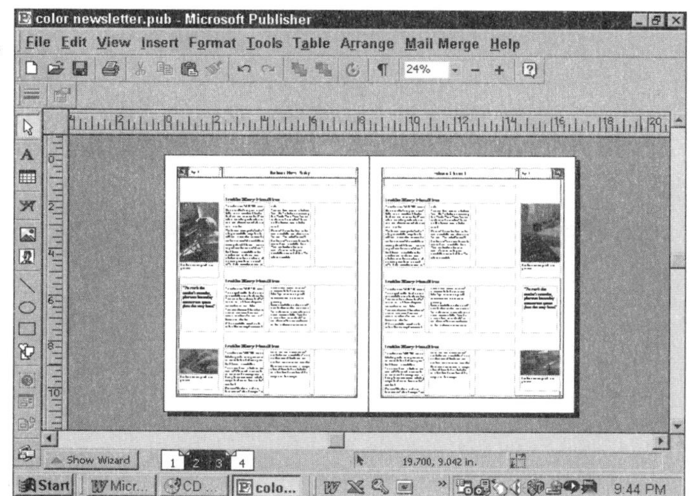

Personal Workbook Answers

Chapter 1

see page 20

1. **When you have Publisher and another program open at the same time, what are two ways that you can switch between them?**

A: To switch between programs in Windows, you can either click their buttons in the taskbar or press Alt+Tab.

2. **What does it mean when a menu option is followed by an ellipsis (. . .)? An arrow?**

A: When a menu item is followed by an ellipsis, a dialog box will open. When it is followed by an arrow, you'll see a submenu.

3. **If you make a mistake in Publisher, what are two ways of undoing the error?**

A: You can press Ctrl+Z, click the Undo button on the standard toolbar, or choose Edit ➪ Undo.

4. **Which mouse button do you click to bring up a context menu?**

A: Right-click to bring up context menus.

5. **How do you bring up the text formatting toolbar? The picture formatting toolbar?**

A: These toolbars are operation-sensitive. That is, when you work with text, the Text Formatting Toolbar appears. When working with pictures, the Picture Formatting Toolbar will replace the current toolbar showing.

6. **How do you show the Help screen and Microsoft Publisher on your monitor at the same time?**

A: By clicking the Show/Hide icon in the Help window, you can keep Help open while working in Publisher.

7. **Can you use the Help system if the Office Assistant is in use? How do you turn off the Office Assistant?**

A: The Help System is not available as long as the Office Assistant is on the job. To deactivate the Assistant, right-click it and choose Hide, or choose Help ➪ Hide the Office Assistant from the menu.

8. **How do you do a keyword search in the Help system?**

A: Press F1 for Help or choose Help ➪ Microsoft Publisher Help. Click the Index tab and enter a keyword in the text box provided. Click the Search button and choose from a list of articles in the lower list box.

Visual Quiz

Q: How did this travel brochure headline get this way? How did we remove the toolbars at the top of the page?

A: The text frame was selected and then the Rotate button in the toolbar was clicked twice. To make the toolbars disappear, either right-click the toolbar and remove the checkmark or choose View ➪ Toolbars and remove the checkmarks from Standard and Formatting selections.

Personal Workbook Answers

Chapter 2

see page 36

1 The Microsoft Publisher Catalog appears each time you start Publisher 2000. How do you turn off this option? How do you turn it back on again?

A: The Catalog may be turned off and on by choosing Tools ➪ Options. In the General tab, place a checkmark or remove the checkmark from the Use Catalog at Startup option.

2 How do you change your personal information in Publisher? Use the Help function to find a second way, not mentioned in this chapter.

A: You can edit your personal information at any time by selecting Edit ➪ Personal Information. The second way to remove personal information is to delete the information from the publication itself. This will not remove it from the stored data, only from the current document.

3 How do you insert an item of personal information into a publication? Use the Help function to find a second method besides the one mentioned in this chapter.

A: To insert any of the personal information that you have stored, you choose Insert ➪ Personal Information and select one of the items from the submenu. Personal information may also be inserted while going through the various wizards.

4 Mention two ways to save your file while you are working. What happens the first time you use either of these methods with a new, unsaved file?

A: You can press Ctrl+S or click the Disk icon in the standard toolbar. The first time you use either method, the Save As dialog box opens and you must enter a name for your publication.

5 How do you print only one business card on a sheet of paper? Why would you want to do this?

A: By clicking the Page Options button in the Print dialog box, you can choose to print only one copy of the business card. You may want to do this for proofreading purposes or as a sample for the professional printer who will print those cards.

6 How do you add a logo to a personal information set?

A: Open the Publication Wizard, if it is not open already, and choose Personal Information in the upper Wizard window. In the lower window, click the Insert Component button and choose Logo from the list.

7 After you have typed in the address on an envelope you are about to print, you decide you would like to print it in a different, larger font. How would you change the font?

A: Select the text to be changed. Choose a different font from the Formatting Toolbar Font drop-down menu. Change the size using the Font Size drop-down next to the Font drop-down.

8 You have to print up 300 brochures on Special Paper from PaperDirect. Would you print them all on your laser printer, or would you use your office copier? Explain your decision.

A: The office copier would be the preferred route to printing that many brochures. Not only would it be faster than printing on your laser printer, but it would also save wear and tear on your laser printer.

Visual Quiz

Q: Does the Borders Business Card shown here require Special Paper or not to print in color? How can you tell?

A: Special Paper is not required to print this business card. You can tell by looking in the Wizard window and noticing that Plain Paper is selected.

Chapter 3

see page 54

1. **How can you save an updated (previously saved) publication without opening a dialog box?**

A: You can either press Ctrl+S or click the Save icon in the standard toolbar.

2. **How can you find the date and size of a file in the Save As dialog box?**

A: By clicking the Views button and selecting Details, all file information is shown in the File List window.

3. **If you want to view all Publisher files (*.PUB) together in a folder that also contains graphics and text files, how would you change the file order in the list?**

A: By clicking the Views button that appears at the top of the dialog box, you can choose Arrange Icons ➪ By Type. This will group all files by the file extension.

4. **For publications that will be updated on a regular basis, what can you create to make subsequent editions quicker and easier to complete?**

A: A Publisher template file will be handy to have when repeating or revising documents.

5. **What Microsoft Windows utility may be used to copy, move, and delete files?**

A: Windows Explorer is a handy utility program that helps you manage your files. You can start Explorer by right-clicking the Start button and choosing Explore.

6. **When using Pack and Go, what three files are created and what are their purpose?**

A: The PUZ file is the compressed document with all the components necessary to make up your publication. A Readme.txt file is included to tell the recipient what is on the disk and how to open the packed file. Finally, Unpack.exe is included to let the recipient open the compressed file and restore it to its original state.

7. **What are the three instances when you would want to use Pack and Go?**

A: Anytime you want to copy or move your file, you should use Pack and Go. Some instances are when you move your file to another computer, when you want to archive the file for use later and remove it from your system to open up space, or to take your document to a commercial printer.

8. **When moving or copying files in Windows Explorer, what key should you press to copy the file?**

A: Hold down the Control (Ctrl) key while dragging the file to a new location. This will place a copy of the file in the new folder.

Visual Quiz

Q: In this figure, name as many ways as you can to start Microsoft Publisher.

A: You can double-click the MS Publisher icon on the desktop, you can click the Start button and choose Microsoft Publisher from the Programs menu, or you can double-click the First Publication icon on the desktop. The latter will open Publisher and the First Publication document.

Chapter 4

see page 78

1. **What is the difference between the Publication by Wizard tab and the Publication by Design tab in the Microsoft Publisher Catalog?**

A: The Publication Wizard is grouped by project — all of the business card designs are together, as are the letterhead and envelopes. The Publication by Design selections are grouped by color-coordinated themes — each design concept has different projects in it.

Personal Workbook Answers

2 While the Microsoft Publisher Wizard is active, are the drop-down program menus available?

A: No. You can't get to the Publisher menus while the wizard is active.

3 How can you change an awards certificate into a greeting card?

A: This is a trick question. You can't change the project, but you can change the design using the Wizard window.

4 When using the wizard, you change from a double-sided publication to a single-sided publication. What could happen and what page could you preview to see if it did?

A: You could lose some of the content. If you're using the wizard, a button labeled Extra Content will appear underneath the top window of the wizard. There's nothing really on a page that would tell you something is missing.

5 What does KISS stand for?

A: Keep It Sweet and Simple, a great motto for beginning designers.

6 Once you have completed a wizard, how do you clear or close the Wizard window that is left open?

A: You can click the Hide Wizard button in the status bar, or choose View ➪ Hide Wizard.

7 When Microsoft Publisher has already been opened and you have closed the Microsoft Publisher Catalog window, how can you open the Catalog window again?

A: Choose File ➪ New from the menu and the Catalog will open again.

8 What is the difference between the circle and arrow bullet in the list of wizards?

A: Clicking an item with the arrow bullet opens a submenu of choices. With the circle bullet, what you see is what you get — no submenu exists.

Visual Quiz

Q: In this figure, explain the steps you would take to change the area in the top right-hand side of the page to a customer address area.

A: This newsletter was created using a wizard. Therefore, to change the area in the upper right-hand frame to a customer address area, you first click the Show Wizard button. Once the Wizard window is open, click the Customer Address option in the upper window. In the lower window, when asked if you want to include a placeholder for the customer's address, change the option button to Yes. To create an address area without the wizard's help, you could delete the text in the frame and type in the address yourself. Just don't forget to format it.

Chapter 5

see page 92

1 When you are ready to print, why should you not use the Print button on the standard toolbar?

A: Using the Print button on the standard toolbar does not give you the Print dialog box and therefore doesn't let you set up the printer preferences.

2 What is the keyboard shortcut to print?

A: Ctrl+P.

3 **If you have a multiple-page document and you want to print several copies, what option can you choose to print them so that each set comes out of the printer in page order?**

A: You can choose to collate the multiple copies in the Print dialog box.

4 **Where are two places that you can specify the printing resolution for your document?**

A: Clicking the Properties button next to the selected printer in the Print dialog box will enable you to specify the print resolution in the resulting dialog box. Also, you can click the Advanced Print Settings button in the Print dialog box to set the resolution in the Device Options tab.

5 **When printing a long document with many graphics, what can you do to speed up printing and save ink or toner?**

A: Set the printer to a lower resolution for speed and conservation of imaging supplies.

6 **When printing a large poster-type document that is too large for your printer, what technique do you use to send the document to your printer?**

A: You can tile the document so that the entire poster will print on several pieces of paper.

7 **What is a Windows .prn file and how can you use it?**

A: When you print to a file, Windows programs automatically give this file a .PRN extension. Though not editable, you can take this file and send it to a printer for the page or pages to print.

8 **What is the difference between the File menu options: Save As Web Page and Create Web Site from Current Publication?**

A: When you select Create Web Site from Current Publication, you will use a wizard to convert your document to HTML. Save As Web Page enables you to bypass the wizard.

Visual Quiz

Q: When you click the Advanced Print Settings button in the Print dialog box, you get the Print Settings dialog box. In the Publication Options tab, most of the settings are unavailable. Why?

A: These settings are for printing to a file for a commercial printer. They will appear when you prepare your file for this type of output.

Chapter 6

see page 114

1 **What measurement units are used predominantly in the United States printing industry?**

A: If you're going to get into commercially printing your documents, you should become familiar with picas and points, the standard measurements in the industry.

2 **What key do you hold while moving a frame to constrain it to either straight up and down or left and right?**

A: Hold the Shift key while dragging a frame to move it in a straight line.

3 **How do you change the beginning page number of a publication?**

A: Choose Tools ➪ Options, and in the General tab you can type a new page number into the Start Publication With Page text box.

4 **Besides the Text and Picture Frame tools, what other frame tools are there in Publisher?**

A: Other frame tools are used to create and hold a table, WordArt, or the Clip Gallery.

5. **What is the maximum number of pages you can add to your document at one time?**

A: You can insert up to 999 pages at one time.

6. **With a frame highlighted, what happens when you press the Control key while dragging a corner handle?**

A: When resizing a frame using the top, side, or bottom handles, you hold the Ctrl key to move the opposite side the same distance. If you are dragging a corner handle, all four corners will move equal distances.

7. **To quickly view your entire page, what keyboard shortcut can you use?**

A: Ctrl+Shift+L displays your entire page in the Document window. If you have Two-Page Spread checked in the View menu, you will see a left and right page together.

8. **When zoomed in on a two-page spread, what key combinations can you use to pan across or up and down a page?**

A: PgUp and PgDn keys, in combination with the Ctrl key enable you to pan across pages.

Visual Quiz

Q: Notice the photo highlighted on the right-side page of this spread. What is the quickest and best way to zoom in on this image so that it is centered in the screen?

A: You can either right-click and choose Selected Objects from the context menu, or click the Zoom drop-down in the standard toolbar and choose Selected Objects.

Chapter 7

see page 140

1. **What type of guides are usually red and blue?**

A: Layout guides, which indicate columns and margins, are red and blue.

2. **If you cannot select an object or group of objects on the foreground layer, what does that mean?**

A: The object is probably on the background layer of the page.

3. **What do you call the information at the top and bottom of a page that can sometimes contain the page numbers or chapter or publication title?**

A: You place headers at the top of the page and footers at the bottom of the page to hold information like page numbers and chapter or publication titles.

4. **When you hold the Shift key and select multiple items, what shortcut key can you use to group the items together?**

A: To group several items, press Ctrl+Shift+G, or you could just click the Group button that will appear when you have several items selected.

5. **What three things can you snap to?**

A: You can snap to guides (both layout and ruler), ruler marks, and objects.

6. **What toolbar comes up when you double-click the status bar that shows an object's dimensions and location on the page?**

A: The measurement toolbar will float onscreen when you double-click the status bar.

7. **To rotate an object at 15-degree increments, what key combination do you use while you drag one of the object's handles?**

A: You must hold the Ctrl and Alt keys down when rotating an object to constrain the rotation to 15-degree increments.

8. **What do you call the gray area that surrounds your page and what is it used for?**

A: The scratch area is the gray portion of the Layout window where you can place objects for later use. Items in this area are saved with the document, but won't print.

Visual Quiz

Q: How can you tell that this is the background layer and not the foreground?

A: Look at the page navigation icons. Because they have an "L" and "R" on them, instead of numbers, it tells you that you are working on the background layer.

Chapter 8

see page 168

1. **How can you import a text file if your word processing file format is not among the list of files that Publisher can import?**

A: You can usually save your file as an ASCII text file from within your word processor. This format will be able to be imported into Publisher. Or, simply highlight the text in your word processor, copy it to the Windows Clipboard, and paste it into Publisher.

2. **Can you edit a text file in Microsoft Word if it was not created in Word to begin with?**

A: Because text that is imported from any other word processor is considered part of Publisher, you can edit it using Microsoft Word.

3. **When fitting copy to a frame, what are the drawbacks?**

A: Sometimes the font size gets reduced, making it inconsistent with the rest of the publication. Also, the font size may get shrunk so badly that it is unreadable.

4. **When do you have to draw separate frames for columns of text instead of assigning a number of columns to the frame?**

A: For documents destined for the Web, you can not have overlapping frames. In this case, use separate frames instead of columns.

5. **What is the default measurement for tabs in a Publisher document?**

A: By default, tabs are set at every half inch.

6. **Once you have wrapped text around a graphic, can you change it back to where it wraps around the frame that holds the graphic? If so, how?**

A: You can click the Wrap Text to Frame button in the formatting toolbar; right-click the frame holding the graphic and choose Change Frame ➪ Picture Frame Properties and click the Entire Frame option; or, access the Picture Frame Properties dialog box by selecting Format ➪ Picture Frame Properties from the menu.

7. **What is the major problem you may encounter when you spell check a document?**

A: Words may be spelled correctly but used incorrectly. For example, using "there" instead of "their."

8. **What is the best way to organize your text styles?**

A: Name text styles in groups so that they appear alphabetically. For example, headlines can be named head 1, head 2, and so on.

Personal Workbook Answers

Visual Quiz

Q: **What do the icons on the top and bottom of this frame tell you? What happens when you click them?**

A: The icon at the top of the frame tells you that this text is continued from another linked frame. The icon at the bottom of the frame indicates that more text exists in this file than will fit into the frame.

Chapter 9

see page 182

1. **What are the two most popular file types of fonts?**

A: You will find both TrueType and PostScript fonts available for Windows applications to be the most popular format.

2. **What point size would you select to make your type one-half inch tall?**

A: Make your text 36 points. This will make your type one-half inch tall from the bottom of the descenders to the top of the ascenders.

3. **Besides the number of lines that a Drop Cap extends down and the size of the letters, what other three elements can you change once the size and position is chosen?**

A: You can change the typeface itself, as well as the font style and color.

4. **What is the difference between tracking and kerning?**

A: Tracking is the amount of space between all characters in a given typeface or text style. Kerning is used to control the spacing between two characters, which, because of their appearance when together, makes it appear that more space exists between them than necessary.

5. **What is leading and how is it used?**

A: Leading is another term for line spacing. When you increase leading, you place more space between the lines in a block of text. Decreasing leading causes the lines to move closer together.

6. **How do you open the WordArt interface once you have created a WordArt object?**

A: Just double-click the WordArt object or frame and you can edit the text or any of its effects.

7. **In order to fill the entire frame with the art, what button should you select?**

A: You can choose Best Fit from the Font Size drop-down and/or click the Stretch button.

8. **If you choose to stretch the WordArt object to fill the frame, what setting has no effect if you are working with a one line word or phrase?**

A: Because you are stretching the WordArt to fill the frame, one-line text is not affected by the alignment indicated.

Visual Quiz

Q: **This headline uses capital and small capital letters. How can you format it with opening only one dialog box one time?**

A: Open the Font dialog box and choose Small Caps in the Effects options.

Chapter 10

see page 202

1. **Tables, like any text or image have to reside in what type of container?**

A: A frame. You have to draw a frame to hold the table.

2. **When you add columns or rows to a table, what do you run the risk of happening to the table?**

A: The frame containing the table could migrate off of the page when you add rows or columns.

3. **What technique does Publisher offer to accommodate headers and subheads that span across several columns?**

A: You can merge cells and use them for headers and subheads, as well as other like text.

4. **When you remove a diagonal line from a cell, what happens to the contents of both halves?**

A: Removing a diagonal, just like merging cells, will cause all of the text to be placed in one cell.

5. **When you resize columns and rows, what useful Publisher feature can you use to ensure that the borders of columns and rows will be placed in an exact location on the page?**

A: Resizing columns and rows is subject to Publisher's Snap feature. You can snap to layout guides, ruler guides, ruler marks, or objects.

6. **To be sure that you are only changing the width of one column or height of one row in addition to the one next to it, what key do you press while dragging the border?**

A: Hold down the Shift key to resize only the row or column selected.

7. **What other program in the Microsoft Office Suite can you use to aid you in creating tables in Publisher?**

A: You can use Microsoft Excel to create tables, and then copy and paste them into Publisher.

8. **When using the Table AutoFormat preset designs, what one element seen in the preview window will not get changed?**

A: The typeface shown in the Preview window will not be assigned to your table text. The style, however, will be.

Visual Quiz

Q: In this calendar, identify all of the places where cells were merged.

A: September 1999 resides in merged cells. Also, the three cells in the first row under the days of the week are merged, as are the last two cells in the last row.

Chapter 11

see page 222

1. **How can you import graphic files from elsewhere on your computer into your publication?**

A: Choose Insert ➪ Picture ➪ From File and browse to the graphic file you want to insert.

2. **How can you easily find clip art that's appropriate for your publication?**

A: Choose Insert ➪ Picture ➪ Clip Art to open the Clip Gallery, and then type words related to your topic into the "Search for clips" box.

3. **How can you make your own clip art easier to find for future use?**

A: Add it to the Clip Gallery by opening the Clip Gallery and clicking Import Clips. You can then type in a short description, assign it to a particular category and assign keywords to it.

4 **How can you use the Internet to expand your collection of clip art?**

A: From inside Clip Gallery, click Clips Online. This automatically connects you to the Internet and takes you to Microsoft's Clip Gallery Live site, where you can find many more clips of all types.

5 **How can you create graphics in another program and insert them into your publication, while still maintaining the ability to use the program you created the graphics in to edit them?**

A: Create the graphic, copy it to the Clipboard, and then choose Edit ➪ Paste Special to insert it into your Publisher publication.

6 **What should you try to eliminate from graphics with the cropping tool to make them look better?**

A: Any extraneous material that isn't directly related to the point of the graphic: for instance, unnecessary figures in the background.

7 **How can you undo cropping?**

A: Activate the Cropping tool, and then drag the frame handles beyond the original edge of the graphic. This will reveal all of it again.

8 **How can you input images from a scanner or digital camera into your Publisher publication?**

A: Choose Insert ➪ Picture ➪ From Scanner or Camera ➪ Select Device to activate the scanner or digital camera you have hooked up to your computer, and then choose Insert ➪ Picture ➪ From Scanner or Camera ➪ Acquire Picture.

Visual Quiz

Q: In this figure of the Clip Gallery, find the places you would click to browse a category of clips, enter keywords to search for clips, add your own art to the Clip Gallery, or look for more clips in Clip Gallery Live.

A: Click the large icons in the main part of the Clip Gallery to browse clip categories. Enter keywords in the "Search for clips" box. Choose Import Clips to add your own art to the Clip Gallery, and choose Clips Online to explore Clip Gallery Live.

Chapter 12

see page 248

1 **How do you open Microsoft Draw so you can draw your own illustrations for your publication?**

A: Choose Insert ➪ Picture ➪ New Drawing.

2 **How can you draw basic shapes using Publisher's own Object toolbar?**

A: Click the Line tool, Oval tool, or Rectangle tool, and then click and drag your mouse pointer inside your publication to draw the shape.

3 **How can you change the shape of an object you've drawn?**

A: Click and drag one of the handles at its edges.

4 **How can you create more complex shapes from simple ones?**

A: Group simple shapes together by clicking each one in turn while holding down the Shift key, and then choosing Draw ➪ Grouping.

5 **How can you draw a perfect circle or square?**

A: Hold down the Shift key while you draw the circle or square.

6 How can you add colors, fill effects, and shadows to objects?

A: Double-click the object, and then choose Fill Color, Line Color, or Shadow from the Draw toolbar.

7 How can you edit clip art in Microsoft Draw?

A: Choose Insert ➪ Picture ➪ New Drawing to open a Draw window, and then choose Insert ➪ Picture ➪ From File or Insert ➪ Picture ➪ Clip Art to insert a picture into the Draw window, where you can use the Draw tools on it.

8 How can you change the color of an object?

A: Right-click the object you want to recolor, and then choose Change Object ➪ Recolor Object.

Visual Quiz

Q: In this figure of Microsoft Draw, find the controls you would click to add 3-D effects, apply a shadow, change the fill color, change the shape to a different AutoShape, and add a new AutoShape.

A: Click the 3-D button at the far right to add 3-D effects. Click the Shadow button to apply a shadow, and the Fill Color button to change the fill color. Choose Draw ➪ Change AutoShape to change the shape, or click AutoShapes to add a new AutoShape.

Chapter 13

see page 260

1 How do you browse the Design Gallery for specific categories of objects?

A: Choose Insert ➪ Design Gallery Object and select the Objects by Category tab.

2 How can you find several different design objects that all share the same style?

A: Choose Insert ➪ Design Gallery Object and select Objects by Design.

3 How can you change a design object to an entirely different style?

A: Select the design object, and then click its Wizard button. Choose the new style from those offered.

4 How can you edit the text in a design object?

A: Click the text box containing the text and edit it as you would text in any other text box.

5 How can you change the graphics in a design object?

A: Click the design object to select it, and then click the Ungroup button to turn it into a collection of separate elements. Double-click the graphic you want to change.

6 How can you turn a group of separate elements in a publication into a single design object?

A: Select them by clicking each one in turn while holding down the Shift key, and then click the Group button. Click the Design Gallery button on the Object toolbar and select the Your Objects tab. Choose Add Selection to Design Gallery.

7 How can you import design objects from another publication?

A: Click the Design Gallery button, select the Your Objects tab, click Options, and then select Browse. Locate the publication you want to import design objects from and click OK.

8 How can you organize your own design objects so you can find them again?

A: When you add them to the Design Gallery, create categories for them that will help you remember where they are.

Personal Workbook Answers

Visual Quiz

Q: In this figure of the Design Gallery, locate the Fall design set, the Fall Masthead design object, and the button you would click to insert the Fall Masthead into the current publication.

A: The Fall design set is listed near the bottom. The Fall Masthead design object is the first item displayed. To insert it into your publication, you'd click the Insert Object button at bottom right.

Chapter 14

see page 278

1. **Can you only create one Publisher Address List?**

A: Because you can save the Publisher Address List file under any name you want, you can create more than one list.

2. **So you can make the Publisher Address List more streamlined for entering data, what should you do to the fields?**

A: Remove any fields that you won't be using. That way, you don't have to worry about skipping fields when entering data.

3. **Name two ways that you can find records in your Publisher Address List.**

A: You can use the Find Entry text box to locate a matching record or you can flip through the records by using the record number arrow button. Additionally, if you know the record number, you can enter it into the text box provided.

4. **What other types of database files can you use to mail merge in Publisher? Name at least three.**

A: You can use Microsoft Outlook, Access, dBase-compatible databases, a Microsoft Word database, an Microsoft Works database, Microsoft Excel, FoxPro, and several types of ASCII files.

5. **What is the name of the Microsoft software program that will help you keep track of contacts, dates, and e-mail addresses?**

A: Microsoft Outlook, which is available on the Microsoft Office CD, or it may be downloaded for free from the Microsoft Web site.

6. **What other special abilities or features does the program in question 5 have?**

A: You can use it as a personal information manager (PIM) because it includes an address book, calendar, e-mail, and to-do list.

7. **What is the function of a Boolean operator when filtering a database?**

A: A Boolean operator creates a relationship between search criteria. Typically, you use "AND" or "OR" to find records that match your search needs.

8. **What are your two choices for sorting a field?**

A: You can sort a field either as ascending or descending.

Visual Quiz

Q: You have 32 Smiths and 44 Jones in your database. How many records will be returned from this filter setting and why? What can you change to ensure you get all of the Smiths and Jones?

A: This query will return no records because "AND" is being used as the operator. You should change the operator to "OR" in order to get all 76 records. This search won't even turn up schizophrenic individuals who may think they are both a Smith and a Jones.

Chapter 15

see page 290

1. **What must you remember to enter between field codes unless they are included in the data in your database?**

A: You should include any punctuation and spaces if they are not part of the data in the record.

2. **How does Publisher know when to begin a new line when you are entering field codes in your publication?**

A: Press the Enter key to begin a new line, just as you would if you were typing the information in from the keyboard.

3. **What menu commands can you use to alternate between seeing the data in your layout and seeing the field codes?**

A: After choosing Merge from the Mail Merge menu, select Mail Merge ➪ Show Merge Results.

4. **In order to change the font that your data will appear in once the document is printed, what must you do?**

A: Select the field codes that you inserted and change the font on the codes. Whatever font you select for the codes will be reflected in the merged data.

5. **What are the four arrow buttons and what are they used for in the Preview Data dialog box?**

A: The Arrow button in the Preview Data dialog box lets you move to different records. From left, they are Go to first record, go back one record, go forward one record, and go to last record.

6. **Besides using the arrow buttons to preview your data in the Preview Data dialog box, what else can you do?**

A: You can enter a record number in the text box provided between the two sets of Arrow buttons.

7. **When printing to a file, where is the best place to put the PRN file and why?**

A: Put the .PRN file on your hard drive. If the file ends up being larger than will fit on your selected removable media, you won't run out of space. Also, your hard drive works faster than most removable disk drives and your file will be done sooner.

8. **How can you print just one page of your multipage merged publication?**

A: You can't. It's an all or nothing proposition. One option is to filter the database to only one record, but you still end up printing all pages of the document.

Visual Quiz

Q: This is the address area of a four-page newsletter. How can you add a custom message in the black diagonal box based on the customer whose address will appear during the mail merge?

A: You can add a field to the database where you can enter custom messages based on the customer data. Insert the field code in the diagonal box and merge print.

Chapter 16

see page 310

1. **What are the two most common ways that a hyperlink will appear on a Web site?**

A: Hyperlinks appear as either underlined text or as a clickable graphic.

2 Hyperlinks can do other things besides take you to a different location on the Internet. Name two of them.

A: You can have a hyperlink to send an e-mail message, download a file, take you to a different page in your Web site, or take you to a different location on the current Web page.

3 What is another term for a large graphic that has several hyperlinks embedded in it?

A: Web professionals call these large images with multiple hyperlinks "image maps."

4 What are small copies of larger pictures called and what is their purpose on a Web page?

A: Smaller images that link to larger images are called "thumbnails."

5 What are animated GIFs called in the Clip Art Gallery?

A: Look for animated GIFs in the Clip Gallery under Motion Clips.

6 What is the difference between check boxes and options buttons?

A: While you can click more than one checkbox in a group, you can only select one option button in a group at a time.

7 Why should you limit the number of characters in a single-line text box?

A: If the information is being stored in a database, limiting the number of characters saves file space. It also limits the visitor in how much they can type into the text box.

8 In order for forms to be e-mailed to you or someone else, what Microsoft product must be installed on the Internet server where your Web site resides?

A: Microsoft FrontPage Extensions should be installed on your Internet server to allow e-mailing of data from forms.

Visual Quiz

Q: This image shows five visible hyperlinks in the page. Can you name them all?

A: The links on this page are 1) Page of links, 2) Café-Anon, 3) Jolt & Bolt Coffee, 4) Pricelist for Jolt & Bolt Coffee, and 5) The image of the coffee cup itself (see the little hand with the index finger up?).

Chapter 17

see page 328

1 What are two ways you can change the background color or texture of your Web pages?

A: If you began your Web pages using the wizard, you can go to the Background Texture selection in the upper Wizard window and then click the Select Texture button. Otherwise, those whose Web pages were started from scratch, not using the wizard, should go to Format ➪ Color and Background Scheme to make changes.

2 When you change or add a background to your Web site, what is the single most important thing to consider regarding your visitors?

A: Loading time. Background patterns that are complicated or are made up of large image files can take awhile to load. Ranked right up there with the download time is readability. Be sure that the text on your Web page is readable on top of the background.

3 What purpose do keywords serve when they are assigned to your Web page?

A: Search engines will use these keywords to categorize your Web pages and list them in their databases.

4 **How can you place Java or ActiveX components into your Web page?**

A: Use the HTML Code Fragment tool and insert the Java or ActiveX component into this frame.

5 **What is the keyboard shortcut for previewing your Web site in your system's default browser?**

A: Ctrl+Shift+B opens your browser of choice and lets you preview your Web documents.

6 **What are the two standard widths that Publisher provides for Web pages?**

A: The default size is 6 inches. However, you can set your Web page up to be 7.5 inches.

7 **Before shortening a Web page, what should you do?**

A: Group or move any items on the Web page that fall below the width that you are going to specify. Otherwise, these items get dropped on the scratch area and will not save to your Web page.

8 **Name two ways that you can upload your Web pages to an Internet server?**

A: You can upload your files using an FTP program, which Publisher has built into it, or you can use the Web Publishing Wizard, which is an external program that can either be downloaded for free from the Microsoft Web site or installed off of the Publisher/Office CDs.

Visual Quiz

Q: This computer is set up for 640 × 480 resolution. Notice that the visitor has to scroll from left to right to see the entire page width. What can you do to your Publisher document to eliminate scrolling left to right?

A: You can set your page width to a lesser value. After ensuring that all elements are on a page in your Publisher document, you can save the file as a Web page again, eliminating the need for scrolling from left to right.

Chapter 18

see page 344

1 **What must you do first in the Commercial Printing Tools menu before you can print four-color separations? Hint: You will not be able to apply printer's marks unless you do this first.**

A: You must first select Tools ➪ Commercial Printing Tools ➪ Color Printing. In the Color Printing dialog box, click the Process Colors (CMYK) option button.

2 **Where can you change the lines per inch of your film?**

A: In the Print dialog box, click the Advanced Print Settings button. Click the Device Options tab and change the lines per inch (lpi) in the lower section of the dialog box.

3 **What are two different ways that you can send your print job to a service bureau?**

A: You can select File ➪ Pack and Go ➪ Take to a Commercial Printing Service, or you can create your own .PRN files from the Print dialog box.

4 **What imagesetting or prepress process uses choking and spreading?**

A: When you choke or spread colors, you are trapping your publication.

5 **Can you embed any font in your publication? Why or why not?**

A: No, not all fonts can be embedded. Because of copyright infringement, some fonts are unable to be embedded in your file. In this case, the printing service should have the fonts available on their systems in order to process your print job.

Personal Workbook Answers

6 What are crop marks and how are they used?

A: Crop marks indicate the trim size of a page when the page is printed on an oversized piece of film or paper. They are small, thin lines placed in each corner of the page.

7 Should you link or embed graphics when they are being sent to a service bureau or film output? Why?

A: This all depends on whether you want anyone messing with the images. If you want your service bureau to be able to edit your images, link the files. For untouchable images (by anyone), embed them.

8 What is the difference between the two Pack and Go procedures: Take to Another Computer and Take to a Commercial Printing Service?

A: Pack and Go for commercial printing will do everything that Pack and Go for another computer does and more. You are also asked what you want to print to give to the service bureau or printer — a composite print or separated prints.

Visual Quiz

Q: Looking at this newsletter inside the spread. Do you need to use bleed marks?

A: No elements extend off the page, so bleed marks aren't necessary to include in this file.

Index

B

Index

Index

G

H

I

Index

J

K

L

Index

M

N

Continued

Index

Q

R

S

Index

T

Index

Continued

Index

X

Y

Z